LAURENCE BERGREEN

CAPONE

THE MAN AND THE ERA

LAURENCE BERGREEN

CAPONE

THE MAN AND THE ERA

M

MACMILLAN

LONDON

First published 1994 by Simon & Schuster, Inc., New York

First published in Great Britain 1994 by Macmillan London Ltd
a division of Macmillan Publishers Limited
Cavaye Place London SW10 9PG
and Basingstoke

Associated companies throughout the world

ISBN 0-333-57040-5

Excerpts from an essay by Eliot Ness reprinted with permission
from The Western Reserve Historical Society.
Excerpts from the diary of H. L. Mencken published by
permission of the Enoch Pratt Free Library in accordance
with the terms of the will of H. L. Mencken.
Excerpts from "Chicago" in *Chicago Poems* by Carl Sandburg,
reprinted by permission of Harcourt Brace & Company.

1 3 5 7 9 8 6 4 2

A CIP catalogue record for this book is available from
the British Library

Printed and bound in Great Britain by
Mackays of Chatham PLC, Chatham, Kent

To Betsy, Nick, and Sara
and
To my mother and father

The evil that men do lives after them,
The good is oft interred with their bones.

—Julius Caesar, Act III, sc. ii.

Contents

ALPHONSE CAPONE
Family Tree

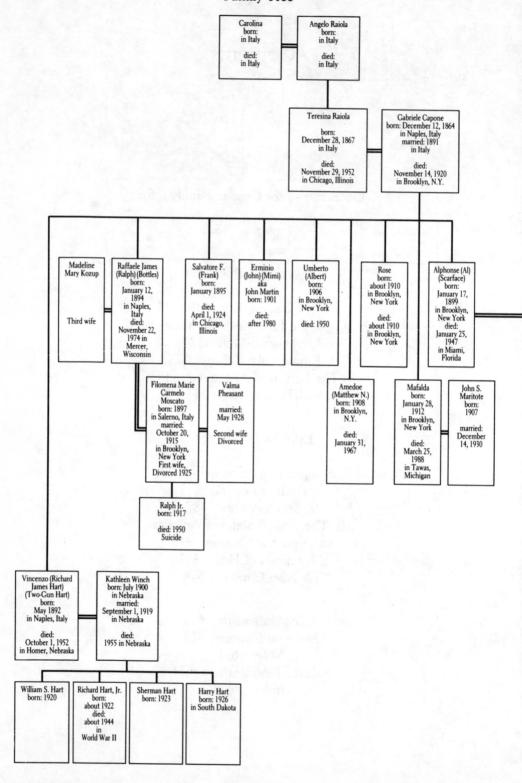

ALPHONSE CAPONE
Family Tree

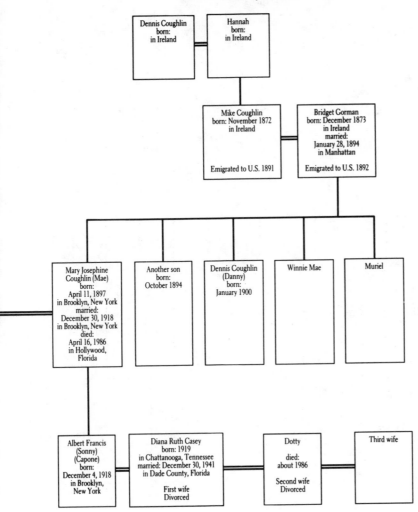

Prologue

ALL I KNOW about Al is that he was extremely kind to me and my family, especially my mother. He just loved my mother to death. Many a time he'd see her and say, "Hi, Mom, how are ya?" put his arm around her and kiss her, and when he walked away she'd have money in her hand, in her pocket. That's the way he was. In my experience with him there was nothing but kindness.

He bought me my first bicycle. He said to me, "Did you go down to the sporting goods store?" I said, "No." He said, "Well, go down there. They've got something for you to pick up." So I went, and there was a brand new bike waiting for me. I was young. Rode it home. And he was sitting on the porch waiting for me. He had a grin from ear to ear. Then he rode the damn bike half the afternoon.

Of course, anytime anything went wrong in Chicago, the newspapers had to have someone to blame. The police had to have someone to blame. But they were never able to pin anything on him. Can you imagine standing seven guys against the wall and running a machine gun and killing all of them? You'd have to be crazy, right? Got to be doped up, no matter what kind of enemies they are. That St. Valentine's Day Massacre was the worst thing that ever happened in Chicago as far as racketeering went.

Anyone ever needed any help who went to him, they got it. He helped those old people in Chicago, those old Italians during the Depression. If it hadn't been for him, half of them would have been on welfare, or worse, but he always had ways of helping them earn a dollar. He never let anyone think he was just giving them something. He'd say, "I'll rent your garage. I may need it." Or, "I'll rent your basement. I may need it." Never using it, but he would pay them anyway. In those days back in Chicago he'd pay 'em $75 a month; it was a lot of money back in 1930. He was just that way. During the Depression he even ran soup kitchens in Chicago. He fed many and many a bum. I don't know what he gained by being kind to those kind of people because they couldn't do anything for him; he was doing it for them. But that's the kind of individual he was. He just liked people.

He always urged me to stay straight. What convinced me was the time we were coming home from the Strand movie theater in Lansing, Michigan. He used to love to get me in the theater and hand me a package of gum. I chewed like crazy watching the movies, see, and he'd say, "I've got old Snorky here." He'd call me by his own nickname. Anyway, we're walking down the street—myself, Al, Frank Nitti, and Jack McGurn. McGurn was a hell of a golfer, you know; he could have been a pro. So we're just walking down the street on a summer evening coming home from the movies, but as we passed this place, this home, we stopped.

The window shades were all up, the lights were on, and there was a family sitting there having dinner. And he says to me, "Boy, what I wouldn't give to be able to sit with my family with the shades up like that, eating dinner." He says, "Boy, don't you ever get involved in this kind of life. If you do, and I'm alive, I'll personally kill you."

That was impressive to me because with all the money he had and all the people around him, his life really wasn't his own. He always had to be on guard, always had to watch. Couldn't even have his hair cut or a shave. The barber had to come to him. Every time they went to a restaurant they practically took it over. Always sat near a window so there was an easy escape if they had to. If you think the president has security it was nothing compared to this. It was always two or three bodyguards in front and a couple on each side and two or three in back. That was a hell of a life. . . .

—Anthony Russo*

* A pseudonym.

Part One
PURSUIT

CHAPTER 1

Campanilismo

HE WAS ATAVISTIC, flamboyant, impossible to ignore. A big fat man with a cigar and a $50,000 pinkie ring. A jowly smiling Satan nearly six feet tall, with two scars across his left cheek. He weighed over two-fifty, yet despite his bulk and the sloppy grin, he could move with lethal speed and force. Not an articulate man, he was nonetheless charismatic: warm, charming, generous. A big tipper. He attempted elegance with an outrageous wardrobe—custom-tailored suits of purple, electric blue, or yellow; pearl-gray fedoras accented by a black band; and diamond-encrusted stickpins. He liked people, wanted them to adore him, and people gravitated toward him, they applauded him, sought his autograph, and as he excused himself as a businessman or a rogue, he submitted to their hero worship and condemnation.

His name was Al Capone, and he was, according to the *New York Times* on the occasion of his death, January 25, 1947, "the symbol of a shameful era, the monstrous symptom of a disease which was eating into the conscience of America. Looking back on it now, this period of Prohibition in full, ugly flower seems fantastically incredible. Capone himself was incredible, the creation of an evil dream."

Incredible. Fantastic. Ugly. Evil. In harsh, censorious language the obituaries attempted to explain, condemn, and, perversely, revel in his life and career. They informed the public that "Alfonso Caponi" had been born in Naples in 1895, as if no American lad could ever grow up to be so evil. They evoked his apprenticeship to crime in Manhattan's Little Italy, in particular, a neighborhood known as the Mulberry Street Bend; reproduced his draft card; mentioned his service during the Great War as part of the French "Lost Battalion" and described the duel—though some accounts referred to shrapnel—which gave him the two famous scars across his left cheek. They confided that his nickname was "Scarface"; explained that the young Capone fled a murder rap in New York and arrived in Chicago one step ahead of the police to work for his cousin Johnny Torrio, vice lord of that city. They portrayed him as the mastermind behind the notorious St. Valentine's Day Massacre on February 14, 1929; in some accounts he even wielded a machine gun himself. They gave as the cause of his death pneumonia or a stroke, or a combination of the two; and, finally, they unanimously claimed his death marked the end of an era of gangsters and murder in Chicago and around the country. Thus his life became a paradigm of the gangster's progress in America.

However, nearly all of this endlessly repeated—and generally accepted—information was erroneous, beginning with the time and place of his birth. So, too, was the story of his military service in the Great War; the often-reproduced draft card actually belonged to another Al Capone, a butcher who resided in New Jersey. The manner in which he received his scar was similarly falsified and romanticized, as was his real nickname ("Scarface" was strictly for the movies and newspapers), the true cause of his death, even the correct spelling of his name. Nor did his demise mark the end of gangland, as his moralizing obituaries predicted; powerful racketeers followed Capone as surely as they had preceded him. "You who only know him from newspaper stories will never realize the real man he is," his younger sister, Mafalda, publicly stated, but her words fell on deaf ears or met with outright derision; was she not blinded by family loyalty? And then there were the movies and later the television programs inspired by his career, which served to increase the confusion surrounding his deeds and reputation, since these dramatizations endowed characters engaged in largely fictional exploits with the names of real people. Ultimately, the Al Capone who became familiar to Americans is a myth: a poisonous but intoxicating blend of the shrill yellow journalism of the 1920s, Hollywood sensationalism, and pervasive anti-Italian prejudice. These multiple distortions transformed Capone into a larger-than-life symbol of evil.

•   •   •

For decades American politicians and writers had been warning the populace about Al Capone—or someone very much like him—as an example of the alien element contaminating clean native shores with disease, throwing the nation's economy into turmoil with cheap labor, and corrupting Anglo-American institutions with rapacious feudal codes. The Capone phenomenon, according to such voices, was the natural and inevitable outcome of the nation's permitting millions of immigrants from around the world to flow into the country during the last quarter of the nineteenth century. Among the most influential critics of unrestricted immigration was a Republican member of Congress from Massachusetts, the Honorable Henry Cabot Lodge. The scion of a wealthy family, a historian, and a former editor of the respected *North American Review*, Lodge personified the political, economic, and financial establishments of his day; well could he presume to decide whom to admit to the United States and whom to exclude. In 1891, three years before Capone's parents arrived in New York, this flower of New England warned that during the previous fifteen years alone, almost 6.5 million immigrants had poured into the country, a number "equal to one-tenth of the entire population of the country," a sum, he warned, that contained "enough voters to decide a presidential election." Lodge wanted them to stay away for precisely the reasons they wished to come, because they were impoverished, uneducated, without a secure place in the world. "We have the right to exclude illiterate persons from our immigration," he insisted, and he proposed screening the millions of undesirables washing up on American shores with a literacy test, a notoriously elastic gauge. "And this test," he concluded, "combined with others of a more general character, would in all probability shake out a large part of the undesirable portion of the present immigration. It would reduce in a discriminating manner the number of immigrants, and would thereby benefit the labor market." Later in the year, Lodge warned that the United States had become a haven for the "paupers and criminals" of Europe. "It is certainly madness to permit this stream to pour in without discrimination or selection, or the exclusion of dangerous and undesirable elements," by which he meant, specifically, Italians, who, he noted, simply came to this country to earn money and then returned home to spend it, enriching their countrymen at the expense of Americans. Despite Lodge's warning and an 1882 federal law excluding paupers and criminals, immigration continued almost unchecked, inhibited only by the Great War. "We are overwhelmed, submerged and almost drowned out by a great flood-tide of European riff-raff, the refuse of almost every nation on the continent, paupers, criminals, beggars and the muddy residuum of foreign civilizations," complained the *New York Herald*. "We don't wonder that they want to come to this country, but the country is not a philanthropic institution or an asylum for the crippled and depraved of the globe. . . . The sooner we take a decided stand and shut down the gates the better." Not until 1924 did Congress finally establish a quota system for immigrants.

Each immigrant group suffered from this intense bias in its own way, but one of the cruelest stereotypes to gain currency—and beyond that, intellectual respectability—was that of Southern Italians like the Capones, who were invariably portrayed as lazy, lusty, stupid, and criminal. Writing in the *Century Magazine* as late as 1914, Edward Alsworth Ross, a prominent sociologist, gave voice to the beliefs of America's ruling class concerning the disreputable new arrivals, especially those who came, like Al Capone's parents, from Naples. "Steerage passengers from Naples," Ross observed, "show a distressing frequency of low foreheads, open mouths, weak chins, poor features, skew faces, small or knobby crania, and backless heads. Such people lack the power to take rational care of themselves; hence their death-rate in New York is twice the general death-rate." Too unintelligent to survive, or so Ross believed, Southern Italians also displayed a want of "mechanical aptitude." In addition, "their emotional instability stands out in sharpest contrast to the self-control of the Hebrew and the stolidity of the Slav." As for their children, their exasperated American teachers agreed that they "hate study, make slow progress, and quit school at the first opportunity. . . . They are very weak in abstract mathematics." Coming to the New World only worsened these problems, Ross believed. They were far better off in their own country, among their own kind, he insisted. "Who can forget the joyous, shameless gregariousness of Naples?" Ross asked, where "the streets are lively with chatter and stir and folks sitting out in front and calling one another." They like it there in the slums of Naples, he supposed, where the illiterate peasants "covet the intimacies of the tenement-house." (Even that observation, intended as a compliment, held sinister implications.) In contrast to the typical Southern Italian, Ross described those national character traits he admired: "The man who 'sweareth to his own hurt and changeth not' is likely to be a German . . . , an Englishman with his ideal of *truth*, or an American with his ideal of *squareness*."

Even the champions of the impoverished immigrants despaired at the inability of Italian arrivals to improve themselves, find employment, become educated, in short, to *assimilate*. Among the most influential was Jacob Riis, himself an immigrant who had abandoned a comfortable background in Denmark to venture to the United States. In his career as a crusading journalist with the *New York Evening Sun* and a social reformer, he displayed righteous anger at the disgraceful living conditions imposed on the newest Americans, especially children, but when he came to Italians, he portrayed them not as casualties of the appalling social conditions afflicting all immigrants, but as victims of their own flawed natures. Unlike Lodge, whose xenophobia was largely an intellectual proposition, Riis based his impressions of Italian immigrants on direct personal observation. In his otherwise progressive book, *How the Other Half Lives* (1890), Riis wrote that the Italian who comes to New York "promptly reproduces conditions of destitution and disorder which, set in the framework of Mediterranean exuberance, are the delight of the artist, but in a matter-of-fact American community become its danger and reproach. . . . The Italian comes in at the bottom . . . and stays there."

The harsh view shared by respected politicians and journalists had as its street equivalent a single word summing up what so many Americans thought of Italians: dago. A corruption of *Diego* (Spanish for James), the derisive epithet originated in the American West and worked its way back East, where it extended to the new Italian arrivals, who were often pitifully unaware of the climate of hatred and resentment awaiting them in America.

As Southern Italians, they had been accustomed to prejudice from the Northern provinces of their own country; indeed Northern Italians could be just as contemptuous of their Southern compatriots as Henry Cabot Lodge and Jacob Riis were. For Northerners, Italy consisted of two countries, the North and the South, or perhaps even three: the North, the South, and Sicily—the latter province being so alien, backward, corrupt, and feudal that the Northerners referred to the Sicilians as Africans, a term that had little to do with the Sicilians' appearance but much to do with fears about their character. (As an adult trying to survive in the fiercely contested rackets, Capone came to share the non-Sicilians' fear of the "Black Italians" who dominated the business; "those crazy Sicilians" became his common complaint.) In addition to the virulent prejudice they faced at home, Southern Italians were also plagued by natural disasters; there were earthquakes, there were droughts, there were even volcanic eruptions—all of which suggested that farmers and other peasants who made their living from the land had best flee for their lives. As a result, they kept on coming despite the extreme hostility they faced in America, and their numbers shot past the levels that had so concerned Henry Cabot Lodge. In 1880, approximately 12,300 Italians came to the United States; only eight years later, the number reached over 51,000, more than a fourfold increase. During the 1890s, Italian immigration averaged about 50,000 souls a year; and in the following decade, the first of the new century, the numbers exploded: 100,000 in 1900, 230,000 in 1903, 286,000 in 1907. The figures remained at these tremendous levels until the Great War impeded civilian transatlantic travel. Nothing—not the threat of war between the United States and Italy or the hovels awaiting them in "Little Italys" around the nation—deterred the Italians from coming to a land bristling with transplanted historical hatred for them. Their willingness to brave these hardships was testament to their desperation, their courage, their naïveté, and their great hopes for life in America—hopes that, more often than not, were to lead to conflict and bitter disappointment.

The youth of Al Capone, as with many other sons and daughters of Italian immigrants, was largely a response to this climate of anti-Italian prejudice. He and his brothers would all devise different responses; some of the strategies would prove more admirable than others, but none of them would escape it.

. . . .

Al Capone always insisted he was an American, born and bred, and so he was, but his Italian heritage formed and informed every aspect of his life and career. He belonged both to the Old World—with its fatalism, corruption of flesh and spirit, and charm—and to the New—with its striving, materialism, and violence.

His mother, a seamstress named Teresina Raiola, and his father, a barber named Gabriele Capone, grew to maturity, married, and started their family in Naples. Italy's third-largest city, located on the western coast approximately halfway between Rome and the boot's toe, Naples sprawls down to the ocean like a brightly colored, tattered and soiled dishrag. Neapolitans are renowned for their ability to improvise and adapt; they have to, living in a city hemmed in by Mount Vesuvius on one side and the Tyrrhenian Sea on the other, a capital that had been changing hands for over two thousand years. At one time or another, Greeks, Romans, Austrians, Spaniards, and the French (in the person of Joseph Bonaparte, Napoleon's brother) ruled the city; for a time during the eighteenth century, it had served as the seat of an improvised nation, the Kingdom of the Two Sicilies. As a result of this ceaseless upheaval, the city had the air of an abandoned capital that had fallen into chaos; where kings once walked, herds of sheep later grazed. "There is nothing . . . quite like Naples in its sordid and yet tremendous vitality," wrote Edward Hutton, an English visitor, of the city in 1915. The noise, dirt, and overcrowding appalled the fastidious Hutton; Naples seemed more "a pen of animals than a city of men, a place amazing if you will, but disgusting in its amazement, whose life is . . . without dignity, beauty or reticence."

However, Neapolitans enjoyed a reputation for being singularly accepting and relaxed in the midst of the dirt and chaos of their city. They had seen too much of history's folly to heed the Catholic Church; resentful of the North, or at least mindful of the North's resentment of them, Neapolitans tended to be antipapist, antimonarchist, antiauthoritarian. The centuries of rulers coming and going, cynically exploiting the region and then carelessly abandoning it, had a profound effect on the Neapolitan and Southern Italian consciousness. Proverbs dear to the peasantry expressed rage at the scarcity of social justice and the abundance of hypocrisy: "The gallows is for the poor man, the law courts for the fool," "He who steals from the king commits no crime," and most tellingly, "The fat pig pays no taxes."

In this richly cynical atmosphere, organized crime flourished openly. Criminal societies were a prominent feature of Neapolitan life and commerce—not in the form of the Mafia, a clannish, closed society with mystical overtones specific to Sicily—but rather the Camorra, a far more open assemblage of racketeers, extortionists, pimps, and gamblers. The Camorra was a secularized Mafia, all business and unencumbered by ritual, operating on the principle of exacting tribute from the populace. A 1912 inquiry into the workings of the Camorra discovered that it "levied blackmail upon all gambling enterprises, brothels, drivers of public vehicles, boatmen, beggars, prostitutes, thieves, waiters, porters, marketmen, fruitsellers, small tradesmen, lottery winners, pawnbrokers, controlled all the smuggling and coined bogus money." The various forms of blackmail, some large, some trivial, were so widespread that *Camorristi* became synonymous with extortionists of any type. The Camorra played a larger role than mere extortion, however; the people got something in return for their money. In the absence of a respected government, it functioned as a subterranean political organization as well; *Camorristi* offered their services as political fixers, and they could work minor miracles in obtaining permits, eliminating unwanted competition, and bringing obstinate public officials to heel.

Attaining this powerful role was an extraordinary accomplishment for an organization that had begun life early in the nineteenth century in the jails of Naples, where it functioned as a force for order rather than a destructive conspiracy. The Camorra succeeded in levying tribute or taxes, depending on one's point of view, on prisoners, for whom it obtained all manner of services and privileges in return. By 1830, the Camorra had moved beyond the prison walls to embrace the remnants of local government, and *Camorristi* were readily identified by their dashing "uniform," which consisted of a red kerchief, sash, and rings adorning every finger. The Camorra assisted the police with keeping order in Naples because it addressed working-class unrest, sometimes blunting it by making vice easily available, and sometimes righting blatant wrongs and offering a rough justice that could not be found in the courts. Anyone who defied the Camorra wound up with a huge scar running along the neck from ear to ear. Naples was said to be filled with people disfigured for this reason, each of them a warning to others not to disobey the Camorrists. However, the real key to the Camorra's effectiveness was its organization. Naples was divided into twelve sections, and the Camorra assigned a *capo'ntrine*, a sectional captain, to cover each one, and the sectional chiefs in turn reported to the *capo in testa*, the head captain. Within each of these sections, various local gangs, or *paranze*, held sway, their powers sharply circumscribed by the Camorrist hierarchy. By 1860, the Camorrist influence was so great that the political establishment entrusted the organization with the task of ensuring public safety.

Despite their quasi-legitimate status, *Camorristi* knew full well they had chosen a dangerous way of life, ruled by the shotgun and the whims of local bosses who jealously guarded their profitable, illicit fiefdoms. A Camorrist knowingly chose *la mala vita*, the evil life: the general term for a life of crime, the underworld. *Camorristi* added to the hazards they faced by their use of prostitutes. Many suffered from venereal disease, and many Neapolitans came to think of Camorrists as ravaged in mind and body by the malady. Though fraught with risks, *la mala vita* was also glamorous, and if a follower survived, he could be assured of becoming a fixture in the community, for the Camorra clung parasitically to the political establishment and offered a measure of social stability.

When Al Capone reached Chicago in 1921, he encountered a city that was in many ways an American version of Naples, for Chicago also had a large working-class population that supported semilegitimate criminal societies working hand in glove with a corrupt local government. Capone did not consciously model the organization he built in Chicago on the Camorra of Naples, and he certainly never called it by that name (or any other name, for that matter); nonetheless, the intricate, hierarchical, civic-minded Camorra served as his prototype.

A thousand years of history demonstrated the futility of life in Naples, but in America anything was possible. Yet before most would-be immigrants set foot on a boat bound for the New World they had already committed themselves to a form of indentured servitude known as the padrone system, an adaptation of the Camorrist way of doing business; even the means of reaching America became an extension of Neapolitan corruption. Under this system, Italian emigrants found themselves instantly reduced to the status of a commodity, and that commodity was labor, *sciabola*—work done with the shovel. The boss or the extortionist who organized the laborers and exploited them was known as the padrone, and life for the Italian immigrant under his regime was extremely harsh. Adult men earned an average of only $40 a year, and children worked as well, hawking newspapers, shining shoes, begging, and then giving the pennies they earned to their padrone. Women often became prostitutes. Writing in the *Bulletin of the Department of Labor* in 1897, three years after the Capones' arrival in New York, John Koren labeled the padrone system a "species of semislavery" exploiting at least two-thirds of all Italians in America.

Italians endured the cruel system because their sojourns in the United States were generally brief. During the mid-1890s, far more Italians *returned* to their native land from the United States than immigrated; the returnees consisted largely of laborers who had worked in America for slave wages under the padrone system and then limped home, exhausted and disillusioned, to the hamlets from which they had come. But that situation was slowly changing. Through exposés such as Koren's, the American public perceived the padrone system as an evil to be wiped out. Under pressure of government scrutiny, the monopoly abated. Now entire families came from Italy, not just individual males to earn illusory "princely wages" and flee home. These families came to seek a new way of life, to settle permanently, to become Americans.

·   ·   ·

Among the 42,977 Italians who arrived in the United States during 1894 was an unremarkable young family from Naples. Their name, as they themselves wrote it on their immigration and naturalization papers, was a fairly common one in their region: Capone (not Caponi, as many published accounts later claimed). The Capones would soon expand into a large, closely knit family, but at the time they arrived in New York, they consisted of only four members: the head of family, Gabriele Capone, then thirty years old; his wife, Teresina (or Teresa, as she was often called), who was three years his junior; and their two small children: Vincenzo, who was born two years earlier, in 1892; and his infant brother, Raffaele, who, having been born on January 12, 1894, came ashore in his mother's arms. They came to stay, not to return to Italy in a year or two, as so many other immigrants had. The timing of their arrival in America meant that they missed the peak of the padrone system; Gabriele arrived on his own recognizance. He was a barber, a humble occupation to be sure, but a trade nonetheless. He was beholden to no boss, and he was still young enough to make a fresh start.

Gabriele had married Teresina Raiola just three years earlier in Naples, and their first priority was starting a family; at the time of their transatlantic crossing, she was pregnant with their third child, Salvatore, who was born in January 1895, a year after Raffaele. Within the family, all the children would always be called by their Italian names, but they acquired and were known to the world by the American names they adopted. Vincenzo became James, Raffaele became Ralph, and Salvatore became Frank. As for their parents, neither of them altered their names to suit American custom. In time, Gabriele learned to read, write, and speak English, while Teresa, who lived a more circumscribed life in the home, never troubled to memorize more than a few simple English phrases.

Once they had passed through Ellis Island and arrived in New York, the Capone family, like other Italian immigrants, gravitated toward neighborhoods sheltering people who had fled the same region, if not the same town. This powerful sense of place was known as *campanilismo*. The word derived from *campanile*, a church bell tower, and it signified the region within the sound of the tolling of the village bell. The pull of *campanilismo* caused Southern Italians to pass their daily lives within their village: to work, marry, live, and die within tightly circumscribed borders. In America, by extension, *campanilismo* came to mean the immediate neighborhood. More than religion, perhaps even more than language, *campanilismo* reinforced the Italian immigrant's alienation from American life, for every neighbor, coworker, or merchant with whom an Italian immigrant dealt came from the same region of Italy. The sameness buttressed the immigrants' identity, but at the same time it cut off the immigrants from a world of *American* possibilities.

Most Americans were oblivious to the nuances of settlement patterns of Italian immigrants; the mere mention of that ill-favored class conjured one neighborhood in particular: the Mulberry Street Bend, near the Lower East Side of Manhattan, an area notorious as a breeding ground of human degradation in all its gaudy variety. Although it was widely assumed in the press that Al Capone grew up in Mulberry Bend and first learned the rudiments of his trade there as a street urchin (he must have, master criminal that he was), neither he nor his family lived there.

The more prosaic truth is that the Capone family followed the path of least resistance, settling in Brooklyn, a borough that had rapidly become home to tens of thousands of Italian immigrants. No mere appendage to New York City, Brooklyn was a world unto itself. In fact, Brooklyn was a separate city until as late as 1898 (four years after the Capone family first moved there), when it finally joined New York City in law if not in spirit. Although it was connected to Manhattan by two immense bridges, the Brooklyn Bridge and the newer Williamsburg Bridge, it was a million miles away. None of the Capones would ever have much to do with Manhattan; nor would Manhattan and its racketeers have much to do with them, except to condescend to them. Manhattan was a noisy, compact environment, frantic, abrasive, and vertical. Brooklyn remained a succession of congenial, low-profile neighborhoods, provincial and insular, as much a state of mind as a borough of New York City.

In Al Capone's Brooklyn, the presence of the Atlantic Ocean was felt everywhere. Sea gulls wheeled, screeching, above empty, sun-splashed streets lined with row houses and gaunt trees. The tang of brackish seawater permeated the air, mingling with the acrid odors of oil, exhaust, and rotting vegetation. The docks—a source of employment for thousands of local inhabitants—were located but a few minutes' walk from the streets of his youth. The presence of shipping and shipbuilding introduced a large transient population of sailors, who in turn attracted gambling houses, bars, and brothels catering to them. Prostitutes were common in the area, especially on Sands Street, which featured the full array of honky-tonk attractions designed to separate sailors from their hard-won pay: tattoo parlors, saloons serving cheap whiskey and the occasional Mickey Finn, dance halls, gambling joints, and whorehouses to suit every taste.

On a hot day in Brooklyn, the stink off the Gowanus Canal—the local River Lethe, a man-made waterway for barges—brought tears to the eyes. Though it was the only unusual topographical feature of the neighborhood, it wasn't much of a canal, just a jagged slash zig-zagging through the marshy

Brooklyn terrain, its water now brownish, now unnaturally green, opaque, gnawing at the hulls of rusty barges, its banks overhung with dense, tangled weeds from which protruded discarded machinery. A short walk from the street where Capone grew up, the Gowanus Canal had long been a magnet for criminal activities of all types. It was not unusual for corpses to turn up in the canal, often mangled, with signs of having been dead for several days before they had been dumped.

The Capones' first apartment was located at 95 Navy Street, in the Red Hook section, "a slum that faces the bay/ Seaward from Brooklyn Bridge," wrote Arthur Miller, another product of Brooklyn, in his drama A View from the Bridge. Their housing was primitive, an unfurnished flat in a block of four-story tenements next to the Brooklyn Navy Yard and its cacophony. The Capone family was poor and had no furniture or decorations to soften and domesticate the surroundings. Heat was provided by a potbellied stove in the parlor and an oven in the kitchen. Cold water was available from a sink in the hallway. Indoor plumbing was unknown. To reach the bathroom, they went down the steps to the yard, where a small shack offered scant privacy. Rents in the district, which was heavily Italian, fluctuated between $3 and $4 a month; even though the figure was low, the prices of food and other necessities such as coal for heating were relatively high and placed a huge financial burden on immigrants like Gabriele Capone. At the time, men in his position were lucky to make ten dollars a week—considerably less, incidentally, than their counterparts were earning back in Italy. From the front of his tenement, Gabriele could see the Brooklyn Navy Yard's black-and-white sign arching over the entrance, but if he thought he might find work within, he was soon disappointed, for at the time Italian immigrants had no foothold there; the Irish, Germans, and other, better-established ethnic groups had made it their preserve. Gabriele had no alternative but to resume his trade of barbering, while Teresina took care of the children and, when she had time, took in piecework to supplement their meager income.

Their new neighbors, virtually all of whom were recent Italian immigrants, recalled the Capones as a quiet, conventional family. The mother, Donna Teresina as she was known, kept to herself. Her husband, Don Gabriele, made more of an impression, since he was, in the words of one family friend, "tall and handsome—very good-looking." Like his wife, he was subdued, even when it came to discipline. "He never hit the kids. He used to talk to them. He used to preach to them, and they listened to their father." Since no photograph of Gabriele survives, the most complete portrait of this man comes from his second son, Raffaele, who more than thirty years later found himself serving a sentence at the U.S. penitentiary at McNeil Island, Washington, for federal income tax evasion. There he talked about his father—and what it was like growing up in the newly transplanted

Capone household—with a pride and affection that survives even the routine notes from the interview.

The subject states that his father received a very good education in Italy. Thinks it must have been at least equal to a high school education. States that his father belonged to several Italian Societies of various kinds and spent considerable of his working time in them. Also gave considerable to duties in the Catholic church. States that his father worked as a barber throughout his entire life, having learned the trade at an early age. The subject thinks his home was equal to if not better than the average American home. States that his parents took great interest in their children and that they always had plenty to eat, good clothes to wear, and a good house to live in.

When it came to Teresa, her second son noted for the record that she "was very devoted to her children and did all for them that any mother could do."

As Ralph's reminiscences of his parents suggest, nothing about the Capone family was inherently disturbed, violent, or dishonest. The children and the parents were close; there was no apparent mental disability, no traumatic event that sent the boys hurtling into a life of crime. They did not display sociopathic or psychotic personalities; they were not crazy. Nor did they inherit a predilection for a criminal career or belong to a criminal society. Criminal dynasties did exist among some Italian immigrants, especially in New York, but the Capones were too modest, too *unsuccessful*, to belong to that particular elite. They were a law-abiding, unremarkable Italian-American family with conventional patterns of behavior and frustrations; they displayed no special genius for crime, or anything else, for that matter.

However, the Capones certainly feared crime. During their early years in New York, the most notorious type of Italian villainy was the Black Hand, *La Mano Nera*. This was a distinctly Old World version of extortion, courtly but deadly. It began with the victim receiving an anonymous, elaborately worded letter that began, often as not, with the greeting "Honored Sir," and went on to demand ransom in exchange for the life of the recipient or members of his family. Illustrations of daggers and skulls accompanied the text. Black Hand threats to murder or kidnap helpless children were carried out just often enough to make victims sure to pay. Although American law enforcement agencies often referred to it as a society, the Black Hand consisted of freelancers. Furthermore, *La Mano Nera* preyed exclusively on Italians, who unanimously feared and despised this vestige of another era. As the Capone children were growing up, the Black Hand symbolized criminal behavior to them. Years later, when a Senate investigation committee asked Ralph Capone, Al's older brother, if he had ever heard of the Mafia as a child in

Brooklyn, he shook his head and replied, "No. I heard 'Black Hand.' I never heard the word 'Mafia.' "

Although they lived a conventional life, and Gabriele practiced his harmless, legitimate trade, the Capone family was several layers removed from the mainstream of American society. First, their religion, Roman Catholicism, set them apart from most Americans; anti-Catholic prejudice ran high and would only increase until the time of the Great War. Their language isolated them culturally and economically from the hoped-for rewards that had lured them to America, and even among other Italian immigrants their Neapolitan dialect presented still another barrier. Perhaps it was better that they were so isolated, for at least they were shielded from their adopted country's dislike and fear of immigrants like themselves.

Responding to the strain of relocating in a foreign land, Gabriel and Teresa Capone had no more children until 1899, five years after their arrival. When they did bring another child into the world, they prayed that God would grant them a daughter after three sons, but their fourth child proved to be another boy. He was born on January 17, 1899. To him, their first child conceived and born in America, they gave the name Alphonse Capone.

•   •   •

From the moment of his birth, the child was exposed to hazard. Italian immigrant communities were notorious for their high infant mortality rate. According to one survey, it was nearly double the amount in other areas of New York. Fatal cases of pneumonia, diarrhea, and diphtheria abounded. The incidence of polio was also the highest in the region, and the foul Gowanus Canal was suspected as the source of the disease.

The infant managed to survive these early perils, and twenty days later, on February 7, the Capone family appeared in St. Michael and St. Edward's Church at 108 St. Edward's Street in Brooklyn for a baptismal ceremony. In the lore that has grown up around Al Capone over the years, several sinister names have been put forward as Capone's godfather, names of other, older Brooklyn gangsters, as if the child were being baptized into a life of crime, but in fact there was no godfather present that chilly day. Instead, a family friend named Sophia Milo assumed the role of the child's godmother.

The ceremony began as the priest, Father Garofalo, met the family at the entrance of the church and asked for the name of the child. After murmuring an introductory prayer, the priest breathed softly three times on the child's face, saying, "Depart from him, unclean spirit, and give place to the Holy Spirit, the Advocate." He then traced the sign of the cross on the child, to symbolize Christ's taking possession of him. "Sever all snares of Satan which heretofore bound him," the priest intoned over the infant, who was not yet three weeks old. The priest placed a pinch of salt in the child's mouth, saying, "I cast out the demon from you, in the name of God the Father almighty." As the godmother held the child, the priest drew water from the baptismal font with a ladle and poured a few drops on him, declaring, "I baptize you in the name of the Father, and of the Son, and of the Holy Spirit."

In the years that followed, St. Michael and St. Edward's Church served as the principal place of worship for the Capone family—especially Teresa, who attended Mass as regularly as Gabriele and his sons avoided it. A modest place, this church offered one of the few legitimate refuges available to the Capones and other Italian immigrants from the dreary routine of their lives. Every year, on May 8, church members organized an extravagant street festival to glorify their patron saints. As many as 200 people marched in a parade through the neighborhood. An immense banner in honor of St. Michael, adorned with an archangel bearing a flaming sword standing above a cowering Spirit of Darkness, led the way, offering one of the few splashes of color and fantasy in the otherwise dismal neighborhood. The parade came to a halt in front of the church, where Attanasio's Brass Band played beloved overtures and arias from the dark, magical operas by Verdi: *Aïda*, *Rigoletto*, and *I Vespri Siciliani*, with its romantic tale of a thirteenth-century rebellion leading to the creation of the secret society known as the Mafia. Opera was often an addiction for the Italians (as it would be for Capone), at once an escape from and a celebration of life, a portal into another, more exalted realm.

· · ·

In June 1900, when Alphonse was about eighteen months old, a U.S. census taker found the entire Capone family living at 69 Park Avenue in Brooklyn, in the building that housed Gabriele's barbershop: a decided improvement over their previous apartment on Navy Street. The information Gabriele gave the census taker provided a concise portrait of the Capone family at the turn of the century:

Capone, Gabriele: head of household; male; 34 years old; married for 9 years. Born in Italy; immigrated in 1894; in US 6 years; citizenship status: Declaration of Intention. Occupation: barber (shop); no unemployment in the previous year. Can read, write, and speak English. Rents home.

Capone, Terresa [sic]: wife; female; 30 years old; married 9 years; mother of 4 children; 4 now living. Born in Italy, immigrated in 1894, in US for 6 years. Can read and write, unable to speak English.

The census also revealed that Gabriele had already taken the crucial step toward becoming an American citizen and attaining his goal to remain permanently in his new home. "Declaration of Intention" meant that he had filed for citizenship, usually known as taking "first papers." He would finally complete this protracted process, formally renouncing his allegiance to the king of Italy and becoming a full-fledged American, six years later, on May 25, 1906.

The crowded Capone household eventually included two boarders, both Italian immigrants. One was a middle-aged musician named Andrea Callabrea, who had recently arrived in the United States, and the other was a young barber by the name of Michael Martino; he was, in all probability, Gabriele's apprentice, working in the barbershop in return for room and board. There was nothing, on the face of it, to suggest that this household was nurturing the most notorious criminal in American history; it was utterly typical of other Italian immigrant families throughout the neighborhood: the men working at trades or crafts, usually self-employed or in small businesses, the women tending the children who swarmed through apartments and would soon choke the schools and streets of Brooklyn.

· · ·

In 1904, when he was five years old, Al began attending Public School 7, located on Adams Street, close to the cramped Capone apartment. P.S. 7 was an old, dreary place, assaulted by the constant rumbling of the nearby elevated railroad, and its student body consisted largely of children from families as poor as his. For many children of immigrants, the public school system became a rite of passage from the old, confining ways into the mainstream of American life. It was in the public schools that many of the children first heard English spoken constantly and met other boys and girls of different backgrounds. It was where they first began to learn about America, to pledge allegiance to the flag, and to eat strange American foods they had never tasted at home. The children in turn passed on some of the knowledge of American customs they had acquired in school to their parents, who, if they did not speak English and had no cause to travel, would not have learned of them. Thus education trickled upward through the immigrant communities, as casual as a rumor. However, the notion of continuing education was a novelty. New York City had begun administering high schools only in 1897, and at the time Capone was working his way through the dregs of the city's public school system, most Italian immigrant families expected their children to leave school as soon as they were old enough to work, usually before reaching the ninth grade. Italian immigrants, especially, were discouraged from seeking higher education. Their Irish Catholic or American-born teachers often viewed them as a nuisance at best, a menace to the American way of life at worst. Even the Catholic Church fostered this attitude. "The Italians are not a sensitive people like our own," an Irish priest advised the archbishop of New York. "When they are told they are about the worst Catholics that ever came to this country they don't resent it or deny it. If they were a little more sensitive to such remarks, they would improve faster."

Schools such as Capone's P.S. 7 offered nothing in the way of assistance to children from Italian backgrounds to enter the mainstream of American life; they were rigid, dogmatic, strict institutions, where physical force often prevailed over reason in maintaining discipline. The teachers—usually female, Irish Catholic, and trained by nuns—were extremely young. A sixteen-year-old, earning $600 a year, would often teach boys and girls only a few years younger than she. The teachers kept order any way they could, usually by shouting and throwing erasers and chalk at recalcitrant students. They resorted to corporal punishment when necessary, often striking a child with a ruler. The teachers also lived with the threat of violence and retaliation from their pupils and rarely went anywhere alone, inside or out of the school building. Still, fistfights between students and teachers were common, even between male students and female teachers. "They were a fighting tribe, those teachers," wrote a veteran of the Gowanus public school system, "and they needed to be to survive." While children such as Al Capone found school a place of constant discipline relieved by sudden outbreaks of violence, their parents could only imagine what was taking place behind the institution's big red doors. There was almost no contact between families and schools.

·   ·   ·

When Al became a little older, around ten, he was drawn to the Brooklyn docks, where the action was. There he could study a 100-ton floating crane used by the Navy and watch the changing of the military guard at the gate of the Navy Yard. The soldiers' marching fascinated the boy, who enjoyed hooting at the men who fell out of step. He was hardly alone in this practice and was usually ignored, except for one revealing instance. Observing a particularly inept guard bungle the drill, Al called out, "Hey, you long-legged number three there! Get in step! You're holding 'em up."

After he was dismissed, the errant soldier charged the Navy Yard gate, preparing to spit at his heckler. Instead of running away, Al held his ground and dared him to fight: a brave and foolhardy thing to do. But just before the boy and the man came to blows, the corporal in charge of the recruits called the soldier off. As he left, the corporal confided to Al, "You got his goat for sure, but if he really spits on you, I'll put him on report."

Instead of being grateful for the gesture, Capone remained defiant. "Don't do any reporting," he said. "Just let the big sonofabitch outside the gate. I'll take care of him."

Capone's bravado impressed the corporal, who later told his sergeant, "If this kid had a good officer to get hold of him and steer him right, he'd make a good man. But if nothing like this will happen, the kid may drift for a few years until some wise guy picks him up and steers him around and then he'll be heard from one day."

The young Al Capone *was* heard from again, at least in the neighborhood. On this occasion, he chose to vent his youthful fury at the Italians' traditional rivals, the Irish. A neighbor, Angela Pitaro,* says, "When Al Capone lived on Navy Street, all the *paisani*, the Italian fellahs, got together, and went to this Irish bar. In fact, every corner had a bar, all of them Irish. Women off the boat from Italy used to wear two or three skirts, and the Irish fellahs would go behind them and pick up the dresses." When the harassment hit closer to home, Angela recalls that Al became involved. "One day, my mother goes out to the hall. She's looking for her tub. She has to wash clothes. 'Angela,' she says, 'they stole my tub. How am I gonna wash my clothes for my kids? Who took it?' My brother said to my mother, 'Ma, don't worry, we'll buy you a new one.' But they couldn't take it no more, the Italian boys. So Al Capone formed a gang. They were young—fourteen years old.

"Then, one day, we heard a noise, biddi-bum-bum-bum, biddi-bum-bum-bum, and then we heard, '*And we are the boys of Navy Street, and touch us if you dare!*' The Irish fellahs came out of the bar. The Italian fellahs, Al Capone, my brothers, the whole gang, they gave those Irish fellahs such a beating. In those days the cops were short and fat, and by the time they came all the boys disappeared. They were on top of the roofs."

In this incident a few outlines of the mature Capone are visible. The vengeance he wreaked on the "Irish fellahs" was not an act of vandalism or desecration; it was surely violent and probably unnecessary, but it was, in its misguided, exuberant way, a gallant and generous gesture designed to secure the return of the missing washtub. It showed that Al, even in early adolescence, acted as a leader, playing the hero, wanting to be seen as a righter of wrongs, even while he perpetrated his own mischief. It also demonstrated his protective instincts, especially where his own kind, especially the women, were concerned. Above all, Al liked to create a spectacle in which he cast himself as the champion of the oppressed and aggrieved. "*We are the boys of Navy Street, and touch us if you dare!*"

As he acquired a taste for the distractions and dangers of street life, Capone's school record, which had once showed promise, gradually deterio-

* A pseudonym.

rated. From P.S. 7 he moved to a larger school, P.S. 133. Located half a dozen blocks from his home, the new school was a hideous Gothic monstrosity, as impersonal and forbidding as its name, a massive building that bore more resemblance to a prison than to a place of learning. There he consistently received Bs on his report card, until the sixth grade, when his grades began to disintegrate. He was often truant, missing school more than half the time, and as his absences took their toll on his studies, he was forced to undergo the humiliation of repeating sixth grade. By the time he was ready to go on to the seventh grade, Al Capone was fourteen years old. That year his adolescent frustration and impatience with school finally exploded. After being scolded by his teacher one time too often, Al lashed out at her. She struck him, and he hit back. Since hitting was common in these schools, the incident might have ended there, but then the teacher took him to the principal, who administered a sound beating to Al. Afterward, the boy vowed never to return to P.S. 133, and he never did.

So ended the school career of Al Capone, as did the schooling of many other children in the Gowanus section of Brooklyn. Although the image of the large and glowering young student striking his young female teacher seems brutal, it is worth noting that such altercations were daily events at P.S. 133. Still, the expulsion was a decisive event in his young life, for it marked his first formal rebuff from an American institution, and by extension, from the mainstream of American life. The overriding message that the educational system sent to Al and to his classmates from Red Hook and Gowanus was that they were insignificant, had nothing to offer, and existed solely on the grudging largesse of the state. For these youths, school was more a tool of confinement than a method of advancement; it was an institutionalized form of punishment, a dead end. At the time of his expulsion, Capone had, at any rate, pretty well run his course in school. He was fourteen, able-bodied, and there was virtually no chance that he would go on to high school, even if he had been a model student.

. . .

By the time Al quit school, the Capone family had abandoned their quarters on Park Avenue for a succession of better equipped apartments on nearby Garfield Place. They lived first at number 38, then moved to slightly larger quarters a few doors up at number 46, and finally settled at number 21, on the other side of the street. Although it was only a ten-minute walk from Navy Street, Garfield Place was in every way superior: a pleasant, quiet, residential street lined with row houses and trees. There was a pool hall at number 20, close to the Capone home, and it was here that Gabriele spent considerable time, and where his son Al, in preference to attending school, learned to play the game, at which he quickly excelled.

The move from Navy Street to Garfield Place was a small one, at most a step or two up the social scale for the Capones, but to Al the relocation would have enormous significance, for his new surroundings placed him in proximity to the most important influences of his life as a young adult. Just up the hill from Garfield Place was a stable Irish neighborhood; here, only blocks from Al, lived the girl whom he would marry. Another local landmark of equal significance for Al was a small, second-story establishment at Fourth Avenue and Union Street, identified by its unprepossessing sign: THE JOHN TORRIO ASSOCIATION. It was here, in these utterly ordinary surroundings, that the first modern racketeer held court.

Everybody in the neighborhood knew Johnny; he was small, shy, precise, almost dainty, and generous—especially with youngsters willing to run errands for him. His wife adored him; years later, when he hovered near death after an assassination attempt, she declared he had always been the "best and dearest of husbands" and described their domestic life as "one long, unclouded honeymoon." To the locals, Torrio appeared to be a fairly successful numbers racketeer, quietly tending his part of the so-called Italian lottery. They would have been disappointed but not really surprised to know that this well-dressed man with the tiny hands and feet also managed a number of local brothels. But they would have been astounded to learn that their Johnny, more than any other individual, was responsible for the development of modern corporate crime—that is, casting traditional Italian racketeering in the American corporate mold, making its vices available to all, not just Italians, and eventually extending its turf far beyond the streets of Brooklyn to the entire nation. "As an organizer and administrator of underworld affairs Johnny Torrio is unsurpassed in the annals of American crime," one of its ablest chroniclers, Herbert Asbury, has written. "He was probably the nearest thing to a real master mind that this country has yet produced. He conducted his evil enterprises as if they were legitimate businesses." If the Black Hand represented the past of Italian crime, Johnny Torrio incarnated its future. But for now that corporate, mainstream type of crime, which so closely resembled legitimate American business, existed in embryonic form in the John Torrio Association. Al Capone walked beneath the sign several times a day.

Torrio usually stood or sat in front of the building, looking for young recruits. He would pay the boys as much as $5 to run trivial errands, and the ones he found trustworthy he would assign more delicate and difficult tasks such as deliveries and payoffs. It was only a matter of time until he struck up an acquaintance with the gregarious Capone boy living right in the neighborhood. Thus Al found his first and most important mentor. Torrio became his Fagin, his link to the world beyond Brooklyn, the vast and glittering world of the rackets.

To win Torrio's confidence, Capone had to pass a simple test. Torrio invited him to drop by headquarters at a certain time, and when Al showed up, Torrio made a point to be absent, but he had left behind a tempting sum of money where it could be easily taken. Many of the boys whom Torrio tested in this way took the money, and that was the last they ever saw of Johnny Torrio, but not Al, who left the money where it was and in so doing won Torrio's trust. From that time forward, the two enjoyed a partnership that lasted over two decades. In the end, it was Al who benefited most from the relationship; Torrio had many aspiring racketeers and hoodlums courting his favor, but Capone had only one Torrio in his life. If any man could be said to have invented Al Capone, to have been responsible for making him into what he eventually became, that man was Johnny Torrio. The proximity of the Capone residence to Torrio's place of business made all the difference to Al, and it would eventually make all the difference to Torrio as well, for what Torrio, with his brilliant, analytical mind was able to conceive, Al would eventually be able to execute.

It is not difficult to fathom Torrio's appeal to Al; the man was everything Gabriele was not: wealthy, successful, respected. He had made it; he was connected. He had ties to Manhattan, especially the notorious Five Points gang, for decades a fixture of that borough's underworld, an army numbering over a thousand young Italians available for hire by politicians, anti-union businesses, or anyone else willing to pay them to create mayhem. If there was a strike, the Five Pointers could break it up; if there was an election, they could enforce voting. Their leader was a small, dapper former boxer named Paolo Antonini Vacarelli. Like most other Italian prizefighters of the day, he had taken an Irish nom de guerre to overcome anti-Italian prejudice; thus he was known as Paul Kelly. His headquarters were located at the thrillingly disreputable New Brighton Dance Hall on Great Jones Street in Lower Manhattan, and his realm included the choicest blocks of southern Manhattan, including City Hall. But Kelly's day was passing; a celebrity in turn-of-the-century New York, he later retreated to a Sicilian district in Harlem, where he was content to organize hordes of ragpickers. Torrio and other racketeers quickly filled the vacuum, learning to work together, realizing that cooperation, not gang warfare, led to real wealth and power. Torrio's bailiwick was the Jane Street mob, a splinter of Kelly's gang, but Torrio rarely resorted to Kelly's strong-arm tactics. Torrio was, above all, a peacemaker; he had no bodyguard, carried no weapon, and always spoke in soft, measured tones. He considered himself a businessman, not a gang leader, and he conducted his rackets in a businesslike way.

So Capone passed through the days of his youth in Brooklyn. Days on the street. Days of running errands for Torrio, who was invariably mild, appreciative, disciplined, and, in his way, unspoiled. A perfect role model for young Al: the pimp and gambler who rigidly segregated business from his personal life, who maintained a wholesome home and a devoted, adoring wife. Whores on the job, a Madonna at home. Working for Torrio brought young Al $5 here, a ten spot there, and he brought all of it home to his mother, who never questioned the source of the money and lavishly praised her little breadwinner. Days of doing sums in his head, of calculating the odds. Days of learning by careful observation what men would pay for, how much they would bet at poker, at craps, on various neighborhood lotteries, on the outcome of the Dodgers game that afternoon. Learning how much they would pay for a drink or a woman.

During his apprenticeship, Capone learned to restrain his youthful bravado ("*We are the boys of Navy Street, and touch us if you dare!*") and to emulate Torrio's approach to organizing the rackets and reconciling opposing factions. From Torrio he also learned the importance of leading an outwardly respectable life, to segregate his career from his home life, as if maintaining a peaceful, conventional domestic setting somehow excused or legitimized the venality of working in the rackets. This compartmentalization was good discipline, but its emphasis on piety, on home and hearth and sentimental platitudes, also led to domestic sterility. In these circumstances, maintaining a "good home" became a crushing burden. But it was a form of hypocrisy that was second nature to Johnny Torrio and that he taught Capone to honor.

· · ·

As he fell under the spell of Torrio, Capone also became familiar with Brooklyn's numerous youth gangs. With its large working-class population and its multitude of immigrant groups, Brooklyn spawned a rich mixture of gangs, all of them in need of willing and bored young boys like Al. The gangs defined themselves by feuds with one another, and the most widespread rivalry existed between the Irish and the Italians. The Catholicism shared by the two groups was, if anything, a divisive factor, for there was a constant rivalry over which group made better Catholics. The Irish, from their cold climate and their repressive homeland, believed they were superior, and they considered the Italians lazy, self-indulgent, prone to all types of excess, and much too sexual. The Irish tended to regard sex with strict disapproval and so were convinced that they, as a group, were God's favorites. From the Irish point of view, the great problem was that the Vatican, through a ghastly historical accident, happened to be located in Rome, while all the world knew the Irish were more virtuous and Ireland more deserving to be the seat of the church.

In combat with their Italian counterparts, Irish gangs proved to be hardy, occasionally murderous, wielding bricks and stones in street combat. In addition to their Irish enemies, the Italian gangs faced constant, bloody internecine rivalry—much of it based on the Italian origins of the gang members, in other words, a continuation of *campanilismo*. The two main factions were the Sicilians, who were fairly visible and congregated in Manhattan, and the Neapolitans, who were more obscure, though more numerous, and resided mainly in Brooklyn.

Among the best-known gangs of Capone's youth were the Red Hook Rippers, the Garfield Boys, and the Gowanus Dukes. Over the years, one gang would spawn another; rival factions would battle over turf. In a world that had rejected them, immigrant children like Al Capone found a refuge in the gangs, a fleeting sense of identity, of belonging. In school, they were nothing, at home they were nuisances, but on the streets they could find other models to emulate, to act out their rage and frustration, to reflect the world's hate back on itself. Too old to run with the Navy Street Boys, Capone now owed allegiance to the South Brooklyn Rippers, a ragtag collection of boys ranging in age from twelve to fifteen. They spent most of the time simply loitering; occasionally they resorted to petty vandalism or theft, but they were too green to be genuinely feared. Capone eventually moved on to another local gang, one consciously modeled on Kelly's outfit, known as the Five Points Juniors. They served as an auxiliary to their adult counterparts, but its members, mainly boys playing hookey, were not necessarily apprentice gangsters, and they drifted away from the group as casually as they had joined it.

·   ·   ·

Despite his flirtation with juvenile gangs, his expulsion from school, and his apprenticeship to Johnny Torrio, Al Capone still aspired to a legitimate career; he gave little indication of consciously preparing himself to be a racketeer. Many boys his age, and with his lack of prospects, were already out of the house, but he continued to live at home. Life in the Capone family continued to evolve, to creep upward. Gabriele progressed from renting his barbershop at 69 Park Avenue to owning it; he had a stake in America now, however small. Teresa continued to bear children. In 1901, she gave birth to still another boy, Erminio, or Mimi, as he was known in the family; later, he would go by the name of John. 1906 saw the birth of another boy, Umberto, who later went by the name of Albert or "Bites." Two years later, Amedoe, later called Matthew, or Matt, or Mattie, was born. Finally, in 1910, into this world of boys came the first female Capone to be born in America. She was named Rose. As if an angry God insisted that there should be no Capone girl, the child died before the year's end.

Two years later, on January 28, 1912 (ten days after Al's thirteenth birthday), Teresa Capone finally gave birth to a daughter who survived. As a symbol of their overflowing gratitude, her parents bestowed an extravagant name on her, Mafalda, after an Italian princess. The youngest child in the family, the only girl, with no less than seven older brothers to look out for her, Mafalda grew up in an atmosphere of indulgence. In fact, compared to her brothers' rude upbringing, she was downright spoiled, and the preferential treatment she always received affected her temperament. The Capone boys, Al included, were generally quiet and respectful toward their parents, especially their mother, but Mafalda's tongue could sting; she lashed out at anyone who crossed her. Thin and high-strung, Mafalda was, within the family circle, the most vituperative and ferocious Capone of all.

· · ·

By the time Mafalda was born, the eldest Capone boy, Vincenzo (James), had abandoned the family. Always strong-minded, he could no longer stand the confinement of Brooklyn, the monotony, and the lack of prospects. In 1908, at the age of sixteen, he ran away from home—not for a week or a month, but for good. A year after his disappearance, his family received a letter from James, postmarked Wichita, Kansas. He was fine, he told them; they needn't worry about him. They read to their amazement that he was traveling around the Midwest—which the Capones of Garfield Place could only imagine as a plain populated with Indians and buffalo and no Italians whatsoever—and that he had joined a circus as a roustabout and wrestler.

Hardy and muscular, James enjoyed living out of doors, rambling from town to town, seeing America: big cities like Omaha, little one-horse towns, whistle-stops, open spaces. He did his best to disguise his New York accent, and in time he came to sound like a midwesterner himself. Although he looked as Italian as his younger brothers, he never revealed his origins, never spoke of Brooklyn or Naples. He passed as a Mexican, or an Indian, or a combination of the two. He became fascinated with guns, which were readily available at the circus, and he spent hours shooting at beer bottles and empty cans with a .32-caliber pistol.

Indians especially fascinated James; he admired their physical prowess and their ability to coexist with nature. He spent time on the fringes of Indian reservations, and he gambled with Indians when they came to the circus. Perhaps, as an Italian immigrant, he was drawn to them because he shared their alien status; he knew what it meant to be an outsider in the white man's world, to be discriminated against, treated as a second-class citizen, and shunted onto a reservation. What was the Gowanus section of Brooklyn if not a reservation for Italian immigrants and other second-class citizens?

During the years of James's wandering, the Great War in Europe slowly engulfed the United States. In April 1917 the United States declared war, and James, still entranced with guns, enlisted in the infantry and went to

France with the American Expeditionary Force. He was the only Capone to enter the armed forces. (In later years, imaginative journalists would claim that Al had seen action in France, where he received his famous scars, but there was no truth to the story.) An able soldier, James perfected his shooting ability and rose to the rank of lieutenant. In France, he received a sharp-shooting medal from the commander of the American Expeditionary Force, General John J. Pershing. A photograph taken of the event shows Lieutenant Capone, standing in a field of mud, saluting, taut, his chest ready to receive the medal from the general's gloved hand. All the while, the Capone family knew nothing of his whereabouts. Nearly two decades passed before they heard from him again.

•   •   •

After James fled, the Capone family looked to the next child, Ralph, to lead the way. Taller, more reserved, and nowhere near as keen as his younger brothers (to say nothing of that spitfire, Mafalda), Ralph followed a far more conventional path, and for many years his younger brother Al followed faithfully behind him. Reliable Ralph quit school at the end of sixth grade, not in a burst of fury as Al had, but simply because it was time for him to go to work and augment the family's income. He found a job as a messenger boy for the giant Postal Telegraph company, delivering telegrams, hustling for tips. Later, he went to work in a nearby book bindery, a position that paid better. At least he was out in the world, employed, and he had, in a modest way, surpassed his father.

At about this time, his prison records reveal, Ralph acquired gonorrhea. This was not a surprising development, given the proximity of prostitutes in the neighborhood, but his condition healed and left no long-term effects on his health. It should be noted that Ralph's interest in women was not con-fined to prostitutes. On October 20, 1915, he became the first of the Capone boys to marry. He was twenty-one, and his wife, Filomena Marie Carmelo Moscato, usually called Florence, was just seventeen years old. Like him, she had been born in Italy, in her case Salerno. They were married in Brooklyn, and two years later they had their first child, a son, whom they named Ralph Jr.

Theirs was not a happy home. Ralph and Florence quarreled constantly, and the arrival of their child, rather than cementing their relationship, aggravated the strains that had existed before his birth. According to Ralph, Florence dishonored the name of motherhood; she neglected both him and the child; one day he came home from work to discover that she had left Ralph Jr. with the neighbors and had run off. Only in America. The es-tranged couple never reunited and eventually divorced. Throughout these years of domestic strife, Ralph functioned as the dutiful breadwinner. He sold life insurance for a year or two, developing an easy manner with his customers, and then he moved on to a clerical job at a street car company. More significantly, he also handled a soft drink route on the side, and everyone began calling him "Bottles." The nickname followed him throughout life as if it were a prophecy: "Bottles" Capone.

Al gave every appearance of trudging along in Ralph's footsteps: responsible if unspectacular clerical jobs, early marriage, and a child. He passed approximately three years working in a Brooklyn munitions factory and another three as a paper cutter. The latter meant mind-numbing, repetitive work, and the pay was equally humiliating, only $3 a week, all of which he dutifully brought home to his mother. That Al was able to hold these jobs as long as he did and to turn the money over to his family demonstrates his tenacity and loyalty, as well as his lack of direction. He remained—and was long remembered—around his neighborhood as likable and well-behaved, not especially prone to violence or other forms of antisocial behavior. A nice boy in tough surroundings. You didn't hear stories about Al Capone practicing with guns; you heard that he went home each night to his mother.

There was another side to the adolescent Capone: he loved to have fun. To dress well, to get out, to enjoy himself, to show off. Al loved to dance, and he was renowned as the best pool player in the neighborhood, a local champion with the cue. These activities suggested that he was gregarious and socially adept and that he possessed a highly developed sense of fine motor coordination—not exactly the characteristics associated with youthful hoodlums. At about this time he came to the attention of another Brooklynite, Daniel Fuchs, one of the first novelists to depict Jewish immigrant life in America. Fuchs was astonished by the bloody reputation Al later acquired, for the writer, known for his unsparing portrayals of Brooklyn life, recalled Capone as a peaceful lad, well dressed and well mannered, hardly the typical neighborhood thug. Al was, in contrast, "something of a nonentity, affable, soft of speech and even mediocre in everything but dancing. Capone, always a well-dressed individual, was like many other Italians an excellent dancer. He frequented a hall called the Broadway Casino." An early friend of Capone, a reporter named Edward Dean Sullivan, seconded this impression of Al as a harmless young man. "Let me say that in my capacity as a newspaper man, I have known twenty men infinitely more vicious than he is," he wrote. "He never drank and the one outstanding trait known about him, in the tough circles where his skill with a cue won him some attention, was that he must be home every night at ten-thirty." Such disarming testimonials failed to tell the entire story, though, for Capone also frequented a far more sinister gathering place than the Broadway Casino; it was called the Adonis Social Club, and it was a magnet for violence. Gunfights had a way of erupting unpredictably at the Adonis, sending its young patrons, who were largely

Italian, scrambling to the floor and out the door. In the basement, guests could take target practice if they liked, blasting beer bottles to smithereens. It was here that Capone learned how to handle a revolver.

• • •

Like his brother Ralph, Al also became familiar with the local prostitutes, and he probably contracted syphilis from them at this time. Throughout his life, Al refused to admit precisely how or when he caught the disease that would shape his future. In his later years, when he was undergoing treatment for syphilis in Baltimore, Maryland, he did reveal to his physicians that he was infected early in his life, *very* early, in fact, which suggests that he contracted the disease not long after he became sexually active. That Al acquired syphilis at such a young age was not evidence of promiscuity, however, since there is a 75-percent chance that engaging in sexual inter-course with an infected partner will lead to transmission of the disease. In other words, just one visit to a contaminated prostitute, the result of a dare or a spur-of-the-moment decision, would have sufficed to give him the disease. At the time, syphilis ran unchecked through the population, but not until the draft of the Great War would public health officials realize how widespread it was; blood tests revealed that approximately 10 percent of the draftees suffered from venereal disease. Estimates of syphilis in the general population of the United States varied greatly, but usually ran from 6 to 10 percent. Millions of Americans suffered from the disease at the time Al contracted it, and tens of thousands were dying of it each year.

Despite its devastating effects, venereal disease remained a secret plague, rarely spoken of, yet it had been devastating populations at least since the fifteenth century. Its origins are traced, interestingly enough, to the city the Capones fled: Naples. It went by several names, depending on who did the naming. The Italians called it the French disease, *morbus Gallicus*, and the French reciprocated by naming it the *mal Napolitain*, the Neapolitan disease. In this way the ancient scourge followed the Capone family all the way from Naples to Brooklyn. The malady acquired the name by which we know it in 1530, when an Italian poet, Girolamo Fracastoro, wrote a poem in Latin in which his hero, a shepherd named Syphilis, insults the god Apollo, who in turn afflicts his genitals with the disease; thus was the name of this fictitious character immortalized in a way his creator could never have imagined.

Because of its varied and exotic presentations, syphilis had long fascinated physicians, though they were powerless to cure it. A great mimic of other physical and mental ailments, it was considered the prince of clinical dis-eases. "Know syphilis in all its manifestations and relations and all other things clinical will be added unto you," declared Sir William Osler, an eminent physician and teacher. What was known about syphilis was that it is caused by a spirochete, a screwlike organism, usually transmitted by genital contact. In its first, most obvious, and least harmful stage, a boil or open sore, teeming with spirochetes, appears on the genitalia; if left untreated, it usually disappears within one to three weeks. The secondary stage is often more difficult to detect because the symptoms mimic the flu: a sore throat, a rash, enlarged lymph nodes. That, too, heals by itself, so it is entirely possible for the sufferer to think he has had a bad cold rather than a sexually transmitted disease. Syphilis then enters a latent stage, free of symptoms, and the final, or tertiary stage does not begin for another two to *twenty* years. It is rarely fatal in the first or even the second stage; only if it returns for the dreaded third (or tertiary) stage can the disease kill, and then in only 20 percent of the cases.

Although he had no way of knowing it, Al belonged to that unlucky 20 percent of syphilis victims. Once his sore and his fever disappeared, he believed he had recovered from his illness, as most people did. As he later told his physicians in Baltimore, the disease simply vanished, and he assumed he had been cured somehow. He had no way of knowing that it had actually gone underground, gradually becoming a form of dementia, similar to Alzheimer's disease; slowly but surely the victim loses his mind. In his case, the disease typically attacks the frontal lobes of the brain, the seat of the personality, and within a short time it begins to alter the victim's behavior. The changes are so subtle as to be undetectable at first. The new, altered personality is closely modeled on the old; it is an exaggeration of it. Dr. Bernhard Dattner, an outstanding syphilologist, described the transformation this way: "Frequently the initial personality changes are so insidious that even close friends of the patient remain unaware of them. How much more difficult it is for the physician to detect these minimal signs of psychic aberration if he has never before seen the patient." The array of symptoms Dr. Dattner observed included "irritability, nervousness, lack of initiative, insomnia, and memory impairment." So it was with Al Capone. Those closest to him and most familiar with his behavior were the least likely to recognize the incremental changes wrought by the disease. Generally affable, he could, on rare occasions, lash out at those who threatened him. As the neurosyphilis slowly took over his brain, however, his mood swings, which had previously been within normal limits, became more extreme. He would act moody and remote, then exuberant. More genial, then more enraged. More passive and withdrawn, then more hostile.

If Capone's syphilis had healed itself, as most cases did, it is unlikely he would have developed into the high-profile, feared gangster he became. It is entirely possible he would have drifted into the rackets under Johnny Torrio's guidance. But of course his syphilis never did vanish, and the special swagger and vehemence associated with Al Capone—the sudden outbursts of violence, as well as his reckless gambling—were the result of his incurable disease. Indeed, tertiary syphilis is usually associated with megalomania; the young Al, quiet and withdrawn, showed little of those tendencies, but the mature Al, with his hallucinations of grandeur and his penchant for brutality, certainly did. The Capone we remember was the creation of a disease that had magnified his personality. Syphilis made Al Capone larger than life.

An early instance of Capone's rage suddenly spewing forth occurred one night when, as he attended a local political rally, a pool-playing pal of his informed him that a "slicker had stopped in . . . and had cleaned out the best of the talent for about eight hundred dollars." According to Capone's friend Edward Dean Sullivan, "Al hurried over to the pool room and at half past ten he had the eight hundred dollars back and a hundred and fifty of the stranger's money. . . . Without a word the stranger reached in his pockets, opened a long bladed knife, and told Al that he'd play another game, or else—!" Capone hit his adversary just once, but the blow was so powerful that it knocked the man out. Capone returned home, always mindful of the 10:30 curfew, but later that evening he heard the man in the poolroom was dead— and that he had killed him. As Al later learned, the report was wrong, and the man survived, but the single blow had done sufficient harm to send him to the hospital for months.

Sullivan's story gave rise to one of the first legends surrounding Capone, that the poolroom confrontation sparked his flight from Brooklyn to Chicago to avoid a murder charge. In fact, when the time finally did arrive for Capone to leave Brooklyn, he would be a young married businessman looking for better career prospects, not a teenage gangster fleeing a murder rap. But the persistent legend demonstrated that an aura of violence—whether deserved or not—clung to Capone from an early age. Try as he did to avoid it, brutality, like syphilis, was fated to follow him through all his days.

•   •   •

Al Capone's first encounter with violence as a tool of business came through his mentor, Johnny Torrio, who, though a peace-loving man himself, knew intimately the uses of force, bribery, and fear. He introduced young Al to influential friends on Coney Island, where the flesh and the flash were to be found. The resort and amusement area was a considerable distance from Capone's home and the headquarters of the Torrio Association, all the way at the other end of Brooklyn. There Al met and came to work for Brooklyn's own Prince of Darkness, Frankie Yale.

Alternately killer and benefactor, he elicited wild and contradictory passions in Brooklyn, but on one point, at least, there was universal agreement: nobody defied Frankie Yale. He was only six years older than Capone, still in his midtwenties, but already famous and feared. He drew stares wherever he went, for everyone recognized the shock of black hair, the pug nose, and the burning black eyes. He was handsome in a menacing sort of way, compact and muscular. The stories about him were impressive; to hear people talk, Yale had killed eight, ten, maybe a dozen men—or more.

Yale was not his real name, of course; that was an affectation. Nor did he originally spell it "Uale," as is often claimed and as it appears on his tombstone. His original name was Francesco Ioele. Nor did he belong to the Mafia, which was an almost exclusively Sicilian preserve. He was born in Calabria, one of the poorest of all Southern Italian provinces, in 1893, and he came to the United States as a child, the first of the influential Calabrians with whom Capone associated. Because of *campanilismo*, it was unusual for Neapolitans like Capone to form alliances with rural Calabrians, who tended to be more suspicious and pragmatic than their urban counterparts. In the years to come, however, Capone would surround himself with Calabrians, who proved dutiful and respectful once he was able to win their trust.

Yale spent his adolescent years in the Five Point Juniors, constantly getting into scrapes. At seventeen, he teamed up with a wrestler by the name of "Booby" Nelson to wreak havoc in a poolroom on Surf Avenue; his victims discovered what a horrendous weapon a cue could be. The melee led to his first jail sentence, and shortly after his release, he was sent to jail again, this time for toting a pistol. More arrests ensued, including a charge of theft of sheep- and goatskins worth $300. Marriage finally accomplished what the courts had been unable to do; it took him off the street and transformed him from a thug into a businessman. He lived the life of a local big shot, ensconced in a large and gloomy brick home at 6605 14th Avenue, owned by his in-laws. The address doubled as his place of business; the legitimate career he pursued was dreadfully appropriate, for Frankie Yale became an undertaker.

He also developed many sidelines. There was the ice route, for one. Ice was a necessity in the days before refrigeration, and icemen, usually from an Italian background, operated strictly as freelancers. The competition among them kept prices and profits low. Once Frankie Yale moved in and organized them, the icemen served assigned districts, for which they paid him a handsome tribute. Prices went up, and so did the profits. Essentially Yale imposed a series of local monopolies, strictly enforced. If you were an Italian iceman, and you bought your supply of ice from Frankie Yale's company and paid him his cut, you had no problem. His collectors' cars announced themselves with horns trilling a distinctive note, and the icemen trotted out to hand over the money, discreetly contained in an envelope. If you bought your ice somewhere else, you received a warning or a broken window in the night, or your child came home from school describing an encounter with a threatening stranger. Frankie understood that it was human nature to make a mistake now and then. If you persisted, however, Frankie shut you down. No one went to the cops, because Frankie had paid them off.

Then there was the laundry business, another profitable sideline in which he displayed his golden touch. To prevent unions from attempting to infiltrate their business, the owners of laundry establishments paid Yale $150 a week to scare off organizers. He exploited the situation by establishing his own union, and he forced workers to contribute a dollar a week out of their modest salaries toward it or face immediate firing, a beating, or worse. Yale's union did nothing to protect or advance the workers' cause, as a legitimate union did; it was a means of exacting tribute from laundry workers. Even cigars became a racket for Yale. He launched a brand featuring his portrait on the box, and the cigars sold for twenty cents, or three for fifty. As with the ice, tobacco shops had better stock them, or harm could come their way. Windows could be broken; necks, too. Brooklyn merchants found that in the long run it was better for business to stock the stinking Frankie Yales, as the cigars were known.

Frankie fancied himself an entrepreneur, and his most ambitious venture—the one that lured Capone into his orbit—was a Coney Island bar and dance hall situated close to the Atlantic Ocean. Established in 1916 with the proceeds of the ice racket, it was modeled on the thriving College Inn, and Yale decided to have a little fun by naming his pleasure dome after a university; thus Yale came to be the proprietor of the Harvard Inn. The Ivy League aura immediately went to his head; he began to part his hair in the center, after the fashion of students. The center part soon led to bigger changes, a flashier wardrobe, brightly colored fabrics, all in the height of gangster fashion, accented with eye-popping jewelry, especially his famous diamond-studded belt buckle. When people asked what the buckle represented, Yale replied with a laugh that it stood for the Championship of the Underworld. His new position meant that he spent many late nights away from his wife, Maria, and their two girls; inevitably, he sought out female friends around Coney Island, choosing from a large transient population of willing and desperate girls. Yale knew how hotheaded their boyfriends could be, and displaying the same cool judgment he brought to his business ventures, he always brought a bodyguard to stand watch during his brief assignations. When the girls became pregnant, Frankie had a solution for that, as well; he found nice young men for them to marry—men who happened to work for him and would not complain if their new brides happened to be pregnant or who assumed that they themselves had fathered the child. Whatever the problem was, the resourceful Frankie Yale had a solution.

Despite its grand name, the Harvard Inn occupied a modest one-story building located on a popular thoroughfare, Seaside Walk. The most imposing feature was the bar, which ran twenty feet, almost the entire length of one wall. There was also room for an orchestra and a small dance floor. Yale loved running the tawdry little place. Every night he sat at his table, whose location was carefully chosen, a little off to the side, near the exit, in case he needed to make a speedy egress. His constant companion was "Little Augie" Carfano, another tough from the Gowanus area. There Yale nursed his tumbler of whiskey and transacted business. Searching for a young man who could double as a bouncer and bartender, capable of combining a winning manner with the threat of force, Yale turned to Torrio for a recommendation, and Torrio sent him Al Capone, who was now eighteen.

Capone and Yale struck up a rapport, and the young man became a fixture there, doing everything from washing dishes to waiting on tables under the proprietor's eye. He made himself a popular figure; the customers paid their respects to Frankie and shied away from "Little Augie," but they liked Al, the jolly way he served up the foamy beer at the bar and occasionally took a turn on the dance floor himself. It was not exalted work, but the job kept him busy and on display. There was plenty of opportunity to mingle with the customers, too.

One night, after he had been at the Harvard Inn for a year, Capone was waiting on a table occupied by a couple about his age. Al could not take his eyes off the girl. She was Italian, and she had a gorgeous figure. He repeatedly buzzed the table, and finally, with the impulsiveness of his age, he leaned over to her and said in a loud voice, "Honey, you have a nice ass, and I mean that as a compliment." Suddenly, the man who accompanied her leaped to his feet. His name was Frank Gallucio, he was the girl's brother, and he was obviously drunk. Capone had just done the unforgivable: he had insulted Frank's sister. Gallucio was nowhere near as big or bulky as Capone, but emboldened by alcohol he punched the man who had insulted his sister. As he later recalled, "A punch was not enough to stop Capone."

Capone's unpredictable rage erupted. Fearing for his life, Gallucio pulled a four-inch knife from his pocket. The sight of the flashing metal sent patrons fleeing. Gallucio went straight for Capone's neck. Undeterred, Capone moved in, and the blade cut into the flesh of his left cheek and his neck, once, twice, three times. There was blood everywhere now, blood on the knife, blood all over Capone, blood on the floor. Terrified, Gallucio grabbed his sister and ran from the Harvard Inn. Capone's wounds looked awful, but the injuries healed cleanly, leaving three large scars: one ran four inches along his left cheek and another followed his left jaw for slightly more than two inches. The third was the least visible but marked the most dangerous injury he had sustained; it coursed down his neck beneath his left ear. As they healed, the scars turned from red to white, and over the years Capone would become increasingly sensitive about them, averting his head from cameras attempting to photograph his left side, refusing to answer questions about them, even resorting to powdering them in a vain attempt to make the pale grooves blend with his olive complexion. But for now, they were a badge of courage, showing that he was a street fighter, and as the years passed, the scars acquired increasing fame until they came to identify Capone in the public mind forever as "Scarface."

Intent on revenge, Al announced he was looking for Gallucio, and he made sure to invoke Frankie Yale's name. Capone's antagonist sought the assistance of a small-time hood named Albert Altierri, who in turn took the issue to a rising young racketeer in Manhattan by the name of Salvatore Lucania. Only two years older than Capone, Lucania had been born near Palermo, Sicily, and had arrived in the United States as a boy of nine, spending the remainder of his bleak youth on the Lower East Side of Manhattan, where he fell in with the Five Points gang. By the age of sixteen he had gotten himself arrested and jailed for running heroin. Later, when everyone called him Lucky Luciano, he would rival Capone in underworld influence and direct a vast racketeering empire, much bigger than anything Frankie Yale ever dreamed of, all run out of a luxurious suite in the Waldorf-Astoria Hotel, where he maintained a full-time residence under the alias "Charles Rose."

Hearing the story of the knife fight, Lucania sided with Gallucio; nobody should insult someone's sister as Capone had. To bring the matter to an end, Lucania proposed a sit-down, a formal gathering, at the Harvard Inn to discuss the issue thoroughly. The principals waited until after hours, after the drunken patrons and chorus girls had departed, and then Lucania, Gallucio, Yale, and Capone engaged in a serious discussion of the slashing and what should be done about it. The elders in their wisdom decided that Al should apologize to Gallucio for insulting his sister, and that would be the end of the matter. Should Al attempt to take revenge, it would be his funeral. No matter how much he disliked the outcome of the parley, Capone had no choice but to obey, for Lucania was already powerful and feared, while Al was still a nobody, a waiter at a Coney Island bar; he had to show respect. And Al did. As long as he controlled his temper, Al always knew what was expected of him and behaved accordingly.

From its bloody beginning to its peaceful conclusion, the entire incident had been an education for him; he had seen the power of the racketeers to intervene in daily affairs and to enforce peace, and he began to learn the potency of restraint. In the years to come, when he had ample opportunity and power, Capone always refrained from attempting to settle the score with Gallucio, who never amounted to anything more than a minor Brooklyn thug. Instead, Capone put him on his payroll as a $100-a-week errand-runner. Of course, if any harm had come to Gallucio, suspicion would immediately have fallen on Capone, so discretion in this instance proved the better part of valor.

The scarring incident, for all its symbolism, was essentially a youthful escapade, and more importantly, Capone managed to keep his job with Frankie Yale despite the uproar he had caused. However, his next violent encounter, less celebrated and far more vicious, became a milestone in his youthful career in crime. After the fight with Gallucio, Al learned to make himself useful to his boss, especially in the always ticklish matter of collections. In Brooklyn in those days, youthful hoodlums were addicted to practicing "the look": a deadly gaze designed to strike mortal fear into the hearts of their enemies. Done right, this Rasputin-like, mesmerizing gaze could be more effective than a blow to the chin, but it was not for amateurs. Trying to give "the look" with just the right degree of menace, it was easy to appear ridiculous rather than intimidating, so the young hoods practiced in their mirrors, often for hours at a time, until they got it right. Yale had the look, as did his bodyguard, "Little Augie" Carfano. Eventually Capone acquired the look, too, and he soon had an opportunity to employ it in the service of his boss.

In addition to his other interests, Yale bankrolled a number of dice games. He told Capone he was especially vexed by one character, Tony Perotta, who had broken a dice game and now owed Yale $1,500: a considerable amount of money in 1919. Perotta's position was especially vulnerable because he was in the United States illegally; if any harm came to him, the police would be unlikely to conduct a diligent investigation. Al knew Perotta slightly and agreed to collect the money.

Capone found Perotta, predictably enough, leaving another dice game. Confronting him in the hallway, Capone demanded payment. "No," said Perotta, "this isn't fair. We've known each other a long time, and now you're doing this to me?" Capone tried again to make Perotta pay, but not even throwing "the look" could make him change his mind. The incident quickly got out of hand, and before he knew what he had done, Al had shot the man. And Perotta died. When he next saw Capone, Yale, greatly displeased, demanded to know why the younger man had killed Perotta. "The guy complained," Al told him. "He had a big mouth. He deserved what he got." Yale stood back, beheld the young man willing to do a "piece of work" (the standard euphemism for murder), and embraced him. From then on, Frankie loved Al; he loved the man who would one day kill him, as well.

.   .   .

Al was nearing nineteen now; though he still lived at home on Garfield Place, he was in every way a man, except in the eyes of the law. Although he had encountered many women at Coney Island, he became deeply attached to a girl who lived right on Garfield Place, in a house nearly within sight of his. Her name was Domenica, but everyone called her Susie. Only thirteen years old, she had already acquired a reputation around the neighborhood for wildness, and Al soon caught the fancy of this impulsive young creature. Her extreme youth posed no obstacle to him, and they were so often in one another's company, and seen together so frequently, that marriage and children, in no particular order, seemed the inevitable outcome of the romance. But at this crucial moment the relationship ran into trouble. Either Al or his parents began formal matrimonial negotiations with Susie's family, only to learn that the girl's parents were utterly opposed to the match. They insisted their daughter was too young to marry, they wanted no part of hoodlums or racketeers, and they did not consider Al Capone a fit husband for their daughter. The romance ended, and Susie, the wild one, went on to marry another Italian youth, who, as it happened, also had connections to the rackets.

To avoid the stigma he had acquired among the law-abiding inhabitants of Garfield Place, Al began to look further afield for a mate. He passed the time at a club located in a basement on Carroll Street—a small place where Irish and Italians could be found. It was here that Al met a young woman to whom, despite everything to come, despite the other women, the violence, the lengthy jail sentences, despite all that, he would always remain devoted. Her name was Mary Coughlin. She was a saleslady in a department store, slender and pretty, and on the strength of these qualifications she became his Madonna. Everyone called her Mae.

Mae was different from the other girls Al had known; she was older than he, not a child but an adult. She was Irish. And her family was more prosperous than the Capones. Though she lived just a brief stroll from Garfield Place and the dank stretches of the Gowanus Canal, she came from another culture, the world of middle-class respectability. At the time Mae and Al met, the Coughlins resided at 117 Third Place, where they occupied a pleasant, substantial row house, three stories tall, with a traditional Brooklyn stoop. The street was broad and lined with trees, in all respects a respectable middle-class Irish enclave. Like her new swain, she was the product of immigrant parents, but hers had fared rather better in America than the Capones. Her mother, Bridget Gorman, was born in December 1873 and emigrated to the United States at age nineteen, and her father, Mike Coughlin, had been born in November 1872 and came to the United States in 1891. He soon found employment with the Erie Railroad, for which he worked as a clerk. Although they had both been born in Ireland, Mae's parents probably met after they came to New York. Before marriage they lived not in Brooklyn but in southern Manhattan (in what is now called SoHo), Michael on Grand Street and Bridget on West Houston. On January

28, 1894, they were married at a nearby church, St. Anthony of Padua, which describes itself as the oldest Italian Catholic church in the archdiocese of New York. As such it was an unusual choice for the wedding of these two young Irish immigrants, but since they lived on the border of Little Italy, St. Anthony was a sensible location. They subsequently moved to Brooklyn, living first at 6 Manhasset Place, and finally on shady, serene Third Place, far from the crowding and corruption of Manhattan. At the time Mae met Capone, the Coughlin family included her parents, two older sisters named Winnie Mae and Muriel, and a younger brother, Dennis, known to everyone as Danny.

There is no record that Mae's parents objected to her relationship with Al, or were aware of his gangland connections, but it is likely that they viewed their daughter's alliance with skepticism, at best. The Coughlins were known as decent and law-abiding folk; there was no taint of gang activity or racketeering about them. Neither they nor their daughter Mae had anything to do with the likes of Frankie Yale, or his Irish equivalents, the so-called "White Hand" gangsters like "Peg-Leg" Lonergan or "Wild Bill" Lovett, who ruled the Brooklyn waterfront. At the same time, the Coughlins' address bordered an Italian neighborhood, so it was not uncommon for their children to become familiar with Italians, despite the antagonism between the two immigrant groups, but romance and courtship were another matter entirely. Believing that Italian husbands routinely beat, cheated on, and degraded their wives, many an Irish father declared that he did not want his daughter marrying an Italian; she must marry a *white* man. In this climate of prejudice, the Coughlins could only have regarded their daughter Mae's relationship with Capone with trepidation. By the standards of the day, theirs was virtually an interracial romance. However, young Italian men of Al's background viewed matters differently, as did some Irish girls. For the Italians, taking an Irish wife meant marrying up the social scale; furthermore, they considered daughters of Hibernia to be sufficiently pious and submissive to make good, devoted, patient wives. They would concentrate on their churches and children and stay out of their husbands' affairs. Capone's mentor, Johnny Torrio, for instance, was married to an Irish girl from Kentucky, and she was devoted to her husband, his interests in vice and racketeering notwithstanding. Italian men in pursuit of Irish mates were also aided by the reluctance of their Irish counterparts to marry at a young age. The Irish male typically waited until the age of thirty before assuming the burden of maintaining a home, while Italians of Capone's background frequently wed before they reached twenty.

Although Al was only nineteen when they met, Mae was fully two years older, a disparity she went to considerable lengths to obscure throughout her life. With Mae leading the way, the romance progressed quickly; by April she was pregnant with Al's baby. She would not have known about his bout with syphilis unless he chose to tell her, and even if he did confide, he assumed he was now healed and the episode over. However, the latent syphilis would eventually have serious consequences for the entire Capone family.

Although Mae was pregnant, the couple did not wed immediately. For immigrant Catholic families, this was an unusual situation, and it suggests that there were great tensions in the relationship at this juncture. It is possible that Al and Mae would never have married, were it not for one external factor: the draft. On September 12, 1918, when Mae was seven months pregnant, Al went down to his local draft board, located between Fourth and Fifth Streets on Seventh Avenue in Brooklyn, and registered with the Selective Service System. This was an action he had been required to take earlier, but he had failed to do so. At the time of his registration, the clerk, Dorothy Wasserman, noted that Alphonse Capone was five feet seven inches, of medium build, with "gray" eyes, and "dark brown" hair. He gave his present occupation as a "paper cutter" at the United Paper Box Company in Brooklyn, and listed his mother, "Theresa Capone," as his nearest relative. (A registration card for one "Alfonso Capone," born in Montella Avellino, Italy, in 1896, living in Atlantic City, New Jersey, and working as a butcher, has been widely reproduced and described as the registration card for Al Capone of Brooklyn. It is, of course, nothing of the sort.) Once Capone had registered with the Selective Service System, he was vulnerable to being sent into combat overseas along with hundreds of thousands of other American boys. However, if Al were married, with a child to support, the likelihood of his being drafted declined. Thus his marrying Mae would, at one stroke, help him avoid the draft and resolve his domestic problems. More than ever, circumstances dictated the path he would follow in life.

From then on events moved forward swiftly, the milestones crowding one another. On December 4, 1918, Mae gave birth to a baby boy, whom they named Albert Francis Capone. He was universally known as Sonny, and his godfather was the man who was virtually a father to Al, Johnny Torrio. That Torrio was willing to stand as godfather suggests that he had counseled Capone through the entire ordeal of courtship and pregnancy.

Sonny was apparently healthy at birth, but as he grew older it became apparent that he was sickly, with a tendency to catch persistent infections. As time went on, he also became hard of hearing. That unusual symptom suggested that Al had transmitted his syphilis to Mae, who in turn transmitted congenital syphilis to their child. At the time of Sonny's birth, the disease was a leading cause of deafness in children. "When deafness occurs in the congenital syphilitic," stated a respected medical textbook of the era, "it should be regarded as syphilitic in origin until proved otherwise." Even though Sonny's deafness did not appear until well after his birth, there was still a high likelihood that congenital syphilis was the cause, for its effects are often delayed for years, with the most common cases in males appearing between the ages of eight and fifteen: precisely Sonny's situation. In addition to deafness, syphilis causes stillbirths and miscarriages. Both Al and Mae came from large families, and it would have been natural for them to have a large brood of their own, but Sonny remained an only child. This raises the suspicion that latent syphilis made it impossible for Mae to carry another child to term, and neither she nor her husband would have known the real reason why this was the case. So it was that the elusive disease continued to exert an invisible but decisive influence on the Capone family. It had already disabled their boy and shortchanged them of their chance to spawn a large family, and its most serious consequences were yet to come.

Al was a father, but not yet a husband. When the couple belatedly applied for permission to wed, they misrepresented their ages, even though the marriage license they signed was a sworn affidavit. On this document, they both gave their ages as twenty, when in reality Al was still nineteen and Mae twenty-one. As his occupation he furnished not "bartender" but the more respectable-sounding "paper cutter." Further embarrassments awaited the young couple. At the time, the law specified that a man came of age at twenty-one; thus Al, who was legally a minor, had to obtain his parents' consent to marry. The law of the day also specified that a *woman* came of age at eighteen, so Mae was spared the humiliation of having to ask her parents' permission to join the father of her newborn child in holy matrimony. If she had, they might well have refused her request.

Finally, there was the matter of syphilis. Had the couple been required to take a blood test, it would have revealed Al's condition, but they circumvented that obstacle. In lieu of a test, their marriage license contained the statement "I have not to my knowledge been infected with any venereal disease, or if I have been infected within five years I have a laboratory test . . . which shows that I am now free from infection." They were not required to respond to these precautions specifically; it was simply a declaration, not a question requiring an answer. Thus the disease continued to elude detection.

Having negotiated the intricacies of the law and shaded the truth according to their whims, Al and Mae wed as soon as the bride was physically able, following the birth of their child. On December 30, when Sonny was just three and a half weeks old, the ceremony took place at the Coughlins' splendid church, St. Mary Star of the Sea, hard by the Brooklyn docks. The church was distinguished by its impressively long transept and its soaring bell tower, which afforded a view across the length and breadth of Brooklyn. It was because of splendid buildings such as this that Brooklyn had acquired its nickname, sentimental but accurate, as "the Borough of Churches."

The Reverend James J. Delaney presided at the nuptials, and Mae's sister Winnie Mae acted as a witness and probably as a bridesmaid as well, but this could not have been a joyful wedding, despite the grand surroundings, not with the parents of the bride predisposed to dislike the bridegroom, and the couple having recently become parents themselves. Still, the ceremony was far removed from the floozies at the Harvard Inn and, for Al, it constituted a giant step toward respectability. Suddenly he had direction in life. Mae certainly exerted a more wholesome feminine influence than the Sands Street whores of his youth had. For the rest of their married life, Mae always represented virtue, conventional morality, and rectitude to Al; her existence legitimized all his ventures, however nefarious and immoral. She was the family member who dutifully attended Mass, and, following the example of Johnny Torrio's Irish wife, remained wholly, willfully ignorant of her husband's business life. Pale, bland, compliant, soft, and silent. Virtue on a pedestal towering over him. Otherworldly. A household goddess. That was just the way Al wanted his wife, but Mae's isolation could only have made for a stultifying domestic life. His constant lip service to the conventional pieties of hearth and home lacked true spontaneity and warmth. By marrying Mae, Al both obeyed and disobeyed his ingrained sense of *campanilismo*. True, she came from the neighborhood and had spent her childhood only blocks from Garfield Place, but she was *Irish*. Mae, for her part, found herself cut off from her family. She had married into the Capone clan rather than the other way around, and she would have to learn to acquiesce to her rather formidable mother-in-law, Teresa, and to acquire the rudiments of the Italian cooking her husband favored. Language posed a more serious barrier, for at home the Capones still spoke Italian in a guttural Neapolitan accent, and Mae often found herself unable to understand her in-laws, whom she thought enjoyed a secret rapport with one another that she would never be able to share. She remained an outsider.

· · ·

Now that he was married, with a wife and child to support, Capone veered toward a legitimate career once again. He gave every appearance of having put his youthful gang experiences behind him and of wanting to return to a quiet, respectable occupation. He quit working for Frankie Yale, and more importantly, he decided the time had come for him to leave Brooklyn, to remove himself and his new family from the gangs, the dangers, and the temptations of his former life.

It is generally assumed that he made a seamless transition from the underworld of Brooklyn to the underworld of Chicago at this juncture, but, in fact, when Capone left home, he went first to Baltimore, where he worked not as a hit man, racketeer, bartender, or pimp, but as a bookkeeper for a legitimate construction firm run by Peter Aiello, who also headed a building and loan organization. Capone's position was purely clerical. Each morning, soberly attired in a suit and tie, Al went to the Aiello offices in the Highland Town section of Baltimore.

It seemed he had put the rackets and the gaudy Brooklyn street life behind him for once and all. He made himself into a valued worker at the Aiello construction firm, displaying a good head for figures and for business in general. He became familiar with accounting procedures and learned to read a balance sheet: essential skills on which he would capitalize throughout his life. "Evidently he was a good employee, and evidently my father liked him," says Peter Aiello's son, Mike. Capone apparently enjoyed the prospect of a secure, respectable future with Aiello Construction.

As Al began to get his life on a secure footing, with a wife, a child, and a reputable career away from the corrupting influences of Brooklyn, his father's health began to decline. He stopped going to the barber shop each morning and, now that his children were getting older and leaving home, eased into retirement. At the beginning of 1920, the census taker came calling and found that the Capone household at 38 Garfield Place had shrunken to just six: Gabriele; his wife, Teresa; their three sons (Erminio, now seventeen and working as a "candymaker," Albert, fourteen and still in school, and Amedoe, eleven); and the lone Capone daughter, Mafalda, who was a schoolchild of eight.

On the morning of November 14, 1920, Gabriele went, as he often did, to a poolroom at 20 Garfield Place, across the street from his home. There he collapsed without warning and died of a heart attack. He was fifty-five years old. A doctor named W. E. Martin took charge of the body at the Capone home at 38 Garfield Place and determined Gabriele Capone had died of "chronic myocarditis," or heart disease. He was buried three days later at Calvary Cemetery in the borough of Queens; Al returned to New York to attend the funeral, as did the entire family, with the exception of Vincenzo, the oldest child, who had ceased to communicate with the family. Emigrating to America had been the great adventure of Gabriele's life; beyond that, he had little to show for all his years of work, but he had left a bounteous legacy in the form of his large family; he was survived by his widow, eight children, plus two grandchildren (from Al and Ralph) about which the family knew and others (from Vincenzo) of whose existence they were ignorant.

The death of Gabriele marked the end of Al's legitimate career. It is possible that the sudden absence of parental authority made the young Capone feel free to abandon his bookkeeping job and his carefully acquired aura of respectability. In any event, he resumed his relationship with Johnny Torrio, who had during the intervening years expanded his racketeering empire with the quiet cunning of a visionary. Torrio had abandoned the hotly contested streets of Brooklyn for the comparatively open spaces of Chicago, where he now worked for the prodigal vice lord there, "Big Jim" Colosimo. The opportunities were enormous: gambling, brothels, and, with the advent of Prohibition, an entirely new profit center based on illegal alcohol. Torrio persuaded Capone that he could make much more money working in the Chicago rackets than he ever could in a legitimate field of endeavor. Capone accepted the offer, for wherever Johnny Torrio went, Al was sure to follow, with his family, his newly acquired bookkeeping skills, his latent syphilis, and his scars.

Torrio's recruitment of Capone was shrewd, for Al had served a dual apprenticeship, learning street crime with Frankie Yale and bookkeeping with Aiello Construction. Now he would be able to combine these experiences in Torrio's new organization, putting his skill with numbers to darker and more lucrative use than he had in Baltimore.

Al's career move had consequences for the entire Capone family. With *campanilismo* still a fact of life, everyone from his widowed mother, Teresa, to his little sister, Mafalda, was poised to follow his lead. His acceptance of Torrio's offer was a bold move for Al, the biggest he had taken in his twenty-one years. With it, he vaulted over his older brothers to assume the leadership of the family, and from this time forth his mother, his brothers, and his sister all pinned their hopes of prosperity in America on him and his relationship with Johnny Torrio.

At the beginning of 1921, the rising young bookkeeper gave notice to his boss. Peter Aiello was surprised and sorry to lose the capable young man, whom he genuinely liked and wished well. As a parting gesture of goodwill and appreciation, Peter Aiello lent Capone $500. Al never forgot the generous gesture; he vowed to repay the loan as soon as he was on his feet in Chicago, a promise he eventually honored in a way that his former boss could never have imagined. "He said that he was cut out to do bigger and better things," Mike Aiello notes of Capone's leave-taking, "and he needed money to go to Chicago because he had some opportunities there."

CHAPTER 2

Where the East Meets the West

SIOUX CITY, IOWA, rises above the banks of the Missouri River like a drowning man struggling to surmount treacherous waters. At its highest point, the city looks across the fast-flowing river toward the Nebraska border and its smaller sister town of South Sioux City. Beyond them, looming as an indistinct shape on the horizon, is a range of mountains; actually, it is more of a ridge, a wrinkle in the immense flatness of the prairie landscape. There, some sixteen miles from Sioux City, near the southern boundary of Dakota County, lies the hamlet of Homer, Nebraska, population 500, give or take a few souls, depending on the weather and time of year. A road runs from Sioux City all the way out to Homer, as does a rail line skirting the tiny town center. Nowadays trains roll right past Homer without hesitation, but in years gone by a few paused briefly at this whistle-stop to take on water or coal, and, incidentally, to discharge the odd vagabond.

In the spring of 1919, one such guest of the railroad alighted at Homer, shook the dust and grime from his clothes, and walked into town. He knew no one, and no one knew him. He was twenty-seven years old, but he looked even older, careful and alert, like a man who had traveled widely, and indeed he had. He was different from the other tramps, however; there was something stiff and military in his bearing. He was short, wiry, and muscular, with a prominent nose—a true Roman nose—dark eyes, a shock of black hair, and an olive complexion. In a region whose sparse population consisted predominantly of immigrants from Scandinavian countries, his dark, striking features set him apart. His name, when he chose to utter it in his flat, nasal voice, gave little clue to his origins: Richard Joseph Hart. This was not his real name; it was, rather, one he assumed in tribute to his hero, the silent-movie cowboy star William S. Hart. On the screen, in popular Westerns such as *Wagon Tracks, White Oak,* and *Three Word Brand,* William S. Hart sat tall in his saddle and fired his pistols with magnificent accuracy and without any remorse. He was tall, handsome, aloof—a man who resorted to violence only in the service of good, to restore the established order and rid the West of its bad men. It was a persona with profound psychological appeal to Richard Hart, who was himself caught in a personal conflict of good and evil, a drama so intense it had obliterated his identity.

His desire to escape his origins and to create a new identity had led him to Homer, whose strangeness and isolation held him as if it were a magnet and his soul iron. He had seen much of America and even something of Europe, thanks to Uncle Sam, but after his years of wandering, he was ready to settle down for good, to raise a family, hold down a job, and make a name for himself. Though he would occasionally leave Homer in years to come, he would live here for the rest of his life. It was precisely the refuge Richard Hart was seeking, a forgotten town where he could be whomever he pleased and spend the rest of his days living out his fantasy of the Wild West as invented by Hollywood and enacted by William S. Hart.

The stranger's real name was Vincenzo Capone.

He was the oldest of Al Capone's brothers, the lost Capone, who had run away from Brooklyn at the age of sixteen, joined the circus, and later served with distinction in the American Expeditionary Force during the Great War. But now the war and its glories were over, and he had been mustered out to return with his sharpshooting medals to the Midwest and the open spaces he had come to favor during his days traveling with the circus. While the rest of his brothers drifted half-consciously into lives of crime, Richard was determined to differentiate himself from them, and not merely by changing his name. If they found themselves on the wrong side of the law, he would make certain to be on the right side, and more than that, and in emulation of his cinematic role model, to *enforce* his idea of the law. So strong was his drive to be right and to do right that he set himself on the path to becoming, without realizing it, a mirror image of the fledgling crime family he had fled. He became, in short, not a good man, but an outlaw's *idea* of what a good man must be: a man as self-assured, aloof, and violent as William S. Hart up on the screen, his guns blazing, his face a mask of self-righteousness. No doubts, no uncertainties, no ambiguities—not with a fast horse and a six-shooter in either hand. In the silent movies, it was always obvious who were the good men and who were the bad, and in the struggle between right and wrong, Richard Hart knew to which side he belonged. Or so he thought.

Once the train had pulled away and turned into a distant puff of smoke, Richard Hart was surrounded by silence disturbed only by a constant, mournful wind. Here and there a sign creaked forlornly on its hinges, and in one or two of the windows facing the street an unseen hand moved a curtain aside to permit a clearer view of the new arrival. In this windswept landscape, the ridge that had beckoned in the distance transformed itself into a gentle, rolling hillside. The little town offered a small café, a post office, and there was even a newspaper, the *Homer Star*, which was widely read in those parts, but Homer was above all a farming community, and the talk centered on agriculture: aerating, composting, fertilizing, and endlessly, the weather, rain being a special obsession with Homer's farmers, like farmers everywhere: the amount of rain, the frequency of rain, the chances of rain. It was all as far from Brooklyn—or any big city—as you could get, which was just as he wanted it.

Richard was an ambitious, even driven man, hungry for a reputation and glory, but he was forced to content himself, at first, with the limited career opportunities available in Homer and the surrounding towns in the northeast corner of the state. He found employment briefly as a timekeeper with a railroad crew, and later he hired himself out as a housepainter and paperhanger, but he did not succeed at these ventures. He did, however, make himself known. He talked of his adventures in the war, displayed the sharpshooting medals, and joined the local American Legion post, where he tried to exploit whatever status would accrue to a veteran. Hart was also fond of boasting of his physical prowess and daring. He would wrestle any man who took up the challenge, and he claimed he drank a pint of warm cat's blood every day, though no proof of the habit was forthcoming.

Folks in Homer might have been tempted to dismiss the newcomer as a braggart, but within weeks of his arrival in Homer, fate presented him with a chance to display his physical courage. Situated at the base of the ridge, Homer and other towns in the area were subject to flash floods, which could be destructive and deadly. On May 19, 1919, an unexpected downpour inundated the neighboring town of Emerson, Nebraska, and Richard threw himself into the rescue efforts, coming to the aid of a girl named Margaret O'Connor. The *Homer Star* related that "Hart pushed little Margaret O'Connor up to a fence where she hung to the barbed wire until rescued by her father. The elder O'Connor had to tread water up to his neck to rescue the girl." As dramatic as the deed was, it paled in significance beside Hart's other rescue that day, which involved an entire family named Winch. Their nineteen-year-old daughter, Kathleen, quickly caught his eye, and the two were soon in love and inseparable. Their courtship continued throughout the summer of 1919.

The Winches had arrived in Homer only a year before their deliverer. They came of German stock, and William, the father, had done a bit of everything: tended bar, worked in a hardware store. He was known as a stubborn man; as one of his grandsons was fond of saying, "He'd argue black is white." It was a trait he shared with his daughter's fiancé. William and his wife, Bertha, were Lutherans, and they regularly attended St. Paul's Lutheran Church in Homer. There were, incidentally, two other churches in town, Methodist, which was a bit higher on the social scale, and Catholic, which was a bit lower, but Richard avoided all three houses of worship and the ties to tradition they represented.

On September 1, Richard Hart wed Kathleen Winch in a small, simple Lutheran ceremony in Homer. Three children—all boys—followed in quick succession. The father named his oldest child after his movie idol, William S. Hart; he would be known to all as Bill. Hart named the second child after himself, Richard Jr. Sherman, the third child, was born in 1923. (A fourth child, Harry, would be born several years later, in 1926.) As a husband and father of three children, Richard Hart Sr. was by now an established presence in Homer, but he continued to conceal his origins. On his youngest son's birth certificate, for instance, he gave his birthplace not as Naples, Italy, where he had actually been born, nor Brooklyn, New York, where he had spent his boyhood; rather, he claimed to have been born in Oklahoma, and he allowed the impression to stand that his dark coloring came from Mexican or Indian forebears.

Hart's burgeoning family offered proof of the new life he had chosen in Homer, as did his career, which suddenly acquired new status with the arrival of Prohibition. The Eighteenth Amendment to the U.S. Constitution was ratified on January 16, 1919, and went into effect exactly one year later. Section I read: "After one year from the ratification of this article the manufacture, sale, or transportation of intoxicating liquors within, the importation thereof into, or the exportation thereof from the United States and all territory subject to the jurisdiction thereof for beverage purposes is hereby prohibited." And Section II: "The Congress and the several States shall have the concurrent power to enforce this article by appropriate legislation." With these words the buying and selling of alcohol became a federal offense.

A watershed in major cities such as Chicago and New York, Prohibition had long been the rule in rural areas such as Homer. In the Midwest, where the Anti-Saloon League, the Women's Christian Temperance Union, and other Prohibition groups wielded great political clout, the populace was already "dry" either by custom or by local ordinance—which is not to say that no one drank, or that liquor was not available. It was indeed, but buyers had to know where to look for it; they had to know which drugstore or café sold alcohol under the counter or for "medicinal" purposes. The illegal liquor trade flourished, though in secret, and gave rise to its own vocabulary. The term *moonshine* had been in use since at least the eighteenth century, referring to the phantom presence of illegal alcohol, or spirits distilled at night, hidden from prying eyes. Those engaged in brewing the stuff became known as moonshiners, and those engaged in selling or transporting it, especially in the Midwest, became known as bootleggers. The term, which became popular in the 1890s, derived from the practice of concealing liquor in the upper part of the leg or boot. Elusive, illegal, self-employed brewers and distillers had long flourished throughout the Midwest and especially in the South, and there were as many regional variations on the process of making beer or whiskey as there were recipes for other staples. Isolated farmers frequently distilled whiskey solely for their own use, or for their families, and often the most effective Prohibition agent was not a federal agent but a wife outraged by her husband's drunkenness.

To wage war on the moonshiners and bootleggers and to enforce the Eighteenth Amendment, the federal government created a new breed of law enforcement official: the Prohibition agent. Carrying state or federal commissions, the Prohibition agents had greater authority than local law enforcement officials. But these men were generally new to their trade, and their lack of experience hampered their effectiveness, for even in the best of circumstances, Prohibition was an extremely difficult law to administer. At the same time, the agents' low wages made them exceedingly vulnerable to bribery. Most bootleggers had a ready supply of cash, and Prohibition agents everywhere quickly discovered they could earn more and escape the hazards of their job simply by accepting bribes. Most, but not all, Prohibition agents succumbed to these blandishments. The job also attracted men with a taste for danger, who were willing to lay their lives on the line for a cause. Among them was Richard Hart.

With his love of guns, his adoration of William S. Hart, and his need of a steady job, Richard instinctively gravitated toward this type of work. In the summer of 1920 he sought and obtained a commission from Nebraska's governor, Sam McKelvie, as a Prohibition enforcer. He had a badge, he had a gun, and he had power. The proliferation of bootleggers courtesy of the Eighteenth Amendment promised to keep Hart occupied for a long time to come.

Within weeks of receiving his appointment, Hart completed his first successful Prohibition raid. In Martinsburg, Nebraska, north of Homer, he captured five stills and began generating both publicity and a reputation as a lawman to be reckoned with. "Pictures of Hart's raid results were taken for publicity purposes," the Homer Star noted, because "it is believed they may some day have historical significance." No one was more acutely conscious of the possible significance of such artifacts than Hart himself, who made a point of being photographed with his booty whenever possible. In an early picture, he is seen standing with two other Prohibition agents between two stills and a ramshackle collection of bottles and jugs. He wears a gun, a six-pointed tin star, and a Stetson that appears to dwarf his compact frame; his left hand rests on the coils of one of the captured stills. This was a relatively restrained pose for Hart; as his career unfolded, he would become more flamboyant, always in costume before the camera, as if he were William S. Hart himself, acting in a real-life Western. However, as Hart quickly discovered, one raid and one notice in the paper did not suffice to rid the area of moonshine. Within the next ten days, he returned to Martinsburg twice to raid more stills, but no matter how fast he worked, the stills spread even faster.

In Morrill County, in western Nebraska, a local newspaper, the *Bridgeport News-Blade*, estimated that between fifty and a hundred stills were in operation, the evidence being "dim lights flitting about at night in the breaks along Pumpkin Creek and in the hills that flank the Platt River where moonshiners were plying their trade." That was enough to draw the attention of agent Hart. The paper's account of his *modus operandi* leading to the arrest of two men was so detailed that only Hart himself could have supplied the particulars.

> The agent went to the Bartling Ranch last Saturday and passed himself off as a returning soldier . . . looking for attractive land in which to file a homestead. There he met McArdle, who after some conversation asked if the agent ever "took anything." The agent admitted that he sometimes indulged, whereupon McArdle invited him to look at his "place," which was situated on the bank of a little creek that runs about 100 yards from McArdle's house. The agent found the "place" nicely situated in the shade of the tree that grew beside the creek. The platform had been erected in the tree on which was resting a gasoline tank from which a feed pipe led to a gasoline stove burning on the earth. The stove was a large pressure cooker from the safety tube of which ran a copper coil that was buried in the water of the creek, the end opening into a jug of liquor. The still was in full operation. The liquor was running into the jug. The agent and McArdle arrived.

The arrest had proceeded according to plan until this point, when matters took an unexpected turn:

> The agent began to question McArdle until McArdle became suspicious and backed off toward the tree in the fork of which a revolver was lying. The agent saw the revolver and at once drew his own automatic on McArdle and ordered him to hold his hands high and get away from the tree. The agent possessed himself of McArdle's gun, phoned to a neighbor for a conveyance and loaded the still and McArdle and came to Bridgeport. Shortly after arriving here the agent arrested John Bartling.

Most of Hart's arrests ended the same way, with a conviction. The guilty party either paid a fine or spent ninety days in jail.

As he gained experience in his new job, and possibly just to vary the routine, this man who was already living under an assumed name began a series of masquerades. On October 28, 1920, he arrived in Randolph, Nebraska, reputed to be a center of illicit alcohol activity, but instead of his badge and crisp Stetson, he wore the shabby overalls of a laborer. In this guise he managed to ferret out enough information to direct a raid on the city's stills. Twenty men, including some of Randolph's best-known names, were among the catch, and the enterprising brother of Al Capone earned himself a headline: "State Agent Hart Cleans Up Randolph!" Several weeks—and raids—later, it was followed by another headline: "State Agent Hart Cleans Up Cedar County!"

The consequences of the latter raid led Hart through enough twists and turns to pack a dime novel. He decided to drive one of his captives, "Slats" Pogonese, to Lincoln, Nebraska, and turn him over to the sheriff. They immediately got lost in a severe rain storm, and instead of traveling south to Lincoln they drove north to the tiny town of Spencer, close to the South Dakota state line. There Hart decided the two of them looked sufficiently scruffy to pass themselves off as outlaws. In this role Hart and his prisoner asked the owner of the garage in which he had parked his car where to buy a quart of moonshine—"white mule" they called it in these parts, on account of its kick. The man told him, Hart procured his moonshine, arrested the seller, and returned to the garage to arrest the informant. Everything went smoothly until Hart discovered that the seller was in fact the marshal of Spencer, Nebraska. Undaunted, Hart decided to turn in both men, but before he could, another marshal attempted to arrest Hart for disturbing the peace. The two fell into a shouting argument, and Hart left with only "Slats" in tow. The violator was duly charged and jailed, and Hart came away from the episode with an abiding mistrust of local law enforcement officials, who often as not operated in cahoots with the bootleggers, offering protection, skimming profits, and preventing honest men like agent R. J. Hart from doing their job.

Several weeks later, Hart devised another disguise; more flamboyant than anything he had previously tried, it revealed as much about the man as it concealed. He turned up in Schuyler, Nebraska, a fair-sized town about fifty miles east of Omaha, disguised as a handicapped veteran. It was the mustard gas, he told the curious; he hadn't been the same since the war. One other thing about this lonely doughboy; he liked to roll the dice. Even better, his pockets bulged with cash. Within days he had managed to ingratiate himself with most of Schuyler's high rollers. He then fed the information to other Prohibition agents, and on December 17 he joined them in a raid on the town's liquor stills, one of which was camouflaged in a soft drink bottling facility. Once again he arranged for the haul to be photographed for the sake of posterity, and the result displayed an assortment of bottles and jugs, all looking harmless enough in themselves. Through these and other exploits, Hart's fame increased weekly, and by the spring of 1921, scarcely more than two years after he had arrived in Homer, he had become known throughout Nebraska as a resourceful and feared lawman. The *Homer Star* marveled that its own R. J. Hart "is becoming such a menace in the state that his name alone carries terror to the heart of every criminal."

His growing reputation and obvious daring brought him to the attention of the Federal Bureau of Indian Affairs, which offered him a far more hazardous appointment: the suppression of liquor traffic among the Indians. Given his identification with the Old West, it was an assignment that Hart was unable to resist. His new duties often took him away from home for days on end. Initially, he spent much of his time in and around the Yankton reservation, just across the border in South Dakota. The Indians were expert at hiding their stills, and he devoted many days on foot or on horseback to tracking their movements with only his horse for companionship. It was hardly the type of work in which a boy from the streets of Brooklyn was likely to excel, much less survive, but Hart quickly distinguished himself in these demanding circumstances. Within months, the superintendent of the Yankton reservation was moved to write to the Bureau of Indian Affairs in Washington, D.C.: "I wish to commend Mr. Hart in highest terms for his fearless and untiring efforts to bring these liquor peddlers and moonshiners to justice. I have tried the county and state officers and even the Federal Prohibition officers in Sioux Falls with very discouraging results. This man Hart is a 'go-getter.' "

While undoubtedly effective, Hart's "go-getting" meant, in practice, using his fists. It must be remembered that he was often dealing with Indians who were armed with knives and guns, extremely intoxicated, and liable to be violent. His way of bringing them to heel was to drive straight to one of their drunken gatherings; as soon he emerged from his car, he would hit the first Indian he could reach, knocking him cold. Hart later explained his method of dealing with Indians this way: "You've got to get in the first lick."

Even as he fought Indian moonshiners Hart steeped himself in Indian lore and took the trouble to learn the language of the tribes he was assigned to police. In time he befriended several of their chiefs, men known as Blackbird and Lone Wolf. Always fond of photographs, he liked to pose for portraits with the Indians. In one, an Indian child is dressed in his most elaborate garb, while Hart, his Stetson firmly in place, tries to stare down the camera. In another, he stands beside three Indians, the four men in a line, equal, warriors all. In time, most of the Indians—drinkers excepted—came to respect him, and they conferred a name on Hart that would stay with him until the end of his life: "Two-Gun." The name was repeated by the whites, as well, and once it began appearing in the newspapers, which could scarcely resist such a colorful nickname, no one called him Richard anymore; it was always "Two-Gun." Wherever he went, "Two-Gun" Hart wore pistols in holsters on either hip to live up to the name—and the reputation—he had won for himself in the West.

Hart was now poised for a major career in law enforcement. A man with his drive, talent, and accomplishments was likely to wind up in the state capital, heading this or that state law enforcement agency, or even spend time in Washington, in a federal job. The future was bright, especially a future containing Prohibition. The identity he had forged for himself out of the legends of the American West continued to hold, and more than that, to carry him to heights he would otherwise not have attained in a country rife with anti-Italian prejudice. As an outsider, he developed a dual identification—with silver screen cowboys on the one hand and Indians on the other. He could play both outlaw and lawman at the same time, endlessly chasing aspects of himself, acting out on the stage of the American prairie the drama of his divided psyche. Yet no one suspected he was anything other than what he claimed to be, an Oklahoma-born veteran who had come to Homer in search of work and made good. No one realized that "Two-Gun" Hart's real name was Vincenzo Capone, not his supervisors, his coworkers—not even his wife knew who he really was.

Until this point in his life—the summer of 1923—Hart's early manhood resembled a saga of the Old West, worthy of William S. Hart himself. A stranger comes to town; he saves the life of a family, whose daughter he marries; and he then makes a name for himself as a gun-toting lawman respected by whites and Indians alike. All the while, he has an assumed identity, a past he refuses to reveal to anyone, not even his wife. But this was no silent movie scenario; this was the extraordinary balancing act Hart managed to maintain with remarkable control until the summer of 1923, when he stumbled into a misadventure that threatened to disrupt his livelihood and to reveal the identity he had so carefully concealed. It involved moonshine, a car chase, bad luck, even worse judgment, and before it ended, a man lay dead, and a mob was threatening to hang "Two-Gun" Hart.

· · ·

On the evening of October 23, Hart and another Prohibition agent named Walter Gumm; two young Winnebago Indians, Walter Tebo and Robinson Smith; and the town constable, Logan Lamert, gathered in South Sioux City. Their mission was straightforward: the arrest of a bootlegger by the name of John Haaker, who was reputed to sell moonshine to Winnebago

Indians. Their plan was routine: the Indians would buy liquor from Haaker
and the agents would move in to make their arrest. But when the two Indians
tried to purchase liquor, Haaker, who probably suspected he was being set
up, refused to deal.

Convinced that Haaker was indeed selling liquor, Hart, Gumm, and
Lamert dropped off the Indians at a nearby filling station and returned to
watch the suspect. At 10:30 that night, the men finally spotted a pair of cars
approach Haaker's place of business and crawl to a standstill. Several men left
the cars, then reentered, and the cars pulled away. Hart, Gumm, and Lamert
decided to follow one, a Buick. "We were satisfied in all probability they had
whiskey in their possession which they had bought at Haakers," recalled
Hart's companion, Walter Gumm, "and I called out to them that they were
under arrest." The words had no effect, and Hart decided to take matters into
his own hands, to play the hero once again. Balancing on the running board
of his car, he shouted at the men in the Buick that they were under arrest.
But the Buick heedlessly continued on its way, and Gumm, who was driving
the agents' car, speeded up until Hart, still on the running board, drew even
with the driver of the Buick. Hart was so close he could practically reach out
and touch the suspect. Just then the Buick speeded up, and the two cars raced
along the darkened streets of South Sioux City. When the Buick pulled into
the lead, Hart and Gumm drew their weapons.

At that point, the two cars were about 150 feet apart, going about thirty-
five miles per hour. The agents' car was traveling along the bumpy shoulder
of the road, and it was pitch dark. Despite these hazards, "Hart discharged
two shots, apparently at the rear tires of the Buick," Gumm recalled, "and
then I reached around the windshield with my right arm and fired one shot
down towards the ground and towards the rear tire of the Buick, although I
could take no aim, and there would be no accuracy to my shooting." The
unmistakable implication was that the darkness, speed, and bumpy road, not
to mention the distance between the two cars, had caused the shots to be
wild.

The Buick came to a standstill, and when Hart reached it, he discovered
the driver had been shot and was bleeding badly. The victim was not an
Indian; he was a white named Ed Morvace—thirty-five years old, married,
and the father of a seven-month-old son. He worked in the area as a mechanic; like Hart, he had served with the American Expeditionary Force
during the war. Later that evening Morvace died. The coroner, in the
presence of Hart, performed an autopsy and "determined the cause of death
to be the gun shot wound and that the bullet entered at the back of Morvace's
neck and came out through the mouth." The death of Ed Morvace was listed
as accidental.

The death of Ed Morvace took place on a Saturday night, and within

hours it polarized the community into vehemently pro- and anti-Hart factions. Gumm recalled, "Hart and I both heard that on Sunday evening after
the shooting there was a gang of bootleggers who got together and got some
rope and talked about going down to the agency and getting Hart and hanging him. On account of Hart's activities in enforcing the liquor laws there is
a very strong feeling against him among bootleggers and law violators generally." A lynch mob was not the only threat Hart faced. On Tuesday, a
warrant was issued for the arrest of R. J. Hart, who immediately surrendered
to the sheriff of Dakota City, Nebraska, where he was formally charged with
manslaughter; bail was set at $7,500.

Now the pendulum swung the other way, in Hart's favor. Among steadfast
Prohibitionists, and especially fervent members of the politically influential
Women's Christian Temperance Union, Hart's arrest made him into a cause
célèbre, a martyr to justice. The *Union Worker* of Lincoln, Nebraska, a
Prohibition propaganda sheet, observed, "Now the bootleggers are filled with
glee because this officer has been arrested and will go to trial. . . . If we do
not stand by our conscientious officers where would the bootleggers place us
in a short time? Would it be safe after sundown?" In the name of the
Constitution, public safety, and all that was holy, dry bankers rushed to put
up Hart's bond, and he thereby avoided the humiliation of being locked up
in jail. He was even allowed to keep his beloved gun. Still, he had to defend
himself against the manslaughter charge, and even if he was exonerated, the
incident would leave a blot on his record. Worse, the scrutiny he suddenly
faced could reveal that "Two-Gun" Hart was in fact an Italian-born immigrant named Vincenzo Capone.

As the controversy grew, Hart defended his actions. He insisted that he, a
decorated sharpshooter, could not possibly have fired the shot that killed
Morvace. The implication was that Gumm, not Hart, had fired the fatal
bullet, but no matter who was to blame, nothing could bring Morvace back
to life. From the viewpoint of the victim's widow, Olga, it scarcely mattered
which agent had murdered her husband. She sued them both for $50,000,
and she further alleged that "the officers accused of the killing gathered
around the dead body and referred to it in vile and obscene names." Newspaper accounts of the pointless killing and the manner in which it occurred
fanned the flames of public anger with Hart. For several nights running,
mobs assembled on the streets of Dakota City, and the threat of a lynching
hung in the crisp autumn air.

The most likely occasion for a lynching would have been when Hart
appeared at the Dakota County courthouse to testify at an inquest, but he
foiled the mob by appearing a day earlier than scheduled. Immediately
afterward, the county attorney declared, "The verdict of the jury at the
inquest was that either Hart or Gumm, the Indian agent, had shot Morvace

while in pursuit of his duty. The law says they are not guilty of any crime and there will be no charge brought against the officers." The resulting headline, "CORONER'S JURY HOLDS SHOOTING WAS JUSTIFIED," further inflamed the anti-Hart contingent, who demanded an eye for an eye. Fearing for his life, Hart went into hiding on the Winnebago reservation.

Militant prohibitionists persisted in their support of Hart. The WCTU took up a collection to pay for his legal expenses. A lawyer named Harry Keefe served as their mouthpiece. "This is not a question of the guilt or innocence of Hart," Keefe argued, "so much as it is the issue of the enforcement of the law. If an enforcement officer is convicted of such a charge, it will materially affect the future operations of other enforcement officers. Many of them are too timid now. If Mr. Hart is eliminated from the field, it is going to make the bootleggers more secure in their position." Keefe's position sounded extreme, and it was; blinded by self-righteousness, the WCTU appeared to advocate the shooting or killing of anyone who was even *suspected* of violating the Prohibition laws. Right or wrong, the influence of the WCTU forestalled further local investigation of the matter.

Meanwhile, news of the shooting reached Washington, D.C., where the Justice Department launched an inquiry that eventually concluded that Hart, whether or not he actually fired the fatal bullet, was "guilty of careless indifference to consequences." James Kinsler, the U.S. attorney for Nebraska, offered the opinion that Hart, being a better marksman than Gumm, was less likely to have shot Morvace, but in any event, "all the shooting, both by Hart and Gumm, was wholly uncalled for." As a result of the Department of Justice's inquiry and the public controversy back in Nebraska, "Two-Gun" Hart's sterling reputation was badly tarnished. He eventually surfaced and resumed his duties policing liquor traffic among the Indians, but the rapid rise he had enjoyed in his profession was now permanently stalled.

In one respect, however, Hart could be grateful. The controversy failed to uncover his true identity. No one had thought to question where he had been before his arrival in Homer, so the fiction of Richard Joseph Hart remained intact—at least for now. However, pressure to disclose his past came from Hart himself, who gradually tired of living a lie, especially now that the lie had let him down. At about the time Ed Morvace was shot to death, Hart—along with the rest of the Midwest—heard startling news of the family he had fled fifteen years ago. The news came not from New York, but from Chicago. Through newspaper headlines and photographs, Hart discovered what had become of the brothers he had deserted fifteen years before. As in his own situation, violence and gunplay were involved. "GUNMAN KILLED BY GUNMAN" read one headline, and the accompanying article made it plain that Hart's brothers were on the opposite side of the law. The Chicago newspapers took to calling Al a "vice lord." Now that "Two-Gun" Hart knew where his brothers were, it was only a matter of time until he went to Chicago to see for himself what had become of his family, and especially his extraordinary younger brother Al, whom the newspapers called "Scarface" and whose career was about to eclipse his own.

. . .

Hog Butcher for the World,
Tool Maker, Stacker of Wheat,
Player with Railroads and the Nation's Freight Handler;
Stormy, husky, brawling,
City of the Big Shoulders:

They tell me you are wicked and I believe them, for I have seen your
painted women under the gas lamps luring the farm boys.
And they tell me you are crooked and I answer: Yes, it is true I have
seen the gunman kill and go free to kill again.

So began Carl Sandburg's famous ode to the city the Capone family now called home. After the congestion of Brooklyn and the quiet, middle-class respectability of Baltimore, Chicago came as an enormous release for Al, his mother, and his brothers, a receptive environment for their growing ambition, for it was a city obsessed with innovation, progress, and wealth. It had always been this way in Chicago; as early as the 1680s La Salle, the French explorer of the Great Lakes region, came upon the site of the future city and prophesied, "This will be the gate of Empire, this the seat of Commerce. The typical man who will grow up here must be an enterprising man. Each day as he rises he will exclaim, 'I act, I move, I push,' and there will be spread before him a boundless horizon, an illimitable field of activity. A limitless expanse of plain is here—to the east water and all other points of land. If I were to give this place a name I would derive from the nature of the man who will occupy this place—*ago*, I act; *circum*, all around; Circago."

Empire. Commerce. Illimitable. Chicago. A vital city, devouring itself by the tail as if it were a mythological snake. Corrupt, hypocritical, and stratified, but bursting with vitality. A competitive, fierce, and unsubtle place, where people thought in headlines and talked in bulletins. Staccato. Blunt.

And they tell me you are brutal and my reply is: On the faces of women
and children I have seen the marks of wanton hunger.
And having answered so I turn once more to those who sneer at this my
city, and I give them back the sneer and say to them:
Come and show me another city with lifted head singing so proud to be
alive and coarse and strong and cunning.

In a city obsessed with quantity, statistics related a tale of wild, almost wanton expansion. In 1850, only a few years after Chicago became an official port of entry (and about the same time a public ordinance outlawed hogs from running loose in its streets), the number of inhabitants stood at barely 28,000 enterprising souls. In the entire city there was but a single "paved" block: a stretch of dirt or mud (depending on the weather) covered with wooden planks. Just a year later, the population, swollen with the ranks of immigrant laborers and entrepreneurs who had migrated west in search of fortune, jumped to 40,000; four years later, the number had doubled. By 1870, the city, cleared of hogs and getting more of its streets paved every day, claimed a population of 300,000—a tenfold increase in two decades. Physically, Chicago still resembled a village that went on forever, an endless succession of low, wooden shanties arrayed along the coast of Lake Michigan. Then the city of Chicago reached the first great crisis in its development, a trauma that its collective psyche still wrestles with and rehearses to this day. It was in one of these wooden structures—according to legend, belonging to a Mrs. O'Leary, whose cow toppled a lamp—that a fire started on the night of October 8, 1871. It burned for days, turning the night sky into day, the smoke visible up and down Lake Michigan. By the time it finally burned out, the city had been gutted. The flames consumed eighty blocks, including 1,600 homes, along with bridges, streets, and public buildings of every description. As many as 100,000 people were suddenly homeless, and the amount of the damage approached the inconceivable sum of $200,000.

The immolation of the old city of Chicago set the stage for the new—buildings made of granite, iron, and steel this time, the advent of city planning, and the skyscrapers. Within three years, the city rose Phoenix-like from its ashes, and the statistics shot up again: half a million inhabitants by 1880, over a million in 1890, 1.7 million at the turn of the century, and by 1920, the year of Capone's arrival, a population of 2.7 million and still climbing; within a few years the population would reach the 3 million mark. As recently as the War of 1812, the site had been a rough-hewn military outpost known as Fort Dearborn, and now, scarcely more than a hundred years later, the city of Chicago was the second largest city in the nation—one of the largest in the world. The unquestioned capital of mid-America. And *all* its roads were paved now; indeed, they seemed to be paved with gold.

In a city twenty-six miles long and fourteen miles wide, with twenty-two miles of lake frontage, covering an area of two hundred square miles, there seemed to be room for everyone—rich man, poor man, beggar man, thief. They were a heterogeneous group, these Chicagoans; the prototypical American city was actually made up of ethnic blocs maintaining close ties to their native lands. The blocs remained separate, occupying distinct districts of the city; there was no such thing as a melting pot in Chicago, not even as a myth.

That wasn't the Chicago way. The Chicago way was to make room for monolithic blocs of inhabitants who preferred not to overlap with one another. Your Poles, nearly half a million of them, in their South Side neighborhoods, your Irish in their precincts, your Russians, Germans, Swedes, Czechs, Bohemians, Jews, and blacks in their respective neighborhoods. Where they belonged. The same applied for the Southern Italian immigrants. *Campanilismo* proved as compelling in Chicago as in Brooklyn, and Capone found Southern Italian immigrants concentrated in two areas: the city's crowded Little Italy, over 100,000 strong, and just as important, the city of Chicago *Heights*. Despite its hopeful-sounding name, Chicago Heights was no leafy suburb, nor did it occupy high ground; it was a separate city an hour or more south of Chicago proper, as supine as the day is long. Chicago *Flats* would have been a more accurate name for the area, which Al Capone would come to know quite well in the years to come, and on which he would leave his indelible mark.

Geographically, Chicago fell neatly into three major sections divided by the meandering course of the Chicago River. The relatively compact North Side (where the wealthy congregated in imposing brownstones or in luxurious high-rise apartment buildings), the sprawling, ethnic, residential South Side, and the West Side, a largely industrial area that gradually blended into the rural Midwest. They all intersected at the Loop, the city's central business district. Here elevated and underground railroad lines entered, described large arcs, and exited, giving the area its name. To pass through the Loop on foot, by rail, or by car was like entering a machine; life coexisted simultaneously on several different levels: the street, the underground, and the overhead railways. Everything crisscrossed—the traffic, pedestrians, trains, and the Chicago River—to form a dense environment rivaling the most crowded neighborhoods of New York. Within its compact area, the Loop presented the archetypal American urban landscape, all sharp corners, piercing shafts of sunlight, and menacing shadows concealing pickpockets or even gunmen. While trains roared overhead, shots could be fired, a woman could scream, and no one would hear. But then you walked a few blocks east, and you were suddenly on the shore of Lake Michigan, an endless blue expanse carrying ships to and from Canada, Detroit, Milwaukee, and other points north.

Port city, prairie metropolis—Chicago presented many aspects, none more startling than the Union Stock Yards. Prior to Capone's arrival, the yards, which covered nearly 500 acres of South Side real estate, had more than any other feature served to characterize Chicago for the rest of the country. There was a simple explanation: you could smell them long before you saw them, a pungent animal odor that made you feel soiled at first and then made you feel alive. The yards were basically a huge outdoor livestock hotel whose vast pens held cattle awaiting the slaughterhouse and the meat market. More numbers to give some idea of the sheer quantity of meatpacking business transacted in Chicago: 17 million cattle, sheep, and hogs passed through the yards each year, their carcasses issuing from fifty meatpacking plants employing 75,000 individuals. How brutal the slaughter, with men wading through blood on the killing floor, but how many mouths it fed. The plants produced both meat and animal by-products: soaps of every description, oils, fertilizer, hides, cattle food, feathers, glycerine, buttons, and wool. This industry was but one of the many engines driving Chicago's economy. There were also railroads and immense lumber yards, and the world's largest mail-order houses, Sears, Roebuck and Montgomery Ward, to count among the commercial glories of Chicago. Twenty-four hours a day, the city's inhabitants transported, sold, slaughtered, auctioned, and bartered the nation's essentials. "All the legal battles—smoke, noise, light, heat, sewerage, pavements, water, side-walks, taxes—have all been fought and conquered," boasted the 1924 *Rand McNally Guide to Chicago*. "Those who seek locations here know exactly what they are to get, what they can do, and what they have to pay. Here may be obtained practically any quality, or grade, or type of labor required."

No matter how big it grew, Chicago remained an unpretentious city with a vernacular culture, open and accessible to all and mighty glad to take your money, but abrasive and constantly in flux. It was "two-fisted and rowdy, hard-drinking and pugnacious," in the words of Robert St. John, among the most enterprising correspondents of the era. "She was vibrant and violent, stimulating and ruthless, intolerant of smugness, impatient with those either physically or intellectually timid. She had her slums, then, too, and her squalor, her smells, and her dirt, but they *did* wash the streets at three or four o'clock every morning in those days and the breeze from Lake Michigan was like a drink of champagne." Another famous graduate of Chicago's rambunctious school of journalism, John Gunther, said simply that Chicago had "the most intense vitality of any [city] I have ever lived in."

What better place for an ambitious racketeer to touch down, to grow rich. This was no Paris. Didn't pretend to be. This was Hogtown. Porkopolis. Chicagoans rejoiced in their city's pride of place in the commercial world, but they were acutely aware that in the cultural and social realms it had rather a dismal reputation; they knew all about it, and they were proud of it. Pleased to be considered square and naïve. A story making the rounds in the 1920s illustrated the point. One day the wife of one of Chicago's overnight tycoons found herself at a proper tea on Boston's Beacon Hill, home of that city's gentry. Cabots and Lodges abounded. Amid the clinking of china, the hostess confided to her guest, "Here in Boston, we lay a great deal of stress on breeding." To which the woman from Chicago responded, "Well, where I come from, we think it's a lot of fun, too, but I guess we just don't talk about it so much." As the Beacon Hill hostess should have known, Chicago's interest in bloodlines was reserved for horses and hogs, not families. Despite its enormous new opera house, designed primarily to be bigger than the Metropolitan Opera in New York and secondarily to accommodate music, it remained a cultural outpost. You want art, try New York. Try Boston. Cross the Atlantic. You want *jazz*, stop by the South Side, where an immense and vital black community was in the making. But jazz wasn't indigenous to Chicago; like most things there, it was imported, from the South, New Orleans, in particular. Even its beer and breweries, arguably the city's greatest gastronomic attraction, were imported from Eastern Europe. The city's coarse, improvised quality could make visitors reel in disgust, especially English writers. H. G. Wells described the place as a "dark smear under the sky," and Arnold Bennett dismissed it as a "suburb of Warsaw." "Having seen it [Chicago], I urgently desire never to see it again," wrote Rudyard Kipling. "It is inhabited by savages. Its air is dirt."

In the absence of high culture, architecture reigned as the city's natural art form, and its preeminence was understandable, for architecture was solid, practical, and sufficiently commercial to matter in Chicago. It was, after all, merely a pretentious name for real estate. To the rest of the world, the skyscraper symbolized Chicago architecture—and Chicago itself. The world's first skyscrapers transformed a provincial settlement into a modern metropolis of somber greens, grays, and blues: a backdrop of immense buildings etched with light. In other cities, architects designed skyscrapers of necessity, and they tried to disguise the resulting structures as traditional buildings, but in Chicago, Louis Sullivan and John Root, to name two of an extraordinary rich field of artist-entrepreneurs, eagerly embraced the requirement to pile one story atop another.

Their skyscrapers gave the city its distinctively modern ambience. In downtown Chicago, the sunshine, leaping from sky to window to street, refracted by the greenish water of Lake Michigan and tinged with smoke and steam, was almost palpable. On the clearest mornings, light sliced through the air, creating a mirage of skyscrapers that vanished as the angle of the sun's incidence changed. In the afternoon, buildings receded into a bluish haze and seemed gargantuan, unreal. By the day's exhausted end, the stench of burning coal and the reek of the slaughterhouses hung in the air, and the city's remorseless, ubiquitous trolleys squealed above the streets throughout the rowdy night. To take up residence in Chicago was to install oneself in a vast, throbbing machine, buying, selling, manufacturing, shipping, hustling. A furnace of commerce.

Laughing the stormy, husky, brawling laughter of Youth, half-naked,
sweating, proud to be Hog Butcher, Tool Maker, Stacker of Wheat,
Player with Railroads and Freight Handler to the Nation.

The price Chicago paid for all its wealth and exuberance was human exploitation. "Civic-minded" was not a term often used in connection with Chicago's leading citizens. An established family was one that had been around for more than twenty years and owned a factory, a business, or real estate. In Chicago, "old money" was an oxymoron, inherited wealth a novelty. The city was built on legends of strong-willed, charismatic men who had arrived penniless, acquired fortunes through hard work, and become pillars of respectability. Everyone in Chicago knew the story of Philip ("I do not love the money, what I love is the getting of it") Armour, who cornered the market in pork. He bought low, sold high, and built a meatpacking empire, which in turn funded a good deal of the city's art and educational institutions. They were also in the thrall of the legend of Potter Palmer, who founded the precursor of the city's best-known department store, Marshall Field, and whose Palmer House hotel was destroyed by the Chicago fire only thirteen days after it had been completed, and was instantly rebuilt, bigger than ever. And there was Marshall Field himself, the department store tycoon, who died a mysterious death during a sex orgy in a posh Chicago brothel. Above all, there was the hydra-headed McCormick dynasty, which appeared to have sprung from the pages of a Booth Tarkington novel, dark, majestic, and cobwebby. One branch—the "rich branch"—held the patent on the McCormick reaper, which, in addition to altering the course of American agriculture, gave rise to the Chicago-based International Harvester. Later on, the "poor branch" (the characterization was strictly relative) came to control the *Chicago Tribune* and its radio station, WGN. (As everyone knew, its nationally recognized call letters stood for "World's Greatest Newspaper": an instance of typical Chicago self-promotion.) During the 1920s, when Al Capone was making his bid to take his place alongside the other Chicago dynasties, the McCormick *Tribune* was not merely an influential newspaper, it was a major power broker in the city's public life, almost a shadow government, whose imperial, eccentric publisher, Robert R. McCormick, had designs on changing the course of national and even international affairs. There were other dynasties, as well: the Florsheims, the McNallys, the Sterns, Smiths, and Ryersons. Each traced its wealth to a single-minded founder who, inevitably, came to Chicago penniless, or nearly so, and rose to great wealth and position through pluck and luck.

In his idle moments Al Capone liked to compare himself to these other self-made Chicago millionaires. He was fond of casting himself in their time-honored rags-to-riches mode, another American success story. "When

I came to Chicago," he once boasted, "I had only $40 in my pocket. I went into a business that was open and didn't do anybody any harm. . . . At least 300 young men, thanks to me, are getting from $150 to $200 a week. . . . I have given work that has taken many a man out of the hold-up and bank robbery business." Al Capone, self-made man, benefactor. A man persevering against all odds. If fame is an index, Capone was right to do so, for his reputation eclipsed all others. In fact, the city was ripe for the taking.

The absence of traditions and widely acknowledged standards of personal conduct and business behavior generated impressive statistics, but it also made for a state of near anarchy. Chicago, said its boosters, was an "open city." Translation: its political establishment was for sale to the highest bidder. Political influence in Chicago was one more commodity to be bought and sold like so many head of cattle or a choice location. The city accomplished its business the easy way, through fixing and corruption. The judges were fixed, the juries were fixed, the reporters (half of them, anyway) were on the take from their sources. It was *expected* that police were on the take; citizens bribed them just to be on the safe side. To be a cop was to be assured of never going hungry. The lawyers bribed juries, and everyone bribed the politicians, who in turn bribed the good citizens of Chicago to vote for them. All over town, the fix was in, and year after year it seeped into the city's core, until doing business in Chicago, any business at all, meant paying protection money, but that was only the start, because the further anyone went in Chicago public life, the more corrupt he became. Only nobodies and a few zealous, wrongheaded reformers were foolish enough to be honest, for to be an honest man in Chicago was to be alone, without allies, vulnerable, impotent.

A mammoth city on the prairie, Chicago brought together urban corruption and Wild West lawlessness, resulting in a volatile and deadly compound. Decades before Al Capone set foot in the city, a large, well-organized, and deeply entrenched syndicate already had its hand in running many aspects of civic life. Its presence was no secret, and it bred social malaise and fierce resentment. "First in violence, deepest in dirt; loud, lawless, unlovely, ill-smelling, irreverent, . . . the 'tough' among cities, a spectacle for the nation," scolded the muckraking journalist Lincoln Steffens, in his popular exposé, *The Shame of the Cities* (1904). "I give Chicago no quarter and Chicago asks for none. 'Good,' they cheer, when you find fault; 'give us the gaff. We deserve it and it does us good.' They do deserve it." Chicago confirmed Steffens's thesis that the alliance of politics and business—which Capone would soon learn to manipulate to great profit—guaranteed civic corruption. Yet even this sternest of critics failed to predict the level of violence this situation would create.

In his exhaustive retrospective of Chicago corruption, *Organized Crime in Chicago*, John Landesco, writing from the vantage point of 1929, observed:

For many years Chicago has been under the domination of the underworld. For many years Chicago has tolerated vice, and now the
underworld and vice have it by the throat. We have complained of
crime . . . , yet we have exhibited to our youth the spectacle of a
policeman in full uniform acting, not only as customers of, but often
as partners in, our brothels, our gambling houses, and our liquor
selling. . . . This is the dark side of Chicago. The measure of crime in
Chicago is the measure of its social selfishness, of its public indifference, and of its public corruption.

Landesco said what everyone in Chicago acknowledged to be the case, and
he explained it as folks in Chicago did, ascribing the pervasiveness of corruption to the fact that the city was, for all its size and apparent sophistication, still a frontier boomtown at heart. "The prevalence of crime in Chicago
is in large measure *due to our very newness and to our very democracy,*"
Landesco observed. "Crime is the problem of adolescent youth and the
failure properly to deal with crime is nearly always a weakness of an adolescent city and of an adolescent nation. *There has always been crime upon the
frontier.* The main trouble with Chicago is that it is too young and that it has
grown too fast." Like many early students of Chicago, he offered mesmerizing statistics to make his point. "With the exception of New York," he
claimed, "Chicago furnishes the richest field for plunder that is to be found
in the United States. In ninety-three years Chicago has grown to be the third
largest city in the world. The bank clearings of the Chicago district for the
year 1927 amounted to the enormous sum of $35,958,216,000. Is it to be
wondered at that the robber is to be found among us?"
    Indeed, criminal organizations had been a fixture of civic life in Chicago
since the beginning of the century, fully two decades before Capone's arrival.
The term *gangster* was already part of the American tongue and initially
denoted organized attempts to stuff ballot boxes and rig local elections; later
the term came to include street gangs and groups of criminals of every sort.
In a 1927 study of Chicago's neighborhoods, Frederic Thrasher found no
fewer than 1,313 active gangs comprising 25,000 members, and this was, in
Thrasher's words, a "conservative estimate"; no doubt hundreds of other
gangs eluded his painstaking research. The gang, Thrasher demonstrated
beyond dispute, was an integral part of Chicago, too entrenched to be erad-
icated by reform, prosperity, or other panaceas. Another, related term, *racketeer*, came into use in the mid-1920s, when Chicagoans suddenly began to
discuss, and their newspapers to cover, the city's more sophisticated gang
members. Within several years the term became popular throughout the
country, and the *Chicago Journal of Commerce* devised a definition as precise
as that slippery expression allowed:

A racketeer may be the boss of a supposedly legitimate business association; he may be a labor union organizer; . . . or he may be just a
journeyman thug. Whether he is a gunman who has imposed himself
upon some union as its leader, or whether he is a business organizer,
his methods are the same; by throwing bricks into a few windows, and
incidental and perhaps accidental murders, he succeeds in organizing
a group of smaller business men into what he calls a protective association. He then proceeds to collect what fees and dues he likes, to
impose what fines suit him, regulates price and hours of work, and . . .
to boss the outfit to his own profit. Any merchant who doesn't come in,
or who comes in and doesn't stay in and continue to pay tribute, is
bombed, slugged or otherwise intimidated.

Racketeers and gangs controlled the other Chicago: the city's flourishing
demimonde, to which the Capone family naturally gravitated. Throughout
the Midwest, in fact, mention of Chicago conjured two images. First came
the wealth, excelled only by New York, and then, close behind, the city's
reputation for licentiousness. In churches and in revival meeting tents,
preachers tirelessly warned of the plight of innocent farm girls who went off
to Chicago in search of a better life and higher wages, and quickly fell prey
to the nets and snares of the modern (and godless) age. Alone, subject to
temptation on all sides, desperate for money, these young women, so the
preachers said, wound up in Chicago's white slave trade; in other words,
they became prostitutes. One of the best-known jeremiads directed against
Chicago was Samuel Paynter Wilson's book, *Chicago and Its Cess-Pools of
Infamy* (1910), in which the author railed against the manifold snares of
Chicago's vice trade. "Sexual commerce may be purchased almost anywhere in the South State street and West Side alleys for the remarkably
low price of ten cents," he warned. "The street boy hunting these underworld sections of our city is first led into sexual sin by one of the crippled,
half rotten, yet painted vampires of the street whose only care or hope is
a crust of free lunch and enough whisky or 'dope' to drown for a time."
Another popular broadside of the day, William T. Stead's *If Christ Came
to Chicago!* condemned Chicago's flesh trade in tones of biblical wrath,
but at the same time his book helpfully included a *map* of all the city's
best-known brothels, ostensibly to warn the unwary of what streets to
avoid. The guide disguised as a diatribe caused a sensation and sold
briskly. With a copy of *If Christ Came to Chicago!* in hand, a tourist could
find his way to a brothel and later return to the book to understand how
terrible the experience had been.

•   •   •

At the moment Al Capone arrived in Chicago, the city's vice trade was undergoing a rapid transformation, emerging from its sordid and celebrated Victorian past. Along with the stockyards, railroads, and other major businesses invoked by Carl Sandburg, vice had long been intertwined with the city's history and political structure, and like those other important businesses, vice had its own district, in this case the infamous Levee. As most Chicagoans knew only too well, the Levee covered the blocks between Clark Street and Wabash Avenue, from Eighteenth to Twenty-second Streets. Brothels honeycombed the streets, pickpockets flourished, and youth gangs caroused. Pimps were so numerous and brazen that they formed their own union, the Cadets' Protective Association, and the madams, not to be outdone, formed theirs, the Friendly Friends.

To those who came to the Levee in search of pleasure, price determined everything. Indeed, the Levee was organized into a rigid caste system determined by the cost of sexual services. At the bottom of the ladder was Bed Bug Row, where black prostitutes sold their bodies for twenty-five cents a throw, and at the top, the celebrated Everleigh Club at 2131 South Dearborn Street. To the rest of the United States, the little prairie towns, and even New York, the Everleigh Club *was* Chicago prostitution; everyone knew about it, including the city's most influential police and politicians, who were regular customers, and who were paid off handsomely to permit it to function, indeed, to thrive. Two sisters, Ada and Minna Everleigh—proper, Kentucky-born daughters of a lawyer—presided over the club, which boasted fifty palatial rooms, a gourmet kitchen, and the most refined women to be found in the entire Levee. Beginning in 1900, the Everleigh Club operated twenty-four hours a day, and the Everleigh sisters became celebrities in Chicago; their picture appeared in the paper, and they went about the city together in their horse-drawn carriage, dressed in splendor. Eventually the forces of reform caught up with the Everleighs, and Chicago's Mayor Carter Harrison, who had vowed to rid the city of vice, shut the place down. The Everleigh sisters had no choice but to comply, but they proved so accomplished at their trade that they retired as millionaires, still in their thirties. Thus they became another Chicago success story.

With the departure of the Everleigh sisters in 1912 and the waning of the Levee as the focus of prostitution, organized syndicates took over the prostitution business, giving rise to a new type of vice lord. James Colosimo was by far the best known of the new breed. He had emigrated from Consenza, Italy, in 1895 and gotten his start in Chicago as a Levee pimp who attracted the backing of two hopelessly corrupt aldermen whose names were always mentioned in the same breath: Michael "Hinky Dink" Kenna and John "Bathhouse" Coughlin. Colosimo made himself useful as their "collector," a euphemism for extortionist. All the while, he maintained a parallel legitimate career as a street sweeper. Within a short period of time, he organized other street sweepers into a union, and he had the beginnings of a power base. In exchange for delivering the union's vote, he won an appointment as a precinct captain. Now part of the city's power structure, he had nothing to fear from the law, and he returned to his first love: prostitution. Big, jolly, handsome, careless, popular, Rabelaisian, Colosimo attained a celebrity of the first rank. His flagship was the gaudy Colosimo's Café at 2128 South Wabash Avenue, one of the most popular nightspots in Chicago. Patrons came to drink at the renowned mahogany-and-glass bar, and to eat in its dining room, whose walls were covered with green velvet and gold filigree. Beneath chandeliers made of solid gold, racketeers mingled with society figures and famous performers. Colosimo adored the opera, and his pal Enrico Caruso regularly patronized the café, as did Clarence Darrow, the distinguished lawyer, and a good part of the city's power elite. "Here they could rub elbows with demimondaines and their pimps, with gamblers, prize fighters, liquor agents and out-and-out sex perverts," wrote former mayor Harrison in disgust, "enjoying the experience as a new fling at life!" In addition to his café, Colosimo maintained "cribs" (minibrothels) all over town; the cribs skimped on luxury, but they brought their services closer to the customers. Despite their dreariness, Colosimo's brothels generated vast profits a trick and a shot of whiskey at a time. Newspapers estimated that Colosimo reaped more than $50,000 a month from his "resorts." Out of this income he built opulent homes for himself and his father, staffed by liveried servants. With his outsized appetites and huge girth, "Big Jim" was very much a product of the Gilded Age; he wore diamonds on every finger, a diamond horseshoe on his vest, and diamond studs in his shirt. Even his belt and suspender buckles glittered with diamonds. He came by his diamonds cheaply, since he acted as a fence for jewel thieves, and the diamonds he did not wear he carried loose in his pockets like so many marbles, which he magnanimously dispensed to grateful policemen and other guardians of the sacred public trust.

Colosimo's partner in love and crime was his wife, Victoria Moresco, a successful madam in her own right. As their family business grew, Colosimo sought a capable, unassuming man who could manage the enterprise without attracting attention. A man who could be trusted. After rejecting dozens of potential candidates in Chicago, Colosimo began hearing about the fine reputation of a low-keyed pimp and racketeer in Brooklyn: Johnny Torrio. In some versions of this tale, Torrio is described as Colosimo's nephew, but in the absence of evidence to confirm the relationship, it is more likely their kinship was spiritual rather than familial. When the two men finally met— Colosimo huge, obvious, and carefree, Torrio slight, subtle, and worried— Colosimo came away impressed, and he offered Torrio the job. Torrio accepted, and from then on he was the driving force behind Colosimo's success. Although he came to exercise great political influence in Chicago, Torrio never flaunted his status. He lived as unobtrusively here as he had in New York. In contrast to the garish excesses of his boss, Torrio, the classic insider, lived in an unpretentious apartment at 101 West Twenty-first Street with his wife, Ann, to whom he remained devoted. Unlike so many other men in the vice trade, including Colosimo and Al Capone, Torrio resisted any temptation to engage in sexual relations with his prostitutes. He made it a point to be home at six o'clock each evening, and he went about the city unarmed, despite the constant threat of danger. Neither did he smoke, drink, or swear. As he entered middle age, he looked exactly like what he was, a prosperous and entirely private businessman.

Even as Torrio assembled an empire of vice, his boss, consumed by a reckless passion, squandered it all. Colosimo's undoing was, not unexpectedly, a woman. Her name was Dale Winter, and she had come to Chicago, like so many other girls, to seek her fortune as an actress and a singer. Unable to find work, she resorted to singing at Colosimo's raffish café, and it was there that "Big Jim" saw and fell in love with her. From that time forward he was infatuated with her and left the running of his business to Torrio, who tirelessly soldiered on. Finally, in March 1920, Colosimo made the decisive break and in the process set the stage for the first modern gangland slaying. He divorced his wife and business partner, Victoria Moresco, and within three weeks he and Dale Winter were wed; at the beginning of May he installed his new bride in his home on Vernon Avenue. The courtship, divorce, and May-December marriage were the talk of Chicago—and beyond. From his vantage point of the Harvard Inn in Brooklyn, Frankie Yale closely followed Colosimo's folly. Still an exceedingly dangerous, vicious man, Yale had watched his former ally, Johnny Torrio, progress from Brooklyn to Chicago, with great success. With the advent of Prohibition, Yale was doing a booming business running bootleg whiskey out of his Harvard Inn, but Yale wanted more. It appeared that Colosimo, old, fat, and hopelessly in love, was vulnerable. So it was that Frankie Yale decided to visit Chicago.

On the last day of his life, May 11, 1920, Jim Colosimo said good-bye to his new bride and rode in his chauffeured car to the café, where he planned to catch up on business he had neglected during the previous months. He went to his office, talked with the secretary and the chef, called his lawyer but failed to get through, and passed the time of day. He seemed impatient and ill at ease that afternoon, for he had an appointment—with whom he did not say—and the man was late. At 4:30, he stepped into the lobby on his way to the street, but he never made it. Pistol in hand, Frankie Yale had concealed himself in an adjoining cloakroom, and when his target came into view, Yale fired twice. The first bullet struck Colosimo at the back of the head; the second shattered the glass of the empty cashier's cage and disappeared into the wall. "Big Jim" Colosimo, Chicago's popular vice lord, fell on his back, dead, assassinated. His hair was soon matted with blood, which seeped into the floor. He was forty-three years old. Covered by a gray tweed suit, a red rose fastened to the lapel and a pearl-handled revolver in the pocket, his massive bulk was truly impressive; in death he somehow seemed larger than he had in life. Yale immediately fled the scene of the crime, but not before at least one witness, a terrified waiter, got a good look at him.

News of Colosimo's assassination astonished all Chicago, and it was immediately seen as a watershed event for the city. The day after, the serious-minded *Chicago Daily News* commented, "The murder of James Colosimo, vice lord on the south side since 1912, . . . marks the ending of one epoch and the beginning of another in the history of vice in Chicago. . . . The old Levee was never dead; it was simply slumbering. With its awakening came the war for power—power to collect money from disorderly houses, to give jobs to henchmen, to gain immunity." Had Colosimo lived out his natural life span, he would have been just another racketeer pursuing his inglorious career, but the assassination conferred a significance on him that he had lacked in life. His funeral on May 15 became a gaudy demonstration more appropriate to the last rites of a powerful political figure or a popular entertainer—both of which he had been, in his own way. In fact, the last rites of James Colosimo became the first of Chicago's great gangster funerals, an event that priests and police captains alike attended to pay their last respects to the sort of man they were supposed to condemn. Colosimo was universally recognized as Chicago's premier pimp, yet his honorary pallbearers included three judges, a congressman, an assistant state attorney, and no less than nine Chicago aldermen—all of them marching in step with racketeers such as Johnny Torrio and Jakie Adler as well as an unsavory assortment of small-time pimps and white slavers. Torrio, who never displayed emotion, wept in public and told the press, "Big Jim and I were like brothers." A procession of 5,000 of the faithful followed the hearse bearing Colosimo's body to Oakwood Cemetery. "It is a strange commentary upon our system of law and justice," remarked the *Chicago Tribune* of the spectacle, which accurately reflected the close alliance between the city's racketeers and political establishment.

Once the body was laid to rest the questions began. The first concerned the disposition of his estate. At the time of his death, "Big Jim" Colosimo, who left no will, was rumored to be worth at least half a million dollars, diamonds included, but in the end, only $75,000 could be located; because of legal technicalities surrounding the circumstances of his marriages, the money went to his father rather than to Victoria Moresco or Dale Winter. The second, and far more troubling, question concerned the identity of his assassin. Since Colosimo had died with his pockets full of money and the jewels he habitually carried, and his seven-carat diamond ring still on his finger, it was apparent that robbery was not a motive. The precise, methodical execution suggested that the culprit was a professional on assignment. The list of suspects included corrupt politicians with whom Colosimo had quarreled; his ex-wife, Victoria Moresco (whose brothers, it was said, were out to avenge her honor); an early lover of Dale Winter's; and even Johnny Torrio. Suspicion also fell on the Black Hand, the freelance blackmailers who sent elaborate letters to extort money on pain of death. Wealthy and visible, Colosimo was a prime target of Black Hand threats, but his method of dealing with blackmail was simple: he paid the money. One faint clue did turn up: a note someone had scrawled on the back of a blank check in Colosimo's dining room that day. It read, "So long, vampire. So long, lefty."

Police investigators soon discovered that the real culprit was Frankie Yale. In an effort to link Yale to Torrio, a story made the rounds that Torrio had paid Yale $10,000 for the job, but Yale was far too prominent to kill on commission. In all likelihood, he murdered Colosimo to satisfy his own expansionist goal of ruling the Chicago vice trade. The police duly arrested him in New York and charged him with the murder of James Colosimo, and they located the waiter who placed Yale at the scene of the crime, but as this witness came to realize, testifying against Frankie Yale was hazardous to one's health. Trembling with fear, the waiter at the last moment claimed his memory failed him, and with that the case against Yale unraveled.

Years after the event, stories began circulating around Chicago newsrooms that the young Al Capone himself hid in the cloakroom and carried out the deed, said to mark the first step of his rise to the summit of the Chicago rackets. But for the young Capone to have carried out the murder of the most powerful vice lord in Chicago, his mentor's boss, would have been suicidal. Furthermore, Al Capone had not yet arrived in Chicago at the time of Colosimo's death. In the end, no one was ever found guilty of the murder of Colosimo, though the Chicago police and racketeers alike continued to insist that Yale had been responsible.

Although he avoided indictment for murder, Yale's attempt to destabilize Torrio's Chicago empire backfired. The removal of "Big Jim" actually consolidated the Torrio organization, which in turn froze Yale out. He remained in New York, plotting the death of rival gangsters closer to home. In February 1922, he himself became the target of an assassination attempt, which occurred the night he traveled from Brooklyn to a racketeers' ball in lower Manhattan. The bullets flew just as Yale, dressed in a double-breasted suit, spats, black patent-leather shoes, a gray Chesterfield coat, and a fedora, was making his way from his Cadillac to the dance hall. The first volley felled his partners, and Yale hid beneath the car, waiting for help that failed to arrive;

the sound of the dance had drowned out the gunfire. Eventually he came out, assuming the assassin had departed, but just as he entered the dance hall, a bullet struck him in the back and tore through one of his lungs. The police believed that a rival Irish gangster, "Wild Bill" Lovett, was responsible.

Yale underwent surgery at Manhattan's Gouverneur Hospital and survived, though he was seriously weakened from the attack. Shortly after he went home to Brooklyn, he happened to attend Mass at a nearby church, St. Rosalia's. It was there that the priest, Father John Costa, found him and began a campaign to persuade Yale to build a new church. Father Costa chose his benefactor well, for the resulting church, the new St. Rosalia's, towered above the neighborhood, an opulent monument to the self-aggrandizing generosity of Frank Yale. He had long been feared throughout Brooklyn; now he had respect as well. Still, he was hated, and "Wild Bill" Lovett was not the last man to make an attempt on the life of Frankie Yale. The next time, his would-be assassins would come not from Brooklyn but all the way from Chicago.

· · ·

Within weeks of Colosimo's funeral, Chicago was again the scene of political pageantry and chicanery. The Republican National Convention came to town in June, and there, in the original smoke-filled room of American politics, the party bosses settled on an obscure Ohio senator named Warren G. Harding as the Republican candidate for president. He proved in harmony with the times, and the chosen candidate of Chicago racketeers, for Harding was a corrupt candidate picked by a corrupt party in a corrupt city. As such he and his running mate, Calvin Coolidge, won an easy victory over the Democratic ticket, which consisted of Ohio governor James M. Cox and Franklin D. Roosevelt, the former assistant secretary of the Navy. The watchword of Harding's presidency was the phrase "return to normalcy," which meant that the federal government, after the imperial pretensions of the administration of Woodrow Wilson, was planning to do nothing, to abdicate its powers and responsibilities, and, always a popular measure, reduce taxes.

The tenor of Harding's relaxed and corrupt administration was echoed in cities and states across the country. The Illinois governorship, for instance, was occupied by Len Small, who was indicted in 1921 for stealing over half a million dollars during his term as state treasurer; Small was acquitted because, it was widely believed, he bribed the jurors. Meanwhile, in Chicago, the administration of the mayor, William Hale Thompson, was proving to be a carnival of corruption. As a public servant, Thompson was a fraud, and everyone knew it, even his backers, who supported him for just that reason. And to his opponents, he was scandal incarnate, the "bad breath of Chicago politics," in one journalist's memorable phrase. Thompson was a political cartoon satirizing corruption come to life. Everything about him was oversized. He did not speak, he declaimed as he pointed upward with one long, bony, crooked finger. Behind the laughable façade lay a certain low cunning. "Big Bill" Thompson, as he was called, knew how to take popular stands, to tell the people what they wanted to hear, and what they wanted to hear most of all was that he would turn a blind eye to the city's vice trade, and, later on, to Prohibition. Thompson obliged; he announced that he was wet, and so was Chicago. There was a small but visible morals squad in Chicago, dedicated to eradicating prostitution; Mayor Thompson, who was married but kept a mistress, shut it down. Every racketeer in town, Torrio and Colosimo included, considered Thompson one of their own. Wherever he went, Torrio carried his membership card in the William H. Thompson Republican Club. Here was a man the racketeers could understand; here was a politician they could work with. They bribed him, and on election night they delivered the votes, whatever it took to keep such a valuable man in power. Even without their help, Thompson demonstrated an ample capacity for low cunning. To enlist the support of Chicago's huge bloc of Irish voters, he constantly railed against King George V and the horrible conspiracies that malevolent sovereign planned to unleash against the United States. Indeed, said Thompson, England was planning to invade the United States at any moment. Thompson's preposterous brand of demagoguery made him a laughingstock across the nation, but in Chicago, where isolationism prevailed and anti-English sentiment ran high among the Irish, his rhetoric struck a chord. Running on this platform, Thompson became the dominant figure in Chicago's rambunctious political life.

The primary voice calling for reform belonged to the newly created Chicago Crime Commission, backed by a group known as the Secret Six, which consisted of prominent businessmen who wished to preserve their anonymity and their safety. The Chicago Crime Commission differed from other elements in the fray in that it had no political ideology and no aspirations to power. Rather than relying on ballots, bribes, or bullets to enforce its will, the Chicago Crime Commission relied on disseminating information and analysis concerning the nature and extent of corruption in Chicago, all of it mercifully free of inflammatory Prohibition rhetoric. As early as 1919, its director, Colonel Henry Barrett Chamberlin, detected a new trend in Chicago's racketeering: the emergence of a sophisticated syndicate patterned after legitimate corporations. "Modern crime, like modern business, is tending toward centralization, organization, and commercialization. Ours is a business nation. Our criminals apply business methods," he observed. "The men and women of evil have formed trusts."

Preeminent among such men and women was Johnny Torrio, who inherited Colosimo's empire amid an atmosphere of corruption that ran from the White House to Chicago's City Hall. Where the Everleigh sisters had controlled one brothel, and Colosimo several dozen, Torrio oversaw the operation of thousands of speakeasies, brothels, and gambling joints. (Thousands more belonged to other syndicates.) Once Prohibition got under way, his organization was making $4 million annually from beer, almost as much from gambling, $2 million from prostitution—and that was only in Chicago. In the new territory, the suburbs, he reaped an illicit harvest of another $4 million. That represented gross profit, and his expenses were equally impressive, not only the constant bribes but the payroll of the estimated 800 men in his employ. Even after he had given the police, the mayor, and various aldermen their due, Torrio's organization cleared several million dollars a year. The organization—which had no name—could take its place beside Chicago's other major industries, and it was growing faster than most. With increased wealth, Torrio found, came increased hazards. Coinciding as it did with the advent of Prohibition and the ascent of Warren G. Harding, Colosimo's death created a vacuum so large that not even Johnny Torrio could successfully fill it, though he made a brilliant, concerted, businesslike attempt to do so. Although Torrio had managed to forge alliances with other racketeers in Chicago, he had much to fear from Yale himself, who was just as capable of killing Torrio as Colosimo.

It was at this critical point in his career—and in the evolution of the Chicago rackets—that Torrio brought the twenty-two-year-old Capone to Chicago. On his arrival in 1921, Capone entered the thriving vice trade, working for Johnny Torrio. His older brother Ralph, who followed him to Chicago a year later, was soon engaged in the same work. The two shared an apartment at the intersection of Farwell and Sheridan Streets while they helped to manage Torrio's volatile empire.

Now that he had committed himself to working in the vice trade, Al Capone turned his back on the legitimate career path he had successfully pursued in Baltimore, but no matter what his line of work, he used many of the same skills in his new business that he had in his old: managing was managing, and bookkeeping bookkeeping. Of all racketeering activities, prostitution carried the greatest stigma, and yet it formed a vital part of his initiation into the rackets, for prostitution was not merely a sideline of the rackets, it was the foundation. Even among the racketeers, it carried an aura of disgrace. Those who derived their fortune from brothels habitually diverted attention from the ugly fact by pointing to the hypocrisy of those who sought to suppress vice, but in the end they could never mount an adequate defense of what they did; they could only insist that people always wanted illicit sexual activity, it was human nature, and since someone was going to make money from it, they might as well be the ones to cash in.

The two Capone brothers managed several small, midlevel brothels, which in practice meant they toiled as shills and janitors. It was routine, even dreary work, neither glamorous nor particularly dangerous. They might just have easily been working in a bathhouse, for their chores were similar—luring customers from the street, making sure the employees were presentable, maintaining a fresh supply of linen on hand, collecting money, and turning it over to the boss, in this case Johnny Torrio.

One prospective customer vividly recalled his first impression of Al as a small-time brothel manager in Chicago: a "swarthy, heavy-set fellow with hairy arms, and with part of a hairy chest also exposed . . . and a long ugly scar diagonally across his left cheek." Although his appearance was threatening, his demeanor was engaging, and he invited the young man, named Irle Waller, to drop by his establishment—or his brother's. Apparently the two places offered the same services at the same prices. Both were decidedly modest, overshadowed by other, better-known, and more expensive bordellos in the neighborhood, bordellos whose girls strolled the streets at lunchtime, not soliciting customers—that would be uncouth—but advertising their wares nonetheless. After a few minutes' hesitation, Waller, accompanied by several friends, decided to inspect the little brothel Capone managed, wherein they embarked on a journey that began in youthful lust and ended with money. "It was an old, brick, two-story flat-building, weatherbeaten and unpainted, as were all the others in that area," Waller related of Al's shabby but efficient whorehouse. Within, the boys confronted

six or seven girls about twenty years old, in flimsy undergarments called "chemises" or "Teddy Bears" in those days. Oh yes, also high-heeled pumps, usually black patent leather, to enhance them sexually. Some even had fancy extra curls attached to their coiffures. All of this for two dollars, and if and when you chose a girl she led you to a small cubicle. . . . Each cubicle contained a very small bed—with linen clean to dirty, depending on when you arrived. There was a table with a cheap bowl and pitcher of water, a towel, a bar of soap, and a small twenty-five watt electric bulb hanging from a cord in the air.

She would ask you did you want the first-class job, which was three dollars, or the two-dollar "trick," also how about venereal protection with a twenty-five cent rubber. When you finished, she would bring out a small coin container for any extra gratuity you might wish to deposit for her alone.

Of this two dollars, she received one dollar, and then a ten-cent deduction was made for "protection" against raids and for bail and legal service.

After less than a year managing small brothels, Al received a promotion to the premier position in Torrio's empire of vice: manager of the Four Deuces. So named because of its address at 2222 South Wabash Avenue, in the heart of the old Levee district, the Four Deuces served as Torrio's Chicago head-quarters. A saloon occupied the first floor where locally produced whiskey sold for twenty-five cents and imported whiskey from Canada or rum from the Bahamas went for seventy-five cents; above, on the second floor, were Torrio's offices and a horse-betting parlor; a gambling den (poker, roulette, faro, blackjack) occupied the third floor; and finally, at the top of the stairs, there was, in the words of one journalist, "a colorless, no-nonsense sex mill designed for results." A brief session with a woman at the Four Deuces cost two dollars, and for five dollars, the customer could watch a "circus": two women going at it with each other. That was the Four Deuces as the world knew it. Then there was the basement, about which horror stories circulated sotto voce. "They snatch guys they want information from and take them to the cellar," another Chicago pimp, Mike "de Pike" Heitler, explained to the police in 1931. "They're tortured until they talk. Then they're rubbed out. The bodies are hauled through a tunnel into a trap door opening in the back of the building. Capone and his boys put the bodies in cars and then they're dumped out on a country road." Mike "de Pike" might have been telling the truth, or he might have been boasting; no one, not even Chicago's law enforcement officials, could say with certainty whether the horror stories were true, but they were sufficient to throw a scare into every racketeer in the city. (Shortly after he told these tales, Heitler was killed, his charred remains recovered from a house that had burned to the ground.)

Once Torrio took Capone into the business and made him a partner rather than an employee, Al no longer had to shill for customers; he was now a businessman, with an annual income approaching $25,000. However, Al Capone had not come all the way to Chicago to be a glorified pimp, and as he made his way in the rackets, he moved quickly to distance himself from the vice trade as practiced at the Four Deuces. He printed up business cards reading: "ALPHONSE CAPONE—Second Hand Furniture Dealer—2220 South Wabash Avenue," but there is no record of the ruse having fooled anyone, at any time. Of greater importance, he opened a new office at 2146 South Michigan Avenue, where he displayed a penchant for camouflage. From the street Capone's place of business appeared to be a doctor's office: "A. Brown, M.D." the sign read. There was even a waiting room with bottles of medic-inal alcohol on display, but a 1924 raid on the "doctor's" office disclosed that it was, in fact, the nerve center of the Torrio-Capone organization. Police seized ledgers that revealed how methodical and businesslike Capone had become in his administration of the organization's enterprises. Each was devoted to a distinct aspect of the business:

- Names of police and Prohibition agents on the organization's payroll
- Itemized income from the organization's brothels
- Names of the organization's breweries
- The names of the organization's biggest customers—individuals as well as hotels
- A list of the speakeasies buying liquor from the organization
- Truck and boat routes used to transport the liquor from the Caribbean and Canada to Chicago

Taken together, the books showed that the Torrio-Capone organization had earned approximately $3 million in each of the last three years. The police estimated that this amount, impressive though it was, amounted to only a fraction of the organization's total earnings, and a U.S. attorney, Edwin Olsen, declared his belief that the syndicate's annual gross approached $70 million, making it one of the largest businesses in Chicago, if not the entire Midwest.

The Torrio-Capone organization offered a $5,000 "reward" for the return of the ledgers, and just before they were to be delivered to the U.S. attorney, a Municipal Court judge by the name of Howard Hayes intervened. Judge Hayes impounded the ledgers, and then, without bothering to inform the city of Chicago, returned the ledgers to Al Capone. The matter, which had briefly threatened to expose the entire Torrio-Capone operation to the scrutiny of the press and prosecutors alike, suddenly dropped from view.

•   •   •

The wonder-working bribe had been arranged by Capone's new associate and fast friend, Jack Guzik, a scion of Chicago's first family of vice. Throughout his life, Guzik maintained he was not really a gangster, for he never carried a gun, never resorted to violence, and cringed at the sight of blood. Nor, at first glance, did Guzik's background seem to fit the gangster mold. He belonged to a large Orthodox Jewish family, one of eleven siblings, some of them talented, others street-smart, and all of them loyal to one another. The Guziks were, in fact, the kind of immigrants who could have succeeded in any one of numerous legitimate occupations, but who happened to earn their living through prostitution and saw nothing wrong with it.

The parents, Max and Mamie, emigrated to the United States from Russia in 1892, along with their children: Harry, Morris, Joe, Fannie, Benjamin, Jack, Rebecca, and Charles. In the New World, Max, the head of the family, followed a traditional Jewish immigrant occupation: he became a cigar maker. Once in Chicago, the Guzik family swelled to include three more children, Mollie, Katie, and Sam. Twenty-three years separated Harry, the eldest sibling, from Sam, the youngest. A cigar maker's wages could not feed the entire family, and Max developed a lucrative sideline as a precinct captain for those politician-pimps, "Hinky-Dink" Kenna and "Bathhouse" Coughlin. In this role Max delivered votes to the machine and collected payoffs in the process; he also made numerous contacts in the vice trade that he was able to pass along to his children. Two of Max's sons, Harry and Jack, eventually joined forces to become, in the words of the law, pimps and panderers. And they became quite successful at it, too. Despite his youth, Jack (born on March 20, 1886) took the lead, running his string of no-frills brothels. As Al Capone discovered, Jack Guzik was nothing like the flamboyant Jim Colosimo; he was devoted to his wife, Rose Lipschutz, whom he married when she was sixteen, and to his children: Charles, Jeannette, and Frank. (Charles became the third generation of Guziks to work in the vice trade. In 1956 he was sentenced to a term of sixty to 100 years for sex offenses involving teenagers.)

Meanwhile, Harry, the eldest sibling, and his wife, Alma, managed a popular brothel at 119th and Paulina Street; it was known as "The Blue Goose." In 1907 they were convicted for white slavery, in the process achieving national notoriety. Indeed, the term *white slavery* first came into widespread use in connection with one of Harry's own whores. Her name was Mona Marshall, and while she was confined to her brothel one night, she wrote the statement, "I am a white slave," attached the note to a key, and threw it down to the street, where a milkman found it and turned it over to the police. Although Mona was not a captive in the conventional sense, since she spent at least as much time outside the brothel as she did within, and although she subsequently denied writing the note, the concept of a white slave inflamed the righteous indignation of a young assistant state's attorney named Clifford Roe, whose oratory roused the entire city to one of its occasional fits of revulsion against the vice trade, and the noise was heard as far as Washington, D.C. In 1910, Congress passed the Mann Act (usually referred to as the White Slave Act), which made it a federal offense to transport a woman across state lines for "immoral purposes." As written, the law had limited usefulness, and within Chicago, little changed. Mona Marshall, the original white slave, returned to prostitution, and Harry Guzik, though sentenced to the Illinois State Penitentiary, received a pardon from the governor, Len Small, who was, incidentally, a protégé of Chicago's mayor, "Big Bill" Thompson. Later, it emerged that Guzik had bribed the governor to obtain his freedom. The pimp knew every man had his vice, and every politician his price.

Although he had been working in the vice trade for years, Jack Guzik managed to avoid legal trouble until December 3, 1917, when he was arrested for disorderly conduct—a charge covering a multitude of sins—and sentenced to eight months in the county jail. After that, his distinctive visage became familiar to police and, later, to the press: a short man, pudgy and pale, hopelessly flabby, with a large neck and jowls that seemed to double the size of his face. Actually, they were more than jowls, they were wattles, and they spilled over his collar, obscuring the knot of his tie, and whenever he spoke, they quivered. Jack favored round tortoiseshell glasses, heavily tinted; he always wore a hat, and the combination of his pear-shaped physique, glasses, and broad-brimmed hat made him look like a big shot with sinister connections.

Although best known as a pimp, he did have aspirations beyond the brothel. He made himself so useful to Torrio that he was rewarded with an interest in the organization's gambling joints. And in 1919, just before Prohibition took effect, Torrio further rewarded him with the ownership of a brewery whose profits were certain to skyrocket once beer was outlawed. Yet Jack Guzik was never really a gambler or bootlegger, except by default; he remained a pimp, the calling to which he had been born. As his reputation grew, he acquired a vivid, mysterious nickname: "Greasy Thumb." No one could say exactly how he came by it; one story had it that as a waiter in a kosher restaurant he had often been careless in carrying plates to the tables and dipped his thumb in the soup. Another insisted that the name referred to his greasing the palms of police and politicians with money. In either case, the nickname conveyed the seamy aura surrounding Jack "Greasy Thumb" Guzik.

Working for Jack, and then with Jack, Al became extremely fond of the man, who was like an older brother to him. Jack made him feel at home in Chicago. As their friendship deepened, Capone picked up a smattering of Yiddish from Jack, as well as fondness for Jewish delicacies such as jellied calves' feet, and, in return, he was glad to demonstrate his cooking skills for the Guziks, donning an apron to prepare spaghetti with the Capone family's special red sauce, extra spicy, the way he had learned from his mother. Jack, in turn, valued Al's bookkeeping skills, and even more than that, his sense of family loyalty and his warmth. Finally, Capone's physical strength and his willingness to use it endeared him to Jack, who was missing a kidney and suffered from chronic bronchial ailments. He seemed to be a perpetual convalescent, and he was an unrepentant coward in all physical activities.

It was Torrio who had brought Capone to Chicago, but it was Jack Guzik who kept him there. Al's primary allegiance in the organization switched from Torrio to Guzik, and the relationship marked an important step for Al, who until this time had worked exclusively for Italians in Brooklyn (Torrio, Yale), Baltimore (Aiello), and Chicago (Torrio again). He was now reaching beyond the Italian milieu with its inward-looking *campanilismo* to the city's—and the rackets'—other important immigrant group, the Jews. There were nearly 300,000 Jews in Chicago in the early 1920s, and they were entering the mainstream of civic life as rapidly as the Irish had a generation earlier, their influence on the city's political and business life growing with every passing year. The attraction the Guziks held for Capone is apparent; although they belonged to a different tribe, they were in many ways a reflection of the Capones—another large, closely knit, immigrant family who dealt in crime but who in their private lives maintained a solid, bourgeois, upwardly mobile façade. Jack Guzik and his family lived in one of the city's better suburbs, in a house which, with its nine rooms and servant, could have belonged to any prosperous businessman of the day. A glance at the externals of the Guziks' lives offered little clues as to the nature of the family business. Children played in the front yard, a dog romped through the bushes, and the future U.S. attorney for Chicago, George E. Q. Johnson, the man who would lead the crusade to put Al Capone and Jack Guzik in jail, lived just down the street. What better proof that the neighborhood was respectable and safe.

.   .   .

Although he was by now a member in good standing with the Torrio organization, the young Al Capone, without the steadying presence of his wife and child, is remembered mostly for his coarse, immature behavior, and his continual drinking. In August 1922, while drunk and at the wheel of one of Torrio's deluxe sedans, he collided with a parked taxi. The young Capone in a besotted rage staggered from his car and pulled a gun on the cabbie, whom he may have suspected of being a rival racketeer attempting to kill him. The incident appeared in one of the Chicago papers, who introduced its readers to a young man named "Alfred Caponi" residing "at the notorious Four Deuces, a disorderly house at 2222 South Wabash avenue."

Early this morning [the account continued] his automobile crashed into a Town taxicab, driven by Fred Krause, 741 Drake avenue, at North Wabash avenue and East Randolph street, injuring the driver. Three men and a woman, who were with Caponi, fled before the arrival of the police.

Caponi is said to have been driving east in Randolph street at a high rate of speed. The taxicab was parked at the curb.

Following the accident, Caponi alighted and flourishing a revolver, displayed a special deputy sheriff's badge and threatened to shoot Krause.

Patrick Bargall, 6510 South Claremont avenue, motorman of a southbound street car, stopped his car and advised Caponi to put the weapon in his pocket, and the latter then threatened him, according to witnesses.

In the meantime, the Central police had been notified and they hurried to the scene, arresting Caponi. Krause was given first aid treatment by an ambulance physician.

It was Capone's first arrest in Chicago, the first time the police became aware of a young man about whom they would be hearing a good deal in the years to come.

The article failed to mention that "Alfred Caponi" was, at the time, drunk, for he was charged with driving while intoxicated, carrying a concealed weapon, and assault with an automobile—all serious violations that might, if proven in a court of law, send him to jail for months or even years, his "deputy sheriff's badge," with which Torrio had provided him, notwithstanding. However, Torrio's well-paid and well-placed connections saw to it that the matter was dropped, and Capone was never indicted.

Capone's drunken behavior figured again later that summer when he encountered a young singer from Kentucky by the name of Rio Burke, who was struggling to establish herself in Chicago. One day, after entertaining an audience of hod carriers, she attended their picnic in a city park. "To this picnic came two brothers," she remembers. "One was rather good looking except for a deep and prominent scar that ran all the way down his left cheek. He had recently come out of New York and everyone seemed to know him and paid him great homage. I was later to learn he was Al Capone, which meant nothing at the time. As the afternoon wore on, Al became very, very drunk and started throwing money around like confetti. Everybody was getting ten- and twenty-dollar bills, and the entertainers went home rich. But he became so drunk and belligerent that his brother Ralph had to persuade him to say good-bye and go home, to everyone's great relief." That was not the last occasion Rio Burke would see Al Capone: "Never could I have dreamed that one day this drunken hulk would be sitting at my dining-room table, dressed to the nines in a silk suit, with princely behavior, or that he would hide out in my home for eight days after a spectacular Chicago murder."

The end of Capone's drunken behavior coincided with the arrival of his family from Brooklyn—not just Mae and Sonny, but his widowed mother, younger brothers, and baby sister. Al was now making enough money from Torrio's organization to be able to buy, in his own name, a home for them all at 7244 South Prairie Avenue. This was an address on a tranquil, middle-class South Side suburban street far from the turmoil of the Loop and the corruption of Johnny Torrio's vice, booze, and gambling empire. Prairie Avenue went on for miles; no less than fifty long blocks separated the house from the Loop. The cushion of distance appealed to Capone's need for safety, but he took further precautions to customize the house, installing iron bars in the basement windows and a large brick garage around the back to house his cars, which were always at the ready should he need to make a hasty departure. Despite these unusual features, the appearance of the house was conventional enough. Built of red brick, two stories tall, it towered over its small lot. Nine stone steps led from the street to the front door, and on the second story, a portal opened onto a small terrace overlooking the street. The front yard contained a single tree, and a vine crawled up one side of the house.

Compared to the life Capone had known on Garfield Place in Brooklyn, the Prairie Avenue residence was a glorious improvement, a sign of having arrived in America, but by Chicago standards it was an ordinary dwelling such as any moderately successful businessman or career civil servant might own. It was one of thirty-four houses on its long block, several of which belonged, interestingly enough, to policemen and their families. In another sharp break with the past, the Capones were the only Italians in the neighborhood, which consisted of a mixture of Scotch, Irish, and German descendants. In fact, just two doors south of the Capones' new home lived a retired Presbyterian clergyman. For a racketeer who sought to present a façade of respectability and legitimacy to the world, and who wanted to keep his family far from the field of battle, 7244 Prairie Avenue was ideal. The unpretentious house would serve as Al Capone's residence of record for as long as he lived in Chicago. Although Capone was often absent for long periods of time—weeks, sometimes months on end—he always returned here, to breathe the unpolluted air, to feel normal again, a man with a wife and a child, even though with the passing of time that normality became an unreachable ideal.

Although the Capones had apparently burst the bounds of *campanilismo*, they lived as they had back in Brooklyn, and as their ancestors had before them in Naples, that is to say, on top of one another, in the same house. No matter how far they had come economically and geographically, they still clung together. Now in her midfifties, Teresa, the honored dowager of the clan, lived on the top floor of the house. On the first floor, in a suite of rooms at the back, lived Al, his wife, Mae, and their boy, Sonny, now in his fifth year of life. Other brothers came and went, using rooms in the house as they needed. They included Frank, now twenty-seven, Mimi, twenty, Albert, sixteen, and Mattie, who was fourteen at the time the family moved to Chicago. Only Ralph, who was approaching thirty, lived outside the home, in the apartment at Farwell and Sheridan he had once shared with Al, but he, too, could often be found on Prairie Avenue. In sum, it was a crowded, noisy, lively household.

The Capones soon became known to the neighborhood. Mae or Teresa often knocked on neighbors' doors to borrow a cup of sugar or flour, and they made a point to return more than they borrowed. Mafalda rode her bicycle in the neighborhood. Later, when she became older, she attended the Richards School, a private institution. Her older brother Al was celebrated at the school for his habit of appearing at Christmas in a large sedan, filled with gifts. Playing the role of the grand seigneur to the point of parody, he would step out of the car and supervise the distribution of baskets of candy, turkeys, and presents for every student and teacher at his little sister's school. Beyond that extravagance, the neighbors had little sense, initially, that Mafalda's big brother, the one with the scars on his cheek, was a racketeer, bootlegger, and pimp. The Al Capone they knew (or thought they knew) said he was a dealer in used furniture, but he didn't seem to hold a steady job. He spent many days lounging around the house, wearing a bathrobe and slippers. He occasionally played with his son in the backyard, gently tossing a ball in the boy's direction. He would cook for anyone in the neighborhood who was willing to come inside and eat with him. Al's spaghetti was known throughout the neighborhood, and as he stood before the kitchen's huge stove, wearing an apron, stirring the sauce, he urged his guests to wash it down with as much Chianti as they could manage.

The house, Mae, and, most of all, Sonny represented Capone's strivings toward redemption. Although he preyed on other people's weaknesses for a living, his reputation and standing in the community mattered deeply to him. The deeper he went into racketeering and all its associated sins, the more he idealized his family, as if they, in their innocence, were living proof that he was not the monster that the newspapers later insisted he was.

· · ·

During the Capones' first few years in Chicago, the city still enjoyed a relatively peaceful environment. Under the influence of Johnny Torrio, local racketeers had neatly carved up the city, and each respected the other's territory, settling matters among themselves without firing shots or leaving corpses for the police to find and the newspapers to photograph. Even the pressures of Prohibition did little to disturb the rackets' smooth operation. However, the low body count told only part of the story, because the city's neighborhoods were rocked by countless gunfights and explosions caused by homemade bombs, generally known as pineapples. You didn't have to be a racketeer to be drawn into the escalating brutality; merchants (often from immigrant backgrounds) increasingly resorted to violence to protect their stores, fruit stands, or warehouses from small-time hoodlums hurling pineapples in the middle of the night from a passing car; the police, ever more deeply involved with racketeers and bootleggers, proved embarrassingly inept at coping with the situation and restoring law and order.

News of the violence, carried to every home through Chicago's six daily newspapers, eventually led to political repercussions. After eight years in City

Hall, "Big Bill" Thompson became the scapegoat for the lawlessness (which he had at the very least abetted), and as scandal engulfed his administration, he withdrew from the 1923 election in the certain knowledge that he would lose. He was succeeded by the well-meaning, earnest, and slightly dull William E. Dever, who intended to enforce Prohibition as it had never been enforced in Chicago. "This guerrilla war between hijackers, rum runners and illicit beer peddlers will be crushed," he declared. "I am just as sure that this miserable traffic with its toll of human life and morals can be stamped out as I am mayor that I am not going to flinch for a minute." With such statements, Dever sowed a whirlwind of violence. The irony of the situation was obvious; under the two corrupt Thompson administrations, the racketeers quietly went about their business. Now, in the reign of the upright Dever, violence broke out across the city, and it came from all directions. Gangsters started feuding with other gangsters, policemen began killing gangsters, and innocent bystanders got caught in the crossfire. Not even Johnny Torrio, who abhorred violence, could find a safe haven.

Facing the prospect of at least four years of Dever's rhetoric and tiresome reform politics, the Torrio-Capone organization decided to move the base of their fast-growing operation to the western suburban town of Cicero. It seemed like the ideal solution, for Cicero was small enough for the organization to control. They could *own* the city government, from the mayor to the dog catcher. Their gambling dens and brothels could function without interference. And Cicero was in Cook County, as was Chicago; indeed, the big city merged almost imperceptibly into its smaller neighbor. Although Cicero was a suburb, it was largely industrial. There were no architectural flights of fancy here, only endless rows of brick buildings squatting beside the town's broad avenues, below the immense, smoke-filled sky. It was an ugly place; you'd have to go all the way to Gary, Indiana, and its hulking gray furnaces to find more depressing surroundings. Until the arrival of Al Capone, Cicero was best known as the site of an enormous Western Electric plant, which employed over 20 percent of the town's wage earners; they assembled, so the company claimed, most of the world's telephones. They were paid handsome wages, these dutiful, hardworking citizens of Cicero, to work for Western Electric, which anchored the town's economy.

Like every other part of Cook County, Cicero had its distinctive ethnic cast. There were few Irish, Italians, or Jews in Cicero, and virtually no blacks; 80 percent of its 40,000 inhabitants came from Bohemia in Central Europe, or their parents had. Cicero's Bohemians were known as quiet, even submissive folk, rather rigid, clinging stubbornly to the ways of the Old World, who wanted one thing that only the bootleggers could give them: their daily beer. No ordinary saloon suds, theirs was a robust, heavy brew, so filling that the men often drank it instead of eating a conventional lunch. It

was made by local breweries according to Old World formulas, and it occupied a central role in their lives. It was the workingman's due, and more,
a symbol of their culture and way of life. To Cicero's citizens, Prohibition
was an inexplicable aberration in an otherwise benign country, and they
deeply resented it as an intrusion on their peaceful, productive way of life.
For all these reasons, the organization's move to Cicero should have been a
happy solution, but it was not to be. From the moment the Capone boys
came to town, gunfire echoed in the once-quiet streets, and violence sub-
verted time-honored custom.

The racketeers' conquest of Cicero began in October 1923, when Johnny
Torrio opened a brothel on Roosevelt Road, staffed with twenty prostitutes.
Police arrested the entire consignment of girls, as well as a second batch
Torrio sent to another location in Cicero, but the real opposition to the
introduction of prostitution came from rival racketeers afraid to be outdone.
Always the peacemaker, Torrio sat down with them and painstakingly worked
out agreements concerning which gang would handle what vice in Cicero.
Once the deal was set, Torrio decided the time had come to move his aging
mother back to Italy. The two of them traveled to Italy, where he squirreled
away the millions he had made in the Chicago rackets and set her up in a
large estate staffed by thirty servants. In his absence, he left the management
of the Cicero rackets to Al Capone, who proceeded to demonstrate a style
completely different from that of his master.

Although he had been in Chicago for more than three years, Al Capone
remained an unknown, with the exception of the brief notoriety he had
gained in his 1922 car accident. He had managed a few brothels, demonstrated a talent for ingratiating himself with Torrio and Guzik, and had
moved the rest of his family to their comfortable, bourgeois home out on
South Prairie Avenue, but beyond that he had little to show for himself. He
was still a small-time hoodlum masquerading under various aliases, most
frequently "Al Brown." But all that changed when he assumed the management of Torrio's Cicero operation. Torrio had been content to build an
empire piece by carefully assembled piece while remaining hidden in the
background; Capone insisted on nothing less than complete control of Cicero, thrusting himself into the foreground at every opportunity. For the first
time, the extravagant outlines of the Capone persona became visible to all
Chicago.

As soon as Torrio sailed for Italy, Capone installed himself in a somber,
redbrick building known as Anton's Hotel, owned by a restaurateur known as
Tony "the Greek" Anton, who had joined his retinue. He was soon joined
by his older brother Ralph, who opened or assumed control of speakeasies
and nightclubs. The best known was the Cotton Club of Cicero, located at
5342 West Twenty-second Street. The files of the Chicago Crime Commis-

sion, which continued to track the spread of the rackets, characterized it as a " 'whoopee' spot where liquor flowed freely and it served as a rendezvous for those interested in night life."

The most visible Capone in Cicero at this time was not Ralph or Al but Frank, who, at twenty-nine, was two years younger than Ralph and four years older than Al. Of all the brothers, Frank seemed by far the most promising. He was certainly the best looking—tall and lean, with thick, wavy hair. His quiet manner and neat business suits gave him the air of an intent young banker. Trading on his respectable appearance, Frank fronted for the organization in its dealings with the Cicero town government. In exchange for Capone's support, they pledged to let the organization's gambling and prostitution rackets function without interference. They were to see to it that no one, not one solitary police officer, stood in the way of Capone's clubs, gambling dens, and brothels. To ensure these worthy men held office, Frank Capone went far beyond the usual Chicago-style politics of importing people from other towns to vote again and again. In his first Cicero election, he organized a show of Capone force, placing a fleet of sedans on the street. He stationed men at the polling places to ask voters their preference; anyone planning to vote for a candidate not controlled by the Capone organization was advised to leave. At day's end, Capone henchmen seized ballot boxes in the precincts considered favorable to the opposition, emptied them, and filled them with new ballots favoring Capone candidates. The inevitable result of Frank's election strategy was that every Capone-backed candidate was elected by an overwhelming margin.

While Frank reorganized Cicero's political scene, Ralph supervised the opening of the organization's new brothel, the Stockade. It was a gruesome choice of a name, conjuring as it did the bygone stockades of the Levee's white slave trade, in which young girls were "broken in" to their new calling. As for location, Ralph chose to place the brothel not within Cicero proper but in neighboring Forest View, a newly incorporated village whose lack of a local government meant that Ralph need not trouble himself with the niceties of rigged elections. Instead, he went directly to the head of the police, Joseph W. Nosek, and announced his intention to build a "hotel" in Forest View. Recalled Nosek, "I saw no harm because I just didn't know who the Capones were." He found out once he saw Ralph's entourage of small-time racketeers. Nosek ordered them out of town. That night two men rousted him out of bed and hustled him to the town hall, where others awaited him. "They told me they were going to kill me," Nosek said later. "They beat me over the head with the butts of their guns and though I was streaming with blood and dazed from pain they kicked me over the floor."

In the end, Nosek was spared his life, and Ralph erected his brothel. It sheltered about sixty girls who worked out of a large old building made of

stone and wood. The Stockade was more than a whorehouse; it also served
as a gambling den, a munitions dump for the Capone organization, and a
hideout for racketeers on the run from the law. A first-class, full-service
establishment, the Stockade catered not to Cicero's working-class population
but to pleasure seekers who came by car from Chicago. The Capone-
controlled Stockade prospered and became by far the best-known attraction
in Forest View, which acquired a new nickname, "Caponeville."

As the Torrio organization strengthened its hold on Cicero, Al developed
a special interest in the operation of a new, state-of-the-art gambling establishment known as the Ship. After his apprenticeship in Torrio's brothels,
gambling was actually a step toward respectability for Al, but managing a
gambling den was a complicated business. To function properly, it required
more than an assortment of roulette wheels and blackjack tables; it also
required a staff of specialists. There were the ropers, who stood outside the
door, trying to lure customers within; the friskers, who were prepared to
relieve patrons of their weapons; the stickman, who controls the dice; the
bankers, who control the payment of money; and, most importantly, the
shills, who were employees of the house posing as patrons. Taking care to
look as legitimate as they could, the shills were responsible for creating the
excitement designed to keep a patron in a game, and who made it unlikely
that the patron would ever win.

In addition to the Ship, the Torrio-Capone organization also came into
control of Cicero's Hawthorne Race Track, which presented fixed races.
Despite Al's increasing involvement with all these varied aspects of gambling,
he himself was an astonishingly reckless bettor, who invariably lost far more
than he gained. Of course, when Al gambled at the Ship, he *was* the house,
so losing was to his advantage, and at the track, he always knew in advance
which horse would win, so he had little incentive to master the fine points
of handicapping. At the same time, his making a point of dropping large
sums of money—at first hundreds and later thousands of dollars on a roll of
the dice—gave the impression that Cicero's gambling establishments were
indeed legitimate.

•   •   •

Although his power was increasing month by month, Al Capone remained remarkably unchanged. When not aroused to fury, he could be as
charming, gregarious, relaxed as he had been back in the Brooklyn dance
halls he frequented during his adolescent years. He spent much of his time
with his landlord and friend, "Tony the Greek," lounging in Tony's restaurant by the hour, and consuming vast quantities of Tony's food. Tony,
for his part, saw only Capone's generous and warmhearted side, and he
was quick to leap to his friend's defense. He would tell of Al's countless

acts of generosity, the lavish tips he dispensed on newsboys and errand-runners.

News of his progress in Chicago traveled all the way back to Brooklyn, inspiring other young Italian immigrants to try their chances in the wide-open western city on the lake. Inevitably, they gravitated to Al Capone, expecting he would give them a job that would make them rich overnight. Although he did not make them rich, Capone did find them jobs, usually back in Brooklyn, where he still had influence. His old neighbors on Navy Street, the Pitaros, with whom he had formed a short-lived gang, were typical beneficiaries of Al Capone's informal employment agency. " 'I'm going to Chicago, I'm going to speak to Al Capone,' " Angela Pitaro recalled her oldest brother, Joseph, declaring one day. "He wanted to get in the gang, my brother."

When he reached Chicago, Joseph Pitaro was warmly received by Al, who took him on a tour of Chicago Heights—Capone territory. "Joseph," he said, "this is my building, this my laundry, and these are my whorehouses." He then took his visitor to the Capone headquarters; there were guns every-where. "Joseph," Capone suddenly warned him, "you go home. Go back to Brooklyn. You got a job there, and don't you ever get mixed up in this." Then Capone gave Joseph a small but significant lead. "When you go back to Brooklyn," the racketeer advised, "you go to Myrtle Avenue, to the movie house, and see Mr. Haskel."

Haskel, it turned out, was a Jew, a novelty for people like the Pitaros, and he gave Joseph a test. "I'll show you something," he said. They entered the movie theater, where a gang of rowdy youths were disturbing the other patrons. "You see that? That's got to stop. If you're man enough to stop these boys, you've got a job." Joseph took his coat off, smoothed his hair, and walked through aisles until he came to the troublemakers. He grabbed one by the neck. "Come here," he said to the boy, "I want to talk to you. Are you gonna stop this? Are you gonna behave? If you ain't gonna behave, you're getting out of here, and you're not comin' here no more to this show." Joseph managed to quiet the boys, and the job, thanks to Al Capone, was his.

As the Capone aura grew, people gravitated to him not just for what he could do for them, but because they wanted to associate with him, and, even more tellingly, to *be* like him.

Among the would-be Capones was a young boxer, a club fighter named Mickey Cohen (you didn't have to be Italian to follow Capone's example), who ingratiated himself with Al's brothers Ralph and Matthew. Soon the brothers invited him to dinner at the Capone home on South Prairie Ave-nue, where, over Teresa's pasta, Mickey fell under Al's spell. From the start, Cohen maintained "a great respect for Mr. Capone, because the guy was such a man and carried himself so nicely." He was also charmed by Al's solicitous manner. "After I got to know him, he always patted me down to see if I had money in my kick—my pocket. I think the least he ever put in my kick was a couple of hundred-dollar bills. I respected his ways, like a kid has an admiration for a great boxer or some idol that you want to kind of follow in his footsteps, or mold your life in his footsteps. . . . Admiring the guy as much as I did, I may have tried to copy his ways. Like somebody may talk in a way that you like, so you try to copy his way of expressing himself."

As Cohen intuitively sensed, Capone's smoothness and his air of civility made the rackets seem as legitimate as any other business, an avenue to self-respect. For an outsider like Cohen, the legitimate world was a country club to which admittance was forbidden and prejudice a white picket fence separating him from privilege and entitlement. But Capone's example made those cruel boundaries seem irrelevant. "See, I was really nothing—a young kid really—when I came to Al Capone, and the guy treated me like I was Frank Costello from New York," Cohen later wrote with something approaching wonder. "He never talked down to me or anything. And he was worried about how I was getting along all right, my comfort. And he even said to me, 'What do you want to box for? It's a tough racket, why don't you get out of it?' . . . He intimated to me . . . if I found something to get into, he would back me up." With Al's blessing, Cohen began running a small crap game in cahoots with Matthew Capone—Mattie, as everyone called him. Cohen financed the crap game in a novel fashion; each night he borrowed several hundred dollars from the cash register of a barbershop in the Loop, and each morning he returned the amount, plus a small additional sum. But money was not Cohen's problem; people were. Mattie and Al were often not on the best of terms, for the younger Capone fiercely resented Al's prominence, and the sibling rivalry eventually brought Cohen into conflict with Jack Guzik. "Greasy Thumb" summoned Cohen to a meeting and delivered a harangue in which he tried to lay down the law, at least as it was understood by racketeers: "Are you crazy? We gave you an OK for poker. We don't have any craps in the Loop, and you come around and you open a fucking crap game. Are you out of your mind?"

"I couldn't make no money with poker," Cohen tried to explain.

Guzik ordered Cohen to shut down his crap game and report to work at a Capone gambling joint going by the name of Chew Tobacco Ryan's. "I'm putting you on the payroll for twenty-five dollars a day," Guzik said, but Cohen insisted this was not enough for him and his assistants. "That's what I was told," Guzik replied. The scales fell from Cohen's eyes. Al was the salesman, the glad-hander and backslapper, who picked pockets in reverse, depositing money rather than stealing it, but once you were on the inside, Cohen discovered, you didn't deal with Al, you dealt with Ralph or Guzik, which wasn't nearly so much fun. They didn't waste time holding hands and making you feel good the way Al did, they didn't cater to your hopes and fears; they told you exactly what they wanted you to do. It was a classic Mr. Inside/Mr. Outside operation, with Al presenting a smiling face to the outside world and Guzik maintaining internal discipline. He was a son of a bitch, accustomed to dealing with other men who fit that description; they were all sons of bitches together. Shouting and posturing, Cohen and Guzik failed to come to an agreement, and Cohen stormed out of the meeting, vowing to reopen his crap game that night, and "Greasy Thumb" Guzik be damned.

Five nights later, Cohen happened to be standing out in front of his joint, where a game was in progress, looking out for meddlesome cops. ("You know, a ten-dollar or twenty-dollar bill would carry the coppers.") The snow was knee-deep, the street quiet, and then, all at once, "I'm a son of a bitch if a black car don't come by with this machine gun and *baroom!*" Thus spake "Greasy Thumb."

Cohen refused to seek safety by falling to the street, for he did not want to sully the flashy camel hair coat he had just purchased from Hill Brothers. Still standing, he watched the black car circle and return; the gunmen fired again, not directly at Cohen, who assumed "they were just trying to scare me." Later, Cohen fancied himself the hero of this encounter: "They were all talking about that crazy little Jew bastard that wouldn't even fall." In fact, the chastened gambler shut down his rogue crap game and began to look for a new racket.

Although Capone could be secretive and brutal, he was also capable of whimsical, self-aggrandizing gestures when the mood came over him. Learning that Peter Aiello was coming to Chicago to attend an engineers convention, Al remembered the Baltimore contractor who had given him his first legitimate job and subsequently loaned him $500 to move to Chicago. Determined to repay the debt many times over, and, not so incidentally, to demonstrate his newfound status in Chicago, Capone decided not to throw a mere banquet for Aiello. No, his heart was so full of gratitude he decided to organize an entire *parade*.

Since Al Capone wanted a parade in Cicero, a parade there was. On the appointed day, the guest of honor beheld hundreds of well-wishers, all of them assembled at the behest of Al Capone and the organization, marching through the streets of Cicero, waving flags and throwing confetti, all in celebration of Peter Aiello, the man who had sent Capone west.

The last time he had organized a parade, Capone had been a boy leading his gang through the hostile streets of Brooklyn, banging on pots and pans as they went and shouting a slogan of defiance: "*We are the boys of Navy Street, and touch us if you dare!*" Now he was a man, but he still had his parade, and the streets were no longer hostile; they belonged to him. He remained faithful to the dreams of his youth as few ever can. Moving through the crowd, greeting the men he had "invited" to turn out, Capone relished the merriment (albeit enforced) in the streets of Cicero. More than any racket, it was a sign that he had arrived. Never again would his enjoyment of *la mala vita* be so innocent, carefree, and childlike as it was on this day.

• • •

Throughout the winter of 1923–24 no one in Cicero dared to defy the Capone brothers, with one crucial exception: the *Cicero Tribune*. This was not the august *Chicago Tribune*, one of the most powerful and autocratic newspapers in the Midwest, with all its financial resources and prestige. This *Tribune* was a tiny new venture managed by an unknown journalist named Robert St. John, who at age twenty-one burned with the reckless optimism of youth and who set out to make a name for himself as a journalist. The son of a pharmacist, St. John had grown up in Oak Park, one of Chicago's most handsome suburban communities, and had been attracted to Cicero for the same reason as Capone: it was a prosperous, quiet, overlooked industrial area offering a promising location for a new business. "I started the paper with a partner named Oscar Palmer," St. John recalled of those early days in Cicero. "He was a businessman and an advertising man, and we both thought there was a great opportunity in Cicero because it was a community composed largely of first- and second-generation Bohemians from Czechoslovakia. They were good, law-abiding citizens who simply wanted their beer. They were very much against crime and prostitution and gambling and all the rest of it, and so we thought there was a great opportunity there for a newspaper that would be on the side of the people and against the Capones."

The *Cicero Tribune* appeared once a week, and it soon attained a circulation of approximately 10,000 copies. On the front page of each issue, St. John, playing the role of crusading journalist to the hilt, ran an exposé of the Capones' growing influence on the town. In response, Capone henchmen "harassed my reporters almost immediately, either bribed them or threatened them. There were frequent telephone threats," St. John says, and as a result, "I had a big turnover of reporters." The harassment only made the young editor more determined and defiant. Within its pages, the *Cicero Tribune*'s editorials continually denounced the Capones' sinister influence.

In advance of the April 1, 1924, primary, St. John uncovered fresh details of the Capone organization's plan to ensure that its slate, which consisted entirely of Republicans, met with no Democratic opposition. Through informants he learned that one of the Capone-backed candidates, unhappy that even the lowest flunky in the Capone organization was making more than he did as a member of the Cicero Town Board, demanded a cut of the Torrio-Capone take in Cicero. In response, St. John wrote, Capone "delivered a speech which . . . could not be reproduced in type, for it was embellished with unprintable profanity and expletives." At the end of his tirade, he turned on his brother Frank, castigating him for choosing such stupid candidates and then giving him a new mandate.

"Why don't you make Cicero a real town?" he bellowed. "Improve it! Fancy it up! Why don't you pave all the streets with concrete? It might cost ten or twenty grand a city block, but my God, these Hunkies [i.e., the Bohemians or "bohunks" of Cicero] make dough at Western Electric, don't they? They can afford it. I know a contractor who'd be happy to give you boys a 20-percent kickback. Pave the streets with cement! Make the dump an up-to-date place!" This was no idle boast; Capone was determined to leave his mark on Cicero as a master builder as well as a hustler. In fact, as the primary approached, it was apparent that Capone had ambitions extending beyond prostitution and gambling; he wanted political power as well. He did not simply want to corrupt or control the powers that be, he wanted to *be* the government, raking in money from the roulette wheel with one hand and spending it on public works with the other. No other racketeer in Chicago, and certainly not the recessive Johnny Torrio, had any ambition remotely approaching Al's; all they wanted to do was get rich quickly and quietly and live to enjoy their wealth.

Al got his way. He ran notices for hearings concerning the proposed pavement in the *Cicero Tribune*'s rival, the *Cicero Life*, in the process squelching any criticism that paper might have chosen to print. Once the plan became public knowledge, no one dared question it. Frank, again representing the Torrio-Capone organization, supervised the bidding on the paving contracts, ensuring that kickbacks were included. "If the other bidders protested," St. John recalled, "it was easy to send Frank Capone to see them and explain that in the interests of their personal health and in view of their natural desire for a happy old age it was not advisable for them to do any future bidding on Cicero paving jobs." The *Cicero Tribune* covered every detail of the rigged bidding, and as the bitter winter of 1924 relented, it seemed possible that the Capone organization's hand-picked candidates might go down in defeat at the polls. The little newspaper's crusade against the racketeers brought favorable mail as well as a flood of glory-seeking job applicants. In fact, all the Chicago newspapers were following the power struggle, and on the eve of the primary, the *Chicago Daily News* reckoned that before the day was over three men would be killed in Cicero.

Robert St. John shook his head in disbelief at the dire prediction.

·   ·   ·

Election day in Cicero.
Fair skies, chilly weather, brisk winds.

Large automobiles paraded up and down the streets, some trailing large, flowing Republican (i.e., Capone) banners, while others sported smaller Democratic regalia. But as the morning progressed, the seemingly festive tone turned ugly. Election workers for the Democrats, men whose job it was to get out the vote, began to disappear. The experience of one unlucky Democratic worker—Stanley Stanklevitch—proved typical; he was kidnapped by men he had never seen, blindfolded, and confined to a cellar until three o'clock the following morning. Finally he was led to a car and tossed out on the streets of Cicero. He went directly to a hospital to treat the wounds he had received during the day.

The threat of harm spread to the voters, as well. "Polling places were raided by thugs and ballots torn from the hands of voters waiting to drop them into the boxes," reported the *Chicago Tribune*, which predicted the election in Cicero offered a taste of things to come for all of Chicago. "Women were frightened away from the polling places and many a voter was sent home with a broken head without having cast his ballot." One voter told of being kidnapped and confined to a basement with eight others whose sole offense was that they intended to vote Democratic in Cicero that day.

Word of the mounting violence in Cicero soon traveled to Chicago, reaching the ears of a county judge, Edmund K. Jarecki. Alarmed, Judge Jarecki burst into the office of Mayor Dever, demanding that Chicago send in its police force to calm the city of Cicero. Dever wearily explained that the Chicago police had no jurisdiction in the town of Cicero, which had its own police force, but, he pointed out, the judge himself could deputize citizens to preserve order in Cicero, if he chose, and there was nothing to prevent him from selecting Chicago policemen for the assignment. Within minutes, the judge conferred with Chicago's chief of police, who assembled a contingent of seventy cops in nine "flivver squads"; their ostensible mission was to protect the 20,000 workers at the Western Electric plant from gunfire in the streets of Cicero. Before departing, the riot squad assembled at Chicago's Lawndale police station, where they were issued shotguns. However, there were several irregularities about this brigade. The policemen were all in plain clothes, and they rode in unmarked sedans. The danger of the situation was that Capone's organization drove around Cicero in precisely the same type of plain black sedan.

From his vantage point across the street from the Western Electric plant, located on the border between Cicero and Chicago, St. John watched the flivver squad enter Cicero, patrolling the street in single file, proceeding at a speed of about fifty miles an hour. Just then, he wrote, "I noticed a neatly dressed man leave a building on the Cicero side of the street." At first, St. John took him for a banker or a store owner, but then he realized the man in the suit was Frank Capone, who had been trying to negotiate a lease on the building he had left. At the same moment, the driver of the lead police car also recognized Frank.

"They tell us at headquarters there's a lot of shootin' and stuff goin' on in Cicero," the driver later told St. John. "I know that if there's shootin' the Capones must be mixed up in it, and the first thing I see when we get here is a man I know is Capone's brother. What's wrong with that?" What *was* wrong became apparent within seconds. The lead police car shrieked to a halt, and the nine sedans behind it quickly followed suit, narrowly avoiding a chain-reaction collision. "It was not difficult to imagine what had gone through his [Frank Capone's] mind in that split second when life and death hung in the balance," St. John wrote. "He heard the screaming of brakes, turned quickly, saw thirty or forty men in ordinary street clothes leaping from a long line of seven-passenger black touring cars. . . . He reached with his right hand for his right rear trousers pocket." Before Frank could identify his pursuers or fire a shot, his slender body was hurled backward by the force of dozens of bullets. Concealed within their cars, the policemen fired their shotguns at him until he fell to the streets of Cicero, and they continued to fire bullets into the lifeless body until their guns were empty. One of the policemen, Sergeant Philip McGlynn, was generally credited as the man who shot Frank Capone, but he was certainly not alone in firing on the victim.

"When we rolled over his corpse," St. John recalled, "his hand was still on his revolver. For the first time I understood that newspaper cliché about a body 'riddled' with bullets. No one ever determined how many shots were fired, but a sizable percentage of the Chicago detectives, seeing a Capone reach for a gun, had acted in a manner generally described by coroners' juries with the expression 'homicide committed in self-defense.' " Privately, St. John held himself responsible for Frank's death; it was his paper, after all, that had run the exposés leading to the death of a man who, while hardly blameless, did not deserve summary execution on the streets of Cicero.

Frank Capone had died about midday, and Al, when he heard the news, went white with fury. Together with his brother Ralph, he went to the Cicero morgue to identify Frank's body. All at once it was apparent that his ambitious scheme to take over Cicero had turned to waste and tragedy. Even Al Capone was astonished at how reckless and overpowering the Chicago police had been. The death of Frank became a turning point in Capone's career as a racketeer. From now on he would become the dedicated outlaw, determined to crush and control. Frank's death also thrust Al even further into prominence. Had he lived, it is likely that Frank, the most businesslike of all the Capone brothers, would have taken a leading role in the family's affairs, and it is entirely possible that he would have become the most influential Capone, a low-profile racketeer in the Torrio mold, but it was not to be. His corpse was soon lying on a slab at the Cook County morgue, photographed by Chicago's newspaper photographers. Thus Frank became the first member of the Capone family whose photograph appeared in the Chicago papers, and it was his death mask.

Before he began mourning for his older brother, Al demanded vengeance in Cicero that day. It was early in the afternoon, and the polls were still open. All across town, Capone henchmen continued to kidnap election officials and steal ballot boxes. One election official who resisted was killed. He was the second man to die in Cicero that day, and St. John realized to his horror that the *Daily News*'s prediction at which he had scoffed might become true after all. He had through his newspaper done more than anyone else to expose the Capone family's racketeering in Cicero; would he be the next man killed?

That night, the votes were counted, and considering the reign of terror the Capone organization had visited on Cicero, the race turned out to be surprisingly close. The Capone-backed Republican candidate for president of the village board, Joseph Z. Klenha, received 7,878 votes, and his Democratic opponent, Rudolph Hurt, 6,993, a difference of less than a thousand ballots. The rest of the Capone-backed Republican slate won over their opponents by similar margins. The people had spoken, the guns had roared, and when the smoke cleared, it was apparent that Al Capone had won his battle for Cicero, but the price—his brother's life—was beyond reckoning.

Once he had absorbed the magnitude of the defeat the Capone forces had dealt him, St. John decided to visit a Cicero saloon to console himself. There, over a glass of beer, he caught sight of one of his valued contacts in the community; he was a garrulous former prizefighter-turned-bootlegger and self-styled philosopher named Eddie Tancl. "When I could get him alone at a table in the corner he would talk about life and death, the theater, music and even poetry with a freshness of approach and expression which was more stimulating than the beer he sold," St. John remarked. However, the place was so crowded that night with men excitedly discussing the election that St. John found conversation with Tancl or anyone else impossible, and he decided to leave. As his hand touched the door, a shot rang out and Eddie Tancl crumpled on the floor, killed without apparent reason by a drunk. It was minutes before midnight, and St. John immediately went to the phone and dialed the *Chicago Daily News*.

"Your reputation is safe," he told the reporter who had written the gruesome prediction concerning election day. "Cicero has just obliged you with its third murder of the day. Good night."

•   •   •

From the moment Frank Capone fell dead on the streets of Cicero, a spirited debate over who was to blame filled the Chicago newspapers. Both sides advanced their arguments. The police pointed out that Frank had been arrested for carrying concealed weapons only five days earlier, but it was equally true that a judge had dismissed the complaint and returned the weapons to Frank for purposes of self-protection. The irony of the situation was apparent; had Frank been *un*armed, he would have lived to celebrate the results of the Cicero elections. Although his plan to preserve order in Cicero had turned into a fiasco, Judge Jarecki refused to accept blame. "Practically all the dirty work was done by Chicago gangsters hired to go there and swing the election," he said in his defense. "Chicago's best gunmen were there to kill or terrorize whatever voters and workers were opposed to whichever candidates were friends of the gunmen." What he failed to mention was that he had been responsible for sending many of those gunmen to Cicero.

At the inquest into Frank's death, Al Capone, using his alias, Al Brown, testified, but he had little to say—or to admit. Photographed by the newspapers, he appeared that day to be a somber-looking young man wearing a dark coat and holding a black fedora in his hands, his eyes cast down. Gangsters? Gambling? Rigged elections? He insisted he knew nothing of these matters; he was only a used-furniture dealer. Frank, said Al, happened to be in Cicero on election day "to buy a coffee shop." Although several eyewitnesses testified that Frank Capone had not fired a shot, the police told a much different story to the coroner's jury, insisting Frank had lured them into a pitched gun battle. They said he fired on them twice as he ran away, and he would have fired a third time had his gun not jammed. It was only then that he suddenly fell to the ground. Robert St. John, who had seen the entire event unfold, knew that it hadn't happened that way, that Frank had been startled by the police, reached for his gun, and was dead before he was able to pull it out of his pocket. But the coroner's jury formed a different impression. After hearing the hastily assembled evidence, the jury returned a verdict that Frank had been killed while resisting arrest, and the police were "justified" in taking his life.

•   •   •

CAPONE—Salvatore Capone, beloved son of Theresa and the late Gabriel, brother of James, Ralph, Alphonse, Erminio, Humbert, Amadea, and Mafalda. Funeral Saturday at 9 A.M. from late residence, 7244 Prairie Avenue.

So read the family's death notice for Frank ("Salvatore") Capone in the *Chicago Tribune* on Thursday, April 3, 1924. His last rites turned out to be the largest, most lavish gangster funeral Chicago had seen since the death of James Colosimo. "GANGLAND BOWS AT SLAIN CHIEF'S BIER," declared the *Chicago Daily News* of the scene at the Capone home on Friday night. "Dressed in their best, bringing their womenfolk and thus tacitly declaring a truce, the kings, princes, nobility, and commonality of the underworld gathered in hundreds yesterday to pay their past respects to their late brother in arms, Frank Caponi," the *Chicago Tribune* reported. For two blocks in every direction the streets were packed with a "curious commingling of those who were simply curious, of those 'in the racket,' of neighbors and friends of the simpler ways of the slain gunman's days," said one reporter of the sight. "There were many hard faces and harder fists in the crowd."

Within the Capone home Frank's body was laid out in a silver-plated coffin engraved with his name. Candles placed at the head and foot of the bier burned steadily, their glow playing over his motionless features, glinting off the coffin's cold, polished surface. In the front hall, Theresa, Al, and Ralph, all of them attired in black, greeted the neighbors, family friends, and members and allies of the Torrio-Capone organization.

The opulence of the coffin was exceeded only by the extravagance of the flower arrangements, estimated to have cost $20,000, all provided by the preferred florist of Chicago's racketeers, Dion O'Banion, of whom it was said, "He could twist a sheaf of roses into a wreath or chaplet so deftly and gently as not to let fall a single petal." The baby-faced, ambidextrous, music-loving O'Banion walked with a limp, his left leg four inches shorter than his right. But there was more to O'Banion than his angelic façade. He had spent his youth in Chicago's Little Hell as a petty thief and singing waiter, and his floral business concealed the fact that he was also a major bootlegger and racketeer in his own right, in many ways Johnny Torrio's Irish counterpoint on Chicago's North Side. In fact, Mayor Dever's chief of police, Morgan Collins, went so far as to describe O'Banion as "Chicago's arch-criminal." O'Banion, the police said, had arranged for the deaths of at least twenty-five of his enemies. Although he was never tried for the murders, he went about the city with no fewer than three pistols on his person at all times concealed in pockets thoughtfully provided by his tailor. At election time, he proved so effective at getting out the vote in his North Side wards that a popular saying went, "Who'll carry the 42nd and 43rd?" Answer: "O'Banion, in his pistol pocket."

O'Banion's lavish floral arrangements for Frank Capone included a six-foot-high heart woven of red carnations and an equally impressive lyre fashioned of lilies and orchids. On the evening before the funeral, the interior of the Capone house on South Prairie Avenue, reported the *Chicago Tribune*, "was banked with a profusion of blossoms. When every nook and cranny from the kitchen to the attic had been fairly choked with these delicate tributes, they were heaped up on the front porch and hung from the balcony. . . . By nightfall the entire terrace was covered with brilliant blossoms. Finally the lack of space made it necessary to festoon the trees and lamp posts in front of the house with wreaths, immortelles and hanging baskets." Within the house, mourners trod across a carpet of 3,000 roses, "ground into powder under the heels of scores that passed the silver-plated coffin." The perfume of crushed blossoms, however sweet, did little to soothe the raw and sullen mood. There had been a festive air about "Big Jim" Colosimo's funeral, but Frank Capone's youth—he was not yet thirty at the time police gunned him down—ensured that the tone of his last rites was entirely tragic; instead of singing, there was wailing. Outside, hundreds of curiosity seekers jammed the street as darkness fell. Not everyone in attendance wished the Capones well. Police Chief Collins dispatched the same cops who had shot Frank to death to observe his funeral.

The next morning brought chilly spring weather, with gray skies and rain threatening. At 9:30 Frank's silver-plated coffin was rolled from the house, transported carefully down the nine front steps to the street and into the back of a waiting hearse. A funeral cortege consisting of no fewer than one hundred cars—fifteen of them bearing flowers—proceeded deliberately to Mt. Olivet Cemetery, where a canopy covered the open grave site. There a priest addressed the throng: "You people here to-day show by your overflowing numbers that you have a great affection for this man. . . . Pray for him and aid him in paying his atonement." As women sobbed, the silver-plated coffin was lowered into the ground, and clumps of earth heaped upon it.

Throughout the wrenching spectacle and afterward, Al refused to talk to reporters covering the event and kept in the background, aware that his relative anonymity afforded perhaps his best defense against the forces of law and order, the same forces that had taken Frank's life without reason or remorse. To judge from the newspaper coverage of his brother's death and burial, there was still considerable confusion about who Al Capone really was or how he spelled his name, and little recognition of his growing influence in Chicago's rackets. The papers gave his first name as "Alfred" or "Toni." He was usually described as the manager of the Four Deuces, and one newspaper, the *Chicago Tribune*, called him "Scarface," the first appearance in print of that sinister nickname. This description was assuredly not of Al's devising; it was the inspiration of an unknown journalist who had just succeeded in coining the most famous gangster nickname of all time. Yet no matter how the press portrayed him or misspelled his name, Al Capone kept a discreet public silence that masked his private agitation. He was not about to forgive or forget Frank's death, and only Johnny Torrio's counseling restraint kept him from mounting a full-scale war against the Chicago Police Department. Finally, a trivial incident triggered all his barely contained fury and frustration, and at a stroke Al "Scarface" Capone abruptly acquired a notoriety that would follow him to the end of his life.

．　　．　　．

Friday, May 8, 1924: a cool, cloudy spring day barely five weeks after Frank's funeral. On the corner of Twenty-second and Wabash, near the Four Deuces, Jack Guzik, Al Capone's partner in prostitution, encountered a small-time hoodlum named Joe Howard. At twenty-eight, Howard still lived with his elderly mother above her fruit stand while he freelanced as a small-time safe blower, bank robber, and whiskey highjacker. Without warning, Howard, who may have been drunk, lurched in Guzik's direction and asked him for a loan. "Nuts to you," the pudgy little racketeer replied, and walked on. Suddenly Howard lunged straight for Guzik, shouting, "You dirty little kike!" and slapped him on the face.

Rather than fighting back, the pudgy, decidedly unathletic Guzik tracked down Al Capone, whom he found at the Four Deuces, told him of Howard's reckless behavior, and the two of them went in search of the offender. They quickly located him in a bar managed by one "Hymie" Jacobs, at 2300 Wabash. Prohibition was then so lax in Chicago, especially on the South Side, that Jacobs did not even bother to pretend that his drinking establishment was anything other than what it was: a saloon.

As the two men entered, Howard, who was drinking with another small-time hood named Tony "Mouth" Bagnolia, glanced up and said, "Hello, Al."

"What's the idea of pushing Guzik around?" Capone shouted.

"Listen, you Dago pimp, why don't you run along and take care of your broads?" *Pimp*: it was the ultimate insult to Capone, because it was true.

His nerves frazzled with anxiety and grief over Frank's recent death, Capone impulsively reached in his pocket, pulled out his pistol, and before anyone could stop him, emptied it; four bullets struck Howard in the face, two in the shoulder, and he fell to the floor of the saloon, still grinning, but dead.

It was now 6:30 in the evening, the light just beginning to fade from the overcast sky, and at this hour, in this busy neighborhood, there was no way to disguise the murder that had just occurred. At least four bystanders had seen Capone shoot Joe Howard. Capone fled the scene of the crime. The police arrived shortly afterward, took charge of the body, and began their inquiries; they were followed by reporters. "I am certain it was Capone," the chief of police was quoted as saying, "and I know just how it was done."

What should have been an open-and-shut case quickly turned into a tantalizing mystery, as one by one the eyewitnesses, realizing that their lives might be in jeopardy if they cooperated with the police, developed a highly selective (and suspect) form of amnesia. On arriving at police headquarters, the saloon proprietor, "Hymie" Jacobs, now claimed not to have recognized either Capone or Guzik. At the moment the shots were fired, Jacobs said, he happened to be "stooping behind the counter with his head in the safe looking for a package of nickels." As for Al Capone, Jacobs claimed he'd heard of him but never met the man. Another eyewitness to the murder, Tony "Mouth" Bagnolia, failed to live up to his nickname, claiming he was in the back of the saloon at the time of the shooting, too far away to get a good look, and while he did admit he heard someone call out "Hello, Al" shortly before the gunfire, he couldn't be certain it was Al *Capone*. Meanwhile, the police undertook a futile search for Capone at the Four Deuces as well as his home on South Prairie Avenue, and by the early hours of the morning, they had decided that Capone himself might not be involved after all. There seemed to be an endless number of men with a motive for killing Howard, who had been in and out of trouble for years, and none of the other suspects enjoyed the protection of Johnny Torrio.

While the police were suspiciously lenient with Capone, the daily papers made the most of the vicious killing, and the following morning bleary-eyed citizens of Chicago were greeted with sensational headlines in huge boldface type, the letters two inches high, introducing an audacious new racketeer to the public, a man known as "Al Brown":

GUNMAN KILLED BY GUNMAN
"FOUR DEUCES" OWNER HEADS MYSTERY FEUD
'Al' Brown Vanishes After Shooting.

"Another murder in the liquor and crime serial was accomplished last night," read the lead in the *Chicago Tribune*, which furnished only a sketch of Capone's identity and role in the rackets, though it was damaging enough: "Alphonse Capone, vice lord of the south side bad lands where he is better known as Al Brown of 'Four Deuces' fame, is sought as the slayer." As if declaring him a murderer was not enough, the *Tribune* published his photograph; his careful grooming announced that he was no longer the roughneck from the Gowanus section of Brooklyn; he looked very much the prosperous young businessman. It was hard to imagine this studious-looking young man harming anyone.

One law enforcement agent was not so easily swayed, however. As assistant state's attorney, William H. McSwiggin had won a reputation as the "hanging prosecutor" of Chicago because of his ability to win death penalties. The young prosecutor, a heavyset man who wore thick glasses, now drew a bead on the man who called himself Al Brown. Over the next few weeks he questioned a series of witnesses, and despite their evasions, he became persuaded that Al Capone had indeed killed Howard, although he failed to assemble a case that would convince a jury to return a death penalty against the malefactor. A month after the killing, when it was apparent the investigation had come to naught, Capone himself suddenly appeared at a Chicago police station, where he declared, "I hear the police are looking for me. What for?" He was immediately taken to the Criminal Courts Building and ushered into McSwiggin's presence. The two bulky young men, each determined to get his own way, confronted one another. The prosecutor was Irish, the suspect Italian; this was an ethnic rivalry Capone understood from his youth in Brooklyn, where the Irish had been the chief rivals of the Italian gangs. Capone hotly proclaimed his innocence to the Irish prosecutor. "I'm a respectable businessman," he insisted. "I'm a second-hand furniture dealer. I'm no gangster. I don't know this fellow Torrio. I haven't anything to do with the Four Deuces. Anyway, I was out of town the day Howard was bumped off." All lies, which Capone figured was just what the Irish prosecutor deserved.

Undeterred by the suspect's denials and the witnesses' faulty memories, McSwiggin insisted he would still be able to indict Capone for the murder of Joe Howard, and the inquest continued, but without the desired result. On July 22, the jury considering the evidence concluded its deliberations with the following statement: "We, the jury, find that Joe Howard came to his death on the premises at 2300 South Wabash Avenue, from hemorrhage and shock due to bullet wounds in the head, face and neck; said bullets being fired from a revolver or revolvers in the hand or hands of one or more unknown, white male persons, in the vestibule of said saloon on said premises." So there would be no indictment, no trial, no conviction of Alphonse Capone for the murder of Joe Howard, but that was not the end of the matter for Bill McSwiggin, renowned for his tenacity. He refused to consider Joe Howard just another casualty of the beer wars, as the police did, and forget the matter. Bill McSwiggin never forgot anything, especially the Italian, Al Capone. Nor would Capone neglect the "hanging prosecutor."

• • •

Once the excitement surrounding the murder of Joe Howard abated, Capone returned to the haven of Cicero, becoming ever more entrenched. He abandoned the modest Anton's Hotel for its more impressive neighbor, the Hawthorne Inn, located at 4833 Twenty-second Street, which the Torrio organization owned. Capone saw to it that the building's windows were equipped with bullet-proof steel shutters, and armed sentries milled in the dark lobby. Security was ubiquitous, the ambience menacing. "Entrance was through a passageway, twenty-five feet long . . . leading to the lobby," recalled a reporter.

The chairs, settees, lounges . . . were so arranged as to front on the passageway. The visitor, therefore, found himself in the center of a kind of stage, undergoing a visual onslaught. His coming had been tipped off by a lookout at the street door who had pressed a warning buzzer. There were never fewer than a dozen ostensible idlers in the lobby—fellows with indigo-stippled chins and eyes as expressionless as those of a dead mackerel; the Capone bodyguard. They gazed from behind newspapers and through a haze of cigarette smoke amid a silence that was earsplitting. The bellhops, the room clerk, and the girl at the telephone switchboard were on the Capone payroll.

The organization's new headquarters also sheltered the Hawthorne Smoke Shop, which served as a gambling establishment and a gathering place for the Capone organization. The liquor flowed, seventy-five cents for a shot of (Torrio-Capone) whiskey, twenty-five cents for a glass of (Torrio-Capone) beer, and the money rolled in; the Hawthorne Smoke Shop Inn handled as much as $50,000 a day on the horses alone, and over at Lauderback's, another gambling joint, it was not unheard of for $100,000 to change hands at roulette. Prohibition-era Cicero could now boast of being home to over 100 saloons and 150 gambling dens, most of them controlled, directly or indirectly, by the vast Torrio-Capone syndicate. The sheer amount of money was something new; Johnny Torrio had never seen anything like it, and Al Capone had never expected to. The economy of the 1920s, inflated by relaxed regulation, increased speculation, and a conviction that the economic bubble would never burst, benefited racketeers at least as much as stockbrokers and speculators. Capone and his lieutenants strolled around Cicero with thousands of dollars jammed in their pockets, more money than they had ever expected to see in their entire lives, with the promise of more, always more, where that came from. "The impecunious hoodlum of 1920, who had thought $25,000 a year a fairly snug salary, was now disbursing, in the booze traffic alone, $25,000 a week in payrolls," marveled one reporter. The racketeers' lingo reflected the inflated amounts of money being thrown around. They called hundred-dollar bills "leaves"; twenty-five dollars was just "two bits." Smaller bills, the fives, tens, and twenties, did not even merit names. The basic monetary unit became the "grand": $1,000.

The Hawthorne Inn became the symbol of Capone's presence in Cicero, but it lacked one essential for a racketeer: privacy. Al's real retreat was a large, handsome building he acquired at 1600 Austin Boulevard, on a quiet, tree-lined residential street in Cicero. Built of tan brick and highlighted by ornamental masonry, the hideaway appeared to be a small apartment building, but Capone was its sole resident. On closer inspection, it became apparent the place was a fortress. An eight-foot-high brick wall surrounded the backyard, a tunnel connected the garage to the building, and the front door was made of steel. It shut with a clang that became a familiar sound in the neighborhood, and a bar within snapped into place to secure it. Bodyguards were posted at the front, and they constantly scrutinized the area. Within, the appointments were solid, middle-class, except for the bedroom. There Al Capone constructed a palatial lair for himself, complete with a mirrored ceiling. Of course this was not a retreat he shared with Mae and Sonny, who remained on South Prairie Avenue. It was here that he came with his pals and all their teenage mistresses to drink, to party, to make love until dawn and sleep to noon.

Al Capone came into his own in Cicero, the city in which he succumbed to the dark lure of the racketeer's life. It was one thing to be Frankie Yale's muscle or Johnny Torrio's protégé, but to rule his own turf, his own *town*, was intoxicating. At twenty-five, up from the streets of Brooklyn, he was besotted with his newfound power, the girls who flocked to the racketeers, the illicit whiskey, and the great white drug, cocaine.

The evidence of Capone's use of cocaine is limited but compelling. Years later, in 1938, just prior to his departure from the federal penitentiary at Alcatraz, he was given the most thorough medical examination of his life, in the course of which the prison's physician noted Capone's "perforated nasal septum." By far the most likely cause for this hole in the wall of cartilage separating his nostrils: cocaine. This was evidence of more than casual use. To burn a hole like that in his septum required his snorting tens of thousands of dollars of the drug. Since Capone had been in jail since 1931 at the time of the medical examination, the most likely time for him to have used the drug was during the early and mid-1920s, when cocaine was the drug of choice among the wealthy and fashionable of the era, and flappers wore little spoons around their necks to scoop the innocuous-looking white powder into their nostrils. It was just a distraction, a harmless high, or so people thought.

As a brothel manager, Capone was surrounded by cocaine users; the drug was his for the asking. So there was nothing unusual about Capone's use of cocaine; it would have been more remarkable for him to avoid the ever-present drug. But it *is* noteworthy that he snorted enough to perforate his septum, an indication of addiction rather than casual or even repeated use. Thanks to the proceeds from the rackets he managed, though, Capone had the financial resources to support the habit, and its effects went far beyond his nasal septum. His behavior also underwent marked changes. Every time he snorted cocaine, he experienced its distinctive, exhilarating rush of self-confidence approaching omnipotence, and the manic restlessness it induced. What better time to dream of controlling not just Cicero but the rackets of the entire city of Chicago. And why stop at Chicago? Why not the entire country? What better time to plot the assassination of his rivals? The term *assassin* originally meant "eater of hashish," referring to the ancient assassins of the East who prepared themselves for battle by ingesting the drug. So the racketeers' assassins nerved themselves with drugs before murdering their modern-day adversaries. As the effects of the drug wore off, he would experience the darker side of cocaine use, the wearying, draining aftermath: depression, a strange wheezing in his nostrils, and a craving for more. For Al Capone there was always more; he could afford anything, including enough cocaine to burn a hole in his nose. If the scars he bore on his cheek bore witness to the external violence of his adolescence, the wound to his septum, internal and hidden to everyone but a physician, testified just as eloquently to the havoc cocaine wreaked on his psyche.

Capone's cocaine habit has escaped notice, in part because he made a point of discouraging any of his organization's men from dealing in cocaine or its even more dangerous cousin, heroin. He hated hopheads (heroin users), railed against them, and insisted that any of his men caught using the drug would be fired—or worse. But Capone habitually took a stand on one issue in which there was some gray area, some dispute about what was right and wrong, to avoid another issue where there was none. He admitted to being a bootlegger and even a gambler, for instance, but never a pimp (which he assuredly was). In the same way he denounced heroin while indulging his own cocaine habit.

• • •

As Al Capone cavorted in his suburban fortress, life in Cicero appeared to return to normal. Even Robert St. John, who had editorialized against Capone, later claimed that Cicero's reputation for violence was undeserved. "Ninety-nine percent of Chicago never saw a gangster, never heard a shot fired, never had any contact with all this to-do," he declared. In reality, however, little had changed; the racketeers were, if anything, even more deeply entrenched. Now, instead of guns, they used their control of the Cicero government to resolve "problems." A merchant who advertised in St. John's newspaper, for instance, suddenly found his property assessment raised, and thus subject to higher taxes. Or inspectors descended on his place of work, finding violations invisible to the naked eye. "No parking" signs appeared like mushrooms in front of his store, warding off the customers. All these headaches disappeared once the offending merchant switched his advertising from St. John's *Cicero Tribune* to the less controversial *Cicero Life*.

Watching his advertising dwindle as a result of the pressure applied by the Capone-controlled government, St. John decided to strike back with his most daring exposé yet: an account of a visit to a Capone-controlled brothel. Knowingly or not, St. John had singled out the area in which his nemesis was the most sensitive and vulnerable, for, as Joe Howard had discovered at the cost of his life, nothing could be more calculated to infuriate Al Capone, the improver of roads and fixer of elections, than to be branded as a pimp.

Although he was well known to the Capone henchmen by now, St. John insisted on doing his own reporting for the story: "One midnight I put on shabby clothes, emptied my pockets of all identification, and set out." He drove to the brothel, which was located in a nondescript frame house on a deserted stretch of road near Cicero's Hawthorne Race Track. Posing as a customer, he lingered in a small bar in the front, then passed through a series of doors controlled by electric buttons. Bullet holes pockmarked the doors, and it seemed that anyone the organization wanted to kill was simply lured into the passageway, trapped between the automatic doors, and shot to death. Passing safely through this gauntlet, St. John entered a larger room, where he sat waiting on a bench as the girls ("All were blasé and businesslike in their attitude, as if they were selling ninety-eight cent sweaters in a department-store bargain basement") slowly entered the room and left with whoever was sitting on the hot seat at the end of the bench. Once a seat became vacant, everyone on the bench shifted one place closer to the end. The atmosphere was not, St. John noted, especially glamorous or enticing. Indeed, the hallmark of Capone brothels was their efficiency, not their luxury; they were thoroughly up-to-date, veritable factories of sin, the carnal equivalent of the Western Electric plant, "the very antithesis of pleasure," in St. John's words.

The undercover reporter bumped from place to place until at last he sat on the edge of the bench, terrified of being recognized (after all, he told himself, "I had undertaken to try, almost singlehanded, to crush . . . one of the most powerful underworld organizations America had ever known") and anxious about what he would say to the girl he selected. Finally, he paid his five dollars and went upstairs with a young girl who introduced herself as Helen. When they were alone in a small room, one of perhaps a hundred in the brothel, St. John admitted he was engaged in research, though he stopped short of specifying his true mission. St. John stealthily interviewed Helen and another prostitute until four o'clock in the morning and, in his own estimation, accumulated "enough material for a modern *Moll Flanders*," including details of Al Capone's visits. He then jumped to safety from a second-story window and drove home to set down his sensational story.

When the exposé ran in the next issue of the *Cicero Tribune*, a great hue and cry went up. Until this time, St. John had stood alone in defiance of Capone. He and his one-horse newspaper had done more to assail the racketeers and expose their nefarious tactics to public scrutiny than all the police and politicians in the entire city of Chicago. Now, at last, St. John had allies. Right-thinking citizens formed committees, ministers denounced the growing tide of sin, and indignant delegations besieged City Hall. "Everywhere they went they were received with the courtesy due groups of distinguished citizens and gentlemen of the cloth," St. John observed. "Everywhere they were given promises of action. Yet the weeks went by and nothing happened." Civic rage at what the Capone organization was doing to Cicero—its reputation no less than its property values—mounted until a minister in a neighboring town arranged to retain the services of an experienced arsonist. One morning, when the brothel St. John had visited was empty of prostitutes and customers alike, the lonely wooden building was destroyed in a fire that had obviously been carefully timed. "Here was another 'crime' for which I was indirectly responsible," St. John wrote, "but as long as no lives were lost in the fire I refused to let it bother my conscience. Alphonse Capone, even if he had no fire insurance, would not have to change his scale of living."

The burning of the Capone brothel had, at a stroke, redefined the terms of the conflict between the racketeers and the good people of Cicero. The anonymous minister's tactics were worthy of racketeers everywhere, and they amounted to something Al Capone could understand. The destruction was a public affront, and Capone had no choice but to arrange for a public retaliation against St. John. Still, as the young editor of the *Cicero Tribune*, St. John was to a certain extent protected from harm by the role he had carved out for himself in such a brief period; it would not do to create headlines reading "Young Journalist Found Dead," which would be certain to bring down the wrath of the newspapers if not the entire city on the Capone organization. For that reason, it was more desirable to humiliate him than to kill him.

Days after the brothel's destruction, Al put St. John on notice. The messenger in this case was Louis Cowan, a bit player in the Capone organization determined to carve out a larger role for himself. Al liked him; Louis could be useful. He stood perhaps five feet tall, and he was a news dealer whose stand happened to be located directly beneath the offices of the *Cicero Tribune* at 52nd Avenue and 25th Street. So Capone took up little Louis Cowan, gave him money and a fancy car, and made him the organization's professional bail bondsman. The arrangement was a clever one, and Capone's use of Cowan revealed the racketeer's newfound sophistication in business matters. In return for the car, money, and status Capone conferred on him, Cowan was required to post bail for any Capone racketeer who was arrested. The plan worked this way: Al Capone transferred perhaps half a million dollars in apartment buildings to Cowan, who owned the real estate in name only. Every man in the Capone organization carried Cowan's business card and was ordered to call Cowan in the event of an arrest. The number printed on the card did not connect with an office; rather, it rang a public phone located in a drugstore near Cowan's news stand; it was here, in this public phone booth, that he conducted his business dealings, with the druggist frequently summoning Cowan to the phone. Once he received his orders, the diminutive news dealer would jump into his limousine and drive to the police station, display proof of the real estate he held in his name, and put up whatever amount was required to get the Capone man out on bail.

Now Cowan's assignment was to threaten St. John on behalf of the Capone organization. St. John knew exactly who Cowan was; every so often the little man would sidle up to St. John to discuss selling the *Cicero Tribune*, always meeting with a rebuff. But this time he wanted St. John to know that Al and Ralph were extremely angry with the *Cicero Tribune*. Cowan delivered the threat with all the posturing he could muster, and when he was finished the indignant journalist told the little man that he was angry, too, "angry that the whole lot of them had not yet decided to get out of Cicero and leave the town alone." As St. John came to realize, his response was "a juvenile and reckless thing to have said."

Two days later, as the young editor was walking to work, he crossed the intersection and saw a black sedan speeding toward him; it was the kind of car that police and gangsters alike favored. "The brakes shrieked, the car stopped, and four men jumped out," he recalled.

> I felt just as Frank Capone must have felt, except that I recognized two of the men coming towards me. One was Ralph Capone himself. The second was Pete Pizak. . . . Pete had a gun in his hand. The others were reaching their pockets.
>
> I had time to do something Frank Capone had not had time to do. Instinctively I dropped to the ground and curled myself up in a ball like a cat, with my head buried.
>
> Pete Pizak, to my relief, did not pull the trigger of the gun. He used the butt as a club. Someone else had a cake of soap in a woolen sock. . . . The third man used a blackjack. Ralph directed the operation. They were trying to aim at my head, but I had it buried. As I wiggled and squirmed, most of the blows landed on my arms and legs. They must have succeeded in hitting me at least once on the head, however, because suddenly everything went black.

Two policemen present at the start of the beating stood by and watched as the Capone organization settled its score with St. John. The only individual who attempted to come to the victim's rescue was the *Cicero Tribune*'s society editor, but the lone, unarmed woman could do nothing to stop the violence.

When Ralph, Pizak, and the two other men had finished their work, they returned to their black sedan and drove directly to the hotel Al Capone called home in Cicero, but the brutality of the Capone organization did not end there. St. John had a brother named Archer, also a newspaper editor. Archer's base was in Berwyn, the town next to Cicero and thus of considerable strategic value to the Capone organization. In emulation of his gallant brother, Archer St. John was preparing to run an exposé of the Capones' designs on Berwyn in his own publication, whose staff consisted of only himself. Just before the article ran, Capone henchmen kidnapped him; they handcuffed, blindfolded, and confined their captive to a remote hovel—all on the same day that Robert received his beating. Archer's captors released him in the woods sometime later, and he eventually found his way home, though he was still badly shaken. His exposé never appeared, but the beatings received by the St. John brothers had considerable shock value; the *Chicago Tribune* ran a banner headline—"BOY EDITORS BEATEN; KIDNAPPED"—above an account of the Capones' skulduggery.

Even after this, the Brothers Capone were not quite done with the Brothers St. John. After the beating he received on the streets of Cicero, Robert spent a week recovering in the hospital. Discharged, he went to the cashier's office where he was dumbfounded to hear that his bill had just been paid in full. "He was rather dark complexioned," the cashier said of St. John's benefactor, "about your height, but much huskier, and he was very well dressed, all in blue, with a diamond stickpin. He didn't give his name. Just said he was a friend of yours."

St. John accepted the anonymous charity, and even before he returned to his office at the *Cicero Tribune* he resumed his quest to rid Cicero of the Capones. He approached a young man in the police department whom he considered his good friend, "as clean-cut as a college basketball player," and demanded that he draw up warrants for the arrest of Ralph Capone and the other thugs who participated in the beating, which could easily have maimed or killed St. John. "Al likes you," said his friend, displaying a surprising intimacy with the organization. "He likes all newspapermen. But he likes Ralph better. So take it easy, kid!" St. John was not about to take it easy on Capone and insisted on the warrants. At length his friend reluctantly agreed, and he instructed St. John to return the following morning at nine o'clock sharp.

The next day, the journalist reappeared exactly on schedule and was shown to an office on the second floor of Cicero's modest police station. As he waited in an office, another man joined him, a man with a scar on his left cheek, a scar he had tried to hide, unsuccessfully, beneath a layer of flesh-colored talcum powder. "He was impeccably dressed in a blue suit, white stiff collar, blue tie pierced by a sizable diamond, black well-polished shoes, blue pocket handkerchief, and black hat at a jaunty angle," St. John recalled. The man extended his arm in greeting.

"Glad to meet you, St. John," said Al Capone. "We'll get this over quick."

So began their tête-à-tête—in the police station, of all places, but this *was* Cicero, where the force was in the employ of Al Capone, and what better way to drive the point home to a hotheaded, misguided young journalist than to meet him in that stronghold of the law. They were both young, these two men discussing the future of Cicero, St. John barely twenty-two, Capone just four years his senior, but both were seasoned beyond their years—battle-hardened soldiers who had seen too much of war to return to innocence.

Capone began by launching into an impassioned defense of his activities in Cicero. "Sure I got a racket. So's everybody. Name me a guy that ain't got a racket," he asked rhetorically. "Most guys hurt people. I don't hurt nobody. Only them that get in my way. I give away a lot of dough. Maybe I don't support no college or build no liberries, but I give it to people that need it, direct." By this Capone meant that his organization employed hundreds of errand-runners and paid off hundreds more not to interfere. "What in the hell good is a college, anyway? I know some guys that went to college. Are they as smart as I am? . . . I even got college men working for me, would you believe it? Yes, and Harding was a college man and see where it got him! He's as dead as Cicero. . . ." Capone hastened to explain he meant "the guy named Cicero, the Greek." He moved on to the substance of his meeting with St. John, which was to insist that the *Cicero Tribune*'s bold exposés had actually helped the Capone interests because they created priceless publicity. "Take the Ship," Capone explained. "How can I advertise? I'd like to buy a page in the *Chicago Tribune* every day. Come to the Ship. Best gambling joint in the country. But I can't advertise. So you guys write stories . . . and I get my advertising for free. Why should I get sore?" Capone let the thought hang in the air as he flourished a gold cigarette holder, inhaled deeply, and apologized, after a fashion, for the beating his brother had administered to St. John, claiming it was all a misunderstanding; the boys had been drunk and forgot their manners. "I tell them, 'Let the kid alone.' And when I tell 'em something there ain't no argument. But the other morning the boys had been boozing it up . . . and they forgot what I told them and they made a mistake and now I gotta straighten it out."

The racketeer produced a fat roll of money—mostly $100 bills, St. John noticed—and made his offer.

"Now look, you lost a lotta time from your office." He carefully removed three bills from the roll.

"I guess you lost your hat." One more bill.

"You had to get your clothes fixed up." St. John watched him peel away two more bills.

"I've taken care of your hospital bill, but there was the doctor." Al continued to peel off the bills, until St. John had lost count.

If Capone thought his stratagem would end their vendetta, he was abruptly disillusioned. "I was suddenly filled with contempt for him," St. John wrote. "It obviously was beyond his comprehension that there existed anyone anywhere who did not have his price." The young journalist, his body still aching from the beating, made no reply. He abruptly left the room, slamming the door after him, spurning Capone and a roll of bills fat enough to choke a horse.

In the end, Al Capone's bankroll prevailed over the power of the free press in Cicero. Once more he sent Louis Cowan forth to warn St. John that the Capone organization viewed the *Cicero Tribune*'s latest exposé with displeasure, and once more St. John rebuffed him, but Cowan's riposte caught the journalist off guard: "Maybe you don't know who owns the *Cicero Tribune* now."

Cowan proved all too correct; St. John discovered to his dismay that Al Capone had pressured the paper's principal investors into selling their interest, which the racketeer promptly placed in Cowan's name, just as he had with the Cicero real estate. St. John held stock in the company, but he was now employed by the same Capone organization he had risked his reputation and indeed his life to condemn. He now found himself subject to the same blandishments to which Cowan had succumbed: a high salary, a sleek new limousine, whatever it took to keep him happy.

The idea of working for Louis Cowan, the cocky, obnoxious little man who had taunted him over the months, was too much for St. John to bear. "Well, Mr. Publisher," he said, "I guess you and your scar-faced friend have won. Say good-by to him for me." With those words he walked out of the *Cicero Tribune*, went home, gathered his possessions, and left Cicero forever. "I telegraphed a newspaperman's employment agency and said I wanted a job as far away from Cicero, Illinois, as I could get and still be in the United States. They offered me a position in Rutland, Vermont, and I accepted." St. John's adventurous career in journalism continued, and he subsequently became a distinguished foreign correspondent (in which capacity he was given to comparing Al Capone's methods to those of Adolf Hitler) and broadcaster, but he never returned to the town where he had gotten his start.

Once St. John departed, Cicero belonged to Al Capone—not every building, of course—nevertheless, it belonged to him in spirit. It had taken two years of struggle, but he had attained dominion over the city. Now that he controlled the city without fear of inquiry from prying journalists, his organization stored its liquor in the safest of all locations: the basement of the Town Hall. Al gave a very public demonstration of his power over the local government when, one day, he got into an argument with Joseph Klenha, his handpicked mayor, and wound up throwing Hizzoner down the steps of the Town Hall and, as the mayor attempted to get to his feet, kicked him aside; all the while a policeman walking his beat observed without interfering.

Under the Capone regime Louis Cowan continued to prosper—for a time. He managed the *Cicero Tribune*; Albert Capone, the second-youngest of all the brothers, served an apprenticeship in its circulation department. Thus the newspaper that had made its reputation attacking the Capones now became the Capones' house organ. Cowan later entered a new racket: slot machines. In time, the former news dealer earned the title "King of the Slot Machines," yet no matter how inflated his reputation became, he remained Al's faithful errand boy. He continued to relish the perquisites of his position until one day in 1932. As he was delivering the proceeds of the day's betting at the Hawthorne Race Track, some $6,000 in cash, a fusillade of bullets blasted him into eternity. The police inquiry into the murder of Louis Cowan led nowhere, nor was the money he carried at the time of his death ever recovered. The investigating detective, it is said, made off with the loot.

•   •   •   •

The Capone family lost a son in 1924, but before the year was out they gained one, as well.

After the Capone brothers became the subject of lurid headlines—first Frank's death at the hands of the police, and later Al's murder of Joe Howard—reporters at Chicago's daily papers became aware of yet another Capone brother. This one did not live in Chicago, as the rest of his family did, nor was he a racketeer. He was, the newsmen were astonished and amused to note, a Nebraska Prohibition agent who had taken the name of Richard Hart—"Two-Gun" Hart, as he was called back home. Even though he was on the opposite side of the law from the rest of his siblings, his burning dark eyes, olive complexion, and determined manner all created an unmistakable family resemblance.

He was now drawn to Chicago by the headlines his brothers had generated, to see what had become of the kin he had abandoned. The Capones in 1924 were a much different family than the one he had left in 1912. So much had happened; his father had died four years earlier, and the entire clan had moved to Chicago, where Hart found them living in the solid, conventional house on South Prairie Avenue. In a sense, everyone was the same, all of them living on top of one another, Teresa still cooking, but everyone was different, too. This was not Brooklyn, and the Capones were no longer just another family of recently arrived Italian immigrants struggling for a foothold on the bottom rung of the economic ladder. They had, for better or worse, made a name for themselves in Chicago. In the Loop, in Cicero, and out on the distant reaches of South Prairie Avenue the Capones were *somebody*, as they had never been back in Brooklyn, or, for that matter, in Naples. As Hart discovered, they were full-fledged racketeers now, in league with Johnny Torrio. They were not members of the Mafia, which even here, in America, remained a stronghold of Sicilians, or the Neapolitan Camorra, which was strictly Old World, but of their new American counterpart, the rackets, the "syndicate," the "organization." No matter what name it was given, it took an up-to-date, businesslike approach to the same old disreputable trades, while benefiting greatly from a new line, bootlegging, thanks to the hypocrisies of Prohibition.

One of the most startling aspects of his brothers' life in Chicago was how freely they went about the city, despite their notoriety. The journalists, many of whom used the Capones' drinking and gambling facilities, treated them as friends, almost as celebrities. So when their brother came a-calling from Nebraska, the Capones were happy to show off the family's black sheep in the white hat. The reporters, in turn, asked Hart the inevitable question: did he, as a Prohibition agent, sworn to uphold the law, plan to arrest his brothers for bootlegging? Hart told the newsmen he certainly would, *if* any of his brothers ever happened to set foot in Nebraska. As long as they stayed in Chicago, they were safe.

Hart also knew his family was still in mourning. The recent death of Frank had done nothing to deter the surviving brothers from entering ever more deeply into a life of crime; if anything, the tragedy increased their determination to pursue *la mala vita* in Chicago, wherever it might lead. His senseless death demonstrated anew what they had always known to be true: that there was no justice for Italians in America, except for the justice they enforced by their own hand. The police, politicians, the mayor, even the governor of Illinois could all be bought with the proceeds of prostitution, bootlegging, and gambling. In this wilderness of corruption, only the gun spoke with absolute authority, as Hart knew better than any of his siblings. He was aware of their criminal activities, and he knew that his younger brother Al had recently taken a man's life, but they were still family.

Despite the obvious differences in the paths they had chosen, what mattered in the end were the blood ties, the unstated sympathies, especially between Hart and his brother Al. Like Al, Hart had been involved in the death of a man just a few months before the Joe Howard murder. He had nearly lost his job and his life because of it. Both men possessed a strong will to power, and both were drawn to the gun and gunplay. The two brothers had a fierce desire to impose their will, and they had both become notorious in the process, as the nicknames they both had earned—"Two-Gun" and "Scarface"—indicated. Each brother personified one aspect of a duality deep in the Capone family's collective psyche, one choosing to become an outlaw, the other a lawman, each a mirror image of the other. It was as if one brother represented a hidden aspect of another, Hart displaying Al's frustrated striving toward respectability, and Al acting out Hart's barely restrained attraction to violence and anarchy. Good and evil inseparably linked by a fraternal tie.

Although he reestablished ties to his family, Hart did not resign his commission as a Prohibition agent; he was not tempted to exchange the marshal's Stetson for the gangster's fedora. He had his own life to lead in Nebraska, his own wife and children, who knew him only as Richard Hart, the lawman, and he had his own reputation to maintain. So after his visit to Chicago, he returned to the wrinkle in the prairie known as Homer, Nebraska, the open spaces, and the Indian reservations, where he felt most at home. It was as though he were leaving the twentieth century, where his brothers dwelled and became wealthy from their collective endeavors, for the nineteenth, where a man lived and died by his own devices and controlled his own destiny. This man who appeared so violently determined to assert himself was actually adrift on the tides of time, a hitchhiker through history.

.   .   .

Thereafter, Hart returned to Chicago at least once a year, generally during holidays. He never told his wife, Kathleen, where he was going, or why; nor did he tell his children about their notorious uncles in Chicago. Still, rumors trailed him back to Homer, and as his children grew older, they overheard their friends whispering that their father, "Two-Gun" Hart, was related to the famous Al "Scarface" Capone. And when Hart's children weren't listening, their friends called them "Capone."

CHAPTER 3

Memento Mori

PIMP, BOOKKEEPER, PROTÉGÉ, political boss, gambler, bootlegger, "used-furniture dealer," mourner, murderer, addict—Capone had played all these roles during his first four years in Chicago: a high-velocity voyage into notoriety. With the help of his brothers and the patronage of Johnny Torrio he had become master of a fair-sized industrial town by the fall of 1924. He was wealthy, he was powerful, he was feared, he was well dressed. He had established his wife, child, and mother in a comfortable home, and he observed the proprieties of home life even as he sought the favors of prostitutes and supported himself with the poisoned fruit of their trade. All this, and he was only twenty-five years old: a legend-in-the-making, another Chicago success story. The racketeer as tycoon. Yet as Capone knew so well, a single well-aimed bullet could take it all from him in an instant, and other racketeers would rush to divide the spoils. After an opulent gangster funeral—the wreaths, the endless cortege, the sobbing at the grave—he would become just another victim of the city's gangster wars, remembered only by his family. Indeed, it was highly likely that he would meet his end in precisely this way, as racketeers in Chicago were doing with increasing frequency all around him.

On Chicago's South Side, the truce Johnny Torrio had carefully put in place with the advent of Prohibition was quickly disintegrating, with lethal results. With some accuracy, the press labeled the struggle a "beer war," although much more than beer and other types of alcohol were at stake; it was actually a vicious battle for political control of Chicago. In just one month, September 1923, the beer war claimed four victims, all members of gangs that had violated Torrio's truce and invaded one another's territories. In December, five more murders occurred in the bootlegging trade, each one dutifully, even lovingly, recorded by the press. Now the smell of gunfire hung over all of Chicago, not just Cicero.

The Chicago Crime Commission, the most reliable source of information concerning the early growth of organized crime in Chicago, compiled a body count of the beer war comprising both the well-publicized, pivotal assassinations, when real power changed hands, and the day-in, day-out deaths of foot soldiers. In 1920, for example, the survey recorded twenty-three "gangland-style" slayings in Chicago; most remained unsolved. The following year, the number of deaths reached twenty-nine, and in 1922 the rolls increased to thirty-six victims. Then, in 1923, as Prohibition took hold and the stakes grew, there were fifty-two casualties, an average of one a week, according to the Commission's survey, and in 1924, the number crept up to fifty-four, with no end in sight.

Although bootlegging-related deaths accounted for only a fraction of Chicago's overall murder rate, they received the majority of the headlines, and the disproportionate attention accorded them prompted one journalist of the period to state, "Two-thirds of the deaths in Chicago are due to the beer-running trade." Statistics failed to support his claim, but the impression gained general acceptance, especially outside the city limits. In Washington, D.C., the Federal Bureau of Investigation, under the leadership of its youthful director, J. Edgar Hoover, refused to interfere in Chicago or anywhere else, preferring to leave the messy business of enforcing Prohibition laws to the beleaguered and often corrupt agents of the Federal Bureau of Alcohol Violations. So the violence in Chicago—all of it widely reported, discussed, and condemned—grew unchecked, tolerated as the inevitable stepchild of Prohibition. "You can hardly be surprised at the boys killing each other," said Clarence Darrow, the eminent trial lawyer, who lived in Chicago. "The business pays very well, but it is outside the law and they can't go to court, like shoe dealers or real-estate men or grocers when they think an injustice has been done them, or unfair competition has arisen in their territory. So they naturally shoot."

By the time gangland violence in Chicago attracted national attention, the figure most often associated with it was Al Capone, whose name was dragged into nearly every major slaying, though never with conclusive evidence. It *was* true that the bloodshed of the early and mid-1920s worked uncannily to his advantage, eliminating his rivals, superiors, and enemies, and making it possible for him to rise to the topmost echelon of the rackets, but he consolidated his power not by plotting murders but by running an organization, taking care to stay well behind the front lines, and benefiting from the mayhem taking place all around him. Nowhere was this better illustrated than by the death of the man who handled the floral arrangements for Frank's funeral: Dion O'Banion.

.   .   .

The angel-faced chief of Chicago's North Side bootlegging had prospered ever since that gray, solemn day in May 1924 when Frank Capone was laid to rest. His business was flourishing, not just flowers, but bootlegging, which netted him nearly $1 million annually, and he supplemented this amount with a series of daredevil hijackings of other bootleggers' finest stock, bonded whiskey being a particular favorite of his. Only recently he had raided a warehouse containing nearly 2,000 barrels of whiskey, which he replaced with water as a jest. Officially, he was allied with the Torrio-Capone organization, which offered him an umbrella of protection from rival bootleggers and numerous freelancers, but even though he had contributed men and firepower to the April 1 election in Cicero that brought Capone to power, he felt slighted, used, misunderstood. Think of the gorgeous flowers he had supplied for Frank's funeral!

Torrio threw O'Banion a bone in the form of a tightly circumscribed piece of territory in Cicero; the grant wasn't worth much, maybe twenty grand a month, walking-around money by the standards of the Torrio syndicate, but it was a presence. O'Banion owed his fortune to being a little crazy and to his talent for business, as he proved anew by increasing the take of this concession fivefold, in part by encouraging speakeasies to move to Cicero. Torrio and Capone were impressed, envious, resentful. "Dion was all right and he was getting along . . . better than he had any right to expect," Al explained later, adding a memorable turn of phrase. "But, like everyone else, his head got away from his hat." Ever the strategist, the peacemaker, and the visionary racketeer, Torrio proposed to give O'Banion a percentage of the organization's income from prostitution in return for a percentage of O'Banion's Cicero operation. The deal was a typical Torrio proposition, linking potential adversaries in a common enterprise. But Torrio made one miscalculation. O'Banion, like many Irish racketeers, was appalled by prostitution; it was a filthy business, and he preferred to leave it to the Italians and the Jews. Let *them* burn in hell for all eternity. Deal refused.

O'Banion's resentment of the Torrio-Capone syndicate's preeminence extended to their allies, especially the six Genna brothers. The "Terrible Gennas," they were called—Angelo, Sam, Pete, Tony, Mike, and Jim—all of them Sicilian bootleggers. They were reputed to be a tough crew, prepared to resort to violence at the slightest provocation, yet the Gennas were also imbued with a certain Old World, fin-de-siècle elegance and ennui, as if they had been exiled from their proper realm and were fated to pass the rest of their days engaged in a futile search for their lost grandeur. They were a tightly knit family, these Gennas, and one of their number, Tony, resembled a poet more than he did a gangster. He did whatever he could to distance himself from his disreputable family, living in the Congress Hotel with his companion, Gladys Bagwell, a minister's daughter who played piano in speakeasies. He aspired to a career as an architect and was fiercely proud of the apartment buildings he had designed to supply decent housing for his impoverished countrymen. No matter how far afield he ranged, however, the family business came first, even for Tony.

The Gennas easily overcame the restrictions of Prohibition by acquiring government authorization to produce "industrial alcohol." Permission in hand, the Gennas became "alky-cookers," that is, they paid impoverished Sicilian families in Chicago's Little Italy to brew whiskey at home in small copper stills, easily moved to avoid detection. The Sicilian families had been accustomed to brewing at home in Italy, and it was natural for them to continue to do so in the United States. The Gennas paid their Sicilian home brewers the astonishing amount of $15 a day, and all they had to do in return was to mind the still and siphon off the residue. Meanwhile, the Gennas' fee for the homemade whiskey quickly became a necessary supplement to each household's meager income. Every week the Gennas gathered the results of the week's alky-cooking, which they stored in a giant warehouse located at 1022 Taylor Street, only four blocks from the Maxwell Street police station. This proved to be a convenient arrangement for the police and the Gennas alike, and the sight of cops entering and exiting the warehouse as they collected their bribes became so common that people in the neighborhood referred to the warehouse as "the police station." The arrangement was so profitable that policemen from distant districts came by to collect bribes— until the Maxwell Street police gave the Gennas a list of their men, the *only* cops to pay off.

It was dreadful stuff, the Gennas' homemade brew. It stank, it was raw, and it was dangerous. Brewed quickly, on the cheap, the Gennas' whiskey teemed with toxins. Real whiskey acquires its distinctive golden hue from the wooden casks in which it is slowly and patiently aged. But the Gennas had no time for the careful distillation of whiskey; instead, they colored it with caramel, or coal tar, and flavored it with fusel oil, a noxious by-product of fermentation normally removed from whiskey lest it cause severe mental disturbance or even insanity. These chemicals were not the only hazards to the health of the consumer. Confiscating a hundred casks of the home brew, the police discovered dead rats in the whole lot.

Nor were the Gennas the only ones selling home brew. Alky-cooking was ubiquitous in Prohibition-era Chicago; the streets of Little Italy reeked with the sickeningly sweet vapors of homemade booze. The phenomenon was repeated all over Chicago, all over the country, in fact. It was one of the saddest aspects of the failure of Prohibition. Good liquor, manufactured by traditional distilleries, was scarce and extremely expensive; in its place cheaply made substitutes flooded speakeasies, poisoning drinkers. As Prohibition wore on, Americans forgot what real liquor was like, how it tasted, the subtle ways it affected the mind and body. Instead, they became familiar with the far more potent effects of bootleg booze. If any type of alcohol deserved to be prohibited, it was this poisoned fruit of Prohibition. The Gennas put their homemade poison in a bottle labeled brandy or whiskey or bourbon, and thus disguised it was extremely profitable. Three dollars a barrel: half the price of O'Banion's high-class whiskey. Each still produced as much as 350 gallons of high-proof poison a week with ingredients costing less than a dollar a gallon. The Gennas grossed over $300,000 a month, of which $7,000 went toward payoffs to the police, who also had the opportunity to purchase the alcohol, wholesale, if they wished. When the Gennas began selling this wretched alcohol in O'Banion's prime territory on the North Side, the florist implored Torrio to send the six Sicilians back where they belonged, on the West Side. Torrio demurred; he knew how dangerous the Gennas were, heavily armed, steeped in Sicilian blood oaths, and well connected to the police. In defiance, O'Banion dared to do what no other bootlegger would: he hijacked a truck bearing $30,000 of the Gennas' rotgut. The Gennas rattled their sabers, but with Torrio acting as go-between, advocating restraint, the animosity between the Irishman and the Sicilians stopped short of outright war.

Already flirting with disaster, O'Banion further tempted fate by betraying Johnny Torrio and Al Capone to the police, with whom he had developed a mutually beneficial relationship. "He was spoiling it for everybody," Al explained and complained: "Where we had been paying a copper a couple of hundred dollars, he'd slip them a thousand. He spoiled them. Well, we couldn't do anything about it. It was his funeral." So it would be, but not just yet. In return for his money, O'Banion received information that he planned to use against his bootlegging partners in a byzantine scheme that demonstrated how clever the florist could be—and how reckless.

Just six weeks after the funeral of Frank Capone, and days after the murder of Joe Howard, O'Banion came to the Hawthorne Inn in Cicero, where he met with Torrio and Al Capone, whom he startled with his announcement that he planned to retire from bootlegging. The Gennas had made life too difficult and dangerous for him, he explained. Indeed, he planned to leave Chicago altogether and retire to Colorado. Torrio and Capone greeted the news with jubilation. The volatile Irishman made trouble wherever he went, and his graceful retirement from the bootlegging scene could only be a blessing. All they had to do was meet his price, and O'Banion had thought about that, as well. The three men jointly owned the Sieben Brewery, and O'Banion offered to sell his share for half a million dollars. He even volunteered to transport their last shipment of beer as partners; it was scheduled for

May 19, 1924. Delighted, Torrio and Capone saw to it that O'Banion received immediate payment in full.

O'Banion's offer to relinquish his share of the Sieben Brewery to Torrio and Capone concealed considerable guile. Prior to the meeting, O'Banion had learned through his police contacts that the brewery was to be raided by police on the night of May 19. Normally, a raid on a brewery was a matter of small import in Chicago—it usually indicated that the right police captain had not been paid off, or wanted more, and nothing was easier to arrange than a quick cash payment to the proper authorities—but this raid, as O'Banion discovered, was to be different. This time federal authorities under the direction of the U.S. attorney were running the operation with Mayor Dever's blessing. Since Torrio already had a prior conviction for violating the Prohibition laws dating back to 1923, a second conviction would probably lead to enormous fines, a jail sentence, and the publicity Torrio abhorred.

On the night of May 19, the raid on the Sieben Brewery occurred exactly as O'Banion had anticipated. As Torrio, O'Banion, and a small army of their henchmen supervised the loading of barrels onto a convoy of trucks waiting to distribute them to thirsty speakeasies across Chicago and the state of Illinois, police swooped down and arrested twenty-eight sullen bootleggers. Torrio was detained, as was O'Banion, to maintain the fiction that he had no prior knowledge of the raid. Only Al Capone himself managed to avoid arrest, for he was not present at the brewery that night. Once Torrio was delivered to the custody of *federal* authorities, he realized that O'Banion had effected an elaborate and humiliatingly successful betrayal. In anger, he refused to post bond for O'Banion, as he routinely did for his other partners and employees. Torrio himself was soon free on bail, but he was later convicted of owning a brewery and received a sentence of nine months in jail and a $5,000 fine—all of it due to the perfidy of Dion O'Banion.

After the raid and Torrio's arrest, O'Banion's days in the bootlegging business, indeed, his days on Earth, were numbered. Not that O'Banion himself displayed the slightest sign of concern about his safety as he bustled about his flower store, cheerfully greeting his customers; of all gangsters he was the most accessible and personable. It was hard to dislike the short, limping, smiling young man—hate him, yes, but not dislike him.

On November 3, O'Banion and his ally, "Hymie" Weiss, arrived at the Ship, Capone's Cicero gambling establishment, to divide the profits with his partners. Business proceeded as usual, except for small but revealing comments the participants made from time to time. Al, for instance, noted that Angelo Genna had racked up a $30,000 IOU, and in the interest of preserving the health of all concerned, he recommended they forgive the debt, but O'Banion would have none of it. He went straight to a telephone, called Genna, and instructed him to pay the debt within a week's time. The demonstration showed Capone and Torrio how serious the rift between the Gennas and O'Banion really was. Al and Johnny were doing all they could to keep the murderous Sicilians happy, but they could not control the reckless O'Banion, who was liable to get them all into trouble. As they left the Ship that day, "Hymie" Weiss cautioned O'Banion to stop antagonizing Torrio and the Gennas. But O'Banion was in a feisty mood; he was not one to take orders from anybody. "Oh, to hell with the Sicilians," he told Weiss.

The bold retort became a refrain among Chicago bootleggers, many of whom felt the same way but were afraid to utter those ominous words: to hell with the Sicilians. Inevitably, the Sicilians said, in effect, "To hell with the Irishman." Together with Capone and Torrio, the Gennas planned the assassination of Dion O'Banion. The murder was to be accomplished the old-fashioned way, which meant the organization would murder O'Banion face to face, at his place of business, in the middle of the day, and everyone in Chicago would know who was responsible, and why.

One matter remained to be resolved before the assassination could be carried out. The Torrio-Capone organization required the blessing of Mike Merlo—Don Miguel Merlo, to give his honorary title—the president of an influential organization known as the Unione Sicilione. Originally a fraternity of immigrant Sicilians who had banded together for self-protection, the Unione had over the years mutated into a racketeering power broker. Under Merlo's direction, the Unione proved adept at manipulating Chicago's racketeers, all of whom needed its support in the bootlegging trade and feared its potential for violence. In Chicago as elsewhere in the United States, Southern Italian immigrants persisted in their fear of and disdain for Sicilians, whom they held to be violent, inflexible, and superstitious. No one—not even Dion O'Banion—dared to incur the opposition of the Unione Sicilione and its 15,000 members. Merlo was opposed to the idea of Torrio and Capone eliminating O'Banion—the murder would be bad for business, bad for everybody—and as long as he remained in office, there would be no assassination. But Mike Merlo, the one man who stood between O'Banion and death, was suffering from cancer; the disease was in its advanced stages, and on November 8 he collapsed and died.

Initially, Mike Merlo's passing proved a boon for O'Banion, who promptly sold $100,000 of flowers to the mourners, including a spectacular twelve-foot- high floral effigy of the deceased. Capone alone accounted for $8,000 worth of flowers. O'Banion also received one curious order, so small that he nearly overlooked it. Jim Genna, one of his sworn enemies, visited the store and bought $750 worth of flowers for Merlo's funeral. He left as inconspicuously as he had come, carrying with him a mental blueprint of the interior of O'Banion's flower store.

The selection of Merlo's successor provoked Frankie Yale to return to

Chicago. As head of the powerful New York branch of the Unione, Yale had considerable influence over the selection of who would fill the corresponding post in Chicago. He conferred with Torrio and Capone, and the three men decided to appoint Angelo Genna, one of the six Sicilians who wanted only to see Dion O'Banion in his coffin. As the new president of the Unione Sicilione, Angelo had no objection to the immediate elimination of a certain North Side bootlegger who had recently humiliated him on the telephone over a little IOU. So it was that the Torrio-Capone syndicate finally arranged for the assassination of Dion O'Banion, which became the most highly publicized and significant gangland slaying of Prohibition-era Chicago, eclipsing even the death of "Big Jim" Colosimo four years before.

· · ·

On Monday, November 10, 1924, only two days after the death of Mike Merlo, O'Banion left the twelve-room apartment where he lived with his wife (the couple had no children) and proceeded directly to his place of business, William E. Schofield's North State Street flower store, where he passed much of the morning preparing a large order for the funeral of yet another beer war victim. He was accompanied by three employees, and they were surrounded by plants and flowers of every description: roses, palms, ferns, chrysanthemums. Outside the window, on State Street, schoolchildren swarmed around a parochial school, and across the street loomed the Gothic Holy Name Cathedral, huge, impressive, and cavernous. O'Banion knew it well, for he had served as an altar boy at Holy Name years before.

At noon, a blue Jewett sedan parked in front of the flower store. The driver remained at the wheel, and as the motor idled, the door opened. An eleven-year-old boy named Gregory Summers watched three men get out of the car. "Two of them were dark and they looked like foreigners. The other man had a light complexion," he would later recall. The three men opened the door to Schofield's flower store.

The proprietor was in the back, lovingly arranging his flowers, but the porter, a black man named William Crutchfield, looked up from his mopping and assumed the group consisted of the racketeers with whom his boss so often did business. However, these men were not well dressed, which was out of the ordinary. O'Banion appeared, genial as always. The night before a man had called to say he would stop by at noon the next day to pick up a wreath. O'Banion assumed this group was collecting the order. "Hello, boys," he said, "have you come for the flowers?" His left hand held a pair of shears, and he extended his right arm, preparing to shake hands with his customers, one of whom clutched O'Banion's outstretched arm and pulled him forward, off balance.

Crutchfield, who may have suspected danger, decided his mopping was finished and retreated to the back room, where he heard five shots, a pause, and then a sixth shot ring out. O'Banion's two other employees, who were also in the back, fled the scene, but Crutchfield ran to his boss, whom he found sprawled on the floor, surrounded by his flowers, his eyes wide open, his body jerking convulsively, and his blood seeping onto the floor. The shots had been fired at such close range that O'Banion's clothing was burned. He had taken five bullets in the body and a sixth in the head. His assassin, the man who had grasped his arm and pulled him off balance, was Mike Genna. With Genna was a notorious team of Sicilians who now lived in Cicero: John Scalise and Albert Anselmi. These men served one and only one function: they killed on the orders of whoever their boss happened to be at the time. They were handsomely recompensed for this job, receiving a cash payment of $10,000 apiece, as well as a diamond ring worth another $3,000. As soon as the three had accomplished their chore, they ran out of the store, dove into the Jewett, and as Gregory Summers continued to watch in amazement, sped off.

Relieved that another racketeer was out of the way, the police did not try too hard to catch O'Banion's killers. As a matter of routine they interrogated Johnny Torrio, Al Capone, and the Gennas, all of whom professed to revere their old companion Dion and to make a convincing show of grief at his death, pointing to the large floral arrangements they had sent to his funeral as proof. They were so beautiful they brought a lump to the throat. The police even suspected that Frankie Yale might have come all the way from Brooklyn to hasten O'Banion to the grave, though Yale excused himself by saying he had come to town to attend the funeral of Mike Merlo, and after making his statement to the police, he returned by train to New York and relative safety. Although the police suspected Yale had killed O'Banion, he had actually come to consult with Torrio and Capone rather than to deprive the Gennas of their revenge. With the death of Dion O'Banion, the Torrio-Capone syndicate appeared to have accomplished a major coup; they had eliminated the most unpredictable and dangerous of all major bootleggers, they had ingratiated themselves with the Gennas, and they had annexed O'Banion's rich North Side territory.

For all these reasons, then, the funeral of Dion O'Banion was not an occasion for mourning but rather a great victory celebration. Torrio and Capone were glad to see him go, and they wanted to give the old boy a magnificent send-off. Not that everyone approved. The Catholic Church, in the person of Cardinal Mundelein, refused to permit a funeral Mass for O'Banion at Holy Name, the cathedral across the street from the murder scene, and forbade his burial on consecrated ground. The ecclesiastical rebuff did little to dampen the festivities. O'Banion's murderers laid on the largest, most lavish gangster funeral ever seen in Chicago, as if to persuade themselves that he really was dead, after all.

For O'Banion's next-to-last resting place they selected a funeral home whose owner, John A. Sbarbaro, led a curious double life. Even while running the mortuary preferred by Chicago's gangland, he served, incredibly enough, as an assistant state's attorney; in fact, he worked with William McSwiggin, the young "hanging prosecutor" who had been so determined to indict Al Capone for the murder of Joe Howard only six months earlier. Sbarbaro personified the affinity between criminals and politicians in Chicago, a phenomenon that so often frustrated the prosecution of even the most blatant crimes. At Sbarbaro's funeral parlor at 708 North Wells Street, O'Banion "lay in state" (in the apt words of the *Chicago Tribune*) in a casket said to cost $10,000, wrought of silver and bronze, surrounded by gold candlesticks, and highlighted with a gold tablet reading "Dion O'Banion, 1892-1924." At thirty-two, he was approximately five years past his prime by gangland's standards, and considering his recklessness, it was remarkable that he had lived as long as he had. Of course Torrio was nearly twice his age, but Torrio was the exception, and he had turned over much of the day-to-day operation of the syndicate to Capone. As musicians from the Chicago Symphony Orchestra played solemn music in the background and the deceased's immediate family cried softly, the mourners filed past the bier to pay their respects to the slain racketeer. The funeral procession was so large that it became the subject of national attention and fascination. It extended for a mile and included three bands and a police escort dispatched by Capone from the village of Stickney. (Only an order from Chicago's chief of police prevented what was certain to have been an embarrassingly large contingent of that city's force from joining the parade.) The pallbearers included "Hymie" Weiss, who had counseled O'Banion to apologize to the Gennas, and who would immediately begin plotting to take over the rich North Side empire O'Banion had controlled; another up-and-coming racketeer by the name of "Bugs" Moran; and four other gangsters (*racketeer* being too polite a term for them): "Schemer" Drucci, Louis Alterie, Frank Gusenberg, and Maxie Eisen ("the Simon Legree of the pushcart peddlers," according to one journalist). More than two dozen cars were required to transport flowers from the funeral home to the cemetery, including a large basket of roses bearing a message of consummate irony: "FROM AL."

The cortege reached awesome proportions; 10,000 people walked behind the hearse, and when they reached Mt. Carmel Cemetery they joined another 10,000 mourners assembled at the grave site, where Father Patrick Malloy, who had known and liked the deceased since O'Banion was a boy, delivered a truncated eulogy. Capone and Torrio were in attendance, although they knew that O'Banion's allies saw past the floral arrangements and realized exactly who was responsible for the death of their friend and leader. When a reporter sidled up to "Hymie" Weiss, asking who the racketeer thought had actually killed O'Banion and suggesting Al Capone, Weiss drew back as if confronted by a snake. "Blame Capone?" he said with heavy irony. "Why Al's a real pal. He was Dion's best friend, too." Feelings ran so high that all mourners were ordered to check their weapons until the funeral had concluded, but Torrio and Capone were obliged to pass a long, uncomfortable day that began at the funeral home and ended at the cemetery, where across O'Banion's grave they confronted the accusatory stares of Weiss, Drucci, and Moran.

O'Banion's stupendous last rites became a remarkable—and, for the political Establishment—humiliating display of the racketeers' influence and power over Chicago. Here was what the Johnny Torrio Association had come to, all the way from a Brooklyn storefront recruiting children to this, the grandest funeral Chicago had ever seen. It was as if a carnival was coming to town, a carnival of death. In the Chicago of the mid- and late 1920s there would be more of these days of the dead, when a gangster funeral brought the entire city to standstill. They were indicative of the hold that men such as Torrio, O'Banion, and Capone were developing on the popular imagination. People were fascinated not because they were criminals—criminals were nuisances, they were dreary—but because they lived by their own rough code and were willing to die in pursuit of their goals. It is always fascinating when people choose to die in public; the sight makes the spectators feel more alive; so it was with the gangsters and their dark allure. Better than any politician, they understood what it took to draw a crowd. The funeral amounted to precisely the show of strength Mayor Dever and the other embattled bureaucrats at City Hall dreaded, a sign for all the world to behold that they were losing the war against the bootleggers, racketeers, and pimps for control of Chicago. "Are we living by the code of the Dark Ages or is Chicago part of an American Commonwealth?" Dever asked in his characteristically archaic diction. "One day we have this O'Banion slain as a result of a perfectly executed plot of assassins. It is followed by this amazing demonstration. In the meanwhile his followers and their rivals openly boast of what they will do in retaliation. They seek to fight it out in the street. There is no thought of the law or of the people who support the law." Such words came as high praise to the bootleggers and racketeers responsible for the situation. Not even the church was capable of exercising authority over the outlaws. O'Banion was laid to rest in unconsecrated ground, as the church had insisted, but this was Chicago, and five months later the body was exhumed and moved to consecrated ground. In disgust, John Stege, a high-ranking police captain, said, "O'Banion was a thief and a murderer, but look at him now, buried eighty feet from a bishop."

•   •   •

For all its pomp and circumstance, the funeral of Dion O'Banion became Johnny Torrio's last hurrah. His vision of peaceful, profitable bootlegging (with a little gambling and prostitution on the side) ended as bootleggers and racketeers became ever more disorganized and combative, shifting alliances week by week. Torrio and Capone, who thought that they would enjoy greater security than they had ever known, became marked men the instant O'Banion went to his grave. Even at O'Banion's funeral each man feared for his life as rumors circulated that gunmen were looking for them, that they were, in Chicago parlance, "on the spot." Their newest enemy was "Hymie" Weiss, the bootlegger who had failed to persuade O'Banion to apologize to the Gennas. Weiss now set his sights on O'Banion's prime North Side territory, and he was determined to take it from the Torrio-Capone organization by force.

In the face of this threat, Torrio concluded it would be wise to absent himself from Chicago and his new enemies. Immediately following the funeral he once again entrusted the organization to Capone, whose main task at this point was simply to stay alive. Death was everywhere, and Capone became obsessed with security. Over the next eighteen months, the gangster associates of Dion O'Banion, including Moran, Drucci, and Weiss, would make a dozen recorded attempts on the life of Al Capone, each one a reminder both of the absolute necessity of security precautions as well as the incompetence of his adversaries. (If ever there was a gang that couldn't shoot straight, it was Moran and company.)

The threat of assassination had a profound effect on the way Al conducted himself and his business. Although he himself was unarmed as a mark of his status, he never went anywhere without at least two bodyguards, one on either side. With the exception of his home on South Prairie Avenue, he was never alone during this period. He traveled only by car, sandwiched between bodyguards, with a trusted, armed chauffeur named Sylvester Barton at the wheel. Even with all this protection, he preferred to travel under cover of night, risking travel by day only when absolutely necessary. Such were the rules of the deadly game to which he was irrevocably committed. The death of Frank—result of a split-second decision—had taught him fear, and fear became his constant companion, caution his watchword, as he shuttled from his lair at the Hawthorne Hotel in Cicero to the fortress on Austin Avenue and his home on the South Side. Even indoors he took security precautions. In a restaurant he sat at the back, facing the door, near a window, in case he needed to effect a quick escape. In his home he never stood in front of an open window; the curtains were always drawn to prevent a sniper from drawing a bead on him. No other racketeer, not even Johnny Torrio, took the same precautions as Capone. Most of them, entranced with their own power and swagger and the fear they could strike into "civilians," went about the city casually, carelessly, assuming the weapon bulging in a shoulder holster offered them all the protection they required. Not Capone. For him security, constant vigilance, and bodyguards were neither an encumbrance nor an admission of cowardice, they were a way of life. Rather than crippling him, this fatalism paradoxically liberated him; if he was going to die young, he might as well enjoy the illicit pleasures available to him while he could. His cocaine addiction made the thought of imminent death easier to accept; under the influence of the drug it seemed as if *la mala vita* amounted to a glorious suicide mission.

As Capone sequestered himself in Chicago, Johnny Torrio traveled south to Hot Springs, Arkansas, which was fast becoming a refuge for racketeers on the lam, but the fear that gunmen loyal to the late O'Banion were trailing him prompted the aging racketeer to move on to New Orleans, Cuba, the Bahamas, and Florida. At each stop he transacted some quick bootlegging business before he fled.

While Torrio contrived to stay a jump or two ahead of the gunmen, Weiss decided to strike at his chief deputy, Al Capone, who had remained in Chicago as the winter settled in and icy winds swept off Lake Michigan across the city's towering, indifferent skyscrapers. On the assumption that the enemy of his enemy was a friend, Weiss formed a loose alliance with two other rivals of the Torrio-Capone organization, "Schemer" Drucci and "Bugs" Moran, both of whom had served as pallbearers for Dion O'Banion. They were long on idiosyncrasy and bravado, this trio, but short on skill and cunning. Their nominal leader, "Hymie" Weiss, was actually named Earl Wajciechowski, but when he shortened his last name, it was generally assumed he was a Jew, and he acquired the nickname "Hymie." In reality, however, he was Catholic. Unlike many racketeers, who let their wives pray for their sins, Weiss was devout and carried rosaries wherever he went, frequently attended Mass, and had no difficulty reconciling his spiritual inclinations with his temporal activities, which now included his determination to assassinate Torrio and Capone. Weiss relished the perquisites of the racketeer's life, especially the sumptuous chorus girl with whom he lived, Josephine Libby. "You'd expect a rich bootlegger to be a man-about-town, always going to nightclubs and having his home full of rowdy friends," she said of their life together, "but Earl liked to be alone with me, . . . listening to the radio or reading . . . histories and law books. He was crazy about children." But their home life was perhaps not quite so wholesome as she maintained. When federal marshals arrested him for violating the Mann Act (prostitution, in other words), they discovered an array of gangster paraphernalia in his apartment: shotguns, revolvers, knockout drops, handcuffs, and enough whiskey to stock a speakeasy. At twenty-six, he was the youngest member of the group, though he was already a veteran of the Chicago rackets, an example of the youngsters coming up fast in a boom economy supercharged by Prohibition.

"Schemer" Drucci, the least-known, least-influential associate, derived his nickname from his propensity for concocting all manner of far-fetched hits, heists, and kidnappings. In reality Drucci was more the dreamer than the schemer, his criminal behavior confined to such prosaic activities as robbing public telephones of their coins. Still, he had a streak of recklessness and daring, and he *looked* the part of a gangster—tough, dark, and menacing, his expression frozen in a tragic mask topped by wild, unkempt hair: a face to haunt the dreams of his enemies.

Of them all, George "Bugs" Moran was the most violent and unstable. (Since there is no justice when it comes to gangsters he would also be among the most long-lived.) They called him "Bugs," even to his dimpled, handsome, smooth-shaven face, because his temper was so horrible people assumed he was "buggy" or crazy. Moran was of Polish and Irish descent, born in Minnesota in 1893, married to a woman claiming to be a Sioux Indian: an all-American combination. He took to a life of crime in his youth on Chicago's North Side, and by the time he was twenty-one he had participated in twenty-six known robberies and had served several jail sentences. As a result, an aura of the repeat offender and the jailbird hung over him. Whenever there was a beer war slaying, the police routinely hauled "Bugs" in for questioning, only to release him hours later. He knew all the judges in Chicago and liked to tweak them. "That's a beautiful diamond ring you're wearing," he once told Judge John Lyle, the self-appointed scourge of gangsters. "If it's snatched some night, promise me you won't go hunting me. I'm telling you now I'm innocent."

The Moran-Drucci-Weiss gang immediately set out to eliminate the man they considered primarily responsible for killing O'Banion: Al Capone. It was a task that would preoccupy them for the next five years, culminating in the most celebrated gangland slaying of all, the St. Valentine's Day Massacre, and even that bloodbath failed to resolve the conflict. Capone proved too careful, too lucky, to succumb to his implacable, incompetent opponents, but even if they had succeeded in killing him, it would have done little to alter the makeup of the Chicago rackets, for Capone was an organization man. Had Al fallen in the line of duty, Ralph was prepared to fill the leadership vacuum, just as Al had taken over when Frank died, and if Ralph was assassinated, there were all the younger Capones waiting in the wings. In addition, the family enjoyed the backing of Jack Guzik and his extensive network of political alliances. There really was little the Moran faction could do to topple the Torrio and Capone organization, though they certainly did not stop trying.

On the afternoon of January 12, 1925, while Torrio was still down south, Moran, Drucci, and Weiss made their initial attempt on the life of Al Capone. They found him—or at least his chauffeured car—parked outside a restaurant at State and 55th Streets. The means they chose to execute the hit were precedent-setting. Until 1925, racketeers and their gunmen had traditionally relied on pistols, shotguns, and homemade bombs to settle their disputes. Now Capone's would-be assassins employed a new, highly deadly weapon known as the Thompson submachine gun.

It was not a new weapon, merely a forgotten one, surplus from the Great War, a "broom for sweeping trenches," as it was called, designed to kill as many men as efficiently as current technology permitted. At the time, no one imagined it would fall into the hands of civilians, much less outlaws. The weapon was intended strictly for war, but war was precisely what the gangs in Chicago had declared on one another—and on the police, should they be tempted to interfere. They used them at first in practice, on dummies or other targets, in basements, but it was only a matter of time until some ferocious assassin decided to see what the tommy gun could do to his enemies. The inventor of this modern, scientific dispenser of death was a retired Army ordnance officer, Brigadier General John Taliaferro Thompson, who in 1916 devised what he called a "submachine gun." It was smaller than its successor, but astonishingly potent, capable of firing 800 rounds per minute. The bullets were stored either in a magazine or a round drum, which gave the weapon its distinctive look. Although it was as large as a shotgun, and the drum made concealment difficult, it was still relatively light, less than ten pounds, yet its .45-caliber bullets could pierce armor plate at a distance of 500 yards. Accuracy was impossible; just holding onto the gun was all that most men could manage. Because the tommy gun recoiled at the rate it spat bullets, it often gave its handler deep bruises.

After the war, the Auto-Ordnance Corporation, based in New York, tried to sell the weapon commercially, and since it manufactured 15,000 of them, it tried hard. Their plan was to equip every major police department in the country, as well as reputable private security forces, with the tommy gun. The New York Herald of January 31, 1922, carried an advertisement for the gun, declaring it a "Sure Defense Against Organized Bandits and Criminals" and proceeded to explain how changing times demanded no less: "The old time safeguards are inadequate to foil the carefully planned raids of heavily armed bandits, whose 'getaway' is assured by high powered automobiles." The gun sold for a modest $175, the drum magazine cost an additional $50.

Since there were no laws to prohibit or to limit the sale of the submachine gun, the Auto-Ordnance company enjoyed a wide-open market. Yet they found few customers, and most of the guns were stockpiled until unscrupulous dealers delivered them into the hands of the very outlaws they were intended to be used against. By then some regulations—too little and too late—had been instituted, and the black market price for a nice submachine gun with the serial number filed off or obscured by a row of little Xs had soared to $2,000. Only gangsters could afford those prices. At first, the Chicago police were at a loss to explain the damage caused by the earliest machine gun attacks. Old-fashioned shots fired one at a time chipped away at masonry here and there; now, hundreds of .45-caliber bullets shattered windows and left distinctive jagged patterns of bullet holes. When the police finally identified the cause of the damage, they, too, equipped themselves with tommy guns, and thus, in the space of a year or two, pursuing a career as a bootlegger became several times more deadly than it had ever been. The machine gun changed the rules of gangster war. No longer was a marksman's skill required; now only brute force was needed to wield the weapon with deadly results.

Armed with their submachine guns, the would-be assassins drove slowly past Capone's car and fired at it. It was a fine show, destined to be repeated often in Chicago over the next six years, but in this case it was a failure. At the time the submachine guns opened fire, there were three men in Capone's car: the chauffeur, Sylvester Barton, who was wounded, and two bodyguards, both of whom eluded the lethal spray of .45-caliber bullets by falling to the floor. As for Al himself, he had left the car only minutes before to enter the restaurant. He returned to find that the tommy guns had stippled his car with bullets, tearing a gash in the hood and ruining the motor.

The new weapon made a mighty impression on its intended victim, as well. "That's the gun!" Capone later told a journalist. "It's got it over a sawed-off shotgun like the shotgun has it over an automatic. It shoots four hundred and fifty shots a minute. Put on a bigger drum and it will shoot well over a thousand. The trouble is they are hard to get. A cop don't want to get hold of one because his shield number gets mixed up in the record of sale. Bank guards ought to be a good spot to get them from."

• • •

As Capone's driver, Sylvester Barton, recuperated from the injuries he had received in the attempt on the life of his boss, a young man named Tommy Cuiringione took over the job. Within days henchmen working for the Moran-Drucci-Weiss forces kidnapped the new man. The weeks passed, and nothing was heard from the missing driver.

A month after his disappearance, a couple of boys walking a horse through the woods south of Chicago paused at a cistern for the horse to drink. The horse refused, backing away from the cistern as if it contained something vile. Perhaps the boys looked in the cistern and saw what the horse had sensed; perhaps they did not bother to investigate. But later that day they brought a policeman to the suspect cistern. The policeman smelled the water, fouled by the stench of decaying flesh. With the help of the boys, he removed a body—pale, bloated, and disfigured—from the drinking hole. Whoever it was, it was obvious he had died horribly, for the skin was disfigured in numerous places with cigarette burns. His wrists and ankles were bound with wire, and at the back of his head there were five bullet holes. It was a death of surpassing brutality, even for brutal Chicago.

The body, when it was identified, turned out to be that of Capone's loyal driver, Tommy Cuiringione.

For the boys who had found the corpse, it was their first encounter with death. For the policeman who had pulled it from the cistern, it was a sickening reminder of the level of violence in his city. And for Capone, who had employed the victim, it was evidence that the assassination of Dion O'Banion had been a mistake of major proportions. But O'Banion had been so sly and infuriating in the way he had double-crossed him that both Capone and Torrio had allowed themselves to be drawn into a contest which, once begun, could lead to the deaths of all the participants.

. . .

Despite the ever present danger, Torrio quietly returned to Chicago after his anxious journey through the South, tanned if not rested. He was still under indictment for the Sieben Brewery raid and would soon be standing trial along with eleven other men, and he had at least as much to fear from the police and federal law enforcement authorities as he did from rival gangsters. Fixed in his ways, he returned to his apartment and his wife. Assuming he was safe because he had turned over the reins of his organization to Capone, he went about the city unarmed, without even a bodyguard.

On January 24, twelve days after the attempt on the life of Capone, Torrio judged the weather mild enough for shopping in the Loop with his wife. When darkness fell they headed home, arriving at their apartment building on Clyde Avenue a few minutes after four. As his wife, Ann, walked from the car to the door, Torrio followed a few steps behind her, carrying packages, heedless of the blue Cadillac rounding the corner and pulling up in front of the building. Two men—"Hymie" Weiss and "Bugs" Moran—jumped out of the car. Weiss held a sawed-off shotgun, Moran a pistol, and they took aim at Torrio's automobile, apparently under the impression that their target was still in it. They fired, wounding the driver, Robert Barton (the brother of Al Capone's chauffeur, who had been similarly afflicted), and then caught sight of Torrio. They fired wildly, in the general direction of Torrio, who was hit twice, in the chest and in the neck. The criminal mastermind, mentor of Al Capone and advocate of nonviolence, fell to the street, helpless, in agony, as his assassins approached. Weiss and Moran stood over him and deliberately fired into his right arm, and then, to destroy him as a man, into his groin. Throughout the ordeal, Torrio remained conscious. The gunmen were following the pattern of O'Banion's killing: a series of bullets to the body, then the coup de grâce administered to the head. O'Banion's avengers wanted Torrio to die the same way. Moran held a pistol inches from the victim's head and prepared to fire, but before he squeezed off the fatal bullet he was distracted by a passing laundry truck. When he did fire, there was silence, a faint click; the firing chamber was empty: a typical Moran miscalculation. The would-be assassins fled, leaving Torrio barely alive on the icy asphalt.

An ambulance transported Torrio to Jackson Park Hospital, where pandemonium broke out. He was rushed into surgery to remove the bullets, but the doctors gave little hope. Police swarmed everywhere. Al Capone in a "loud, checked suit," accompanied by a delegation of fifteen members of the organization, many of them armed bodyguards, confronted the cops, crying, "The gang! That gang did it!" over and over, but when pressed to identify the members of the gang, he fell silent, obeying the racketeers' code never to divulge information about other racketeers, including one's enemies, to the police. Even *Mrs.* Torrio was there, a "slim-shouldered figure in a blue serge tailored suit," her diamonds glittering, preparing herself to become a widow, albeit an exceedingly wealthy one.

An attempt on the life of Chicago's leading racketeer was a scoop of major proportions for the city's dailies, and the *Herald and Examiner* dispatched Patricia Dougherty to the hospital with the idea that Ann Torrio would be more likely to talk with a woman. "I know you are a reporter," Ann said when Dougherty appeared at her side in a waiting room. "And I know what you people are saying about my husband. . . . I'll tell you about him. He's a wonderful man. Thoughtful. Considerate. Our married life has been 12 years of unbroken happiness. He has given me kindness, devotion, love— everything that a good man can give a woman. Look what he did for his mother! Just last year he took her back to her birthplace in Italy. She left there a poor peasant. She came back the richest woman in the village."

"I understand," Dougherty whispered, gently returning to the matter at hand. "But I was wondering about Capone. I saw him here. Isn't it true your husband and Capone are good friends?"

"They are business associates," Ann replied. "I never met Capone before tonight. He has never been to our home."

Realizing that she had already said too much, Ann Torrio turned her attention to her husband. As the anxious hours crept by, the doctors sent word he was expected to live, after all. But for a racketeer who is "on the spot," as Torrio was, a hospital can be a dangerous place. Take what happened to Frank McErlane, the man the Illinois Association for Criminal Justice once called the "most brutal gunman who ever pulled a trigger in Chicago." When he was in the hospital recovering from an attempt on his life, his rivals stole into his hospital room and opened fire, but before they finished him off, McErlane reached under his pillow, produced a pistol, and began firing enthusiastically until his attackers fled. So there was nothing to stop the Moran-Drucci-Weiss faction from striking again even here, in Torrio's room. Capone, always security-conscious, doted on Torrio, and during his recuperation slept on a cot in Torrio's room to ensure that the helpless older man had round-the-clock protection.

The Chicago police also interested themselves in Torrio's welfare and became unusually diligent in tracking down his assailants. They assigned one of their senior detectives, William Schoemaker—"Shoes," everyone called him—to the case. John Sbarbaro, who led a curious double life as a racketeers' undertaker and an assistant state's attorney, attempted to question the victim, but Torrio, a supremely disciplined man, refused to name his attackers. "I know who they are," he said to Sbarbaro as he lay in agony. "It's my business. I've got nothing to tell you." Detective Schoemaker and the police subsequently located a boy of seventeen who had witnessed the attempted assassination of Johnny Torrio, and he soon faced a lineup of suspects, including "Bugs" Moran, whom Detective Schoemaker had suspected all along. The youth immediately identified Moran as one of the gunmen. "You're nuts!" Moran snapped, but his accuser remained adamant: "I saw you shoot that man." By uttering those words, the boy had instantly put both his life and the lives of his parents in jeopardy, so a judge kept Moran in jail as long as possible. Ultimately the police failed to build a case against Moran, and without Torrio's assistance their inquiry, which had seemed so promising, was destined to fail.

Although the unexpected misfiring of the gun had spared Torrio's life, everything was different for him now. It should have been the best of times for the Torrio-Capone organization; Mayor Dever's plan to reform the city and enforce Prohibition was at best an empty promise, and there was more money than ever to be made from brothels, bootlegging, and gambling. Instead, it was the worst of times. Torrio was in the hospital, and his lofty, apparently secure position in the Chicago rackets had come to a woeful end, as he himself was the first to recognize. Moran, Drucci, and Weiss had struck twice, and it was inevitable they would try a third time, or as many times as necessary. There was no way to stop them short of killing them, an act bound to give rise to further retribution. So Torrio was caught in a vicious cycle of bloodshed, and he knew he was caught.

After almost four weeks in the hospital, Torrio was at last able to rise from his bed, and the first order of business demanding his attention was the trial stemming from the Sieben Brewery raid. Torrio astonished police and prosecutors by appearing in federal court on February 9, 1925, though he was obviously frail, and he still wore the bandages on his wounds, most conspicuously on his throat. There Torrio pleaded guilty to the charge of operating a brewery, and Federal Judge Adam Cliffe sentenced him to pay a fine of $5,000 and to serve nine months in the Lake County Jail in Waukegan, Illinois.

Bringing all his influence to bear, Torrio had an easy time of it in jail. He was soon on cordial terms with the warden, Sheriff Edward Ahlstrom, who provided the prisoner with a clean, private cell equipped with oriental rugs and posh furniture. The sheriff thoughtfully installed bulletproof shutters on the windows to forestall further assassination attempts, and he assigned two deputies to watch over Torrio twenty-four hours a day. An eminent—and generous—bootlegger such as Johnny Torrio deserved no less. A gentleman. So refined. An opera devotee. Nothing like your typical gangster. As the weeks of confinement passed, Torrio grew so close to Ahlstrom that the two men often dined in the sheriff's home, and after dinner Torrio sat on the porch, greeting visitors such as Al Capone until it was time to return to his cell. Despite his privileged status, Torrio recognized that he had reached the end of his days as a racketeer, at least in Chicago. Once he regained his freedom, he would still be the target of die-hard O'Banion loyalists, and if convicted of violating Prohibition laws a *third* time, he would likely be sent to jail for the rest of his life. Perhaps the most damaging aspect of the trial was the publicity it generated; he was too well known in Chicago now to conduct business as usual. This was not the way he preferred to operate. Everything was too violent; no one listened to reason anymore. All the treaties he had painstakingly negotiated among the differing racketeering organizations had been violated. As for the machine gun, he had an absolute abhorrence of the weapon. Its use would lead to the end of racketeering, he suspected. On the other hand, he was wealthy; the newspapers were saying he was worth ten, twenty million, but they neglected to include the money he had stashed away in Italy. The rewards were no longer worth the risks.

After pondering his situation for several weeks, Torrio sent for Capone. Overcoming his resistance to entering a jail, especially one located outside his territory, Al reluctantly traveled to Waukegan in March. What happened next was a passing of the torch. Torrio announced that he was going to retire from Chicago if not from racketeering, and not unexpectedly he was leaving the entire organization to the Capone *family*, not just Al. Together, the brothers controlled nightclubs, gambling establishments, several breweries, dozens of brothels in Cicero and the surrounding areas, the Four Deuces, as well as lucrative arrangements to supply liquor to thousands of speakeasies in

Cicero and the South Side of Chicago. At the same time, they incurred immense obligations: the responsibility of paying off police and other public officials, security measures for themselves and the men who worked for them, and the menace posed by Moran, Drucci, and Weiss.

.   .   .

Torrio served his jail sentence without incident, and when he was freed in the latter part of 1925, a convoy of cars assembled by the Capone organization whisked him away to safety and anonymity. After several years abroad, Torrio quietly returned to New York, where he eventually lost whatever visibility he had acquired in Chicago, and he pursued an exceedingly low-profile career as a bootlegger, just one of many in a city that did not make an issue of Prohibition the way Chicago did.

As for the "Terrible Gennas," the Sicilians who had prodded Torrio and Capone into killing O'Banion, they proved tragically vulnerable. In May, the Moran gang assassinated Angelo, and several weeks later, they attacked Mike, the one who had killed O'Banion in his flower store. Later, Tony, the architect, fell victim to another Italian racketeer. The surviving brothers went into hiding, their reign of terror ended as quickly and as violently as it had begun. Several years later, the *Chicago Tribune* caught up with Jim Genna in Rome. No longer a feared ganglord, he operated a modest vacuum cleaner agency located in the Piazza di Spagna and yearned for America. The fate of the Gennas served as an object lesson to the six surviving Capone brothers. If they were not exceedingly careful, they would finish as the Genna clan had, either dead or disbanded.

.   .   .

Once he assumed control of the entire syndicate from Torrio in the spring of 1925, Capone had real power in Chicago, and power changed him, and just as importantly, it changed the way everyone regarded him. He was no longer just another hoodlum or racketeer; he was *Al Capone*, a name to be reckoned with. No longer did he lurk in the shadows of the Hawthorne Inn, going about his business in the secrecy on which Johnny Torrio always insisted. He did all he could to make himself visible, and more than that, respectable, at least by the standards of Prohibition-era Chicago. Thus, in the spring of 1925, immediately after taking the reins from Torrio, Capone moved to the Metropole Hotel. Today the remains of the Metropole stand amid the detritus of a once-bustling neighborhood, a stopping point for the occasional tourist bus, but in its day, the hotel offered a bustling, thoroughly cosmopolitan environment in a thriving neighborhood. It was an impressive structure, seven stories high, prominently situated at 2300 South Michigan Avenue, close to the Loop and the Four Deuces. Only four years earlier,

Capone, completely unknown in Chicago, had worked as a pimp at that establishment. Now he occupied a lavish hotel suite in Chicago, another hotel suite in Cicero, a hideaway in Cicero, and a house on South Prairie Avenue: such were the generous wages of sin.

Capone's suite at the Metropole consisted of five rooms, numbers 406 through 410; in addition, he maintained two "guest rooms" on the sixth floor and two more on the seventh. The tab for all these rooms came to $1,500 a day. The focal point was his office, in room 406, located in a turret at the corner of the building. Gazing through the broad Chicago windows he could survey his entire South Side domain sprawling beneath him, as orderly and as flat as a map. The Metropole also contained another feature of interest to Capone; a series of tunnels connected its basement to other buildings in the immediate vicinity. The tunnels' intended purpose was to haul small trucks of coal during the bitter winter months, but for Capone and his men the burrows could also double as escape routes or hiding places in the event of the emergencies that inevitably befell men in their hazardous line of work. Capone's quarters included other unusual features. Several rooms were devoted to a gym, where his men could toss a medicine ball or work out on a rowing machine or punching bags. (Capone himself rarely used the athletic equipment, however.) There was also an ample supply of girls available to service the men. "When a guy don't fall for a broad, he's through," Capone was supposed to have said by way of explanation. The hotel served as his base of operations until 1928, when he moved across the street to another luxurious hotel, the Lexington.

From the moment Al Capone moved to the Metropole, all Chicago was aware of his presence. It was as visible an address as there was in the city. The increased visibility was part of his new strategy, one he had begun to deploy cautiously in Cicero, but now, with Torrio out of the way, he pursued with gusto. Tony Berardi, a young photographer for the *Chicago Evening American*, recalls watching the transformation of Al Capone from a publicity-shy hoodlum to a gregarious emissary from the underworld: "The first time I ever saw the man was at a police station, and naturally, at the beginning, he used to cover his face with his hands, a newspaper, whatever. He never posed for pictures at that point. More than once or twice I saw him try to beat up photographers. He never bothered me, though; I was just a skinny little kid. Every editor wanted to get close to the guy so that they would get firsthand news. Our city editor, Harry Read, was the one who became very close with Capone." The two men formed an unusual partnership. Capone supplied Read with exclusive stories and interviews likely to draw readers, and Read, in turn, groomed the rising young gangster for success. "Read educated the guy in this respect. He said, 'Al, look, you're a prominent figure now. Why act like a hoodlum? Quit hiding. Be nice to people.' After that, Capone would go to the ball park to see baseball games. He'd go to fights. He became, if you want to put it this way, kind of a gentleman," Berardi recalls. "That was the one thing about gangsters in those days, they wouldn't hold up people. They wouldn't rob a bank. If you got into their territory, you were in trouble, but the public didn't fear those people because they were never harmed." Capone made a point of publicizing his relationship with Read as an emblem of the legitimacy to which the racketeer aspired. To set the seal on their mutually beneficial relationship, Capone appeared at the editorial offices of the *Evening American* one day to bestow on Read a jewel-encrusted pendant with a gold chain. Proud of the gift the city's most notorious racketeer had just given him, Read responded by inviting the young journalists standing around gawking to come over and shake Capone's hand, which they did. The close relationship between Capone and Read inevitably gave rise to rumors that the journalist was accepting more than gifts and favors from the racketeer in exchange for favorable coverage, but Berardi, for one, was convinced this was not the case: "There was a lot of talk that he was on the payroll, but Harry Read died a poor man. He only used Capone to get news. Never, never would I believe that he took one nickel from any hoodlum."

Even as Capone courted the press he took care to conceal the less acceptable aspects of his life: the guns, the army of enforcers who used them, his drug use, and prostitution. "I never saw him with a woman, nor did any other newspapermen," said Berardi. "At least fifteen of us got together, and the subject came up, and not one of us ever saw Al Capone with a woman. As far as I know he was a good family man. Much as I didn't like the guy, I have to admit he was good with kids. He sure helped a lot of people that I heard about when they were in arrears with their rent. He was a charitable guy." Like Berardi, the gentlemen of the press saw what Capone wanted them to see: a well-dressed, generous, gregarious fixer and bootlegger supplying a thirsty public. "He was one hell of an organizer," Berardi came to realize. "He was no dummy. He knew how to pick people for certain positions in certain categories. He had people who met with the mayor, with the chief of police, and so on. And they were not all Italians. He had people of every nationality you could think of: Irish, Swedes, Poles, Germans, and Jews, like 'Greasy Thumb' Guzik."

Although Berardi appreciated Capone's administrative abilities, the photographer harbored no illusions about the man. He believed Capone harmed the reputation of all Italians in Chicago by giving them an undeserved reputation as criminals. The racketeer's effort to build a political base among Italians in Chicago struck Berardi as a sham, a disgrace. "There were roughly 500,000 Italians in the Cook County area," Berardi says, "and out of that entire group maybe 500 admired Al Capone. Italians were and are honest, hard-working people, and they had no respect for him. I myself didn't have respect for him. I knew what he was and what he did. He didn't help the Italian-American people. Christ, if your name ended with an *e*, *i*, or *o*, everyone thought you were a member of Capone's mob or one of his relatives. He hurt the Italian people, and I didn't like that because even though I was born and raised in this country I'm damn proud that my family came from Italy."

Berardi and Capone frequently eyed one another at a gymnasium where Berardi, an amateur boxer, trained. "I used to work out there every day," the photographer recalls. "It was a pretty large gym. On Thursday night they'd put on a show, with seating for anywhere from 300 to 500, and Al Capone would come there damn near every Thursday. He was a sports nut; he loved sports. So he knew me, he saw me boxing. I don't think he wanted to tangle with me."

The two nearly came to blows when they finally met. The occasion was an assignment from Harry Read to photograph Capone in his new office. From the moment he entered the door, Berardi encountered Capone's elaborate security precautions. "As I got into the elevator carrying about forty-five pounds of photographic material in a large bag," Berardi recalled, "three or four hoods wanted to know where I was going, and I told them I was going to see Mr. Capone. 'What have you got in the bag?' one of them asked. So I took all my photographic equipment out to show him, and then I had to put it all back. I get up to the floor where his office was, and as I enter a couple of other guys wanted to know what the hell was in this bag. I went through the whole thing again. Then, when I got in to see Capone, I said, 'Did you put those bastards up to do this to me?' He said, 'Oh, they were just having some fun.' "

Remembering Berardi from the gym, Capone issued a challenge: "I hear you're a pretty tough guy. Do you think you can lick me?"

"Al," said Berardi, "let's cut out the shit. Let me take your picture and get the hell out of here. If you want to find out how tough I am, why don't you come by the gym?"

With that Berardi went about his assignment and left the Lexington unharmed.

Henceforth the two men had an uneasy rapport. Berardi was now in the awkward position of earning his livelihood photographing a man he despised, and Capone did whatever he could to ingratiate himself with Berardi. Assigned to cover a horse race at the Hawthorne track Capone controlled, Berardi was surprised to find Al himself at the race that day, accompanied by his usual retinue of five bodyguards. "Kid, how you doing?" he called out.

"I'm doing fine," said Berardi.

"Why don't you bet on number 6?"

The odds against the horse Capone recommended were exceedingly long:

ninety-nine to one. Before Berardi could reply, one of Capone's attendants rushed over and stuffed a slip of paper in his jacket pocket. "I looked at it," Berardi remembered, "and it was a five-dollar ticket on this number 6 horse. When I looked at the *Racing Form*, I saw he was a steeple chase horse! He'd never run on a flat track. How could this horse win? Well, he broke out in front and stayed out in front, and I don't think anyone dared catch him. The goddamn horse won by a block. He came down from ninety-nine to one to sixty to one so I collected $300. Capone didn't bribe me; he just put $300 in my pocket. The following week, they ran the horse again, and he won, and then I heard they destroyed the horse."

Buying favorable publicity, Capone knew, was only half the game. Political influence was the other, and the new Al Capone did more than bribe journalists and pose for photographers. Almost every day he drove to the complex that served as both City Hall and the county building, where he would walk up and down the street, shadowed by five bodyguards, two in front, two in back, and one walking beside him. He did all he could to make himself seem available, a man with nothing to fear. Always beautifully dressed, quiet, another political fixer going about his daily rounds. He paused to converse with city officials who were on his payroll—or wanted to be. "He did that damn near every afternoon. He'd talk to people just like he was running for office," Berardi noted in amazement.

Judge John H. Lyle, a self-proclaimed scourge of gangsters, recalled the galling spectacle of Capone working the crowd:

> The first time I saw him was in front of City Hall, prior to my election to the bench. I was talking with a City Council colleague, Walter Steffen, and the then Chief of Police, Charles C. Fitzmorris. Capone got out of an automobile accompanied by his bodyguards. We saw aldermen swarm around him to shake his hand.
>
> "Well, Chief," Steffen said in jest, "looks as though Scarface has come down to take over City Hall." Fitzmorris flushed and left without a word.
>
> Warren Phinney, a newspaper reporter friend of mine, followed Capone. He told me afterward that the mobster went to the City License Bureau and shook hands with a long line of men waiting to buy licenses for "soft drink parlors." Then Capone went into the adjoining County Building for another round of handshakes.

To his dismay, Lyle had glimpsed the future of Chicago, and it was Al Capone. If Capone had his way, he would become mayor of Chicago himself, or so the Establishment feared, but they miscalculated. Al wasn't all that interested in attaining political power, which was too confining. As a racketeer just now hitting his stride, he knew that political office could be bought and sold; no, Capone didn't want to be the mayor—he wanted to *own* the mayor, which was a much better arrangement, allowing for more flexibility. If the current mayor, William Dever, that apostle of Prohibition, couldn't be bought, why, his term would be ending the following year, and already there were rumblings that "Big Bill" Thompson was preparing for a comeback, and he was a politician much more sympathetic to Capone's inclinations, as wet as Lake Michigan.

Capone's political flair, his urge to be seen in public, was unique among racketeers, who as a rule abhorred publicity; none of his brothers had any use for it. In contrast to Al's incessant politicking, his older brother Ralph, for instance, continued to shun attention and refused to change his public demeanor, which was often surly and boorish, more in keeping with the stereotypical gangster. Berardi was left with the impression that Ralph "was a miserable sonofabitch. He was a hood. If he saw you with a camera he'd say, 'I'll flush your goddamn camera down the toilet.' Al was a saint compared to him." The other, younger brothers, those just serving their apprenticeships, maintained an even lower profile, and as a result, few in Chicago realized that behind Capone's rise to power and fame stood an extensive family network backing him up at every turn, allowing him the luxury of appearing at City Hall each day while they tended to the routine of the syndicate's vice, prostitution, gambling, and bootlegging enterprises.

•   •   •

Even as Capone sought to establish a respectable public presence, events constantly undercut him. In the early months of 1925, a young minister named Henry C. Hoover of Berwyn launched his campaign against Al Capone. Inflamed by the exposés in Robert St. John's little *Cicero Tribune*, Hoover had helped to form a vigilante committee calling itself the West Suburban Ministers' and Citizens' Association, which attempted to harass Capone by setting fire to his Cicero brothels. After St. John fled Cicero, Hoover continued to pursue Capone, and his efforts culminated in a raid on the Hawthorne Smoke Shop on May 16, 1925. There Hoover, who personally conducted the expedition into Satan's domain, discovered an array of gambling paraphernalia, just as he expected.

The daytime raid roused a grouchy Al Capone from a sound sleep, and the two men, after months of circling each other, finally came face to face. "This is the last raid you'll ever pull," Capone warned Hoover. Later, when he calmed down, he appealed to the minister to "come to an understanding." The minister refused, of course, and left the premises with his group. Outside the Hawthorne Smoke Shop, Capone's men broke the nose of one raider and assaulted another, named David Morgan. He recovered from the beating only to be shot at a later date by four gunmen believed to work for Capone. Morgan survived the shooting as well, but it served to frighten off other would-be vigilantes. In sum, the affair generated exactly the type of publicity Capone wanted to avoid. Although Hoover relented, the memory of the raid would return to haunt Capone six years later, when the minister confronted the mobster in federal court.

By the following month, June 1925, Capone had reached the conclusion that his line of work was so risky (albeit profitable) that he tried to obtain life insurance, but this stab at respectability only led him into an embarrassing quandary. An agent called on him in his office at the Metropole Hotel and began to ask the usual questions:

"What is your occupation?"

Capone gave his usual answer. "Dealer in secondhand furniture."

At the end of the interview, the agent, who knew full well that Capone had as much to do with secondhand furniture as Johnny Torrio had, advised that he would be hearing from the company. Inevitably, Capone's request was rejected. Capone subsequently approached six other insurance firms, all of whom refused to underwrite his life, each rejection driving home his special, hazardous status. He could buy police captains, aldermen, sumptuous women, but he couldn't purchase life insurance at any price.

Still obsessed with his personal safety, he adopted a new, state-of-the-art security measure in the form of an armored Cadillac sedan built to his specifications. "The body was of steel construction, the windows of bullet-proof glass, and the fenders nondentable," wrote a reporter, William Pasley, who covered Capone for the *Chicago Tribune*. "It had a special combination lock so that his enemies couldn't jimmy a door to plant a bomb under him." The car cost $20,000—a small fortune in 1925—and weighed seven tons. Capone rode in the car constantly; it became his toy, his status symbol. Pedestrians along Michigan Avenue or Lake Shore Drive became familiar with the sight of Capone's bulletproof limousine purring along the pavement. They stopped, turned, and hoped to catch a glimpse of its celebrated occupant. Each one said the same thing: "There goes Al." No one needed to mention his last name. By now everyone in Chicago knew who Al was, and the bulletproof limousine had done more than its share to establish his identity and status. To add to the spectacle, his limousine was always accompanied by a convoy for additional security, as if any were needed. "Preceding the portable fort was a scout flivver," wrote Pasley, "which darted in and out of traffic, keeping a distance of a half-block, and performing somewhat the same duties as a destroyer to a battleship. Immediately following the fort was a touring car containing the Capone bodyguard. This convoy seemed superfluous considering the invulnerability of the new equipage, but Capone was taking no chances." No wonder the parade always drew a crowd; Capone had acquired an aura, a mystique. Anyone seeing this convoy pass realized at once that it contained a very important person, indeed. Chicago had seen some flashy gangsters over the years, but none possessed Capone's flair for conspicuous consumption.

•   •   •

Capone's sole respite from the pressures of running his business enterprises these days was the *schvitz*, a traditional Jewish steam bath. He began to frequent the 14th Street Bath House, located near Chicago's Jewish ghetto on Maxwell Street. It was Jack Guzik who introduced Capone to the place, and Capone usually came with the Guzik brothers and as many as a dozen other friends and hangers-on. They normally appeared on Wednesdays; the owner posted a sign reading "closed for boiler repairs," and Al and the boys would have the place all to themselves. Clad only in large towels, they indulged in innocent horseplay, hurling buckets of ice-cold water back and forth. They also used a traditional whip made of birch leaves to flagellate one another's backs, another old-country custom. To the proprietor of the steam bath, Capone and his gang seemed more like high-spirited kids than dangerous lords of the underworld.

Al also liked to receive an invigorating massage at the *schvitz*, and this meant placing *bonkes* on his back. A *bonke* was a small, wide-mouthed glass jar, and the masseur would begin by inserting a lit match in the *bonke* to remove the oxygen, then quickly apply the little jar to Al's broad back. According to custom, the *bonke*'s gentle suction helped to stimulate the circulation and drew impurities from the skin, or so the masseur insisted. Capone came to love this Russian-Jewish version of a massage, and he always tipped the masseur lavishly for his services. He also liked to tease the owner of the bath house. "Come on," he would say during a massage, "we're going to *cheder*." In Yiddish, the term meant school, but to Capone it was a euphemism for one of Guzik's brothels.

Afterward, Al was always hungry, and before he left the *schvitz* he sent out to a nearby delicatessen for sandwiches—fragrant mounds of brisket of beef. Capone consumed several of these himself and earned a reputation as a *fresser*, a big eater. Only then, when his body was clean and his belly was full, did he go to *cheder*.

•   •   •

Less than a year after taking over from Johnny Torrio, Al Capone was the most important racketeer in Chicago, a city that was fast becoming the nation's most important center of racketeering. He enjoyed a limitless income from his organization's management of gambling, vice, and bootlegging activities, and he had achieved a measure of fame in his adopted city.

He had access to women and drugs, and he still controlled Cicero. Despite these myriad distractions, he managed to maintain a stable family life. His wife, Mae, rarely ventured far from their home, and his mother, who continued to live with the family, was happiest when she was in the kitchen, cooking large meals for the extended Capone family. His chief source of concern at home was his only child, Sonny. Now eight years old, Sonny was a sickly child whose health was a perennial source of concern in the Capone home. Neighbors saw little of Sonny, who, ill with one infection after another, was generally confined to the house. The fact that he was the only child made every challenge to his health loom large in his father's mind. Eventually he developed a mastoid infection in his left ear. In the era before antibiotics, mastoid infections often led to surgery, which, even if successful, often left the sufferer with impaired hearing. In search of a cure for his son, Capone contacted prominent doctors in Chicago, but they warned him that a mastoid operation would leave Sonny permanently deaf. In growing desperation he decided to look beyond Chicago to specialists in New York, eventually coming across an ear, nose, and throat specialist by the name of Dr. Lloyd, whose office was located on St. Nicholas Place; Capone, it is said, promised to pay the impressive sum of $100,000, but the surgeon took Sonny Capone as a patient for the customary fee of $1,000. The operation was scheduled for December, and Al traveled with the boy to New York. There was more on Capone's agenda than this matter; he also planned to do some serious negotiating concerning alcohol shipments with his former employer, Frankie Yale. It promised to be an eventful trip.

The medical procedure was a success insofar as Sonny's life was spared, though he remained hard of hearing. Relieved of this burden, Al turned to negotiating with Frankie Yale. At issue was Chicago's supply of bootleg whiskey. Although Chicago received vast amounts of alcohol from Canada, there was never enough whiskey, especially imported whiskey, to meet the demand. Yale happened to be one of the largest importers of whiskey in the East; in "wet" New York, his rum-running operations ran relatively unimpeded by the Coast Guard and elected officials. In fact, his vast warehouse in Brooklyn was overflowing with cases of Scotch and Irish whiskey. So it was mutually beneficial for the two men to arrive at an agreement, which they did. Yale agreed to sell his alcohol to Capone and guarantee safe passage in the New York area; the dangerous business of transporting the alcohol a thousand miles from Brooklyn to Chicago would be Al's responsibility. Capone was willing to run the risk, and so laid the groundwork for the most important interstate route for alcohol during the Prohibition era. His business arrangements successfully concluded, Capone could have taken the train back to Chicago at that point, but since he was in New York, Yale invited him to attend a celebration on Christmas day. Capone accepted, and in the process he happened upon the most violent and bloody episode in his career.

The plan was for Al to join Frankie on Christmas night at the Adonis Social and Athletic Club, located on Twentieth Street in Brooklyn. Its grandiose name notwithstanding, the Adonis Club was actually a speakeasy frequented by Italians, including many Brooklyn racketeers, who held their convocations in a small room at the back lit by dim orange bulbs. Capone himself had frequented the club in his youth. The Christmas gathering was an annual event, a rowdy stag party featuring the best champagne and chorus girls Yale had to offer. Still, this year promised to be different. At the time, Brooklyn was in the midst of gangland strife, with Yale's Italians, generally though inaccurately referred to as "Black Handers," in one camp, and their rivals, the Irish "White Handers," led by their chief, the murderous "Peg-Leg" Lonergan—so named because he had lost his right leg in a railroad accident. At issue was control of the jobs and payoffs available on Brooklyn's lucrative waterfront. It had long been an Irish stronghold, though Italians were constantly threatening to move in; every so often, both sides would sit down and arrive at a truce or accommodation, but the grievances ran so deep and tempers so hot that all attempts at peacemaking between the two groups disintegrated into gang warfare.

It was not at all surprising, therefore, that on the day before the party in honor of Capone, Yale received a tip that his arch rival, Richard "Peg-Leg" Lonergan, accompanied by a crew of gunmen, planned to strike when the Christmas bash was at its height. At first Yale intended to cancel the party, but when he heard of the threat, Capone would have none of it; he was determined to go, to let himself be seen. It was important that he not be deterred by threats, especially on his home turf. But first he made preparations, sending for the Gennas' vicious Sicilian gunmen, John Scalise and Albert Anselmi, the men who had been hired to kill Dion O'Banion for $10,000 apiece, plus a diamond ring.

Capone, Scalise, and Anselmi arrived at the Adonis Club early on the evening of December 25. There they found over fifty *paisani* deep in revelry—men with names such as "Chootch" Gianfredo, "Frenchy" Arlino, and "Glass-Eye" Pelicano. An hour later, Yale signaled Capone that Lonergan and his men were in the vicinity, preparing to enter the club. Rather than hide, Capone summoned all his bravado and rushed forward to greet "PegLeg" Lonergan. Recovering from his surprise at discovering Al Capone, of all people, in the Adonis Social Club, Lonergan rudely pushed by and headed for the small room at the back, dragging his peg leg across the wooden floor, calling the Italians "dagos" and "wops," demanding to be served a drink.

As Lonergan and his thugs filled the club, fifty pairs of eyes observed, and fifty hands tightened around fifty barely concealed pistols. Suddenly he called out, "Everybody freeze!" The owner of the club, "Fury" Argolia, doused the lights, and the Italians disappeared beneath their tables.

It was only a matter of seconds until the shooting began. Suddenly, there was the sickening thwack of a meat cleaver sinking into bone and flesh. Argolia himself had buried the cleaver in the skull of a Lonergan man, who fell to the floor in a lifeless, bloody heap. Then more shooting broke out, shots spraying through the dark. By accident or design Lonergan and his men stood in a faint light cast by a chandelier as Capone and his hired assassins, each of them equipped with a .45-caliber revolver and shielded by a sturdy mahogany bar, fired on the Lonergan group from the darkness. After two or three minutes, the shots stopped, and Capone called for "Fury" to turn on the lights. Three bodies that only minutes before had been Lonergan's hand-picked assassins lay on the floor, but Lonergan and two others were still at large. Capone found "Peg-Leg" himself hiding under a piano. Lonergan started to blast away; all the shots were wild. Al moved in to deliver the coup de grâce: three well-aimed shots at Lonergan's head, and the most feared Irish gangster of the day was dead, his body sprawled over the piano stool. His wooden leg became a trophy cherished by the Italian gangsters who were there that night.

In all, four of the White Handers died in the ambush, while Capone, Scalise, and Anselmi emerged unscathed. The gun battle came to be known as the Adonis Club Massacre; this was the first time, though not the last, that the term *massacre* would be associated with Capone. The gun battle had important implications for Brooklyn's thriving rackets. It broke the Irish grip over Brooklyn's waterfront. Henceforth, the Italians, led by Frankie Yale, were in the ascendancy. And it demonstrated that Al Capone was still a force to be reckoned with in Brooklyn; indeed, he was now more important than his former boss, Frankie Yale.

The police investigated, but not surprisingly they turned up little of value; anyone who had heard the shots or who had been party to any aspect of the shootout pleaded ignorance or a faulty memory. "Peg-Leg" Lonergan's sister Anna did her best to imply that Italians were responsible for the slaughter without actually breaking the underworld code and saying so: "You can bet it was no Irish American like ourselves who would stage a mean murder like this on Christmas Day." Capone, who had engineered the ambush, nonchalantly told the police, "I was visiting my mother for Christmas, and as a favor I was working as the doorman at the club." Given his preposterous explanation, it was not surprising that he was charged with homicide, but the judge, Francis McCloskey, dismissed the indictment on December 31, 1925, and Capone was free to return to Chicago to greet the New Year.

The Adonis Club Massacre did more than alter the balance of power between Irish and Italian gangs in Brooklyn; it also had a decisive effect on the balance of power between Brooklyn and Chicago. Until this time, the Gem of the Prairie had been an outpost of the Brooklyn rackets; Johnny Torrio had led the way, followed by Frankie Yale, who had remained in Chicago just long enough to kill "Big Jim" Colosimo, and finally Al Capone had built his empire there. Throughout this process, Chicago had remained within Brooklyn's sphere, a child that had outgrown its parent. With the Adonis Club Massacre, the Brooklyn rackets henceforth became an adjunct to Chicago. Although Brooklyn was still Frankie Yale's turf, Capone's influence there was now decisive, and in the years to come it would only grow. Capone maintained his sway over Brooklyn, as well as Chicago, not simply because he was quick with a gun in a shootout but also because of his bootlegging. Yale, Lonergan, and the other Brooklyn racketeers led gangs, but Capone administered an *organization*, which made all the difference in the world.

"Chicago is the imperial city of the gang world, and New York a remote provincial place governed by a proconsul. Even Philadelphia has passed New York in importance in this gunman's universe," wrote Alva Johnston in the *New Yorker* of the new criminal order. Think of it: *even Philadelphia* was bigger than New York when it came to gangsters; "New York can't have everything," Johnston lamented. He noted that New York's second-rate gangsters "have copied certain technical effects, such as the use of the machine-gun and the sawed-off double-barrelled buckshot pistol, from the progressive Westerners, but they have made no headway in the direction of welding all gang interests into one big combination." Meanwhile, out in Chicago, "Beer has lifted the gangster from a local leader of roughs and gunmen to a great executive controlling a big interstate and international organization. Beer, real beer, like the water supply or the telephone, is a natural monopoly."

Explaining how Chicago came to its current prominence, Johnston introduced readers residing elsewhere to a man whose name they probably had not encountered until now:

> After Dion O'Banion, Hymie Weiss, and other Chicago independents had perished in a hopeless struggle against economic law, one man stood out as the greatest gang leader in history—Alphonse Capone, sometimes known as Big-hearted Al because of his extravagance in buying floral pieces, but usually called Scarface Al because of a pretentious scar down the left side of his face. Otherwise he has soft, fat, sentimental features, large red lips with exaggerated curves of sympathy, large eyes with active tear ducts, black eyebrows which contract rather fiercely when certain ideas strike him.
>
> Al travels in a bullet-proof car. He surrounds himself with eight men

selected for thickness of torso who form an inner ring about him when he appears in public. They are tall and he is short, a precaution against any attempt to aim at him through the spaces between their necks. For Al's protection, the eight men wear bullet-proof vests. Nothing smaller than a fieldpiece could penetrate his double-walled fortress of meat.

No one had ever accorded Capone the status that Johnston did—the greatest gang leader *in history*—but it was a judgment that the annals of crime would confirm.

There had never been a criminal quite like him before. Capone did not operate outside the law, but from within, corrupting it as he went. He was no outlaw, loner, or renegade. He was not antisocial; he was, if anything, ferociously prosocial. He was a businessman, an organization man, but more than that, he was now part of Chicago's power structure, a mover and shaker in his own right, able to dispense patronage and charity. Of course, he drew a great deal of his strength from the hypocrisy of the political Establishment, especially concerning Prohibition. Unchecked, his rule might well become the law of a corrupt and cynical land.

Accounts of Chicago's preeminence in racketeering reached all the way to the nation's capital. In February 1926, Vice President Charles G. Dawes brought to the attention of the U.S. Senate a statement prepared by a group of concerned prominent citizens in Chicago—lawyers and civic boosters and such—asking for federal assistance to end Chicago's "reign of terror." Like nearly all reformers, the group placed the blame not on Prohibition and its blatant hypocrisies but on the convenient scapegoat of the Italians, "a colony of unnaturalised persons," they called them, "feudists, Black Handers and members of [the] Mafia." Together, they had created a

supergovernment of their own in Chicago which is levying tribute upon citizens and enforcing collection by terrorising, kidnapping and assassinations. . . .

Many of these alien outlaws have become fabulously rich as rum-runners and bootleggers, working in collusion with the police and other officials, building up a monopoly in this unlawful business and dividing the territory among themselves under penalty of death to all intruding competitors.

Evidence multiplies daily that many public officials are in secret alliance with underworld assassins, gunmen, rum-runners, bootleggers, thugs, ballot box stuffers and repeaters, that a ring of politicians and public officials operating through criminals and with dummy directors are conducting a number of breweries and are selling beer under police protection.

The Senate listened respectfully to this alarming account of a criminal "supergovernment" and did nothing about it beyond referring it to the Immigration Committee for further consideration.

·   ·   ·

Capone returned to Chicago at the beginning of 1926 in buoyant spirits. On both personal and professional fronts, his trip to New York had been hugely successful; the immediate threat to Sonny's health had been removed and his own status in the racketeering world had been greatly enhanced. From his home base, Capone anxiously awaited delivery of his first shipment of alcohol from Frankie Yale's Brooklyn warehouse, following the agreement they had struck. However, the trucks transporting bootleg whiskey across state lines faced formidable challenges from both Prohibition agents and rival gangs. The poor conditions of the roads, often unpaved, presented additional hazards to inexperienced drivers. It was indeed a risky business.

Capone entrusted the job of overseeing the transportation of the whiskey to one of his lieutenants with all precautions to be taken in the strictest confidence. No one—especially members of rival Chicago gangs, itching for a chance to interfere—was to know the details of the complex arrangements to deliver Yale's whiskey to Chicago. "The first shipment was four trucks," this Capone lieutenant later recalled. "The convoy was to keep in touch by telephone every day so we would know their progress and where they were at all times. We figured it would take them six or seven days—without any major truck repairs or breakdowns—to make the trip. We knew all the gangs in Chicago . . . knew about our convoy, and we figured out of all of them Hymie Weiss and his Northsiders would probably try to hijack our trucks. That is why on that day in the early spring of 1926 a carload of body guards and I drove to South Bend, Indiana and met our trucks. It was late in the day when we met them and even though the drivers were tired we decided to drive on through the night to get into Chicago as soon as possible." The most dangerous part of the journey was "that stretch of road between Gary and Michigan City that runs along the Lake Michigan sand dunes. The hijackers would wait on the side roads back in the dunes and when you came by with your truck load of booze they would come roaring and at gunpoint force you to stop. Then they would place their driver in your truck and leave you standing by the side of the road—that is, if they didn't kill you. Which happened more than once." Throughout Prohibition, the Indiana State Police became accustomed to finding a burning truck laden with bootleg alcohol and the charred remains of the unlucky driver.

To avoid that plight, three of the Capone trucks sped into Chicago along Route 6 and the Lincoln Highway, while the fourth truck traveled at a slower rate in order to lure the rival Northsiders into an ambush. The lieutenant, heavily armed, rode in an ordinary car far behind the last truck. "A few miles east of Gary a touring car came out of a side road and drove up . . . to the side of our truck," the lieutenant recalled. "It started shining a spot light on it. Up ahead another car pulled out in front of our truck and stopped in the middle of the road. In the car, we knew it was a heist and we surprised the Northsiders by coming up on them with our guns blazing. . . . Two of the Northsiders were left there [for dead] that night."

This shipment got through, as did many others, and soon all Chicago reveled in Frankie Yale's imported whiskey. Eventually the Capone organization employed so many truck drivers that the legitimate interstate trucking industry was transformed. Until that time, drivers had shunned the "northern route" linking New York and Chicago, but now they took to saying: "If Al Capone can haul illegal booze from New York City to Chicago, we can haul legal cargo over the same route." Many young men with a taste for adventure were willing to run the risks of delivering alcohol for Capone across the northern route because the pay was so generous. Thus Capone came to employ a small army of highly paid, expendable truck drivers, able-bodied young men who had no criminal inclinations but who suddenly found themselves working for gangsters.

Among them was Jack Richie. He had grown up on a farm in Tiffin, Ohio, and gravitated to Chicago, like so many other young men in search of a bigger and better future, only to find that he could earn no more than $35 a week driving a delivery truck. He lived in a dreary hotel; his chief amusements consisted of listening to *Amos 'n' Andy* on the radio, taking in an occasional White Sox game, drinking bootleg beer at fifteen cents a glass in a speakeasy, and playing poker in the back room. Richie happened to live a few blocks from the Metropole Hotel, Capone's headquarters, and in time he met various Capone employees in the local saloons. One man offered him a job as a truck driver on the northern route. The pay could run as high as $300 a week: nearly ten times Richie's salary. One morning, Richie reported to Jack Guzik at the Metropole Hotel, who assured him that he would be paid even during the weeks he did not work, and he could live rentfree in the Calvert Hotel. Richie took the job. "You are now among friends," Guzik told him as the interview came to a close.

Richie began making the New York to Chicago runs in February 1926; a round trip required about two weeks. He never traveled alone; a Capone guard, armed with a .45-caliber Colt, machine gun, or sawed-off shotgun always accompanied him. As winter yielded to spring, Richie was constantly reminded of the hazards of his high-paying job; he was often fired at, and one night he was ambushed right on Western Avenue in Chicago but managed to escape. Although his trucks were constantly held up, Capone himself did not bother with the high-risk hijacking game; instead, he put the word out that he would pay the hijackers handsomely for the booze they captured. One way or another, then, he had most hijackers on his payroll. Richie lasted in his job for more than two years, until the day he received an anonymous letter pushed under his door, warning that he might be killed at any time in a hijacking attempt, possibly by Capone's own men. Taking the threat seriously, he withdrew all the money he had saved from the bank and took the next bus out of Chicago, fortunate to have escaped with his money and his life. His days of driving a truck for Al Capone on the northern route were over.

•   •   •

MCSWIGGIN—William H. McSwiggin, beloved son of Anthony and Elizabeth F. McSwiggin, nee Fitzpatrick, brother of Mary, Helen, Emily, and Margaret McSwiggin. Funeral Saturday, 9:30 A.M., from residence, 4946 Washington-blvd, to St. Thomas Aquinas church. Burial Mount Carmel cemetery.

For every Jack Richie who managed to survive his dealings with Capone, others were swept into a whirlwind of violence. Among them was William McSwiggin, the youthful "hanging prosecutor" who had vowed to indict and bring Al Capone to trial for the death of Joe Howard in 1924. His murder threw Chicago into its greatest crisis of conscience concerning the spread of gangsters' power and the threat of violence. It occasioned an outpouring of sympathy, analysis, conspiracy theories, and promises to clean up Chicago (and Cicero); although everyone involved in the investigation believed the so-called "Capone gang" was behind it, no one was ever arrested, much less tried for the murder. Of all Chicago's gangland killings, the death of Billy McSwiggin remains one of its most complex and intriguing mysteries.

What *is* known for certain is that on the last day of his life, April 27, the twenty-six-year-old Billy McSwiggin, as he often did, ate dinner at the home of his parents at 4946 West Washington Boulevard. His father, Sergeant Anthony McSwiggin, was a veteran detective with the Chicago police force with thirty years' experience. He was honest, widely respected, and in the words of his friend Judge John Lyle, he "idolized his brilliant son." At about six, "Red" Duffy, also the son of a cop, rang the doorbell and announced he had come to pick up Billy, who left before finishing the evening meal. "I have an appointment with Duffy," McSwiggin explained. "We are going to Berwyn to play cards." Though this seemed an unlikely pastime for a tough young prosecutor, gambling the night away in one of Al Capone's strong-holds, it had become a habit for McSwiggin, who in the process developed a nodding acquaintance with members of the Capone organization and even with Al himself, the gangster he had once vowed to indict for the murder of Joe Howard. But time had softened McSwiggin's desire for vengeance, and he was content to sit and drink Capone's bootleg booze, while Al, quick to seize the advantage, began referring to "my friend, Bill McSwiggin." Capone was apparently sincere in his liking for the hanging prosecutor; they were, after all, about the same age, and Capone needed McSwiggin's goodwill, or at least his indulgence, to conduct business.

Duffy was not the only one with McSwiggin that night; the third man was another son of a cop, Jim Doherty. A bootlegger and political hack, it was Doherty who was to bring the expedition to grief, for he had incurred the enmity of Al Capone, who held him responsible for the recent assassination of his sometime ally, "Samoots" Amatuna.

The night that McSwiggin, Duffy, and Doherty set out to play cards in Berwyn found Al Capone at the Hawthorne Inn, brooding on the latest gang war, this one involving two rival bootleggers, brothers named William "Klondike" and Myles O'Donnell. The bitter feeling between the Capone organization and the O'Donnells, which had been building for several months, had become so intense that it could burst into the open at any time.

Meanwhile, McSwiggin's expedition to Berwyn did not proceed according to plan. The car carrying the young prosecutor, Duffy, and Doherty broke down almost as soon as they pulled away from McSwiggin's home. Doherty, who owned the car, deposited it at a garage, and the group, which now included a retired policeman named Edward Hanley, changed vehicles—a change that would prove fatal. The sleek new Lincoln in which they now rode belonged to "Klondike" O'Donnell; it was the kind of car that bootleggers and gangsters drove, not prosecutors. Rather than playing cards in Berwyn, the men decided to head straight for the heart of Capone's territory, Cicero, where for the next two hours they were engaged in a raucous pub crawl. Everywhere they went in Cicero that night, the boisterous Irish lads made themselves known, and at some point they were joined by the other O'Donnell brother, Myles.

At a quarter after eight, the Lincoln sedan pulled up in front of a speakeasy known as Harry Madigan's Pony Inn located in a nondescript two-story brick building at 5613 West Roosevelt Road, not far from the Hawthorne Inn, where Capone was having dinner. " 'Scarface' was at another table," a man who gave his name as "Henry Armstrong" later told a reporter. "At about 7:15 an excited, pale stranger came in. He whispered something to Capone. Then they went together to an alcove. Capone gave him a rifle with a big round magazine on it. The stranger went out." What Capone heard was that the O'Donnells' Lincoln had been seen cruising around Cicero, a violation of Capone's territory that amounted to an act of provocation. But Capone did not know that among the men accompanying "Klondike" O'Donnell was Billy McSwiggin, the prosecutor Al liked to call his friend. The "rifle with a big round magazine" that Capone had bestowed on his associate was, of course, a machine gun. Several other Capone henchmen joined the man who had warned Capone. Together they walked to the back of the hotel, entered their waiting automobiles, and formed a five-car convoy consisting of a lead car, two cars following to block traffic if necessary, Capone's chauffeured limousine trailing at a distance of fifty feet, and finally another car well behind the limousine. The convoy arrived within moments at the Pony Inn. At half past eight, McSwiggin, Hanley, Doherty, Duffy, and the O'Donnell brothers staggered out of the Pony Inn, heading for the Lincoln and the next stop on their spree, and as they did so Capone and his men watched from the safety of their five-car convoy.

That was when McSwiggin's night on the town with the boys ended, and the nightmare of blood and terror began. As McSwiggin's group came into view, Capone's gunmen let loose, and the unmistakable rhythm of a machine gun firing split the night. Whether Al himself had fired any shots was not clear, and it would soon become the matter of impassioned debate. As the convoy rolled past, the victims fell to the street; the entire attack had taken only seconds to execute, and over fifty shots had been fired. ("I saw a closed car speeding away with what looked like a telephone receiver sticking out of the rear window and spitting fire," said one elderly witness of her first look at a machine gun in action.) Red Duffy, his body nearly cut in two by the bullets, and Jim Doherty were gravely wounded. The O'Donnell brothers and Edward Hanley were lucky to survive; they had reacted quickly enough to dodge the hail of bullets. As for Billy McSwiggin, the "hanging prosecutor" whom Al Capone had called his friend, he was writhing on the sidewalk, his body riddled with twenty bullets lodged in his back and neck.

Fearing another attack, the O'Donnell brothers hastily dragged Duffy to a tree and left him. ("Pretty cold-blooded to leave me lying there," he remarked just before he died the following day.) They then carried Doherty and McSwiggin to their Lincoln sedan and sped to "Klondike" 's house on Parkside Avenue. By the time they arrived, both McSwiggin and Doherty were dead.

Panicking, the O'Donnells hauled the bodies inside, removed the contents of their pockets, ripped the labels from their clothes, as if these precautions would change anything, and returned the corpses to the car. The O'Donnells drove away from the city and its lights to the black prairie extending from the outskirts of Berwyn. They came to a halt along a deserted stretch of road, shoved the remains of McSwiggin and Doherty out the door, and fled. At ten o'clock that night, the driver of a passing car noticed the bodies. He stopped to investigate and discovered they were still warm. He informed the police, and by midnight the corpses had been delivered to the city morgue, where they were positively identified as those of James Doherty and William McSwiggin.

Only six hours earlier McSwiggin had been eating dinner with his parents, and the news of his death wreaked havoc on his family. "Mrs. McSwiggin was so grief-stricken that a physician's care was later needed," it was reported. "The father, Sergt. Anthony McSwiggin, returned this morning from a trip to Des Moines, Iowa, to get a prisoner. He had left home just after his son started out last evening on the ride that took him to death. A message calling him home reached him at Davenport. Sergt. John Murphy, Sergt. McSwiggin's partner at the detective bureau, met him at the station to help him bear the shock. Then the father went home with his daughters—Helen, twenty-six years old; Emily, twenty-three; Nellie, nineteen; and Marjorie, seventeen—and tried to comfort the stricken mother."

"Those bullets couldn't have been meant for him," the grieving father said. "The assassins were out for someone in the group, someone they thought were their enemies."

"Dad was so brave and wonderful," added his youngest daughter, Marjorie. "He's trying not to show how hard it hit him. He was so proud of Bill."

Even before the slain prosecutor was laid to rest, the Chicago newspapers were howling for justice. The banner headline in the *Chicago Tribune* for Wednesday, April 28, proclaimed:

Gangsters Turn Machine Gun on William McSwiggin
2 OTHERS OF AUTO PARTY SLAIN IN CICERO KILLING
Booze Feud is Back
of Crime—Police
Raid Village
Resorts.

Wednesday's *Daily News*, not to be outdone, claimed to have solved the case and laid the murder at Capone's doorstep:

BARE MCSWIGGIN DEATH TALE
CAPONE IS ACCUSED OF IMPORTING GANG;
DEATH QUIZ OPENED
Torrio Also Suspected; Police Charged Young Assist-
ant State's Attorney Was Shot Down in Cicero
by Gangsters by Mistake.

Gunmen brought to Cicero from New York by "Scarface Al" Capone and John Torrio at primary time killed William H. McSwiggin,

assistant state's attorney, and the two other victims of last night's gang
battle in Cicero. . . .

James J. Doherty, who was killed with McSwiggin, had been cutting
in on the Torrio-Capone monopoly in the Cicero beer business. "Red"
Duffy, the third man killed, was thick with both McSwiggin and
Doherty.

Torrio and Capone recently got eleven automatic rifles (one-man
machine guns) of the type used in the murder of McSwiggin, Doherty
and Duffy.

These facts Capt. John Stege, assistant chief of detectives, uncovered
to-day, after eighteen hours of high-pressure work on the triple murder
mystery. Armed with those facts he sent his two best detective teams out
to find Capone and Torrio on the one hand and . . . Myles O'Donnell,
the beer-gang leader, on the other. O'Donnell was McSwiggin's fourth
companion, according to Stege.

As the police quickly discovered, many of their "facts" concerning the
murder were inaccurate or badly out of date. The notion that Capone had
imported an assassination squad to battle rival bootleggers was discarded, and
of course Johnny Torrio had left Chicago months before. In his absence, the
police began to search for Al Capone, who proved maddeningly elusive.
Frustrated, squads of plainclothesmen drove to the Hawthorne Smoke Shop
in Cicero, where they wielded sledgehammers and destroyed every slot machine and roulette wheel in sight. "The only thing we left was the ceiling,"
said one detective who had participated in what he called the "kick-over."
For all their exertions, the raiders found no clues to Capone's whereabouts
or McSwiggin's death.

Failing to capture Torrio or Al Capone, the police turned their fury on his
brother Ralph. Swooping down on Ralph's home at 1924 South Forty-ninth
Court, they discovered a small arsenal: three shotguns, two pump guns,
seven revolvers, and parts of a Thompson machine gun, "such as was used
in the McSwiggin murder." This was damning evidence, and the police
immediately arrested Ralph, along with his wife and a cousin named Charles
Fischetti. This lead, though promising, turned up nothing relevant to Mc-
Swiggin. The police then invaded Capone's home on Prairie Avenue, where
they arrested his younger brother John and inspected furniture they believed
belonged to Al. Again, the arrest yielded nothing beyond a sense of Al
Capone's elusiveness.

The next act of this predictable, tragic story concerned the funeral of
McSwiggin. His mother, who had fainted on learning of her only son's
death, sobbed hysterically throughout the ceremony. "Let him stay with me
a little while," she pleaded as the pallbearers came to move her son's coffin

from the house to the hearse. "Oh, why did they kill him?" she wailed. It was a question that no one was capable of answering. The turnout at his funeral service at St. Thomas Aquinas Roman Catholic Church was impressive, numbering several thousand mourners including the city's top officials, but for all the solemn display of strength it was not the equal of the great gangster funerals the city had witnessed. There were "only" three or four thousand observers, at most, and "only" eight carloads of flowers to accompany the body of the slain prosecutor.

After the funeral Mass, William McSwiggin was buried in Mt. Carmel Cemetery, outside of Chicago; a plain, solid tombstone marked his grave. As the firing squad gave her son a military salute, Mrs. McSwiggin, perhaps remembering the machine-gun bullets that had taken her son's life, collapsed. Even here, amid these tranquil surroundings, there were reminders of the violence afflicting Chicago, and which had claimed the young prosecutor's life. "On the way [to the grave site]," noted the *Chicago Tribune* of the procession of mourners, "they passed . . . the granite shaft that marks the last resting place of Dean [sic] O'Banion, the most colorful of the gangsters killed by enemies in the alcohol business." And not far from O'Banion's grave was that of Mike Merlo, the late head of the Unione Sicilione. In fact, the graveyard was filled with the bodies of racketeers and gangsters, all casualties of Prohibition and their own greed. In later years, Mt. Carmel would also become the site of the family plot for the entire Capone clan. Even in death, then, were these blood enemies forced to abide together within the all-knowing, all-forgiving embrace of the church.

· · ·

During the next few days, as more details of the circumstances surrounding the murder emerged, the integrity of McSwiggin himself was called into question. Here was a man who had once vowed to get Capone for the murder of Joe Howard, yet on the last night of his life he was in the company of those well-known bootleggers, the O'Donnell brothers. Deep in Capone territory. Drinking bootleg booze. There was no evidence that McSwiggin was actually on the take from the O'Donnells, but the *appearance* was highly suggestive. The more the press and police dug, the more it looked as though McSwiggin had unwittingly conspired in his own death. Still, the manner of his murder had been so brutal that public sympathy, which wavered at first, came down firmly on the side of young Billy McSwiggin, the brilliant prosecutor whom gangsters had viciously murdered.

His father fanned the flames of sympathy. "I thought my life was over, but it's only begun," he declared. "I'll never rest until I've killed my boy's slayers or seen them hanged. That's all I have to live for now." Chicagoans learned that little "Mac" was the apple of his father's eye, the delight of his four sisters, a graduate of De Paul University, where he had compiled a fine record, and a good Catholic. Influenced by such comments, public opinion was inclined to forgive Billy McSwiggin's lack of judgment on account of his age. "He was only twenty-six years old and had the riotous blood of youth in his veins, and he enjoyed himself with youthful gusto in his own way," wrote a reporter. Within days a cry was repeated in the pages of the daily newspapers: *Who killed McSwiggin?* Thus McSwiggin, in death, did more to torment and harass Capone than McSwiggin, alive, had ever done.

The slain prosecutor's boss, Robert Emmet Crowe, the state's attorney, responded to the outcry with a show of vigorous action. "It will be a war to the hilt against these gangsters," he declared, and he offered a reward of $5,000 to anyone providing information leading to the arrest of the men responsible for McSwiggin's death, the money to come from his own funds. This was the kind of grandiose gesture and rhetoric for which Crowe was known. Born in Peoria, Illinois, and educated at Yale, he had held his post since 1919, the year that "Big Bill" Thompson became the mayor of Chicago and Len Small the governor of Illinois, but even as these men sank into the murky waters of corruption, he managed to keep afloat with deft bureaucratic maneuvers. He was particularly adept at distancing himself from the men who had helped to bring him to power. Where Thompson and Dever made empty promises calculated to appeal to their constituencies, Crowe emphasized that Prohibition had created an impossible situation in Chicago. "The town is wet and the county is wet, and nobody can dry them up," ran one of his characteristic exculpatory utterances. "For every dive in the county there are two in the city, and everybody knows it except [Mayor] Dever. Why don't I get busy and stop it? For the simple reason that I am running a law office, not a police station."

McSwiggin's murder presented Crowe with the fight of his political life. From the start the press questioned his ability to act independently. "Everybody knows that the curse of criminal investigation, the blight of protection from crime, is political factionalism. The 'beer war' is mixed up from top to bottom with politics," began the *Herald and Examiner*'s critique. "Robert E. Crowe is not only the state's attorney, he is the head and front of a political organization. Politics ties his hands. Many of his own lieutenants and their privates might be involved. . . . So far as crimes of violence are concerned, this city is in danger. Why blink [at] the fact? Mr. Crowe cannot help us." Crowe overcompensated for such public doubting by deputizing no less than three hundred detectives, a small army dedicated to raiding speakeasies and gambling dens throughout Chicago, especially in Cicero. One of the first pieces of information their reign of terror yielded was that Harry Madigan, the proprietor of the speakeasy where McSwiggin had downed his last drink, had recently switched sides in the simmering Capone-O'Donnell feud.

"When I wanted to start a saloon in Cicero," he said, "Capone wouldn't let me. I finally obtained strong political pressure and was able to open. Then Capone came to me and said I would have to buy his beer, so I did. A few months ago Doherty and Myles O'Donnell came to me and said they could sell me better beer than Capone beer. . . . It cost me fifty dollars a barrel, where Capone charged me sixty. I changed, and upon my recommendation so did several other Cicero saloonkeepers." The implication was that Capone—or his men—were seeking retribution for Madigan's changing sides, so investigators again raided the Hawthorne Inn; on this occasion they seized ledgers detailing the organization's gambling and bootlegging operations. The documents would have all been very interesting in another context, but they shed no light on McSwiggin's death, and the police failed to make an arrest.

Despite the confusion and finger-pointing, Crowe, who needed to appear decisive, declared that he had reached a determination about who was responsible for the death of Billy McSwiggin. On May 5, all the Chicago dailies carried the following statement:

> It has been established to the satisfaction of the state's attorney's office and the detective bureau that [Al] Capone in person led the slayers of McSwiggin. It has become known that five automobiles carrying nearly thirty gangsters, all armed with weapons ranging from pistols to machine guns, were used in the triple killing.
>
> It has also been found that Capone handled the machine gun, being compelled to this act in order to set an example of fearlessness to his less eager companions.

It was a bold thesis, but there was still no *proof*. By this time everybody who was anybody in Chicago law enforcement had an opinion as to who killed McSwiggin and why, and all the theories implicated Al Capone. "All of the investigators agreed with Sgt. McSwiggin that Capone was responsible for the slaying," noted Judge Lyle, going to the issue of motive, "but it's my opinion that Capone was solely after the O'Donnell crew and had not known McSwiggin was in the party. Capone would have foreseen the heat that was raised by killing the prosecutor. . . . Capone would not have killed McSwiggin unless the prosecutor had angered him beyond reason and no evidence to this effect was produced." The investigators gradually came to realize that the young prosecutor had been in the wrong place (the O'Donnells' car) at the wrong time (in the midst of the Capone-O'Donnell feud). As Lyle implied, Capone had a compelling reason *not* to kill McSwiggin, since the lad was a prosecutor and the consequences would be dreadful for Capone. Prosecutors, policemen, detectives, even the wives and children of rival gangsters were all off-limits in the gangland wars. The most likely explanation for his death is that Capone had not known he was with the O'Donnells when he struck. The irony was that his intended victims, the O'Donnell brothers, escaped with their lives, while the bullets intended for them took McSwiggin's life instead.

In an effort to fathom the reasons behind the shooting, the state attorney's office convened one grand jury after another. Since a special grand jury could remain in session for no more than a month in the state of Illinois, there would eventually be six in all, stretching over a six-month period, until October 1926. Their failed efforts to obtain an indictment against Capone or anyone else for the murder of McSwiggin became a civic embarrassment of major proportions.

There was no shortage of reasons for the breakdown. Foremost was a lack of reliable witnesses; once called before the grand jury, the witnesses, afraid for their lives, disappeared. One of the grand juries summarized the situation in this manner: "A conspiracy of silence is evident among the gangsters, and intimidation of all witnesses is clearly evident, also. There is an element of fear involved because anyone who aids the public officials by giving facts is very likely to be 'taken for a ride.' " The assessment concluded, "Silence and the sealed lips of gangsters make the solution of that crime, like many others, thus far impossible." At the same time, the jurors were afraid to convict, afraid for their lives, in fact. There was no secret about their identities; the papers had taken care to print their full names, occupations, addresses, and in some cases, even their *photographs*. In these circumstances, only the most foolhardy juror would insist on issuing an indictment, for in all likelihood he would meet the same end as McSwiggin.

The balance of terror created enormous public frustration as the fruitless investigation stumbled along through the summer of 1926. Although this was not the first time a machine gun had been used by gangsters in Chicago, the murder of McSwiggin did much to establish it as the gangsters' and bootleggers' weapon of choice. People didn't know which to blame for the death of McSwiggin, the gangsters or the machine guns. In the *Daily News*, a cartoon cynically detailed the escalation of violence in Chicago. The first panel depicted a blackjack; in the next, a hand gripped a revolver, "providing," said the caption, "a satisfactory result by killing one person." In the following panel, a masked gunman fires a tommy gun to "kill more people with little exertion," and the final panel predicted: "In the future they will probably get a 'Big Bertha' and shoot up a whole town to get just one or two men."

Still lacking hard evidence linking Capone to the murder, investigators proceeded to pillage Capone-controlled brothels in the Cicero area. They wreaked havoc on the most notorious establishment, the Stockade, and on another occasion, an unidentified group burned a brothel in Forest View. When firemen arrived on the scene, they stood by, watching the blaze. "Why don't you do something?" asked a Capone employee.

"Can't spare the water," a firefighter told him.

Joseph Z. Klenha, the president of Cicero's town council, complained that he was sick and tired of the Chicago Police Department's habit of raiding his peaceful little city and creating bad publicity. "Why not blame the Boer War on Cicero?" he asked. "The constant patrolling of our streets by Chicago squads is making a burlesque of the whole thing." Klenha's protest fell on deaf ears. Meanwhile, a grand jury in Chicago was investigating Klenha's alliance with Capone; in fact, they were about to return an indictment against the two, along with a score of other racketeers and town employees, for violating the National Prohibition Act. The grand jury cited the presence of enormous amounts of bootleg alcohol in Cicero: "10,000 gallons of un-colored spirits, and 50,000 gallons of cereal beverage, fit for use for beverage purposes." Capone himself was charged with selling alcohol at the Ship. The indictment listed "2,000 pints of cereal beverage, 205 gallons of alcohol, and 4 barrels of cereal beverage" at that gambling establishment. Although Capone's network of bribery ensured that he would never be convicted of these charges, the existence of the indictment gave the police an excuse to continue their raids.

The next wave of assaults turned up interesting evidence in a brothel known as the Barracks. This was a typical Capone operation, a gambling, drinking, and whoring establishment located in Burnham, a suburb the syndicate controlled in cooperation with Johnny Patton, known as "the boy mayor of Burnham" because he had operated a saloon ever since he was a lad of fourteen. For the week of September 6, 1925, the ledger revealed, the slot machines took in $906, the piano player received $55.25 in tips, the bar took in $2,677.10, gambling earned another $1,800, and finally prostitution, by far the biggest contributor to the establishment's earnings, accounted for $5,891. These figures made for a gross income of $11,329.35, out of which 10 percent automatically went to payoffs. There were also sizable expenses, $8,540 worth, leaving a profit for the week of $1,746.35. The Stockade earned several times as much, and assuming this was a representative week, the entire group of Capone-controlled brothels in the Cicero area took in $4 million annually. The ledgers afforded police their first clear picture of how much business the brothels actually did, and the information prompted a federal grand jury to indict Al Capone, Ralph Capone, the O'Donnell brothers, and several others for violating the Volstead Act. Once again, the charge came to nothing, and worse, it was a symptom of how seriously the case, if any, against Capone for the murder of McSwiggin had become sidetracked. If only the police could actually find Capone and question him, then the murder of McSwiggin might be solved.

•   •   •

Throughout the crisis-ridden days of early May, Capone successfully avoided the press and police by taking refuge in the home of one of his lieutenants, Dominic Roberto, who was married to Rio Burke. A singer with a singularly sweet disposition, and not inclined to look too deeply into her husband's business dealings, Rio remembered Capone for his drunken behavior at a picnic four years earlier. She found it difficult to believe that the young boor she recalled now led Chicago's most powerful racketeering organization. His transformation within the span of a few short years was remarkable, for he was now a sober, even grave presence in her home, always well dressed, clean, and polite.

At the time Rio and Dominic lived in Chicago Heights, an area which, with its large Italian population, was to become increasingly important in Capone's organization. During these days, the wife of another Capone lieutenant, Jimmy Emery, stayed with them, treating the illustrious fugitive from justice to her delicious cooking. "She was the best cook in the country," Rio Burke recalled, "and he ate whatever was set before him. In fact, all I ever saw of Al Capone while he was hiding out in our house was a perfect gentleman. Most of his suits were silk; he was impeccably dressed, always well groomed. I would say he was a rather handsome man, but I never thought of him as sexy, and I don't believe women hounded him. He didn't seem to be a womanizer, but I'm sure he had mistresses. *I* never looked upon him that way because he was all business. He didn't smile much, he didn't laugh much. He was always all business."

Despite Capone's calm demeanor, Burke was alert to signs of danger, especially the guns stored in their otherwise proper house. "One day my maid called me and said, 'Mrs. Burke, come down here. I'm cleaning out the front room.' We pulled a gunny sack into the light, and it was filled with all kinds of revolvers. And I asked Dominic, 'What in the *world* are all those guns doing in the closet?' But all he said was, 'Some of the boys are going hunting.' I didn't dare ask what that meant, but I do recall that Dominic never went to bed without a gun under his pillow. And one time, when I went to put clean handkerchiefs in his drawer, I found one of those fountain pen guns. It was round and black and looked like a fountain pen, but it was really a gun." Her entire life was like that little device: it seemed ordinary enough on the surface, but a closer inspection revealed it to be filled with danger.

To relieve the monotony of these eventless, anxious days, Capone and

Dominic Roberto took long drives in the country, often tracing the shore of Lake Michigan to Milwaukee and back in a single day, letting the time pass, trying to escape the monotony, the two of them just driving, hardly talking, watching out for cop cars. And as the sun slipped from the sky and shadows lengthened, they drove on, into the midwestern night. The police wanted him, but they could not find him; he was a lost man, in search of himself. Under pressure from all sides—the police, the press, and rival gangs—Al feared for his life as he never had before. The cops had shot his brother Frank on the streets of Cicero, and he was convinced they would come after him during one of their fact-finding raids. And if they missed their mark, it would be only a matter of time until the O'Donnells retaliated. Even though he had managed to sidestep an indictment for McSwiggin's murder, he knew that the public and law enforcement authorities held him responsible for the atrocity. And when the next policeman or prosecutor was killed, the murder would be laid at his feet, even if he had never heard of the victim's name.

In fact, he was fleeing not just the murder of McSwiggin but the entire series of murders beginning with the death of his brother Frank on April 1, 1924, his killing Joe Howard, his complicity in the murder of Dion O'Banion, and so on through two harrowing years, with McSwiggin's death coming as the culmination of a rising tide of police and gangland violence. Capone was sick of living with the fear of imminent death, the presence of guns, the taste of terror constantly on his tongue. For over two years he had not been able to spend more than a few days at a time in one place, whether it was the Hawthorne Inn, his home on Prairie Avenue, or the Metropole Hotel. He was exhausted from the relentless tension and anxiety, and he was desperate to escape the gathering sense of doom, the conviction that he would meet the same end as his brother Frank. The women, the cocaine, and the food in which he indulged made the fear go away, but for only a little while, until the next dead body turned up, and the headlines started to scream again.

For all these reasons, emotional as well as practical, Capone decided to remain in hiding—not for days or weeks, but for three months. During that period none of the three hundred detectives assigned to the McSwiggin case had any idea what had become of him; they combed New York, hiked through the woods of Michigan, and descended on the hamlet of Couderay, Wisconsin, where Ralph had acquired a hunting lodge, all to no avail. Rumors circulated that Al Capone had fled to Indiana, to Canada, to Italy. A rather large gap always appears at this point in the chronology of Capone's life, and it is often assumed that nothing of significance occurred during this period. The assumption is wrong; the summer of 1926 was an absolutely critical period in his life. As they stretched on, these three "lost months" formed a crucible from which he emerged a far different man.

The truth is that Capone, after spending eight days with Dominic Roberto

in Chicago Heights, journeyed west to Lansing, Michigan, where he was
sheltered by friends and moved in circles about which the newspapers and
the police knew nothing. As the months passed, his clandestine travels
throughout the Midwest became a journey into himself, a time of introspec-
tion and soul-searching from which he emerged with a new, yet strangely
familiar vision of what he wanted to do with the rest of his life.

CHAPTER 4

Round Lake Refuge

TO REACH LANSING from Chicago in those days meant a leisurely drive of slightly more than 200 miles through green, rolling countryside. The further from Chicago Al Capone went, the fresher the air, the cleaner the towns, the less likelihood that he would be recognized. He proceeded east along the southern rim of Lake Michigan, past Gary, Indiana, past Michigan City, and then drove along the shore, bustling and pleasant at this time of year, to Benton Harbor, Michigan, a resort town where several of his partners in crime were buying land and building substantial, secluded vacation houses. Just beyond Benton Harbor, the highway left the lake and pointed east to Kalamazoo and Battle Creek, then angled north into Lansing. From the bootlegger's perspective, the city occupied a highly strategic location, since it is located in the center of lower Wisconsin, approximately eighty-five miles from Detroit, at the confluence of the Grand and Red Cedar Rivers. Thus situated, it served as a checkpoint and clearinghouse for much of the Capone organization's imported, high-class alcohol as it came into the country across a narrow stretch of water from Windsor, Canada, opposite Detroit. The trucks carrying Capone's booze paused briefly in Lansing, then proceeded to Chicago, New York, and points south and west.

For all its geographical advantages, Lansing did pose certain problems for Capone and his small army of bootleggers. It is, for one thing, the state capital, teeming with the sort of government and legal officials that racketeers normally avoid. Lansing is also a company town, the company in this case being Oldsmobile, the nation's first major car manufacturer, founded by Ransom E. Olds. Lansing's Oldsmobile plant was immense and employed thousands of workers. The concentration of manufacturing and government jobs introduced a measure of sophistication and wealth to Lansing. However,

Capone and his men avoided the city, its factories, and its money, preferring the Michigan countryside, with its rolling hills, large lakes, innumerable hiding places, and its sizable Italian community, which consisted of immigrant families that had fled the crowding and confusion of Chicago's Little Italy and the dreariness of Chicago Heights. It was here, in the heartland, that Italian immigrants became Americans in a way that was not possible in Chicago Heights, where a combination of prejudice from without and *campanilismo* from within stalled the process of assimilation. Compared to the Heights, Lansing was a promised land, and when Italians managed to reach Lansing they felt they had made it. The lucky ones owned their own businesses, especially produce markets and stores, and they lived the good life, the American dream to which they all aspired.

Among the Italians who had abandoned the danger of Chicago Heights for the opportunities of Lansing was Capone's good friend Angelo Mastropietro.* He was a young husband and father who had once worked for the Capone organization in various minor capacities connected with the liquor trade, supplying clubs and overseeing local distribution. Then Angelo, like so many young men in Chicago Heights, became involved in a deadly altercation. The event proved a turning point in Angelo's life, for soon after the murder he fled Chicago Heights for Lansing, where he started his life anew. "Life was very hard for the Italians in Chicago Heights," Angelo's daughter, Grazia,* recalls. "It was a dead, ugly town. You can go out to the cemetery there and see a mother's grave, surrounded by five or six sons, all dead in their twenties. Murdered by gangsters. That's why the Italians came to Lansing. My father, Angelo, ran a fruit and vegetable market at 120 South Washington Avenue in Lansing, and it was legitimate. It was in a fine location downtown, and there were always trucks coming and going full of fruit, and my father made a lot of money selling to all the big restaurants, Greek coffee shops, and cafés."

Angelo's decision to leave the rackets was perhaps the only course more dangerous than entering *la mala vita* in the first place, for spurned gang members threatened to track down and kill the renegade before he could betray his former colleagues. But Angelo was one of the lucky ones whose life was spared, in part because he left Chicago, and in part because he continued to perform favors for the Capone organization. He occasionally allowed Capone to use the Washington Avenue market as a front for his bootlegging operations. "The men who worked there had these trucks, and they used to go down to Florida and pick up fruit, and they also delivered booze here, running it from Canada," his daughter notes. But Angelo never made ref-

---

* A pseudonym.

erence to the rackets or to the unpleasantness back in the Heights, though everyone around him, including his family, knew why he had left home. He had succeeded in building a new life for himself in Lansing, running a thriving produce market, and becoming, at least in the eyes of his *paisan*, a wealthy man. Even better, he now earned his living legitimately, through hard work and vigilance and good judgment, and it became clear that perhaps the best decision he had ever made was to quit Chicago Heights and all it represented.

Then Angelo was asked to perform the biggest favor of all, to shelter Al Capone during the summer of 1926, when the most notorious racketeer in Chicago was wanted for questioning about the murder of McSwiggin.

When his former employer, Al Capone, came to Lansing, Angelo Mastropietro identified and understood. He, too, knew what it was like to live with the fear and tension; he understood how it corrupted a man's life, and he offered to protect Capone for as long as necessary. With Angelo's help, Capone became a fixture in Lansing during the summer of 1926 and for four subsequent summers. The city became his summer home away from home, and with Angelo's sponsorship he made many new friends in the local Italian community. However, Capone did not attempt to control or alter Lansing's political landscape as he had changed Cicero's. He wanted nothing from Lansing beyond the one thing he could never find in Chicago: peace of mind.

The Al Capone the Italians of Lansing came to know was nothing like the "Scarface" whose evil deeds regularly made headlines in the Chicago dailies. When the people of Lansing considered Capone, they did not think of beer wars, drive-by machine-gun shootings, and a rat's nest of urban corruption. They did not shudder at the thought of a powerful racketeering organization dealing in vice and death. The Al Capone they knew in Lansing was a soft-spoken, impeccably groomed man burdened by concerns about which he rarely spoke and given to intoxicating bursts of charity. To them, he was neither a pimp, gambler, murderer, or racketeer. He was a friend, a benefactor, and in some cases a savior. It was one thing to be outside the rackets looking in, but to be on the inside, to feel Capone's warmth, to be the recipient of his superhuman generosity, was as close to being at home as the Italians of Lansing had ever felt in the strange, wealthy, bigoted land in which they lived. Capone, in turn, reveled in their approbation. In Lansing he could walk the streets without fearing for his life; here, if nowhere else, men were not out to kill him, and the knowledge that one such refuge existed made him feel human and offered a measure of redemption from the corruption and violence he had sown in Chicago.

The Mastropietro family was among the first to appreciate and to profit from Capone's attempt to rehabilitate himself. Beginning in 1926 he virtually became a member of their family, and he stood as *compare*, or godfather, to Angelo's two daughters, Grazia and Catherine,* on whom he lavished presents such as jewelry and especially a cherished lavaliere. With such gifts he purchased their love and goodwill. "Al Capone and his family were all good people," Grazia insists. "They were respected in the community. And they weren't ignoramuses, like in the movies. He spoke very well. He'd walk into a room and you wouldn't even know he was there until suddenly everyone else had stopped talking, and you'd turn around and see that Al had come in. And when he spoke you could hear a pin drop because he spoke so softly, nobody could make any noise while he was talking, very softly, but with such authority. He was a very refined man. Years later, when that movie in which Rod Steiger played him with a loud, roaring voice showed up on television, I remember my aunts and uncles, who all knew Al, laughing, and my mother and grandmother, who had adored him, were outraged because he had been so quiet, and they resented showing him involved with killing, violence, and revenge. Oh, they hated it. Capone was not loud, flashy, and coarse. Capone had class. More than that, he had grace."

Although Capone did not resort to violence in Lansing, he nonetheless took care to import his two principal bodyguards, "Machine-Gun" Jack McGurn and Frank "The Enforcer" Nitti, who took up residence with him outside Lansing in a secluded area known as Round Lake. This is a small, peaceful region. The lake is modest, hardly more than a large pond ringed with weather-beaten cottages connected by a network of dirt paths leading to a narrow beach. From his small cottage, Capone enjoyed a view of rolling hills, farmhouses, and barns.

Here, beside Round Lake, Al lived the simple life. He spent his days lolling on the beach, alternately swimming and resting. Occasionally he played with the children who came to frolic at the water's edge. "We were all thrilled when Al Capone rented those cottages at Round Lake," says Grazia's cousin Giovanna Antonucci* of those bygone summer days. "We kids had our own cottage with the ladies, and the men had another cottage, and the bodyguards had another cottage. So there were three cottages in all: men, women, and bodyguards. When we were all there Al loved to swim. You can't believe the way that old man would swim. He was a wonderful swimmer. He'd take his friends, who all wore those straw hats they had at the time, way out, and they'd say, 'The wind blew my hat,' and he'd swim to it, like a game they were playing. He would swim underwater, and when he came to the surface he made a noise like a sea lion." Besides swimming, she remembers, Al and his companions "mostly talked, played records, drank,

* A pseudonym.

and read a lot. They had books, you can't imagine all the books they had. I sneaked into Al's cabin once, and I looked through all the books, and I found this one book, *The Mark of Zorro*, and it interested me because in the picture on the cover he was wearing a cape and a black hat."

After the children departed, Al returned to his cottage, where he watched the sun slip from the sky and the lake water turn glassy and fade into the night. The only sounds he heard were the regular croaking of frogs and the occasional cheep of a bird. For once his nights did not reverberate with the rattle of the roulette wheel, the squeal of tires, and gunfire. The loudest sound heard at Round Lake was thunder. After a humid day, the gathering storms of night split the sky with jagged streaks, and then the rain would fall, beating incessantly on the cottage's flimsy roof, which amplified the sound into a drumbeat. Sometimes the rain on the roof sounded like distant engines growling, as if automobiles lay in wait; at other times it subsided into a peaceful drone.

When he grew restless, Capone found diversion in a spacious roadhouse, an isolated dancing-and-drinking establishment overlooking the lake. Originally the site was a stage coach stop; the roadhouse was built in 1913; in 1920, with the coming of Prohibition, it became a dance hall. Later on, in the 1930s, it was known as the Club Roma, a nightspot renowned for its hot jazz, but for now the house policy was ten cents a dance, and the sound of laughter, high girlish squeals, ricocheted across the floor. It was not a place where married women ventured; the girls who went there were looking for men to buy them drinks, and they were looking for a good time, an improvised encounter, makeshift hilarity. It was here, in these unpretentious surroundings, that Al drank and danced; it was also where he met a pretty young woman who later became his companion in the little cottage down by the lake.

. . .

As Capone's stay in Lansing stretched on, an ever-increasing number of the city's Italians became aware of his presence, and many became involved in sheltering him, either actively by providing such essentials as food and accommodations, or passively by not informing the wrong people of his presence or whereabouts. Capone, for his part, proved eager to purchase the goodwill of his hosts, yet he remained aware of the unfathomable gulf separating him, the racketeer and outlaw, from the rest of society, both Italian and non-Italian.

No one felt that gulf between Capone and the rest of the world more keenly than a sixteen-year-old named Anthony Russo, who became a surrogate son to the racketeer. The Al Capone he knew was a warm, endearing, generous presence, a man who seemed larger than life but at the same time haunted, vulnerable, and doomed. Like many other Italians in the area, the Russo family had become acquainted with Al in Chicago, and from the first young Anthony basked in the reflected glory shed by the racketeer. He remembered how Al gave $200 cash gifts to his mother and had surprised him with a shiny new bike, then spent the afternoon riding it himself. But Anthony was not so naïve that he was ignorant of the sense of danger with which Capone lived; he knew of Capone's yearning for the life of ordinary families, who could gather beside an open window, eating dinner, without fearing for their lives. He vividly remembered the way Al cautioned him never to get involved with the rackets. "If you do," he once told the youth, "and I'm alive, I'll personally kill you."

Despite this warning, Anthony made himself useful as an errand boy for Capone at Round Lake. The young man found his boss to be moody, troubled, but self-contained. "When he was angry at something," Anthony remembered, "he wouldn't talk, and of course everybody stayed clear of him. Everybody shut up, too. His mood was their mood. And when he opened up and started to talk they started to talk. But I never saw him talk in anger. I'm sure that there were times when he said, 'Hey, get out there and beat the hell out of that SOB,' but no matter what went wrong, when he calmed down he talked very reasonably to everybody. They knew him well enough that when he spoke he meant what he said. He was basically a happy-go-lucky guy, and, hell, we used to have more damn laughs.

"Even at Round Lake, though, he always wore a tie and a white shirt. He used to send me into Lansing when he needed socks. Told me exactly what to buy. They were seven and a half dollars a pair. One-hundred-and-fifty-dollar silk shirts. That was a lot of money then. He'd give me a $100 bill, and I'd go out and buy him five pairs of socks, come home, go to give him the change, and he'd tell me, 'No, keep it.' I made more money this way than his bodyguards were making. Frank Nitti and Jack McGurn, I mean. McGurn was a hell of a golfer, a two-handicapper. He could have been a pro, but being on Capone's payroll at $150 per week was a hell of a lot better then being a pro golfer in those days." These were meager salaries for Al, who boasted he was making $33,000 each *week* and who showered $200 gifts on the adults. Nor did McGurn and Nitti get a cut of the organization's gambling and profits, although Capone dangled the possibility before them, as long as they remained obedient and loyal. "It was just like working for a big organization," Anthony observes. "You know, if those people had put their mind to a legitimate business as much as they had put their mind to that type of business, they could've made a fortune legitimately. Dummies don't run those organizations. The dummies were the ones found in the gutter. The smart ones always knew how to keep their noses clean. No, Capone and his guys were highly intelligent businessmen with a lot of ideas. But even a big businessman was not making the kind of money he could make in the booze business, and of course the nice part about that business is that it's an all-cash business.

"It worked like this: Capone's people would walk into a saloon, and they would say to the owner, 'You oughta handle Ace Beer,' which was Capone's beer, and the guy would say—you always found a wiseass—'Get outta here, you punks. I'm not gonna handle your beer.' And Capone's people would say, 'You know, it might help your business.' 'Naw,' says the owner, 'get the hell outta here. Don't bother me.' Well, that was the wrong thing to say because the next morning he'd show up and the whole front of his place would be blown out. The owner would be standing there scratching his head and wondering what he was gonna do next, and the guy that was trying to sell him beer would say, 'Gee, if you'd had Ace Beer I don't think that would've happened to ya.' Then he'd walk away. Now the owner doesn't have the kind of money to rebuild, so he goes back to the Capone group to get money. From there on, he only does what they tell him."

Learning his way around the Capone organization, Russo recognized that one other man wielded immense power, more power, in certain ways, than Al; this was Frankie La Porte. Says Russo of La Porte: "He even controlled Capone. He was a very suave individual, he commanded a lot of respect, and as a result he quietly got all of this power to a point where anybody wanted to get into Capone's confidence, Frankie was the guy they'd call. And he ended up being the one who would say to Capone, 'This is what you'd have to do,' 'This is what I would want you to do,' because of his connections throughout the whole United States. He became the go-between for Chicago, New York, Kansas City, St. Louis, Los Angeles. Frankie didn't ever deal with the lower echelon. His dealings were always with the top guy in every town."

La Porte's influence over Capone was of particular interest to Russo because Frankie had almost married the youth's sister. "In those days all marriages were fixed in the Italian groups," Russo explains. "If a fella liked the girl, he'd talk to the parents. In fact, he didn't even talk to the parents himself, he would send a representative. The parents had to approve first, and the daughter didn't have a hell of a lot to say about it. Now Frankie was a good-looking kid, but there was an argument, and the engagement got broke up. My sister was brokenhearted over it." The end of the courtship meant more than broken hearts; it also affected the future of racketeering in Chicago. Shortly before they were forced apart, Frankie had vowed to Russo's sister, "If you don't marry me, I'm going to go into a life of crime." *La mala vita.* And Frankie La Porte kept his word.

As he fell under Capone's spell, Russo became convinced that two factors—the hypocrisy surrounding Prohibition and virulent anti-Italian prejudice—were largely to blame for Capone's vicious reputation. Russo was especially sensitive to these concerns because his own family had suffered from them. His father, who had emigrated from Italy, had been a stonemason in Chicago Heights. When Anthony was a small child, his father had taken a job constructing a chimney. During foul weather, the other laborers, a mixture of Germans, Poles, and Italians, stayed home because of the danger posed by the high winds. But Anthony's father had a family to support; his wife was pregnant, and he needed the money badly, so he went to work that day. The wind blew the chimney over, and it crushed him to death. A week passed before the others cleared away the rubble and removed the body. As compensation for the death, his employers offered his widow— Anthony's mother—the sum of $100 for her child and $100 for the child she was carrying. There was a condition: the money was to be held in trust until each child turned twenty-one. "It's for your own good," the employers told Anthony's mother. "Everyone knows you can't trust Italians." Shortly afterward, the widow gave birth to her second child, and two weeks later she went to work in the onion fields outside Chicago Heights with her newborn infant strapped to her back in order to earn money to feed her children. Picking onions was arduous, backbreaking work, but it was one of the few jobs available to unskilled laborers. The pay could be as little as five cents a day. She somehow managed to keep from starving, and when her son Anthony became a teenager he found employment in the local fruit markets, and later on he went to work for Angelo Mastropietro in Lansing. "Angelo was a real high-class gentleman, and Al Capone recognized it," Anthony recalls. "He wasn't the ordinary hoodlum who was always cussing and drunk. He was always very straight about everything. He was one of those people you could trust. He would have been a terrific salesman for IBM. Let the customer do the talking, and you sit there and listen."

Anthony's new job brought him face to face with the severe anti-Italian prejudice that existed outside Lansing, especially in the South. He often traveled to Tennessee to obtain sweet potatoes for resale in Chicago and Detroit. It was arduous labor, but it paid $150 a week. One night, a friend invited him to a pool hall in a little town called Dresden. When they arrived, Russo discovered to his surprise that the place was filled with men. His friend explained they had come to see *him*, for they had never seen an Italian before. "They think, if he's Italian, he's gonna kill ya on sight," Russo says. "They expected me to walk in with a gun on each hip, and it was kind of comical to see."

Given this climate of prejudice combined with a certain fascination with Italians, Russo could understand how Al Capone had acquired a diabolical reputation, but the young man from his own experience judged that impression to be false. "In my personal opinion he was always a gentleman. He always urged me to stay straight. He helped those old people in Chicago, those old Italians. If it hadn't been for him half of them would have been on welfare, or worse. Anyone ever needed any help and who went to him and asked him for help got it. He was just that type of individual. Nobody ever gave him any special title, they never referred to him as 'Godfather,' they just called him Al. Except for the old Italians, that is. They respected his power, and when they were in his presence and he'd go over to shake their hand, they would kiss his hand because deep down they were afraid of him, see. To them he was always *Signore Capone*. They looked up to him as the Boss; they had to have a leader to look up to because that was the way it had been in Italy. Capone was more important to them than the president of the United States because they couldn't go to the president for help. Al was the one that they always went to. Someone was sick, they didn't have money to be taken care of, you could always depend on him to take care of those things. Say that you and your wife had a daughter whose husband was giving her a bad time. Al was the one you'd get to help straighten out the problem. I don't know what he gained by being kind to those kind of people because they couldn't do anything for him; he was doing it for them."

According to Russo, Capone differed from the stereotypical gangster in one other critical way: "He never carried a gun. He didn't have to; he had all those bodyguards. What'd he want to carry a gun for? The only time I *did* see him with a gun in his hand was when McGurn, Nitti, and I were driving out to his cottage at Round Lake one night. Al was already there. We were in a big Studebaker touring car, and McGurn says, 'Boy, what a pretty moon tonight' just as we come to a curb. We were going so fast we tipped right over. These guys all carried big .45s, which they gave to me. Now I'm just a kid. It's a lonesome little road out there, but you never know when someone is gonna come around, so I was going to walk to the lake, to Al's cabin, but Nitti says, 'No, no, this is wrong.' He says, 'Al will kill us if Anthony shows up over there with all this stuff, he'll kill us. I'll go with you.' I never forgot this. Now instead of me walking on my knees he loads a couple of guns on himself, and off we go. We aren't too far from the lake. We walk over. Nitti knocks on the door. And he's shaking. He knows that Al does not want to see this. He knows we are in trouble. I mean here's a guy who's wanted in Chicago and here're all of his bodyguards in a wreck. So the police know that he's in the neighborhood. Nitti knocks on the cabin door. Al says, 'Who's there?' And Nitti's so goddamned scared he can't answer. Nitti knocks on the door again, and Al says again, 'Who's there?' And Nitti *still* doesn't answer. He's too damn scared and I'm too damn dumb to answer. All at once the door flies open and there's a big .45 pointed right at Nitti's forehead. He got his voice back in a hurry.

" 'Jesus Christ, Al, don't shoot! It's me! Jesus Christ!'

"And Al says, 'Come on in here. What in the hell happened? What is this?' "

Nitti and Anthony entered Capone's cabin. Once inside, Anthony saw someone else partly concealed behind Capone. It was a girl, a good-looking blonde. Not Italian. Her name was Virginia, and she was Al's mistress at Round Lake. Virginia impressed the young Russo as a "beautiful gal, as nice as you can be and still be involved with that group. Al met her in the roadhouse. You'd get all kinds of types in that place. She was a very well-proportioned gal. Wasn't tall. Good-looking. But you know she meant nothing to him. The wives thought they had the best of everything, and they did. Men like Al always treated their wives with respect. The gals knew that as long as they kept their mouths shut and their noses clean everything was gonna be okay. And they only came around when they were asked, and if they weren't asked they'd stay in their room or wherever they were. Al's wife never complained about the girlfriends. Now whether she didn't dare to complain or she was smart enough to keep her mouth shut nobody knows. You could ask a woman in her position a question about her husband, and she never knew anything about his business. All she knew is that her husband was in the fruit business or he had a flower store or a meat market somewhere, and that's *all* she knew. Most of the men were highly respectful of families, and Al would sometimes get melancholy and talk about how he hadn't seen his family for awhile. He loved his son, and he was afraid for him. Once you get into that kind of life you really don't want a lot of liabilities. The amazing thing was that nobody ever bothered Al's wife. But then those people never bothered women. You never heard of wives getting hurt. They had a code of ethics no one ever understood."

•   •   •

After several weeks in seclusion by the shores of Round Lake, Capone felt more secure in Lansing, and with the help of the Mastropietros he began to establish ties to the Lansing police force. Although he was wanted for questioning in Chicago, little more than 200 miles distant, the Lansing police conspired to keep his presence a secret, at least from the Illinois authorities. The pivotal figure in this conspiracy of silence was Lansing's chief of police, John O'Brien, whom the world knew as a respected law enforcement officer. For him, the situation was simple; all he had to do to earn the money he accepted was to remain silent. The Mastropietros, for their part, lauded O'Brien's behavior. "John O'Brien came to parties at our house," Grazia Mastropietro says. "He knew Al Capone was in Lansing, but he didn't bother him because Al was our friend. O'Brien was one of those to whom friendship is the first thing, and he protected his friends. For instance, if he had a friend who was a gambler and who was about to be raided, he told the man, and the man got out of town in time. It wasn't corruption to warn a friend, was it?"

Anthony Russo recalled that Al's new ally, Chief O'Brien, "could be tough when he wanted. Boy, he could be tough. But he was always nice to us, of course. We were friends. We were family. He got his little piece out of knowing that Capone was in town. He got a few bucks out of it, just like any other police protection that you get. All he's got to do is keep his mouth shut and keep the police away from the area." But it wasn't quite that simple, for several years later, when Capone no longer had need of his services, O'Brien's profitable arrangement with the racketeer was discovered. "He retired in disgrace," says Grazia. "By that time I was in high school, and my family sent me there to keep him company because he was so depressed. We were all afraid he was going to kill himself. He always liked me so much, and I used to talk to him a lot. He didn't kill himself after all, but his career as policeman was finished."

Enjoying both Italian hospitality and police protection, Capone felt secure enough to leave his Round Lake hideout and to move freely and openly about the city of Lansing. He took a suite in Lansing's Downey Hotel, where he held court with politicians and newspapermen. "When I first met Capone I was a boy of seventeen working at the office of the *State Journal*," recalls Lloyd Moles, a veteran Lansing journalist. "I always knew what to expect when I started hearing 'Uncle Al' is coming. He would take over the second floor of the Downey, where he renewed friendships. Yet I had no knowledge of who he really was, even when I was introduced to him. He seemed to enjoy children and always had gifts for them. As a news reporter years later I asked the police if they knew that he had ever visited the Lansing area." Not only did the police know that the nation's most notorious racketeer was virtually a summer resident, Moles learned, but "Capone always notified them that he was in town."

Although Capone conducted his business at the Downey Hotel, he lived with the Mastropietro family in their house on Saginaw Street, where he vicariously enjoyed the domestic tranquillity he would never be able to purchase with any amount of money or blood. He played with the Mastropietro children and their friends and relatives by the hour, and he loved to toss babies high into the air and catch them in his big strong arms. He lavished small presents on the older children. Giovanna Antonucci was one who recalled those innocent shopping sprees with Capone: "He took us kids by the hand downtown, in Lansing, Michigan. We went to a big department store, and he got us all clothes; he dressed us from head to toe. I got a taffeta dress, white patent leather shoes, everything. And my brother got a new bike and new clothes. People knew him in Lansing; he wasn't hiding. I remember walking down the street and the people would stop and say to him, 'Hi, Al!'

People would go by in a car, and they'd stop and say, 'Hi, Al!' They all knew him. Nobody was afraid of him. We liked him. He was good to us. We wished he would never go home. He talked soft. You could barely hear that man talk. And he wasn't a criminal, not at all. To tell you how nice he was, he had a young fellow, one of his young bodyguards. We all knew him. Next door to us lived a pretty girl, an American girl—I mean not Italian, we were American, too—and he was going to take her out on a date. But before he did, Al said to the young man, 'Are you taking this girl out?' And the young man said, yes, he was. And Al told him, 'You take her out and bring her home the same way you're taking her out.' Meaning, don't get funny. Don't mess around. That's the way Al was, a perfect gentleman."

Yet life with "Uncle Al" Capone on Saginaw Street was not quite so tranquil as it appeared. A sense of menace permeated the household, and even the children sensed it. "I remember him sitting on the porch," recalls Grazia Mastropietro of Capone's stay in her home, "and at that time, I knew the Chicago police were looking for him. And there were two local policemen sitting in the window of the house across the street. They were there the whole time he was here. And then there were cars that drove by the house very slowly."

Giovanna Antonucci remembers the secrecy with which Capone and his men cloaked themselves; they lived in a world that children and other innocents were not permitted to enter. "My brother and I were curious about Al and his men so we opened the doors to peek at the men. All the men were playing cards, drinking. They all wore guns in holsters, and we were scared. We shut the door right away. Then we'd peek again, to see how they were talking and playing cards. Meanwhile, Grazia would crawl under the table and untie everyone's shoes, and the men would pretend not to notice. They always kept all the window shades down. No window shades were up, ever, because, you know, somebody could walk by or drive and shoot them. But since we were kids, we were left alone. Nobody bothered us; they were nice to us, and we liked them. When all of us children were playing out of doors, Al would call me: 'Come here, Giovanna,' and he'd give me five dollars, or maybe even more. 'Go buy ice cream for all these children,' he'd say, meaning the ones I was playing with. And I would go to the drugstore and buy our ice cream. So of course we liked them, especially Al."

Although Capone, the compulsive extrovert, paraded about the streets of Lansing, the elders warned their children to keep his presence a secret. The last thing they wanted was for one of their children to start talking about their summer guest, Al Capone, in front of friends and strangers. "You were brought up with fear," Grazia remembers of that time. Decades later, the stigma of association with Capone persists. Grazia's daughter, now a young mother, recalls, "When I was a child I would ask my grandma to tell my girlfriends about Al Capone, but instead of saying anything she would pull me into another room by my sleeve and say, 'Don't you tell those girls that we knew him.' " Her mother solemnly observes: "That was the one thing. They would kill you if you opened your mouth."

If "Uncle Al" introduced an element of danger into the Mastropietro home, he was also instrumental in dispelling another menace that Angelo had long endured in Lansing. At the time, many of the Italian merchants were being victimized by the last of the Black Handers, the freelance Italian blackmailers who preyed exclusively on other Italians. "All the merchants were told that they had to kick in protection money every week, or else," Grazia notes. "But they didn't have it. Many of them were starving during those years in the early twenties. All they had were their businesses. They used to threaten to beat them up or blow up their businesses if they didn't give them tribute. Even then it wasn't killing, it was beating them up or blowing up their store, which was bad enough. They got together, these merchants, and went to see my father and petitioned him for help, and my father went to Capone to help. Capone told my father, Angelo, to tell the Black Handers: 'Al Capone says leave these Italians in Lansing alone.' And he did the same thing to the Purple gang in Detroit: 'If you bother these people in Lansing you deal with me.' Capone got word to the Purple gang, and they did lay off, and that was one more reason the Italian merchants respected my father and loved Al Capone."

Capone opposed the Black Hand partly for selfish reasons, because they threatened his own rackets, and partly because he wished to be seen as a hero to his people. In this quest he succeeded, at least in Lansing. Grazia Mastropietro says, "My mother would say to me about Al Capone, 'Don't ever let anybody tell you he was a killer or some sort of thug. He is a beautiful gentleman.' " Grazia's mother felt justified in saying these words to her daughter because in a world of corruption and prejudice, Al Capone stood as a force for law and order and self-respect. He was capable of bringing justice and even a measure of prosperity to the Italians of Lansing. To them he was no gangster, and his bootlegging activities were a source of pride rather than shame. He was an employer, a friend, and an arbiter of justice. This new role was immensely flattering to Capone's ego; it afforded him the respect he had never been able to buy with any amount of money or bullets in Brooklyn or Chicago. In those urban centers he was constantly branded with terms such as "pimp," "gangster," and "murderer," but in Lansing he was regarded as a fixer with important connections, a man in a position to help people. Even today, the Italians of Lansing who knew Capone remain quick to leap to his defense. They are neither naïve nor blind; they are bitterly realistic and pragmatic people who have struggled to survive in their adopted home. The uncomfortable fact was that Capone helped them achieve their version of the

American dream. Furthermore, he was, at least to them, polite, charming, generous, loyal—all those things a criminal mastermind is not supposed to be.

Yet the Al Capone who took children into town for ice cream in Lansing was the same Al Capone who impulsively pumped five bullets into Joe Howard in Chicago. He cultivated extremes of good and evil, and according to the racketeering code by which he lived, he accomplished his good works through evil. His crimes only intensified his desire to purchase redemption at any price. For Capone, giving away money or gifts was often the cheapest way to feel good. For instance, he beseeched his friend and protector Angelo Mastropietro to accept a shiny new car as a token of gratitude, but Angelo refused these and other blandishments from Capone, explaining that he was motivated by friendship and loyalty, not by the expectation of material reward. Yet most other Italian families in Lansing could not afford Angelo's noble gesture. They knew Capone was always good for a touch, sometimes cash for household expenses such as food, but more a gift for a special occasion. "There was one family so poor that they could not afford a wedding dress for their daughter when the time came for her to be married," says Grazia Mastropietro. "Capone not only bought her the dress, he paid for the wedding, and he gave her a *dòte*, a dowry. He also gave money to high school kids for college. I can't say it was the equivalent of four years' tuition, but it was a start."

As a result of his generosity, Capone began to see himself in a new light. If he could do the same back in Chicago, perhaps people there would regard him with the affection and respect he had won in Lansing. If only he could be more like his friend Angelo Mastropietro, to whom traditional values such as friendship, loyalty, honor, and family mattered more than anything else in life. To accomplish this lofty goal, Capone knew he would have to resign the role he had inherited from Johnny Torrio, but he was ready to walk away from the precarious position of power in which he found himself, as well as the headlines that smeared his name. If nothing else, he might live longer. As a practical matter, he could turn over the day-to-day operation of the organization to Ralph and to Jack Guzik. Indeed, they were already running it in his absence. Then he could devote himself to clearing his name. Of course, the obstacles he faced seemed insurmountable, beginning with the murder of McSwiggin, but how wonderful to live without that dry lump of fear at the back of his throat, to walk about Chicago as freely as he went about the streets of Lansing, where people, when they saw him, called out, "Hello, Al!" and waved instead of firing a machine gun or plotting to poison the very pasta he ate.

His brother Vincenzo, he knew, had transformed himself from a potential gunman into the lawman everyone called "Two-Gun" Hart. He had even made himself famous as a marshal and Prohibition agent. Of course his transformation, which meant partially concealing his identity, had been extreme and bizarre, and Al could never go that route, but he felt the temptation to legitimacy to which Vincenzo had succumbed. As the tranquil summer weeks passed, it was a temptation on which Capone meditated. Should he reform? Leave behind his life of crime? More importantly, *how* would he accomplish this transformation? It was impossible.

No, Angelo counseled him. With God's will anything was possible.

•   •   •

Although he delighted in the company of children and consoled himself in the arms of Virginia, perhaps Capone's greatest pleasure during these summer months was listening to his opera records, the big stacks of glistening black 78-rpm discs he purchased in Lansing. "Al loved music," recalls Grazia Mastropietro. "He bought a phonograph, and he bought every Caruso record he could find in Lansing. He would play them by the hour." What a luxury it was to sit in the Mastropietros' living room, listening to the gorgeous music unfold. Capone was obsessed with opera as only an Italian could be. Although he adored Ruggiero Leoncavallo's violent and melodramatic *Pagliacci*, whose tormented souls are consumed by infidelity and retribution, he loved the musical epics of Giuseppe Verdi most of all—*Aïda* with its pageantry, the tragic inevitability of *La Forza del Destino*, and finally, late at night, when the children were asleep, the harsh, rich, dark strains of *I Vespri Siciliani*, the Sicilian Vespers, Verdi's romanticized version of the uprising that gave birth to the Mafia. Here was an opera to inflame Capone's imagination with its portrayal of the clash of historical forces, pressures he fancied having confronted in his own struggle against the authorities in Chicago. In his reveries, he saw himself not as a racketeer or a pimp, but as a champion of the freedom and dignity of Italians in the United States; like the ancient Sicilians, he was prepared to resort to violence when provoked, to assert his dignity as an Italian-American and as a man. He found many cues for such flights of fancy in the opera's libretto, written by Eugène Scribe, which told of the thirteenth-century patriotic uprising by the Sicilians against their French oppressors and the birth of Sicilian statehood.

The oppression and prejudice that Al Capone faced in contemporary America had its origins in a far more recent historical event: the assassination of the superintendent of police in New Orleans, Louisiana, in 1890. The aftereffects of this murder were felt by all Italian-Americans trying to make their way in their new home. At the time, New Orleans, renowned for its flourishing prostitution industry, was also a city rife with anti-Italian prejudice. The mayor, Joseph A. Shakespeare, spoke for many citizens of New

Orleans when he declared, "Our genial climate, the ease with which the necessities of life can be obtained, and the polyglot nature of the population unfortunately has singled out this part of the country for the idle and emigrants from the worst classes of Europe: Southern Italians and Sicilians. . . . We find them the most idle, vicious and worthless among us. . . . They are without courage, honor, truth, pride, religion or any quality that goes to make good citizens." Not long after he uttered these words, the city's youthful superintendent of police, David C. Hennessy, was assassinated. As the hunt for Hennessy's murderers began, the police found a so-called "Mafia gun" near the scene of the crime. "The weapon was of the murderous Italian make," noted the *New Orleans Daily Picayune*. Mayor Shakespeare ordered the police to arrest "every Italian you come across."

A month later, in November 1890, a grand jury indicted eleven principals and eight accessories to the crime. Newspaper headlines carried the story to every corner of the country; it was the first time most Americans heard of the "secret organization styled 'Mafia.' " In the streets of New Orleans men regularly taunted Italian immigrants with the question, "Who killa de chief?" and walked away laughing. After four months of turmoil, the trial for the murder of David C. Hennessy commenced on February 16, 1891, at old St. Patrick's Hall. Ultimately, the jury declared a mistrial in the case of three of the accused, and found all the others not guilty. In the morning, the citizens of New Orleans were confronted with the intolerable headline in the *Daily Picayune*: "NONE GUILTY!"

A month later, the White League, a white supremacist organization, held a rally to protest the verdict. The meeting attracted hundreds of irate people, who listened to a procession of speakers intent on whipping them into a frenzy. Eventually the mob raced to the prison where the Italians had been confined since the conclusion of the trial. Arriving at the prison, the mob met with no obstacles; neither the police nor the sheriff dared to offer resistance. As twenty armed men entered, guards obediently opened the cells holding the Italians, all of whom tried to flee for their lives. Although each vigilante carried a list of the eleven Italians who were supposedly guilty of killing Hennessy, the angry mob indiscriminately shot Italians to death. Meanwhile, outside the prison walls, other vigilantes strung up two more Italians. The mob also hanged another man, Antonio Bagnetto, from a tree in front of the prison, and during the next few hours women stopped by to immerse their handkerchiefs in the blood of the two corpses. The lynching— mass murder is a more accurate description—claimed the lives of eleven Italians in all, five of whom had played no role in the trial.

Astonishingly, both the New Orleans authorities and the press hailed the vigilantes responsible for the deaths of innocent men. Even the *New York Times*, while deploring the lynching, conceded it was a "terribly effective method of inspiring a wholesome dread in those who had boldly made a trade of murder." The leader of the lynch mob, a lawyer named William S. Parkerson, became a hero, receiving congratulatory telegrams from all over the nation, and he later undertook a speaking tour around the country, insisting that his lynching demonstrated that southerners were the most patriotic of all Americans. Meanwhile, Mayor Shakespeare stirred up a fresh quarrel with the city's Italians, telling them, "I intend to put an end to these infernal Dago disturbances, even if it proves necessary to wipe every one of you from the face of the earth." Faced with such threats, Italian immigrants to the United States, who had once favored New Orleans, avoided the city where they were greeted with the taunt "Who killa de chief?" and would be for decades to come. Instead, they congregated in northern cities such as New York and Chicago, where they hoped American society would accord them a more benign reception. But it was not to be. In the decades to follow, shotguns gave way to pistols and machine guns, and lynchings yielded to jail, and the deadly rivalries repeated themselves in the manner of a Greek tragedy, strophe after bloody strophe.

Such were the origins of the historical nightmare in which Al Capone found himself in the summer of 1926. Prejudice, hate, revenge, and economic need had been the controlling facts of his life, but he yearned to escape these conditions, if only to save his own neck. Capone spent many hours discussing his options with his friend Angelo Mastropietro. The easiest choice was to continue to hide out in Lansing, secure among his friends and allies who controlled the police. Another option, also relatively easy to accomplish, was to slip across the border to Canada, his family following shortly afterward. And then there was the idea of returning to Chicago. Of all the choices, it was the most hazardous, the most likely path to his becoming an assassin's victim. But if he survived, if he submitted himself to the authorities who wanted him in connection with the shooting of McSwiggin and managed to clear his name, he might begin to embark on a new life. Capone chose the last option, the riskiest and most difficult of all. In the end, it was the only one worth pursuing.

He began holding conversations via long-distance telephone with law enforcement officials in Chicago, and soon the word spread throughout Lansing's Italian community: Al Capone was thinking of turning himself in. The negotiations between the Chicago law enforcement authorities and the notorious racketeer required great delicacy. When Capone had second thoughts about proceeding, his friend Angelo urged him to continue. Otherwise, Angelo argued, Capone would have to spend the rest of his life on the run, and sooner or later he would be caught. It was better to surrender in a situation over which he had some control, some chance for rehabilitation, if not vindication. Eventually Capone realized he could not walk away from his allies, enemies, and the corpses, and the bloody memories; he would have to own up to some, if not all, of the consequences.

The outcome of surrender was impossible to predict. Within him stirred the potential for redemption as well as the lust for fast money, deceit, and murder. Yet to be known as the former manager of the notorious Four Deuces, to be called "Scarface" for the rest of his life, was intolerable. The opinion of other people always mattered deeply to him; he craved their good opinion, in fact. He had his whole life before him; he was only twenty-seven—old for gangsters, who tended to die at about that age—but he was young according to the standards of the legitimate world. So, after much anguished indecison, Capone chose to return to Chicago to seek exoneration and ultimately, to abandon the rackets in which he had made his name and his fortune in favor of a legitimate career. To choose legitimacy, then, was to choose life. He would leave the rackets forever.

• • •

After four months of rest and reflection, Al Capone called the Chicago authorities to tell them he was returning to Illinois at last. According to the agreement he worked out with State's Attorney Crowe, Capone planned to deliver himself into the custody of federal officers led by Pat Roche, the chief investigator, at the Illinois-Indiana state line.

On July 28, 1926, in sweltering midday heat, a car slowly approached the state line and deposited a bulky, well-dressed figure, instantly recognizable as Alphonse Capone. A contingent of reporters on hand to cover the proceedings approached and listened intently as Capone explained the arrangements. "I will go with Mr. Roche to the Federal Building [in Chicago]," he said in a matter-of-fact tone indicating his careful preparations for this moment. "We have been talking by long-distance phone, and I think the time is ripe for me to prove my innocence of the charges that have been made against me. I've been convicted without a hearing of all the crimes on the calendar. But I'm innocent, and it won't take long to prove it." A reporter asked why Capone had gone into hiding if he truly believed himself innocent, and the elusive racketeer responded, "The police have told me a lot of stories. They shoved a lot of murders over on me. They did it because they couldn't find the men who did the jobs, and I looked like an easy goat."

With these words Al Capone launched the campaign to clear his name.

CHAPTER 5

The Return of Al Capone

HIS CHRYSALIS OF PRIVACY TORN ASUNDER, Al Capone reentered Chicago to face accusations of murder. The unhurried pace of his summer sojourn in Lansing gave way to a series of bureaucratic shocks to his system; he was suddenly public property, deprived of his freedom, in police custody. Only now did the abhorrent implications of his situation become real. The police had gunned down his brother Frank with impunity, and they would seize any pretext to do the same to him. But Capone fought back the rage and fear the police inspired and put on an amiable façade, as if he were completely unconcerned about being surrounded by coppers who held him responsible for McSwiggin's death. There would be no charming these coppers, no bribing them; his only course was to submit. The hour of judgment was at hand, and Capone, his immaculate fedora in place, his tie knotted precisely, readied himself to meet it.

On July 29, 1926, the morning after his surrender on the Illinois-Indiana state line, Capone was scheduled to appear before Judge Thomas Lynch, the chief justice of the Criminal Court of Chicago. The outcome would reveal whether Capone's decision to emerge from hiding and confront the accusations concerning his involvement in the death of McSwiggin was the shrewdest or the most foolhardy of his career; it was certainly the riskiest. If he handled the situation well and kept his wits about him, he might succeed in avoiding the snares of the law, but if he lost his temper, he could lose his life in the process. Reporters awaited him on the courthouse steps, where he paused to try his case in the press by making a statement that qualified as a minor masterpiece of innuendo. "Of course I didn't kill him," Capone said of McSwiggin, as the journalists frantically scribbled in their notepads, trying to keep pace with the words uttered by the man who had mysteriously vanished for three months and had just as mysteriously returned to their midst. "Why should I? I liked the kid. Just ten days before he was killed I talked with McSwiggin. There were friends of mine with me. If we had wanted to kill him, we could have done it then and nobody would have known. But we didn't want to; we never wanted to. Doherty and Duffy were my friends, too. I wasn't out to get them. Why, I used to lend Doherty money. I wasn't in the beer 'racket' and didn't care where they sold. Just a few days before that shooting, my brother Ralph and Doherty and the O'Donnells were at a party together."

To another reporter, Capone offered his most precious revelation: "I paid McSwiggin. I paid him plenty, and I got what I was paying for." Thus Capone made several points: the first was that he knew and liked McSwiggin, the second was that McSwiggin frequented Capone-controlled speakeasies in violation of Prohibition, the third was that the deceased's *father* was a drinking pal of Al's, and finally, and most tellingly, he routinely bribed McSwiggin.

Having delivered his artful self-defense, Capone entered the courtroom to face the moment of truth, the charge of murder. He was accompanied by his lawyer, Thomas Nash, who had built a thriving practice on guiding racketeers such as Al Capone through the maze of the Chicago court system. It was whispered in the halls of the Federal Building that Nash managed to get his clients off with such frequency because he knew whom to bribe, and, when it came to jurors, whom to threaten. On this instance his preparations paid off, for no sooner did an assistant state's attorney named George Gorman announce the warrant for murder than the judge dismissed the case, explaining, "This complaint was made by Chief of Detectives Schoemaker on cursory information and belief. Subsequent investigation could not legally substantiate the information." After months of controversy, civic uproar, and the newspapers' determination to call him to account, Capone was a free man.

The swift decision vindicated Capone's delayed return to face questions and accusations concerning the murder of William McSwiggin; in fact, it proved to be a masterstroke, for the elusive racketeer had contrived to purchase the most precious commodity of all: time. In his absence tempers had cooled, and the continuing investigation into McSwiggin's career had turned up a great deal of suspicious behavior. So open were McSwiggin's alliances with various Irish bootleggers and men who could reasonably be called "gangsters"—alliances rooted in the neighborhood, going all the way back to their childhoods—that he was posthumously revealed to be a thoroughly sullied and compromised public servant who had at the very least placed himself repeatedly in harm's way. He was, in short, an accident waiting to happen. Only a remarkably foolish and reckless prosecutor would routinely gamble and carouse with bootleggers, as McSwiggin had. And if McSwiggin was flouting Prohibition, the law he had sworn to uphold, and not merely taking a nip in the privacy of his home but racing from one bar to the next all across Cicero and doing so in the company of some of the city's biggest bootleggers, and not merely drinking with them but accepting rides in their car and gambling with them, and telling his father about it, who, although a police sergeant, seemed to think nothing of such behavior—if McSwiggin was capable of such behavior, then what kind of prosecutor was he? More than that, what kind of *example* was he? As the public mulled over his behavior, it became apparent that Capone and McSwiggin were not on opposite sides of the law; they were, in fact, locked in an alliance—perhaps conspiracy is a more accurate description—*against* the law of the land. They were not at opposite ends of the moral scale; they were separated by only a few indistinct shades of gray. Each was using the other, and the public be damned. Ultimately, McSwiggin was using the law against itself. In light of these revelations, which had appeared throughout the summer of 1926, he was no longer the martyred public servant he had seemed that night in May when machine-gun bullets cut him down.

As Capone and his counsel left the courtroom, they passed Sergeant Anthony McSwiggin, a gaunt, tragic figure, there to bear witness for his slain son. After the man he believed to be his son's killer left, McSwiggin said bitterly, "They pinned a medal on him and turned him loose," and he went on to mutter, "They killed me, too, when they killed my boy."

The enmity between Capone and Anthony McSwiggin did not die in court that day. In a lonely, quixotic quest, the old policeman wandered the jails of Chicago, seeking to interview prisoners who might supply clues as to the identity of his son's murderer. Although none gave Capone's name, the elder McSwiggin went to the papers and claimed he now knew who had killed his boy, but he could not reveal the murderers' identity because the information was too dangerous for public consumption. Soon he reversed himself and said he could, after all, name the men who had killed William McSwiggin. The killers were Al Capone; two of his lieutenants, Frankie Rio and Frank Diamond; and a bootlegger by the name of Bob McCollough. Few heeded the words of a profoundly troubled old man, and Anthony McSwiggin's attempt to reopen the case came to nothing.

Not long afterward, the story of a new confrontation circulated through the newsrooms and speakeasies of Chicago; it told how the veteran police officer, incensed and obsessed, tracked down Capone in the lobby of the Hawthorne Hotel and shouted "Murderer!" to his face, at which point Capone produced a revolver and handed it to his dumbfounded accuser with these instructions: "If you think I did it, shoot me." But Anthony McSwiggin could not bring himself to pull the trigger at the crucial moment; he fled the lobby, and Al

Capone returned to a high-stakes poker game in progress in one of the rooms upstairs.

In the end, Capone was never fully exonerated in the death of McSwiggin, but the finger-pointing and the blame-shifting moved past him, to new targets, including the office of the prosecutor himself, Robert Crowe, who appeared too comfortable with racketeers to prosecute them. Crowe, after all, was McSwiggin's boss and had profited from the same unwholesome alliances in which McSwiggin had been entangled. The more prosecutors investigated the McSwiggin killing, the closer they came to indicting themselves. As the investigations droned on, all pretense of secrecy, of "closed-door" hearings evaporated, and the findings suggested the real culprits were not the racketeers but the entire city government of Chicago, now revealed as an entrenched bureaucracy far more interested in protecting itself and preserving its hard-won perquisites than in responding to public issues, needs, and concerns.

Ultimately, the real victim of the McSwiggin shooting was Chicago's established political order. William Dever, "Decent Dever," the reformist mayor, stood on the sidelines, wringing his hands, a picture of impotent indignation and self-righteousness. All his antigangster, Prohibition rhetoric remained just that. It was apparent that no city, county, or state agency was capable of launching an impartial investigation into McSwiggin's death or any other serious matter involving racketeers and bootleggers; the final recourse, a federal inquiry, did not as yet exist. From now on the situation would either get a lot worse or a lot better. Corruption would either become so far-reaching and so accepted, and men like Capone so powerful, that no one would waste the breath to challenge them, or the federal government would be compelled to step in, if only to preserve its own credibility in the face of the threat posed by gangsters run rampant. The question remained, however: of all the laws that Capone and other racketeers broke as they went about their business, what crime would finally lure the Feds into the fray?

•   •   •

All Chicago was aware of Capone's highly public campaign for vindication in the McSwiggin shooting. Meanwhile, he waged a secret war—a conflict as intense as any beer war battle in the streets of Chicago—in the outlying city of Chicago Heights. At the time, the town was a century old; originally known as Thorn Grove, and later Bloom, it finally became incorporated in 1892 as Chicago Heights. Italians began moving to the Heights in large numbers soon after, and by 1920 the city's population had risen to 20,000 and would double within a decade. They settled in a town of broad, straight streets lined with modest, single-story homes and two-story shops. The railroad cut a swath through the center of town, beneath an immense western sky. Although Italians found employment in the factories and onion fields of Chicago Heights, many never found a reliable path to self-advancement. A typical Chicago Heights factory, ran one account of the time, "was a place of heat, grime, dirt, dust, stench, harsh glares, overtime, piece work, pollution, no safety gadgets, sweat, etc. The workers were, as the Italians called them, 'Bestie da soma,' beasts of burden." Even their neighborhood was known as "Hungry Hill," a cruelly appropriate name.

The Battle of Chicago Heights seemed an extension of the brutality of life there; at the time it occurred few understood the reasons behind the bloodshed; indeed, it has never been fully understood until now. This was a fight for control of Chicago Heights, an area of ever increasing importance in the Capone organization. It was here, in this community where alcohol was brewed in so many Italian homes, that Capone faced opposition not from the usual enemies, the police and the Drucci-Moran-Weiss gang, but from other Italians. And it was here, in Chicago Heights, that Capone's associates implacably subdued the opposition of their countrymen. Three ambitious members of the Capone organization were chiefly responsible for the campaign. They were Dominic Roberto, who had sheltered Capone shortly before he fled to Michigan; Jimmy Emery; and Frankie La Porte.

The oldest of this ruthless trio was Jimmy Emery, who had been born Vincenzo Ammarati in Cosenza, Italy, on November 2, 1892. He did not reach the United States until he was twenty. Shortly after, he settled in Chicago Heights with his wife, Josie, with whom he had five children—four sons and a daughter—within a span of eight years. The Emerys lived at 2606 Chicago Road, and when he applied for naturalization in March 1922, Jimmy listed his occupation as "grocer." Even by this early date, perhaps before he had even heard of Al Capone, Jimmy Emery knew Frankie La Porte, who witnessed the petition for naturalization. On *his* petition, dating from May 1926, La Porte also declared he was a grocer and stated that he had been born in Sambiase, Italy, on October 7, 1901, arriving in the United States in 1913. His address in Chicago Heights during this period was 212 East 22nd Street, and he was not yet married, which was unusual for a man of his age. La Porte also witnessed Dominic Roberto's petition for naturalization, which was filed on January 1, 1921, and was eventually dismissed on account of the petitioner's "bad character." Thus La Porte and Roberto were acquaintances of long standing. Roberto had been born, like La Porte, in Sambiase, Italy, on January 15, 1896; he had arrived in Canada in 1913 and immediately entered the United States. He lived at 2415 Chicago Road in Chicago Heights, close to Jimmy Emery's home, and like his two colleagues listed his occupation as "grocer."

Roberto claimed he was single when he applied to become an American citizen, but there was a good deal of wishful thinking in that statement.

Before he arrived in the United States he had indeed married, and his wife
still resided in his hometown of Sambiase. When he emigrated to the United
States, she became a "grass widow," the name given to the wives who were
left behind when their husbands emigrated to America. Like many of these
wandering husbands, Roberto later took another wife in the New World, the
singer Rio Burke. They met in Chicago Heights, where she was performing.
Fleeing his advances, she returned home to Kentucky, but he chased her all
the way there, enlisted the support of her family, and in the end his suit
was successful. They were married on April 14, 1924, in the home of a
Methodist minister in Jeffersonville, Indiana, a small town on the Ohio
River, not far from Louisville, Kentucky. Because of the improvised nature
of the marriage and the absence of a priest, Dominic Roberto regarded his
union to Rio as something less than binding. Jaunty, well dressed, charming,
and generous, "Dom" continued to maintain his Italian wife throughout his
marriage to Rio. Even as he lavished presents, including a grand piano, on
Rio, he funneled money to his Italian wife in Sambiase, keeping both women
happy. "Dominic made a good husband," Rio says. "He had a soft heart."
Roberto's double life was an open secret among Italians in Chicago Heights,
though Rio, who was not Italian and therefore an outsider, did not learn of
it until years later.

During her years as Roberto's American wife, Rio became accustomed to
having Capone as a frequent guest in their house. She remembers his constant concern over Sonny's health, which remained precarious, although by
"health" Capone probably meant personal safety. "Of course Al bought him
every toy under the shining sun," Rio says. "He didn't have one bicycle, he
had four or five. He didn't have one train, he had four or five. He would play
with them awhile and then tire of them. Then Al would get a pickup truck
and bring all the stuff out to Jimmy Emery's house." Observing Capone's
lieutenants at close quarters, she became aware that Jimmy Emery was not
the smiling paterfamilias he appeared to be. If Dominic had a soft heart,
"Jimmy had one like stone. He had a mean streak, a real mean streak. He
would call Josephine, his wife, in the middle of the night, one or two o'clock
in the morning, and say, 'Get up, Josie, and cook for six, cook for eight.' And
she had to get up and cook a big meal. Of course, Al Capone would often
be among them. One night Jimmy caught her putting butter in something,
and he didn't like butter. I saw him pick up one of these great big glass
cigarette holders and throw it at her; it cut her mouth open. She was in bed
a couple of weeks. And I've seen him bat her around. He had an ungodly
temper."

Although Rio appeared to be a compliant racketeer's wife, she nearly
became the undoing of the men who ruled Chicago Heights. "While we
lived in Chicago Heights," she recalls, "Jimmy was grooming Frankie La

Porte to take his place in the organization. And Frankie was somewhere near my age—very young and very handsome. We practically took La Porte into the family; he was there most of the time. Now, after I married Dominic, I could never go anywhere alone. Italian men are very possessive and watchful of what the wife does, you know, and of course I was considered a very beautiful girl, I had opportunities, so I wasn't ever allowed out by myself. Frankie had to take me. Every time I went to the doctor to take care of a little lung trouble, Frankie took me. Every time I went shopping downtown, Frankie took me. We were thrown together almost daily, and after a while, it got a little sticky. But we were both smart enough to know the consequences if we were to let it go on, so we cooled it. I didn't want to get stabbed in the back when I was making love." So far as Rio could tell, neither Dominic nor Jimmy Emery was ever aware of the romance taking root in their midst.

For four years, Dominic Roberto managed to have it all, a career as an important racketeer and two wives, but his career and his American marriage began to unravel in 1928, when he was indicted for violating the Volstead Act. Shortly after, he "divorced" Rio and went into hiding, only to surface in 1931, when the case against him was dropped. Applying for a passport, he claimed he had never been married, which landed him in trouble with authorities again. His luck had finally run out. He did a stretch in Leavenworth federal penitentiary, where his ex-"wife" faithfully visited him, but if she hoped to win him back, she was to be disappointed, for soon after his release in 1933 he was deported to Italy. On his last night in Chicago, the city where he had made his fortune, he took Rio to dinner and gave her a good-bye present of $1,000; then he sailed for Europe, and she never saw him again, though he continued to be ever present in her thoughts. Disgraced but wealthy, he returned to Sambiase and his Italian wife. Whereupon, Rio notes, "I became the grass widow."

·   ·   ·

Such was the background and precarious social status of the three men responsible for directing the Battle of Chicago Heights. Since Capone spent the summer of 1926 among Italians who were nearly all former residents of Chicago Heights, his ties to that community became stronger than ever, and he was determined to annex this area to his empire. And yet, despite its large Calabrian population, the Chicago Heights rackets were controlled by a group of old-fashioned Sicilian gangsters grown complacent with age. Their leader was Tony Sanfilippo; the spelling varies depending on where his name appears—in a newspaper, a police blotter, or a federal file. He was assisted by Joseph Martino. Sanfilippo, who had emigrated to the United States from Palermo, Sicily, had served briefly as an alderman from the Third Ward, been a member of the local draft board during the Great War, and now worked as a druggist; Martino managed a poolroom. However, what these men actually did for a living was to shake down Chicago Heights' numerous alky-cookers, demanding tribute on pain of death, and there were more than enough shootings in the Heights to lend credence to their threats. In return, the Sicilians promised to provide the still owners with protection, but that meant bribing the police, and the Sicilians preferred to keep all the money they extorted. As a result, the poor alky-cookers of Chicago Heights found themselves subject to both extortion *and* arrest.

This was the situation in Chicago Heights when Emery, Roberto, and La Porte arrived. They promised the alky-cookers and Italians of Chicago Heights a better deal: little or no tribute, and guaranteed protection from the police. In exchange, they dealt solely with the Capone organization. Once the battle lines were drawn, the confrontation between the Capone organization and the Sicilians turned lethal. The front page of the local newspaper, the *Chicago Heights Star,* carried terrifying accounts of the deaths of Sicilians, but no one perceived the method to the madness; no one understood who was ordering the killing of the Sicilian racketeers and why. No one realized that, ultimately, Al Capone, acting through his three lieutenants, was responsible for the rash of mysterious deaths in Chicago Heights.

Tony Sanfilippo, the local Sicilian boss of the rackets, became their first victim. On April 3, 1924, he was found dead in his car, a Jordan brougham, parked on 17th Street. It was early in the evening, and the lights were on, the motor idling. According to police, Sanfilippo had been "shot four times in the head, the bullets entering from behind. All of them went through the skull. The hair and skin were powder burned, showing that the revolver, a .38, had been held near the head when the shots were fired." His pockets contained $446 in cash, a check for $1,000, and a loaded .38 revolver. He was forty-six years old and left a wife and three small children: the most respected blackmailer in Chicago Heights. The police could not say precisely why Sanfilippo had been murdered, although the local press speculated that he might have been dealing in drugs, and no one outside the Italian community realized Roberto, La Porte, and Emery had ordered the murder and that Al Capone had sanctioned it.

With the departure of Sanfilippo, another Sicilian, Phil Piazza, took over the leadership of the Chicago Heights rackets. Beginning in 1926, the Piazza gang found itself the target of assassination attempts from unseen enemies. On June 2, 1926, while Capone languished in Lansing, Jim Lamberta, a member of the Piazza gang, was shot to death. He had been going from party to party that night in Chicago Heights, accompanied by two women married to other men. One of the women was shot dead, the other seriously wounded, and their involvement with these gangsters became the focus of concern.

Again, no one suspected the involvement of Emery, Roberto, and La Porte, let alone Al Capone, in this bizarre incident, but it was generally recognized that the assault had been badly botched. The intended victim, Phil Piazza, the big boss himself, had been present but unharmed by the bullets. About seven weeks later, on July 23, the *Chicago Heights Star* carried a headline many had expected: "PHILIP PIAZZA IS MURDERED IN MAFIA MANNER. Shot Dead Outside Cafe on Lowe Avenue—Assassins Escape—WAS A POWERFUL BOSS." Once again, no one could say who had pronounced the death sentence on the Chicago Heights racketeers. "All over Cook County Philip Piazza's power was well known. . . . He had a very good appearance and had a manner which made him many friends. He was said to be worth $200,000," noted the *Star* in a tone of regret more appropriate to the passing of a wealthy mainstay of the community than a gangland execution. Of all the deaths plotted by the Emery faction, this was the most crucial in establishing their dominance in Chicago. With Piazza out of the way, they now moved quickly. Just ten days later, on August 3, the *Star* headlined: "SHOT GUN SLUG BARRAGE DROPS YOUNG SICILIAN—Murderers Fire from Passing Auto on Fourteenth Street—Murder Unexpected?" The murder was definitely *not* unexpected, for the victim was another Sicilian, twenty-three-year-old Joe Salva, the nephew of the late Jim Lamberta. Once again, four shots felled him. Once again, no one knew who was responsible for the killing. And once again, Capone's lieutenants had eliminated another rival for control of the Chicago Heights rackets without being caught, without even incurring suspicion. They were waging the gangland equivalent of guerrilla warfare.

For all its mounting ferocity, the Battle of Chicago Heights attracted little attention in Chicago itself. Though both cities were in Cook County, the Heights lay an hour-and-a-half drive distant from its larger namesake. Since the victims (with the exception of the two women) were all known to be racketeers, the authorities were notably lax in their efforts to determine who was responsible for the deaths. The coroner's jury investigating the death of Phil Piazza, for instance, decided that he had been killed by a bullet and left matters at that. No one was charged with the crime, let alone convicted; the *Star's* headline concluded: "Murder . . . Fades Into Unsolved Darkness." Of the old guard, only Joseph Martino was still alive, and the Capone organization would eventually catch up with him as well.

Within several weeks of his return from Lansing, Al Capone, with the blessing of La Porte, Roberto, and Emery, assumed control of the Chicago Heights rackets, whose gambling dens, stills, and speakeasies became his to enjoy and exploit. Once again, Al Capone had demonstrated that he was the law. He was also the town's major employer of Italians, for alky-cooking drew on many different skills. There were farmers to supply grapes, grocers to supply sugar needed for fermentation, plumbers to construct and repair stills, and truck drivers to handle deliveries. According to Dominic Candeloro, a historian of the region, "Even grandmothers and favorite aunts got into the act, making a little moonshine for a niece's wedding or for a little extra money to pay for piano lessons."

Triumphant, Jimmy Emery, Dominic Roberto, and Frankie La Porte established their headquarters at the Monroe Hotel, at Seventeenth Street and East End Avenue. Now that the bloodshed was over, Capone visited almost every week, usually on a Sunday, to participate in a traditional Italian picnic with his men. This was an elaborate affair requiring several days' preparation. On the day of the picnic, the odor of meat sizzling on an open-air grill wafted across the outskirts of town. Neither Capone nor any of his men attended Mass, but their wives did, and when it was over everyone including bodyguards and children gathered for the feast. To demonstrate his solidarity with his Chicago Heights comrades, Capone boldly posed for pictures with them all. In one particularly revealing shot, he sits on the grass at the center of his inner circle, seeming to dominate them all with his bulk and expansive manner. He has removed his jacket, and his tie is coming undone. With revealing body language, Capone extends his right arm toward Frankie La Porte, who stares intently at the camera, while Vera Emery, who is Jimmy's daughter and Capone's goddaughter, snuggles with her dog between the two racketeers; to their left, Emery himself reclines on the grass, a faint smile playing about his lips. (Vera Emery's life would not be as secure as it seemed on this sunny afternoon. Years later, her husband's head would be blown off as he sat in his living room, reading a newspaper: one more reason why racketeers *always* took care to keep their curtains closed.) Behind the group stands a phalanx of five formidable bodyguards including Louis "Little New York" Campagna and "Fur" Sammons. Another picnic photograph, this one without Capone, reveals an impressive lineup of his "soldiers," including La Porte, Roberts, and Emery, and in the middle, given pride of place, "Machine Gun" Jack McGurn. There is a sense of finality about this picture, as if these men were soldiers pausing to commemorate their recent victory.

As these photographic records suggest, Capone was now the city's leading figure, and he won the loyalty and admiration of the Italians living there with a combination of intimidation and extravagant gestures the likes of which had never been seen in Chicago Heights. He contributed heavily to the local church, Saint Rocco, located at 315 East Twenty-second Street, on Hungry Hill. He rode through the main streets of the little city, throwing silver dollars from the window of his Cadillac. The coins flashed in the sunlight, and as they struck the sidewalk with a satisfying metallic clunk, young boys set upon them and brought them home to their grateful mothers. The carelessly distributed cash filled many hungry mouths and earned considerable loyalty for Capone. Neither Philip Piazza nor any of the other Sicilian blackmailers had done that, or anything like it, and compared to their brutal regimen Capone seemed a benefactor, a Robin Hood, especially to the boys in the Heights. Among them was John Pegoria, who later became a newspaper photographer for the *Chicago Sun*. Born and raised in Chicago Heights, he went to school with the sons of the owner of a local tavern called the Milano Café, formerly the headquarters of the Piazza gang before Capone wiped them out. "I was in the saloon," Pegoria recalls of a day in 1926, "and Mr. Capone came in there, and he got a root beer for me. He seemed like a very nice, affable fellow. He never bothered anybody unless you bothered him." Pegoria later saw him again at a wedding in the Heights. "There was a custom at Italian weddings to have chairs arranged all around the dance floor, and older people would sit on those chairs and watch the others dance while they served cookies, nuts, and so on. When Capone came, he had a handful of money, and he passed out bills to the old ladies who were sitting around."

Another Chicago Heights boy, Sam Pontarelli,* became almost a second son to Capone. "Al came to the Heights two or three times a month, usually on Saturday or Sunday," he remembers. "He would have dinner, then play cards and dice with the boys. He was the world's worst gambler. An uncle of mine beat him out of $20,000, and he picked up a whole stack of $100 bills and threw them at Capone, telling him, 'You've got no business playing this game!' At the horse track, Lincoln Fields, in the Heights, Capone was also a lousy bettor. He placed three bets on each horse, to win, place, and show." Pontarelli, too, profited from his association with Capone. "When my cousin was baptized, Al gave me a $1,000 bill, and I was just a kid." By conventional measures, that money would be worth more than ten times as much today. But to the boys who came from poor immigrant families struggling to survive in the Heights, the real value of the dollars that Capone capriciously bestowed on them was incalculable.

· · ·

Now that it belonged to him, Chicago Heights served as Capone's principal refuge from Chicago itself, yet few realized he had anything to do with the Heights except for the small circle of Italian colleagues stationed there. The city afforded him a useful hideout, for it was closer than Lansing, Michigan, and populated with loyal, protective Italians who revered Capone and guarded his welfare as if their lives depended on it, which they did. And yet this prize further complicated his life. It was no longer possible for him to quit the rackets, to walk away from gangland—not as long as he lived in

* A pseudonym.

Chicago and controlled the Heights. Even if he changed, Chicago would not change. Since the beginning of the year, the beer war had claimed the lives of more than a hundred men, and dozens more had fallen on the streets of Chicago Heights. The greater Chicago region was in a state of siege, an even more violent place now than when he had left, and if he wanted to stay alive, the chaotic situation compelled him to respond in kind. As he knew, his worst enemies were not the police, who could be controlled with bribes, but other gangsters, who were as eager as ever to see him dead.

Capone had returned to Chicago intending to attain respectability at any cost. He had already skillfully rebutted the charge of murdering McSwiggin. Now he faced a far more difficult challenge: to return the rackets to the stability of Johnny Torrio's era, when men sat down to settle their disputes at the table rather than murdering one another on the streets of Chicago. If Capone could meet this goal, he would be able to achieve his goal and retire from the rackets, perhaps as soon as the end of the year. He envisioned spending Christmas at home on Prairie Avenue with his wife and child, a wealthy former bootlegger. But he was temperamentally ill-suited to this daydream, too gregarious to spend the rest of his days sitting in dark back rooms, wheeling and dealing, overseeing payoffs, and pulling strings. He needed to be in the limelight himself, making the speeches, pressing the flesh, seizing the initiative.

On August 10, he dispatched one of his gunmen, Louis Barko, to harass two of his three principal rivals, "Hymie" Weiss and "Schemer" Drucci, who had prospered in Chicago during the months Capone had hidden in Lansing. Barko caught up with his prey shortly after nine o'clock in the morning as the men were on their way to a meeting with Morris Eller, a ward boss with ties to the city's Sanitation Department, and John Sbarbaro, the gangland undertaker who doubled as an assistant state's attorney. Drucci was carrying $13,200 to be used as payoff money. As they approached the Standard Oil Building, where the meeting was to occur, Barko and three other men drew their pistols and launched their assault.

Bullets flew. Pedestrians on their way to work scattered. A police car arrived. More bullets. Weiss ran into the building, and Drucci tried to escape by jumping onto the running board of a moving automobile. The police apprehended both Drucci and Barko, took them down to the station house, and grilled them. Since this was Chicago, the potentially deadly shootout metamorphosed into a farce. The suspects, who were well known to the police, supplied bogus names and addresses to the befuddled chief of detectives, William "Shoes" Schoemaker. True to the gangsters' code of honor, Drucci insisted that he had never before seen the man who had fired on him. On second thought, Drucci admitted, maybe he *had* seen him, but in any event, there hadn't been a shootout, just a few stray bullets, and he had no idea why they had been fired. Perhaps the other fellow was after Drucci's money. Yes, Drucci insisted, he had been the unfortunate victim of a routine holdup. He didn't know anything about gangs, and neither did the other fellow. "Shoes" rubbed his jaw in dismay, and the men were set free.

Through Barko, Capone had sent a message to Drucci and Weiss that he was back in town, as ferocious as ever, and they conveyed their reply in spectacular fashion. Six weeks later, on September 20, Capone was eating lunch at the Hawthorne Inn with Frankie Rio, one of the bodyguards suspected of killing McSwiggin. They sat, according to custom, with their backs against the wall, at the end of a line of fifteen white, tile-covered tables, at the rear of the restaurant. It was a lovely fall afternoon, the trees beginning to show their fall colors, a sense of excitement in the crisp air, for this was the day of the fall meet at the Hawthorne Race Track. From across the length and breadth of the land bootleggers had sent their best horses to Capone's monument to the sporting life, and their massed silks made a brilliant display. Capone was looking forward to spending the afternoon at the track, occupying his seat of honor, presiding over the festivities. That would come a little later, at 2:30 P.M. The hands of the clock over the cash register seemed to pause forever at 1:15 P.M. Passing the time, Al lifted a coffee cup to his lips, but before the liquid reached his mouth, he suddenly plunked the coffee cup down on the saucer. He had heard something out of the ordinary, something deadly.

Everything happened at once: sixty patrons shrieking, Capone sliding under the table, Rio waving his gun and standing, his gaze riveted on the double doors leading from the restaurant to the street. The sound grew louder, until it became recognizable as the lethal drumming of machine-gun fire approaching along the broad expanse of Twenty-second Street from the west. The waiters fled the restaurant, and the other patrons—gangsters, businessmen dawdling over lunch, mothers with their children—screamed, and those with the most presence of mind joined Capone on the floor, beneath the tables. Then the sound, which had been growing louder, abruptly disappeared. The car from which the bullets had been fired sped up and disappeared. Silence reigned. Strangely enough, nothing had been broken, despite the unmistakable chatter of machine-gun bullets.

The patrons began to stir, though no one ventured to stand, except for Capone, who realized that his attackers, whoever they were, had fired blanks. Of course. No one, not even a gangster, would fire into a crowd of innocent bystanders with a machine gun. Determined to show that he had not been intimidated, Capone got to his feet and began marching toward the doors, but his progress was halted by a human form flying through the air at him and wrestling him to the ground. Before he had time to react, Capone was pinned to the ground; his assailant was Frankie Rio, who was only doing his job. "It's a stall, boss," Rio said, gulping for air. "The real stuff hasn't started. You stay down." Capone looked at him, blinked, and relented. Down he stayed, waiting for the next development.

Half a minute later, a convoy of seven closely spaced cars rolled past the U-shaped façade of the Hawthorne Inn. As they drew even with the hotel, machine guns concealed within the cars began to fire on the restaurant containing Capone, his lips pressed to the floor. This time they were firing real bullets, which drilled a deadly design into the hotel's façade. The lead car came to a halt at the far end of the Hawthorne, and five more behind it appeared to park in front of the hotel, one after the other, without a gap, and from every car came a stream of machine fire aimed at the Hawthorne and its neighbor, the Anton Hotel. Then two more cars pulled up, and during a brief lull in the firing, a man whom witnesses later described as wearing brown overalls and a khaki shirt emerged from the second-to-last car and walked to the main doorway of the Hawthorne, carrying a machine gun in his right hand. He knelt and started firing continuously, reloading when necessary, raking the exterior and interior with hundreds of .45-caliber bullets in orderly rows about the height of a man's heart. When he was finished, he stood and walked back to the car. The car blew its horn three times, and the convoy rolled down the street and out of view.

The marauders had fired more than a thousand shots at the two Capone-controlled hotels, destroying every single pane of glass, reducing doors and other wooden fittings to splinters, chiseling grotesque shapes into bricks and mortar. Despite the ferocity of the attack, not one person had been killed, including the intended victim: Al Capone. There were several injuries, however. Clyde Freeman, his wife, and their five-year-old son, Clyde Jr., all of whom had come from Louisiana to see the races, were trapped in their car parked near the Hawthorne when the attack began. When the smoke cleared, Mr. Freeman discovered a bullet hole in his hat and another in his son's coat. More seriously, one bullet had grazed his son's knee, another had entered his wife's arm, and a shard of glass from the shattered windshield had landed in her right eye. Capone rushed to the Freemans' car, which was pockmarked with bullets from one end to the other, and when he discovered what had happened, he offered—no, *insisted*—that he pay all their expenses. He did, and they eventually came to $10,000.

The other victim was none other than Louis Barko, the Capone gunman who had opened fire on Drucci and Weiss the month before. He took a bullet in the shoulder, a wound that brought him to the attention of the chief of detectives, William Schoemaker, who once again uttered oaths and subjected Barko to a prolonged grilling, along with Weiss, Drucci, and "Bugs" Moran. Once again, all that Barko would say was, "Never saw them before." The police dropped their investigation of the incident, even though a thousand bullets had been fired in Cicero in the middle of the day. Had "Shoes" and his embattled and corrupt police department bothered to jail any of these men, the next bloody episode in the history of Chicago's gang war would never have occurred. In the absence of such measures, Capone demonstrated once again his flair in settling scores with his enemies, especially the man who had dared to humiliate him as "Hymie" Weiss had that brilliant fall afternoon in Cicero.

Before Capone struck, he decided to give Weiss one last chance to live. In the spirit of his resolve to quit the rackets, he invited Weiss to a meeting at the Morrison Hotel on Monday, October 4. Capone hoped to lure Weiss into a business alliance, thereby ending their lethal rivalry. Determining that his own presence was too inflammatory, Capone selected Tony Lombardo, the current boss of Chicago's Unione Sicilione, to negotiate on his behalf. "Capone is very anxious for peace," Lombardo was reported to have said at the meeting. "Few men will be left alive on either side if this fighting keeps up. Both you and Capone are under thirty. There is no reason why either of you should die. All this killing is insane. There's plenty of business for both." Lombardo then presented Capone's deal: in exchange for peace Weiss would manage all the beer concessions in Chicago north of Madison Street. This was an extravagant offer, for Madison cut through the heart of the Loop, and the territory comprised thousands of speakeasies. It was the equivalent of handing Weiss, murdering son of a bitch though he was, an exceedingly lucrative distributorship. Such was the price Capone was willing to pay for peace—and his life.

Weiss angrily refused the offer. "He's a snake," he said of Capone. "His favorite stunt is to smile in your face and kill you. There's more in this thing than business. Capone hasn't paid yet for O'Banion's murder."

"That was two years ago," Lombardo replied. "You fellows have done your share of killing."

"Capone will have to prove to me he means peace," said Weiss.

"He'll give you any proof in his power."

"Scalise and Anselmi killed O'Banion," Weiss noted. "Tell Capone to put Scalise and Anselmi on the spot. That's the price of peace."

Lombardo excused himself from the meeting and called Al to tell him of the condition. How should he reply to Weiss?

"I wouldn't do that to a yellow dog!" Capone shouted.

Lombardo relayed that message to Weiss, who stormed out of the meeting, and the effort to arrange peace between the warring factions fell into disarray. With the failure of these negotiations, it was only a matter of time until Capone reacted to the humiliation Weiss had inflicted on him. Either he would have to kill Weiss, or Weiss would surely kill him. So the nightmare of blood and terror returned, raising the possibility once more that he would soon be laid to rest beside his brother Frank in the Capone family plot in Mt. Carmel Cemetery.

* * *

The following day, October 5, a man calling himself Oscar Lundin rented a second-story room at 740 North Street for $8 a week. The location happened to be across the street from Schofield's flower shop—the same shop in which Dion O'Banion had been assassinated two years earlier, and which continued to serve as the headquarters for his successors, "Schemer" Drucci, "Bugs" Moran, and "Hymie" Weiss. The room Lundin rented afforded an unobstructed view of this shop; in fact, it made for an ideal machine-gun nest, and throughout the following week its constantly changing occupants staked out the site. Finally, on the afternoon of Monday, October 11, a Cadillac bearing Weiss himself came into view, gliding to a stop across the street from Schofield's flower store.

Two men observed Weiss from their vantage point in the second-story apartment at 740 North State Street. The floor was littered with their cigarette butts, but when they saw his car pull up, they put down their cigarettes and picked up their tommy guns. They watched carefully, for, if they were lucky, they would be able to pick off not only Weiss but also his four companions: W. W. O'Brien, a criminal lawyer; Benjamin Jacobs, a corrupt politician; Patrick Murray, a bootlegger; and Sam Peller, their chauffeur.

Weiss waited until a Buick arrived; he then left his Cadillac and began to cross the street, apparently in a state of excitement. He was in the midst of a complicated transaction, having just left the Criminal Courts Building, where he had just obtained a list of the jurors selected for the trial of "Polack Joe" Saltis, a South Side racketeer charged with murder; Weiss intended to bribe or threaten the jurors. Meanwhile, the assassins hidden in the second-story apartment lifted their machine guns to the window, and as Weiss jumped across the trolley tracks in the middle of the street, they opened fire. Within seconds the gunmen killed Murray and wounded Jacobs, O'Brien, and Peller. As for Weiss himself, he fell dead on the sidewalk with ten bullets in his body. He was twenty-eight years old, middle age for a racketeer.

Holy Name Cathedral stood as a silent witness to the shootout, and it bore the scars. Before the bullets flew, the cornerstone was inscribed with a quotation from St. Paul's Epistle to the Philippians:

> At The Name Of Jesus Every Knee Should Bow
> In Heaven And On
> Earth.

Afterward, the inscription read:

Every Knee Should
In Heaven And On
Earth.

For years the cathedral did not repair the damage, preferring to leave it as a monument to Chicago's violence, of the day when, in the words of the *Tribune*, "Gangdom literally shot piety to pieces."

Weiss received a predictably lavish gangster funeral. The undertaker who organized his last rites was John Sbarbaro, who had so ably touched up the bullet-ridden corpses of other gangsters. The casket was bronze with silver fittings, and the body was laid to rest at Mt. Carmel Cemetery, final resting place of both gangsters and their victims. Capone was not brazen enough to attend the funeral, but Moran and Drucci were there to mourn their slain comrade in arms, wondering whose funeral they would attend next: Capone's, each other's, or their own. Since it was late October and election day was fast approaching, a number of the politicians who turned out to pay their respects to the city's second-biggest bootlegger rode in cars festooned with garish campaign posters, transforming the funeral into a campaign rally. Speeding toward the cemetery, automobiles in the cortege proclaimed their urgent messages:

KING-ELLER-GRAYDON FOR SANITARY DISTRICT TRUSTEES
JOE SAVAGE FOR COUNTY JUDGE
JOHN SBARBARO FOR MUNICIPAL JUDGE

In the Chicago of the late 1920s, politics and funerals, especially gangster funerals, increasingly had a way of overlapping, the distinction between them growing ever more faint with every new murder.

Although every indication pointed to Capone as the man who had planned Weiss's death, the killers were never found, their identities never discovered, despite an intriguing array of evidence they left behind. Detectives investigating the murder found one of the tommy guns used in the shootout only a block from the scene of the crime. In the second-story room rented by "Oscar Lundin" they discovered depleted shotgun shells strewn across the floor. There was even a gray fedora on the bed; within, the label was that of a Cicero merchant whose store was located close to the Hawthorne Inn. Despite these and other clues, as well as dozens of potential eyewitnesses to the shooting, the police failed to arrest or charge anyone with the murder. Instead, the chief of police, Morgan Collins, substituted rhetoric for action, announcing that he held Capone personally responsible for the latest slaughter in the streets of the city. "Capone played safety first by importing the killers, expert machine gunners, and then hurrying them out of town,"

Collins explained. Furthermore, Collins admitted, "Capone has an alibi. He was in Cicero when the shooting occurred. If we bring him in it will be because we have the goods on him cold, but there is no use putting him on the grill until we do." A reporter commented, "The Chicago Police Department surrendered to Capone—unconditionally."

This time Capone had no need to flee. Instead, he held a press conference. "I'm sorry Weiss was killed," he declared, concealing his glee, "but I didn't have anything to do with it. I telephoned the detective bureau I would come in if they wanted me to, but they told me they didn't want me. I knew I would be blamed for it, but why should I kill Weiss?" Unlike the McSwiggin killing, the police and prosecutor's office did not even attempt to question Capone about the assassination of Weiss, let alone try him for it, although they suspected he had engineered it. But then, McSwiggin had been one of their own, and Weiss was but another hoodlum. In a sense, Capone had done the police a favor by eliminating him.

Capone's confident handling of the situation reflected his increasing sophistication in fending off murder inquiries. Walter Trohan, a reporter covering the police beat for the City News Bureau, a press pool that served as a training ground for many of Chicago's best-known journalists of the era, recalls Capone's techniques for dealing with Chicago's law enforcement agencies, techniques more reminiscent of a powerful politician than a gangster: "If there was a gang killing, the police used to bring in Capone just for questioning and to look him over. . . . At the time the court was located above the South State Street police station. One morning, as I went up these wide steps leading into the court, where Capone was, two fellows frisked me. I became highly indignant. I went downstairs to complain to the captain of the police station. They were largely Irish in that police station, and since I was a Notre Damer I was a hero there, and all the people were generally very kind to me. The captain looked at me and said, 'Those aren't my men, those are *Capone's*.' "

•   •   •

Meanwhile, the murder of "Hymie" Weiss occasioned the city's worst crisis of conscience since McSwiggin's death six months earlier, and it revived talk everywhere of Chicago as the nation's murder capital, a city ruled by machine-gun-wielding gangsters whom the police were powerless to control. According to one account, during the previous four years 215 gangsters had killed one another, and the police had taken the lives of an additional 160 booze-runners and racketeers. Throughout the city, cries of revulsion at all the killing went up. Chicago, declared the *Literary Digest*, "is sick today with poison, . . . at least from the political and governmental point of view, as any drunkard poisoned in the liver, kidneys and heart by alcohol itself," and the publication summed up the situation in Chicago as "murder galore and crime unpunished." This was a sentiment widely shared across the nation, and the coverage was even more shrill than it had been in the past, if that were possible, the tone more frantic, more desperate, as the papers realized that Chicago's law enforcement agencies really were powerless to intervene in the gang wars; no amount of prodding in the press or bloodshed on the streets could inspire the police or even the state attorney general's office to take action. There was a great deal of talk about what the killings would do to Chicago's "image," a word used even then, and that concern became the dominant theme of public discourse—not safety, not corruption—no, the issue of the day ran along the lines of, "Good heavens, what must other people *think* of us, carrying on as we do with machine guns and such? People must be made to realize that Chicago is filled as it has always been with decent, God-fearing citizens, and these hoodlums are only a tiny minority, an *aberration*."

Amid the clamor few thought to examine the underlying cause of the violence and corruption: Prohibition. The corruption and hypocrisies created by the unenforceable law had become an integral part of the city's economic and political life. The police enriched themselves from the graft, and even the newspapers, so quick to vilify gangsters, were often in secret sympathy with them, as this reminiscence by a crime reporter for the *Chicago Tribune*, James Doherty, reveals: "The *Trib* was a wet paper and its staff were wet too—we were a hard-drinking, hard-working bunch, and we were against Prohibition because of the methods of enforcement." Competition among Chicago dailies was intense, and as a result, Doherty noted, "Crime was important news then and we used to give it full coverage. . . . I spent a lot of time with the mob and saw Capone often. I can't say I especially liked the guy, but he was always nice enough to me. I wrote hundreds of stories about him. I'd accuse him of murder today and meet him tomorrow, and neither of us would mention the subject. I'd see him at a funeral, or in a speakeasy, or down at the DA's office, and he'd always give me some quotes. He wasn't very good company, not a very articulate guy. He'd exchange commonplaces but he didn't volunteer information. Still, the more I wrote about him, the more he liked it. He loved the limelight and was always willing to yak a little with reporters. He liked the advertising. It made better business for him. It made it easier to intimidate the customers. We built him up as the big shot in the gang world. They were all racketeers and they liked to be known as good ones—like the politicians used to say: 'Just spell my name right and say what you like.' I can't feel he was all evil, like he's been painted since then. Sure, he was a cold-blooded killer, but he had his good side. I see him as a victim of his time and circumstances. Capone was tolerated by the public because—let's face it—he was giving them a service they wanted. No one minded about them trading booze; it was all the killing that brought about their undoing." So the reporters wrote their stories condemning violence, then went to their speakeasies to drink their bootleg booze to forget about it, while their bosses, the newspaper owners, went home at night and uncorked choice vintages from their wine cellars, and they, too, forgot all about it—until the morning brought news of fresh carnage during another night ruled by the unenforceable law.

The frantic tone of the newspaper coverage of the killings and violence obscured many of the reasons behind it. Strangely, no one had as yet paused to analyze the overall structure of Chicago's gangs and their battles with each other, but if they had, they would have discovered that the assassination attempts were not as random or arbitrary as they seemed; they in fact were highly predictable. They were often preceded by threats and warnings (if anyone had cared to pay attention), and they were all accomplished for specific reasons—usually revenge. The skein always went back to the killing of Dion O'Banion, and the subsequent competition between his successors, the Moran gang and the Capone organization. Nearly every major shootout contributed to the vendetta between these two groups. These were hardly the only gangs in Chicago, but they were so large and influential and had formed so many alliances with smaller gangs and bootleggers that the Capone-Moran rivalry defined the racketeering environment in Chicago and throughout much of the country. With every murder this pattern became clearer, and it was obvious to everyone that the killing would beget more killing. The pattern told a tale of greed and revenge; it was only a matter of time until the vendetta led to a massacre.

Even Capone could not resist adding his voice to the debate over Chicago's gangster problem. He seized on the mounting public hysteria to portray himself as the city's savior rather than its scourge. For the first time he was attempting to carry out at least some of the decisions he had reached over the summer in Lansing; perhaps he even thought he could be hailed as the savior of Chicago, as certain citizens in Lansing were prone to think of him. Although he was unwilling to give up his massive, lucrative bootlegging empire, he delivered a grandiloquent, emotional plea to other bootleggers to give up their violent ways (and incidentally to let him run the industry untroubled by competition). With the skill of a politician carefully gauging the symbolic value of his surroundings, Capone chose to hold his press conference not in his lavish suite at the Metropole, where his words would seem self-serving and hypocritical. Instead, he returned to a far less opulent setting, his former base in Cicero's Hawthorne Hotel, where he would seem more the victim than the perpetrator, for only weeks earlier he had been the intended victim of the spectacular drive-by shooting, from which hundreds of holes drilled by machine-gun bullets were still plainly visible. Even there he took care to meet the gentlemen of the press in a small, shabby room furnished with only a bed, a dresser, and several chairs, "the one object indicative of the man who is reported to have made more than two million dollars in the booze game," a reporter noted, "being a magnificent diamond brooch tie-pin with a four-carat amethyst in its center."

"There is enough business for all of us without killing each other like animals in the streets," he said. "I don't want to die in the street punctured by machine-gun fire." As he spoke, Capone clutched a photograph of his son, now seven years old, and insisted that he wanted only to make the city a safe and decent place for the child whom he loved beyond all else. "They all got families, too," he said of his rivals. "What makes them so crazy to end up on a slab in a morgue with their mothers' hearts broken over the way they died? If anyone will get those fellows together—what's left of the North Side gang—and anyone else that thinks they're bucking me in business will take their guns away and sit them down to listen to me I'll make peace with all of them. I'll tell them why I want peace—because I don't want to break the hearts of people that love me—and maybe I can make them think of their mothers and sisters, and if they think of them they'll put up their guns and treat their business like any man treats his—as something to work at and forget when he goes home at night. . . . I talked to 'Hymie' Weiss and the others, saying, 'What do you want to do, die before you're thirty? I don't.' We started over. We kept our bargain, but they broke theirs. I sent word to those fellows to stop while some of us were left alive. They wouldn't listen. A couple of weeks after that eleven cars drove past this hotel at noon and gave us a machine-gun fire that made this street look like a battlefield." The oratory revealed Capone's growing confidence that he could, after all, control the entire city and turn it into a bootlegger's paradise.

On October 20, nine days after Weiss's death, he arranged an extraordinary "peace conference" between the two opposing factions. This was no secret underworld convocation held in a smoke-filled basement; it was, rather, a well-publicized meeting scheduled to take place at the Hotel Sherman, located but a stone's throw from City Hall and across the street from the office of Morgan Collins, the chief of police. Above all Capone wanted to give the conference a sense of legitimacy. To this end he dispatched an emissary to Judge John Lyle, of all people, who now found himself the target of Capone's latest attempt at gangland diplomacy. The Capone emissary explained his proposition: since Chicago's rival syndicates were constantly warring with each other, Al wanted to hold a meeting to divide Chicago among them and thus bring peace to the city, and he wanted Lyle, who had declared himself the implacable enemy of the city's racketeers, to act as the arbiter.

Astounded by the audacity of the idea of asking a judge to preside at a

meeting of racketeers trying to settle their turf disputes—all of which concerned illegal activities—Lyle was moved to ask himself, Is there anything in
the world as weird as the gangster mind?

"What's my cut?" he inquired, kidding the emissary, who was at a loss for
a reply.

"The boys didn't think you'd take their money."

"Here's a message to take back to the boys," Lyle said, turning serious.
"We're not going to give them the town. We're going to take the town away
from them."

To which Capone's emissary replied, "You mean you won't do it? Think
of the prestige! Judge, this could make you a big man. You could run for
mayor!"

Lyle habitually portrayed himself as the hero in his encounters with racketeers, and the record does show that he resisted the temptation to become
a "big man" in this fashion. Spurned by the judge, the Capone organization
promptly offered its backing to their second choice, the blustering former
mayor, "Big Bill" Thompson. Ever since William Dever had defeated him,
"Big Bill" had been spoiling for a comeback, and now that his rival's anti-
racketeer policy had proved a dismal failure, Thompson was more than
willing to cooperate with Capone in order to win the election, which would
be held the following year.

In the meantime, Al Capone's vaunted peace conference took place as
scheduled in the Hotel Sherman—the Sherman House, as Chicagoans called
it. On Capone's side of the table, the roster included Harry Guzik, Jack's
brother; Maxie Eisen, a racketeer loosely affiliated with the Guziks; Tony
Lombardo of the Unione Sicilione; and Ralph Sheldon, a bootlegger. Across
from the Capone group sat the distinguished representatives of the Moran-
Drucci gang: "Bugs" Moran; "Schemer" Drucci; William Skidmore, a saloon keeper turned political fixer; and Jack Zuta, who served as their
equivalent of Jack Guzik. Those were the living. Given the circumstances
that had led up to this meeting, the dead figured even more prominently; the
shades of "Hymie" Weiss, Dion O'Banion, and Frank Capone hovered over
the conference, as did the ghosts of dozens of other, lesser-known racketeers
and hundreds of their departed henchmen. "Here they sat," wrote an indignant journalist of the gathering, "thieves, highwayman, panders, murderers,
ex-convicts, thugs, and hoodlums—human beasts of prey, once skulking in
holes as dark as the sewers of Paris, now come out in the open, thrust up by
Volstead and corrupt prominence to the eminence of big business men. Here
they sat, partitioning Chicago and Cook County into trade areas, covenant-
ing against society and the law, and going about it with the assurance of a
group of directors of United States Steel."

For those in attendance, more than business was at stake; they were negotiating survival itself. Capone attempted to dominate the meeting through sheer force of personality. Afterward, he described the arguments he had employed to persuade his rivals of the importance of peace: "I told them we're making a shooting gallery out of a great business, and nobody's profiting by it. It's hard and dangerous work and when a fellow works hard at any line of business, he wants to go home and forget it. He doesn't want to be afraid to sit near a window or open a door. Why not put up our guns and treat our business like any other man treats his, as something to work at in the daytime and forget when he goes home at night. There's plenty of beer business for everybody. Why kill each other over it?" He then switched to his more personal concerns for wanting peace. He recalled that he told the racketeers how he wanted to stop the killing "because I couldn't stand hearing my little kid ask why I didn't stay home. I had been living in the Hawthorne Inn for fourteen months. He's been sick for three years . . . , and I've got to take care of him and his mother. If it wasn't for him I'd have said, 'To hell with you fellows! We'll shoot it out.' But I couldn't say that, knowing it might mean they'd bring me home some night punctured with machine gun fire."

Capone's harping on his concern for his only child swayed the other racketeers, and once Al fell silent, business was transacted swiftly. The results of the extraordinary meeting were immediately announced to the reporters waiting just beyond the closed doors. Of greatest importance, there would be a "general amnesty" among the gangs, which vowed to refrain from beatings or murders. As a corollary, all past murders were to be considered closed cases, as if they were so many debts to be wiped off the books. In addition, the gangs would refrain from feeding malicious tidbits of information concerning rivals to the press. Anyone who was caught violating these standards would be reported immediately and "disciplined" accordingly. The gangs' fierce territorial disputes were resolved, at least on paper. Moran and Drucci retained their strongholds, the Forty-second and Forty-third Wards, while Capone formally acquired control of all territory south of the Madison Street boundary, as well as the territory to the west and south down to Chicago Heights.

Once the meeting broke up, the participants filed out of the Sherman House and reconvened in the Bella Napoli Café to toast the new era in Chicago's rackets. A reporter whom Capone had invited to the feast witnessed once-mortal enemies taunting each other as if they were children running loose on a playground. "Remember that night when your car was chased by two of ours?" asked one.

"I sure do!" said another.

"Well," said the first hoodlum with a laugh, "we were going to kill you, but you had a woman with you." And with that lighthearted jest all the men collapsed with laughter.

As the booze took hold, the men grew sentimental, lachrymose, and united against their common enemy—not the police, not the DA's office, but the press. "I'd never have had my boys shoot any of yours if it hadn't been for the newspapers," said one, who spoke for the others. "Every time there'd be a little shooting affair the papers would print the names of the gang who did it. Well, when any of my boys were shot up and the papers came out with the right hunch as to who did it, I just naturally decided that I'd have to have a few guys bumped myself." After a night of drinking the men straggled home and awoke to greet the new day in Chicago.

The conference proved to be a success. "Just like the old days," Capone said. "They stay on the North Side and I stay in Cicero and if we meet on the street, we say 'hello' and shake hands. Better, ain't it?" Before the treaty, the beer war had claimed a dozen lives each month. For seventy days following the conference, not a single man was murdered in connection with the bootleg trade: the longest stretch of peace Chicago had known since the advent of Prohibition nearly seven years before.

· · ·

Capone had managed to survive another year of attempts on his life. Against all odds, he had brought about a cessation of the beer war, though no one could say how long the fragile treaty among the racketeers would last. As New Year's revelers hailed 1927 by uncorking bottles of bootleg champagne, Capone began to talk publicly about his plan to retire from the rackets, in fulfillment of the promise he had made to himself in Lansing. The first short winter days of January found him not at the Metropole Hotel or the Hawthorne Inn, but at the little house on Prairie Avenue, busying himself with family pursuits and greeting the New Year with resolutions to mend his ways and live up to the noble promises he had made to himself and Angelo Mastropietro during the summer. As he looked forward to 1927, Capone had reason to hope that the truce in Chicago would endure.

Despite his newfound conversion to the cause of nonviolence, rumblings of gangster warfare resumed, some of them unnervingly close at hand. The bitter cold night of January 6, 1927, found Al in the restaurant of the Hawthorne Inn, which was deserted with the exception of his friend Tony Anton, the owner. A bell rang, signifying the arrival of patrons downstairs. "Customers coming up. I'll get their order and be back in a second," said "Tony the Greek." Al waited, but Tony did not return. Nor did he hear any sound of patrons from the doorway. Al eventually went downstairs himself to look around, but Tony had disappeared.

The following night, Al returned to the restaurant in search of his friend, only to learn that Theodore Anton, a.k.a. "Tony the Greek," had been taken for a ride. His body, frozen solid, had been found in a ditch, partly covered with several inches of ice that had to be chipped away to free the corpse. On hearing the news, Al broke down and cried, inconsolable at the death of his friend. The murder remained a mystery, never avenged. Had "Tony the Greek" been murdered at any other time, the event would have led to a new cycle of gangland violence, but with Capone subscribing to the Sherman House peace conference and resolved to end the killing, he did no more than shed tears for his loyal friend. After all, he had retired from the rackets, hadn't he?

And yet, Capone being Capone, he could not resist leaving the field of battle without managing to generate a little publicity for himself. So it was that he invited reporters to visit chez Capone on January 23, 1927, when he planned to make an announcement of interest. The Al Capone who greeted the distinguished members of the press that day appeared the picture of domesticity and contentment as he padded about the house in ornamented bedroom slippers. A bright pink apron completed the disarming picture of the racketeer in repose. There were no guns, no bodyguards in evidence. He had celebrated his birthday twelve days earlier, but he looked at least a decade older than his twenty-seven years. His mature appearance came partly from his thinning hair and partly from his bulk, carrying as he did over 215 pounds on his five-foot-seven frame, but there was more than that. The five violent years he had spent in Chicago had marked him deeply; he had lived harder and faster than most men, and he was already embarked on a premature middle age.

In between greeting his guests he busied himself preparing a large quantity of spaghetti, glancing occasionally at a huge pot in which several gallons of water boiled furiously. "I am out of the booze racket," he told the journalists as he emptied the scalding water in which he had boiled the spaghetti, and then he invited them all to join him for a good, old-fashioned Italian meal, complemented by a fine bootleg wine. "I positively have retired," he reiterated as the reporters toasted his health and began to twirl their forks around the steaming coils of spaghetti heaped on their plates. At that moment Al probably believed what he was saying. It did seem like the right thing to do, to quit the rackets as if he were a champion prizefighter retiring from the ring before he was humiliated by a knockout blow. So he indulged his penchant for playacting, carrying out one last grandiose gesture. But when the afterglow faded he became bored within the confines of his house. No amount of cocaine or bootleg booze could slake his thirst for power and attention. And there was still so much money to be made in the rackets. What had begun in Lansing as a solemn promise to his honorable friend, Angelo Mastropietro, devolved into a ruse designed to protect his position.

Once the effects of Capone's wine wore off, the reporters became more than a little skeptical of his declaration. They knew him as a feared killer, the

head of an immensely lucrative racketeering organization, and one of the
nation's biggest bootleggers, if not *the* biggest. What, exactly, had he retired
from? Who would succeed him as head of the organization? And what would
he do next? As subsequent events demonstrated, Al Capone had no more
retired from the rackets than his enemy "Bugs" Moran had. But Al, who
knew the uses of publicity, wanted to give the *appearance* that he had retired;
he hoped thereby to deflect police scrutiny and, even more importantly, to
make his enemies, the ones like Moran who still wanted him dead, believe
that he was no longer worth killing. As Capone and his audience knew, no
one left the rackets voluntarily, especially not the leaders. So the reporters
weren't fooled, and they resumed their campaign (which happened to sell
thousands of newspapers) to convict him of some final disgrace from which
he would never be absolved. "Capone lives on in luxury," wrote a *Tribune*
reporter in a swoon of despair. "He lives on because—surrounded by Italian
gunmen who are little known, since they are kept out of the limelight—he
is scrupulously guarded and because his killers have exterminated most of his
rivals. Meanwhile Chicago stands bedraggled and mocked at before the
world. As Daniel Defoe wrote long ago:

> *We have been Europe's sink, the jakes where she*
> *Voids all her offal outcast progeny."*

Such was the contempt that Al inspired, even in "retirement," as the *Pax
Capone* descended on Chicago.

• • •

Tell 'em, cowboys, tell 'em! I told you I'd ride 'em high and wide!
                                   —"Big Bill" Thompson, April 5, 1927.

Capone may have mended his ways for the present, but Chicago's political
life continued to follow its old crooked path. Although the beer war had
abated, folly continued to rule public life. Corruption remained the order of
the day, with or without Capone's money, influence, and firepower behind
it. Mayor Dever's political fortunes had continued their decline, and his
campaign to enforce Prohibition had lost its credibility. His lot could be
compared to that of a hapless substitute teacher assigned to a particularly
unruly classroom on which he vainly tried to impose order by shaking his fist,
but his behavior only served to aggravate the anarchic situation, and he was
on the verge of being laughed out of his classroom by the troublemakers he
had vowed to subdue.

"Big Bill" Thompson, awaiting a comeback since he had dropped out of
the race four years earlier, found this volatile political climate ideal, and he

exploited it with showmanship reminiscent of P. T. Barnum. Better than any other figure on Chicago's political scene—with the possible exception of that quasi politician, Al Capone—Thompson knew the uses of publicity. He never missed an opportunity to grab a headline, to remind voters that they need only turn to him to restore the city to its former luster.

A true child of the jazz age, Thompson had been born in Boston in 1867 to a family of considerable means. Detesting school and the confines of the East, he went west in search of adventure and worked as a brakeman for the Union Pacific Railroad, a ranch hand, and a self-styled cowboy. He gravitated toward Chicago to indulge his taste for lavish living and subsequently entered politics, it was said, on a fifty-dollar bet. Scandal pursued him wherever he went. During one campaign, he was forced to admit he had frequented Chicago brothels. Sexual hypocrisy came naturally to him; he married a proper dowager, who lent him an aura of Victorian respectability even as he kept an attractive Jewish mistress. He ate and drank with abandon. Flamboyance was his trademark. During the Dever administration, for instance, Thompson built himself a $25,000 yacht, christened her *Big Bill*, arranged for a figurehead depicting none other than the ship's owner, and, to the vast amusement of the press, declared his intention to lead an expedition to capture a certain fish reputed to climb trees. He traveled down the Mississippi River on the *Big Bill*, pausing at towns along the way to make political speeches and to do whatever he could to attract attention to himself.

He never did find his tree-climbing fish, but he did manage to start a Thompson-for-mayor boom, which he cultivated carefully on his return to Chicago. There the race already included two of his protégés, Fred Lundin and Dr. John Dill Robertson, who had served as the city's health commissioner. Thompson viewed their entry into the mayoral race as treachery, and he was greatly annoyed. To exhibit his displeasure, he rented the Cort Theatre, where he staged a political vaudeville in the form of a Rat Show, in which he appeared on stage bearing a cage holding two rats. One, he told the audience, was called Fred and the other Doc, after his rivals. "Fred," he addressed one of the rats, "wasn't I one of the best friends you ever had?" And to the other rat, he said, "I can tell this is Doc because he hadn't had a bath in twenty years until we washed him yesterday." (This was a reference to Robertson's position as health commissioner.) Thompson ended his demonstration by explaining that the cage had formerly held *six* rats, but Doc and Fred had devoured the others. The audience loved the show, and Thompson suddenly became a viable candidate for mayor. His opponent was, once again, William E. Dever, whom Thompson began denouncing as that "left-handed Irishman." Wherever he went, he whipped up anti-Catholic prejudice against Dever. The articulate, decent Dever was by no means an easy target, for he enjoyed immense prestige, though much of it came from *outside* Chicago. In fact, he was widely regarded as the nation's ablest mayor, the man Chicago required to defeat its gangsters. As the campaign wore on, Dever took the high road, and a dull journey that proved to be, while Thompson took the low, and far more entertaining, route to power.

As the race narrowed in the early months of 1927, Thompson deftly shifted from vaudeville stunts to outlandish demagoguery. Once again he lambasted the tyrannical King George and attained new heights of absurdity when he criticized the number of pro-British books in Chicago's libraries; "treason-tainted histories," he labeled them. To rid themselves of this menace, he urged the citizens of that fair city to pillage the treacherous libraries and burn the offending books. Thus did Thompson distract the populace and inflame their imaginations with spurious campaign issues of his own devising.

Attempting to parry Thompson's fatuous remarks, Mayor Dever threw up his hands in frustration. "How can I campaign against a brain like that?" he complained. Even he had to admit that his commonsense, literal-minded campaign paled before the fanciful guile Thompson spouted, especially on the subject of Prohibition. Ever the harlot of the voting booth, Thompson insisted that he was "wetter than the middle of the Atlantic Ocean," and to prove his point, he vowed to allow every speakeasy Dever had shut down to open once again and to add 10,000 new speakeasies to the already-sodden Chicago landscape. To lend credibility to this promise, the Thompson campaign headquarters served some of the best bootleg booze to be had in the entire city.

Chicago's reputation as a crime-ridden haven for gangsters inevitably became an important issue in the campaign, perhaps the only real issue. Although Dever could lay claim to honesty, if not effectiveness, in this regard, Thompson quickly seized the initiative by blaming the city's criminal atmosphere on his opponent. He took out a large ad in the *Chicago Tribune* in which he warned, "The city is overrun with morons and other vicious elements. The papers teem with accounts of murders and other horrible lawlessness. *Thompson* pledges himself to change these conditions and make life and property once again secure in Chicago." "Big Bill" saw nothing inconsistent about condemning gangsters even as he sought backing from Capone and other racketeers. The only thing that mattered to him was getting the vote, even if it meant creating a carnival of hysteria.

For all his anticrime propaganda, it would be difficult to imagine a politician better suited to further the aims of Chicago's racketeers than Thompson, but Capone, becalmed in a premature retirement, resisted Thompson's sweaty overtures. They were both Republicans, it was true, but even though Thompson was infinitely corruptible, Capone considered him a fool, untrustworthy and unreliable. The racketeer preferred the public servants he controlled to be low-profile, no-nonsense types, like his man in Cicero, Edward Z. Klenha. Capone valued discretion, the appearance of honesty, but Thompson was a walking scandal, altogether too messy, provocative, and colorful. When Thompson courted the favor and financial backing of racketeers, he received an outpouring of cash from saloon owners, who were understandably delighted with his determination to ignore Prohibition, and he attracted the support of "Schemer" Drucci and Jack Zuta, who oversaw vice and gambling operations for "Bugs" Moran and came forward with a $50,000 contribution.

Not to be outdone by his dimwitted but dangerous rivals, Capone secretly contributed $260,000 to the Thompson campaign, more in self-defense than from a genuine desire to see the man elected. This was strictly a cash transaction, casually dispensed during the campaign. According to the Chicago Crime Commission's investigation of the election, the "money was ladled out to Thompson workers from a bathtub in the Hotel Sherman, filled with packages of $5 bills." The money naturally came with various strings attached. The first concerned territory: "Capone should have the undisputed right to houses of prostitution and gambling houses, to operate slot machines, and control the sale of beer and booze in all the territory of the city south of Madison street," the *Chicago Tribune* revealed. The second quid pro quo involved people. The Thompson Republican Club soon numbered various Capone cronies such as Morris and Emmanuel Eller, a father-and-son team who paid men to vote twice, and Daniel Serritella, who represented the Unione Sicilione. All of them received influential appointments under Thompson. When news of the Capone contribution eventually leaked out, Thompson's political rivals and the press outdid one another to denounce the arrangement.

As the April election approached, the Chicago police braced for an outbreak of gangland violence. Election eve found the deputy chief of police, John Stege, carefully instructing his men on the use of the tommy gun. Two hundred fifty "flivver squads" patrolled the length and breadth of the city on election day, but police encountered little of the wanton slugging and kidnapping associated with past elections. It was true that one or two election judges were kidnapped and beaten within an inch of their lives, and five shots were fired, and a couple of Democratic clubs were bombed, but considering this was a Chicago election, these incidents barely registered. Voters joked nervously whenever a passing automobile backfired; no, they reminded themselves, it was not a shotgun blast.

Everyone from the police to the Dever supporters expected Capone to send his troops into battle, but unenthusiastic about Thompson and determined to preserve his "retired" status, Capone and his men were nowhere in evidence. "Schemer" Drucci, however, could not resist throwing himself into the fray.

To help out his man, "Big Bill," Drucci decided to kidnap a Dever supporter, Alderman Dorsey Crowe, on election day, April 4, and hold him overnight. But Drucci wasted precious time destroying the office and pummeling Crowe's secretary and never did accomplish his goal. He and two colleagues were caught on the corner of Diversey Parkway and Clark Street the same day. The police relieved Drucci of his .45 and held him in custody. Eventually his lawyer, Maurice Green, came forward to demand his client's release, and four policemen were assigned to escort Drucci to the Criminal Courts Building, where Green waited. The police detail included Danny Healy, a tough cop who had once dared to beat up "Polack Joe" Saltis, the bootlegger. As the police car sped through the streets of Chicago, Healy taunted Drucci until the gangster was in a rage, restrained only by the gun the cop aimed at his heart. Healy later gave this account of the ensuing struggle: "Drucci said, 'You—I'll get you. I'll wait on your doorstep for you.' I told him to shut his mouth. Drucci said, 'Go on, you kid copper—I'll fix you for this.' I told him to keep quiet. Drucci said, 'You take your gun off me or I'll kick hell out of you.' He got up on one leg and struck me on the right side of the head with his left hand, saying, 'I'll take you and your tool. I'll fix you,' grabbing hold of me by the right hand. I grabbed my gun with my left hand and fired four shots at him.' " Drucci collapsed, and by the time the car arrived at the Criminal Courts Building, he had died.

Drucci's lawyer cried for Healy to be arrested for murder, but on hearing the demand, William Schoemaker, the chief of detectives, replied, "I don't know anything about anyone being murdered. I know Drucci was killed trying to take a gun away from an officer. We're having a medal made for Healy." The police could barely conceal their amazement that "Schemer" Drucci was dead and that one of their number had killed him. A cop actually killing a gangster—not taking his money, not drinking his bootleg booze, not looking the other way—this was a rare event in Chicago. In fact, Drucci was the first racketeer of significance to die at the hands of the police since the shooting of Frank Capone three years earlier. Another day in Chicago brought another gangster funeral, this one with a military flourish ("Schemer" Drucci was a veteran), another silver casket at Sbarbaro's Funeral Home, and another burial at Mt. Carmel Cemetery, fast becoming the Arlington National Cemetery of Chicago's gangland wars. His widow, who stood to inherit his $400,000 estate, was not especially grief-stricken. Cecilia Drucci—the picture of a flapper—sighed sweetly and said to a reporter, "A policeman murdered him, but we sure gave him a grand funeral."

If Cecilia Drucci was strangely heartened and the chief of detectives delighted by Drucci's death, Capone's pleasure at hearing the news can only be imagined. At a stroke, Drucci was gone. Weiss was gone. Everything was breaking Capone's way. Of his worst enemies, only "Bugs" Moran was left, along with his ragged crew of bootleggers and gunmen, and they were no match for Capone's well-heeled, experienced organization. But anyone with a machine gun and sufficient nerve was dangerous, and Capone maintained a healthy fear of Moran and a mounting conviction that something would have to be done about him at the right time and place.

.   .   .

To no one's surprise, William Hale Thompson carried the election, receiving 515,716 votes to Dever's 432,678. That night the Thompson forces held their victory celebration in the opulent Louis XIV Ballroom at the Sherman House, where they shouted their hero's campaign anthem until they were hoarse, and "Big Bill" himself cavorted in a ten-gallon hat. Later that night he invited his supporters to toast the victory aboard his yacht, the *Big Bill.* The crowd accepted his offer in such numbers that his ship of fools sank to the bottom under their weight. Thompson scrambled to safety, as wet, cold, and boisterous as ever. Vowing to discharge the responsibilities of his office with the same gusto he had brought to his campaign, he took the oath of office on April 13, 1927. Shortly afterward he established the custom of driving around the streets of Chicago at night in an open touring car with a spotlight trained on him. "The people like to see their mayor," he explained. And so they did.

Now that Thompson was back in office, Capone realized that his contribution had been the best quarter of a million dollars he had ever spent. Without lifting a finger or exposing himself to criticism, he had gotten rid of the detested Drucci, and Thompson, bigoted oaf though he was, removed all local obstacles to the smooth operation of Capone's organization. Indeed, one of the mayor's favorite nightspots was Ralph Capone's Cotton Club in Cicero, which became the common ground of racketeers and politicians alike. With the return of "Big Bill" to City Hall, Chicago politics underwent a rapid transformation; Dever's impotent fury at gangsters and Prohibition violators yielded to Thompson's easy indulgence and pandering. He took care to pay off his backers; Capone's ally, Dan Serritella, received an appointment as city sealer, and as the inspector of weights and measures he was ideally positioned to receive an endless supply of bribes. (Several years later, he was convicted of defrauding the city.) He also became Republican committeeman in the First Ward and as such Capone's principal link to City Hall.

Buoyed by his success, Thompson developed ambitions extending far beyond Chicago. He interpreted his victory as a mandate to launch a national campaign. When President Coolidge declared he would not run for reelection in 1928, Thompson promoted himself—and, even more remarkably, people began to consider him—as the next Republican candidate for president. If Warren G. Harding could make it to the White House, why not William Hale Thompson?

To whip up enthusiasm for his presidential candidacy, "Big Bill" invited his friends and a Police Department quartet to accompany him in a private railway car, and the troupe set off on a ten-thousand-mile cross-country speaking tour, stopping at state fairs and prairie towns to denounce such infamies as the League of Nations and the World Court, anything that threatened, in Thompson's view, the idea of "America First." Thompson was greeted with affection and respect throughout the Midwest, as far west as San Francisco, and as far south as New Orleans, where the Kingfish himself, Huey Long, soon to become the governor of Louisiana, held a banquet in Thompson's honor. At a loss for conventional words to describe the boom, the *New York Times* coined the term "Bigbillism."

• • •

In May 1927, the U.S. Supreme Court handed down a ruling that was but a whisper amid the din of "Big Bill"'s Chicago, although eventually it would have profound consequences for that beleaguered city. "DECIDES BOOTLEG-GERS MUST MAKE TAX RETURN," the headline in the *New York Times* neatly summarized. "Supreme Court Holds They Are Not Immune Because of Violating Dry Law." The decision had come about as a result of a case that arose in Charleston, South Carolina, where lawyers argued that the Fifth Amendment to the Constitution forbidding self-incrimination protected their client, a bootlegger named Manley Sullivan, from the necessity of filing a tax return and paying taxes on his ill-gotten gains. In response the Court amended the law in a small but significant way by ruling that from now on income derived from *illegal* sources of revenue must also be reported and was subject to income tax. The author of the opinion, Associate Justice Oliver Wendell Holmes, wrote, "We are of the opinion that the protection of the Fifth Amendment was stretched too far," and he proceeded to explain, "It would be an extreme if not extravagant application of the Fifth Amendment to say it authorized a man to refuse to state the amount of his income because it had been made in crime." In other words, income was income, whether legitimate or not. The ruling was aimed at two large shadow industries that had grown mightily during Prohibition; one was gambling, such as betting on horses, and the other was bootlegging. What the ruling said, in effect, was that bootleggers such as Al Capone must pay taxes on their entire incomes.

The Supreme Court ruling caused a brief flurry. The *Times* commended the decision and emphasized its application to bootleggers who "make fabulous profits, but . . . must pay their taxes just the same as less favored mortals." At first, the ruling did little to change the status quo, and bootleggers did not start inundating the IRS with their returns. However, the

Internal Revenue Service took the ruling as a legal basis to demand that gamblers and bootleggers pay taxes on their ill-gotten gains, and they were prepared to prosecute to achieve this goal. The racketeers scoffed; none of them was foolish enough to pay taxes on their illegal gains. They might just as well walk into the office of the U.S. attorney general and surrender. Like every other racketeer, Al Capone would no more dream of filing an income tax return than he would allow an honest race to be run at the Hawthorne Race Track.

At first glance, the ability of the IRS to catch Capone or any other boot-legger of consequence appeared extremely limited. Ever since Congress first began imposing a federal tax on income in 1913, the IRS had faced the problem of compliance, especially when it came to tax dodgers such as Capone. Under the stewardship of a former Post Office stenographer named Elmer Irey, the agency set up a Special Intelligence Unit designed to catch these offenders; despite its exalted title, which often struck other government bureaucrats as more than a little pompous, the unit toiled in the shadow of the Federal Bureau of Investigation; few people were aware of the unit's existence and even fewer cared. Furthermore, Irey's enemies constantly dep-recated him and spread groundless tales of drunken behavior. Now, at a stroke, the Supreme Court decision gave the IRS and its Special Intelligence Unit real power. Irey, a prickly, self-effacing civil servant, rolled up his sleeves and began to investigate the most visible racketeer in the country's most corrupt city: Al Capone.

• • •

For the moment, "Bigbillism" flourished in Chicago, and Capone emerged from his self-imposed retirement to exploit it. The entire political system with its patronage and rigged elections became the ultimate racket. Of course from the racketeers' perspective, the whole country was a series of overlapping rackets. What was the insurance business but a giant racket, and a legal one at that? What was John D. Rockefeller's Standard Oil monopoly but the most lucrative racket in the country, and Rockefeller himself the biggest racketeer of them all? And in Chicago, the financier Samuel Insull— "Emperor" Insull, they called him—had over the years built up a vast web of power and utility companies, in the process appearing on the cover of *Time* magazine not once but twice, becoming a hero to businessmen and the common man alike. Insull was the president of eleven companies, a director of eighty-five more, and the chairman of another sixty-five. He employed as many as fifty thousand people, and from his office high above Wacker Drive he controlled an empire worth $3 billion, all of it arranged in a complex pyramid requiring the economic boom to sustain it.

For all his immense wealth and Establishment credentials, Insull's life

contained a number of parallels to Capone's. Capone's constituents bet on
fixed fights; Insull's invested in rigged stocks. Capone's gambling empire
became a pseudoeconomy for diversion and entertainment, what he called
the "light pleasures," a shadow of the stock market, but not necessarily more
sinister. Both men possessed a perverse genius for exploiting the tenor of the
times, which blurred the distinction between legitimate and illegitimate.
They lived in constant dread of assassination; both traveled about the city in
armored cars equipped with bulletproof glass and gun ports. On several
occasions, while driving through the streets of Chicago in his sixteen-cylinder
Cadillac, Insull was fired on. His chauffeur was shot in one instance; in
another, he and his wife were nearly kidnapped by gunmen as they drove
home. After several brushes with would-be assassins, Insull turned to the
man most capable of providing security. Glad to be of service, Al Capone
offered Insull the use of several of the organization's bodyguards, but Insull,
who was as stingy as he was wealthy, refused to pay their salaries. Insull also
had concerns about appearances. It wouldn't do to be seen with a phalanx of
Sicilian gunmen, and Insull instead raised a small army of security guards
drawn from the ranks of his employees. Beyond the need for security, the
modus operandi of both men had much in common, for Insull and Capone
were determined to build monopolies to control their product. Insull contributed $100,000 to Thompson's campaign, almost as much as Capone had,
but few bothered to criticize Insull for doing so or to divine sinister motives.
As Capone knew, people outdid themselves to worship the wealthy, as long
as they did not have Italian surnames.

Determined to purchase and flaunt whatever status he could attain, Capone expanded his Chicago headquarters at the Metropole; he and his men—
and the women they kept—now occupied more than fifty rooms, virtually
the entire hotel. Liquor flowed, and prostitutes came and went undisturbed.
Gambling flourished around the clock. In this topsy-turvy reflection of conventional life, weekdays at the Metropole were devoted to the pursuit of
pleasure and Sundays to business. On Sunday mornings, the lobby teemed
with the lawyers, judges, and politicians who came to deal with Capone; they
traversed hallways staked out with armed security guards until they reached
rooms 409 and 410, where he held court. The petitioners ushered into his
presence were invariably impressed by the patriotic portraits of three great
Americans displayed on the walls: George Washington, Abraham Lincoln,
and William Hale Thompson. Thus Capone publicly aligned himself with
the new mayor, even while he continued to disparage him in private.

With little to fear from the police and with the tacit cooperation of City
Hall, Capone became more of a man about town than he had ever been, a
public figure who regularly appeared at major civic functions symbolic of the
day. It was the age of dashing, daring aviators, and on May 15, days before

Charles Lindbergh completed his transatlantic flight, an Italian pilot, Commander Francesco de Pinedo, hopscotching the globe on behalf of Mussolini, landed his hydroplane on Lake Michigan, where he was besieged by a party of official greeters and well-wishers including the Italian consul, the chief of Chicago's fascists, Air Corps officers, a judge, and Al Capone, who leaped forward to shake Pinedo's hand. Capone's presence was duly noted by the press, which occasioned some grumbling about the propriety of a gangster representing Chicago, but the police promptly explained that they had *invited* Capone in case they needed to call on him to help quell an antifascist riot.

.   .   .

Secure in the knowledge that he had earned his place in Chicago's public life, Capone overcame his fear of assassination and began to appear regularly in public, especially at sporting events of every type. He had much to choose from, for it was an era of legendary athletes: Babe Ruth in baseball, Bill Tilden in tennis, Red Grange in football, and Jack Dempsey and Gene Tunney in boxing. Capone became a regular at Chicago Cubs home games, always in the company of several bodyguards, and occasionally a young boy that everyone, including the newspapers, assumed was his son. But Capone was not so foolish as to display his only child before 30,000 members of the public. Sonny Capone remained secluded in the safety of the family house on South Prairie Avenue, and this boy was a stand-in. He was Sam Pontarelli, another of Capone's surrogate sons.

Not everyone considered the gangster welcome. When Tony Berardi photographed Gabby Hartnett, the Cubs' centerfielder and later a member of the Hall of Fame, autographing a baseball for Capone, the fleeting incident caused respectable voices in Chicago to insist that Capone by his mere presence was dishonoring the great American pastime. In response, the commissioner of baseball, Kenesaw Mountain Landis, forbade the players from fraternizing with the fans.

Although he adored the company of sports figures and frequented gyms almost as much as he did brothels, Capone was no athlete. He had excelled at pool in his youth, but since much of his life consisted of eluding his enemies and hiding indoors, he had little interest in exercise. He made an exception when it came to golf, another sport winning new devotees in the 1920s; indeed, golf became something of a craze among the racketeers of Chicago, and Capone was especially devoted to it. As his experience with the sport demonstrated, even *golf* could be hazardous.

Capone's preferred links naturally belonged to his syndicate. The course was located in suburban Burnham, home of the "Boy Mayor," Johnny Patton, who ran a country club inevitably known as Burnham Wood. Its nine-hole course opened in 1925 and soon began attracting a following among Capone's gunmen, including "Machine Gun" Jack McGurn and another tommy gun virtuoso called Fred "Killer" Burke, who was as coarse and ugly as McGurn was sleek and handsome. They were later joined by Capone, who played there as often as twice a week. There he became friendly with his twelve-year-old caddie, Timothy Sullivan, who fell under the sway of Capone's charm and generosity. Much later, Sullivan recalled the first time he saw Capone: "He was wearing a white silk shirt with his monogram, no tie, gray plus fours and a belt with a diamond buckle, and he was surrounded by his gangsters," including McGurn; Jack Guzik, who was even less athletic than Capone; and a grim little toad of a bodyguard known as "Banjo Eyes."

The foursome one day consisted of Capone and McGurn against Guzik and Burke, playing for $500 a hole. "Capone teed off first. He fetched the ball a whack that would have sent it down the fairway, only he hooked it, and it curved way off to the left into a clump of trees. I scrambled around on all fours for about 10 minutes trying to find it, scared to death Al would lose his temper and hit me or maybe shoot me, but all he did was grin, pat me on the head and call me Kid." Relieved, Sullivan decided that Al Capone was nothing like his reputation; he seemed gentle and patient, though he played deplorable golf. "I don't think he broke 60 for the nine holes. He could drive the ball half a mile, but he always hooked it, and he couldn't putt for beans." At the end of the afternoon, Capone lost almost every hole, including side bets. Sullivan calculated that the gangster foursome exchanged about $10,000 during that game, and then, to complete his astonishment, Capone tipped him what seemed an incredible sum: $20.

Sullivan, Al's constant caddie, subsequently learned that gangsters played golf like no other people played the game. All the boys wore hip flasks, which clinked with every step they took, and they drank as they went, so by the time they approached the ninth hole they were in an uproarious mood. Drunk, they dug divots the size of trenches, especially "Killer" Burke, who wielded a golf club as if it were a lethal weapon. Without warning they fell into playful wrestling matches. The agile McGurn would turn somersaults or walk on his hands, or the four of them would line up to play leapfrog, McGurn hurtling over the back of Burke, who would in turn jump over Capone, and so on toward the tee, where they would play a game called Blind Robin—Al's contribution to the game of golf. In Blind Robin one of the men reclined on the grass, stuck his face in the air, balanced the golf ball on his chin, shut his eyes, and prayed as the others teed off. When it was Al's turn to serve as a human golf tee, the boys put away their drivers and used a putter, swinging softly—very softly, lest they leave a mark on his round face.

Being racketeers, they constantly cheated on each other, which led to bitter fights. When McGurn caught Burke moving the ball to a better lie, the two men had it out. Burke was much bigger, but McGurn, younger and stronger, knocked down his antagonist a dozen times as a crowd of golfers paused to watch the spectacle. The brawl lasted half an hour, and when it was done, McGurn, bloody but upright, stood in triumph over Burke, who lay on the ground in defeat. "The boys made a stretcher of their hands and carried him to the clubhouse," Sullivan recalled.

During another outing, Guzik vented his wrath on his young caddie. The blowup occurred on the sixth hole, when his ball landed in a sand trap. Using a club suggested by Sullivan, Guzik swung at the ball, only to watch in disgust as it rolled back into the trap. On the third unsuccessful attempt to escape the trap, Guzik suddenly lost his temper. "He grabbed the driver like a bat and went for me, yelling every dirty name you could think of," Sullivan remembered. "I ran zigzagging across the fairway. Luckily, he was too fat and slow to catch me or I think he would have killed me. He stopped finally, out of breath, broke the club across his knees and threw the pieces at me." And so another afternoon on the links with the boys came to an end. The following day, Capone made himself a hero in Sullivan's eyes by humiliating Guzik. "What do you mean treating the Kid here like that?" he shouted at "Greasy Thumb," who mumbled his feeble excuses. He then insisted that Guzik tip the caddie, and when Guzik proffered a measly dollar bill, Al snatched the wallet, extracted twenty dollars, handed the money to the Kid, and threw the wallet at the feet of Guzik, "who picked it up and waddled away without a word."

Becoming wise to the ways of racketeers, Sullivan began cheating to help his friend Al. "I would keep a couple of extra balls in my pants pocket, drop one near the spot where his disappeared, and pretend I'd found it. He caught on pretty quick, but he just laughed and said, 'You're okay, Kid.' " For Capone, betting existed to be fixed, but when "Banjo Eyes" discovered the sleight of hand, he became enraged, called Capone a liar to his face, and the men got into a shouting match on the course. Finally, Al roared: "On your knees and start praying!" He suddenly plunged his hand into his golf bag and pulled out a revolver, at which point Sullivan burst into tears, pleading with the man he had come to admire so deeply not to execute "Banjo Eyes" on the Burnham Wood golf course. Softened by the young caddie's plea, Capone's rage dissipated as quickly as it had come, and the game continued without loss of life or injury.

Although this episode concluded peacefully, Capone's habit of bringing a weapon onto the links continued to present a hazard. During a game with Johnny Patton, the "Boy Mayor," Capone casually picked up his golf bag, and the .45-caliber revolver concealed within went off. Wounded, Al shrieked in agony. "The bullet plowed down through the fleshy part of his right leg," the *Tribune* reported, "narrowly missed the abdomen and then embedded itself in his left leg." Although he had narrowly escaped inflicting permanent damage on himself, Capone urgently required medical assistance. Patton rushed him to St. Margaret's Hospital in Hammond, where a medical examination disclosed a serious wound in Capone's groin. The hospital's chief physician refused to allow him to remain overnight out of fear that the presence of "Scarface" Al Capone would attract other gangsters, who would use the patients for target practice. In the end Capone was allowed to register under the name of Geary. He took a suite consisting of five rooms, one reserved for his use, the others devoted to sheltering his round-the-clock bodyguards, including Tony "Little New York" Campagna. "Pistols are not flashed around the corridors," said a reporter of the scene, "but the sentinels remain at all times ready to care for unwelcome visitors." Within a week Capone was discharged, and he immediately returned to the golf course. "After that," his caddie, Tim Sullivan, observed, "the boys double-checked to make sure the safety catch was on before they deposited any gun in a golf bag."

Young Tim Sullivan's initiation into the racketeers' life eventually comprised matters extending far beyond the game of golf. "One afternoon on the links they kept talking about some kind of party they were going to throw at the clubhouse that night. An orgy, they called it. I'd never heard the word before," Sullivan wrote, "and I was burning with curiosity. So after supper I went back to the clubhouse. The bouncer at the door laughed fit to bust when I asked to join Al's party. 'Better go home and get your diapers changed,' he said. I pretended to go but instead sneaked around to the back of the building." He climbed to a second-story window, through which he "saw about 20 couples, most of them naked. Not Al, though. He just stood on the sidelines, watching and laughing."

After that incident, Sullivan not unexpectedly announced that he wanted to join the Capone gang when he was older. What better life than tearing across a golf course, veering recklessly between leapfrog and murder? Al just smiled and tousled the Kid's hair. "You're part of it now, aren't you? You're my caddie," he told the Kid.

"I mean for real," Sullivan said, "and carry a gun like the other guys."

This time Capone spoke more directly. "Nothing doing, Kid. I want you around a long time all in one piece. You might get hurt. Most guys in my line of business do."

Although the Kid never did join the gang, his older sister, Babe, got even closer to Al. Babe was hardly more than a kid herself, only sixteen years old, with dark eyes and dark hair: an Irish beauty. The two met in the clubhouse, where she worked as a waitress. Serving a cup of coffee to the famous Al

Capone, she became so nervous that she spilled it over his suit. Capone jumped to his feet, hollering at the poor dumb waitress, but when he saw how young and sweet-looking she was, he immediately regained his composure, apologized, and tenderly put his arm around her. "I didn't mean to scare you," he said softly, "but that coffee is pretty hot." He gave Babe a $10 tip and never stopped thinking about her. Soon he started seeing her regularly, showering her with jewelry, diamonds, gaudy bracelets, necklaces, and other sparkling trinkets of doubtful provenance. Afraid of being identified as a gangster's moll, Babe carefully hid the treasures from her mother, but Al proved to be a persistent suitor who saw in the youthful Babe all the innocence he had irrevocably lost. Whenever he was in Burnham he stopped by the Sullivan house, home of his best caddie and his best girl. He ingratiated himself with Mom and Pop Sullivan, who cast aside their reservations and found him absolutely charming, not at all the way the newspapers described him. He had the twin scars, they could see, but his manners were perfect. Eventually Babe stopped trying to conceal their affair. "He kept telling Babe how much he loved her," her brother recalled, "that he'd get a divorce if she'd marry him." Divorce *Mae*? None of the Sullivans took Al's talk seriously, but under the circumstances it sounded rather gallant. In the end Babe refused him, politely but firmly. "She said she was satisfied with the way things were."

As the affair continued, Al often took Babe and her kid brother for drives, casual excursions to nowhere. It was so luxurious, so peaceful inside Al's limousine, except for the machine gun installed beside the driver's seat. "Nothing to worry about," Al said airily when he saw his passengers gaping. "Just a little insurance. Look out the windows." On another occasion, he took a small party consisting of Al, Babe, the Kid, and two bodyguards to see Al Jolson in his latest movie, *The Singing Fool*. It was here, at the movies, that Capone could finally relax and briefly forget the danger with which he lived. When the lights came up, Sullivan was surprised to see tears coursing down the gangster's broad cheeks.

As the Kid discovered, Capone reserved his real passion not for women but for boxing, a sport that ran deep in gangster culture. For years he had spent his idle moments in gyms, encountering old pals, winking, shaking hands, but mainly watching the mesmerizing display of muscle crashing against bone. No other sport was as direct and violent as boxing, so close to actual combat; it was a metaphor, an extension, of the gangster's life: short, brutal, occasionally glorious, but not really glamorous. Nor was it a mainstream sport; it was too sweaty and primitive to earn the acceptance accorded baseball; furthermore, it was illegal in many areas. McGurn and other Capone gunmen had been professional boxers at one time, and many of the fight promoters and managers were closely aligned with racketeers or were racketeers themselves. "Throughout my career," wrote Barney Ross, a Chicago pugilist whom Capone befriended, "I was to find that the most rabid fans in the fight business were the gangsters on the one hand, and the society crowd on the other. And whenever they met at parties honoring this champ or that one, they got along like brothers under the skin. However, the society people sometimes got drunk and nasty, but the gangsters were always gentlemen."

Even if the racketeers refrained from coercing the fighters themselves, they exerted considerable influence over the sport through gambling. Whenever Ross fought, for example, many people from his neighborhood hocked their valuables in order to place the largest possible bet on him. "Al told me I was his good-luck charm," Ross recalled. " 'I made a lot of money betting on you, kid,' he said. 'I'm gonna keep betting on you every time you fight.' " When Ross cautioned that he couldn't win them all, Capone shrugged. " 'So what? You're our neighborhood boy. We gotta back you, win or lose." But once, when Al thought Ross was dogging it in the ring, he took the boxer aside and lectured him: "What the hell's the matter with you, kid? I hear you spend your nights running to every lousy joint in town. Take it from me, you're a goddamn dunce." Ross heeded the warning and won his next decision.

Although Ross and the other fighters hotly denied that the gentlemanly racketeers or the managers they controlled ever fixed fights, evidence to the contrary abounded, especially in Chicago, where the Capone syndicate often dictated who fought whom and what the outcome would be. Their principal connection to the fight world was Joe Glaser, best remembered for managing the career of Louis Armstrong. In an earlier incarnation Glaser was an influential fight promoter in Chicago. From his two-room office in the Loop, Glaser ran his boxing empire and zealously protected his turf. When a gambler and part-time journalist named Eddie Borden denounced Glaser in print as a front for the Capone organization, Glaser had the man run out of town and swiftly returned to business as usual. Glaser's power to fix fights earned him a reputation as the sage of boxing, especially among reporters. Vern Whaley, who covered boxing for the *Chicago Evening Post*, recalls that "on the day of a big fight card at Mills Stadium, Comiskey Park, Cubs Park, even at Guyon's Paradise Ballroom on the west side, Glaser would give me the names of the winners in advance, even the round of a knockout in some bouts that were obviously fixed." Equipped with the leads supplied by good old Joe, Whaley developed a "sensational record" for picking probable winners in his newspaper column.

Among the fighters in whom Capone took an interest was his former caddie, Timothy Sullivan, who had matured into a young boxer of promise. Capone came to watch him work out in local gyms and later on arranged fights for Sullivan—nothing major, no real money involved, just club fights. He eventually compiled a respectable but hardly spectacular 22-19 record.

. . .

The custom of fixing fights went from being the scuttlebutt of newsrooms and gymnasiums around Chicago to an issue of national concern in September 1927. The occasion was the Jack Dempsey-Gene Tunney bout for the heavyweight championship of the world. It promised to be the biggest boxing spectacle ever held in Chicago, and Capone, who loved boxing, was in the thick of the action. Al had become acquainted with Dempsey shortly after the Manassa Mauler (after his hardscrabble birthplace, Manassa, Colorado) had decked Jess Willard to win the title in 1919. And Dempsey considered Al to be "one of my number one fans." Their relationship had been conducted in secret, however; when Capone visited Dempsey's training camp, cameras were averted and reporters put down their notebooks. But Dempsey felt comfortable with Capone, who earned his qualified admiration: "He was a rough customer who wanted to be accepted as a man, not a racketeer."

Dempsey became a controversial figure not for associating with Capone but for refusing to defend his title between 1923 and 1926 against a worthy challenger, Harry Willis, who was black. Instead, Dempsey chose to fight Gene Tunney, who was white and weighed the same as Dempsey: 190 pounds. The New York Athletic Commission withheld its blessing because Dempsey had refused to fight Willis, so the Dempsey-Tunney bout took place in Philadelphia. Tunney prevailed and became the new heavyweight champion. Soon after, Dempsey asked for a rematch. Tunney agreed, and the bout was scheduled to take place at Soldiers Field in Chicago on September 22, 1927. It was to be among the most publicized and controversial contests in boxing history.

Weeks in advance stories swirled through Chicago that Capone was making every effort to ensure that his pal won this time out. It was said that Capone bet $50,000 on Dempsey. He also bought one hundred ringside seats at $40 apiece for his friends and colleagues, and his organization bankrolled countless other bets on the fight. Stories of Capone's involvement with Dempsey became so widespread that the Manassa Mauler was forced to address them publicly; he explained that he asked his friend Al to keep his distance in the name of "sportsmanship." For the sake of appearances Capone reversed himself; now all bets were off. "He'd better get a square shake," he told another fight promoter, "Doc" Kearns, concerning Dempsey. "Nothing preferential, understand, but a fair shake." At the same time he sent Jack and his wife a lavish bouquet bearing a message: "To the Dempseys, in the name of sportsmanship."

This being Chicago, Dempsey arrived at Soldiers Field on the day of the fight in a bulletproof car under heavy police escort. Capone arrived in the company of a taciturn journalist. The man was carefully attired in an understated suit, his face highlighted by wire-rimmed glasses and a narrow, thin-lipped mouth. Few recognized his face, but everyone there read the columns he wrote for the Hearst papers and instantly recognized his name: Damon Runyon. Preferring to talk with his typewriter rather than his mouth, Runyon was fond of observing gangsters at close range, not to expose them, but to view the world with the moral astigmatism of the inveterate racketeer. Damon Runyon was himself a Damon Runyon character—a hard-bitten, hardworking, hard-boiled man who held the world at arm's length. Isolated from friend and foe alike, he was in the midst of transforming himself from a columnist and sportswriter into one of the most highly paid short story writers of the day, using his gangster pals as models. Runyon's colorful gangsters reeked of romance and cockeyed charm, and his suave amorality became his trademark. Thus Al Capone—with his big mouth, his cigar, his bizarre flights of generosity, megalomania, and paranoia—became one of the best Damon Runyon characters Damon Runyon ever met.

Runyon and Capone were joined that night by 145,000 other boxing fans. As Dempsey's emphasis on "sportsmanship" suggested, boxing was aiming for respectability and the Jazz Age was prepared to confer it; this was, for instance, the first major bout at which women formed a significant part of the crowd. "They came in, smiling a bit self-consciously, made themselves pretty, chatted through the preliminary bouts, bit their lips and twisted their mouths," observed the reporter for the *Chicago Tribune*, Genevieve Forbes Herrick. "They wanted a knockout, O, without too much blood, but a knockout."

The great event was preceded by the appearance of the three most powerful elected officials in Illinois: Governor Len Small, Mayor William Hale Thompson, and State Attorney Robert Crowe. "They stood in the white glare of the forty-five huge lamps that made ring and ringside a blaze of daylight and smilingly received the cheers of jubilant men and women," wrote a breathless reporter. At his ringside seat, Al Capone joined the applause, and although the officials ignored him, it must have been comforting for him to reflect that he, the man in the dark, owned all three of the men looming above him in the light, and through them exercised greater influence than any other individual in Illinois.

At 10:00 P.M. the pudgy politicians at last yielded the ring to the fighters, and a sense of expectation at the great contest that was about to begin energized the crowd. The gong sounded, and the fight finally commenced, Dempsey in the dark trunks and Tunney in the white. Dempsey had let his beard grow, and he looked, said one reporter, "savage." The two started sparring, more concerned with not losing than with winning, and as the fight proceeded there was a faint murmuring of disappointment in the crowd as the hoped-for knockout punch failed to appear. But it was clear that Tunney was outfighting Dempsey, the man whom Capone had befriended and backed.

In the middle of the seventh round, Dempsey smacked Tunney's jaw three times in brutal succession, and Tunney, a "crazy, glassy look in his blue eyes," fell to the floor, "like a drunken man." As Tunney grasped one of the ropes to try to steady himself, Dempsey, arms outstretched, towered over him. Tunney gave no sign of returning to his feet. The referee, Dave Barry, tried to wave Dempsey away so the count could begin, but Dempsey, who was himself disoriented, spent perhaps five precious seconds hovering above Tunney, inadvertently delaying the count. Finally he lumbered to his corner, and the referee began the ritual, which was overwhelmed by the deafening howls of the crowd. "By the time the count was under way Gene's head was beginning to clear and before it had progressed half way he had managed to raise himself to sitting position, ready to get up when the count of nine was reached," noted a ringside observer. This moment of suspended animation became known as the legendary "long count," subject of endless debates and hairsplitting over the rules, but in the end all that mattered was that Tunney did get to his feet. Fighting cautiously, he managed to knock down Dempsey in the eighth round, and he was still standing at the end of ten. Tunney won the match by a unanimous decision and retained his title as the heavyweight champion of the world.

After the fight, Capone returned to the Metropole, where he threw a lavish party at which senators and congressmen mingled with journalists eager to drink Al's free booze and with society figures who were in turn desperate to rub elbows with real gangsters. There was a band, of course—this was the Jazz Age, and there was always a band—conducted by Jule Styne, a former child prodigy who had abandoned the strictures of classical music for the popular realm. Later known for his Broadway songs and Hollywood scores, he was now leading a dance band. After the musicians warmed up, Capone took over from Styne, prepared to display his familiarity with Gershwin's "Rhapsody in Blue," the sinuous anthem of the Jazz Age itself.

Al Capone planned to conduct. He had a baton, he had the sheet music, and he had the attention of everyone in the room. He waved his arms with a confident flourish—as if to say conducting was easy, anybody could do it—and the band played. Under the gangster's direction a clarinet soared, the piano trilled, and a recognizable rendition of Gershwin's famous music filled the Metropole. And when his rhapsody ended, Capone took a bow and surrendered his baton. It had been a memorable fight, and for the audience at the Metropole that night, an even more memorable concert.

For Capone the fight marked another glorious night in Chicago, a night to make the twenties roar, but for Jack Dempsey, the loss marked the end of his championship aspirations. He was still useful to Capone, however. When the Manassa Mauler retired from the ring, he went to work promoting fights for the Capone organization. But fixed fights were still the order of the day in Chicago, and as Dempsey later wrote, "I quit because I was being used as a front, a promoter in name only. . . . Capone's mob wound up telling me who was going to fight and how much I had to pay them. When they started giving orders who was going to win and who was going to lose—and naming the round—I got out." Although Dempsey broke with the Capone organization, he later entered into a partnership with Meyer Lansky and Longy Zwillman, two prominent Jewish racketeers, to run the Dempsey-Vanderbilt Hotel in Miami Beach, Florida.

• • •

Closer than ever to attaining the respectability he craved, Capone expanded his organization. Within months of Thompson's arrival at City Hall, the Chicago Crime Commission discovered, "Capone took over the south side, with all privileges. His man [Jimmy] Mondi opened a gambling joint on Clark street, south of Madison street. . . . Capone took over the beer territories from the Saltis and O'Donnell gangs. The slot machine racket later involved the indictment of six police captains. Capone got more than the $260,000 back." He exercised greater control than ever before over the Police Department; the upper echelons of the force aided the racketeer in maintaining a continuous flow of whiskey, even as cops on the beat conducted raids designed mainly for show. William Pasley, a reporter covering Chicago's renewed corruption, grumbled, "Watching an official with a gold star on his chest comfortably downing snits of whiskey while his men are out dry-raiding the city is a rare experience." Capone's near-monopoly of Chicago gambling and bootlegging, the booming economy, and the complete disregard of Prohibition drove the organization's revenue to new heights. In 1927, the U.S. attorney's office estimated, the Capone combine took in approximately $105 million. The amount broke down as follows:

Alcohol manufacture and sale	$60,000,000
Gambling	25,000,000
Vice and resorts	10,000,000
Other rackets	10,000,000

1927 had been a good year for the Capone organization, even with Al in retirement much of the time, and 1928 promised to be even better.

Violence returned to Chicago, for Thompson's new order upset the fragile truce among racketeers engineered by Capone. In May, hardly a month after Thompson took office, a series of murders—there would be four in all—stymied the police. In every case, the victim was attired in the snappy garb favored by racketeers and carried a substantial bankroll, which had not been disturbed. In addition, each victim was Italian, and each came from out of town, one from New York, two from St. Louis, and one from Cleveland. More peculiar still, the right hand of each victim held a nickel; the coin had apparently been placed there after the shooting. The police interpreted the placement of the coin to be a gesture of utter contempt, as if to say the victim's life wasn't worth a nickel.

Suspicion fell on three men associated with the Capone organization: Scalise and Anselmi, who always worked as a pair, and "Machine Gun" Jack McGurn. Notorious assassins, Scalise and Anselmi made likely culprits, but the nickel suggested a flourish beyond their primitive methods for dispatching their victims. Jack McGurn, now a rising star in the Capone organization, strenuously denied any knowledge of the murders. Yet McGurn's word was never reliable. Of all Capone's gunmen, he was the most complex and unpredictable, more of a lethal prankster than a hired assassin: able, smart, and mercurial. Vincenzo Gebaldi (McGurn's real name) was a Chicago boy, the oldest of six, a product of Little Italy, where he distinguished himself both as a student and as a pugilist. He rose through the ranks of amateur boxing clubs, shed his Italian name in favor of a more commercially acceptable Irish nom de guerre, and as Jack McGurn established himself as a welterweight with promise. At about this time, McGurn's father, Angelo, a grocer, developed a sideline selling sugar to the Gennas, the leading alky-cookers of Little Italy. Although this alone did not make Angelo a gangster, he was dealing with exceedingly dangerous men, and in January 1923 he was shot to death. Jack McGurn was nineteen at the time. He turned to a life of crime soon after his father's death, and the police became familiar with him through a variety of violent escapades; he was even wounded by machine gun fire, but he survived to become known as "Machine Gun" Jack McGurn and to carve out his bloody niche in the Capone organization. Despite his reputation, he avoided arrest, and he maintained his innocence throughout the police investigation of the four well-dressed men found dead with their bankrolls intact and nickels pressed into their palms. Although the police ultimately failed to tie McGurn to the murders, they remained deeply suspicious. Had they known him just a little better, they would have realized that when his father, Angelo, was found dead on the streets of Little Italy, he, too, clutched a nickel in his right hand.

All the corpses found during this period had one thing in common: they had once been men who had tried to win the bounty placed on the head of Al Capone. It had not been put there by the police, of course, but by yet another rival, Joseph Aiello, rushing to fill the vacuum created by the death of "Hymie" Weiss and "Schemer" Drucci. Aiello came from a large Sicilian family; in fact, the Aiello clan was in many ways the successor to the Gennas in the Little Italy alky-cooking trade, which is to say they were extremely dangerous. Capone feared them, for the Aiellos had put a bounty on his head: $50,000, they said, for the life of Al Capone. As McGurn eliminated one would-be assassin after another, the Aiellos tried a different approach. They kidnapped the cook at one of Capone's favorite restaurants, the Bella Napoli, and offered him a simple proposition: either be killed or poison Al's next meal in the restaurant with prussic acid. Should the cook accept the latter proposition, Joseph Aiello offered $10,000 to show his appreciation. The cook displayed keen business sense by agreeing to the plan, insisting on payment up front, and then rushing to tell Capone of the Aiellos' perfidy at the first opportunity, thereby endearing himself to his best-known customer. In response, Capone immediately declared that Aiello must be eliminated. Now desperate, Aiello devised another, far more serious attempt on the life of his adversary.

To the casual observer, 311 South Clark Street was a nondescript cigar store in a crowded, unpretentious Chicago neighborhood. But as Aiello and every other racketeer knew, the store served another function as the headquarters of corrupt politicians who controlled the First Ward. It was at this address that "Hinky Dink" Kenna managed his network of payoffs, and it served as a meeting place for politicians and racketeers, including Capone. Across the street stood the small Atlantic Hotel, where, in room 302, Aiello established a machine-gun nest, which meant, in practice, two or three gunmen sitting barely concealed behind draperies in front of a window, scanning the street hour after hour, waiting for their prey.

Capone's obvious move would have been to send his men in after Aiello's crew, but the notoriety resulting from a gun battle between two rival gangs was exactly what he wished to avoid. Instead, he employed his connections in the Police Department to deal with Aiello. In place of Capone henchmen appearing at the Atlantic Hotel, a group of policemen broke up the machine-gun nest, then arrested Aiello in his home in Rogers Park on November 22, 1927. The cops brought him to the Detective Bureau at 1121 South Street for questioning; shortly after he arrived, however, the police tipped off Capone. As Aiello prepared to leave the building, a fleet of cabs raced to the Detective Bureau, and when they arrived, their brakes squealing, over a dozen Capone gunmen hit the street, some equipped with machine guns, others with .45-caliber automatics. So efficient and organized did they seem that policemen observing the sight took the arrivals to be detectives, not gangsters. Only when one of the men entered the Bureau and was recognized as Louis "Little New York" Campagna, a Capone gunman, did the cops realize the truth.

Now the police descended en masse and captured Campagna as well as two other Capone gunmen, but the conflict did not end there. Demonstrating a perverse flair for incompetence, the police locked the Capone crew into a cell adjacent to Aiello's.

"You're dead, friend, you're dead," Campagna whispered through the bars to Aiello, in Sicilian dialect. "You won't get to the end of the street still walking."

"Can't we settle this?" Aiello pleaded. "Give me fourteen days and I'll sell my stores, my house and everything and quit Chicago for good. Can't we settle it? Think of my wife and baby."

"You dirty rat! You've broken faith with us twice now. You started this. We'll finish it."

Freed by the machinations of his lawyer, Aiello implored the police to protect his life, and a detective told him, "Sure, I'll give you police protection—all the way to New York and onto a boat." That night Joseph Aiello and two of his brothers fled Chicago and spent the next two years in remote Trenton, New Jersey, plotting the death of Al Capone.

Had the Keystone cops staged the Aiello drama, the spectacle would have had them rolling in the aisles. Only in Chicago, it seemed, was this sort of law-and-order farce possible, with the police dashing through the streets in their flivvers, pretending to investigate crimes that their superiors had no interest in pursuing, actually hoping the whole thing would blow away before it implicated cops and prosecutors alike.

With the removal of the latest threat to his life, Capone could not resist the temptation to hold a press conference and boast that he was now the most powerful as well as the most brazen racketeer in all Chicago. "When I was told Joey Aiello wanted to make peace, but that he wanted fourteen days to settle his affairs, I was ready to agree," he explained. "I'm willing to talk to anybody any place to bring about a settlement. I don't want trouble. I don't want bloodshed. But I'm going to protect myself. When someone strikes at me, I'm going to strike back. I'm the boss. I'm going to continue to run things. They've been putting the roscoe on me now for a good many years and I'm still healthy and happy. Don't let anybody kid you into thinking I can be run out of town. I haven't run yet and I'm not going to. When we get through with this mob, there won't be any opposition and I'll still be doing business."

It was an emotional, foolish outburst, completely at odds with his earlier resolution to quit the rackets. Events would later compel Capone to take back every word he said.

• • •

Richard Hart placed his three sons in a row. He then distributed cigarettes, and each of the young boys stuck one in his mouth, unlit. Their father stepped back several paces until he stood even with the row of boys. He then drew his revolver and took aim. From a distance, it seemed as though he aimed straight at the boys' heads, but his real target was the cigarette each held between clenched teeth.

The boys closed their eyes as their father cocked his trigger eye and the moment of firing approached. The gun went off with a loud crack, but the boys knew not to move, not to react in any way. One by one, the cigarettes broke in two; half fell to the ground, and half stayed in the boys' mouths. When the last shot died away, the boys opened their eyes, and their father, his pistol returned to its holster, walked toward them, smiling.

They were good boys.

• • •

The Hart family had moved around quite a bit over the last few years, as "Two-Gun" Hart, now a special agent of the Bureau of Indian Affairs, pursued Indian bootleggers on various reservations. The oldest brother of Al Capone was still a hero back in Homer, Nebraska, the wrinkle in the prairie to which he faithfully returned between assignments. Although the Morvace shooting had tarnished his luster, the newspapers still considered him good copy, an authentic if controversial legend in their midst. At the Winnebago Indian reservation south of Homer, ran one account, Hart displayed his courage by cornering three men, probably drunk, who had held up a deputy marshal. "Drop those guns," he ordered, and for once he prevailed through words alone. The administration of justice was not always that clean and simple. In tiny Walthill, Nebraska, just beyond the Winnebago reservation, an Indian stole two horses. "Hart was notified," ran the account, "jumped into his flivver and gave chase, caught sight of the red man and gained steadily on him. He began firing. . . . Hart shouted 'Stop or I'll kill you.' By this time the chase had covered many miles and the horse fell exhausted. The Indian jumped off and ran up the hill. Both men ran out of cartridges but neither knew the other had no more. Hart pursued the Indian up the hill with level revolver and the Indian surrendered."

Wherever he went, he was effective, if violent, but everyone knew how mean Indians could get, especially when they were liquored up, so Hart had more latitude in dealing with them than with whites. At the same time, he liked the Indians, though he never trusted them. He had seen what life on a reservation did to the Indians, often reducing a capable individual to a helpless ward of the state, drifting from one monthly government check to the next, drinking away the money he had done nothing to earn. Hart had no idea how to solve the Indian problem, but he believed he knew best how to handle them, drunk or sober.

In the summer of 1926, when Al sought refuge at Round Lake, the Hart family moved to the Cheyenne River Indian reservation located in central South Dakota. The government quarters consisted of ten houses beside the river, surrounded by tall piles of chopped wood necessary for getting through the cold months. On August 19, his son Harry was born there, the last of Richard Hart's four children. Soon after the family returned briefly to Homer and then moved farther west as "Two-Gun" resumed his quest for glory.

Hart accepted an assignment in Coeur d'Alene, Idaho, close to the Washington State border and the Spokane Indian reservation. Once again his exploits enlivened the local papers, who found Hart ready to give extended interviews detailing his exploits. The dispatches followed him across the state line to Spokane, Washington, site of another Indian reservation:

"TWO-GUNS" SLEUTH PACIFIES NORTHWEST INDIANS

(A.P.) "Two-Guns" Hart, picturesque chief of Indian reservation police, once again proved that he performs as the hero of any good thriller should. On Uncle Sam's payroll the name appears as Richard J. Hart, special federal officer, but the Indians on the reservations that know him as the representative of the "Great White Father" long ago named him "Two-Guns" thanks to his ambidexterity with a six-shooter. . . .

Hart has had a hand in the capture of more than 20 murderers while covering 12 reservations. In the last year he brought in three Indian killers. He has been a cowboy soldier and police officer. A "beat" of more than 200 square miles with supervision over more than 800 is Hart's domain. He travels by foot, in car, horseback, on snow shoes and skis. In summer he has tracked men by the imprints they made in soft pine needles in forests and in winter he has followed them through snow. Under him are three Indian police. His work is different from that of his regular officers or detectives for the criminals he captures are outdoor men and there are a few informers who aid him. "The Indian who kills a man is different from the white," Hart says. "For he will not talk about it and has no regrets. He usually feels that he was justified and forgets and he rarely has a guilty conscience."

Throughout this period, "Two-Gun" Hart was in the papers as often as his brother Al, but the papers were local, not the huge Chicago dailies, and the stories told not of his latest murder charge or indictment; instead, they extolled his derring-do in rounding up drunken Indians and recalcitrant bad men, and no one reading them would have guessed that the heroic "Two-Gun" Hart, who "performs as the hero of any good thriller should," was kin to the man who was emerging as the nation's most notorious racketeer.

At home, his wife, Kathleen, pasted these and other articles detailing his exploits into her scrapbook, along with photographs of Hart on the job or pretending to be, for the one thing he loved better than telling reporters about his adventures was posing for pictures. "He loved to dress up," his son Harry remembers. "No doubt about it. And he loved to be photographed." One striking photograph taken at a carnival shows him attired in Western regalia, holding an absurdly long revolver in his hand, holding up four female "bootleggers" dressed in furs. The women all have their hands in the air, and they appear to be squealing through their barely suppressed laughter. It was all in fun, "Two-Gun" Hart's idea of a joke. Another photograph found him posing insolently beside a moving picture marquee advertising Buck Jones in *The Branded Sombrero*. Let others act, his expression seemed to say; Hart lived a true-life Western. There are others: Hart on horseback, twirling a lasso. Smoking a cigarette, posing with an Indian. He was also proud of his muscular physique, and in several photographs he poses as a bare-chested wrestler in black tights about to engage a rival. Through his constantly changing costumes he expressed the various facets of his nature: menacing, heroic, victimized, haughty.

Wherever he went, his behavior gave rise to oft-repeated stories. "I got to know a fellow in Sioux City," Harry Hart says, "and when I told him who I was, he said, 'Heck, I used to ride horses with your dad. I knew him real well. The first time I met him was in a hotel downtown, and he was real cruddy looking, all dirty and all that stuff. He was with some guys, and he told these guys, "I know you're bootleggers. I'm going to go upstairs now, and when I come back down you'd better be here because I'll git you, I'll find you." And they stayed there. Meanwhile he went upstairs, and when he returned, here he comes in a nice fancy white suit and a big ten-gallon white hat, all dressed up, with two guns on the sides. That was your dad. That was him.' "

                              •   •   •

In the summer of 1927 President Calvin Coolidge and his wife decided to flee the heat and pressure of Washington, D.C., for a summer vacation in the Black Hills of South Dakota. A state-owned game lodge consisting of twenty rooms became the summer White House. They arrived on June 15;

uppermost on Coolidge's mind at the time was the question of whether he should seek reelection the following year. As he pondered his decision amid the natural splendor, the president inadvertently created a furious local controversy by declaring that he did not use a fly when fishing, as local custom dictated; he preferred a hook and worm. He again raised eyebrows when the Sioux Indians adopted him as their "Leading Eagle," and he posed for photographs in an elaborate cowboy costume, complete with chaps engraved with the letters C-A-L. This was not what the American public had come to expect from the man from Vermont, who eventually reached the conclusion that he would not, after all, run for reelection.

During his sundry misadventures out west, the hapless Coolidge was accompanied by several bodyguards drawn from the ranks of the finest law enforcement officers to be found in that wide-open part of the country. Among this elite group was Richard "Two-Gun" Hart, who had received a special commission to serve as Coolidge's bodyguard during the trip. It was a signal honor for Hart, evidence that he had managed to overcome questions about his conduct raised by the shooting of Ed Morvace in 1924. Of all the roles he had played during his career, this was the most satisfying to his vanity and to his desire to live out the mythology of the Wild West. Had anyone troubled to check Hart's past a little more deeply, they would have realized the extent of the fictional identity he had created. Had Coolidge known that one of his trusted bodyguards was Al Capone's brother, he would have been horrified, and the nation would have been horrified. But no one checked, and no one knew.

So it was that each Capone brother subscribed to opposing notions of crime, punishment, and justice. While "Two-Gun" Hart spent his days tracking down bootleggers in the wilderness or safeguarding the president of the United States, his brother Al Capone dodged attempts on his life, ruthlessly expanded his racketeering empire, and forged a new antihero for the Jazz Age: the urban gangster, the man who was a law unto himself.

CHAPTER 6

The Jazz Age

AL CAPONE ADORED OPERA, but the real music of his time and place was jazz. As he maneuvered and blasted his way into prominence as a bootlegger, jazz musicians—many of them capable and a few of them absolutely brilliant—gravitated to Chicago, where they delighted audiences with their effervescent music. Thanks to this migration of talent, Chicago was by 1927 the center of the jazz world, and as a by-product of his control of the nightclubs and saloons on the South Side, Al Capone and his brother Ralph became Chicago's most important jazz impresarios. Despite the existence of Prohibition, their nightclub empire flourished openly. Perhaps their best-known establishment was the Cotton Club, the Cicero nightspot where every jazz musician of consequence aspired to entertain. At the Cotton Club and most other nightspots, the musicians were mainly black and the audience entirely white, and the patrons included Mayor Thompson as well as numerous aldermen, judges, and other public officials. As for the police, they came as guests, not to make arrests. So effective was the Capones' control of local government that Prohibition seemed not to exist on their turf, except as a rumor or an echo of distant gunfire.

Al Capone had never planned a career as a jazz impresario, but he took to the role with enthusiasm largely because it brought him into contact with some of the best-known and most capable performers of the day, all of whom, he was flattered to note, depended on him for employment. To the musicians burning to make names for themselves or simply desperate for work, the Capone brothers, Al and Ralph, were the men to see. Although the majority of the musicians were black, Al, unlike Ralph and all other racketeers, extended himself to them and gradually won their respect and admiration. His behavior was all the more remarkable because at that time

Chicago's black community was invisible to most whites. The six Chicago dailies refused to cover the Black Belt, as it was called, although the leading black newspaper, the *Defender*, did an able job for its constitutents. Compared to other ethnic groups such as the Jews and Italians, to say nothing of the Irish, the Black Belt's political clout was insignificant. However, Capone, as an equal opportunity employer and corrupter, drew no racial distinctions. Everyone was welcome to join his coalition.

Among the young musicians of Chicago's Black Belt who owed their careers to Al Capone was Milt "Judge" Hinton, a renowned jazz bassist often described as the most recorded musician of all time. The Capones gave Hinton his start as both a musician and as a bootlegger, and one memorable day Al himself saved Hinton's career from disaster. Hinton's story was emblematic of many blacks who fled the intense prejudice of the South and came to Chicago in search of a better life. Born in Mississippi in 1910, he moved with his family to Chicago's South Side because, he recalls, "Everybody came to Chicago. There was a tremendous need for unskilled labor at the stockyards, for porters in the hotels and for redcaps at the railroad stations. And these were good jobs, better than what black folks had in the South. So they migrated by the thousands, like my family."

Once these families found apartments and employment, usually at wages higher than they had ever known in the South, Hinton continues, "we wanted our kind of music. We had all these great nightclubs all over the South Side. Louis Armstrong, Jelly Roll Morton, King Oliver from New Orleans, and Duke Ellington from New York—all these guys were working in the clubs and big hotels in Chicago; that's what made Chicago the center of jazz. If you were in Texas and a good musician, you tried to get to Kansas, but the big jazz was in Chicago." Soon-to-be-famous musicians abounded; Hinton's mother was a piano teacher, and her pupils included Nat King Cole. When Hinton grew older, he attended the predominantly black Wendell Phillips High School, whose music director, Major N. Clark Smith, trained any number of ambitious and talented students. "Out of this school came a lot of great musicians who made names for themselves in Duke Ellington's band and Cab Calloway's band," says Hinton. "Major Smith even organized a youth band outside of the school to represent the *Chicago Defender* in the hope of going around the country to play. Lionel Hampton and Nat King Cole were in that band."

Meanwhile, Hinton struggled to find a job playing his instrument of choice, the violin. "When Al Capone opened the Cotton Club in Cicero, he wanted all black musicians and all black entertainment, so he got a fellow from Mississippi, Walter Bond, a young clarinet player, to get the band together," Hinton remembers. "All my peers had a chance to get in this band, but they were not using violins." Unable to find work at the Cotton

Club, the young Hinton delivered newspapers instead, earning $9.25 a week "while all my friends playing trombones and saxophones had a chance to get into Al Capone's band and make $75 a week. I was very much discouraged. I didn't know if I could get me a horn, so I eventually decided to get a bass. After all, what is a violin but a bass with four strings?" With his musical ability and training, he proved a quick study on the bass, and before long he was playing one-night stands in his neighborhood while maintaining his paper route. "All the big black bands had bass players in them, and if one of the bass players got drunk and didn't show up, it was 'get the kid,' and that's how I got my apprenticeship. By this time I was getting to know the bass well and getting to know musicians. Then, one day my mother said to me, 'Now listen, you can't come in here at five o'clock in the morning from playing a gig and change clothes and go deliver those newspapers. You've got to go to school.' " The young Hinton was at a crossroads, but just then Ralph Capone opened up a a new nightclub, and he gave Hinton a job there as a bass player. "Ralph was a pretty tough guy, really mean and cheap, not like Al," Hinton observes. "Ralph was always hitting porters and slapping people around. He wasn't very likable, as Al was. I never had any problems with Ralph, but you could see what he would do if some girl got out of line."

After a stint in Ralph's club, Hinton found work in a cleaning and pressing shop run by his uncle. Hinton soon discovered that this modest establishment was a front; his uncle's real business was delivering "alcohol and whiskey to all the apartment houses in the neighborhood. When it was time for the tenants to pay their rent, they would give a party on a Saturday night and invite all their friends to come over and fry up a lot of chicken and have whiskey. People would come and pay for the food and drink, and that way they got their rent money together. And they bought their whiskey from us, from my uncle. Al Capone saw the potential in this, and he came over to my uncle and a guy named Jim Thomas, who had connections with the numbers racket. Capone told these guys: 'You buy all the alcohol from me for six dollars a gallon and sell it for eighteen dollars. You keep twelve dollars for every gallon of alcohol. I'll handle all the police, you won't have to worry about protection. I'll furnish the transportation. All you have to do is deliver the alcohol and collect the money. Just don't buy from anybody but me.' " Hinton recalls that Capone would appear at the cleaning and pressing shop every Saturday. "He was sort of plump, and he'd walk in with several guys. The police would all be standing around, waiting for him. They would line up just like they were waiting for a bus. He would come in with a bag of money, and he'd pay every policeman five dollars."

Such payoffs greased the wheels of the bootlegging business, but the primary reason for Capone's success was his ruthless elimination of all competition. No other outsiders supplied the neighborhood, but Capone did permit his local distributors to distill their own concoctions. In fact, Hinton's uncle's partner, a man named Pete Ford, built and maintained a still with Capone's blessing across the street from the cleaning and pressing shop. Says Hinton, "Capone kept his gallon cans of alcohol in the back of the place. We would take a case of bottled whiskey, pour it in the tub, mix it with alcohol, and make three cases." Before they sold the result, they carefully disguised it to look like bonded whiskey. "A black guy with a funny eye used to come with a big sheet of stamps to go over the top, sealing the bottle of whiskey. We'd sit back and clip these sheets into strips, and we'd fill the bottles and put this strip over. And we sold this for five dollars a pint. Everybody was making lots of money. My uncle wore a silk shirt, and he kept almost $1,000 in his breast pocket. He was a big eater, and he'd sit back there and eat and just answer the phone as people ordered his whiskey. Then we'd fill up this truck and go deliver it. And he would let me drive. That was how I learned to drive a car. I was fifteen years old, and I was delighted to be involved."

Hinton's brief, highly paid career as a bootlegger came to a brutal end the day he drove Pete Ford to a delivery at Forty-sixth and Drexel. As they approached their drop-off, a car suddenly plowed into them, hurling Hinton through the windshield in a shower of glass and throwing Ford to the street. The two of them lay in a pool of blood and bootleg alcohol, waiting for an ambulance. "They took me to the hospital. Police came but nothing happened because Al Capone had covered the whole thing," Hinton recalls. "Everything on my right side was broken. One of my fingers on my right hand was hanging off, one I used to play the bass. The doctor said, 'I'd like to cut that finger off.'

" 'Please don't cut my finger off,' I screamed. It was just hanging. Al Capone got my mother and brought her down to the hospital. He said to the doctor, 'Don't cut that finger off, don't cut it off.' And what Al Capone said, went. So they put it back together all wrong, but I've never had any problems with it. He took care of all the hospital costs."

Hinton was discharged from the hospital with his finger and his hopes for a career as a musician more or less intact, thanks to Al Capone. Hinton's boss, Pete Ford, was not so lucky. He died from the injuries he had sustained, and soon after that a black "strong-arm" named Slim Thompson, who was also affiliated with the little bootlegging operation, turned up dead. No one knew why he had been killed, but his death was said to be connected with the accident. The ordeal and its aftermath roused Hinton from his reverie of bootlegging glory. He left the business and its promise of fast money, and he never again drove a car. In the years to come, Milt "Judge" Hinton went on to play in several of Ralph Capone's nightclubs and later on with performers as diverse as Charlie Parker, Mahalia Jackson, Bing Crosby, and Aretha Franklin.

Capone's sense of rapport with blacks, to say nothing of the protectiveness the teenage Hinton experienced, was singular for Italians of his generation, most of whom dismissed blacks as *melanzane*, and who cautioned their children not to play with *them*. Yet here was Capone, organizing the black bootleggers, protecting them from the police, and increasing their profits at the same time. And for all these services he laid down but one inviolate condition: "Just buy your alcohol from me." As a result Capone became, if not quite the hero he was to certain Italians, a benign figure; he was the only racketeer to exploit the outsider status common to both groups, each of them oppressed, shunned, thrown back on themselves. Capone's willingness to become involved with blacks, to look after them even while profiting from them, displayed yet again his ability to build a broad-based economic coalition, which in turn made him a potent political force. In contrast, the Chicago Establishment based its authority on excluding the blocs Capone welcomed. The city fathers attempted to enforce a caste system, declaring themselves the ruling class while subjecting the lower orders to Prohibition, which they themselves felt free to ignore.

·   ·   ·

More than bootlegging attracted Capone to blacks; he was also enthralled by their vital music. But as another jazz musician, Fats Waller, discovered, playing for Capone could be an experience in terror, a command performance before a volatile tyrant. A product of Harlem, Waller was a lyricist, vocalist, and pianist of immense talent; best known for his song "Ain't Misbehavin'," he possessed an ability to laugh, joke, leer, pun, and parody his way through the songs he played. When Capone first heard of him, the "harmful little armful," as Waller called himself, was holding court at the piano in the Sherman House, a favorite gathering place for many of Capone's men. One night a Capone gunman stopped the show by waving a machine gun at the crowd; he warned the audience to sit still while he searched for a "friend." During the sweep, the Capone forces herded the audience and Waller into the men's room, and Waller, petrified, refused to come out until police arrived and assured him he was safe. (Given the conditions under which jazz musicians played, was it any wonder that Chicago jazz came to be known for its distinctive edge and bite, a nervousness never felt down in New Orleans?)

Not long after this incident, Waller himself was kidnapped at gunpoint as he left the Sherman House; four men bundled him into a waiting limousine, which sped off into the night. That Waller was black and his captors white added to his terror, and during the drive his imagination was inflamed with the horror of violent death. Instead, the limousine proceeded to Cicero and pulled up in front of the Hawthorne Inn, where the four men ordered Waller out of the car and shoved him into a lounge where a party was in progress. There they ordered him to sit down at the piano and play. Waller sensed he would live a while longer, and he eventually realized he was at a birthday party in honor of Al Capone. In fact, Waller himself was the present Capone's men gave to their boss. Giddy with relief, Waller played on and on. Capone in turn expressed his pleasure by plying Waller with champagne and filling his pockets with bills whenever he played a request. Waller claimed this was his first taste of champagne, and once he recovered from the shock of his enforced ride to Cicero, he had a marvelous time, for Waller loved a party as much as Capone did, so much so that the party lasted for three days, after which Waller went home exhausted and hungover, his pockets bulging with thousands of dollars.

No matter how generous and charming Capone was, the violence inherent in his milieu was always there, intimidating the jazz musicians who worked for him, and if they were not celebrities on the order of Fats Waller, they had to rely on their wits and luck rather than their reputations, to protect them. Among the latter group was Milton "Mezz" Mezzrow, a young Chicago-bred saxophonist with a taste for the low life. As he played his way through "Capone's University of Gutbucket Arts," a campus of brothels and nightclubs, Mezzrow became familiar with Capone himself: "Al always showed up surrounded by a gang of triggermen—they sat in a corner, very gay and noisy but gunning the whole situation out of the corners of their eyes. Al's big round face had a broad grin plastered on it and he was always good-natured." In contrast to his genial but businesslike older brother, young Matthew Capone, whom Mezzrow knew as Mitzi, hung around, trying to make himself useful. "His job was to follow the beer trucks out to Burnham, riding in a small Ford coupé with . . . another protection man, to make sure the load wasn't hijacked. Their cute little Ford tagged along behind those big trucks like a harmless pup, nobody ever guessing that it was loaded up with tommy guns."

When he was not escorting beer deliveries, Mitzi spent much of his time chasing the women who performed in Capone's jazz clubs, but when he fell for a girl singer named Lillian, "a sandy-haired, pleasant girl who was more sedate than the other chicks," Al stepped in. "Fire that girl," he ordered Mezzrow. "Get her out of here. If I hear any more stuff about her and Mitzi you're booked to go too."

"I won't fire her," Mezzrow said, doing the unthinkable, defying Al Capone. "Why don't you keep Mitzi out of here, if that's the way you feel about it?"

"She can't sing anyway," said Al in disgust.

"Can't sing? Why you couldn't even tell good whiskey if you smelled it and that's your racket, so how do you figure to tell me about music?"

Mezzrow reminded himself he was "talking to Mr. Fifty Caliber himself" and quickly fell silent. Normally, defiance from a Capone subordinate would have occasioned a beating, shooting, or even a one-way ride, but Mezzrow occupied a privileged position in the kingdom of Capone, akin to a court jester. Al indulged his musicians.

After an awkward interval, he burst into laughter. "Listen to the Professor," he cried. "The kid's got plenty guts." Mezzrow caught his breath, but Al suddenly lowered his voice. "But if I ever catch Mitzi fooling around here it won't be good for the both of you, see."

"Mezz" saw—and lived.

Like Milt Hinton, Mezzrow, though primarily a musician, also dabbled in bootlegging. Ordered to appear in a large circus tent, Mezzrow expected to play his saxophone. Instead, he was confronted by barrels of beer stacked in rows, and the next thing he knew a Capone henchman handed him a brace and bit and a galvanized pail. "Mezz" wasn't going to make music that day; he was going to make beer. "One of you guys drills holes in these barrel plugs and let three-quarters of a pail of beer run out of each barrel," the henchman instructed. "Then another guy plugs up each hole with these here wooden sticks, to stop the beer from running out." Mezzrow did as he was told, acquiring the rudiments of the brewer's art as it was practiced under the Capone regime:

> After we let out the right amount from a barrel, another guy came along with a large pail that had a pump and gauge attached to it. In this pail was a concoction of ginger ale and alcohol, just enough to equal the amount of beer that was drawn off. This mixture was pumped into each barrel, plus thirty pounds of air, and you had a barrel of real suds. I think they got as high as seventy-five bucks a barrel for this spiked stuff.

Although Capone liked to brag about the quality of his beer and whiskey, the stuff was, as Mezzrow, Hinton, and countless others knew from experience, highly adulterated. The musicians who drank it as they played the night away suffered from the effects of home brewed alcoholic poison, and they had seen others go blind or insane from booze. Perhaps the best-known jazzman to succumb to the effects of bootleg alcohol was Bix Beiderbecke, a horn player who was never without his hip flask of whiskey, and who died of its effects in 1931, when he was only twenty-eight. In time, the musicians, seeking a safer high, began to experiment with marijuana, which they believed was less damaging than rotgut, and compared to some of the toxic booze concoctions they drank, it probably was. Eventually, one of the best-known dealers in jazz circles was "Mezz" Mezzrow himself, who specialized in a potent weed imported from Mexico.

Although Mezzrow managed to flit past the Capone flame without scorching his wings, another performer in the Chicago scene was not so lucky. In the latter months of 1927, a story began to circulate through show business circles throughout the country. The story sowed more terror than any number of newspaper accounts of grim bootlegging murders, largely because the victim was a performer himself, Joe E. Lewis, who had fallen afoul of Capone's prize gunman, Jack McGurn. More than that of any other show business figure, Lewis's career afforded an object lesson in the perils of working for the Capone organization, indeed, of doing business with racketeers in general.

A comedian and singer who had risen from poverty on New York's Lower East Side, Lewis had become a fixture at the Green Mill, a popular speakeasy located on Chicago's North Side, where he was paid $650 a week, much of which he squandered on booze, for Lewis was an alcoholic. In Prohibition-era Chicago most speakeasies belonged to one syndicate or another, and the Green Mill happened to be the particular favorite of Al's debonair bodyguard, Jack McGurn. As McGurn had risen through the ranks in the Capone outfit, Al had rewarded him with a share in the Green Mill, in which McGurn took inordinate pride; no longer just a $150-a-week bodyguard, he was a somebody, a boss in his own right, and he jealously guarded his employees. Then, in August 1927, a rival speakeasy, the Rendezvous, offered Lewis $1,000 a week, plus a cut of the joint's profits from gambling. Although the offer came through the manager, an established bootlegger called John Fogarty, the Rendezvous actually belonged to the Capone syndicate's principal rival, the Moran-Drucci-Weiss gang. Employees did not jump from one place to the other without repercussions.

Only a day after he had agreed to bolt the Green Mill, as he was leaving his suite at the Commonwealth Hotel, Lewis was accosted by McGurn; since the two men knew each other, Lewis was not unduly afraid. Although McGurn had impressed the folks in Lansing, Michigan, as the well-mannered, subservient, soft-spoken bodyguard of Al Capone, here in Chicago, Illinois, he was known as "Machine Gun" Jack McGurn, the assassin reputed to have sent twenty-two men to their deaths without a trace of remorse. As the two men strolled along Diversey Parkway, McGurn asked Lewis why he was leaving the Green Mill, and his simple question received a simple answer: "My contract's up. I'm not renewing." McGurn quietly informed him otherwise. "I'm sorry," Lewis said, "I start at the Rendezvous on November second."

"You'll never live to open," McGurn murmured.

Disbelieving his ears, Lewis replied, "I'll reserve a table for you," and walked on alone.

More than a contract was at stake. The two men were also rivals for the same girl, who was first attracted to Lewis but subsequently abandoned him for McGurn, who, after he was done with her, assigned her to a cheap Capone brothel. Stung by her betrayal, Lewis refused to take orders from the man who had stolen and degraded his girl.

On the second day of November Lewis made good his threat to move to the New Rendezvous. The joint was packed that night, and Lewis took care to enter with a bodyguard, only to receive a threat not from a hoodlum but from a police captain (such was the extent of Capone's control of the Chicago Police Department) by the name of Joseph Goldberg, who told Lewis he would live much longer if he returned to the Capone fold. Lewis ignored the threat, and the show opened with an appearance by a dozen strippers, called "Daughters of Eve," who warmed up the audience until Lewis appeared onstage in a white suit, clutching a drink. After an hour of harmless patter and songs, he ventured to ridicule McGurn before the audience. The show ended uneventfully, and Lewis went home to the Commonwealth. He returned to the New Rendezvous every night for a week, and it appeared that he had succeeded in facing down McGurn's threat. As Lewis knew, as everyone knew, gangsters only kill gangsters. Deciding there was no further need for protection, Lewis dismissed his bodyguard.

The morning of November 9 found Lewis asleep in his room at the Commonwealth Hotel. A knock on the door roused him. Still groggy, Lewis opened the door, and three men rushed in, one armed with a .45-caliber automatic, who whispered, "Just one favor, Joe. Don't yell." Another man, this one carrying a .38, struck Lewis on the back of the head. The comedian, still conscious, slumped to the floor at the feet of the third man, who wielded a hunting knife. More blows to the head, and when Lewis was unconscious, the man with the knife inserted the blade into the victim's jaw as deeply as the blade would go. He removed the blade and dragged the tip of the knife across Lewis' neck. He then tore the skin on Lewis' face and scalp and peeled back the flaps. When he finished his butchery, the comedian was covered with blood seeping from his neck; every beat of his heart pumped more blood from his body.

The attackers fled, taking care to shut the door after them. Their modus operandi suggested they had done this before. No matter how brutal the attack on Lewis, and it was exceedingly brutal, it was not intended to kill him; one bullet would have accomplished that goal. Rather, he was supposed to survive and to serve as a warning to others who contemplated defying the dictates of the racketeers.

Thirty minutes later, Lewis regained consciousness. He was in excruciating pain as blood continued to flow from the wounds in his head and neck. He attempted to get to his feet, but he immediately slipped to the floor. He next tried to use the telephone to summon help, but when he reached for it he knocked it off the table, out of reach. His last hope was to open the door and crawl into the corridor, and after an intense struggle he managed to drag himself into the hallway, where a bellboy discovered him on the verge of death. He was rushed to a hospital, where a surgeon, Dr. Daniel Orth, spent seven hours sewing up the wound and saved Lewis's life. The patient recuperated in the hospital as two Drucci-Moran-Weiss gunmen stood guard.

The *Tribune* of November 9, 1927 carried the earliest detailed explanation for the savage attack:

CABARET MAN'S FEARS TOLD AS STABBING CLEW
Policeman Says Lewis Was Threatened.

Joseph Lewis, the cabaret singer and comedian who was so seriously wounded by knife thrusts yesterday in his room at the Commonwealth hotel, 2757 Pine Grove avenue, that physicians hold little hope for his recovery, had lived for months in constant dread that he would be assassinated.

This was reported to Assistant State's Attorney Joseph Nicolai last night by Police Captain Joseph Goldberg, a close friend of Lewis. ". . . Lewis mentioned Jack McGurn, who has quite a reputation as a strong arm man, as one who had threatened him if he made a change. The way Lewis put it was that McGurn had an interest in the Green Mill and was going to take him for a ride if he went to the other café. . . ."

Mr. Nicolai and Assistant State's Attorney Emmet Byrne tried to talk to the victim at the Columbus Memorial hospital last night, but he was unable to articulate or write. He communicated to them by nods that there were three assailants.

He also nodded assent when he was asked if he could tell the name of one of the assailant, but was unable to write his name.

Under the tutelage of a priest, J. A. Heitzer, Lewis gradually regained his powers of speech, but when police finally presented him with one of his attackers and asked the victim to identify the man, Lewis refused to cooperate. In disgust, the police let the suspect go, but the matter did not end there.

Six days later, gunmen opened fire on Lewis's attacker and on McGurn; the thug died, and McGurn, though wounded, lived. Lewis, now more or less recovered from his wounds, declared his intention to return to the New

Rendezvous. The joint was sold out within an hour of his announcement, and the night Joe E. Lewis appeared there after his attack was unforgettable. He staggered on stage with his head still bandaged, his right arm in a sling, his voice garbled. But the audience cheered him on, and he returned to the New Rendezvous night after night, going through this same bizarre routine for three weeks. There were those who considered Lewis's determination to perform despite his injuries a magnificent display of courage, and there were those who considered it a pathetic display of drunkenness. In either case, he acquired the sobriquet "The Man the Mob Couldn't Kill," and he became one of the more extraordinary sights of Chicago, a symbol of what gangsters like Al Capone had done to the city; everybody who was anybody in vaudeville came to watch Lewis stumble through his comedy act, and the sight struck fear in them, for they all became convinced that the gangsters could do to them what they had done to Joe E. Lewis.

At the end of his stint, a group led by Al Jolson, Sophie Tucker, Tom Mix, representing show business, and "Bugs" Moran, representing gangland, held a benefit in Lewis's honor that netted $14,000. He was supposed to use it to retire from the stage and open a secure little business, but Lewis drank more than ever and recklessly gave the money away.

Seeking to blunt the horrible publicity McGurn had brought to his organization, Capone intervened. "Why the hell didn't you come to me when you had your trouble?" he told Lewis. "I'd have straightened things out." Mollified, Lewis returned to his original habitat, the Green Mill, on the same terms as Moran had offered him, and he began to frequent the Capone-controlled dog track in Cicero, another place where Al could give him money by suggesting which dogs to bet on. There Lewis accidentally encountered his nemesis, Jack McGurn. On this occasion the two men glared at one another. They belonged to the same organization now; both worked for Capone. After a tense interval, McGurn yielded by looking away. Not a word had been uttered, yet Lewis convinced himself that he had the upper hand. Given McGurn's psychopathic personality and fierce pride, that was unlikely, but Lewis did enjoy the protection of Al Capone, whom he continued to serve faithfully for the remainder of his liquor-sodden career.

As the story of Joe E. Lewis gained currency, other performers who came through Chicago lived in mortal terror of Capone. Among the most celebrated of that era was Harry Richman, a vaudeville headliner who sang in a low, tuneless growl and oozed a smarmy charm unique to the period. Richman's source of concern about Al Capone involved the performer's first wife, who had later married Frankie Lake, a Chicago bootlegger. Richman did not know whether Lake was an ally or enemy of Capone; either way, Richman believed his life was in jeopardy. "Gangsters were known to be very touchy about their girls," Richman told himself. "They could get instantly, murderously sore at *anybody* who had had anything to to do with the girls, even if it had been years before."

At the time, Richman was starring in a popular musical revue, *George White's Scandals*, a blend of music, topical satire, and chorus girls. Each year the revue offered a new edition, which opened on Broadway and later embarked on a lucrative national tour. When the *Scandals* brought him to Chicago in 1927, Richman's fear of Capone turned to absolute terror. "On opening night I was so nervous I could hardly tie my necktie," Richman wrote. "I must have spilled forty dollars' worth of imported cologne after I shaved. They had told me that Capone was going to be out front. I immediately went to the asbestos fire curtain and, looking through the peephole, I scanned the audience to see if Capone was there. Sure enough, there he was in the first row, . . . and on either side of the stage I could see his hired guns sitting with their hands inside their coats, ready for action."

Richman refused to go on. George White, the producer of the *Scandals*, materialized to instruct his star, "The show must go on." To which the entertainer replied, "If I'm alive." White pushed him through the curtains onto the stage, as Richman told himself, "If I'm going to get killed, I'll sing my last song better than I ever did it before." Richman sang his opening number from start to finish and lived to hear the crowd roar in approval. But he was still terrified, having decided that Capone's gunmen were preparing to shoot him down during his next number. He was exhausted by the intermission, when the stage manager hurried to his side and said, "Harry, Al Capone wants to see you!"

"If you bring him back," Richman warned, "*I'll* kill *you*."

"You'd better kill me now. He's got thirty-eight bodyguards out there, and if he wants to he can blow up the entire theater."

Before these words had died away there was a knock on the door, and Richman speechlessly beheld the "the ruler of the underworld." Capone rushed forward, gripped the entertainer under the arms, and bellowed: "Richman, you're the greatest!"

"My knees knocked and tangled in a mixture of fear and relief," Richman recalled of the moment. Despite Capone's jolly tone, he was convinced that gangster would shoot him at any time. Summoning his courage, he asked about Frankie Lake, who had married his first wife.

"Frankie Lake," Capone hastened to explain, "don't mean a damn thing in this town. If he ever bothers you, you let me know. If *anybody* ever bothers you, let me know." And he proceeded to invite Richman to a party after the show.

"Mr. Capone," Richman stammered.

"Call me Al."

"Al," said Richman with immense relief, "I'm your boy."

Richman tagged along at the party, which he discovered was populated in roughly equal measure by bodyguards and chorus girls. "After five or six glasses of champagne I began to think he was a likable person," Richman recalled of Capone that memorable night. "It was hard for me to believe that this man had been responsible for all the horrible things I'd heard about him. He was so nice to me."

This shift in perception of Capone from homicidal monster to a generous fan was a refrain echoed by an ever-increasing number of entertainers, but Richman's reaction was particularly extreme. He had expected Capone to kill him at any moment, yet now he was unable to resist the man's charisma. "My champagne-induced infatuation with Capone overcame me to such an extent that I even followed him into the can," Richman continued. "While he stood at the urinal he kept strewing twenty-dollar bills on the floor. The attendant, picking them up, kept saying, 'Yes, *suh*, Mr. Capone, you the greatest man in the world.' " After Capone washed his hands and departed, the attendant confided, "Mr. Richman, I pray to God he come in here and pee every twenty minutes." With such gestures Capone reassured himself as well as those around him that he was not a monster, that he was, after all, a beneficent man, everybody's pal.

At the conclusion of the party, Capone, in his limousine, escorted Richman, who rode in his champagne-colored Rolls-Royce, to the Metropole Hotel, the two luxury vehicles flanked by Capone's convoy of four scout cars. When they arrived at the hotel, Capone bade goodnight to Richman and ordered the scout cars to accompany the entertainer to the Drake Hotel, where he was staying. "Instead of going home in a casket," Richman noted with relief, "I was going home in my own automobile."

Nor did Richman's dealings with Capone end that night; he soon had occasion to sense the power of the Capone mystique. A man for whom ostentation was a way of life, Richman liked to go about town with a $1,000 bill in his pocket, trying to use it in coffee shops and restaurants. Not surprisingly, he soon found himself the victim of holdups; night after night, as he roamed the city in his conspicuous Rolls-Royce after the show, a group of small-time hoods would force his car to the side of the road and fleece him of his money and his jewelry. After several of these episodes, Richman telephoned Capone for help and received an invitation to the Hotel Metropole, where the racketeer continued to hold court.

Richman discovered that Capone ran the hotel like an armed camp. There was a guard posted on each floor, checking off guests as they entered and exited the elevator, and Richman was forced to run a gauntlet of three bodyguards who energetically frisked him. Only after these preliminaries were concluded was he finally ushered into Capone's presence. "There was an American flag on the wall behind Al's desk, showing his love for his country," Richman noted, "and apparently commemorating some battle, too, for the wall was riddled with bullet holes."

"Harry, my boy, what can I do for ya?" Capone boomed. Richman explained that he was sick and tired of being robbed. Capone responded, "I'll fix that," and invited the entertainer to go for a drive with him. Taking a ride with a racketeer in Chicago was a risky proposition at best, but Richman had nothing to fear on this occasion. They went downstairs to Capone's waiting limousine and, trailed by the four scout cars, drove along the streets, admiring the brilliant autumn foliage. Overcome by the sight, Capone remarked, "Ain't that the most beautiful son of bitch you ever seen in your life?" They then drove back to the hotel at a leisurely rate and returned to Capone's office. Al sat heavily in his seat, pressed a button with one chubby fingertip, and an assistant entered, carrying a small package. "There's your stuff," Capone explained. Astonished, Richman tore through the contents; there were his $1,000 bills and his gaudy jewelry, all restored to him as if by magic. He looked up and tried to thank the magician who had accomplished this feat, but Capone halted him. "Forget it, kid. You're a great entertainer, Richman. I love ya like a kid brother." He summoned another assistant, who brought a note that Capone signed. "Put this in yer pocket," Al instructed, "and if you get into any trouble, use it." Richman carefully folded the talisman, placed it in his pocket, and departed.

Richman was held up again that night; a gang of men stopped his Rolls-Royce, ordered him out, and robbed him at knifepoint. "You can take anything I have," Richman told them, "but before you do, will you reach into my inside coat pocket and take out the piece of paper in there and read it?" But his assailants refused to do as he asked; they took his wallet and jewelry and fled. As Richman suspected, that was the not the last time he would see them. The following night they robbed him again, following the same modus operandi. Finally, on the *third* night, Richman recalled, "I used a magic word: 'Capone.' " The men did read the letter, as Richman insisted. It said, "Anybody who harms Mr. Richman in any way, shape, or form will have to account to me," and it was signed, "Yours truly, A. Capone."

The letter had its intended effect on the robbers, who gathered to marvel at the contents and especially the signature. One by one they made their apologies to Richman, praising the *Scandals* and explaining that they had no idea he was a friend of the great Al Capone, of whom they were as terrified as Richman himself had once been. They returned to their car and prepared to drive off, but not before one of them called out, "Hey, how about a couple of tickets?"

"What names shall I leave them under?" Richman asked.

The men, on second thought, decided not to call attention to themselves in this manner and disappeared into the Chicago night, leaving Richman alone with his money and his jewelry. It was as though he had come to a kingdom ruled by a legendary potentate, who took with one hand and gave with the other, and then mixed up the taking and the giving until they merged in a flurry of self-aggrandizement.

Capone deployed the same combination of intimidation and seduction to win the trust of another rising young entertainer who was just making his name in Chicago, the comedian Milton Berle, who received a summons from a stranger to make an unscheduled, private appearance before an invited audience at the Cotton Club in Cicero. This was Ralph's place, a popular nightclub the Chicago Crime Commission had labeled a notorious " 'whoopee' spot." Berle respectfully demurred; although he was not actually afraid for his life, he knew if he went to Cicero he would be forced to miss one of his scheduled performances at the Palace Theater in Chicago, so he offered to appear when he was finished, near midnight. "That's too late," the messenger told him. "They'd really like you a lot earlier. The mayor's a busy man. He can't stay out late at night."

Even the idea of performing before "Big Bill" Thompson failed to persuade Berle. "I've got to be on stage here at ten o'clock—I got a contract with the Palace—and it's at least twenty miles each way right through Chicago to the Cotton Club. It can't be done," he insisted, exaggerating the distance to make his point.

Berle's mother accompanied her son on his tours, and when she heard of the invitation, she insisted he make the time to comply, partly because she was afraid of the consequences if he did not and partly because she herself wanted to meet the famous Al Capone. Berle acquiesced, and soon he and his mother were riding to Cicero in a bulletproof limousine sent by the Capone organization. "I don't know how fast the driver was going," Berle recalled, "but I know we never stopped for one traffic light."

Arriving at the Cotton Club, Berle went directly to the stage, trying vainly to discern who was in his audience as he went through his routine. As he finished, he was approached by a "heavy-set man with thick lips."

"I really want to thank you for making time for us in your busy schedule, Mr. Berle," the man said.

Berle grasped his outstretched hand and felt a wad of bills migrating into his palm. "That's when I realized the polite, soft-spoken man was Al Capone," Berle remembered. He studied his hand, which now held perhaps twenty C-notes, $2,000. "No thanks, Mr. Capone," Berle said. "I don't need this."

"I don't need it either," Capone replied. "And you did a great job. The mayor really got a boot out of you."

Berle held his ground. "I was asked to come out here. I wasn't hired. And besides, I might need a favor from you some day." Capone relented and allowed Berle to return the money as deftly as he had received it. Mrs. Berle then had her opportunity to shake the hand of Al Capone, and the comedian and his mother returned to the limousine for the return trip at breakneck speed to Chicago. Berle made his ten o'clock appearance at the Palace with five minutes to spare.

•   •   •

Many other rising young performers who passed through Chicago on their way to fame found themselves drawn into Capone's orbit for a brief, giddy whirl. Even if they were too green to recognize him for who he was, Capone was drawn to them with a bizarre urgency. Such was the experience of Larry Adler, who played the harmonica with a virtuosity previously unknown for that modest instrument. At the time he encountered Capone, Adler was just a kid, fifteen years old, in the midst of a frenetic vaudeville tour, and his itinerary brought him to Chicago's Oriental Theatre.

At a cast party a man approached Adler, asked him a little about himself, determined that he was Jewish—"You're a Yid, right? Thought so, I can always tell. . . . Ya go to *shule?*"—and suddenly began lecturing him on the importance of going to synagogue every Saturday. The stranger explained that he was a Catholic, and he found the time to attend Mass. Adler, who was young and not especially interested in religion, protested that he had half a dozen shows on weekends; it was impossible to take time off and go to *shule* even if he wanted to. Scowling, the man lectured Adler about the importance of writing to his parents. But I *do* write, Adler protested. How often? Every week, Adler replied—well, maybe every other week. "Look, kid," the man said, "getcha coat, gowwan back to your hotel, this ain't no party for a kid like you anyway. When ya get back, siddown and write a letter your mother and father, right?" The astonished Adler found himself agreeing to the order—he seemed to have no choice—and before he left, the stranger offered a final word of advice: "This Saturday you're gonna go to *shule*, I don't give a damn how many shows you got to do, right?"

At last Adler managed to tear himself away from this insistent man who had started playing the role of his conscience. He asked a friend the identity of the man who was so quick to remind him of his filial and religious obligations. "Come, on," his friend said. "You're kidding." No, Adler told him, he wasn't kidding. Who was the man who had extracted a promise from him to attend *shule*?

"Al Capone," his friend said.

If Adler thought he was through talking with the most feared gangster of the day, he soon discovered he was mistaken, because Capone, after circulating through the crowd, returned to Adler and started boasting about how he attended Mass every Sunday, and he always made a point to send his mother flowers. Didn't Adler do as much for his mother? Well, Adler said, the fact was that his mother lived in Baltimore.

"So?" Capone said, "Ya never heard of Western Union, ya can't wire 'em?"

For Adler and many other stars, a meeting with Al Capone was one they never forgot, and many wound up in his thrall against their better judgment. He exerted his dominion over them in the same way as he did other men, the racketeers and politicians, only he was even more obvious with the performers, who lived in the arena of the ego. He came to dominate them not by shouting, overwhelming, or bullying, although the threat of physical violence always loomed, but by appealing to the inner man, his wants, his aspirations. Whatever cherished self-image he carried around with him and which the world callously ignored or discounted Al Capone claimed to recognize and value, and the legion of friends and allies he won this way never paused to question his motives or his sincerity. Instead, by making them feel valued, they gave unstintingly of their loyalty, and loyalty was what Capone needed and demanded; in the volatile circles through which he moved it was the only protection he had from sudden death. The highest compliment other men could pay Capone was to call him a friend, which meant they were willing to overlook his scandalous reputation, and to pretend along with Al that he had nothing to do with violence or sexual degradation, that he had never been a pimp or a murderer. Capone's ability to evoke this suspension of disbelief was a skill normally belonging to an expert politician; like a candidate running for office, Capone encouraged others to project their needs and fantasies on him, which he in turn claimed to acknowledge. The resulting phenomenon was akin to a mass hallucination, for he managed to replace, at least temporarily, the terrible things they said about him in the newspapers with a new version of the truth in which he was no pimp, no murderer, no gangster; he was a man-about-town who knew how to get things done, a man you could go to if you needed a favor—Al Capone, the happy bootlegger. Since he could be generous and effective when it suited him, and the papers often did malign him, there was just enough truth to support the myth and to make it real for those he persuaded to believe in it and in him.

·   ·   ·

On November 8, 1927, the *Chicago Daily News* declared: "CICERO CLEANS UP IN GAMBLING LULL—Lid on Tight in City, Al Capone's Places Jammed by Gamboleers" and went on to explain, "Scarface Al Capone's gambling houses came into their own last night as the lid was slammed on Chicago. Lauderback's, the Ship, the Radio Inn and other Cicero gaming establish-

Al Capone: Public Enemy Number 1. (*Collection of the American Police Center and Museum*)

James Colosimo's popular Chicago nightclub, where young Al Capone served his apprenticeship in vice. (*Collection of the American Police Center and Museum*)

A novelty shot of Al Capone (left, partly obscured by hat) posing with his brother Albert and Albert's wife, Dorothy (right), and another couple behind a sign advocating repeal. (*Collection of Maxine and Mona Pucci*)

Al Capone's younger brother John—"Mimi" to his family and friends—with his wife, Mary. *(Collection of Maxine and Mona Pucci)*

A novelty shot of Al's younger brother Albert (second from right) posing with bodyguards and a girlfriend in front of a mock saloon. *(Collection of Maxine and Mona Pucci)*

Al Capone's younger brother Albert, known as "Little Al" in the family, was handsome and popular with women; he chose to live in relatively safe obscurity until his death in 1981. *(Collection of Maxine and Mona Pucci)*

Albert Anselmi and John Scalise, Al Capone's most vicious assassins, in 1927. *(Chicago Historical Society, DN-82640)*

The victims of the St. Valentine's Day Massacre, planned by "Machine Gun" Jack McGurn on behalf of Al Capone. *(Chicago Historical Society, ICHi-14406)*

Capone's archenemy George "Bugs" Moran, in the leather jacket, at one of his many arraignments. *(Chicago Historical Society, DN-93634)*

Jack McGurn and his girlfriend, Louise Rolfe, the "blonde alibi," in court in 1929. *(Chicago Historical Society, DN-88600)*

Al Capone (left), Dorothy Pucci Capone, and her husband, Albert Capone, in Florida at about the time of the St. Valentine's Day Massacre (1929). *(Collection of Maxine and Mona Pucci)*

Al Capone's primary Chicago residence, 7244 Prairie Avenue, under police surveillance. He lived in this modest dwelling with his wife, mother, son, and an ever-changing cast of brothers and bodyguards. The house still stands today, looking very much as it did here, in 1930. *(Chicago Historical Society, DN-91356)*

The 1929 funeral of "Hymie" Weiss, another rival gangster whom Capone sent to his grave. This was one of many lavish gangster funerals that dazzled Chicago and appalled the nation during the 1920s. *(Collection of the American Police Center and Museum)*

The hugely corrupt mayor of Chicago, "Big Bill" Thompson (left), and his rival, William E. "Decent" Dever (right), with their wives. *(Chicago Historical Society, ICHi-10024)*

Al Capone's oldest brother, Richard "Two-Gun" Hart (right), posing with stills he captured as a Prohibition agent. *(Harry H. Hart)*

Hart (left) poses with three Indian chiefs whom he befriended in the course of his duties as a Prohibition agent. *(Harry H. Hart)*

Ralph "Bottles" Capone (left) lived his life in the shadows of his younger brother Al. Ralph is shown here with Anthony Aresso, another member of the Capone organization. *(Chicago Historical Society, DN-D8763)*

Johnny Torrio, the inventor of modern racketeering. He was Al Capone's first— and most important—teacher. *(UPI/Bettmann Newsphotos)*

Dion O'Banion, florist, bootlegger, gangster, and early rival of Al Capone. *(UPI/Bettmann Newsphotos)*

ments were jammed to the doors, getting a play such as they have never had in the three lean months when Chicago gambling houses were operating full blast under the Thompson 'wide open town' policy. Meanwhile nearly every gambling house of note in Chicago was closed. . . . The average man seeking to take a chance with Lady Luck was met with the explanation that 'the lid is on and on tight.' "

Appearances to the contrary, the Chicago Police Department was not responsible for "keeping the lid on" the city's gambling establishments. It was *Capone*, demonstrating his control of the city's economic life once again by withholding this hugely profitable activity. He had not suddenly turned reformer; on the contrary, this action was the first sign of his plan to drive Chicago's rackets into the open and thus embarrass the Thompson administration into increased cooperation. Capone had put the squeeze on rivals, even on the police, but now, for the first time, he was putting the squeeze on an entire city. Investigating the extent of Capone's control of Chicago at the time, the *Chicago Daily News*, normally a restrained voice, evoked "the amazing spectacle of a city of 3,000,000 people yielding tribute to a dictator of the underworld."

Amid the tumult Capone once again disappeared, but this time there was no secret concerning his whereabouts. On the day before his departure, Capone and a retinue of gunmen appeared at Marshall Field, the prestigious Chicago department store, not in the guise of racketeers or holdup men but as customers. There they spent, according to one journalist, nearly $5,000 "for the latest suggestions on what the well dressed hunter should wear when taking a rest from the gang wars." They left early the next morning for northern Wisconsin, and in the days that followed, reports trickled back to Chicago that "no better turned out duck shooters ever scratched their expensive leggings on briars. If it rained, they were protected by waterproof coats and breeches." Not surprisingly, "Their marksmanship and the quality of their firearms was all right, too." Al and the boys were gone for one week—long enough for him to decide anew that he must abandon the rackets at all costs.

He returned from his north woods adventure on December 5, equipped with this resolve as well as several braces of duck, hare, and even a bear slain by one of the hunting party. Capone was so eager to trumpet the news of his "retirement" that on the day of his return he summoned reporters to his suite at the Metropole Hotel, where they found him "sitting comfortably in an easy chair, . . . clad in the ultranifty hunting suit he bought for the recent jaunt to the north woods. His jowls still carried the six day beard growth cultivated while he and his companions tramped after bear and deer and hare." His eyes roving across the room, Capone announced he was abandoning the bootlegger's trade, and not only that, he was abandoning Chicago. The thoroughly skeptical press corps reacted to these revelations with intense amusement. "I'm leaving for St. Petersburg, Florida, tomorrow," Capone said above the reporters' chortles. "Let the worthy citizens of Chicago get their liquor the best they can. I'm sick of the job. It's a thankless one and full of grief. I don't know when I'll get back, if ever. But it won't be until after the holidays, anyway." No, he said in answer to a question, he hadn't bought a house there, not yet, but he would at any moment, and he expected to welcome the New Year far from the frigid shores of Lake Michigan. This was the second time Capone had made such an announcement—perhaps the declaration had become an annual rite—except that this time Al spoke in anger. This time he *meant* it.

"I've been spending the best years of my life as a public benefactor," he insisted, ever the servant of a pleasure-seeking public. "I've given people the light pleasures, shown them a good time. And all I get is abuse—the existence of a hunted man. I'm called a killer. Well, tell the folks I'm going away now. I guess murder will stop. There won't be any more booze. You won't be able to find a crap game, even, let alone a roulette wheel or a faro game." Referring to Chicago's chief of police, who had recently called for more uniformed men to combat the city's racketeers, Capone added, "I guess Mike Hughes won't need his 3,000 cops after all. The coppers won't have to lay all the gang murders on me now. Maybe they'll find a new hero for the headlines. It would be a shame, wouldn't it, if while I was away they would forget about me and find a new gangland chief?

"Public service is my motto," Capone continued with bitter irony. "Ninety percent of the people in Chicago drink and gamble. I've tried to serve them decent liquor and square games. But I'm not appreciated. It's no use. I wish all my friends and enemies a Merry Christmas and a Happy New Year. That's all they'll get from me this year. I hope I don't spoil anyone's Christmas by not sticking around." Here Capone alluded to the huge Christmas "bonus" that corrupt cops and city officials had come to expect from him. Al would not be handing out wads of cash this year, and the *Chicago Daily News* estimated he would save himself at least $100,000 through this one economy measure.

He suddenly turned serious and self-pitying. "I could bear it all if it weren't for the hurt it brings to my mother and my family. They hear so much about what a terrible criminal I am. It's getting too much for them and I'm just sick of it all myself. I'm known all over the world as a millionaire gorilla. The other day a man came in here and said that he had to have $3,000. If I'd give it to him, he said, he would make me a beneficiary in a $15,000 insurance policy he's taken out and then kill himself. I had to have him pushed out. Today I got a letter from a woman in England. Even over there I'm known as a gorilla. She offered to pay my passage to London if I'd kill some neighbors she's been having a quarrel with. The papers have made me out a millionaire, and hardly an hour goes by that somebody doesn't want me to invest in some scheme or stake somebody in business. That's what I've got to put up with just because I give the public what the public wants. I never had to send out high pressure salesmen. I could never meet the demand!"

Swept away on the tide of his own words, Capone declared he had no police record. This was far from the truth, as was his next statement: "I've never been convicted of a crime nor have I ever directed anyone else to commit a crime. I have never had anything to do with a vice resort. I don't pose as a plaster saint, but I never killed anyone. I never stuck up a man in my life. Neither did any of my agents ever rob anybody or burglarize any homes while they worked for me. They might have pulled plenty of jobs before they came with me or after they left me, but not while they were in my outfit." As proof of the honest, aboveboard, and legitimate nature of his business, Capone cited Cicero, which he memorably termed "the cleanest burg in the U.S.A. There's only one gambling house in the whole town, and not a single so-called vice den." This was completely untrue, of course, but no one bothered to correct the lord of Cicero.

Capone went on in this vein for a long while; it hardly mattered what he said, how many lies he spread. In the Chicago of 1927, black was white, truth was falsehood, everything was public relations, even the gang wars. When a reporter asked how a bootlegger can justify murdering his rivals, Capone instantly replied, "Well, maybe he thinks that the law of self-defense, the way God looks at it, is a little broader than the law books have it. Maybe it means killing a man in defense of your business—the way you make the money to take care of your wife and child. I think it does. You can't blame me for thinking there's worse fellows in the world than me." Such was Al's way of displaying contempt for "Big Bill" Thompson and his entire administration. The balance of power had shifted decisively in Capone's favor, away from legitimate institutions, which had become too compromised and ineffectual to cope. He had bought and bullied his way to power with bullets, booze, broads, and bucks, but now he behaved as if he were the Pied Piper, about to forsake Chicago to the rats. The Pied Piper of legend had stolen away the children—the future—from the city he had been hired to cleanse because he hadn't been paid the money he was promised. Capone was leaving Chicago because he hadn't been paid *respect*. Even a fraud like Thompson refused to give him his due.

Capone had called himself a "hero for the headlines," and as he antici-pated, his unusual press conference received wide play in the Chicago dai-lies. " 'YOU CAN ALL GO THIRSTY,' IS AL CAPONE'S ADIEU," the *Chicago Tribune* headlined, while the *Daily News*, emphasizing Al's vow to eliminate his Christmas "bonus" payoffs, said simply, "CAPONE PACKS BAGS AND SANTA

WEEPS." Mike Hughes, the chief of police, greeted the announcement with glee. "I feel almost like sending him and his boys a basket of roses," the chief quipped, adding that he still wanted his 3,000 additional policemen.

Mayor Thompson, however, was strangely silent on the topic of Al Capone's sudden departure; no expressions of relief or delight were forthcoming from City Hall. The damning fact was that Thompson needed Capone more than Capone needed Thompson. Indeed, the entire city of Chicago required the services of the Capone organization in one form or another. The press needed him to sell papers; the police needed him to supplement their meager pay and to help keep order (as did the local Prohibition agents); the city's speakeasies and their customers needed him to keep them wet and content; and Thompson needed him most of all to keep a semblance of the peace in Chicago and to help him remain in power. Without Capone, speakeasies would dry up and gang war would erupt. But the mayor could not come out and implore the city's most notorious crime figure to reconsider his decision and stay. Instead, Thompson greeted the announcement with silence, as he would the defection of any powerful supporter.

·   ·   ·

A blast of frigid air descended on Chicago, bringing with it snow and temperatures hovering around the ten-degree mark. Capone managed to avoid the sudden advent of winter, for the day after his press conference, he abandoned Chicago's dangerous streets for a warmer and presumably safer climate. Yet he failed to find the tranquillity he expected. Even when he came under attack in Chicago, Capone was in his element, instinctively aware of what moves to make, how to get things done, which usually meant whom to bribe and, occasionally, whom to eliminate. He had adapted to the city, and the city had in turn adapted itself to him. Once Capone left Chicago, however, he instantly became an outsider, and more than that, an outcast, an object of scorn. Thus his pilgrimage in search of peace quickly turned into a bizarre exile from the one city sufficiently corrupt to appreciate Al Capone.

On December 10, Al, accompanied by his brother Ralph and a contingent of armed bodyguards, boarded a train bound not for St. Petersburg, Florida, as he had announced, but for Los Angeles. It was an odd choice, for Capone had few allies in that city. In addition, Mae and Sonny remained in Chicago. Al planned either to send for them at a later date, or, if Los Angeles did not prove hospitable, to return home. At the time of the journey, he was a month short of his twenty-ninth birthday, and he had seen relatively little of the country. His travels had been limited to Brooklyn, Chicago, and Lansing, Michigan. Although he ceaselessly prowled the greater Chicago region, his attachment to place outweighed his wanderlust. He felt much more at ease within the confines of a bulletproof limousine than exposed to the open country where his older brother, "Two-Gun" Hart, was so much at home. Now this rail excursion gave Al his first opportunity to sense the magnitude of the country and to glimpse, however fleetingly, the other America, in opposition to which his own racketeering empire had been founded. The America Capone saw through the window of his car during that December of 1927 was a land of striking social contrasts and incongruities. Its big cities were the most modern in the world, wholly of the twentieth century, while its prairie hamlets adhered to a manner of living firmly rooted in the previous century. The fault line running between these two Americas—the urban and the agrarian—was Prohibition. Banning the sale and consumption of alcohol signified so much more than simple abstemiousness; it signified an entire way of life: rural, God-fearing, Protestant, middle-class, virtuous, restricted, suspicious, and self-reliant. It was a world in which Al Capone had no place.

If he expected to receive a warm welcome in Southern California, or at least an absence of resistance to his presence, he was disabused of that notion immediately upon his arrival. The Los Angeles chief of police, James E. Davis, warned the notorious racketeer, "You're not wanted here. We're giving you twelve hours to leave." The Capone party spent only a bit more time in Los Angeles than that; they stayed the night at the Biltmore, where Capone gave interviews concerning the state of gangland in Chicago ("This gang war stuff is greatly overdone, and I get tired of it. I'm strictly against gang wars of any kind and I just want to get along with everybody") and spent the following day touring a movie studio. "I never saw them make pictures before," Al commented, "that's a grand racket"—a racket that would soon make millions out of gangster movies inspired by his life story. He also found time to drive past the homes of the stars, notably Pickfair, Mary Pickford's magnificent dwelling. The excursion into celluloid fantasy came to a rude conclusion with the arrival of "Roughhouse" Brown, a detective dispatched by the chief of police to escort Capone out of town. "Why should everybody pick on me?" Capone asked reporters as he prepared to leave. "I thought that you folks liked tourists. I have a lot of money to spend that I made in Chicago. Whoever heard of anybody being run out of Los Angeles that had money?"

Shadowed by the Los Angeles police, the Capone party returned to the Los Angeles rail terminal, where they boarded the Santa Fé Chief on December 14. Their journey east took them through Kansas City, the very heart of the drys. "The police in the station were so thick that some of them were pretending to sell apples," Capone remarked. For the moment, the police let him continue his journey.

Meanwhile, in Chicago, Michael Hughes, the chief of police, and William E. O'Connor, the chief of detectives, announced an ambitious plan to put every gangster in that city under house arrest. "I will place guards at once around the homes of all the hoodlums in Chicago," O'Connor said. "If we can't keep them in our regular jails, we'll bottle them up so as to serve the same purpose." The order would, at the very least, make it difficult for Capone to return to his family in Chicago and subject to arrest if he were seen within the city limits. Anxiously awaiting her husband's return to their home on South Prairie Avenue, Mae was so outraged that she broke her customary silence to complain publicly and to plead that everybody leave him alone, if only for the sake of their child. When printed, her interview had the opposite of its intended effect, reminding the public of Al Capone's vulnerable young boy. "CAPONE'S SON FINDS SINS OF FATHER HEAVY," the *Chicago Herald and Examiner* headlined, "Mother Pleads for Lad, Victim of Schoolmates' Torment." Mae explained that little Sonny came home from school each day in tears caused by his classmates' taunts that his father was a gangster and a murderer. "It's more than he can stand. It's more than I can stand," Mae said, "and it's not fair. He's broken-hearted, and he can't understand it. I'm a true mother, and I suffer with him. Can't something be done?" As the years ahead would reveal, the answer was no, nothing could be done; in fact, Sonny was only beginning to comprehend the stigma that would plague him throughout his life.

En route to Illinois, Al brooded over the implications of being placed under house arrest in Chicago and the dishonor he had brought to his family. At this time, a journalist whom he knew boarded the train: Alfred "Jake" Lingle of the *Chicago Herald and Examiner*. Lingle was no ordinary journalist. These were the days of reporters and rewrite men; the reporters spent their time doing legwork, then phoned in their often scattered findings to their editorial office, where a rewrite man shaped them into a coherent article. As a reporter, Lingle rarely visited the offices of his paper, preferring to spend his time in the company of Capone or one of Capone's henchmen, and he wore the same diamond-studded buckle Al bestowed on his friends. Indeed, Lingle was more of a racketeer than a journalist, as anyone who saw his luxury automobile or visited his lavish suite at the Stevens Hotel realized. (Lingle also maintained his wife and child in a comfortable home.) Working as a reporter gave Lingle excellent cover for his real occupation and unparalleled access to Capone, who unburdened himself during the final phase of the train ride. "It's pretty tough when a citizen with an unblemished record must be hounded from his home by the very policemen whose salaries are paid, at least in part, from the victim's pocket," he told Lingle. "You might say that every policeman in Chicago gets some of his bread and butter from the taxes I pay. And yet they want to throw me in jail for nothing when I seek to visit my wife and my little son." Capone paused to sigh dramatically. "I am feeling very bad—very bad. I don't know what all this fuss is about. How would you feel if the police, paid to protect you, acted towards you like they toward me?" Another pause as Capone's attention wandered to the dreary winter landscape sliding past his window. "I'm going back to Chicago. Nobody can stop me. I've got a right to be there. I have property there. I have a family there. They can't keep me out of Chicago unless they shoot me through the head. I've never done anything wrong. Nobody can prove that I ever did anything wrong. They arrest me, they search me, they lock me up, they charge me with all the crimes there are, and when they get me into court I find that the only charge they dare to book against me is disorderly conduct—and the judge dismisses even that because there isn't any evidence to support it. The police know they haven't got one black mark against my name, and yet they publicly announce that they won't let me live in my own home. What kind of justice is that? Well, I've been the goat for a long time. It's got to stop some time and it might as well be now. I've got my back to the wall. I'm going to fight. It'll be a good fight, too."

Lingle phoned his story in to his paper. Once again, the publicity worked to Capone's disadvantage, for the police were waiting for him on the morning of Friday, December 16, as his train arrived in Joliet, Illinois (which happened to be home to the state penitentiary). As Capone stepped off the train, he pulled his fedora over his brow and turned up his collar to ward off the chill. He looked up to see six policemen fixing him in the sights of their shotguns. "Pleased to meet you," Al said to their leader, Police Chief Corcoran. The guns were still trained on him. "Well, I'll be damned," he muttered. "You'd think I was Jesse James and the Youngers, all in one. What's the artillery for?" Without being asked, he yielded a .45-caliber revolver he was carrying, adding as an afterthought a smaller weapon, and, as a goodwill gesture, the ammunition. The police responded by arresting him for carrying concealed weapons and took him down to the jail. Only days before he had been lolling about his lavish suite at the Biltmore Hotel in Los Angeles, hoping to meet movie stars, but now he found himself confined to a chilly cell in Joliet with several derelicts.

In Chicago, his lawyers, Thomas Nash and Michael Ahern, sprang into action. They arranged to post bail, and after eight hours' detention Capone was free once more. "I am not mad at anybody," he declared on his release. "I am going to make a good big donation to the worthy charities of Joliet." Then he jumped into a car, and a group of the boys drove him to the safety of Chicago Heights, the one city where he could be certain the police would not harass him. By the time he returned to his family on South Prairie Avenue, the police had called off their scheme to place every gangster in the city under house arrest. "Well," said Chief Detective O'Connor of Capone's return, "if he's back, he's back. That's all there is to it." However, O'Connor continued his cat-and-mouse game by placing a round-the-clock police guard in front of the Capone homestead. No one troubled to bring hot coffee or stronger fortification to the cops as they sat shivering in their flivver during the late December storms.

Although he had successfully defied the police, Capone realized that his trip had turned into a fiasco. Everywhere he had gone, he played into the hands of local police chiefs eager to win publicity at his expense. Even worse, he had generated a flurry of unfavorable press coverage across the country. For the first time in his career as a racketeer, he had to endure the uncomfortable sensation that people were laughing at him, and the ridicule followed him all the way back to Chicago, where the dailies continued to heap scorn on him. To present his side of the story, Al Capone held a press conference at the Metropole Hotel and publicly admitted that he was what everyone knew he was: a bootlegger. He did so not because he had decided the time had come to confess and repent, but merely to point out the hypocrisy of those who criticized him. "They call Al Capone a bootlegger," he began. "Yes, it's bootleg while it's on the trucks, but when your host at the club, in the locker rooms or on the Gold Coast hands it to you on a silver salver, it's hospitality. All I've ever done is supply a public demand. You can't cure a thirst by law. They say I violate the prohibition law. Who doesn't?" This was an unanswerable argument, as far as it went, but it conveniently ignored his other, more sinister activities: the gambling, the pimping, the murdering. By admitting to the lesser evil of bootlegging, Capone hoped to obscure his other endeavors, though they all contributed to his preeminence as a bootlegger.

The next morning, December 22, he returned briefly to Joliet for a secret hearing to answer the charge of carrying concealed weapons. On the advice of his lawyers, he pleaded guilty and paid $2,601 in fines and court costs. Unfazed by the size of the fine, the racketeer dug into his pocket, produced a large wad of cash, and peeled off the amount in $100 bills. When the clerk tried to give him change, Al declined, advising the man to give the money to a Salvation Army Santa Claus—"and tell him it is a Christmas present from Al Capone."

•   •   •

Capone spent a subdued holiday season with his family in Chicago, where his foul mood was matched by the weather. Shortly after the New Year, Capone, his wife, and child boarded a train, and they actually did go to Florida. They arrived in Miami on January 4, 1928, only to confront approximately the same reception they had been given in Los Angeles. By now the story of his cross-country wanderings had become well known, and everywhere he went the police followed him and the press delighted in harassing him. The arrival of the homeless gangster-in-exile, as he was inaccurately portrayed, inspired Miami's civic leaders—the churches, the women's clubs, the boosters—to raise their voices in a chorus of righteous protest.

This time, Capone was determined not to be run out of town. As the clamor continued, he praised Miami as "the garden of America, the sunny Italy of the New World, where life is good and abundant, where happiness can be enjoyed even by the poorest." And he explained his intention to become a pillar of the Miami Establishment: "I am going to build or buy a home here and I hope many of my friends will join me. Furthermore, if I am permitted, I will open the finest restaurant anywhere in the state and if I am invited I will even join your Rotary Club." Despite these grandiose ambitions, he remained, in his words, "only another sucker." As it happened, Miami was suffering from one of its periodic busts in the real estate market. A hurricane the previous year had devastated the area, destroyed millions of dollars worth of property, and left 50,000 people homeless. For once Capone's timing favored him. Suckers were most welcome in Miami, and from the moment he uttered the magical words "real estate," he acquired standing in the community. A sale was a sale, even when the buyer happened to be Al Capone, and salesmen descended in droves, eager to reap a fat commission in an otherwise depressed market. "CAPONE HUNTED IN MIAMI," read the headline in the *Chicago Tribune*, "BUT BY REALTY MEN."

As the business community rushed to fleece the newest sucker to blow into town, the city's elected officials, fearful of Capone's turning their fair city into another Chicago, or at least giving that impression and scaring away tourists, issued impressive-sounding statements condemning the racketeer and asking him to leave immediately. Capone countered by arranging a meeting at which he told the city fathers: "Let's lay the cards on the table. You all know who I am and where I come from. . . I have no intention of operating a gambling house or any other illicit business." After the meeting, Miami's mayor, J. Newton Lummus, sounded peculiarly respectful toward Capone, whom he termed "one of the fairest men I have ever been in conference with." Capone sidestepped the obloquy by moving to Miami *Beach*, a smaller community that was virtually a part of Miami but technically a separate city. It was a shrewd move, giving the politicians their breathing room while allowing Al to stay close to the action.

Now that he had introduced himself properly, Capone found that he fit into the Miami scene rather well, largely because the city and its money were even newer than Chicago's. And Florida had yet to be tainted by development. Early visitors from the north described the region as drunk on warmth and light. "Sea gulls floated in it, white shadows," said Marjorie Stoneman

Douglas, an early conservationist. "Bay or sky, it was all dazzling, diamond-edged." When she wrote those words, in 1915, Miami Beach was better known as a failed coconut plantation than as a haven for millionaires, would-be millionaires, and gamblers. Then the Lummus family (to which the mayor belonged) began to develop the area as a resort. Although their Ocean Beach Realty Company got off to a fast start, World War I slowed its progress; not until 1920 did the pace of development recover real momentum. It was still a fragile society, one that could not yet afford to be choosy about its members, and desperate for the support of men with deep pockets—men like Al Capone. In Miami itself, one mammoth building after another went up, many of them in a distinctive style reminiscent of Moorish-Spanish architecture, but on a scale that was wholly and outlandishly American. Helped along by the stock market boom, the city became a playground for the wealthy, many of whom arrived in private railroad cars. Eventually a millionaire named Carl Fisher, who hailed from Indianapolis, led the drive to develop Miami Beach, which, with its imported birds, polo grounds, tennis courts, and golf courses, resembled an oceanside theme park, effectively banishing reality. Thus it proved a receptive environment for a racketeer like Capone who wanted to make it in society, for in Miami, "society" was whatever people said it was.

Capone quickly installed himself in a penthouse suite at the city's premier residence, the Moorish-style Ponce de León Hotel. In addition, he leased a waterfront home for $3,000 for the season. Mae and Sonny moved into the house, and Al shuttled between his family and the hotel. Now that he had paid his dues to Miami, criticism of him suddenly died away. Miami's chief of police, H. Leslie Quigg, went so far as to say of Capone, "If he's here for a good time and behaves himself, he can stay as long as he likes." With those words, Capone appeared to enjoy the complicity of the Miami police in his new ventures, but the extent of cooperation he received from the city's power structure went far beyond that conciliatory statement. It so happened that J. Newton Lummus, the mayor of Miami who considered Al so fair-minded, was also a real estate agent, and a clever one at that. He knew that Capone wanted to purchase a house without starting a new public outcry, and the mayor thought he had a solution to the problem. Even as he publicly denounced Capone, J. Newton Lummus quietly went to work for him.

Lummus located a large, luxurious home he thought would be an appropriate domicile for an upwardly mobile racketeer. It was located at 93 Palm Island, in the midst of a small artificial island built beside a long, low causeway extending across Biscayne Bay from Miami to Miami Beach. This area was worlds apart from Al's other homes in working-class Cicero and Chicago's Prairie Avenue. A chic address, Palm Island was as heavily guarded and as carefully tended as a country club. Most of its homes belonged to prominent figures in Miami's social scene. The home Lummus had set his sights on had been built in 1922 by Clarence Busch, who belonged to the St. Louis brewing dynasty, and it featured fourteen rooms, a small gatehouse, a spacious backyard, 300 feet of frontage on the bay, and a dock. It was the closest to paradise a boy from Brooklyn could hope to get. From the beige tones of its exterior to its graceful Spanish-style arches and sheltering palm trees, everything about the villa said "millionaire." Even better from Capone's point of view, it was secluded, and a high wall enclosed the property, making it difficult for intruders to trespass. Although Clarence Busch had subsequently sold it to one James Popham, the home's association with the Busches was enormously flattering to Capone, for they represented everything to which he aspired: wealth, respectability, and power. Like him, they had built their fortune on booze, but where Prohibition had made Capone's rise possible, it had left the Busches financially hard-pressed.

As Lummus and Capone were keenly aware, if the racketeer were to purchase the Palm Island villa in his own name the transaction would unleash a storm of unfavorable publicity. An intermediary was required, and Capone soon recruited one. His name was Parker Henderson Jr., son of Miami's *former* mayor, and he made an ideal patsy. At twenty-four, young Henderson was a plump young man-about-town with a fondness for the high life. By day, he managed the Ponce de León, where Capone maintained a suite, and he rapidly succumbed to Capone's formidable charm and hospitality, which included an introduction to Miami's leading brothel keeper, Duke Cooney. Within days of Al's arrival, Henderson was proudly wearing one of the racketeer's diamond-studded belt buckles as a token of their new friendship. In fact, Henderson liked everything about the gangster life—the guns, the glamour, and especially the girls—and he was delighted to help when Al asked for his assistance in buying the Palm Island villa. Capone then referred him to Lummus, who said, "If anyone sells property to Capone, you and I should do it," implying that Henderson would receive a commission, although it was hardly necessary by this time to persuade him. The naïve Henderson had already begun to run risky financial errands for Capone. On no less than eighteen occasions between mid-January and April 2, Henderson received money orders sent to Miami from Chicago. They were addressed not to Capone but to a fictitious "A. Costa." Accompanied by a Capone gunman, Nick Circella, who made certain there would be no monkey business, Henderson forged a signature to suit this alias and promptly turned the money over to Al. When the transactions were concluded, Capone had stockpiled $31,000 under his alias, sufficient for a generous down payment on the house of his dreams. In March, Lummus closed the deal on behalf of Capone. Thanks largely to the mayor's skillful maneuvering, Capone finally had a respectable base outside Chicago, should it be necessary to seek refuge. What's more, it was right on Biscayne Bay.

• • •

Although it appeared that the racketeer and the mayor had accomplished their goal to keep the real estate transaction out of the public eye, Capone's acquisition of the Palm Island villa actually gave the federal government its first important lead in its effort to prosecute him for income tax evasion. In Washington, D.C., Elmer Irey's Intelligence Unit of the IRS had been attempting with little success to investigate Capone's tax situation. The plan was to demonstrate that he had not complied with the 1927 Supreme Court ruling which specified that even illegal income was subject to taxation. As expected, Capone had not paid his taxes. "No record of the filing of any return for any year was found," an internal Treasury Department memorandum concluded. Irey's Intelligence Unit subsequently began an investigation to determine how much money Capone was *spending* as a way to estimate how much taxable income he was earning.

To lead this part of the investigation, Irey selected Frank J. Wilson, who had successfully uncovered the financial chicanery of lesser bootleggers. Wilson looked every bit as much a civil servant as Irey; he was about forty but he looked a decade older, with his bald head and his eyes framed by severe wire-rimmed glasses. Of greater importance, he was an obsessive investigator. Despite the danger of the assignment, Wilson and his wife, Judith, moved to the Sheridan Plaza Hotel in Chicago, where he passed himself off as a tourist. He did not tell his wife the precise nature of his investigation; all she knew was that her husband was looking into the affairs of someone named "Curly Brown." It was 1928, and Wilson would spend the next three years digging for the elusive information that could be used to send Capone to prison. "The task," in his words, "was to find gross income in excess of $5,000 (the standard exemption at the time) accruing to Capone for any one year in which he had filed no tax return at all and/or income exceeding the insignificant amounts he did report for other years." Given Capone's vast income and lavish spending habits, this sounded easy enough to accomplish; in fact, it proved nearly impossible. As Wilson discovered, Capone was "completely anonymous when it came to income. He did all his business through front men or third parties. To discourage meddlers, his production department was turning out fifty corpses a year."

Early in the investigation, Wilson sought the help of Art Madden, the IRS's local agent, who warned that attempting to convict Capone for income tax evasion "would be as easy as hanging a foreclosure sign on the moon." Later, Wilson oversaw a small staff, but he was still woefully underequipped.

"For a base of operations the government gave me and my three assistants an overgrown closet in the old Post Office Building with a cracked glass at the door, no windows, a double flat-topped desk, and walls that were peeling as if they'd been sunburned. I could hardly scratch my head without sticking my elbow in somebody's eye."

Escaping the confines of his office, Wilson spent days familiarizing himself with Chicago. He visited Cicero a number of times, took note of the city's gambling joints, saloons, and brothels, but still he failed to find a paper trail leading to Capone. An agent working with Wilson on the investigation complained, "His sources of income are known to us. We believe he could cash in for $20,000,000. But where has he hidden it? Our men get so far, then they find themselves in blind alleys. Just as an example we discovered $100,000 in cash which his brother, Ralph, had secreted in a safety-deposit box. Pin money." Evidence of Capone's financial dealings proved elusive largely because gambling, vice, and bootlegging—the entire spectrum of Capone's rackets—were all-cash businesses. In the rare instances when the organization used checks, these were signed not by Capone but by Jack Guzik or other surrogates. Despite these tantalizing clues, Wilson failed to grasp how the financial arrangement worked. The paradox of Capone's being among the wealthiest men in Chicago while leaving no record of earning any income drove the investigator to distraction. "It was common talk that he [Capone] got a cut of every case of whisky brought into Cook County," Wilson wrote of that fallow period, "that he ran a thousand speakeasies, a thousand bookie joints, fifteen gambling houses, a luscious string of brothels; that he controlled half a dozen breweries. . . . He tore around in sixteen cylinder limousines, slept in $50 French pajamas, and ordered fifteen suits at a time at $135 each. His personal armed forces numbered 700, equipped with automatic weapons and armored automobiles. And I couldn't show that this satrap of Chicago earned more than $5,000 a year!" Meanwhile, Wilson's wife wondered why he was agonizing. "You're certainly making a mountain out of this Curly Brown case," she told him. "He can't be such a big shot. I never see a word about him in the papers."

Because of Capone's acquisition of the former Busch villa, the IRS had better results in Miami. This tangible asset was evidence that he did, in fact, enjoy a substantial income. The nature of the transaction revealed Capone's growing financial sophistication, as the Treasury Department memorandum explained:

In the course of the investigation of Al Capone, it was reported that he had purchased a magnificent home in an exclusive section of Miami, Florida. An investigation in Florida disclosed that the original owner sold the place to a real estate operator [Henderson] for $40,000: $2,000 in cash was paid as a binder and upon delivery of the deed $8,000 in one thousand dollar bills was paid to the seller by the real estate operator, leaving a mortgage of $30,000 due on the property. It was then found that the deed was in the name of "Mae" Capone, the wife of Al. When this fact was learned, the insurance companies withdrew their policies on the basis that the Capones were not a good risk.

As Irey and his IRS investigators continued their efforts to unravel the complex and hidden tangle of Capone's finances, the appointment of a new U.S. attorney in Chicago marked the beginning of a fresh effort to prosecute the racketeer. At first glance, the changing of the guard in the federal prosecuter's office seemed an event of little consequence, and the appointee, George E. Q. Johnson, appeared as unlikely an adversary of Al Capone as Elmer Irey. Born on July 11, 1874, in Harcourt, Iowa, and reared on a farm on Wisconsin, George Emmerson Q. Johnson—the Q. stood for nothing, it was designed solely to distinguish him from all the other George Johnsons— had put himself through law school and risen through the ranks of the prosecutor's office in Chicago, helped along by its Scandinavian-American old-boy network. In February 1927, President Coolidge appointed him a U.S. attorney. At fifty-four, Johnson was tall, wiry, and slightly rumpled. With his unruly hair parted in the center, his round wire-rimmed spectacles, and his tweedy suits, he might have been mistaken for a poet or a perhaps a drama critic—that is, until he opened his mouth, when it became apparent that he combined a scholarly demeanor with an unlimited capacity for indignation in the face of injustice. That last quality set him apart from nearly every other cynical, battle-weary veteran of Chicago's futile war on gangsters, and it came directly from his rural, frugal background. For a lawyer of Johnson's status, the appointment entailed a financial sacrifice (though not by the standards of most people). At the time, federal judges made about $10,000 a year, a state's attorney or district attorney slightly more, and a U.S. attorney such as Johnson earned $15,000. These salaries paled in comparison to what corrupt public officials could reap. One of the most sought-after posts was the sheriff of Cook County; the pay was low, but it was rumored the holder of that office could make a quarter of a million dollars from bribes and shady deals on the side.

Ethnic rivalry gave extra heat to Johnson's zealous prosecution of Capone, for Johnson believed his rural, Swedish roots accounted for his incorruptibility. "I come of Swedish farmer stock," Johnson remarked, "and my bringing up made the thought of taking money when in office abhorrent. . . . It merely had no attraction for me." By the same token, he could not help but note that the racketeers he prosecuted were overwhelmingly Italian, which he assumed accounted for their criminal proclivities. An element of class warfare was also present in the prosecutor's campaign against Capone. There was, on one hand, the urban immigrant class from which Capone had sprung, which was predominantly Italian, Irish, and Jewish; then there was the rural Scandinavian class in which Johnson and many other federal and state investigators had their roots. (Not the police, however, whose immigrant, urban backgrounds resembled those of the gangsters.)

Eventually, however, Johnson came to respect his adversary's formidable abilities. "My father said many times that Al Capone could have been a brilliant businessman," his son, George E. Q. Johnson Jr., notes. "My father meant that he had the organizational ability, cunning, intellect, and street smarts it took to succeed." Beyond that, the U.S. attorney came to realize he also shared an unnerving set of characteristics with Capone. Both men sprang from large families—nine siblings to be exact. Both required bodyguards to protect their safety from constant threats. And both had only one child, a son, and the boys were the same age. "It became a joke—not a very funny one—that some day I would grow up to prosecute Sonny," the younger Johnson recalls. It was as if Capone were Johnson's inverted image, with one family dedicated to doing good and the other to perpetrating wrong.

From the moment he took office, it was apparent that Johnson took his responsibilities with the utmost seriousness. Unlike his predecessors, he refused to fight his battles against the racketeers in the press. He had heard enough of William Dever's unfulfilled promises and "Big Bill" Thompson's blatant lies to know that he would accomplish nothing by making his plans public. In addition, he refused to tolerate Chicago's traditional complicity in underworld activities. He distanced himself from the corrupt elements of law enforcement—the police captains, aldermen, and assistant district attorneys who participated in the profits of the Capone organization in return for protection. Instead, he began to educate himself about Chicago's underworld by reading newspaper accounts covering the last several years. Chicago's dailies, he came to realize, provided highly reliable information on all the players and their rackets, *better* information than the police had collected. He retained a journalist to compile an index-card file of all the men and their organizations, and with this database at his fingertips, Johnson, a man of keen analytic powers, became the first person in a position of authority to gain a thorough knowledge of Chicago's gang structure and gang warfare.

What particularly galled Johnson about Capone and his organization was their pretense at respectability. "Organized crime was a business and the gangsters worked with a great deal of arrogance," he said later. "Some of them posed as political leaders and they had the temerity to go to public banquets where public men were." Above all there was Al Capone, whom Johnson described as a "man of unbelievable arrogance," his brother Ralph, who, Johnson learned, handled most of the organization's brothels now that

Al was so interested in becoming respectable, and their right-hand man, Jake Guzik. Johnson was a man of principle, and the prominence of "Greasy Thumb" Guzik, that *pimp*, offended him deeply, and he reacted on a personal level. "I live in a quiet neighborhood, where there are homes and home-owning people," Johnson explained, "and he established himself just around the corner from me, and nearly all the gangsters, strange to say, are married and bringing up families. He is the conniver and corrupter of the crowd. Al Capone represents the force and spectacular leadership." Not only that, but the Guzik family dog and the Johnson family dog, an English pit bull, got into fights whenever they crossed one another's paths. It was bad enough that Al Capone wanted to control Chicago's government and Ralph Capone managed its brothels, but to have Jake Guzik and family living around the corner—that was the ultimate indignity, an affront to all right-thinking citizens. For all these reasons, George E. Q. Johnson bent every effort to exposing these men to the scrutiny of the law.

• • •

Oblivious to the government forces quietly massing against him, Capone remained in Miami, but his attention was focused on Chicago. The city was convulsed by a violent, no-holds-barred primary election scheduled for April 8. Months in advance of that date, the corrupt administration of Mayor Thompson had begun to reap a whirlwind of civic discontent. Although Thompson himself was not up for reelection until 1931, many significant city offices were at stake, and the primary was generally considered a referendum on his administration. To the surprise of absolutely no one, his new administration had wreaked havoc on the city. Rackets flourished as never before. Near the end of 1927, the Employers' Association of Chicago compiled a list of twenty-three businesses susceptible to racketeering; they included cleaning and dyeing, dental laboratories, window-cleaning, groceries, garbage removal, drug stores, florists, shoe repair stores, glaziers, bakers, butchers, fish vendors, even photographers. "Any man who dares to oppose certain kinds of racketeers or refuses to pay tribute to them is in actual physical danger," the Association concluded.

The increase in racketeering was matched by an increase in violent crime. In 1928, "Big Bill" 's first full year in office, the city was the scene of 367 murders, approximately one a day. (In comparison, 200 murders were committed in New York during the same period.) Although the Chicago police managed to make some arrests, the death penalty was never carried out despite a rising public clamor to use this ultimate threat to deter crime. Thompson's financial record was equally disastrous. Ordered to testify before a grand jury about the source of Thompson's campaign fund, Homer K. Galpin, the fund's manager, went into hiding for eighteen months. As the

Thompson administration wore on, the city was tardy in collecting taxes, neglected to pay its bills, and ran up nearly $300 million in debt. Thus Chicago became, a journalist wrote, "a panhandler on the doorsteps of its bankers."

Despite the civic emergency and sense of crisis, no one dared to step forward to try to rescue the city. Popular opinion held that gangsters ruled Chicago, and popular opinion was correct. Chicago got the gangsters it deserved; they were flashy, extremely wealthy, and up-to-the-minute in their methods as they learned to imitate America's corporate culture. There was no longer any serious opposition to them in Chicago. William Dever, once the city's preeminent voice for reform, never returned to the political arena. He toiled quietly as a bank executive, and two years after his defeat, he died from cancer, briefly mourned and then forgotten, a man of principles who was profoundly at odds with his time. Even in the absence of effective opposition to his administration, Thompson remained vulnerable simply because so many people despised him. Although he was the anti-Prohibition candidate, a stance that should have endeared him to voters, he had failed to anticipate that voters and newspapers alike held him accountable for Chicago's ever-increasing crime rate and its reputation as a center of crime—a reputation that was not limited to the United States. The city under Thompson had become known across the land as a haven for gangsters, the mayor himself the butt of endless jokes:

To the Editor of The New York Times:

GARRETT, Ind., Jan 9 [1928].—Just passed through Chicago today. Wanted to go up and see my old friend Mayor Thompson, but had English breakfast tea for luncheon and was afraid he would smell it on my breath.

You can kid about Chicago and its crooks, but they have the smartest way of handling their crooks of any city. They get the rival gangs to kill off each other and all the police have to do is just referee and count up the bodies. They won't have a crook in Chicago unless he will agree to shoot at another crook. So viva Chicago!

Yours unhit,
WILL ROGERS

There was worse to come. In late January, the home of the city controller, Charles C. Fitzmorris, was bombed, followed by a similar attack several days later on another public official. Then, on February 17, the *New York Times* carried a headline that was to be repeated over the next six weeks with minor variations: "CHICAGO BOMBERS WRECK JUDGE'S HOME—Explosion Throws

Him and Wife From Bed—Third Official Attacked." The victim in this instance had especially interesting connections, for he was John Sbarbaro, *Judge* Sbarbaro, who, as will be recalled, served as the undertaker of choice to slain racketeers. Lately his involvement in their activities had increased— his garage doubling as a drop-off for bootleg booze—and what better and more secure storage place than a judge's garage? No longer would it serve as the scene of shady transactions, however, for the blast had demolished it. Judge Sbarbaro himself claimed to be mystified by the bombing; perhaps, he said, he had been too tough on some of the criminals who had come before him in court, and they were intent on revenge. Many reporters quoted this explanation; no one believed it.

In March, the intensity of the violence increased several notches. Early on the twenty-first, "Diamond Joe" Esposito, a Republican ward boss, received a threatening telephone call; that night, as he was walking home between two bodyguards, a car pulled alongside him. As it slowly rolled past, several men concealed within the car began firing on Esposito. Riddled with bullets, he collapsed on the sidewalk while his wife and three children looked on in horror. The men in the car flung their weapons out the window and sped away. By the time his wife reached him, he was dead. Curiously, his body-guards escaped unharmed; perhaps they had received a warning of the as-sassination. In any event, the men who killed Esposito were never found. Soon after, another prominent political figure, "Big Tim" Murphy, a rack-eteer and bootlegger, was assassinated.

The next round of violence attracted nationwide attention, for the victims were not gangsters or even quasi-gangsters and thus fair game according to the generally accepted rules governing Chicago's rackets. The first was a U.S. senator, Charles S. Deneen, who led a faction of dry reformers determined to oust the Thompson administration. A bomb exploded in Deneen's home and partly destroyed it; only by chance was no one killed in the blast. The second victim was a judge, John A. Swanson, the Deneen-backed candidate for state's attorney, whose home was also blasted on the same night. There were many other bombings of lesser figures—sixty-two such attacks in six months, according to one tally; in all, 115 bombs would rock Chicago that year.

Fear of bombings inflicted additional psychic damage. For instance, all Chicago was transfixed by the news that a bomb consisting of seventeen sticks of dynamite had been found at the busy Water Street Market. The fuse was charred along half its length, testimony to what might have occurred had it not been extinguished by an unexpected snowfall. If the bomb had exploded, the blast would have damaged an entire city block and taken countless lives. At about the same time, George E. Q. Johnson, the new U.S. attorney who was quietly pursuing Capone, became the victim of bomb threats. One morning his wife answered the phone; a strange voice told her that her house would be "blown to bits" if her husband did not "curtail his activities on behalf of the Deneen faction." At about the same time the wife of Thomas O. Wallace, a Deneen candidate for clerk of the Circuit Court, answered her phone. "You tell your husband he'd better get out of politics, for if he don't we'll blow his house up," a voice told her. Telephone threats to kidnap the children of candidates likewise abounded.

The violence—as well as the threat of violence—was all the more frightening because no one knew who was responsible; as Sbarbaro's comment suggests, even the victims were afraid to name names. Confusion reigned. The police did nothing. "There are fifty places in the city where dynamite can be purchased just as a person buys a package of cigarettes," Chief Hughes said in an attempt to shrug off criticism, but neither he nor anyone else attempted to shut those places down.

The mayor, displaying his characteristic guile and cynicism, held the Deneen camp responsible for all the violence, although most of the bombs' targets happened to be politicians who opposed Thompson. "The bombs are the work of the Deneen faction, because they expect defeat," Thompson claimed, and he went on to insist that Deneen's men had also gunned down Esposito, that fine man and loyal Republican. "Big Bill" speculated that Deneen, a committed dry, had imported a cadre of corrupt Prohibition agents who directed attacks on wet candidates: "Deneen is filling this town with Dry agents from Washington, who run around like a lot of cowboys with revolvers and shotguns. Our opponents would have us believe we don't know how to run our town. Vote for the flag, the Constitution, your freedom, your property, as Abraham Lincoln and William Hale Thompson would like to have you do." Thompson's crony, Robert E. Crowe, the state's attorney, further muddied the waters by insisting that Deneen and Swanson had planted the bombs in a vain bid for political advantage. "The public is not going to be fooled by their dangerous methods of campaign," he claimed. "After having bombed the homes of friends of mine and having made no headway, they are now bombing their own homes to create the impression that the forces of lawlessness are running the town."

The public saw through these lies, and discontent with the Thompson administration mounted. The voters realized that the forces of lawlessness *were* running the town with the assistance of Thompson and Crowe, yet the mayor remained adept at deflecting criticism from himself. He continued to divert attention from his own failings by attacking imaginary enemies— especially the tyrannical King George. To hear Thompson tell it, King George was doing more harm to Chicago and the United States than any other individual on the face of the earth. As an example of royal malice, Thompson cited the price of bootleg bourbon, which, he said, had increased tenfold, to $15 a bottle: "King George's rum-running fleet, 800 miles long, lies twelve miles off our coast, so every time you take a drink you say, 'Here's to the King!' " Such was Thompson's idea of a campaign issue, and the preliminary polls showed that his strategy worked; everyone expected the reformers to go down in defeat once more.

When Thompson was forced to address a realistic concern, such as crime, it was only to utter more nonsense. Shortly before the election, the mayor took his ease in his lavish office at City Hall, where he told the Associated Press that Chicago was the "most maligned of all cities." As he spoke, noted the reporter, "a gesture of his great right arm swept to encompass the north, west and south sides of the throbbing municipality . . . and, continuing his movement, he thrust his gold-rimmed spectacles athwart his florid forehead." He scowled when the reporter had the temerity to raise the issue of crime. Crime in Chicago, Thompson informed the Associated Press, has decreased 67 percent during his administration; Chief Hughes told him so only a little while ago. "Sure, we have crime here," Thompson continued. "Chicago is just like any other big city. You can get a man's arm broken for so much, a leg for so much, or beaten up for so much. Just like New York or any other big city—excepting we print our crime here and they don't."

As election day approached, public outrage found vent in political rallies. At one, Edward R. Litsinger, a candidate for the Cook County Board of Review, asked a throng, "It costs $243,000,000 to run Chicago. What are we getting?"

"Bombs!" came the response. "Pineapples!"

Thereafter, Chicago's primary election of 1928 became known as the "Pineapple Primary," in memory of the homemade bombs—"pineapples"—thrown during the contest. They immediately entered the emerging folklore of the era, as Capone's friend Damon Runyon, writing from the relative safety of New York, noted in his story "Gentlemen, the King!" In the tale, a child and a mobster named Jo-jo discuss the notorious Al Capone; one thing leads to another, and the child asks Jo-jo about the famed pineapples. "And what does this Jo-jo do," writes Runyon, "but out with a little round gadget which I recognize at once as a bomb such as these Guineas chuck at people they do not like, especially Guineas from Chicago. Of course I never know Jo-jo is packing this article around and about with him, and Jo-jo can see I am much astonished, and by no means pleased. . . . Well, the next thing anybody knows . . . Jo-jo . . . is telling lies faster than a horse can trot about Chicago and Mr. Capone, and I hope and trust that Al never hears some of the lies Jo-Jo tells, or he may hold it against me for being with Jo-jo when some of these lies come to pass."

Although Runyon's tale dismisses the pineapples with wry humor, they were, in reality, a source of dread in Chicago. Through the smoke and shouting of the primary campaign, the name of one man was constantly invoked as the cause of all the evils afflicting that city. He was not a candidate, he was not even present in Chicago; he was, in fact, over a thousand miles away that winter, lolling about in his Palm Island villa. Despite his absence and his silence on public issues, everyone in Chicago from Senator Deneen to Mayor Thompson held Al Capone personally responsible for the city's crime and violence. Thus he became a campaign issue despite having no role in the election. Furthermore, there was no proof of his involvement with the bombing incidents, nor was his ubiquitous organization ever shown to be involved. Rather, the bombs appear to have been the work of local freelancers who offered themselves to the politicians, especially in the Thompson camp, whose careers were at stake in this election and who felt free to resort to them because Capone made a convenient scapegoat.

The election itself was, in the words of one newspaper correspondent, "a day of sluggings, ballot-box stuffing by shotgun squads, and kidnappings." The chief outrage was the murder of Octavius C. Granady, a black lawyer running against Morris Eller, a Capone ally, in the "Bloody" Twentieth Ward. Machine-gun-wielding thugs chased Granady's car, and when it finally crashed into a tree, they shot him to death. In this case, there were arrests; seven men were subsequently tried for murder—three hoodlums and four policemen, all of whom were acquitted.

Despite the violence of election day, public indignation created by the bombs and Thompson's self-serving lies sent voters to the polls in record numbers. In the most significant contest, they voted out Robert E. Crowe, who had shown himself to be thoroughly corrupt and devious, and replaced him with Judge Swanson. The rout of the Thompson machine amounted, in the words of one observer, to "ballot rebellion." Before the election, Thompson had vowed to resign if his man Crowe lost, but in the wake of defeat, he was, predictably enough, having second thoughts: "Why should I resign?" he inquired. "You'd think I'd lost the whole fight." Thompson remained in office, but he never recovered from the trouncing his administration received in the primary. Newspapers everywhere hailed the defeat of his corrupt political machine. "The primary brought results that are gratifying to the entire country. It was a mighty blow for the restoration of law and order in Chicago," the *Washington Post* commented. The *Kansas City Star* put it even more succinctly: "There is a God in Israel." The humiliation Thompson suffered at the polls shattered his presidential campaign. Thereafter he lost all interest in Chicago, indeed in politics itself. During the next few months, he was nowhere to be seen; when reporters asked for his whereabouts, they were told the mayor was in the Wisconsin woods, hunting.

·   ·   ·

Throughout the election Capone maintained a dignified silence on the recommendation of his friend Harry Read, the city editor of the *Chicago American*, who continued to advise Capone on the best way to handle himself in the press. Once the winds whipping off Lake Michigan had dispelled the smoke of Chicago's Pineapple Primary, Read left Chicago for Miami. He checked into the Ritz Hotel on April 20 with the stated purpose of recovering from pneumonia. In reality, Ralph Capone greeted him on his arrival and immediately spirited him away to Palm Island. In the days to come, Read was in attendance at the Capone villa nearly every day. To establish an image of Capone in exile and in retirement, he arranged for the racketeer to pose for photographs that showed him fishing; they appeared in the *American*. Read was able to get away with that much, but he went beyond the limit when Capone invited him aboard a flight to Cuba. With considerable embarrassment, the *American* later published an account of the excursion, which began on April 23:

> The party flew to Havana, arrived without incident, and registered at the Seville Biltmore Hotel. Mr. Read had lunch, joined the party on a trip to the Tropical Garden, where beer is given away, stopped at a restaurant where dinner was had, and returned to the hotel.
>
> The Capone party went to several cabarets that night, but Mr. Read was in bed at 8 o'clock. . . .
>
> On the following morning at 6 A.M. emissaries from the Cuban secret police came to the hotel and told Capone they had been asked by the American embassy to question him and the persons who had arrived on the plane with him. Capone and the others, including Mr. Read, accompanied the secret police emissary to headquarters, where it developed that the questioning had to do with reports that Capone intended bombing some public buildings as part of a May Day labor demonstration.
>
> On hearing this Capone laughed heartily. After the arrival of the chief of secret police Capone was asked what he was doing in Cuba. He said he came over to spend some money and drink some wine. The chief stated that the Cuban Government was glad to have him as a visitor and hoped his stay would be a pleasant one.

Notwithstanding the warm good wishes of Cuba's chief of secret police, Capone flew home to Miami immediately following their little chat. From this point forward, everything about Capone's life in Miami was dedicated to establishment of a legitimate persona. If he was wholly a creature of the dark, lurid, obscure underworld during his early years in Brooklyn, he now played the heliotrope in Miami Beach, always seeking the sunlight of legitimacy.

For the moment, he gave the appearance of living in permanent, comfortable retirement. He enrolled Sonny, now nine, at the Gesu Catholic School, which offered a cloistered, safe environment for his only child, as well as a veneer of respectability. In addition, he supervised the renovation of the Palm Island villa to his precise specifications. For the sake of security, he enlarged and reinforced the concrete wall running around the perimeter of the property and installed a telephone by the front gate to announce callers. For the sake of luxury, he arranged for the installation of an oversized swimming pool, and when it was finished, Al could tread water in the pool while gazing at the waters of Biscayne Bay, a pleasing prospect accented with white sails and the wakes of power boats churning past. At one end of the pool he built a Moorish-style two-story cabana. He also added a decorative rock pool stocked with tropical fish and renovated the dock fronting the bay. Capone kept two boats tied up to his dock: a speedboat named *Sonny* (later *Sonny and Ralphie*, after his nephew) and a thirty-two-foot cabin cruiser, which he used for fishing expeditions. The renovations cost $100,000, more than twice what Capone had originally paid for the house, but they transformed what was already a comfortable, dwelling into a secure luxury residence.

Within, a large portrait of Al and his son dominated the living room. The second floor was somewhat less spectacular, but considerably homier. A narrow staircase led to a landing providing access to three bedrooms. In the largest, Capone slept on a king-sized bed; the other important piece of furniture in the room was a substantial wooden chest in which he stored his spending money. "Don't keep your money in a bank. Keep it like I do," he advised his men. This habit was both a vestige of his immigrant past and a necessity for racketeers seeking to avoid paying taxes.

Mae did her part to rehabilitate the Capone image. She decorated the Palm Island villa with a vengeance. It was the first home that was truly hers, that she did not have to share with her mother-in-law and Al's brothers, and she embarked on a furious shopping spree. Mae favored Louis XIV replicas, an ornate style in which scrolls, curved armrests, and gilded decorative motifs abounded. She also bought a number of dinner services trimmed with gold, a set of thirteen spice jars, a brass and enamel vanity set, an art deco cosmetic tray and jeweled bottle set, ivory miniatures, a silver-plated juicer, a pair of glass torchères, and a set of four metal elephants—their trunks held high in a traditional sign of good luck and potency. Devoid of taste, reeking of money, this was exactly the kind of opulent decor that the wife of any newly rich magnate might be expected to purchase. Everywhere she went, she left a trail of thousand-dollar bills, to the delight of local merchants. To the extent that respectability could be bought, Mae did so, and she paid for it in cash.

She was also exceedingly careful about the impression she made on her Florida neighbors, although the gestures she made to demonstrate that she was *not* some uncouth gangster's moll were as unintentionally revealing as a shoot-out would have been. Although Al could be reckless with human life, Mae was exceedingly respectful of property. For example, when the lease ran out on the house rented by the Capones, the owner, a Mrs. Stern, expected the place to be riddled with bullet holes. Instead, she found her home in immaculate condition, even better, in fact, than she had left it. In the cabinets she discovered a dozen new sets of silver and china, all of it glistening, untouched. And on the day the Capones' last phone bill, bloated with $500 in long-distance calls, arrived, Mae Capone herself pulled up in her Cadillac. Her platinum hair glistening unnaturally in the sunshine, Mae walked up to the front door, rang the bell, and told the owner, "I came to pay our telephone bill." She withdrew a thousand dollar bill from her pocket book and handed it to the astonished Mrs. Stern. "Keep the change," said Mrs. Capone, "I'm sure we must have broken something while we were here and I hope that will cover it." She bade her former landlady farewell and drove off into the Miami sunshine. Al himself wouldn't have handled it any differently, and her behavior suggests he had told her exactly what to do.

While Mae decorated, Al shopped for clothes, which were becoming something of an obsession for him, as well as a way to meet people who would otherwise cross the street to avoid him. A flash of green, he knew, never failed to bring such people around to his side. One day his new friend, Parker Henderson, brought him around to Sewell Brothers, a men's clothing store on East Flagler in downtown Miami. Al immediately won over Sewell, who found the racketeer surprisingly good company and great for business. On that first visit, Capone purchased dozens of $35 silk shirts and $12 sets of silk underwear—over $1,000 in merchandise, all paid for in cash. Dressed in his new garb he looked, said the owner, "like a tourist," which was precisely as Al wanted it—with one small exception. "He was wearing a belt with a diamond-studded buckle," Sewell remembered, "but the belt didn't match his clothes, so I asked him to let me give him a new one. Then I put on a $100 Panama hat on his head and cocked it down over the scar that started on his left forehead and creased his face. 'This is a gift from me to you—and the belt, too,' I told him. He reached out with his hand and said, 'Let me shake your hand. This is the first time anybody ever gave me anything.' "

There was more to this glad-handing than Capone's love of fancy tourist attire. Jack Sewell happened to be the son of one former mayor of Miami, John Sewell, and the nephew of another, E. G. Sewell; the latter was among those calling for the immediate departure of Al Capone from the community. So this particular merchant was extraordinarily well connected in Miami, and Capone's patronizing his store and purchasing his goodwill carried distinct political overtones. In befriending Sewell, Capone displayed the same strategy that had worked so well for him when he joined forces with Mayor Lummus to purchase the Palm Island villa.

Capone did more than patronize Sewell's store. He directed all his visitors from Chicago to buy their resort wear at Sewell Brothers. And Jack Sewell himself became a frequent visitor at the Capone's villa, where he was startled to hear Capone complain (or was it boast?) that he had just dropped $250,000 in a poker game. Sewell found it next to impossible to dislike Capone. Like so many others before him, he was overwhelmed by the racketeer's genuine charm, his staggering generosity, and his uncanny knack for finding common ground with relative strangers. It might be a fondness for gambling, Italian food, bootleg booze, or women; in Sewell's case, it was boxing. When Al learned that his great friend Jack was a boxing enthusiast like himself, he immediately arranged a sparring session. This was a testimony to Sewell's mettle, for few men were willing to step into the ring with the most notorious racketeer of the day. "When I looked at him, standing there in his bathing trunks and puffing on a cigar, I thought, 'This fellow should be easy,' " Sewell remembered. "We had no gloves, so we just slapped at each other with open hands. I found out right away that he wasn't easy. He was as hard as nails, strong and quick, and he had a very good defense. Four tough bodyguards stood about watching us in silence. They always made me feel uneasy. Later Capone told me he had fought professionally under the name of Al Brown." This was fiction of course; "Al Brown" was the alias Capone had employed in Chicago to elude police investigation of his racketeering activities.

On another visit to the villa, Sewell met Capone's chief pimp and accountant, Jack Guzik, whom Al termed "the father of the syndicate." As Sewell later recalled, "it was the first time I ever heard the word 'syndicate' applied to the mob."

Sewell was under no illusion about the nature of Capone's activities, nor was anyone else in Miami who dealt with Capone, as Sewell later explained when IRS investigators questioned him. "I don't believe there was a politician in town who didn't solicit Capone's aid, his financial aid," he said. "I've seen a lot of them around the hotel. . . . There were all kinds of people up there, Catholic priests on down."

·   ·   ·

In May, Capone finally ventured north to Chicago, slipping quietly into Cicero, where disturbing news awaited him. For well over a year his bootlegging arrangement with Frankie Yale had been unraveling. Yale complained that a growing number of trucks were being hijacked along the great northern route from Brooklyn to Chicago, but Al suspected that Yale himself was responsible for the disruptions. Because this pipeline provided Capone with one of his principal sources of revenue, he took Yale's chicanery seriously. To learn more, he dispatched a crony, James "Jimmy Files" De Amato, to Brooklyn, charged with the mission of reporting back to Chicago on Yale's activities. A month after his arrival in Brooklyn, where he ran a crap game on Coney Island, De Amato was shot to death on the street. In Brooklyn, the demise of "Jimmy Files" was regarded as just another minor gangland murder, but Capone realized that his ruse had been discovered. The "hijackings" of Capone's bootleg booze continued, and his concerns about Yale grew. In the early months of 1928, Yale survived two mysterious attempts on his life, and he began making noises about retiring.

Capone returned to Miami on June 17, having decided it was time to take action. As a young man, he had once killed for Yale; now he decided the time had come to eliminate his business partner and former boss. At forty-three, Yale remained as violent as ever, and any plan to eliminate him posed grave dangers. Whether it was actually necessary to kill Yale was another question. It was likely that Yale was chiseling on their bootlegging arrangement, yet that was not in itself grounds to assassinate him. But Capone was growing more sensitive to slights these days, whether they were real or imagined, as his syphilis gradually eroded and distorted his personality, and he was capable of manufacturing any number of reasons why Yale ought to be killed. The Capone who wanted to execute "Banjo Eyes" for cheating at golf was perfectly capable of planning the death of Frankie Yale for more serious offenses. Once he had decided to act, he summoned six colleagues from Chicago to plan the assassination. They included Jack Guzik and Dan Serritella; the others Capone called "bodyguards," although they were actually hit men: "Machine Gun" Jack McGurn, Scalise and Anselmi, and Fred "Killer" Burke. He then approached his friend Parker Henderson Jr. for another favor. Claiming that his life was in danger, he asked young Henderson to procure some weapons for the "bodyguards" who had just arrived from Chicago, and Henderson, as always, was glad to oblige. He contacted a gun dealer in Fort Worth, Texas, and ordered six revolvers and six shotguns; he paid for them himself and left them in an unoccupied room at the Ponce de León Hotel, from which Capone's men retrieved them. Their plans complete, Capone's six men, now armed, boarded the Southland Express for Chicago on June 28. To avoid harassment by Chief Hughes or any other glory-seeking police chiefs, they disembarked in Knoxville, Tennessee, and drove off in a used automobile, heading not for Chicago but for New York.

When the assassination hit the newspapers, Capone wished to be seen in "retirement," fishing in Biscayne Bay and gambling at Hialeah. Even as he awaited consummation of his plan to kill Frankie Yale, however, a fresh scandal broke, this one much closer to home. The crisis began when the *Miami Daily News* exposed the details of the Capone-Lummus-Henderson conspiracy to purchase the Palm Island villa and even published copies of some of the legal instruments involved in the transaction. The revelation that Capone's real estate broker had been none other than Mayor J. Newton Lummus reignited the anger of Miami civic organizations, who once again clamored for Capone's expulsion. The infuriated members of the City Council of Miami Beach passed a resolution declaring Capone an "undesirable resident, and, by reason of his reputed connection with the Chicago gangsters and underworld, . . . a menace to the community." If he remained, he and his underworld connections "would prove a tremendous detriment, both from a moral and monetary aspect" to the community.

There were angry calls for Lummus to resign, but he bluntly told the council that as the mayor of Miami he had no intention of obeying the dictates of the City Council of Miami *Beach*. There were many other men in the community as bad or worse than Capone, he said, but his argument did little to placate his critics. However, Lummus adroitly lent his name to the resolution condemning Capone, knowing that it lacked any legal force. The mayor returned directly to his real estate business, and Capone once again found himself beset by bad publicity. His name was by now known everywhere, and the local controversy became a national issue. "MIAMI BEACH SEEKS TO DRIVE OUT CAPONE," readers of the *New York Times* learned. "HE REFUSES TO LEAVE CITY—Authorities Appoint Policemen to Tail Him Constantly if Defiance Is Continued."

Capone remained in Miami, but no matter how lavishly he furnished his home or how much cash he distributed in the community, he was constantly confronted with the brutal reality of the rackets. In Chicago, he had managed to keep his family and his career in crime separate; his office in the Metropole Hotel was miles from his house on Prairie Avenue. Whenever he wanted to avoid the police or a rival gangster, he could move from one hideout to the next. But in Miami, he was forced to conduct business in the villa where he lived with his family. Without his brothers to protect him, he had to bring strange bodyguards—and their weapons—into his home. Visitors were startled by the sight of guns displayed atop Mae's Louis XIV furniture. She complained about the unwelcome guests, but Al realized the necessity of maintaining security. He created a spectacle wherever he went. When the Capones dined in a Miami restaurant, for example, they arrived with a retinue of thugs, one of whom lugged a large bass fiddle case, which contained the gold-rimmed plates Al favored and a cache of machine guns, should a show of force become necessary during the meal.

Capone's Florida "retirement" turned out to be more stressful than he had anticipated, and there were telltale signs of the pressure. His temper was likely to erupt at odd times and places, and he was given to destroying his clubs at the golf course for no apparent reason. At the same time, his compulsive need for contact with people grew even stronger in Miami. His career as a racketeer made ordinary human relationships all but impossible, and when he could not win a friend, he was prepared to buy him at any price. As his dealing with Sewell suggests, he would go to any lengths to establish an ordinary relationship, which to Capone meant one over which the fear of death did not hover. Yet the social acceptance he craved could never be his. He could inspire fear, earn limitless amounts of money, and satisfy his lust with numerous prostitutes, but just beyond the glittering rim of his racketeering empire, beyond the clubs and whores and endless money and bootleg booze, there was the terrifying prospect of death and darkness waiting to pluck him at an early age. To forget his troubles, and to make the time in Miami pass more quickly, he began to gamble obsessively. Capone's losses at gambling had already become part of gangland's lore, but in Florida his losses at the Hialeah race track increased exponentially. Every week he gambled away hundreds of thousands of dollars, making the bookies with whom he dealt extremely happy but also a little suspicious; they could not understand why Al shrugged off the losses as if they were inconsequential.

Capone was losing touch with reality because of his advancing case of neurosyphilis—not all at once, and not consistently, but he gradually retreated into episodes of megalomania and paranoia. Under the influence of the spirochetes gnawing at his nervous system, he became ever more temperamental—by turns gloomy, ebullient, and violent—without apparent cause. He suffered from a dimly perceived but keenly felt need for greatness or grandeur lurking just beyond his reach, tantalizing him, driving him on, tripping him up. He was a Caliban driven mad by syphilitic voices and visions he could scarcely comprehend, the proverbial beast who, delighted by the beauty of a butterfly floating through his field of vision, snatches at it, only to crush the insect in his brute fist, and is overwhelmed by his innate clumsiness, violence, and guilt.

· · ·

Sunday, July 1, was warm and sunny in Brooklyn, and the borough's neighborhoods reverberated with the tolling of church bells. One of the most conspicuous sights in Brooklyn that placid morning was a large, gleaming, dark brown Lincoln coursing slowly through the streets. At the wheel was Frankie Yale, out for a Sunday morning spin. Yale drove alone, but he had little to fear, for his brand-new car featured a bulletproof chassis. As he pulled up to an intersection, he failed to notice a black Buick following him.

The Buick held four men, and they did not look like churchgoers. One was "Machine Gun" Jack McGurn, Capone's trigger-happy assassin; the others were Scalise, Anselmi, and Burke. When Yale finally did catch a glimpse of the car in his rearview mirror, he instantly realized what it meant.

Stepping on the gas, Yale turned onto Forty-fourth Street, tires squealing, as the Buick gave chase and rapidly drew even with Yale. The two cars raced along a residential street lined on either side with trees and identical rows of brownstones. At 923 Forty-fourth Street, Solomon and Bertha Kaufman were hosting a party celebrating their son's bar mitzvah. The sound of the speeding cars attracted the attention of the guests, who looked out the large street-level window to see shotgun barrels protruding from the Buick, aiming directly at the head of the driver of the Lincoln. There was a blast, and Frankie Yale slumped at the wheel, dead. His car's body had been bullet-proofed, but not the windows. His attackers did not stop there; they had come to do a job, and they wanted to make sure it was done thoroughly. One of them raised a machine gun and began firing into Yale's body as the Lincoln continued to roll along the street, out of control. This was the first time that weapon had ever been used in a gangland hit in New York. As the sound of gunfire faded, the Buick gained speed, turned a corner, and disappeared. The assassins later abandoned the car, leaving behind a Thompson machine gun, a sawed-off shotgun, and two revolvers. Yale's Lincoln proceeded along the street, rolling up onto the sidewalk, heading toward Mrs. Kaufman's home, and colliding with the stoop in front of the house. As it came to a standstill, the door flung open, and Frankie Yale's corpse, beautifully attired and bloody, fell out onto the street before the appalled guests.

Although Frankie Yale had died on a Brooklyn street and not in Chicago, his murder was among the most significant gangland hits of the decade, for next to Al Capone, Yale had been the best-known, most feared racketeer of the Prohibition era. Yet for all his prominence, no one knew why he was dead or who had killed him; the press and public reacted only to the grue-some circumstances of his murder and the biggest gangster funeral New York had ever seen. The funeral took place on July 5, and 100,000 people turned out to pay their last respects to Yale and to gape at the floral arrangements; perhaps the most outlandish consisted of a large heart fashioned of roses pierced by a dagger, all of it surrounded by a clock of white and blue violets pointing to the time of day when Yale was hit, and underneath, the legend: "We'll see them, kid." It became a source of local pride that the number of mourners, the length of the motorcade, and the cost of the floral arrange-ments for Frankie Yale's funeral exceeded even that of Dion O'Banion's funeral, which had long been considered Chicago's grandest display of the underworld in mourning.

Once Yale was laid to rest, his widow Maria expected to come into a great deal of money, but she was disappointed. Only $3,000 turned up, most of which Frankie had been carrying at the time of his death; desperate for cash, she was reduced to auctioning his renowned diamond-studded belt, but it fetched only $75. Soon Maria Yale, widow of the most powerful ganglord in Brooklyn, was working ten hours a day sewing pants in a factory to support her family.

Once the shock of Yale's assassination wore off, the finger of suspicion pointed at Capone. His emissaries of death had been remarkably careless about covering their tracks. Their Buick carried Illinois license plates and was traced to Chicago. The weapons they had used to kill Yale and then discarded were found and traced to Parker Henderson, who was now as eager to cooperate with the police as he had once been to do Capone's bidding. He explained how he had purchased some of the guns used to kill Yale for Capone. Employing a machine gun also proved to be unwise, for police later recovered it and traced it to a Chicago arms dealer, Peter von Frantzius, who had the distinction of supplying weapons to all the major Chicago underworld figures. The evidence, though circumstantial, was so convincing that Capone might as well have pinned a note to Frankie Yale's corpse, admitting guilt.

The newspapers, if not the police, closed in on him: "YALE DEATH TRIO TRACED TO CHICAGO," declared the Chicago Tribune only days after the murder, and several weeks later added: "CAPONE'S GUN KILLED YALE, SAYS INFORMER." New York's police commissioner, Grover Whalen, announced that Capone was responsible for Yale's death, and made a highly publicized journey to Chicago for a fruitless meeting with the Chicago police, who were not about to get in the middle of a dispute between rival hoodlums; as far as they were concerned, "Scarface" had done them a favor. For the record, Capone denied any involvement; he said he had always liked Frankie Yale and had even sent a small wreath to the funeral, for the sake of appearances.

• • •

Throughout much of the summer Capone was in and out of Chicago Heights and Lansing, Michigan, where he attended to his bootlegging business in the post-Yale era. When Michael Hughes, the Chicago police chief who had threatened to place all Chicago gangsters, including Capone, under house arrest, stepped down, Al returned to Chicago itself to catch up on business. The visit was meant to be brief, for Sonny and Mae remained at the Palm Island villa. However, Al still had important family ties in Chicago. His mother continued to live in the house on Prairie Avenue, accompanied by several of the younger Capone brothers. And his older brother Ralph, now thirty-four, had finally remarried in May 1928 and now lived on the South Side with his new wife, the former Valma Pheasant, and continued to manage nightclubs. Although Al Capone's return to his mother and brothers in Chicago marked at least the second time he had broken his pledge to retire from the rackets, no newspaper or policeman troubled to remind him of his promise. By now it was apparent that Capone would "retire" whenever it suited his convenience and reemerge at an equally convenient opportunity.

Accompanied by a retinue of bodyguards, Al made his first public appearance in Chicago at the Minerva Athletic Club on South Halsted Street. This was actually a gambling joint run by a member of the Capone organization, "Dago" Lawrence Mangano. For the benefit of the journalists who were present, Capone bemoaned the death of Frankie Yale, and once he had unburdened himself of his grief, he "eased his bank roll out of a pocket and went into action with hoarse imprecations." After several unlucky rolls of the dice, "Mr. Capone removed his coat, showing a mauve silk shirt, and went to work again. His luck switched for a few moments, but the dice again went against him, and his loss, with many cluckings of sympathy from his bodyguard, was chalked up at ten grand."

Capone did more than gamble during his stay in Chicago. On July 30, he moved his Chicago offices from the Metropole Hotel to larger quarters at the Lexington, located at Twenty-second Street and Michigan Avenue, only a block away. At first he took a suite of ten rooms under the name "George Phillips." Within several months, Capone and his men had the run of the place, which became indelibly associated with him. The Lexington was an imposing hotel with pretensions to architectural grandeur; its façade combined Moorish and Italian elements with broad "Chicago windows." Within, Al's new office, perched in a corner of the uppermost floor, offered a commanding view of Chicago's South Side—Al Capone's empire—which he surveyed from a chair equipped with a bulletproof back: a gift from Dominic Roberto and the boys in Chicago Heights. He took other safety precautions, preferring to ride a freight elevator to his floor, always in the company of his bodyguards. "The Lexington was a fabulous place, filled with all kinds of traps and escape routes," recalls Vern Whaley, a reporter who visited shortly after Capone moved in. There were alarms, hidden panels, moving walls, everything a security-conscious gangster required, and no one was more security-conscious than Al Capone. Whenever he spent the night at the Lexington, Louis "Little New York" Campagna camped out on a cot strategically located beside the door leading to his master's boudoir. To prevent another attempt to poison his pasta, Capone arranged for his meals to be prepared in a private kitchen under the supervision of his men, and before a room-service cart was wheeled into his presence, the meal underwent the scrutiny of a food tester, usually the chef himself.

Capone was less fastidious about his sexual behavior. His girlfriend of the moment lived in a small suite at the hotel, always on call should her services be required. She was blond, Greek, and young, probably no more than sixteen. When she noticed a sore on her genitalia, she went to a physician, Dr. David V. Owen, whose practice included members of the Capone organization. The girl took a Wassermann test, which was positive, and began a series of injections. There was still no cure for the disease, so the treatment was of limited value. Even though his mistress was diagnosed as syphilitic, Capone refused to take the Wassermann test himself. Ralph's case had gone away on its own (as syphilis does four-fifths of the time), and Al expected the same resolution. So there would be no test, and no treatment for him. In any event, Capone had, in all likelihood contracted his case of syphilis years before, as an adolescent in Brooklyn.

He was far more sensitive to a new threat to discipline in his ranks—not prostitutes, not drinking, but heroin. Harry Read dropped by the Lexington one day, where he found a group of Capone's men searching a bodyguard's room for evidence of the drug. They dismantled furniture, removed and inspected the brass knobs on the bedpost, unscrewed and inspected electric switches, and hammered away at the floor in search of hollow hiding places. Capone told Read that the man who had occupied the room had been addicted to heroin, a discovery that prompted the racketeer to administer a thrashing and to send him off for a "rest cure" in Kentucky. "I love the son of a bitch," he said, "but if he ever goes back on that stuff he'll wind up in a cement overcoat."

• • • •

Although Capone's insistence on security appeared extreme, violence was ever present. The end of summer brought with it a response to the slaying of Frankie Yale. In Chicago's Italian community, September 8 marked the festival of Our Lady of Loreto; in expectation of the event, the poverty of Little Italy was temporarily hidden behind a façade of brightly-colored ornaments, paper lanterns, banners, and parades. The air was filled with the sounds and smells of sizzling sausage and fried dough dusted with powdered sugar. This year, anxiety lurked behind the gaiety, for days earlier, a kidnapping had shocked the community. The victim was the ten-year-old son a wealthy sewer contractor, A. Frank Ranieri, and the ransom was set at $60,000. Frantic, Ranieri did what most Italians in his place would have done; he went to Antonio Lombardo, Capone's handpicked chief of the pivotal Unione Sicilione, for help. Just before Ranieri arrived, however, Lombardo decided to go for a walk in the Loop in the company of his two bodyguards. It was rush hour, and the streets were jammed. Lombardo liked that; a dedicated self-promoter, he wanted to see and be seen. He had recently published a biographical sketch describing how he had overcome hardships facing immigrants and had risen to his eminent position. In reality, he supervised alky-cookers and funneled money extorted from racketeers to local politicians, but that was not how he described himself. "Like most successful men," his biographical sketch concluded with unintended irony, "he has received much, but has given more to the community in which he lives. It is to such men that Chicago owes her greatness." Al Capone himself could not have said it better. As Lombardo walked through the community to which he claimed to owe so much, two men fell in step behind him, pulled out .45-caliber revolvers, and fired dumdum bullets into his head.

Although dozens of passers-by witnessed the murder of Lombardo, and many offered detailed descriptions of the assassins to the police, no arrests were made. Old "Shoes," the chief of detectives, claimed to know who had killed Lombardo and how Capone was involved. "Lombardo paid the penalty for having instigated, with Alphonse Capone, the murder of Frank Uale, alias Yale, in Brooklyn on July 1," said Schoemaker, as if to explain why the police need do nothing. Like so many gangsters before him, Lombardo was laid to rest in Mt. Carmel Cemetery. Despite the impotence of Chicago's law enforcement officials, it was generally assumed Lombardo's death was revenge for Yale's killing, and no event could be more calculated to upset the fragile equilibrium among Chicago's gangs than the assassination of the head of the Unione Sicilione.

The new outbreak of violence in the streets attracted the attention of the Chicago Crime Commission. Under the direction of its seventy-six-year-old leader, Frank J. Loesch, the CCC was attempting to move beyond mere fact-gathering to a more muscular campaign against crime in general and Al Capone in particular. Loesch had practiced criminal law years before in Chicago and later became a prosecutor investigating corruption and election fraud in Chicago when Al Capone was still a child in Brooklyn. In 1928, Loesch sought and received a commission as a special state's attorney to investigate that year's primary in all its manifold corruption. Initially his mission appeared doomed, for the County Board, protecting itself, refused to appropriate money for his investigation, but civic outrage proved so fierce that a popular subscription raised money to run his office, and Loesch accumulated a $150,000 war chest. Eventually the County Board was embarrassed into providing additional funds. The investigation gained momentum, and within months sixty-three men were under indictment. Nearly all the culprits were convicted and fined, but their transgressions only served to whet Loesch's appetite for battle. Antonio Lombardo was hardly cold in his grave, his memory still crowned with a martyr's halo, when Loesch denounced him as the head of the Chicago "Mafia": "All the kidnappings, blackmail, terrorism, murders and countless other crimes committed in the name of the dread Mafia sprang from the minds of Lombardo and the men who are now fighting to take the place vacated by his death. . . . Capone, partner of Lombardo, ruled in other ways. Through him the family tree spreads to take in the names of Jack Guzik and Ralph Guzik. Guzik runs the brothels and the beer and booze syndicates [while] Ralph takes to moonshining." Although the Unione Sicilione drew his ire, Loesch was absolutely obsessed with Al Capone, whom he designated "the head center of the devilment" afflicting Chicago.

Loesch was determined to meet the man who appeared to control the city—all of Cook County, in fact—while holding no official capacity himself. Al at first resisted the idea, but once he received assurances that Loesch came not to prosecute but to negotiate—"I told him I was not there to investigate his criminal record, because I had no power to do that, that I did not care to investigate his Prohibition violations, because that was not my business"—he eventually agreed to a meeting at the Lexington Hotel. With his air of respectability combined with a certain macabre sense of menace, Capone was like no one Loesch had ever met in his long experience as a criminal lawyer. "I found him in an officelike room with half a dozen of his non-English speaking guards standing with their hands on their guns. Over Capone's desk hung three oil portraits. They represented George Washington, Abraham Lincoln, and 'Big Bill' Thompson," Loesch recalled. "That alone was enough to flabbergast me."

"Mr. Capone, gunmen will get you or me whenever they want to," Loesch began. "The gunmen or the law will get you at one time or another."

"He replied," said Loesch, "that he would always best the law, but that he expected his demise some day at the business end of a shotgun."

Given the recent spate of gangland deaths in Chicago, not to mention his own brother's fate, this was a reasonable assumption on Capone's part. "But they'll only get me when I'm not looking," he added.

Then Loesch got down to business. "I am here to ask you to help in one thing," he said. "I want you to keep your damned Italian hoodlums out of the election this coming fall." Loesch was referring to the November 1928 election, which involved more than local politics; with Coolidge out of the race, the country was going to elect a new president.

Capone listened in silence to this request and the slur on his Italian heritage. He thought for a while, then rose to his feet and offered Loesch a drink. The inquisitor declined, and Capone said, "Sure, I'll give them the works, because they are all dagoes up there, but what about the Saltis gang of micks over on the West Side? They'll have to be handled different. Do you want me to give them the works, too?"

Loesch later recalled his reaction to Capone's reply: "I was overpleased with Mr. Capone's apparent willingness to help on the west side and I expressed myself as being grateful."

"All right," said Al, laying out the terms of the deal and flexing a certain amount of racketeering muscle for Loesch's benefit, "I'll have the cops send over the squad cars the night before the election and jug all the hoodlums and keep 'em in the cooler until the polls close."

Recalled Loesch: "It was a grateful handshake that I gave Mr. Capone at this proposition."

Capone proved as good as his word. "On the specified day," Loesch said as he lapsed in Al's gangster lingo, "seventy police cars were used to jug the hoodlums. It turned out to be the most successful election day that Chicago had in forty years. There was not one complaint, not one election fraud, not one threat of trouble all day. What is the answer to that?" For Loesch, the answer was Capone, the most powerful man in Chicago. For this reason the august Chicago Crime Commission came crawling to *him* for help. "Crime is highly organized," Loesch explained. "Capone's men work with the same precision as does a captain of industry, except in Capone's organization the penalty for failure is a charge of shotgun slugs." In his position, Capone paradoxically became a force for stability, doing more to deter street crime than the entire police force managed to do. For instance, he liked to portray himself as the scourge of pickpockets: "A pickpocket once crowded next to my mother on the State Street car and took the wallet out of her purse. I've got no use for a dip. They prey on working people, the scrubladies coming from Loop office buildings in the morning and the tired clerks at night." He preferred the working people of Chicago to spend their wages on his bootleg booze, or in one of his gambling joints or brothels.

Loesch recognized he had crossed an invisible line in going to Capone to beg for peace on election day, and he kept the meeting a secret for nearly two years, until he finally revealed the details in a speech to the Southern California Academy of Criminology and again before a Senate subcommittee. Eager for autumnal glory, Loesch thought of himself as the savior of Chicago's civic virtue, but the revelation of the deal he had struck with Capone caused a shudder of revulsion, for the spectacle of the grand old man of the Chicago Crime Commission going to the Lexington Hotel on bended knee to negotiate a cease-fire from a gangster offered further proof, as if it were needed, of Capone's control over Chicago. The result was that Loesch's reputation was tarnished and Capone's enhanced. The older man's willingness to go public also meant the end of their working relationship. It was only a matter of time until Frank Loesch, like so many others with whom Capone had arrangements, turned on him.

·   ·   ·

The chain of killings set in motion by the assassination of Frankie Yale ended with the murder of Pasqualino Lolordo, who had succeeded Antonio Lombardo as the head of the Capone-controlled Unione Sicilione, on January 8, 1929. Lolordo's three assassins were sufficiently familiar for his wife to admit them to her home and to serve them food and liquor. As they drank to his health they pulled out their revolvers and fired. Mrs. Lolordo claimed she saw nothing, and they, like so many other Chicago assassins, were never apprehended.

By this time, Capone had returned to his family in Miami Beach, where he planned to spend the winter in gangster heaven, fishing from his boat and furnishing his home. He believed he had earned a brief respite from the terrors of gangland, for the last half of 1928 had been especially violent. Capone had plotted the death of Frankie Yale, and he had suffered the loss of his Sicilian allies Antonio Lombardo and Pasqualino Lolordo. On balance, however, his assassination of Yale had accomplished its aims, and Capone believed his selective use of violence had been justified, his judgment vindicated. But the calm was deceptive. Shortly after the New Year, he planned an even more ambitious offense, one that promised to eliminate *all* his enemies in Chicago and end gang warfare in that beleaguered city forever.

Part Two
DESCENT

CHAPTER 7

Slaughter and Sanctuary

IF THERE WAS ONE MOMENT in Al Capone's racketeering career when he appeared absolutely invulnerable, it was now, as he approached his thirtieth birthday on January 17, 1929. The racketeering coalition he had built reached across ethnic boundaries to include Jews, Italians, Poles, blacks, and any other bloc of significance. He was not the only bootlegger in Chicago, but he dominated the business; there was Al Capone, and there was everyone else. The same held true for the vice trade and for gambling. He maintained bases at the Lexington Hotel on the South Side of Chicago; at several locations in Cicero and Chicago Heights; as well as a winter retreat in Miami Beach, Florida, and a summer hideout in Lansing, Michigan. He oversaw an organization of skilled racketeers and gunmen, but the terms *gangster, racketeer,* or *hoodlum* were no longer adequate to describe or contain him. "Bugs" Moran was a common hoodlum, "Greasy Thumb" Guzik a racketeer, but Capone had evolved beyond them into a feared political boss—the de facto mayor of Chicago. His economic influence extended far beyond the city limits. The Capone bootlegging network reached from New York's Long Island to Lake Michigan, and he controlled the flow of alcohol from Europe, Canada, and the Caribbean. Newspapers estimated his income exceeded $100 million a year, but that was the gross amount; as Capone said repeatedly, he had tremendous overhead. No one, not even Capone, could say how much he pocketed, for he avoided banks and saved nothing beyond the stash of cash at the foot of his bed at the Palm Island villa. He was, rather, a pipeline through which huge quantities of money passed; when he needed funds, he dipped into the stream and helped himself. Political circumstances continued to favor him: the mayor was afraid of him, he had bribed the Chicago Police Department into a state of compliance, and Prohibition, the chief cause of his good fortune, was entering its tenth year, turning millions of otherwise law-abiding Americans into lawbreakers.

Many drinkers had come of age during Prohibition and could not remember a time when it had not existed. Thanks to Prohibition, a casual disregard of the law became part of the American way of life. Many Americans realized, perhaps for the first time, that the law of the land could be misguided, or even downright wrong, and therefore should be ignored. In 1929, Mabel Walker Willebrandt, who had served as assistant attorney general, wrote in despair: "No one who is intellectually honest will deny that there has not yet been effective, nation-wide enforcement. Nor will it be denied that prohibition enforcement remains the chief and in fact the only real political issue of the whole nation. No political, economic, or moral issue has so engrossed and divided the people of America as the prohibition problem, except the issue of slavery." Capone had made the most of the situation, riding to fame and fortune on its ironies and hypocrisies. When people referred to him, it was usually in conjunction with the word *big*. Refer to "Big Boy" or the "Big Fellow" and everyone knew whom you meant; there were many gangsters in Chicago, but only one "Big Fellow." Some feared him, others loved him, and given the hypocrisy born of Prohibition, many despised him and rooted for him at the same time. Chicago's power structure drank his booze even as they condemned him as a dago thug, and his ability to circumvent a ridiculous law earned him the sneaking admiration of countless citizens. The career of Al Capone showed it was still possible for a man to come to Chicago with little or no resources and strike it rich in this most commercial of American cities. And Capone had managed to rise to his position of eminence within a span of only seven years, before he turned thirty. Morality aside, his was the grandest success story Chicago had seen in a generation.

It was at the apogee of his power and influence that the government forces that were to bring him down began to gather momentum. Compared to the clout Capone wielded, the Feds were an insignificant presence in Chicago. To Capone and his allies, they seemed harmless, nothing more than a small group of nearsighted clerks poring over ledgers and sorting through yellowing newspaper clippings in cramped, dusty offices borrowed from the postal service. Yet Capone's failure to take them into account proved to be a distinct advantage, for they were free to pursue their goal without interference.

Driven by his sense of moral outrage, George E. Q. Johnson, the newly appointed U.S. attorney, was the first to comprehend the role Chicago Heights played in the Capone bootlegging empire as a refuge, staging area, and arms depot. The Heights had drawn his attention shortly after its police chief, Leroy Gilbert, made a routine arrest of two men ferrying bootleg booze through the town. Chief Gilbert was scheduled to testify against the bootleggers before a grand jury. Then, on the evening of December 6, 1928, as Gilbert sat in the parlor of his home, reading a newspaper, his head was blown off. The police determined that two unknown men with shotguns were responsible, but they were never apprehended.

In retaliation for the outrage, Johnson's office, in cooperation with the Chicago Police Department, raised a posse numbering 100 men, mostly police officers, and deputized them all. This was the first time that a significant number of federal, county, and city law enforcement authorities had put aside their turf squabbles and combined forces against racketeering in Chicago. The results were to prove more dramatic than even they hoped.

Exactly one month after the murder of Police Chief Gilbert, the posse staged the largest raid Chicago Heights had ever seen. In the early hours of January 6, 1929, the streets of Chicago Heights were deserted, the saloons filled. On Hungry Hill, the Italians dutifully tended their stills and tried as best they could to protect themselves from the stinging, piercing cold. The police cars arrived under cover of darkness; in itself, this was not an unusual or threatening sight in Chicago Heights, where the Capone organization controlled the local Police Department, but these police cars had come all the way from *Chicago*, and eventually there were twenty of them on the streets of the Heights, their motors idling, their headlights dark. Their first destination was not, as might be expected, a still or saloon or gambling joint populated with hoodlums and flappers and a jazz band; no, the cars headed toward the Chicago Heights jail, which the raiders regarded as an enemy outpost to be invaded and captured. And that was precisely what they proceeded to do. First, they surrounded the building. Next, a delegation of raiders marched in the front door, telling the startled sergeant dozing at his desk that he was being relieved of duty; they were now in charge here. Surprised and overwhelmed by the invaders, the docile Chicago Heights police yielded. Thus the "good cops" temporarily seized control of the building from the "bad cops."

With the police station secured, the posse executed the next directive. The raiders fanned out across the Heights, breaking into breweries, smashing stills, and seizing huge quantities of alcohol. This was to be expected. However, when the deputies descended on the estate of Oliver J. Ellis, who they believed managed the Subway, one of Capone's lucrative Cicero gambling dens, they finally struck pay dirt. In a building behind the main house the raiders discovered over 400 slot machines; Chicago Heights, they suddenly realized, was the center of the organization's slot machine racket. As day broke, the townspeople came out of their homes to watch the raid on the Ellis estate. As the deputies took sledge hammers to the slot machines, small children chased after the nickels and dimes that scattered across the floor. At the conclusion of the raid, the posse took more than twenty men suspected of complicity in the murder of Chief Gilbert to the Chicago Heights' jail and locked them up, along with the sergeant on duty.

In the span of a few hours, the raid had permanently altered the face of the conflict between the racketeers and law enforcement agencies. The battle lines had suddenly been redrawn, or, considering the history of police corruption, drawn for the first time. Each side had massive resources at its disposal. The Capone organization, for its part, relied on the tremendous revenue generated by bootlegging, and it used the money to buy political power and loyalty throughout Chicago and the state of Illinois. The money also bought the racketeers weapons, headquarters throughout the city, a ready supply of young men willing to risk their lives in return for high wages, and the silence of grand juries. As long as Prohibition continued, this revenue and all it purchased was secure. In addition, the organization had the benefit of the leadership of Al Capone and the allegiance of a broad spectrum of immigrant groups.

But George E. Q. Johnson, representing the U.S. government, was also in a powerful position, with potentially unlimited assets at his disposal. If he needed more investigators, he would have them. If he needed to reach judges to obtain warrants, he could. Most important, he had the law on his side, which was obvious but easy enough to overlook in Prohibition era Chicago. Capone himself overlooked that fact, assuming he could ignore or buy his way out of the law, but he had never before encountered federal authorities, and as he was to discover over the next two years, the Feds worked slowly and clumsily, but they never stopped working. And their incessant probing and analyzing eventually permitted the Feds to reach the weak links in the Capone organization, beginning with Ralph Capone.

The most significant finding of the raid on Chicago Heights was not the booze or the stills or even the hundreds of slot machines; it was a set of ledgers the police had confiscated when one of their men picked the lock of a safe in the Ellis estate. A cautious man who valued his life, Ellis himself refused to say anything to the investigators about the ledgers, but his silence did not end the matter. The ledgers were to provide a mother lode of information for Capone's antagonists. In a rare display of cooperation, the police shared the records with the attorney general's office in Washington. Reviewing the books, Mabel Walker Willebrandt discovered that "the revenue over a period of three years, according to the records kept, was approximately $725,000 a year from the machines . . . in an area where there reside not more than one hundred thousand people."

The records also came to the attention of the IRS, whose Intelligence Unit feasted on them. The IRS investigators determined that the organization's slot machine racket was even more profitable than Willebrandt realized, clearing as much as $1.5 million a year—not bad for an invisible business. By carefully checking every item in the ledgers, no matter how small, the IRS then came up with one of the biggest breaks in the case. The IRS clerks located a list of checks Ellis cashed, and they investigated every transaction until at last they came up with a prize: a check for $2,130, dated June 27, 1928. It seemed a relatively small amount, but the signature gave it special significance. It was signed by Ralph Capone.

The Intelligence Unit had over the past two years come to know Ralph well; their man in Chicago, Eddie Waters, had held several conversations with him concerning the necessity of paying taxes on his entire income. But "Bottles" always maintained he was not a wealthy bootlegger, just a racehorse owner of modest means who made the odd bet now and then. Under pressure he eventually admitted that he owed a total of $4,086.25 in back taxes for 1922 through 1925. In September 1927 Ralph had offered to pay $1,000, claiming his financial situation was so straitened that he would have to borrow even that amount. Sounding as though he had stepped from the pages of a Damon Runyon story, Ralph's lawyer told the IRS, "My client has sustained considerable loss as the result of the sickness and death of his race horses throughout the past year. He has also lost a great deal gambling. All he has left is a half-interest in two race horses and at the present time he is using up practically all his income trying to get them into shape." Neither Ralph nor his counsel seemed to realize that they were admitting the rack-eteer must have made a "great deal" of money in order to gamble it all away. Deeply suspicious of Ralph and convinced he would trip himself up, the IRS refused to settle. Ralph kept offering higher amounts, but even his final offer of $5,000 was refused.

Now, with the telltale $2,130 check in hand, the Intelligence Unit looked more deeply into Ralph's finances. Two of their investigators, Nels Tessem and Archie Martin, scrutinized the books again, as well as all the other supporting documents the IRS had accumulated, almost 2 million items in all. Tessem, in particular, was one of the unsung heroes of the federal government's efforts to smash the Capone organization. His background was Scandinavian, like so many of the investigators, and he possessed a genius for detail. He set to work with a will, and after two months of painstaking examination of the documents, he arrived at several startling conclusions. The first was that even as he was pleading poverty to the IRS, Ralph Capone actually had $25,000 on deposit at the Pinkert State Bank in Cicero under an assumed name, James Carter. That discrepancy was merely the start of a long trail of perfidy. In a report summarizing his findings, Tessem noted,

The investigation further disclosed that [Ralph] Capone was doing a thriving business in connection with the sale of beer at Cicero, . . .

that he was connected with large scale gambling operations and that he was involved in the operation of disorderly houses [i.e. brothels] and other ventures in violation of the law. He employed various means to conceal his activities, among which were the use of aliases, such as James Carroll, James Costello, Jr., James Carter, James Carson, Harry Roberts and Harry White. Deposits which he made in the Pinkert State Bank, under those names, totaled more than $1,850,000.

As Tessem discovered, when Ralph closed out an account in one name, he simultaneously opened a new one in another name for the *same amount*. Tessem and the other IRS agents had already come to the conclusion that Ralph was no financial wizard, but they hadn't realized he was quite that dumb. Tessem also noticed that many of Ralph's bank deposits happened to be in multiples of 55, and as everyone in Chicago knew, a barrel of beer cost exactly $55. So it wasn't very difficult to guess the source of Ralph's income. It was now apparent that Ralph had earned far more income than he ever admitted to the IRS.

The agent's report included more than financial records; Tessem's character sketch of Ralph Capone was laced with contempt: "Ralph J. Capone is a brother of the notorious Alphonse Capone, and for some years has been one of the principals in the so-called Capone organization. He is a man of exceedingly bad repute. . . . In none of the investigations has any evidence been produced tending to show that Ralph J. Capone, at any time in recent years, has been engaged in a legitimate business, unless it can be said that horse racing in some states is a legitimate business."

On the strength of Tessem's findings, the U.S. attorney's office in Chicago indicted Ralph Capone for income tax evasion. Despite the mountain of evidence Tessem had gathered, however, not even the U.S. attorney knew if he could make his case stick, especially in Chicago, where impartial judges and juries were scarce. Furthermore, Ralph's failure to pay taxes seemed a minor sin compared to his bootlegging and other illegal activities, but the obscure and technical nature of the violation actually worked to the Feds' advantage. Only they understood the seriousness of the charge; Ralph, in contrast, was inclined to dismiss it as a ploy to obtain bribes. So Ralph became a test case for the IRS; once they got him, they would go after another linchpin in the Capone organization, Jack Guzik. And once they nailed Guzik, they would go after the "Big Fellow." That, at least, was the plan. But plans had a way of going astray.

•   •   •

In Miami Beach, Al Capone appeared oblivious to the government's strategy to bring him to justice. He displayed no concern over the Chicago

Heights raid, and he refused to trouble himself with Ralph's tax problems. His sole concern remained the threat posed by rival gangs, especially "Bugs" Moran's unsophisticated but tenacious little band, to his safety and to his rackets. Determined to maintain the appearance of living in retirement in Florida, Capone himself could not launch a new gang war, but his vicious bodyguard, "Machine Gun" Jack McGurn, yearned to do battle on behalf of his boss.

In the last three years, McGurn had risen from an obscure, $150-a-week bodyguard to a partner in the Capone organization. Though he retained his superficial charm, the dapper, athletic little man had become more violent and self-confident as he rose through the ranks. He was now a feared presence in Chicago, widely known in his own right. He was often seen at his favorite sporting event, the six-day bicycle races. They were a distinctly twenties phenomenon, these bicycle races, all frenzy and flash. Two-man teams competed on a banked indoor track around the clock. Most of the time, the pace was slow, if not lazy, but occasional heats determined the order of the teams. When they were not pedaling, the racers slept in small, coffinlike boxes behind or even in the middle of the track. Disdaining the mingled odors of sweat and cigar smoke, McGurn and other hoodlums usually waited until the final day to put in their appearance, and then they showed up in force, with a retinue of gunmen and girls attired in furs and diamonds. For McGurn, a six-day bicycle race offered the perfect occasion to strut and to place breathtakingly large bets with an air of nonchalance.

Constantly placing himself on display, McGurn eventually attracted the attention of "Bugs" Moran, who had repeatedly failed to assassinate Capone. Moran assigned two brothers, Pete and Frank Gusenberg, the task of killing him off. One night, the brothers followed McGurn to a phone booth in a hotel on Rush Street and opened fire with a revolver and a machine gun. Glass shattered and wood splintered. McGurn collapsed before he could return the Gusenbergs' fire. The brothers fled, certain that they had eliminated Al Capone's principal lieutenant. They were wrong, as it turned out. Dead wrong.

An ambulance rushed McGurn to the hospital, where doctors removed the lead from his body. He later returned to his suite at the Lexington Hotel, where he lived with his girlfriend, a platinum blonde named Louise Rolfe. McGurn's survival amounted to a death sentence for the Gusenberg brothers, whom he had recognized. Retribution was inevitable, and McGurn had previously shown himself capable of murder on a grand scale. He had taken four lives trying to avenge his father's death, and countless others protecting Capone's life, and he advised Capone to eliminate not just the Gusenberg brothers but the entire Moran gang.

As even McGurn knew, murder on the scale he imagined required plan-

ning. At the beginning of 1929, after he had recovered from Moran's bungled assassination attempt, McGurn went to Capone to ask his blessing for a
counterattack. This Al gave, setting the stage for the most notorious mass
murder in the history of Chicago, a bloodbath that would eventually do as
much to end Capone's career as the combined might of the U.S. government. Of course, no one would have predicted that outcome. At the time,
Capone, who was still in Florida, saw the retaliation as a private matter
among rival gangs. He realized his name might be dragged into it, even if
McGurn masterminded the project, yet if Capone could get away with the
murder of Moran's confederate "Hymie" Weiss with only token complaints
from the press and police, it was tempting to try again with Moran himself.
The man was so widely detested that the press and police would thank
Capone for ridding the city of him. Thus he willingly agreed to pay McGurn
$10,000 plus expenses to accomplish the mission. For the record, however,
Capone wanted no part of the assassination—none whatsoever. He planned
to be in Miami Beach when it occurred, and he wanted McGurn to handle
the whole bloody business himself.

During the next several weeks, McGurn studied the movements of the
Moran gang. They were nothing like the Capone organization, these boys.
They did not control luxury hotels or hold press conferences. Their headquarters were located in a garage behind the offices of S.M.C. Cartage
Company, located at 2122 North Clark Street, then a dreary, nondescript
stretch of storefronts and small businesses. It was in this garage, McGurn
discovered, that the Moran gang took delivery of their booze and distributed
it to their local outlets. As the only locale where all the important gang
members assembled, the garage seemed a promising place to stage the mass
execution McGurn craved. He next assembled an assassination squad comprising some of the finest talents in the underworld. The selection of assassins
required considerable care and diplomacy. The first rule was to import killers
from out of town, killers whom the victims, should they survive, would not
be able to recognize. Since murder was not a federal offense and police
departments in different cities often had difficulty coordinating their investigations, it was advantageous for the killers to leave town as soon as the deed
was done. There was no second rule. Capone's plan to assassinate Frankie
Yale had worked well for just this reason, and it served as McGurn's inspiration. He imported Capone's occasional golfing partner, Fred "Killer"
Burke, from St. Louis to lead the group. Burke was associated with the
Egan's Rats gang, which was in turn affiliated with the Capone organization's
bootlegging network. Although Burke spent much time in Chicago and in
Benton Harbor, the nearby Lake Michigan resort, few associated him with
Capone. "Killer" Burke was better known in his own right as a ruthless bank

robber wanted in at least four states. Aptly named, Burke was glad to participate in another hit, for which he was paid $5,000, and he enlisted the services of an Egan's Rat gunman named James Ray.

They were joined by Joseph Lolordo, the brother of the slain leader of the Unione Sicilione, and two veterans of the Yale assassination, John Scalise and Albert Anselmi, each of whom received $1,000 for their services. This inseparable duo played a unique role in the evolution of Chicago's gangland, for Capone had sent them to kill time and again. They had been notorious in Chicago ever since they had helped to assassinate Moran's predecessor, Dion O'Banion, in 1924. The following year, they had taken the life of Angelo Genna, who had once employed them, and they had even killed a detective and later a policeman; for that last murder they had served brief jail sentences and were now at large once more.

McGurn decided on a novel twist to the assassination. His gunmen would gain access to the garage in the guise of Chicago policemen conducting a routine Prohibition raid. The plan required a police car and realistic police uniforms, including caps and medals. To carry out the ruse, he turned to another Capone associate, Claude Maddox, who obliged by stealing a police car complete with gong as well as several police uniforms for the gunmen to wear on the appointed day. McGurn also brought in two members of Detroit's Purple gang, another Capone affiliate, to act as lookouts. They were two brothers named Harry and Phil Keywell, complete unknowns in Chicago. The gunmen then rented an apartment near the garage, at 2119 North Clark, paying a week's rent in advance to the landlady. They hung their uniforms in the closet, and waited for their moment. Capone, meanwhile, rejoined his family at the Palm Island villa but kept in constant touch with McGurn over the phone until a few days before the event was scheduled to be carried out. Thus he was able to orchestrate events at a distance of a thousand miles.

Timing was everything. To lure the Moran gang to the garage, McGurn carefully set them up. He supplied one of the many booze hijackers working the area with a shipment of Old Log Cabin whiskey; this was a desirable commodity because it was reputedly distilled in Canada, not in a South Side bathtub. McGurn instructed the hijacker to sell the whiskey to Moran at a good price. Moran arranged to purchase another shipment from the hijacker, who called the garage on the night of February 13 to explain that he had just hijacked another load of booze "right off the river" separating Canada from Detroit; not only that, he would sell it for only $57 per case. Moran took the bait. They arranged for the hijacker to deliver the booze to S.M.C. Cartage Company garage, where Moran would pay for it in cash. They set the date for 10:30 A.M. on Thursday, February 14.

St. Valentine's Day dawned cold and windy. The thermometer stood at eighteen degrees, and few pedestrians ventured forth. McGurn had no intention of being placed at the scene of the crime that morning, and he went to considerable lengths to establish an airtight alibi. He arranged to be in the company of his girlfriend, Louise Rolfe, on Wednesday night and throughout most of Thursday. The couple avoided the Lexington Hotel, which would link him to Capone; rather, they checked in at the Stevens Hotel, McGurn making a point to sign his real name, Vincent Gebaldi, to the register to establish his alibi. These maneuvers were to prove singularly effective when McGurn eventually did face police scrutiny.

At 10:30 on Thursday morning, the Keywells spotted a man they thought was "Bugs" Moran arrive at the S.M.C. Cartage Company; the lookouts notified Burke and the other gunmen, who immediately donned their stolen police uniforms and jumped into a stolen police car. Its gong clanging, the black-and-white pulled up in front of 2122 North Clark Street, and four men rushed out, two wearing overcoats and two police uniforms. They gave every appearance of cops engaged in a routine raid. The four men entered the storefront and walked rapidly through a passageway to the bare, unheated garage at the back, where they came upon seven men. Included were the Gusenberg brothers, who had tried to kill McGurn; a safecracker named John May; Albert R. Weinshank, a saloon keeper; James Clark, a bank robber whose real name was Albert Kashellek and who was Moran's brother-in-law; and Adam Heyer, a utility racketeer who served as Moran's "business manager." The seventh member of the group was Dr. Reinhart H. Schwimmer, twenty-nine, a suspiciously prosperous optometrist. Because he alone had no police record, it has generally been assumed that Schwimmer was nothing more than a dapper young doctor who liked to socialize with gangsters for harmless amusement. However, Schwimmer had known Dion O'Banion and was actively involved in bootlegging; he lived in the same hotel as "Bugs" Moran, and he been known to boast that he could arrange for the murder of whomever he wished. So Schwimmer did, in fact, belong to the Moran gang. They were a well-dressed, prosperous-looking group of second- and third-tier gangsters, their diamond stickpins and rings glinting in the morning light. Dr. Schwimmer wore a carnation in his lapel. Their security consisted of Heyer's German shepherd, named Highball, who was tied to a pipe. Each man carried several thousand dollars in cash to pay for the shipment of Old Log Cabin, and they expected to be joined by Moran and two other associates, Willie Marks and Ted Newberry.

At that moment, McGurn's "cops"—actually Burke, Scalise, Anselmi, and Lolordo—entered the garage. They ordered the seven men gathered there to raise their hands and to line up against the wall. Fooled by the disguise, the men, some of whom carried weapons, obeyed. They offered no struggle, no resistance. After disarming their victims, the four executioners suddenly opened fire on them with two machine guns, a sawed-off shotgun, and a .45. The bullets ripped into the bodies; May and Clark received a blast from the shotgun, and within ten seconds the seven men slumped to the floor of the garage, dead. All except for one man, that is: Frank Gusenberg. Made frantic by the noise and the blood, Heyer's German shepherd sent up a piteous howl heard throughout the neighborhood.

As the four executioners left the scene of the crime, they staged a dumb show designed to confuse witnesses. The men in overcoats placed their hands in the air, while the "cops" followed with their guns trained on them. The four walked deliberately to the stolen police car, got in, and sped away. Witnesses believed they had seen two policemen arresting two suspects, not four assassins escaping the scene of the crime. The ploy was as effective as it was clever, but the same could not be said for the results of the assassination.

As they left North Clark Street, McGurn's gunmen were convinced that they had accomplished their goal of wiping out the Moran gang. They were greatly mistaken, for "Bugs" Moran himself, their main target, was *not* among those in the garage. The Keywell brothers, who thought they had identified him entering the building, had mistaken Al Weinshank for "Bugs" Moran; indeed, the resemblance between the two had often been noted. A few minutes late to the meeting, Moran happened to be coming down North Clark Street on foot just as the stolen police car pulled up in front of the S.M.C. Cartage Company. Fearing a raid, Moran, in the company of Marks and Newberry, kept on walking past the garage to safety. By taking this simple precaution, they managed to escape with their lives. Had they been on time to the meeting, the execution would have claimed the lives of ten men. The stolen police car designed to confuse witnesses and victims alike instead scared Moran away; McGurn's plan, brilliant though it was, had proven too clever by half.

The first *real* policeman to arrive at the garage was Sergeant Thomas Loftus, who discovered that Frank Gusenberg, who had received twenty-two bullet wounds, was still alive—but barely. Within minutes, Gusenberg was taken to a nearby hospital, where another policeman, Sergeant Clarence Sweeney, interrogated him.

"Who shot you?"

"No one—nobody shot me," the dying Gusenberg replied.

For a racketeer, this response was perfectly understandable, for if Gusenberg talked and survived, he would surely be killed at a later date.

"Which gang was it?" Sergeant Sweeney pressed, and when no reply was forthcoming, he added, softly, "Want a preacher, Frank?"

"No," Gusenberg whispered. "I'm cold . . . awful cold . . . Sarge . . . it's getting dark."

Sergeant Sweeney turned up the electric heater in the room, then bent over Gusenberg. "Who was it, Frank?"

Gusenberg's lips tightened, but he refused to speak. At 1:35 P.M., his body shivered. It tensed a bit, and relaxed. Three hours after the shooting, Gusenberg was dead. By then word of the appalling event that had taken place at 2122 North Clark Street had begun to spread across Chicago.

At first, no one knew who the victims were or why they had been killed. Witnesses in the neighborhood—and there were many—testified to seeing policemen entering the garage and leaving with two suspects, but police had no record of any such raid. No one realized, at first, that the executioners wore police uniforms as a disguise. The sense of dismay and confusion was overwhelming. No one knew why seven men had been shot to death. It seemed, that raw St. Valentine's Day, to be just another eruption of mayhem on the streets of Chicago. For this reason, Chicago reporters, tired of racing to the scene of every gangster hit, were slow to arrive at the 2122 North Clark Street garage.

The exception to the lethargy afflicting the press was Walter Trohan, the young reporter for the Chicago City News Bureau. He was assigned to the coroner's office, a gruesome beat that brought him dismayingly close to the results of Chicago's gang wars. In one instance his boss ordered him to find out whether a murder victim had been killed by bullets fired by gangsters or by guards, and when the coroner's physician refused to investigate, Trohan clutched the corpse by the hair and sawed off the top of the head to get at the bullets. Not even that experience prepared him for his first sight of the results of the mass execution in the garage of the S.M.C. Cartage Company. "I was in the press room when the call came through that six men had been reported killed in a garage at 2122 North Clark Street," as he recalled. "Johnny Pastor, who usually collected information on births, marriages, and deaths, was the one who actually called it in. I said to the other reporters, 'Johnny's got a hell of a story.'

" 'Well, he's excited, he doesn't know what it's all about,' said the head of the City News Bureau. His name was Isaac Gershman, and he had a complex: he thought he was a great man and a great editor. Well, he wasn't a great man or editor, but I could always laugh. Gersh always wanted to write the great American novel but never got anything down on paper; he was always talking about it. Anyway, he dictated the lead to me: 'Five men are reported to have been injured in a fight at 2122 North Clark Street.'

"I wrote the first bulletin, which turned out to be one of the greatest understatements in gang history. I didn't think much of it either, at the time. I called each paper with the bulletin, and while I was doing that, Johnny called back and said, 'Honest to God, it isn't five men, it's six, and they're dead all over the place, and one more's going to hospital. Honest to God, it's true.' Then Gersh said to me, 'Go up there and take a look.' I asked if I could take a cab, and he said, 'The Clark streetcars run in front of the door every five minutes. Take a streetcar.' So I climbed in a streetcar and went. Fortunately, it was about noon, and most people just didn't believe it for awhile. North Clark Street was just across the lake and up the hill and the streetcar went pretty fast, and I was there within five minutes, ahead of everybody except one or two policemen. I went on in, said, 'City Press,' and walked through a small office with a desk and telephone, bare of furniture, a very poor looking place, and approached the door that led to the garage.

"I opened the door and walked in. There were just pools of blood everywhere and the dead guys spread out all over as in the movies. I'd seen dead guys before—it was part of my job—but one at a time. I'd never seen that many before. They were sprawled all over and there was blood all over and this wild German shepherd was barking and crazy and lunging on a heavy chain. I was impressed, but I was also interested in running to a phone, calling the office, and getting this story in. By that time Gersh was trying to hide the fact that he made me go in a streetcar.

"I was in charge of the case for the City News Bureau, turning in yards of copy, everything was something, and I had a young fellow named Kelleher helping me. I sent him across the street from the garage to inquire at rooming houses who had rented rooms there and to lay in wait to watch and see. He failed to find out that somebody had, in fact, rented a room across the street, and instead the police found out about it the next day. I did know that the victims belonged to the Moran gang, and I knew that Moran himself wasn't among them, and I wondered why they hadn't gotten him, but we found out later he had overslept. In any case, I knew Capone was behind it because they were rival gangsters fighting for chunks of the rope.

"There used to be a great row as to who was the first man at the scene. I was, but it didn't seem to give me any kudos, because sooner or later every reporter who was worth anything came by, and it was really by accident that I got there first, through no willpower, no brilliance. I remember arguing with Mike Fish, a photographer, and he said, 'I was the first one there.' I said, 'No, you weren't.' Well, he said, 'Except maybe for the City News Bureau kid.' And I said, 'I was the kid.' But what difference does it make?"

As word of the slaughter spread across the city, shocked recognition of the enormity of the event followed—seven men, all of them shot to death in the middle of Chicago, on St. Valentine's Day, no less. Police descended on the scene in force. Highball, the German shepherd, continued its insane baying, the garage's brick walls echoing and distorting the noise. Several cops wanted to shoot the animal, but others intervened, declaring that there had been already been too much slaughter. One policeman untied the dog, which immediately bolted for the street. John H. Lyle, the crusading judge who liked to be in the thick of big news stories whether they concerned him or not, decided to see the death and destruction for himself. He masked his revulsion at the spectacle of the dead bodies with sententious pronouncements. "The corpses at the base of the red-splattered wall were the inevitable result of the franchise to kill and plunder public officials and a tolerant citizenry had given gangland by default at Prohibition's beginning nine years earlier," he grumbled.

Soon, the mass execution came to be seen as the most vicious slaughter in the history of Chicago, if not the nation. There had been executions involving greater numbers of victims, but none could match the carnage in the garage of the S.M.C. Carting Company for its horror. After his visit, Willis O'Rourke, who wrote for the *Chicago Evening American*, managed a ghastly joke—"I've got more brains on my feet than I have in my head"—but the sight made even the most hardened veterans of Chicago's gang wars blanch. "I tell you, I've never seen anything like it," said one stunned detective after viewing the spattered blood and tangled bodies at 2122 North Clark Street. "Nothing that's ever happened in this town since Prohibition can compare with it." Patrick Roche, a federal investigator, went further: "Never in all the history of feuds or gangland has Chicago or the nation seen anything like today's wholesale slaughter. I've seen Chicago's booze and vice rackets for years, but never before have seven men been lined up and shot down in cold blood. Never," he concluded, "has there been such a massacre."

That was the word that would always be employed to describe the mass execution in the garage of the S.M.C. Cartage Company: massacre. The St. Valentine's Day Massacre, as it soon became known across the country and throughout the world. "Machine Gun" Jack McGurn's failed attempt to assassinate "Bugs" Moran turned into the biggest story to come out of Chicago during the 1920s, perhaps the biggest story ever to come out of that vital, windswept, brawling, city—an event that crystallized Chicago's entire bloody history into an instant of horror. Newspapers across the country devoted an unprecedented amount of space to coverage of the mass murder of seven men and in the process sold millions of copies. The event impressed itself into the consciousness and the history of the nation like a dark fly caught in gleaming amber.

Newspapers across the country carried muddled and contradictory accounts of the events in the garage of the S.M.C. Carting Company on the morning of February 14. The most sinister aspect of the confusion was the theory that the Chicago police had been responsible for carrying out the mass murder, a notion propagated by many newspapers:

WISCONSIN NEWS
February 15, 1929

CALLS CHICAGO POLICE KILLERS OF GANGMEN
FEDERAL DRY CHIEF EXPECTS SLAYERS NAMED TODAY

CHICAGO—Maj. Fred D. Silloway, assistant prohibition administrator, today advanced the theory that police officers themselves killed
six gangsters and one of their guests herded into a North Side gang
stronghold yesterday and shot to death, and declared that he believed
the names of the actual slayers will be known before night.

The *New York Times* edition of the same day offered a more accurate and
disturbing account:

7 CHICAGO GANGSTERS SLAIN BY FIRING SQUAD OF RIVALS,
SOME IN POLICE UNIFORMS

VICTIMS LINED UP IN A ROW

Hands Up, Faces to Wall of Garage Rendezvous,
They Are Mowed Down.

ALL TOOK IT FOR A RAID

Machine Gun Executioners, Wearing Badges,
Made Swift Escape in Automobile.

MORAN'S STAFF WIPED OUT.

Liquor Gang Chief Head Missing—
Police Chief, Roused by 'Challenge,' Declares 'War.'

CHICAGO, Feb. 14. Chicago gangland leaders observed Valentine's Day with machine guns and a stream of bullets, and as a result
seven members of the George (Bugs) Moran–Dion O'Banion, North
Side gang are dead in the most cold-blooded gang massacre in the
history of this city's underworld....

Gang warfare in Chicago began with the slaying of Dion O'Banion
in November 1924. In the fifty months since then, thirty-eight murders, most of them attributed to the enmity between the North Side
band founded by O'Banion and the West Side syndicate established by
John Torrio and turned over to Al Capone, have been recorded.

Today's massacre marked the end of the proud North Side dynasty
which began with O'Banion. O'Banion yielded to Hymie Weiss who

was replaced by "Schemer" Drucci, who was succeeded by "Bugs" Moran. And Moran tonight was missing while seven of his chief aids lay dead....

"It's war to the finish," Commissioner Russell said. "I've never known of a challenge like this—the killers posing as policemen—but now the challenge has been made. It's accepted. We're going to make this the knell of gangdom."

The spectacle of a squad of hit men masquerading as police was especially galling to law enforcement authorities, who angrily denied the outlandish assertion. Of course, in Chicago, anything was possible, and the fear that rogue cops were on the loose persisted. McGurn, the evil prankster who had planned the disguise, had done his work well, sowing confusion and discord everywhere. Newspapers, ordinary citizens, lawmen, and bootleggers all clamored for retribution for the mass murder. In Chicago, civic groups posted huge rewards for information leading to the conviction of the perpetrators: $50,000 from the Chicago Association of Commerce, $20,000 from the City Council, another $20,000 from the state's attorney, and $10,000 from public subscriptions. Despite the reward money, the best efforts of the Chicago Police Department, an ample supply of eyewitnesses, and several damning pieces of evidence, no one would ever be convicted for carrying out the St. Valentine's Day Massacre.

                                    •   •   •

As the police, the press, and the public sifted through the conflicting details of the massacre, Al Capone was at first mentioned only in passing. His long-standing rivalry with "Bugs" Moran was a matter of record, but as the police discovered when they descended on his suite at the Lexington Hotel and on his Prairie Avenue home, Capone was not in Chicago at the time. He remained in Miami Beach, living quietly, perhaps too quietly, with Mae and Sonny at the Palm Island villa. Examining Capone's phone records, police discovered he had neither made nor received any calls from Chicago for several days before or after the event. And on the morning the seven murders occurred, Capone himself happened to be in the office of the Dade County solicitor, Robert Taylor, who had summoned the racketeer for a brief chat about his dealings in Miami.

Taylor began their meeting by asking Capone about his relationship with Parker Henderson Jr., the gullible manager of the Ponce de León Hotel. "You were getting money sent to you under the name of A. Costa," Taylor said, revealing what the IRS investigators had learned of Capone's dealings in Miami. "Didn't you ever send Parker Henderson to the Western Union office to get it for you?"

"No," said Capone.

"Then Henderson never got any money for you?"

Capone changed his answer. "Well, he did when I bought my home."

"You left money with Henderson, $1,000 to $5,000 at a time, didn't you?"

"I don't remember," said Capone, obviously cornered.

"You didn't receive any money by Western Union from Chicago?"

"I don't remember."

The interview was an embarrassment for Capone, but that scarcely mattered. By inviting the racketeer to his office, Taylor had unwittingly furnished Al Capone with an impeccable alibi for the morning of the St. Valentine's Day Massacre.

During the next two days Capone was highly visible in Miami, betting on the horses at Hialeah, visiting a dog racing track, stopping in at the McAllister Hotel, doing all he could to look relaxed, unconcerned, at ease. Everywhere he went, he was smiling. On Saturday night, two days after the shootings, Capone threw a large party in his villa. One hundred guests attended, including some of the most powerful men in Miami, and the affair was a model of decorum. In sum, Capone had not acted like a man with something to hide. To be more precise, he acted like a man trying too hard to convey the impression he had nothing to hide. Take the matter of the lack of calls to Chicago. Capone normally placed calls to Chicago every day; why did they stop around the fourteenth of February?

The whispers of Capone's role in the massacre turned to shouts when the police finally caught up with "Bugs" Moran, now a former gang leader. When they asked him who he thought was responsible, Moran replied, "Only Capone kills like that." On hearing the remark, Capone mocked, "The only man who kills like that is 'Bugs' Moran." Despite all his efforts to feign innocence, Capone was unable to dissociate himself from the St. Valentine's Day Massacre as he had earlier gangland hits. Instead of ending gang warfare in Chicago, the mass execution sanctioned by Capone and carried out by McGurn would only serve to prolong it. What was intended as the final reckoning between the Moran gang and Capone organization became another pointless, bloody slaughter.

Fearing a new bloodbath, other racketeers fled Chicago in droves. On the afternoon of February 18, the train from Chicago to Miami discharged no fewer than fifty hoodlums from Chicago, including such bootlegging notables as Frankie Lake, Terry Druggan, and Barney Bertsche. The *Chicago Tribune* estimated that at least 500 hoodlums flocked to Miami in the wake of the massacre. Asked about the sudden influx of Chicagoans, several admitted there had been considerable heat of late in Chicago; that violent city was no place to be, not when they could enjoy the Florida sun. Everyone knew the climate down there was better for their health. The influx of wealthy refugees from Chicago revived Miami's lagging hotel trade. Rates for rooms doubled, then tripled. And all the customers paid in cash.

• • • •

On February 23, Dr. Herman N. Bundesen, the coroner of Cook County, held an inquest on the bodies of the seven victims of the massacre. In unsparing detail it showed that each man had been shot at least fifteen times, most frequently in the back and head. Furthermore, judging from the angle of the bullets, it was possible to deduce that some of the men had been shot while they were on the floor. The description of the wounds suffered by the optometrist, Reinhart Schwimmer, was typical of the others and ran as follows:

> There are sixteen bullet wounds of entrance in the middle of the back, twelve of which are in a small group just to the left of the spinal column, and are each about one-fourth inch in diameter. And the perforations were . . . about the size of buckshot. There were seven of these buckshot recovered from the chest cavity. There is a ragged perforation of the scalp and skull with inverted edges resembling a bullet wound of entrance, located on top of his head, about four inches above and posterior to the left eyebrow.... The track of this bullet from its entrance is backward and to the right, with extensive laceration of the brain substance, with exit to the right side of the head. It came out in a large hole.

After examining the bodies, the investigators turned their attention to the bullets themselves. The massacre happened to occur at the moment when the science of ballistics was just gaining acceptance. The nation's recognized authority on the subject, Major Calvin Goddard, demonstrated that each weapon left a distinctive "fingerprint" on the bullets it fired. Thus a trained investigator could match scratches on the surfaces of bullets and shells with distinctive marks inside the barrels of the weapons from which they had been fired. Goddard was based in New York; learning of his work, a group of wealthy Chicago businessmen induced him to move to Chicago, where they financed a laboratory for him at Northwestern University. At first, his mission was to demonstrate that the Chicago police were *not* the gunmen in the St. Valentine's Day Massacre. To this end he tested every machine gun captured by the police (although it was highly unlikely that the police, had they been culpable, would have been foolish enough to return the murder weapons). Just as Goddard was coming to the conclusion that police weapons had not been employed in the massacre, he was presented with a rare opportunity to demonstrate his ballistic science. His benefactor was Fred "Killer" Burke, the gunman in the St. Valentine's Day Massacre.

During most of 1929, Burke remained in the Chicago area, living quietly with his wife under an assumed name, Fred Dane, in a small suburban house located right on Lake Shore Drive. He might have resided there indefinitely, had he not become involved in a drunken driving accident. One night in December 1929 Burke sideswiped another car on Main Street in nearby St. Joseph, Michigan; insult led swiftly to injury as Burke, drunk and enraged, fired four shots into a young police officer, Charles Skelley, who was attempting to arrest him. Skelley later died in the hospital, and the police launched a manhunt for his killer. At that point Burke vanished for over a year. During this time, Major Goddard studied the bullets and shells employed in the Skelley shooting; under the microscope, their markings matched those on the bullets retrieved from the body of Frankie Yale as well as the victims of the St. Valentine's Day Massacre. The identical markings meant the same weapon had been used in all three assassinations, and after protracted labor the police managed to trace the weapon to Burke, who they belatedly realized had been masquerading as "Fred Dane."

Finally, in March 1931, police discovered that he was hiding out at his father-in-law's farm in Milan, Missouri. Although he had grown a mustache to cover a telltale scar on his lip, his distinctively ugly mug was still eminently recognizable. At the farm he took the precaution of sleeping in a bed next to an open window; an escape car was parked just outside. None of these precautions helped when the police descended on the farmhouse early on the morning of March 26, while he was fast asleep. Like other gangsters, Burke had little fear of the police, but he was absolutely terrified of rival gangsters. His first thought on seeing strange men encircle his hideout was that his captors were hoodlums masquerading as cops, just as Burke had disguised himself for the St. Valentine's Day Massacre, and he fully expected the impostors to "take him for a ride." He demanded that they produce their credentials. They did so, and Burke, relieved that mere cops had come for him, went along quietly. Extradited to Michigan, where he was wanted for the murder of Charles Skelley, Burke stood trial and was sentenced to life in prison. Although justice had been served, Fred "Killer" Burke was never tried, much less convicted, for his leading role in the St. Valentine's Day Massacre.

The evidence linking Jack McGurn to the St. Valentine's Day Massacre proved even more tantalizing than the evidence linking Burke. The police arrested McGurn in his hotel suite and brought him down to headquarters, where two eyewitnesses placed him at the scene of the massacre. McGurn was held without bail. At this point the inventive McGurn produced one of the most famous alibis in the history of American crime: he insisted he had nothing to do with the seven deaths on St. Valentine's Day because he had been with his girlfriend, Louise Rolfe, at the Stevens Hotel from nine o'clock the previous night until three o'clock in the afternoon of the fourteenth. Thus it was impossible for him to have been in the vicinity of North Clark Street. Police and prosecutors devoted months to breaking what the newspapers came to call McGurn's "blonde alibi," and when they appeared close to achieving their goal, McGurn trumped them all by marrying Rolfe. Now that she was his wife, Rolfe could no longer testify against McGurn. On December 2, 1929, all charges against him were dropped, and he was freed from jail. McGurn had contrived to outwit the police, but his pivotal role in the Capone organization had come to an end, and he spent the remainder of his years on the fringe of the rackets, his income and his fame steadily dwindling. Never again would he have occasion to perpetrate the mayhem that had marked the St. Valentine's Day Massacre, and the next time he made headlines, it would be as a victim rather than a suspect.

•   •   •

As the police investigation into the St. Valentine's Day Massacre continued throughout the winter and spring of 1929, the public's concern with Chicago's gang warfare in general and Al Capone in particular intensified. Prior to the massacre and the subsequent investigation, Capone had generated headlines and inspired editorials across the nation; now he attained the status of a national phenomenon, a fixture in the public consciousness, the best-known gangster of the era. His involvement with the massacre endowed him with a certain grisly glamour. His gregarious, flamboyant persona inspired much of this fascination; he was not at all the grizzled fugitive from justice that people expected of a murderer. There had never been an outlaw quite like Al Capone. He was elegant, high-class, the berries. He was remarkably brazen, continuing to live among the swells in Miami and to proclaim his love for his family. Nor did he project the image of a misfit or a loner; he played the part of a self-made millionaire who could show those Wall Street big shots a thing or two about doing business in America. No one was indifferent to Capone; everyone had an opinion about him and what they thought he represented. The drys condemned him as the archenemy of Prohibition, and wets pointed to the Capone phenomenon as the inevitable outcome of the unenforceable law.

In New York City, editors began commissioning articles about Capone, paying fifty cents a word, then seventy-five, and finally the unheard-of sum of $1 a word. (This was 1929, and the engine of the American economy was still racing.) Overnight, writing about Capone became a cottage industry. Suddenly every journalist in Chicago was at work on his own I-was-at-the-scene-of-the-crime-and-the-body-was-still-warm reminiscence, and each account made Capone the personification of that city's culture of crime. No longer was his name a synonym for bootlegging, gambling, and prostitution —the "light pleasures," as he liked to call the services he provided; now it was a synonym for murder.

In the pages of *Harper's Monthly*, John Gunther, one of Chicago journalism's brighter stars, declared, "Crime in Chicago has been so psychologically successful, one might say, that it takes such a romantically excessive episode as the recent St. Valentine's Day massacre to stir the citizens at all." He then reckoned the cost of racketeering, not in lives but in dollars. "Murder in Chicago costs from $50 up," he announced. "To kill me, a newspaper man, would probably cost $1,000. To kill a prominent business man might cost $5,000, a prominent city official, $10,000. To kill the president of a large corporation, or a great power magnate, would cost a great deal more, probably $50,000 or $100,000." All this, he insisted, was a matter of "recorded, public fact," and no one doubted him. He listed no less than ninety-one rackets flourishing in Chicago, and concluded, "three million people are being held up by 600 gangsters. What the hoodlums are hitting at is the very essence of business enterprise in the United States."

Nearly all these postmassacre accounts pointed to Capone as the most prominent and elusive of all racketeers. No one else approached his power and influence over daily life in Chicago, or perhaps anywhere in the nation. "Probably no private citizen in American life has ever had so much publicity in so short a period as . . . Capone," the *New York Times* observed on May 26. By then Fred D. Pasley, a veteran reporter with the *Chicago Tribune*, was at work on the first book devoted to the career of the thirty-year-old racketeer. *Al Capone*, he called his exposé, adding a cynical subtitle: *The Biography of a Self-Made Man*. Fearing that the book would do further damage to his image, Capone reacted with characteristic vanity and bravado. He declared that he would write his autobiography or sponsor an authorized account of his life designed to portray him in the best possible light as a family man, a successful entrepreneur, and a public benefactor.

Despite the danger inherent in excessive publicity, Capone reveled in the attention he received and his newfound celebrity status. He invited gossip columnists and journalists into his home for "off-the-record" chats designed to cultivate sympathy and to convey the impression that he was just another retired millionaire living quietly in Florida. He encouraged Damon Runyon, who wintered on Hibiscus Island, close to Capone's villa, to act as his press agent and apologist. Runyon came to the role quite naturally, for he had no qualms about his friend's criminal activities. He liked Al, he could use Al in his articles and stories, and that was enough for him. He advised Capone to give the impression that he had retired from Chicago and bootlegging. At the moment, Jack Sharkey was in Miami training for a prizefight with Young Stribling in Flamingo Park. The event drew Capone like a magnet. To cultivate a new image for Capone, that of a benign and peaceful retired bootlegger, Runyon deftly arranged for his pal to visit the Sharkey training camp and, breaking a taboo, to be photographed with the fighter. Runyon's paper, the *New York American*, ran the result, which showed Capone standing between Sharkey and Bill Cunningham, a former All-American football star. Al, tieless, grinned as he held a straw hat in his gloved hands and strained at the seams of his suit. Runyon also wrote the carefully worded text accompanying the picture: "The somewhat portly person is none other than 'Scarface' Al Capone, once a well-known Chicago gangster, now residing quietly in Florida, who has never been photographed. Although the police have lately mentioned his name in connection with the Chicago rum massacre—which Capone says he knows nothing about—the hitherto shy Al consented to pose with—guess whom?—Jack Sharkey, the sunshine of Miami Beach."

The photograph was just the beginning of Capone's involvement with the Sharkey-Stribling bout. Days before the fight, the promoter, Tex Rickard, suddenly died from an attack of appendicitis. Capone, Jack Dempsey, and other Miami boosters rushed to fill the vacuum. With Runyon's assistance Al threw a memorable prefight party for sixty sportswriters who had converged on Miami to cover the fight. Westbrook Pegler, Paul Gallico, Sid Mercer—all the big names were there. And Runyon, of course. The party itself was in Capone's image. As soon as the guests arrived at 93 Palm Island, they were searched for weapons, and when they entered the house they encountered a dance band, the best imported liquor, and the main attraction, Al Capone, who impressed all with his reserve. At one point during the festivities, he excused himself to give Runyon and several others a tour of his wine cellar. Meanwhile, the wife of Jack Koefed, a sportswriter for the *New York Post*, decided to take a dip in the pool. She went to the women's changing room, located in a small building at the far end of the pool, close to the bay, and sat on a bench to take off her shoes. Instead of the smooth surface she expected, the bench was hollow and appeared to contain a number of sharp objects. She raised a corner of the tarpaulin cover and beheld a small arsenal of shotguns and machine guns. She screamed, and Capone's henchmen swooped down and removed the offending weapons. In the confusion someone wandered into Mae's bedroom and stole her jewelry. Estimated value: $300,000. Mae complained bitterly—surely her husband could use his powers to ensure the swift return of her diamonds and rings—but Al proved far more reluctant to harm a sportswriter who stole from his wife than a rival racketeer who stole from his business. Gallico and Pegler alluded to the theft in their columns, suggesting that the thief should come forward, but Mae's jewelry was never returned.

The next day, there was another uproar at 93 Palm Island when a small airplane circled over Biscayne Bay, approached the house, and released a bomb, which exploded in midair. The great noise sent Al and a bunch of his henchman fleeing into the yard; several men attempted to shoot down the plane, which began to circle back. On the second pass, the plane released a small parachute. The thugs dove for it as it fell to earth. They discovered it contained a note. Speculation as to its contents ran rampant; this could be the start of gangster war in the air over Miami Beach. However, the note demanded neither blood nor money from Al Capone; instead, it demanded tickets to the Sharkey-Stribling fight. It turned out that Eddie Nirmaier, the pilot of the plane, had flown Al and his friends to Bimini Island in the Bahamas for a picnic several weeks earlier. Capone had paid for the flight and promised the pilot complimentary tickets to the boxing match—tickets he had forgotten to deliver. Irked, Nirmaier retaliated by dropping fireworks on Palm Island; that explained the noise and the lack of damage. Capone's response to the airborne reminder was swift and sure. "By the time I got out of my plane," Nirmaier said, "Capone's chauffeur was driving up with my tickets."

On the night of February 27, 40,000 fans—"the most picturesque mob in fight history," in the words of Damon Runyon, who was qualified to pass judgment—converged on Flamingo Park. Capone made every effort to present a *bella figura* in his new tuxedo as he distributed $100 bills with a grin and a handshake. He startled observers by sitting with his old friend Jack Dempsey, who ostentatiously cleaned Capone's seat in the manner of an usher. Westbrook Pegler later described Dempsey's behavior as an "exchange of amenities between two professionals having much in common." Then the crowd watched Sharkey take Stribling in ten lackluster rounds. It wasn't much of a fight, but the event helped to boost Miami's image as an up-and-coming city. Capone's visibility gave many the distinct impression that he had not retired after all. In fact, only one day after the fight, the *Chicago Tribune* proclaimed, "MIAMI DESTINED TO BE RULED BY KING SCARFACE—Capone Making Things Hum at Winter Resort." "King Scarface," the story charged, "controls most of the slot machines in Florida." And an unnamed Miami resident commented, "He is putting his profits into solid concerns. They tell me one of the biggest hotels in Miami Beach is owned by Scarface, and he will invest in other ventures. . . . If Capone gets to control enough of the interests in this resort isn't it natural to assume that he will some day swing the whip?"

•   •   •

In newspapers across the country a consensus formed that Al Capone was no longer Chicago's problem, he was now a national issue. Despite a newly invigorated IRS Investigative Unit and the presence of a zealous U.S. attorney, George E. Q. Johnson, in Chicago, the fact remained that Capone and other racketeers flourished as never before. Something had to be done about them at the highest levels. The outgoing president, Calvin Coolidge, had not lifted a finger, and his successor, Herbert Hoover, gave no indication as to his views on the matter. As the public clamor to do something about Capone and Prohibition grew, Colonel Robert McCormick, the imperious publisher of the *Chicago Tribune*, journeyed to Washington to pay a call on Hoover. Although McCormick was a fanatical Republican, he was also an ardent foe of Prohibition, which he held responsible for atrocities such as the St. Valentine's Day Massacre. As McCormick knew, Prohibition agents were hopelessly ineffectual, and he advised the president that the Department of Justice should cease victimizing ordinary drinkers and instead concentrate on the principal bootleggers who were the source of corruption of Chicago. For instance, McCormick said, "they're not touching Al Capone."

Hoover's response caught McCormick by surprise:

"Who is Al Capone?"

The newspaper publisher hastened to provide the president with a thumbnail sketch of the nation's most capable and elusive bootlegger and to summarize the sorry attempts of Chicago's local law enforcement agencies to bring him to justice. In McCormick's opinion it would be futile to attempt to convict Capone for violating Prohibition. Only the scheme to apprehend him for failure to pay his income tax offered a realistic chance for success. "At once I directed that all the Federal agencies concentrate upon Mr. Capone and his allies," wrote Hoover in his memoirs. "It was ironic that a man guilty of inciting hundreds of murders, in some of which he took a personal hand, had to be punished merely for failure to pay taxes on the money he had made by murder."

One morning soon after, Hoover happened to be heaving a medicine ball—his preferred form of exercise—with the members of his cabinet in a prebreakfast ritual that became known as the "medicine cabinet." Among the participants was Andrew Mellon, the secretary of the Treasury. "Have you got this fellow Capone, yet?" asked Hoover between tosses of the ball. Mellon shook his head. "I want that man in jail," said the president, resuming the game.

• • •

Within days of that conversation on the White House lawn, Capone was served with a subpoena to appear before a federal grand jury in Chicago on March 12. Thus began an intricate game of cat and mouse between Capone and the U.S. attorney in Chicago, George E. Q. Johnson, with each side making subtle but telling missteps. Capone's initial response to the subpoena was to plead poor health as a result of a bout of influenza. On March 5, his Miami doctor, Kenneth Phillips, signed an affidavit stating, "Since January 13, 1929, said Alphonse Capone has been suffering broncho-pneumonia pleurisy with effusion of fluid into the chest cavity and for six weeks was confined to his bed at his home." As anyone who troubled to read the newspapers knew, this was preposterous; Capone had been peripatetic, especially since the St. Valentine's Day Massacre; he had attended Hialeah and the Sharkey-Stribling fight, given two well-publicized parties, and had even visited the office of the Dade County solicitor. And yet, Dr. Phillips continued, "Capone's physical condition is such that it would be dangerous for him to leave the mild climate of southern Florida and go to the City of Chicago. . . . There would be a very grave risk of a collapse which might result in his death from a recurrent pneumonia."

By avoiding a subpoena to appear before a *federal* grand jury, Capone unwittingly gave the government an opportunity, and the Feds exploited it to the hilt. For the first time, J. Edgar Hoover, the director of the Federal Bureau of Investigation, took a personal interest in putting Capone behind bars. The FBI had previously refused to tangle with Capone—or any other racketeer—for a variety of bureaucratic reasons, all of which had to do with the prickly, fiercely defended personality of its director. Hoover had occupied his position since 1924, and throughout the Prohibition years he had avoided bootleggers and racketeers because he feared they would bribe and corrupt FBI agents as they had corrupted Prohibition agents. Fighting urban gangsters was not a battle Hoover thought he could win, and it was not a battle he wanted to fight. Until as late as the 1950s, he argued that racketeers were not breaking federal laws; it was only when FBI agents broke up a nationwide racketeers' conference in Apalachin, New York, in 1957 that Hoover finally declared that the racketeers had crossed state lines to do business, and thus their activities were subject to FBI scrutiny. Until that time, Al Capone was one of the few exceptions to this rule, and Hoover pursued him, in part, because he was afraid the Treasury Department might actually get there first in prosecuting Capone and so rob the FBI of glory. The other reason Hoover took an interest in Capone was that the assistant attorney general, Mabel Walker Willebrandt, urged him to do so, "as a personal matter of great importance to me." Willebrandt continued, "It would be a tenstrike on a huge case if you are able to prove the falsity of this affidavit so that we can punish Capone and the Doctor for contempt. May I rely upon you to do so secretly and soon?"

J. Edgar Hoover had no choice but to comply with her request, and once he committed himself, the FBI did a thorough job of discrediting Dr. Phillips's assertion Capone was too sick to travel to Chicago. FBI agents descended on Miami and rounded up their own affidavits, twelve in all, from witnesses who had seen Capone during the time in question. In one affidavit, Dr. Samuel D. Light, Capone's physician, testified that his patient had indeed been a sick man during the first half of January. Dr. Light noted that he had made seventeen house calls during that period, and Capone had required the attention of two nurses to care for a case of influenza that had turned into "double pneumonia." Then Capone apparently made a rapid recovery, for eight witnesses placed him at the Hialeah racetrack on twenty-four days between late January and early March. And Eddie Nirmaier, the pilot who had "bombed" Palm Island to get tickets to the Sharkey-Stribling fight, swore that on February 2, when he flew Capone and some pals to Bimini, Al "appeared to be in good health," strong enough to make the round-trip flight without any ill effects.

Of special interest, an FBI agent named J. J. Perkins learned of another offshore trip Capone had taken just prior to the St. Valentine's Day Massacre. The party included Capone; his younger brother Albert; Philip D'Andrea, a bodyguard; three Miamians; and William Kelly, a Prohibition agent. As might be expected, Capone paid for all of Kelly's expenses on the trip. The party left Miami on February 8 aboard the steamship *New Northland*. "Previous to the SS New Northland sailed," agent Perkins reported to Hoover, "Captain Tremblay of the SS New Northland, asked Mr. H. V. Perry [manager of the steamship line] who Capone was, as a friend of the Captain's had introduced Capone to him and requested that Capone be given special attention on the trip from Miami to Nassau. Mr. Perry recommended to the Captain of the SS New Northland not to fraternize, and if necessary to stay in his quarters in order to avoid Capone." The Capone party returned from Nassau on the morning of February 13, a little more than twenty-four hours before the St. Valentine's Day Massacre. Such was the precise and detailed fieldwork of which the FBI was capable when Hoover chose to take an interest. As a result of its investigation, the FBI concluded, "There is no doubt that Al Capone was ill during the first part of January, 1929, and was confined to his bed with influenza or possibly pneumonia. However, the evidence . . . proves that he had sufficiently recovered therefrom to be up and about." In short, Dr. Phillips had lied about Capone's health.

The investigative effort required cooperation among the bureau, which was doing the fieldwork; Mabel Walker Willebrandt, who was overseeing the enforcement of Prohibition laws for President Hoover; George E. Q. Johnson, the U.S. attorney who would use the affidavits to instigate contempt proceedings against Capone; and finally, Judge James H. Wilkerson, the federal judge who had issued the subpoena Capone had ignored. On this occasion, the activities of all these agencies and personalities in Chicago and in Washington, D.C., meshed and meshed quickly. "It would be dangerous for him [Capone] to come to Chicago," Judge Wilkerson said, mocking the racketeer's excuse for his absence. "I wonder what kind of danger he means?" Days later the judge charged the racketeer with contempt of court. George E. Q. Johnson was delighted with the outcome. In a letter of thanks to J. Edgar Hoover, the U.S. attorney boasted, "In dealing with persons like Capone my policy is to prosecute vigorously for every violation and this prosecution for contempt will be helpful in other ways"—ways that would become apparent if and when Capone went to trial.

Johnson's assurances were not enough to satisfy the highly competitive director of the FBI, who thought that the bureau's brief investigation would lead to the downfall of the Capone organization. "Capone is popularly viewed as the over-lord of the underworld and there is no doubt but that he wields a tremendous amount of control," Hoover remarked. "I believe that many of his followers, who are controlled by fear and not by sincere loyalty to him, and certainly the innumerable enemies that he has made, would be more inclined to furnish information to the Government authorities concerning Capone's activities if he were once placed in the penitentiary even though it be for Contempt of Court." Hoover's expectations were unrealistic and self-serving. His attempt to jump to the forefront of the government effort to get Capone came to nothing, and Johnson continued to pursue his tedious but far more sophisticated strategy.

While his pursuers jockeyed for position, Capone remained ignorant of his powerful new antagonists; indeed, he still failed to understand the exact nature of his troubles. "They say the police of Chicago want to see me about the gang massacre," he glumly noted on March 6. But it was not the police who wanted to question him, it was a federal grand jury; and the subject under investigation was the not the St. Valentine's Day Massacre but findings of the bold and successful raid on Chicago Heights in early January. Federal prosecutors thought they had come up with evidence linking Capone to mail robbery. Indeed, the Feds were so eager to question him in Chicago about that raid that they offered him protection and held out the possibility of immunity in exchange for his testimony. Even the Chicago Police Department announced they would refrain from questioning Al Capone about the St. Valentine's Day Massacre if he appeared before a federal grand jury. "As things stand now, we don't want to talk to Capone at all," said the deputy police commissioner, John Stege. "He was in Florida at the time of the Clark Street murders."

Capone had faced a similar situation in 1926, when the police wanted to question him about the murder of William McSwiggin. After hiding out in Lansing, he had appeared in Chicago and had managed to wriggle out of that tight spot. Given the assurances the police and federal prosecutors were making, he was willing to try the maneuver again. On March 19, he traveled to Indiana, remaining just on the other side of the Illinois border, fifteen miles from Chicago, where his appearance before the grand jury had been rescheduled for 10:00 A.M. the following morning. At this delicate moment, George E. Q. Johnson, the U.S. attorney, declared, "Capone will be handled like the hoodlum he is." Johnson's outburst nearly wrecked all the carefully laid plans to lure Capone back to Chicago. However, the racketeer did appear as scheduled, testifying before the grand jury for over an hour, during which he reluctantly traced his career in Chicago and admitted he might have neglected to pay his income tax. Always willing to make a deal, Capone, according to one newspaper account, offered to "split any difference he had with the government and might pay the salary of several prohibition agents for a year or two." Afterward, Judge Wilkerson ordered him to return on the twenty-sixth, and Capone's lawyers, William F. Waugh and Benjamin Epstein, demanded the federal government make good its implied promise of immunity. Meanwhile, the police refrained from asking him about the massacre, and rival bootleggers refrained from shooting at him. Capone remained sequestered until his next appearance before the grand jury as the Feds suddenly seized records at both the Lexington and the Metropole, the hotels where he had maintained lavish quarters. Capone professed to be ignorant of Johnson's motive. The U.S. attorney explained he had learned of Capone's lavish hotel accommodations, documented by the records they had seized. If Capone could pay hotel bills running to thousands of dollars every week, surely he earned enough to pay income tax.

Capone had always been extremely careful about hiding his sources of income, a lesson he had learned well from Johnny Torrio; he had not endorsed a check in years, maintained no bank accounts, and left his accounting to his brother Ralph and Jack Guzik. But *spending* was another matter. Capone had spent prodigiously, and he had spent publicly, at hotels, racetracks, restaurants, wherever he went. He had given away money to wealthy politicians and poor widows alike, and his actions had always seemed harmless enough. He knew how to steer clear of murder charges and how to explain his way around bootlegging. If a killer such as Jack McGurn could avoid being charged with the St. Valentine's Day Massacre murders, surely Al Capone, who was infinitely more subtle in his use of violence, would be able to avoid conviction for tax evasion. Judges could be bought, jurors threatened—that was the Chicago way. He could not conceive of the government successfully prosecuting him for tax evasion. "The income tax law is a lot of bunk," he insisted. "The government can't collect legal taxes from illegal money."

Just before Capone was scheduled to testify again, Johnson announced to everyone's surprise that the racketeer was free to go. No further testimony was

required of him at this time. However, on March 27, Capone, who was
packing to return to Florida, was arrested for contempt of court, the fruit of
the FBI investigation into his avoidance of Judge Wilkerson's subpoena.
Capone was incensed, for the government charged him with avoiding testimony he had belatedly given, and after the U.S. attorney himself formally
excused him. As Capone was learning, the law was whatever the government
said it was.

"This is a disgrace!" Capone snapped when he appeared at the Federal
Building in the Loop to answer the charge. Learning that he could leave
once he posted a $5,000 bond, his round face broke into a broad, confident
grin. "That's easy," he said. "My lawyers have that all fixed." The bond
materialized instantly, and Capone donned his fedora. "See you later, boys,"
he said to reporters as he headed out the door.

· · ·

Baffled by the federal government's inconsistent behavior, Capone scur-
ried back to Miami Beach, where he tried to decide on the best course of
action. He explored the possibility of seeking sanctuary in the Bahamas, to
which he had made frequent excursions by boat and air. "My hydro-
aeroplane makes the water jump from my back door here in the bay to my
Bahama island in an hour, and I've been accustomed to flying over several
times a week and then back for supper," he boasted. "We can go over there
and have a quiet highball or two under the British flag without violating the
Prohibition laws of the United States." Furthermore, the Bahamas could
serve as a convenient base for offshore bootlegging. Capone was serious about
purchasing an island to use for this purpose—thus the talk of "my Bahama
island." He visited Nassau several times, planning to make his purchase in
anonymity, but even there he was recognized, and knots of curious tourists
followed him along the street. The crowds were not, it should be added,
hostile; people wished him well and expressed the hope that he would move
to the Bahamas. A real estate agent escorted him to three comfortable houses,
and Capone was particularly taken with one, for which he subsequently
offered $500,000—a staggering amount, indicative of his desperate resolve to
flee the net of American justice slowly encircling him. However, his offer
was refused, as were two bids on other homes, and to make matters worse,
Bahamian officials branded Capone an "undesirable alien." He had been
called many things in his career—pimp, murderer, dago—but his actions
had always spoken louder than epithets until now. This term had the force
of law. If he ever set foot in that British colony again, he would be subject
to arrest or deportation.

In the end, Capone was left with no alternative but to return to Florida,
where he gave his side of the story to the most famous columnist of the day,

Walter Winchell. In the peculiar, staccato style for which he was known, Winchell transcribed his impressions of the racketeer in midcareer:

WALTER WINCHELL ON BROADWAY
Portrait of a Man Talking to Capone

A mutual friend asked me if I would like to meet Capone, and I said I would . . . Might have made a lot of coin from all those magazines that asked for an article on the visit with "The Capones at Home" . . . But I told Capone I wouldn't go commercial on the call—and I didn't . . . He said that he didn't care whether I did or not—that he never met a newspaper man yet who didn't cross him . . . Wonder is it true what I heard about him? . . . That before retiring each night he cried like a baby.

I had always pictured him as a small and fat person. . . He's over six feet! . . . When I was entering his place, he saw me coming up the three steps leading to the parlor. . . He was playing cards with three huskies. . . Their backs were to the door—Capone faced it! . . . "Oh, come in," he called as he saw me, and in the same breath he must have said to the others, "Scram" because they disappeared quicker than the birds. . . He was sweeping the table clean of cards and chips as I sat down on a settee near his side of the table. . . "Sit over here," he said. . . "No, this is all right," I countered. . . "No, sit over here, please." He persisted but I didn't move. . . My orbs had caught sight of the largest automatic I ever saw. . . He covered the gun with one of his immense paws and hid it on the other side of the table. . . . "I don't understand that," I said, "Here you are playing a game of cards with your friends, but you keep a gun handy". . . "I have no friends," he said as he handed me a glass of grand beer.

Among other things I learned during that call was that every time you referred to it as his gang, he corrected you with "my organiza-tion". . . He argued long and loud about being blamed for every-thing—most of which he never did. . . "All I ask is that they leave me alone," he said once. . . I didn't tell him so, but I thought of a lot of people who wished he would leave them alone. . . His beautiful man-sion was really another prison for him. . . He couldn't leave it without a heavy guard. . . When he moved it was done secretly—by plane or boat—both of which were anchored in the waters adjacent to his home there. . . He told me of a doctor down in Miami who crossed him for the Government—who told the officials he wasn't sick at all when all the while he thought he'd die from pneumonia. . . "Once," he was saying, "I was so sick I fell down a whole flight of stairs!". . . The

doctor's fee, he thought, was too stiff, and he paid him only half. . . .
"So he told the Government," said Capone, "that I was never sick". . . .
He sighed heavily, and, with a prop smile, added: "That's the funniest
thing. Anybody I have wined and dined right in my own house crossed
me". . . He handed me the third beer. . . Swelegant!

• • •

At the end of April, evidence suggesting that Capone was still using drugs
came to light when his dentist, Dr. Frank L. Brady, was murdered in his
Chicago office. Two gunmen entered while the doctor was seeing a patient;
one pressed a gun to his white coat and fired, and the doctor slumped to the
floor. An investigation by "Shoes," Captain William Schoemaker, revealed
that Dr. Brady, though a qualified dentist who treated a number of patients,
including Capone, also dealt in a particularly hazardous sideline: he supplied
narcotics to gangsters. It was possible that he obtained Capone's cocaine; the
transactions could easily be camouflaged as routine visits to the dentist. As
with so many other investigations conducted by "Shoes," this one failed to
turn up a suspect or a motive, but the dentist's death exposed another chink
in Capone's armor.

Several days later, at the beginning of May, Capone returned to Chicago.
The next several weeks would prove extraordinarily eventful for him, even by
the exaggerated standards of his life. What brought Capone back against his
better judgment was an appalling rumor that Scalise and Anselmi, the Sicilian gunmen who had helped to carry out the St. Valentine's Day Massacre, had suddenly shifted their loyalty away from Capone and toward the new
head of the Unione Sicilione, Joseph "Hop Toad" Guinta, who had formed
an alliance with another enemy of Capone, Joseph Aiello. Worse, Capone
heard that Scalise had taken to boasting, "I am the most powerful man in
Chicago." These words could only be regarded as a Sicilian challenge to
Capone's preeminence. Capone had always been careful to keep that volatile
stronghold, the Unione Sicilione, in his camp. Any disagreement with the
group was liable to be lethal, and Scalise and Anselmi, unlike the incom-
petents in the now disbanded Moran gang, were capable of killing Capone on
the first attempt, if they so desired.

Before Capone acted to break up the conspiracy forming against him, he
decided to submit Scalise and Anselmi to a loyalty test. He invited the men
to dinner along with Frankie Rio, a Capone lieutenant of unquestioned
devotion. At the dinner, Rio and Capone became embroiled in a shouting
argument. To the astonishment of Scalise and Anselmi, Rio actually slapped
Capone on the cheek before rushing out of the restaurant. Impressed, the
Sicilian gunmen secretly met with Rio the next day, offering to involve him
in a plot to kill Capone and seize control of all his rackets. What Scalise and

Anselmi did not know, however, was that the argument between Capone and Rio had been staged for their benefit. Without realizing it, they had taken Capone's bait. Rio spent the next three days negotiating with Scalise and Anselmi and then reporting to Capone on their treachery. At the end of that time, Capone had decided precisely how he would dispose of the Sicilians and their colleague, Guinta. He would throw a banquet to honor these distinguished gentlemen.

On May 7, Capone, his inner circle, and the three traitors convened for a banquet at a roadhouse in Hammond, Indiana, yet another small town he controlled. That Capone wanted to cross state lines for the gathering should have sent up a red flag to the prospective guests; anyone who committed a crime, say murder, in Indiana and quickly slipped across the state line into Illinois would be considerably harder to catch. Yet Capone's colleagues were compelled to attend; their absence would be taken as a sign of betrayal. So the guest list was lengthy, consisting of nearly a hundred of Capone's closest allies in Chicago. The feasting and toasting lasted well into the night, until Al's mood suddenly turned sour and full of recrimination against Scalise, Anselmi, and Guinta. He accused of them of being traitors, which was the equivalent of passing a death sentence on them. "This is the way we deal with traitors," he said, and before the three men could move, they were bound to their chairs. Capone approached them with a baseball bat in hand and methodically battered each man within an inch of his life.

Savage as the beating was, it was not the end. Once Capone finished, a group of gunmen appeared, their weapons at the ready. Subsequent events were reconstructed by Dr. Eli S. Jones for the coroner of Lake County, Indiana:

> Scalise threw up his hand to cover his face and a bullet cut off his little finger, crashing into his eye. Another bullet crashed into his jaw and he fell from his chair. Meanwhile, the other killers—there must have been three or four—had fired on Guinta and Anselmi, disabling them. Anselmi's right arm was broken by a bullet. When their victims fell to the floor, their assailants stood over them and fired several shot in their backs.

Thus did Capone demonstrate that he, and he alone, was still the most powerful man in Chicago.

In the morning, the three disfigured corpses were found on an empty stretch of highway near Wolf Lake, Indiana. Scalise and Guinta were heaped in the back of an abandoned car, while Anselmi's body lay on the ground nearby. Dr. Francis McNamara, who examined the bodies, stated that never in his thirty years as a jail physician had he seen such damage done to a human body. Scalise and Anselmi were transported home to Sicily for burial, while Guinta, in his tuxedo and dancing pumps, was buried in the final resting place of so many other Chicago gangsters and their victims, Mt. Carmel Cemetery.

Within days of the murders, word began to circulate through Chicago that Al Capone had been present and somehow involved. In fact, Chicago law enforcement authorities and Judge John H. Lyle, who had become a student of Capone, became convinced that Al himself had carried out the executions, bludgeoning his victims with a baseball bat and then shooting them in the head in full view of his lieutenants to serve as an object lesson concerning the consequences of betrayal. Although Capone left the actual shooting to others, the triple murder of May 7 ranks as the most inhuman and violent episode of his entire career. It was true that he believed that Scalise, Anselmi, and Guinta were about to kill him, and he struck in self-defense. Nevertheless, the grotesque manner in which he arranged for them to die displayed sadistic behavior new to Capone, and the entire episode suggests that his neurosyphilis was having ever more drastic and unpredictable effects on his personality.

As the story of the triple murder spread, Capone's associates and family members who were not present at the banquet denied that Al would have been capable of such monstrous behavior. That was not the Al they knew— quiet, courteous, respectful, generous. They liked to believe that he tolerated the violence and brutality of life in the rackets solely as a means to an end and was not himself a sadistic person, certainly not a cold-blooded killer. The triple murders put the lie to the legend of Capone as a benevolent tyrant who protected his own from the depredations of outsiders. He had long insisted he was better than a common hoodlum, yet the events of May 7 argued that he was far worse, and far more dangerous.

· · ·

Three days after taking a baseball bat to Scalise, Anselmi, and Guinta, Capone slipped out of Chicago, ostensibly to attend a prizefight in Atlantic City, New Jersey, then a fashionable beach resort attracting celebrities who pretended to be annoyed whenever journalists spotted them strolling along the famous boardwalk. On this occasion Capone's interest in sport served as a pretext for his real mission, which was to attend a nationwide gathering of racketeers who had convened to form a commission charged with the responsibility of resolving disputes among its members in a peaceful, businesslike fashion. At least, that was the stated reason for the gathering. As Capone would discover over the course of the next several days, there was also a hidden agenda: his jealous rivals wanted to strip him of his power and his profits, and the ill will generated by the St. Valentine's Day Massacre provided them with just the excuse they needed to do so.

"From what I hear there is plenty of shooting going on between these mobs, and guys getting topped left and right," wrote Capone's friend Damon Runyon in a story called "Dark Dolores," a lightly fictionalized account of the gathering that first appeared in *Cosmopolitan* magazine, of all places. "Also there is much heaving of bombs, and all this and that, until finally the only people making any dough in the town are the undertakers." In Runyon's version, a character named Black Mike Marrio, who is a "Guinea, and not a bad-looking Guinea, at that, except for a big scar on one cheek which I suppose is done by somebody trying to give him a laughing mouth," runs the show, insisting that someone above the fray must act as mediator—Chief Justice Taft, perhaps, or maybe President Hoover. Unable to interest these men in the proceedings, the assembled hoodlums finally settle on Dave the Dude—Runyon's fictional version of Frank Costello, who was, next to Capone's boyhood acquaintance Lucky Luciano, the most powerful racketeer in New York. "You see," Runyon writes, "Dave the Dude is friendly with everybody everywhere, and is known to one and all as an alright guy, and one who always gives everybody a square rattle in propositions of this kind." Just as Runyon's merry gangsters settle down to business, they are distracted by various "dolls" circling the conference, and soon several of them, including Black Mike, are attracted to one doll in particular by the name of Dolores Dark. It seems that her admirers had been responsible for killing her boyfriend, and to get revenge, Dolores flirtatiously leads them down to the beach one night and into the water, where they all swim after her toward extinction.

Runyon's fanciful retelling of the conference glosses over the serious business that was transacted among the racketeers who had assembled in Atlantic City that warm spring weekend. Preceded by a reputation as a mass murderer, Al Capone was by far the most notorious. The atrocity of the St. Valentine's Day Massacre was still fresh in everyone's mind, and it was compounded by word of three more barbarous murders that he lately supervised. The moment he was sighted in Atlantic City, the city's director of public safety, W. S. Cuthbert, issued an order "to pick up Al Capone if he is found . . . and arrest him as an undesirable." To appear less conspicuous Capone came with but a single bodyguard, a face new to the racketeering scene. A graduate of the Circus gang, Tony Accardo eventually assumed the leadership of the Chicago organization. That was years later, after Capone's death; for now Accardo betrayed his lack of experience by taking time off from the conference to visit a tattoo parlor, where he had a bird imprinted on the back of his right hand. When he moved his fingers the bird appeared to flap its wings. "Kid," Capone advised, "that will cost you as much money and trouble as it would to wear a badge with the word 'thief' on it."

Capone and Accardo eluded arrest because the boss of Atlantic City's rackets, "Nucky" Johnson, had the foresight to pay the local police not to do their job. ("Nucky" was short for Enoch as well as "Knuckles," Johnson's other nickname.) "Nucky" was not so lucky in his choice of hotels. He had booked his guests at the posh Breakers, a restricted hotel, and the management there refused to allow the Jewish gangsters, of which there were many, to register. Capone was so offended by the insult that he got into a shouting match with "Nucky." "I think you could've heard them in Philadelphia," Luciano said later, "and Capone is screamin' at me that I made bad arrangements. So Nucky picks Al up under one arm and throws him into his car and yells out, 'All you fuckers follow me!' " Using all his clout, "Nucky" arranged for the visitors to stay at the equally plush Ritz, but when Capone reached the new hotel he was still furious enough to tear portraits adorning the walls of the hotel and hurl them at the hapless "Nucky" Johnson. Luciano later commented, "Everybody got over bein' mad [at the Breakers] and concentrated on keepin' Al quiet. That's the way our convention started." The outburst was highly unusual for Capone, who normally prided himself on his restrained behavior in public. Taken with the fact that only days before he had bludgeoned three men with a baseball bat, it was apparent that he had reached the limit of his inner resources. His undiagnosed neurosyphilis was slowly but inexorably advancing on his brain, exaggerating his behavior. What had been mood swings now became terrifying homicidal outbursts.

Capone's violent behavior confirmed the worst suspicions of the other participants. A virtual Who's Who of racketeering in America, they included Jack Guzik from Chicago, "Boo-Boo" Hoff and "Nig" Rosen from Philadelphia, Moe Dalitz and Chuck Polizzi (real name—Leo Berkowitz) from Cleveland, Longy Zwillman from Newark, and John Lazia from Kansas City. The most influential crowd came from New York, and although they quarreled fiercely among themselves, the men from New York believed they, not Capone, stood at the center of the gangster world, and they were united against their common enemy, Al Capone, whose excesses and thirst for publicity were making it so difficult for every other racketeer in America. They also harbored one special grudge against Capone: he was the man who had killed Frankie Yale, and what was worse, he had done it on their turf, in Brooklyn, without consulting them. Even if they had silently cheered Yale's death, they could never condone Capone's arrogance. So the New Yorkers came to bury Caesar, not to praise him.

In addition to Luciano and Costello, the boys from New York included "Dutch" Schultz, Albert Anastasia, Louis Lepke, Meyer Lansky, and, most surprisingly, Johnny Torrio, who had emerged from his quiet retirement. The gangster's gangster, Torrio was the only man who maintained friendly relations with both Capone and the New York mobsters; as such he played a pivotal role in the gathering. Many of those assembled would have dearly loved to draw their revolvers and shoot one another on sight; instead, they turned to Torrio, the éminence grise of racketeering, to mediate their ferocious disputes. It was Torrio's judgment that the time had come for Capone to step aside. His penchant for violence had jeopardized business for all of them, and Torrio remained convinced that racketeers would prosper through negotiation rather than assassination. "There are two ways to power," he explained. "A Capone can rule for a while by blood and terror, but there will always be some who fight him with his own weapons. On the other hand, the man who can make money, big money, for others will eventually be regarded as indispensable."

The groundwork for the conference had been laid the year before at a meeting in Cleveland. Many of the same racketeers now in Atlantic City had attended the earlier gathering, where they had vowed to beat their automatic weapons into slot machines and stills. Capone had given some thought to attending the Cleveland conference but decided against it at the last moment because he believed, probably correctly, that the group would try to limit his unfettered control of Chicago. The thought of other racketeers conspiring behind his back made him uneasy, and he later regretted his decision. Thus, he made the effort to appear in Atlantic City, although the conference could not have come at a worse moment for him.

The conference, running from May 13 to May 16, offered a startling commentary on the depredations of Prohibition and the chaotic state of American society at this moment. The gathering offered dramatic proof that racketeering was no longer a local issue. Furthermore, it conjured up the specter of a national criminal network functioning as a shadow government with huge financial resources and vast political influence at its disposal. However, it was not a conference in the conventional sense. Most of the business was transacted not in smoke-filled rooms or at banquets but out on the windswept boardwalk, where the "delegates" rented rolling chairs equipped with canopies; seated two abreast, the racketeers conversed as an attendant gently pushed them. Alighting at the end of the boardwalk, they removed their shoes and socks, rolled their custom-tailored pants up to their knees, and strolled along the sand beside the gently lapping waters of the Atlantic Ocean, discussing how to apportion the rackets in cities across the country. This was Johnny Torrio's vision of racketeering: a cartel of businessmen coming together to discuss common concerns in a peaceful, dignified manner.

Shunned by jealous rivals, Capone found himself excluded from most of the wheeling and dealing, but he did renew one alliance when he encountered Moses Annenberg on the boardwalk. Moe Annenberg had made his name as a brutally effective circulation manager for the Hearst papers in Chicago; he later moved to Milwaukee and San Francisco in roughly the same capacity. Seven years earlier, he had seized control of the *Daily Racing Form*, the bookies' Bible, and began to build an empire of his own. By 1926 he had left Hearst to manage a network of wire services and racing sheets; eventually, the *Philadelphia Inquirer* would become his best-known, most prestigious holding. Despite the respectable façade, Moe Annenberg did business with racketeers as an equal. Indeed, he was, according to some accounts, the most powerful non-Italian racketeer in the nation. A singularly unattractive and unpleasant man, he excelled in a difficult, often dirty business. The ultimate realist, Annenberg realized he could not afford to ignore Capone, even when the racketeer was in disgrace.

Annenberg's presence at the conference aided certain favored journalists, who received a detailed, if self-serving account of the meeting's accomplishments and resolutions. Indeed, one of the reasons for the conference was the need to generate some favorable publicity and to cultivate a lenient attitude in the public. The gangsters who strolled the boardwalk in Atlantic City and huddled in the corridors of the Ritz during those mild days of May wanted to leave the impression that they were as civic-minded as the characters in a Damon Runyon story, harmless purveyors of the "light pleasures." They selected Robert T. Loughran of the United Press to announce the accomplishments of the fledgling racketeers' commission to the world. He was told that the merry gangsters had agreed to forget their grievances and had adopted a fourteen-point plan that sounded like a racketeer's version of the Treaty of Versailles. The major resolutions relevant to Capone included the following:

- All killings were to be abolished. Henceforth, all controversies were to be settled by the Commission. Members must relinquish all machine guns.
- Johnny Torrio will manage the new Commission.
- Al Capone's organization will be disbanded immediately.
- Torrio will be in charge of finances, paying Commission members each week.
- Joseph Aiello (Capone's sworn enemy) will head the Chicago branch of the Unione Sicilione.
- Capone will surrender the Ship and all his other gambling establishments to the Commission.

Each of these points was, of course, an insult to Capone, and each was motivated by the other racketeers' desire to reprimand him publicly as they helped themselves to portions of his enormous income. The big winner of the plan was Torrio, who, according to the Commission's estimates, would receive annual revenue as high as $15 million a year from the former Capone holdings. These included earnings at three racetracks, which each generated approximately $1 million a year; nearly $7 million from gambling establishments in Cicero and Chicago; $2 million from prostitution; and another $3 million from beer.

Had the Commission's ambitious scheme been carried out, it would have established Johnny Torrio as the preeminent racketeer in the nation, and it would have meant the end of Al Capone's career. However, the intricate set of rules and regulations on which the racketeers agreed proved impossible to enforce. Although Capone left Atlantic City humiliated by his professional rivals, he had no intention of relinquishing control of the Chicago rackets to his former mentor. He had long wanted to retire, but only when *he* decided, on his *own* terms; it was unthinkable for jealous rivals to push him aside. He was still a young man, hardly more than thirty. At the same time, he was shrewd enough to realize that the Commission's plan was a veiled threat against his life. Should he attempt to violate its provisions, he would probably be killed as mercilessly as he had killed Frankie Yale. So he had come, when he least expected, to a major turning point in his career. He could attempt to retain control of his organization, which meant certain death; or he faced oblivion. Neither choice was acceptable, and so he contrived a third course of action. He would wait. Perhaps better than anyone else he recognized how volatile the rackets were. The cast of characters and their alliances changed constantly; nothing was engraved in stone, not even the Commission's edicts. Facing the question of where to wait, Capone selected a place that came as a shock to his family and colleagues, but would prove to be the safest place of all for a gangster in disgrace: jail.

•   •   •

Capone left Atlantic City believing that the instant he set foot in New York or Chicago he would be "on the spot," that is, marked for death. In a desperate ploy to elude both the rival gangsters who wanted to kill him (or so he thought) and the federal authorities awaiting him on his return to Chicago, Capone arranged to have himself arrested on a minor charge. He began by telephoning two detectives, James "Shooey" Malone and John Creedon. Officially, the men were employed by the Philadelphia Police Department, but in fact they spent a fair amount of time in Miami, where Capone had given them tickets to the Sharkey-Stribling fight and entertained them at his home on Palm Island. Now he told Malone and Creedon that he would pass through Philadelphia on May 17, carrying a weapon. According to a report which Malone and Creedon hotly denied, each man would receive $10,000 in return for the favor of arresting him. This was a generous sum, as much, in fact, as Capone paid to have someone *killed*.

What followed was one of the most bizarre interludes in Capone's entire career. On the appointed evening, the detectives waited in the lobby of a downtown movie theater while Capone and his bodyguard, Frankie Rio, amused themselves within. When the boys emerged, Malone declared, as agreed, "You're 'Scarface' Capone."

"My name's Al Brown," answered the racketeer, following the script. "Call me Capone if you want to. Who are you?"

"I extended my right hand, showing the badge," Creedon said later. "Capone put his hand in his coat pocket and pulled out a gun, which he handed to me." In addition to the .38-caliber pistol, Capone reportedly handed Malone a roll of bills in the amount of $20,000—the payoff to the detectives for performing this "arrest."

Thereafter, events—all of them carefuly choreographed in advance by Capone—moved at an astonishingly rapid pace. Creedon and Malone immediately took Capone to City Hall, where police questioned him until two o'clock in the morning. His demeanor throughout was subdued and cooperative; he was nothing like the brash, tough-talking hoodlum they had expected to encounter. "I had a most interesting discussion with Capone shortly after his arrest," said Philadelphia's director of public safety, Lemuel B. Schofield, who talked with Capone in the early hours of the morning. "His manner was in great contrast to the snarls of . . . his bodyguard. . . . Capone quieted him and said: 'Listen, boy, you're my friend and have been a faithful pal, but I'll do the talking.' " And talk Capone did. "I've been in this racket long enough to realize that a man in my game must take the breaks, the fortunes of war," he told Schofield. "I haven't had peace of mind in years. Every minute I was in danger of death. Even when I'm on a peace errand we must hide from the rest of the racketeers. You fear death every moment, and, worse, worse than death, you fear the rats of the game, who would run around and tell the police if you didn't constantly satisfy them with money and favors. I'm tired of gang murders and gang shootings. I spent the week in Atlantic City trying to make peace among the various gang leaders of my city. I have the word of each of these men that there will be no more shootings." His contention that he was simply "trying to make peace" in Atlantic City was, of course, a fiction woven with shreds of truth.

By dawn, the district attorney, John Monaghan, assumed control of the case. A grand jury indicted Capone at 10:30 A.M. on a charge of carrying concealed weapons. One hour later, he and Rio pleaded guilty as charged. At 12:15 P.M. Judge John E. Walsh sentenced the men to one year in prison, and thirty minutes after that, they began serving their sentences. The process of catching the elusive Al Capone, from arrest to incarceration, had taken just sixteen hours—a record for Philadelphia jurisprudence. The entire legal charade in Philadelphia was, as the *Chicago Tribune*'s headline aptly characterized it, "QUAKER JUSTICE IN JIG TIME."

In his career as a racketeer, Capone had, among other crimes, killed several men himself, ordered dozens more to be eliminated, violated the Prohibition Act, bribed thousands of police and Prohibition agents, and he had engaged in large-scale prostitution, yet despite widespread public knowledge of his activities and a string of arrests, Al Capone had never been sentenced to jail—until now. It was Al's habit to admit to a lesser crime in place of a major one. In the past, he had admitted he was a bootlegger but not a pimp, he had condemned heroin while snorting cocaine, and now, when he was suspected of planning the St. Valentine's Day Massacre, he confessed to carrying a concealed weapon, hoping the public would be satisfied that justice would be done if he spent a year behind bars. Such was Capone's plan; the reality of doing penance in prison proved somewhat grimmer than he had anticipated. Capone and Rio were transferred to the nearby Holmesburg County Jail, where Capone was ordered to exchange his custom-made suit for ill-fitting blue denim prison garb. He received a brutal prison haircut and a prison number: 90725. Finally, he relieved himself of the eleven-and-a-half-carat diamond ring he wore on his pinkie—estimated value: $50,000—and entrusted it to his lawyer with instructions that it was to be given to Ralph Capone. The passing of the ring symbolized the transference of power; Ralph would be the acting head of the Chicago organization until Al's return. Meanwhile, the two detectives who had arrested Capone furiously denied they had conspired with the prisoner. "It's enough to make anybody want to quit being a copper," Malone complained. "Here we take a chance and pinch two of the most dangerous characters in the racket. They have guns on them and know how to use them. Then everybody hollers 'Frame up!' "

Malone protested too much, and a consensus formed that Capone's Philadelphia escapade was nothing more than a show trial staged not by the prosecutor but by the accused. The bizarre circumstances of his arrest and imprisonment stirred controversy across the country. The various law enforcement officials in Chicago and Washington who had been trying in vain to get their man greeted the news with restrained enthusiasm masking their utter incredulity. Al Capone in jail, just like that. How could the Philadelphia Police Department succeed where all of them had failed, and succeed so quickly, in just sixteen hours? The shrewd ones, such as George E. Q. Johnson, preferred not to look this particular gift horse in the mouth. "The Capone conviction speaks for itself—and says a lot," he commented. The remark could be interpreted in any number of ways. For those who wanted only to see Capone in jail, it suggested that Johnson was heartened by the sudden development; and for those whose suspicions were raised by the manner in which Capone had been caught, it suggested that it was a frame-up. In either event, Johnson continued to pursue both Al and Ralph Capone for tax evasion.

For John Stege, Chicago's deputy police chief, Capone's arrest in Phila-delphia was a source of profound embarrassment. Why, reporters angrily demanded, hadn't *he* thought to jail Al Capone for carrying a gun in Chi-cago? "I've arrested Capone a half-dozen times, and many times found guns on him. The same goes for a hundred other gangsters around town," Stege blustered, but, he added, "the minute you get them before a municipal court judge, the defense attorney makes a motion to suppress the evidence. The policeman is cross-examined, and if he admits he didn't have a warrant for the man's arrest on a charge of carrying concealed weapons, the judge declares the arrest illegal and the hoodlum is discharged," and so on and so forth. Stege's excuses only served to persuade the public, if further proof were needed, that the Chicago Police Department was hopeless in dealing with the likes of Capone.

In contrast, Capone had demonstrated convincingly that he knew how to get things done. For its speed and daring, the maneuver was especially impressive, for he managed to evade his racketeering rivals and the federal government at the same time. Whether it was actually necessary for him to go to the extreme of placing himself in jail for a year is another matter. One of the reasons Capone had survived as long as he had was his obsession with security; even if he faced the prospect of certain death in New York or Chicago, he could have returned to his Miami Beach retreat, where he had been living in "retirement" for over a year. It is more likely that he simply panicked after the Atlantic City conference, and his scheme to seek a safe haven in jail was yet another symptom of his dwindling grasp of reality—the result of neurosyphilis silently overtaking his reasoning abilities.

• • •

In Chicago, the Capone family rallied and showed they knew as well as Al how to mount a public relations offensive. Rather than hiding in disgrace, his mother, Teresa, now a vigorous fifty-nine; his sister, Mafalda, who had recently graduated from Lucy Flower High School; and various younger Capone brothers took the bold step of inviting reporters into the Capone family home on Prairie Avenue. Teresa wore an elegant black silk dress for the occasion, and she spoke to her guests in a charming mixture of English and Italian through which she managed to make herself understood. "Their living room, with its soft light and velvet rugs, was full of friends talking in high Italian voices of Al's capture and sentence, but the mother was neither too busy nor too excited to talk of her son and tell of his kindness," noted the man from the *Chicago Tribune*, as his gaze fell on the Dresden candelabras, luxurious tapestries, and a large gold crucifix. Mafalda, at eighteen, seemed to use the occasion to announce her availability for matrimony. Confined to her bed with a cold, she invited the reporters into her boudoir, where, dressed in a green silk negligee and reclining beneath a canopy of rose-colored satin, she greeted the men. Mafalda made, in the words of one reporter, "a radiant hostess," and an eloquent one. Of course her brother carried a gun, she said, coyly arranging her negligee over her alabaster shoulders. "Would anyone expect him to walk the streets anywhere without protection?" she asked in purring tones made all the more seductive by her upper respiratory congestion. "If people only knew him as I know him, they would not say the things about him they do. I adore him. And he is his mother's life. He is so very good, so kind to us. You who only know him from the newspaper stories will never realize the real man he is."

Meanwhile, the object of Mafalda's unqualified love and admiration turned restless and irritable. In interviews given through the bars of his deluxe cell, Al Capone stridently repeated his claim that *he* had convened the Atlantic City conference (when in fact he had been summoned) and that *he* had insisted the other racketeers make peace with one another (when in fact they had convened with the purpose of removing him from the rackets). And as the weeks in jail turned into months, Capone denied the rumors that he had arranged for his arrest to save his own skin. He found few believers, especially because his life in jail bore too much resemblance to his life on the outside. At the time he entered prison, there was much talk about what a dirty, overcrowded place Holmesburg was, strictly for hard cases, but Capone was soon transferred to Eastern Penitentiary, where he lived in a section of the jail known as "Park Avenue," in a large cell equipped with rugs and comfortable furniture. He had a supply of liquor at the ready, he could make long distance calls whenever he wished, his food was brought in from the outside, and he received as many visitors as he desired in the privacy and comfort of the warden's office. His guests included Ralph, Jack Guzik, and Frank Nitti, who were all engaged in overseeing the organization in Al's absence. Capone made himself a popular if not beloved figure at Eastern Penitentiary when he purchased $1,000 of handmade crafts from the other prisoners. All prisoners had to work, and Capone drew the most undemanding job available, as a library file clerk. He subscribed to magazines and passed the idle hours reading. He continued to give interviews to the press with almost the same frequency as he had on the outside, but now, instead of proclaiming his innocence, he waxed philosophical, musing about that little fellow Napoleon, the greatest racketeer of them all, in Al's view, and yet, "I could have wised him up on some things. The trouble with the guy was he got the swelled head. . . . He should have had sense enough after that

Elba jolt to kiss himself out of the game, but he was just like the rest of us. He didn't know when to quit and had to get back in the racket. He simply put himself on the spot. . . . If he had lived in Chicago, it would have been a sawed-off shotgun Waterloo for him. He didn't wind up in a ditch as a coroner's case, but they took him away for a one-way ride to St. Helena, which was about as tough a break." Even if the reporter who wrote this story helped Al touch up his phrases a bit, Capone was still colorful copy, whether or not he was behind bars.

As the summer drifted into the fall, and fall into winter, Al became impatient with the year-long jail sentence he had given himself. He grew restless and longed to seize the reins of power again. Headlines told of his numerous appeals to win an early release from prison:

"CAPONE CRIES 'ENOUGH,' BEGS FOR A PAROLE"
"CAPONE LOSES PHILADELPHIA FREEDOM PLEA"
"SCARFACE AL'S LAWYERS FILE NEW PETITION"
"CAPONE IN SIXTH LEGAL MOVE TO GET OUT OF JAIL."
"CAPONE LOSES ANOTHER FIGHT FOR FREEDOM"

No matter what arguments his lawyers made on his behalf, Capone remained caught in a trap of his own devising.

•   •   •

At the beginning of October, the Capone organization suffered a new setback. A grand jury returned seven indictments against Ralph Capone, who had been serving as the acting head of the organization. The charges resulted from Nels Tessem's relentless scrutiny of Ralph's dealings at the Pinkert State Bank in Cicero. In addition, the Treasury Department had recently become familiar with a bootlegging operation he managed; its shipments between Ontario, Canada, and Chicago totaled more than $1 million. Then there was the matter of his large diamond ring and the two limousines he owned while he was pleading poverty to the IRS, not to mention the handsome suite he maintained at the Western Hotel, as the Hawthorne Hotel was now called. The evidence of his wealth was overwhelming. Six of the indictments were to be expected; they concerned his failure to pay taxes. The seventh invoked an ancient statute originally designed to punish profiteers during the Civil War. Now it was applied to Ralph's hiding his $25,000 bank account while claiming he was nearly broke. As a result of that maneuver, he stood accused of defrauding the U.S. government.

The Treasury Department arrested Ralph in a highly public manner, as if to send a warning to all other racketeers. On the evening of October 8, he attended a boxing match. As he took his ringside seat, Special Agent Clarence Converse, who worked with Tessem, approached Ralph, arrested him, and led him away in handcuffs. The hour was late, which meant that Ralph would have to spend the night in jail; in the morning he went free on a substantial bail of $35,000. The trial was set for the following May before Judge James H. Wilkerson.

Unlike his younger brother, who had willingly gone to prison on a minor charge, Ralph faced grave federal charges, not to mention a hostile judge and the wrath of the Chicago press. Furthermore, he was burdened by the stigma of being the brother of the notorious "Scarface" Al Capone. In his dealings with the IRS over the years, Ralph had shown himself to be both dishonest and dumb. Nonetheless, he eagerly sought vindication. He had spent his entire career in the shadow of his younger brother Al, profiting greatly as a result, but he had never commanded the respect, loyalty, and admiration that Al had. If nothing else good came from the trial, it would at least give Ralph a chance to stand on his own. For the first time since he had been indicted, he did something smart: he hired the best defense lawyers money could buy. If the government wanted a fight, a fight he would give them.

Unfortunately for Ralph, he resumed his blunders. Now that he was under indictment, he attracted a fresh contingent of investigators prepared to apply new techniques to law enforcement. He drew their attention when he carelessly resumed his bootlegging business from his suite at the Western Hotel and from a nearby saloon called the Montmarte Café without realizing that the telephones were tapped. At the other end of the line, hanging on his every word, was a daring, even reckless young Treasury agent. His name was Eliot Ness.

CHAPTER 8

Public Enemies

HE WAS A MAN WHOM DESTINY, like a temptress, alternately beckoned and scorned. Today, thanks to several decades of television shows and movies depicting his exploits, Eliot Ness stands as the archetypal sleuth of the Prohibition era, the man who finally brought Al Capone to heel and cleaned up Chicago. The appeal of the Ness legend is obvious, for it simplified the complexities and ambiguities surrounding Prohibition, and it condoned violence and anti-Italian prejudice, for Ness was nothing if not the scourge of that particular immigrant group. Because he was clean-cut, handsome, and boyish, he made these darker impulses seem healthy, normal, and wholly American. If Capone personified what Americans, especially rural Americans, hated and feared about the big cities in the 1920s—the crime, the slums, and especially the immigrants—the legendary Ness appeared to be the remedy: an all-American boy who had grown up amid green lawns and white picket fences, and who represented a nation whose citizens respected the laws and spoke the same language. America the way all Americans, immigrants included, wished to see it.

Ness himself was the first to promote this wildly exaggerated and distorted version of his career to the public. Near the end of his life, when he was forgotten, broke, and drinking excessively, he sought to resurrect some of the glory of his youth and to extricate himself from debt by writing a book recounting his adventures in Prohibition-era Chicago. In the book, he portrayed himself as a real-life Sherlock Holmes stalking a real-life Moriarty in the person of Al Capone. Ness collected himself sufficiently to assemble a short memoir of his early career, which he then turned over to his collaborator, a journalist named Oscar Fraley. When it emerged from Fraley's typewriter, Ness's straightforward, accurate, if undramatic version had taken on the frenetic tone of a Mickey Spillane novel. The result, called *The Untouchables*, finally appeared in 1957, too late to help Ness, who had died two years earlier. It was overblown and often inaccurate both in regard to Ness's original, unimproved version and the historical record, but for good or ill, the book's version of events made a considerable impression, giving rise to the legend of Eliot Ness. To cite but one instance, his account shrewdly fed the mythical notion that one man—not a legal system, not tax laws, and certainly not a bunch of dry-as-dust IRS accountants—was responsible for bringing down Capone. Ness and Fraley had done their job all too well; as a result, the role of the IRS and its Intelligence Unit were forgotten, and the public embraced the legend of Eliot Ness. To read *The Untouchables* is to forget, briefly, that no matter how many stills Eliot Ness smashed or bootleggers he arrested, nothing he did contributed to the government's case against Al Capone.

Yet the truth about Ness was equally fascinating, if less spectacular, for in many ways he did serve as a remarkable foil to Al Capone. The gangster controlled a national crime network generating $75 million a year; the honest young Prohibition agent's annual salary came to just $2,500. Capone was often flamboyant and vicious; Ness was boyish, vague, hard to read. Capone was fat and dark; Ness stood six feet tall, and he was rather gangly, with sleepy blue eyes. Capone's shiny custom-made suits shouted "gangster"; Ness dressed conservatively and parted his cornsilk hair in the middle. Capone's gray eyes and dark hair, not to mention his double scar, gave him an aura of implacable menace; Ness, in contrast, was genuinely handsome, Gary Cooper handsome. Capone raged against his enemies and even took a baseball bat to three of his victims; Ness never lost his temper and always contained his emotions.

Although the real Ness was intelligent, well educated, and ambitious, he was also a publicity hound, impenetrably naïve, and insecure—a lonely, melancholy, haunted man who bore scant resemblance to the self-assured character played by Robert Stack in 114 episodes of *The Untouchables* on television. Ness's worst enemy was not Al Capone, who was assuredly the best thing that ever happened to him, but Ness himself, who was plagued throughout his life by his problems with women and with alcohol. Indeed, his drinking problem was so serious that it eventually destroyed his marriages and his career.

The external circumstances of his early years give little hint of the turmoil that was to trouble his adult life. Ness was a son of Chicago; he was born there on April 19, 1903. He was the son of Norwegian immigrants, Peter and Emma (King), who named their son after George Eliot, the English novelist, without realizing they had bestowed the pen name of Mary Ann Evans on the child. Ness's father operated a Scandinavian bakery in the Chicago suburb of Kensington, working long hours, never wealthy but never poor. The Chicago Scandinavian community was, like other ethnic enclaves, a cohesive group, and early in life Ness formed connections that would determine the shape of his career. The family of his future boss, George E. Q. Johnson, lived close to the Ness home, and it is possible, indeed likely, that the young Ness knew Johnson. So from the start Ness was connected to the men and the ethnic group who would become Capone's primary antagonists, the men who believed in America because America believed in them. In addition, Ness's sister, a decade older than he, was married to Alexander Jamie, an FBI agent. Jamie also taught Ness marksmanship, in the process becoming a glamorous, potent presence in the young man's life and subsequent career.

However, the most important figure in the life of the young Ness was neither his father nor Jamie. The most important figure was his mother, and to understand the special relationship between Emma King Ness and her youngest child is to come close to unraveling the mystery of Eliot Ness. Emma adored Eliot; in later years, when some measure of fame descended on him, she was fond of reminiscing about what a good boy he always was. It was not at all surprising to her that he became a federal agent because as a son, he was more than good; he was, she believed, incapable of doing wrong. Night after night, while Peter Ness was absent, tending his bakery, the young Ness was at home with his mother and occasionally his sister, and he remained attached to them both, so attached that he was still living at home when he was a twenty-six-year-old Treasury agent.

As a result of his overprotected youth and young adulthood, he became accustomed to women identifying completely with him, and he, in return, seemed to identify completely with women. "The ladies loved Eliot," says Louise Jamie, who was related to him by marriage. "He was handsome and personable and understated. He never carried a gun. He was very private. He was typical of the English-Norwegian, the backbone of America. Even the gangsters knew it. There is honor among thieves, you see, if they respect you. Nobody ever shot Eliot for that reason." Indeed, throughout his life, women found him inordinately attractive. Perhaps they were drawn to the inner sadness they thought they glimpsed lurking beneath his pleasant exterior. Or perhaps it was simply his good looks. Throughout his adult life, women lured him from one romantic interlude to the next, but none of the marriages and affairs and romantic entanglements and flirtations in which he became involved came out right in the end.

In an age when a college degree was a rare credential for a detective, Ness attended the University of Chicago, where at different times he majored in law, business, and political science. He cut a fashionable figure on campus, wearing snappy sport coats, playing tennis, double-dating, pledging the

Sigma Alpha Epsilon fraternity. Only his continuing fascination with jujitsu, which he studied diligently in preparation for future combat, was at odds with convention. Ness graduated in 1925, when he was twenty-two, in the top third of his class. In the normal course of events, a bright young man like Ness would have gone on to law school, but Ness, driven, perhaps, by a desire to emulate his brother-in-law, Alexander Jamie, was attracted to the aura of law enforcement.

To continue the story of his early career in his own words:

> In about 1928, I was employed by the Retail Credit Company, . . . a national investigation company devoted entirely to investigations of persons applying for insurance. This was during the Prohibition heyday. My brother-in-law, Alexander Jamie, was at that time an F.B.I. agent, which, of course, was part of the U.S. Department of Justice. I believe the Prohibition Bureau was then transferred to the Department of Justice, and Alexander Jamie was drafted to become Chief Investigator with the Prohibition Bureau. It was his job to make conspiracy cases. I came in presently to work on personnel.
>
> Corruption was apparently a continuous problem with the department trying to handle the enforcement of the Prohibition Law, and soon another division was organized to make conspiracy cases and also to investigate corruption with the Department itself. This agency was called the Special Agents of the U.S. Department of Justice, Prohibition Department . . . , and soon I was drafted into this unit. This is where my connection with the Mafia began.

Though it fielded a staff of 300 agents in Chicago alone, the Prohibition Bureau was overwhelmed by Capone's army of over 1,000 soldiers and its network of 20,000 speakeasies, as well as a lack of popular sympathy. Even Ness acknowledged that he had waged a losing battle against the Capone organization and all the other bootleggers. "The trouble with the Prohibition Law," he wrote, "was that such a large section of the public did not believe in it, they either were against it in its entirety or figured it was for the other fellow." Amid this dismal climate, the U.S. attorney in charge of the operation, George E. Q. Johnson, hired Ness on the recommendation of Alexander Jamie. Ness was a safe choice, because he was a neighbor of the former and related to the latter. At the same time, there were liabilities, for Ness was young, and more than that, he was callow. At the time he first challenged the most dangerous and powerful gangster of the era, Ness was all of twenty-six, four years out of college, still living with his parents.

Ness went to work for Johnson at the time that federal and local law enforcement agencies were coming together for the first time in their effort to dismantle the Capone organization, and he participated in their numerous early raids on Chicago Heights, but he was still an unknown quantity, his name mentioned in the newspapers in passing if at all, and usually misspelled ("Elliott Ness"). Ness was assigned to a partner, Dan Koken, whom he came to idolize, the first of several apparent infatuations Ness had with the men with whom he worked. The two occasionally teamed up with a fellow known as "Nine Toed" Nabors, who was, in Ness's words, "the handsomest man I have ever seen. He was built like a Greek God, with natural, light wavy hair."

Late in 1928, Ness and Koken, posing as corrupt Prohibition agents, began frequenting a Chicago Heights saloon called the Cozy Corners, where, Ness recalled, "rum-runners from Iowa, southern Illinois, St. Louis, and as far away as Kansas City would come. They would leave their cars with the bartenders, and the cars would be driven away by members of the Chicago Heights alcohol mob. The drivers from out of town would stay at the bar, drinking, or avail themselves of what the brothel located on the second and third floors had to offer"—their reward for delivering booze. Ness enjoyed hanging out with the small-time bootleggers; it was glamorous, fun, exciting. Ness played the role of bootlegger to the hilt, and another agent, Burt Napoli, who spoke Italian, pretended to be his chauffeur. In short order the little band became well known to the racketeers of Chicago Heights, who paid Ness $250 a week in bribes—all of it duly reported to his superiors.

Emboldened, Ness and other special agents began shaking down the bootleggers of Chicago Heights still more aggressively. "One time two truck loads of merchandise were coming in," recalls Sam Pontarelli, a longtime resident of the Heights and confidant of Al Capone. "Ness and his men stopped the trucks, grabbed the drivers, squeezed their balls, and beat the shit out of them. Hit them with clubs. It looked as though the shipment would not be delivered, but then money changed hands, and the trucks got through." This behavior convinced the racketeers that Ness "wanted to be a fifty percent partner in the stills and the whorehouses" maintained by the organization. "He was on the take," Pontarelli insists.

On his next visit to the Cozy Corners, Ness insisted on meeting the boss of the alcohol racket in the Heights. This was Joe Martino, the last surviving member of the old Phil Piazza gang, the Sicilian bootleggers and blackmailers who had once terrorized Chicago Heights. Two years before, in 1926, the Capone forces under the direction of Dominic Roberto and Jimmy Emery had killed off or driven out the Sicilians, and only one still walked the streets of Chicago Heights: Joseph Martino. The Capone organization allowed him to live because he was the president of the local branch of the Unione Sicilione, and Capone was reluctant to stir up that hornet's nest. However, the arrival of the reckless young Eliot Ness upset this delicate balance of power. Ness was dangerously ignorant of the recent history of the Chicago Heights rackets; he lumped the Capone organization together with the Sicilians, assuming they were allies when in fact they were often mortal enemies. He also assumed, mistakenly, that Martino occupied a powerful position in the Capone organization when in fact the organization was using Martino to gather intelligence on Ness, much as Ness wanted to use Martino to gather intelligence on Chicago Heights bootleggers.

In his original manuscript, Ness offered a vivid, if awkward, account of his initial encounter with Martino:

Martino was smooth faced, round and short, with very dark hair and complexion. He spoke English well grammatically, with a very heavy accent. It was explained that Joe was the head of the "organization," which turned out to be the Chicago Heights chapter of the "Unione Siciliano". I asked where all the still owners were, and Joe explained that they had already had a meeting, and that the still owners had commissioned himself . . . to pay us to refrain from raiding the stills. We had quite an argument about the amount to be paid. I was the main objector and the hungry one; of course it made no difference what they paid, as the money was marked and turned over to the District Attorney. . . . We brought up questions about how much they paid other law enforcement officials, and who, but they were careful not to bite too hard on these leads. . . .

At this meeting, in the same room, but sitting apart from the group, we noticed a swarthy, silk-shirted Italian, who apparently did not understand a word of English nor did he speak any English. We agreed on a weekly sum, which I think was in the neighborhood of $500.00. As the meeting broke up, Burt Napoli [an agent posing as Ness's chauffeur] turned white, and pulling me aside, said, "The silk-shirted Italian has just asked whether or not he should let you have the knife in the back!" . . . We later learned that this man was one of the killers, imported to do the bidding of the leaders of the gang after the finger had been pointed.

Ness left the meeting convinced he had just spoken with the bootlegging kingpin of the Heights, and on that basis he obtained search warrants for eighteen stills. He subsequently participated in the raids on them, capturing "prisoners, machinery and alcohol," but as he celebrated his first triumph, he learned to his horror that Burt Napoli, the agent who had posed as his chauffeur, had been murdered. Seeking revenge, Ness's unit arrested a suspect, but before they could interrogate him, "he hanged himself by his necktie in his cell. The evidence on him was positive enough to make us feel that the person who had gotten Burt had been brought to justice."

Now that his cover had been blown, Ness's brief career as an undercover agent came to an end, but he was more eager than ever to smash all the stills in the Heights. Henceforth, "we always travelled with sawed-off shot guns in our pockets, and when we went into a restaurant, we always took a corner table as the danger of our undertaking was becoming more imminent." He joined forces with another agent, Marty Lahart, a "tall, happy Irishman," who led a memorable assault on the Cozy Corners. "As he entered the saloon, he yelled, 'Everybody keep their places, this is a federal raid.' As he uttered these words, four revolvers and one shot gun hit the floor," Ness wrote. "After taking control of the first floor, he went to the second floor which was the brothel. He again made the announcement that the federal raid was on. One of the girls quickly looked up, eyed Marty, and shouted, 'Look who's here, Tom Mix.' "

Despite the success of the Cozy Corners raid, Ness sensed he was, in Chicago parlance, "on the spot." One day he picked up the phone, and a rough voice warned: "I got a message for you. You've had your last chance to be smart. Just keep in mind that sometime soon you're going to be found lying in a ditch with a hole in your head and your wang slashed off. We'll keep reminding you so you won't forget to remember." This threat seemed appallingly likely to be carried out the night Ness noticed a suspicious car following him. He forced the car off the road and frisked the driver, who was carrying a gun with the serial numbers filed off and a supply of dumdum bullets. Shortly afterward, Ness spoke with an informant who reported that he had recently overheard men in Chicago Heights plotting to kill the young agent; their plans included using dumdum bullets "so that they would make a large hole in the body they entered." Since Ness still lived with his parents, police placed the Ness family home under twenty-four-hour guard, and Eliot later moved into a nearby apartment with two other agents. The threat was in its own way gratifying because it made him feel different, special—he was so important that men actually wanted to kill him—and as long as he felt that way, he could continue to function in his job, which translated into more professionally sanctioned thrill seeking. He did not have to wait long for more excitement.

"By this time we had successfully gathered enough evidence to make an iron-clad conspiracy case," wrote Ness, "and early one Sunday morning the U.S. District Attorney's Office, plus ourselves aided by about 100 Chicago detectives, went to Chicago Heights, and raided haunts of every known gangster in that area." Ness reserved for himself the honor of arresting the presumed kingpin, Joe Martino. "We read the warrant to him and he went to the closet to pick up a top coat, and at the same time he threw a weapon on the floor. He became deathly sick and we had trouble getting him to the station." He spent the night in jail and, free on bail, returned to Chicago Heights the following afternoon. It was then that the Capone forces struck. Late on the afternoon of November 29, as Martino loitered in front of his saloon on East Sixteenth Street, a passing car fired over a dozen bullets at him. Martino fell to the pavement dead. "He apparently had not been in the Heights for more than two minutes when he was mowed down by machine gunners," Ness wrote. "That was the end for Joe Martino."

The neighborhood immediately reverberated with news of the latest gangland slaying. "His hands are still clasped in the pockets of his working trousers," wrote a *Chicago Heights Star* correspondent who dashed to the scene of the crime. "Reports were that the slaying had been accomplished in the usual gangland manner. A large motor car containing four or five men shrouded behind the curtains drew up at top speed, paused for a minute to deliver a death-dealing volley, and passed out of sight." Martino, forty-five, fell less than a hundred feet from the Milano, where his former boss, Phil Piazza, had met his bloody end. In fact, the block was so dense with scenes of gangland slayings in recent years—half a dozen by one count— that it had acquired the nickname of "Death Corner." Overall, Chicago Heights had been the scene of more than twenty shotgun deaths, and when the *Star* launched an inquiry into the town's rackets, the newspaper's offices were bombed by person or persons unknown, and the investigation came to an abrupt end.

To the end of his life Ness never understood why Martino had been assassinated, or the role his investigation had played in hastening the Sicilian's violent death. To the Capone forces, the forces who had let him live in order to preserve peace with the Unione Sicilione, it seemed Martino had inexplicably betrayed them to Ness. As a traitor, Martino deserved death. By helping to create the misleading impression that Martino was cooperating with the Feds, Ness had inadvertently sent that hapless soldier of the bootlegging wars to his grave.

As a result of Ness's blunder, the legal outcome of the Chicago Heights raids, though splashy, was ultimately frustrating. Early in May 1929 the *Chicago Herald and Examiner* declared: "81 INDICTED IN $36,000,000 RUM RING AT CHICAGO HEIGHTS." Brought by a federal grand jury, the indictments were the result of the raids in which Ness had participated, but the coverage was quick to emphasize that " 'Scarface Al' Capone, reputed head of the ring, escaped indictment. Government prosecutors explained they could not get enough evidence against him." The reason was simple: Ness and the other agents had been chasing the wrong racketeer; they had focused on Martino, the decoy, rather than the obscure but powerful members of the Capone organization. By hastening Martino's death, Ness had actually helped Capone strengthen his hold on Chicago Heights.

. . .

On the strength of his spurious success in Chicago Heights, Eliot Ness received a promotion; he moved his field of operations from Chicago Heights to Cicero, the better to concentrate on Capone. Since Al was in jail in Philadelphia at the time on a charge of carrying a concealed weapon, Ness went after Ralph Capone, who was already under indictment for income tax violations. His assignment was to gather enough evidence of bootlegging to persuade a grand jury to indict Ralph for violating Prohibition laws as well. To accomplish his mission, Ness had to demonstrate conclusively that Ralph was indeed handling liquor shipments. As the Feds knew to their profit, Ralph was no genius; he bought and sold liquor as carelessly as he handled his finances. Each day, late in the afternoon, he was on the phone from the Montmartre Café, placing orders and taking deliveries. It was Ness's idea to tap Ralph's phone and record the conversations, which would be sure to offer a ready supply of leads.

In recent months, wiretapping had proved extremely effective in tracing liquor shipments throughout Chicago. "After a time it became almost impossible to deliver beer without a good risk of being knocked off by us," Ness boasted. However, placing a tap on the phone used by Ralph Capone in a corner of the shabby little Montmartre Café proved considerably more challenging, because, he wrote, "It was necessary to get a man up the [telephone] pole in back of the Montmartre, but the neighborhood was never without a guard, or several guards." To accomplish his goal Ness decided to create a distraction: "In desperation I got my Cadillac touring car out, took down the top, and put my four biggest special agents in the car and started to circle the block. . . . In ten minutes a great deal of interest had been aroused, and the guards got into their cars and followed my four agents from a distance." Meanwhile, Ness's tapping expert, another special agent named Paul Robsky, shimmied up the pole, pretending to be a lineman engaged in repair work. Ness's secretary simultaneously placed a call to the Montmartre. While the secretary bantered with the bartender, Robsky frantically combed the junction box for the correct connection, and when he found it, signaled Ness. "The bridge was made and the telephone tap on the Cicero headquarters of the mob established. This tap was kept alive for many, many months, and we learned a great deal about the operations and personnel of the gang through it."

Poring over the transcripts of Ralph's telephone conversations, Ness and his cohorts found two leads worth pursuing. In the first, a man identifying himself as "McCoy" told Ralph, "I've got two real big orders I want to place."

And Ralph replied, "You know I don't take orders here. Call Guzik at the Wabash Hotel." From this exchange, Ness deduced that "Greasy Thumb" actually ranked higher in the Capone organization than Ralph, which made sense since Guzik was considerably smarter than Ralph. The transcript of the second call was, if anything, even more revealing. In it, a man identifying himself as "Fusco" told Ralph, "I think it's safe now to reopen that spot in South Wabash Avenue." Ralph replied, "I don't know how safe it is, but if you think so, go ahead." At which point, Fusco asked, "What do you hear from Snorky?" meaning Al Capone, who still languished in Pennsylvania's Eastern Penitentiary. "Not much new," Ralph told him. "He'll be back soon." Now Ness realized he finally was getting closer to Al Capone himself, and he took the reference to "South Wabash Avenue" to mean that the organization was about to reopen one of its largest breweries, which federal agents had previously raided and closed.

The information gathered from the wiretap proved reliable. A week later, Ness and several other agents surrounded the brewery, then rammed the front door with a truck equipped with a snowplow (which doubled as a bullet shield). "We arrested six men, took two trucks and destroyed beer and equipment valued at one hundred thousand dollars," Ness recorded with satisfaction.

The raid led to a perilous sequel. The following evening found Ness and his girlfriend driving at a leisurely pace through the Illinois countryside when he noticed "a pair of headlights fixed steadily in my rear-view mirror." He drove his girlfriend home, walked her to the door, and returned to the car. In the hairy-chested prose of The Untouchables, he recalled, "there was a bright flash from the front windows, and I ducked instinctively as my windshield splintered in tune with the bark of a revolver. Without thinking, I jammed the accelerator to the floor. As my car leaped ahead, there was another flash, and the window of my left rear door was smashed by another slug. . . . Driving madly, I circled the block, taking my gun from the shoulder holster and holding it in my left hand as I doubled back to get behind the car which had ambushed me. Now I wanted my turn, but the would-be assassin had faded into the night." Driving home, Ness speculated that the attack "had been planned as a 'welcome home' present for 'Scarface Al.' "

When Capone finally did leave jail and return to Chicago, Ness expected to find himself in further confrontations of escalating intensity. He did not shrink from them; on the contrary, he eagerly anticipated the gangsters' assaults. Doing battle with gangsters, "offered a lot of excitement," in his words. "Besides, I don't think I could stand the monotony of an office." This devil-may-care attitude did not endear him to his colleagues. Many of the men with whom he worked considered him a phony, an amateur who belonged in a classroom, gripping a piece of chalk in his hand, not a weapon.

Ness's colleagues especially disliked his self-consciousness, the way he always seemed to be asking himself how his exploits would look, could he get them into the newspapers, what would the girls think. Ness always wanted to play the hero, with emphasis on the word *play*. Catching Capone was always a game to him, an activity subject to exaggeration and even frivolity. The greatest fraternity stunt that ever was. "It's funny, I think, when you back up a truck to a brewery door and smash it in. And then find some individuals inside that you hadn't expected," he said.

Eliot's idea of fun was doomed to failure. He was trying enforce a law for which popular support had long vanished, and the victories he did win came about largely because Al Capone remained in a Philadelphia jail cell, isolated from his bootlegging empire. Ness's job would become much less fun, and far more frustrating, once Capone gained his freedom and returned to Chicago.

•   •   •

"I can't believe all they say of him. In my seven years' experience, I have never seen a prisoner so kind, cheery, and accommodating. He does his work—that of file clerk—faithfully and with a high degree of intelligence. He has brains. He would have made good anywhere, at anything. He has been an ideal prisoner."

The speaker was Dr. Herbert M. Goddard of the Pennsylvania State Board of Prison Inspectors. The subject was Al Capone.

Goddard had come to know the model prisoner while performing a minor operation on his nose in mid-August 1929 and, two weeks later, removing his tonsils, which, the doctor explained, had been troubling Al for years. Now the doctor could not lavish enough praise on his patient. "I cannot estimate the money he has given away," Goddard said in September 1929. "Of course, we cannot inquire where he gets it. He's in the racket. He admits it. But you can't tell me he's all bad, after I have seen him many times a week for ten months, and seen him with his wife and his boy and his mother."

The public heard no more about the racketeer until he lurched back into the headlines on March 17, 1930, the occasion of his release from the Eastern Penitentiary in Holmesburg, Pennsylvania. Granted two months off for good behavior, Capone had spent ten months behind bars. The manner of his release was every bit as suspect as his confinement had been. To avoid a crush of reporters descending on the prison, Capone was liberated one day ahead of schedule. A car belonging to the warden took him to another prison, Gratersford, where he was held in custody for another twenty-four hours; only then did he actually go free. He immediately took the Broadway Limited to Chicago, where he was met by his brother Ralph and Jack Guzik. The press knew none of this, and to further confuse them, prison officials

went to the trouble to stage a mock release at Holmesburg. Police roped off
the block in front of the penitentiary, and patrolled the streets, while the
warden's office distributed tidbits of manufactured news to waiting reporters.
Although Capone had left the premises the day before, the bulletins conveyed the impression that he was still confined within its stone walls, awaiting the signature of the governor of Pennsylvania on the release papers,
although the signature had already been obtained. With such tactics, the
prison sustained the ruse until after dark, when the warden, Herbert "Hard-
boiled" Smith, appeared before the milling reporters and said, "We certainly
stuck one in your eye that time. The big guy went out of here yesterday at
dusk in a brown automobile to Gratersford prison. . . . Try and find out
where they've gone."

Disgusted by the chicanery surrounding Capone's release, one reporter
called out, "How much did you get for this, warden?"

"You get the hell out of here and stay out," came the reply.

The next day, in a punning allusion to the racketeer's chief occupation,
the *Chicago Tribune* headlined: "WARDEN SPIRITS GANGSTER OUT; CAUSES
UPROAR." This was more than a local story. Capone's release landed him on
the cover of *Time* magazine, an honor normally reserved for tycoons with
whom the magazine's publisher, Henry Luce, was enthralled. But then,
what was Alphonse ("Scarface") Capone, as the magazine called him, if not
the leading tycoon of bootlegging and racketeering in the United States? And
Capone certainly looked the part in his cover photograph, with his hair
neatly combed, his collar just so, and a rose in his lapel. Only the prominent
scar on his cheek spoiled the impression of prosperous respectability. Within,
the magazine presented a somewhat different story, labeling him the "No. 1
underwordling of the U.S." but emphasized that he was more of a businessman than a murderer, a man who "wears clean linen, drives a Lincoln car,
leaves acts of violence to his hirelings."

He was even the subject of a new book, *Al Capone: The Biography of a
Self-Made Man*, by Fred D. Pasley, the *Chicago Tribune* rewrite man who
had spent the previous six months furiously typing his semicoherent account
of Capone's role in Chicago's gangster wars. "Poor little rich boy," the book
concludes, "the Horatio Alger lad of prohibition, the gamin from the side-
walks of New York, who made good in a Big Shot way in Chicago—General
Al the Scarface, . . . creature of the strangest, craziest fate, in the strangest,
craziest era of American history. The story ends—unfinished, like his life—
the red thread still unspun by the gods amuck." Claiming she was completely
unbiased, the *Tribune's* reviewer called Pasley's rambling compilation "a
book that has more thrills to the paragraph than anything written in our
decade." Although it contained scant biographical information about its
thirty-one-year-old subject, its mere existence testified to Capone's stature;

no one troubled to publish books devoted to "Bugs" Moran, "Hymie" Weiss, or Frankie Yale.

In Chicago, the police immediately dispatched a squad of black-and-whites to stake out the Capone home on Prairie Avenue, where they waited three days and nights in the vain hope of catching a glimpse of the elusive racketeer. Only Eliot Ness, still on the case, had any idea of Al Capone's whereabouts, thanks to the wiretap on Ralph's hotel. This way Ness learned of a phone call Ralph placed to summon help in dealing with Al. "We're up in room 718 at the Western," Ralph said, "and Al is really getting out of hand. He's in terrible shape. Will you come up? You're the only one who can handle him when he gets like this. We've sent for a lot of towels." Apparently Al, in celebration of his freedom, had drunk too much and gotten sick in Ralph's suite. Ness had also tapped the phones at the Capone family residence on Prairie Avenue. One call in particular caught the attention of the young agent. It was placed by Jake Lingle, the reporter who was known to be friendly, perhaps too friendly, with Capone, and it was answered by Ralph, sounding more beleaguered with every passing day. Like everyone else in Chicago, Lingle, now at the *Tribune*, wanted to know the where-abouts of Al Capone, and when Ralph unconvincingly claimed he had no idea where the Big Fellow was, Lingle growled, "Jesus, Ralph, this makes it very bad for me. I'm supposed to have my fingers on these things. It makes it very embarrassing with my paper. Now get this, I want you to call me the minute you hear from him. Tell him I want to see him right away." Ralph promised he would, but when Lingle called again, he was infuriated to learn that Ralph refused to produce his brother. "Listen, you guys ain't giving me the runaround, are you?" Lingle challenged. "Just remember, I wouldn't do that if I was you." Lingle's tone of menace struck Ness as curious, to say the least. What kind of reporter dared to threaten Al Capone's older brother?

The instant the police guard around his home dispersed, Capone surfaced, fully recovered from his raucous homecoming party at the Western Hotel. He did not seek refuge in his family's home, nor did he hide out in Cicero or Chicago Heights. Instead, he chose to return to the most visible of all his addresses, the Lexington Hotel on South Michigan Avenue, in the heart of Chicago. He took his seat beneath the framed portraits of that civic trinity—Washington, Lincoln, and "Big Bill" Thompson—and resumed administer-ing his far-flung racketeering enterprises, not only the booze shipments and payoffs but also the brothels and gambling dens, all of which required at-tention after his ten months' absence. He was wearing a bandage on his right hand, a legacy of his drunken behavior at the party, but when asked about the injury, he said only, "I burned it on a piece of roast beef." Reclaiming his racketeering throne, Capone demonstrated that he remained the most pow-erful, important, and controversial figure in Chicago.

Chicago's bumbling deputy chief of police, John Stege, loudly insisted that Capone would be arrested on sight, and the racketeer was only too happy to call Stege's bluff. To demonstrate that he feared no one, not the police, not even the Feds, Capone appeared at police headquarters, taking care to bring a lawyer with him. He asked if the Chicago police wanted to see him for any reason. No, he was told. What about the chief of detectives? No. Then how about John A. Swanson, the state's attorney? Again, no. Finally, did George E. Q. Johnson, the U.S. attorney, wish to ask him any questions? Absolutely not. Johnson was too shrewd to answer a public challenge from Capone; the prosecutor knew the time would eventually come—in court. But Al had proved his point. If the government was planning a major effort to "get Capone," he could find no evidence of it.

He then walked to the Federal Building under police guard; once there, he engaged in heated verbal sparring with the assistant state's attorney, Harry Ditchburne, and Deputy Chief John Stege:

> DITCHBURNE: Al, what do you know about the Valentine day massacre of the seven Moran fellows?
>
> CAPONE: I was in Florida then.
>
> STEGE: Yes, and you were in Florida, too, when Frank Yale was murdered in New York.
>
> CAPONE: I'm not as bad as I'm painted. If you sift everything I was ever accused of you'll find I didn't do it. I get blamed for everything that goes on here. . . . All I want is not to be arrested if I come downtown.
>
> STEGE: You're out of luck. Your day is done. How soon are you going to get out of town?
>
> CAPONE: I want to go to Florida some time next week. I don't know when I have to go to the federal court for trial on the contempt case.
>
> STEGE: You can go because no one wants to put a complaint against you today. But next time you go into the locker.
>
> NASH: [Capone's lawyer] Lenin and Trotsky and others rebelled against that kind of treatment.
>
> STEGE: I hope Capone goes to Russia.

By the time the argument ended, evening shadows were spreading across Chicago. A weary Capone shrugged his shoulders and told the reporters who had followed him on his rounds, "It's kind of hard trying to find out who wants me." Small chuckles. "I made it easy for them. I was willing to face any charge anyone had to make." He began defending himself before his receptive audience by pointing out the hypocrisy of his accusers. "All I ever did was to sell beer and whiskey to our best people," he maintained. "All I ever did was to supply a demand that was pretty popular. Why, the very guys that make my trade good are the ones that yell loudest at me. Some of the leading judges use the stuff." For once Capone spoke the truth. "They talk about me not being on the legitimate. Nobody's on the legit. You know that and then so do they. Your brother or your father gets in a jam. What do you do? Sit back . . . without trying to help him? You'd be a yellow dog if you did. Nobody's really on the legit when it comes down to cases. The funny part of the whole thing is that a man in this line of business has so much company. I mean his customers. If people did not want beer and wouldn't drink it, a fellow would be crazy for going around trying to sell it. I've seen gambling houses, too, in my travels, you understand, and I never saw anyone point a gun at a man and make him go in. I never heard of anyone being forced to go to a place to have some fun. I have read in the newspapers, though, of bank cashiers being put in cars, with pistols stuck in their slats, and taken to the bank, where they had to open the vault for the fellow with the gun. It really looks like taking a drink was worse than robbing a bank. Maybe I'm wrong. Maybe it is." It was now one of his boasts: he did not rob banks as common gangsters did. That, he knew, was a sure way to bring down the full wrath of the federal government on his operation. In closing, he explained, "People come here from out of town, and they expect when they're traveling around, having a good time, that they will take a little drink, or maybe go to a night club. They had better not get caught at it, because if they are—in the jug and see the judge the next morning." With those words, the impromptu press conference concluded, and he returned to the Lexington Hotel, having finally generated some favorable ink for himself.

• • •

Capone's penchant for publicity drew the attention of Ness and a small group of agents, who staked out the Lexington, looking for trouble. They found it when they ran into a minor hoodlum named Frankie Frost, who led the agents on a wild car chase through the streets of Chicago. Ness and his men did manage to capture Frost, but even when he was subjected to intensive grilling and, one suspects, physical abuse, Frost refused to divulge anything of Capone's operation. The episode suggested the futility of Ness's quest, for now that Capone himself was back in Chicago, no one dared talk to an honest cop; it was just too dangerous. "Acquiring the poise which comes with power, Capone had become even more dangerous," Ness was forced to admit, and he proceeded to echo what so many other of Capone's antagonists had come to realize: "Together with his ruthlessness, he had the quality of a great businessman. Under that patent leather hair he had sound judgment, diplomatic shrewdness and the diamond-hard nerves of a gambler, all balanced by cold common sense."

Although Ness endowed Capone with superhuman attributes, Capone, for his part, took little notice of the young agent. Only in Ness's recollections does the racketeer appear to be aware of Ness's existence. If Capone loomed as the ultimate villain in Ness's mind, Ness was, at most, an annoyance to Capone. Befitting his lowly status, Ness never received an invitation to sit down with Capone in the big suite at the Lexington Hotel, never had a chance to confront him directly. Ness kept expecting his adversary to behave like a gangster and make large, crude moves; instead, Capone behaved more like a businessman—insulated and subtle.

Unable to penetrate Capone's stronghold at the Lexington, Ness decided to shift tactics. If he could not get to Capone, he would attempt to cripple his breweries. Relying on information gathered through wiretaps, Ness and his men planned a large-scale raid using a ten-ton truck outfitted with a battering ram. On the night of June 13, they drove their ungainly truck to a suspected Capone brewery at 2108 South Wabash Avenue. As Ness rode shotgun, the truck smashed through the doors. The agents jumped down from the truck, arrested five men, and spilled as much bootleg beer as they could. Soon after, they employed their battering ram truck to shut down another Capone brew-ery. It appeared that Ness had finally found a reliable way to thwart Capone, and he planned a new series of raids.

Then, nothing. Ness raided what promised to be a functioning brewery, only to find a deserted warehouse. He tried again, relying on what seemed to be reliable information supplied by the wiretaps, only to face another "dry hole." In time he began to suspect that if he could tap Capone's phone lines, Capone (or his lieutenants) might be doing the same to him. For once, Ness guessed correctly. As nimble as ever, the Capone organization had lately begun to bribe telephone and electrical workers, who obligingly installed sophisticated taps on the agents' phone lines. Through them, the organiza-tion had been receiving advance warning of the raids and had shut down the breweries before Ness appeared. Thus Capone had contrived to beat Ness at his own game.

Soon after, the Capone organization dispatched a young man known as the Kid to have a chat with Ness. (He was not Tim Sullivan, the caddie whom Capone called "the Kid.") This was a clever choice for a go-between, because Ness had previously used the Kid as an informer and was inclined to believe the Kid's information. On this occasion, the Kid sauntered into Ness's office in the Transportation Building. As they began to talk, Ness revealed his frustration with the unsuccessful raids on the Capone breweries. The Kid explained that since Al had returned to Chicago, the word had spread that anyone who tipped him off to a raid would receive a $500 reward. As Ness absorbed this piece of information, the Kid produced a large enve-lope and gingerly placed it on Ness's desk, apologizing as he did so. Ness opened the envelope, and, as he expected, found money—a pair of crisp new thousand-dollar bills, to be exact. "They said that if you take it easy, you'll get the same amount—two thousand dollars—each and every week," the Kid informed him.

Incensed, Ness shoved the envelope and its contents into the Kid's pocket so roughly that the young man feared Ness was about to hit him. In his reconstruction of events, Ness told the Kid, "Listen, and don't let me ever have to repeat it: I may only be a poor baker's son, but I don't need this kind of money. Now you go back and tell those rats what I said—and be damn sure you give them back every penny or so help me I'll break you in half." Perhaps Ness was not quite so bold and eloquent in reality, but in any event he refused the bribe. Still, the attempt forced him to realize anew how difficult it would be for him, or for *anyone*, to subdue Al Capone.

As he left work that evening, Ness, already profoundly disturbed by the day's events, experienced one final humiliation: his car had been stolen. He believed he knew who was responsible.

·   ·   ·

Although Al Capone had rather easily outwitted Eliot Ness, the racketeer was still unable to resume business as usual. Other law enforcement officers who were considerably more seasoned and effective assailed every corner of his empire.

In Miami Beach, police arrested "Machine Gun" Jack McGurn. The irrepressible triggerman had unwisely called attention to himself by emptying a machine gun into cans of soda pop floating in the bay behind the Capone estate. Shortly afterward, a sheriff's posse equipped with a search warrant raided Capone's Palm Island estate, seizing whiskey and champagne and arresting two of Capone's young brothers, John and Albert, as well as four Capone employees, including his Cicero operative, Louis Cowan.

Meanwhile, in Chicago, Ralph was about to stand trial for income tax evasion. And on March 23 a federal grand jury indicted yet another Capone aide for income tax evasion. He was Frank Nitti, the so-called "Enforcer" who had assisted Jack Guzik in running the Capone organization during the ten months Al had spent in jail. Like the charges against Ralph Capone, the Nitti indictment came about as a result of Nels Tessem's unequaled talent for snooping through financial records. Once again, Tessem began with a single piece of evidence, in this instance a check for $1,000, endorsed by Frank Nitti. Although the check had been cashed at the Schiff Trust and Savings Bank, that institution strenuously disclaimed any knowledge of Nitti. Undeterred, Tessem audited the bank's books for the day on which the check had been cashed and discovered that they were exactly $1,000 short. "Who told you about this?" asked Bruno Schiff, the president of the bank. "No one," said Tessem. Realizing the game was up, Schiff admitted that Nitti had indeed banked with Schiff Trust. As he produced a secret ledger of all the Nitti deposits, Schiff explained that Nitti had insisted on keeping his transactions off the books.

Tessem now had his evidence of Nitti's concealed income. In the end, Nitti had proved to be smarter than Ralph in his financial dealings, but not smart enough to elude Special Agent Tessem's scrutiny. According to the indictment, Nitti owed nearly $160,000 in back taxes on an unreported income of $742,887.81 for the years 1925 through 1927. Nitti immediately went into hiding, but it was plain that he would have to give himself up soon to face charges, just as Ralph was about to do.

With both Ralph Capone and Frank Nitti indictments to his credit, Tessem turned his attention to the most important financial partner, Jack Guzik. Familiar with how the racketeers attempted to conceal their money, Tessem made short work of turning up Jack Guzik's aliases, but he was baffled when he learned of a new wrinkle Guzik had added. Instead of making his withdrawals in cash, Guzik received cashiers' checks, and these had been prepared by a Fred Ries. This was no alias; Ries was in fact a cashier employed at one of the Capone gambling dens, and he frequently made both deposits and withdrawals for Guzik. Of all the leads Tessem had uncovered, Ries seemed the most tantalizing, the most likely to lead to Al Capone himself. Tessem turned over his findings to Frank Wilson of the IRS, who continued to scour financial records in search of Al Capone's income. Tiring of his cramped office, Wilson took it upon himself to track down Ries, only to discover that the cashier had inexplicably disappeared. It was vital to find him, for the government's case against Capone hung in the balance.

Finally, in Washington, D.C., the White House was focusing on Capone with renewed vigor provoked by the outburst of publicity surrounding his release from jail. Johnson's boss, G. A. Youngquist, the assistant attorney general, began pressuring George E. Q. Johnson to resume his tax evasion case against the racketeer. Johnson didn't need to be told; he had been pursuing the matter all along, but nothing would be worse than getting Capone all the way to trial only to see the racketeer acquitted. To gather sufficient evidence to obtain a conviction would take time. This was Al Capone they were dealing with after all, not his clumsy brother Ralph, and Al knew enough not to leave any fingerprints on his financial dealings. On the last day of March, Youngquist reported to the White House: "In reference to Al Capone, I called up Johnson in Chicago and got in touch with the Internal and Prohibition bureaus here, and asked that they start immediately, both of them, to see what they could find. . . . There is a possible prospect of getting a tax evasion indictment against him, but they haven't got enough yet. He is very clever. He is three or four times removed from the actual operation. There is just one small item. That is some money transmitted to him by telegraph in Florida in 1928, but even that was transmitted to some-one else down there for him."

Although Capone continued to elude an indictment for tax evasion, other, more subtle challenges to his economic power loomed. America was enter-ing an era of wrenching social disruption. Capone had gone to jail at the end of the Roaring Twenties and come out at the beginning of the Great De-pression; in his ten-month absence, society had changed drastically. During the next four years, the aggregate value of all goods and services produced each year in the United States would decline from approximately $104 billion to $56 billion. In Iowa, for example, the price of wheat plummeted to eight cents a bushel, and a severe, prolonged drought dealt an additional blow to the farm economy. The economic collapse dealt a devastating blow to millions of Americans. Families broke up and a ghostly army of vaga-bonds, hoboes, and drifters roamed across the country in a futile search for work, a meal, a chance, anything. A popular song of the day, "Brother, Can You Spare a Dime?" evoked the bleak fellowship of sudden impoverishment, a sense of hopelessness and dread growing in the hearts of Americans. "What was this gray lipless shape of fear that stalked their lives incessantly—that was everywhere, legible in the faces, the movements and the driven frenzied glances of the people who warmed on the streets," asked Thomas Wolfe, in his 1935 novel, *Of Time and the River*. "What was this thing that duped men out of joy, tricked them out of all the exultant and triumphant music of the world, drove them at length into the dusty earth, cheated, defrauded, tricked out of a life by a nameless phantom, with all their glory wasted?" For millions of unemployed, disillusioned Americans, the unavoidable answer was the Depression.

Chicago's corrupt and incompetent politicians left the city especially vul-nerable to economic disaster. A task force investigating the financial crisis reported, "Mismanagement by Mayor Big Bill Thompson and his friends, and lethargy on the part of the public have reduced Chicago to bankruptcy." The chairman of the group, Silas Strawn, offered no hope of a recovery. "I'm at my wit's end," he said. "This is the most serious situation ever confronting an American city—and everybody stays asleep." The lack of money meant that schoolteachers, policemen, and firemen could no longer be paid. Thou-sands dropped from the city's payroll into unemployment. Hundreds of vagabonds filled its parks each night.

At the same time, the newspapers estimated the wealth of the recently freed Al Capone to hover around the $40-million mark, and they claimed racketeering cost Chicago $150 million a year in uncollected taxes and lost business, but Capone himself found little consolation in these statistics when he confronted evidence of the toll the Depression was taking. A few days after his return to Chicago, he visited Burnham, the suburb whose government he controlled, and where he had spent so many carefree afternoons playing golf with his pals. In all of Burnham, he discovered, only three people (excluding those employed by City Hall) still held their jobs; one was the milkman, the other was the mailman, and the third was the schoolteacher, and she was getting paid only one month for every three she worked. When he checked up on the Sullivan family, he discovered that Tim, his former caddie and boxing protégé, earned a few pennies shining shoes, Mrs. Sullivan toiled as a scrubwoman, and Babe, Al's former girlfriend, had vanished along with the jewelry he had lavished on her. "We practically lived on the three-day-old bread dad brought home from a bakery," Timothy recalled.

As for Capone, he himself appeared to be unusually depressed. "He looked worn and tired," in Timothy's words. "All he could talk about was how the government was trying to destroy him." No longer was he greeted as a popular Robin Hood figure; the workingman cared little whether Capone was "legitimate" or "illegitimate." His picture beaming from the cover of *Time* magazine, Capone appeared to be another tycoon exploiting the masses. Conditioned by his months of confinement, he remained oblivious to the Depression and obsessed with his own predicament. "I'm sick of being shot at, sick of being trailed around by a bunch of hyenas watching for a chance to kill me," he complained. "If I go to a race track or drop out to see the greyhounds run, I don't know whether I'll get back alive. If I step into a joint to buy a pack of cigarettes it's even money I get a load of buckshot instead. Do you think I'd be fool enough to read a paper by a window in my own home? If I did, the chances are I'd be dead before I had time to glance over the headlines."

Giving voice to concerns on which he had brooded for countless hours in jail, Capone lashed out at the press, in particular. "I've been accused of all the murders that have happened in Chicago in the last ten years," he complained. As a result, people have "got me pegged for one of these bloodthirsty monsters you read about in story books—the kind that tortures his victims, cuts off their ears, puts out their eyes with a red-hot poker, and grins while he's doing it. Now get me right—I'm no angel. I'm not posing as a model for youth. I've had to do a lot of things I don't like to do. But I'm not as black as I'm painted. I'm human. I've got a heart in me. I'll go as deep in my pocket as any man to help any guy that needs help. I can't stand to see anybody hungry or cold or helpless. Many a poor family in Chicago thinks I'm Santa Claus. If I've given a cent to the poor in this man's town, I'll bet I've given a million dollars. Yes, a million."

He emphasized one facet of his character calculated to appeal to the public: Al Capone, the devoted family man. "Ask my wife about my private life," he challenged the press. "I live like any other businessman. Home every evening for dinner. Then smoking jacket, slippers, an easy chair, and a good cigar. I don't chase around with women. And I'm not much of a drinker. . . . I'm nuts about music. Music makes me forget I'm Al Capone and lifts me up until I think I'm only a block or two from heaven. With me, grand opera is the berries." But when a reporter asked him why, if life as a racketeer was so dangerous and loathsome, Capone did not simply retire, as he frequently promised in years gone by, Al replied from bitter experience: "Once in the racket, you're in it for life. Your past holds you in it. The gang won't let you out. And me settle down? Don't make me laugh. If I did, I'd get mine so quick at the end of sawed-off shotgun it would be nobody's business. . . . Murder, murder—that's all this racket means. I'm sick of it. I'd give half my fortune to get out of it. If I could go to Florida and live quietly with my family for the rest of my days, I'd be the happiest man alive."

• • •

The trial of Ralph Capone for income tax evasion commenced on April 9, three weeks after Al's release from prison. The name of the presiding judge had become all too familiar to the Capones: the Honorable James H. Wilkerson of the U.S. District Court. Although George E. Q. Johnson, who masterminded the government's case, did not advertise it as such, the trial was intended as a test case for Ralph's younger brother Al, who was yet to be indicted. As such, it proved eminently successful, at least from Johnson's perspective. The trial took just two weeks, during which the government prosecutors efficiently presented their evidence that Capone had failed to file income tax returns for the years 1922 to 1925. They also had the benefit of Nels Tessem's damning analysis of Ralph's financial misdealing at the Pinkert State Bank in Cicero. The four-foot stack of Ralph's bank records uncovered by Tessem was so heavy that it had to be wheeled into court on a cart. In the face of the overwhelming evidence against him, Ralph was forced to admit that he had opened accounts under assumed names, but he tried to excuse his behavior on the grounds that it was a necessary procedure for a gambler to follow. And, by the way, he said, he was no bootlegger. He did admit that he was related to a certain Al Capone, also known as "Scarface," "Snorky," and the "Big Fellow," but he could not say how Al earned his money. If the government wanted to know, they would have to ask Al himself about it.

Despite Ralph's obvious lies and evasions, the government prosecutors pressed their case. In the courtroom, the technical, nonviolent, noninflammatory nature of the charges proved an asset. The prosecution did not accuse him of being a gangster, a bootlegger, a gambler, or even a pimp; instead, the government focused narrowly on the nonpayment of federal income tax. There were no shades of gray in this area; either he had paid or he had not—and evidence of the latter was overwhelming. The government was betting that tax evasion would prove to be a convictable offense in Chicago, unlike murder or Prohibition violations. Experience had shown that jurors involved in a murder trial feared revenge, often with good reason. Nor was violating the Prohibition laws a convictable charge, for jurors tended to sneer at Prohibition. It was a smart, if unspectacular strategy to stick with the noncontroversial tax evasion charge. The case was sent to the jury on April 26, and after two and a half hours of deliberation and six ballots, they returned a guilty verdict on all counts. Ralph now faced a total of twenty-two years in prison and a fine of up to $40,000. "I don't understand this at all," he grumbled, and that may have been the one truthful remark he made during the entire proceeding.

Although convicted, Ralph was not led from the bar in manacles to begin serving time—at least not yet. His lawyers initiated a series of time-consuming appeals, and until they were resolved, he retained his freedom. He was forced to endure one more public humiliation, however. At the conclusion of the trial, Al threw a small, subdued party for Ralph, taking the occasion to deliver a stinging rebuke to his older brother. "You got caught because you weren't smart," Al said. "You talked too much and you put too many things in writing. You gotta be smart, Ralph, and I hope you will be when you get out." Al had good reason to be concerned, for he was acutely aware that Ralph's trial was merely a rehearsal for his own, and if the government could produce a four-foot-high pile of evidence against Ralph, how much more would they be able amass against the "Big Fellow" himself?

Despite its enormous implications for Al Capone and all other racketeers, the outcome of Ralph's trial rated only cursory mention in newspapers out-side Chicago, and public reaction to the verdict was muted. However, the conviction did send shock waves through Chicago's racketeering fraternity. Bootleggers, extortionists, and gamblers of every description hastened to the Federal Building, where they waited in line to pay whatever back taxes the IRS said they owed. By May, George E. Q. Johnson reported that the government had received more than a million dollars from the delinquent hoodlums of Chicago, but that amount was only a fraction of what they actually owed.

One other party taking a keen interest in the outcome of Ralph's tax evasion case was President Hoover, who continued to oversee the effort to put not just Ralph but Al Capone behind bars. The guilty verdict prompted Elmer Irey's IRS Intelligence Unit to redouble its efforts to obtain evidence against the "Big Fellow," evidence that proved maddeningly elusive. Two days after the end of the trial, Arthur Madden, the Intelligence Unit's Chi-cago field man, was forced to concede to his boss, "There is nothing of much interest in connection with Al Capone." But he did report a few leads, whose significance was not yet apparent. "I have no doubt that Al Capone and his associates received substantial income from the dog race track operated near

Cicero," Madden noted. "As a matter of fact, there is fairly convincing proof that substantial sums were paid to Frank Nitto," that is, Nitti, now under indictment, "who is one of the principals in the Capone organization. One of the banks involved in these transactions has apparently been very obstinate or fearful, or both. I think that some of the bank's officers and employees will have to be thoroughly examined by the Grand Jury before the facts can be brought out." The most telling section of Madden's report concerned an effort by a lawyer Capone had just hired, Lawrence Mattingly, to settle Al's tax obligations. "Mr. Mattingly has called at the office of the Internal Revenue Agent in Charge on several occasions. He has another appointment this afternoon. Evidently he wants to reach a settlement, but the indications are that he desires to accomplish it in a way that would prevent the prosecution of his client." In other words, unlike the treatment accorded every other racketeer at the time, Johnson *refused* Al Capone's offer to pay up; indeed, the government would later portray Mattingly's efforts on behalf of his client as evidence of Capone's guilt. There was only one reason that Johnson singled out Capone for this treatment: the government, and that meant everyone from the president down, was determined to convict Al Capone—if only they could find the evidence.

• • •

Reeling from Ralph's conviction for income tax evasion, Al Capone was dealt a fresh blow from an unlikely opponent: Frank J. Loesch, the seventy-eight-year-old head of the Chicago Crime Commission. From Capone's perspective, Loesch was a toothless dragon backed by a bunch of rich gin-swilling hypocrites whose campaign against racketeers carried distinct overtones of racial and ethnic prejudice. "The American people are not a lawless people," Loesch had recently stated in an address at Princeton University on March 22, 1930. "It's the foreigners and the first generation of Americans who are loaded on us." His audience knew exactly whom he meant—those Italians, Jews, Poles, and Irish—and Loesch took some heat for his remarks, but he refused to back down. Pressed for an explanation, he insisted, "The real Americans are not gangsters. Recent immigrants and the first generation of Jews and Italians are the chief offenders, with the Jews furnishing the brains and the Italians the brawn." (It is worth noting that Loesch himself was a first generation American, the son of German immigrants.)

On his return to Chicago, Loesch decided to take matters into his own hands, not by resorting to violence or instituting legal action against Capone but by launching a program to stigmatize Capone and others. His idea was a simple one, but it worked better than Loesch could have imagined, so well, in fact, that it continues to this day. "I had the operating director [of the Chicago Crime Commission] bring before me a list of the outstanding hoodlums, known murderers, murderers which you and I know but can't prove, and there were about one hundred of them, and out of that list I selected twenty-eight men," said Loesch. "I put Al Capone at the head and his brother [Ralph] next, and I ran down the twenty-eight, every man being really an outlaw. I called them Public Enemies, and so designated them in my letter, sent to the Chief of Police, the Sheriff, every law enforcing officer." The primary object of Loesch's ire was of course Al Capone—"not that I hold Capone responsible for all the crime in Chicago, by no means, but he is head and shoulders in the matter."

Ranking the Public Enemies in declining order of significance, Loesch's list had its share of lacunae and distortions. For instance, he neglected to include the boys from Chicago Heights, and to ignore Chicago Heights was to ignore the innermost circle of racketeering in Chicago and throughout the Midwest. At the same time, he attributed undue significance to comparatively minor figures. Despite these flaws, the list did present a fairly comprehensive *Who's Who* of the underworld. Among the public enemies, in the order Loesch ranked them, were:

Alphonse Capone	Edward "Spike" O'Donnell
Ralph Capone	Joe "Polack Joe" Saltis
Frank Rio	Myles O'Donnell
Jack McGurn	Frankie Lake
Jack Guzick	Terry Druggan
George "Bugs" Moran	William "Klondike" O'Donnell
Joe Aiello	James "Fur" Sammons

"The purpose," Loesch said in a letter explaining his list, "is to keep the light of publicity shining on Chicago's most prominent, well-known, and notorious gangsters to the end that they may be under constant observation by the law enforcing authorities and law-abiding citizens." Even as he stigmatized the gangsters, Loesch challenged the police and everyone else concerned to discharge what he insisted was their civic duty. Had Loesch been even more forthright, he would have placed Mayor "Big Bill" Thompson at or near the top of the list; had he possessed a larger historical vision, he would have cited Prohibition, on which all the Public Enemies thrived.

Although Loesch's Public Enemies List covered only Chicago and ignored racketeers of equal or possibly even greater menace in cities such as New York and Kansas City, its significance extended far beyond the borders of Cook County. On April 24, the *Chicago Tribune* announced the list in an eight-column front-page headline, and it was reproduced in newspapers across the country. Suddenly Chicago's racketeering elite found itself exposed to unprecedented scrutiny—none more than Al Capone. At a stroke, Loesch had defined Capone in the boldest possible outlines. Until this time, the public's impression of Capone was fuzzy, constantly shifting. He was known as the man who might have engineered the St. Valentine's Day Massacre, but then again, he might not have been involved. He was held responsible for the murder of William McSwiggin, a corrupt young prosecutor, but no one could say for certain what his role in McSwiggin's death had been. Although everyone knew Al Capone the bootlegger, few realized he was also a pimp. Now, courtesy of Frank J. Loesch, everyone knew exactly who Capone was: Public Enemy Number 1.

The label struck a chord in a nation racked by the Depression, and Capone now became the scapegoat for all sorts of social ills. No longer was he indulged as a symptom of these ills; he was now perceived as the *cause.* Thanks to Loesch's publicity stunt, Al Capone became the first great American criminal of the twentieth century, and as befits a modern criminal, he was an organization man, not a highway robber or lone killer, but a racketeer, the leader of an illegal fraternity. Conventional wisdom decreed that he and his organization had corrupted society as a whole, and the corruption was spreading fast. As Public Enemy Number 1, Capone redefined the concept of the criminal and by extension crime in the popular mind. Before Capone and the Prohibition era, the public and law enforcement agents clung to notions of criminals—their motives, their personalities—dating back to the previous century. Criminals, it was believed, chose to be evil; indeed, they relished their wickedness, their depravity, and cruelty. And they were loners, outcasts. In the 1920s, however, criminals such as Capone entered the mainstream of society, acquiring vast economic power. They espoused bourgeois values, built homes, took care of their families, tried to teach their children the difference between right and wrong. Some, like Capone, hoped to rise above their line of work. They were not necessarily evil, wicked, or depraved (though some were); they became Public Enemies because they were in an illegal line of work. Their organizations mimicked the customs and structure of conventional businesses. They practiced a rudimentary form of charity. They could deliver social services to people with no access to the legitimate political system. Their very success in business and with their constituents made them menaces, Public Enemies.

Other law enforcement luminaries were quick to echo Loesch's brilliant public relations ploy. In Chicago, Robert Isham Randolph, "The Colonel," as he insisted on being called, wrote a sizzling condemnation of Capone for *Collier's* magazine. At the time Randolph was the head of the Secret Six, a group of some of the richest men in Chicago, including Julius Rosenwald, the president of Sears, Roebuck, and Samuel Insull, soon to be revealed as a racketeer in his own sphere, public utility companies. Their idea was to purge Chicago of its gangsters and thereby improve business conditions, especially for themselves. To this end they gave several hundred thousand dollars to the Chicago Crime Commission, and they even donated $75,000 to Elmer Irey to assist the work of the Intelligence Unit of the IRS.

In his article, Randolph warned of the danger of Al Capone's becoming a model for the nation's underprivileged—that is, immigrant—youth. "To an energetic youngster, born into a civilization that provides him with insufficient playgrounds, gangster life has a natural if disastrous lure. He cannot be relied upon to see through the pretense of Al Capone, master of brothels, posing as a hero. He may only feel the infantile thrill of carrying a gun—playing cowboy—and so blunder into a gang and take up its tragic career as his own. Such a boy meets the poor, weak-brained harlots who serve the gangs and who heap admiration upon youths who wear pistols." Isham's warning ended on an especially contemporary note. "He learns to use drugs to bolster up his courage for assassination assignments and, as like as not, winds up, face down, on some lonely suburban road, 'taken for a ride.' "

Another member of the Chicago Crime Commission, Henry Barrett Chamberlin, used the radio to spread his anti-Capone propaganda. In a broadcast devoted to the subject of organized crime, he tried to whip up public frenzy against the great menace they faced. "Capone is the most dangerous, the most resourceful, the most cruel, the most menacing, the most conscienceless of any criminal of modern times. He has contributed more to besmirch the fair name of Chicago than any man living or dead," he declared. "Beginning as a little ruffian in Brooklyn, by stages, through pandering, traffic in women, and murder, he has reached a place never before occupied by any kind in this country." Even as he portrayed Capone as an omnipotent monster, Barrett tried to assure his listeners that law enforcement authorities were equal to the task of bringing Public Enemy Number 1 to justice. "This lone gorilla of gangland is being cornered. . . . The end is certain; his notoriety, for a time the secret of his strength, promises to be the instrument of his undoing."

Adding his voice to the chorus of condemnation, Billy Sunday, the Evangelist advocate of Prohibition, rented a theater in the Loop where he preached against Al Capone every day for a week. "I'm going to Chicago to do my level best to give Al Capone and his gang of cutthroats the hot end of the poker," he said. "The agencies for good that are at work in Chicago aren't going to be the goat much longer, and if I can be of any help in their battle against Old Man Devil and his crowd I'll stand up and preach him out of Chicago or drop in my tracks in the effort."

In Washington, D.C., President Hoover lent the prestige of his office to this new campaign against Capone by inviting reporters to attend an off-the-record conversation in which he explained that the federal government had already gotten Ralph Capone, and it was only a matter of time until they were able to "reach" his younger brother Alphonse. At the FBI, J. Edgar Hoover also took note of the Public Enemies List. Always jealous of publicity, he adapted Loesch's list into an FBI register of the nation's "Most Wanted" criminals, to be updated as circumstances dictated. In time, the concept of a Public Enemies List became so closely identified with the FBI and Hoover that Loesch's role as the originator of the concept was all but forgotten.

· · ·

On April 20, three days before the Public Enemies List appeared, Al Capone took a train from Chicago to Miami, where he once again tried to disappear into the quiet routine of domestic life at his Palm Island villa. He had been out of prison for over a month by this time; always fearful that other gangsters were planning to assassinate him, Capone wanted to disappear behind the walls of his retreat even sooner, but several weeks earlier the governor of Florida had announced that Capone would be expelled if he set foot in the state. Capone responded to the challenge by hiring two of Miami's leading attorneys, J. F. Gordon and Vincent C. Giblin, who maintained that their client was entitled to enter Florida because he owned a home there. As soon as Capone's lawyers persuaded a federal judge to grant an injunction preventing the sheriffs from "seizing, arresting, kidnapping and abusing" their client, the racketeer boarded a train for Miami Beach. On arrival he held yet another press conference in which he emphasized his intention of living peacefully. "I am here for a rest which I think I deserve," he said in language obviously chosen for him by his lawyers. "All I wish is to be left alone and enjoy the home which I have purchased here." He even claimed to have worked out his income tax problems with the federal government, but he was deceiving himself on that issue. In Chicago, Johnson's office pursued the matter with increasing vigor while avoiding all publicity.

Reunited with his family at last, Capone amused himself by taking his son on boat rides across Biscayne Bay, beholding azure vistas denied him during the long months in jail. But the holiday was cut short once the list of Chicago's Public Enemies hit the newspapers. He quickly discovered that going through life as Public Enemy Number 1 was going to be difficult and humiliating—exactly as Loesch and the Chicago Crime Commission had intended. Other than the Philadelphia escapade, the racketeer had yet to be convicted of anything—had yet, in fact, to be *indicted*—but wherever he went he was treated as if he had already been pronounced guilty of heinous crimes and had no business going forth in society. Bowing to public pressure, the city of Miami announced that Public Enemy Number 1 would be subject to arrest on charges of vagrancy whenever he set foot outside the door of his home. And the city managers kept their promise. Police followed Public Enemy Number 1 wherever he went, and they arrested him whenever they could. He was locked up not once but twice in the same week. On both occasions he was freed on a writ of habeas corpus after spending the night in jail.

During May, Public Enemy Number 1 was in and out of court on at least three occasions as he found to his dismay that bearing the label "Public Enemy" became a self-fulfilling prophecy. In years past, he had successfully eluded the bullets of rival gangsters, but he was not equal to the war of words that had been declared against him. House-bound on Palm Island, he became listless, moody, withdrawn; he seemed to be passing through life as if he were a ghost, and perhaps he was; he could live with being Al Capone, no matter what they said about him, but being Public Enemy Number 1 was unendurable. Beneath the brooding, he was furious. Why, they didn't understand the first thing about him, these hypocritical gentlemen of the Chicago Crime Commission. Men like them paid him for booze on Saturday and condemned him on Sunday. In his own mind, Capone saw himself as a hero to his people, and he had endeavored to play that part since the days he ran with the Navy Street boys in Brooklyn. Now they called him a supercriminal, Public Enemy Number 1. The label was overwhelming, it was insulting, and there was nothing he could do about it.

Although Capone lived quietly in Miami Beach during the spring and early summer of 1930, his every action became newsworthy—reported and dissected in newspapers in the United States and England. Everything he did acquired sinister overtones. If he stayed indoors, he was holding secret meetings; if he went shopping, it was to distract attention from his nefarious activities. If he belched, the roar was reminiscent of machine guns. When he flew to Cuba for the day, the local newspapers warned against the possibility that he would turn Havana into another Chicago. Each day the Chicago newspapers gleefully described the legal net inexorably tightening around Public Enemy Number 1.

FLORIDA SUES TO OUST CAPONE; FIGHT HIM HERE

CAPONE DENIED WRIT TO STOP MIAMI ARRESTS

MIAMI JURORS HINT CAPONE IS A BAD INFLUENCE

CAPONE SEIZED IN MIAMI

MIAMI POLICE ARREST CAPONE FOR THIRD TIME

AL CAPONE ARRESTED AGAIN; FACES TWO PERJURY CHARGES

SET AL CAPONE'S MIAMI PERJURY TRIAL FOR JULY 8

CAPONE HIRES LAWYERS AS U.S. PROBES INCOME

LAWYERS CALL CAPONE'S MIAMI TRIAL "FRAMEUP"

CAPONE EAGER TO QUIT MIAMI AND COME HOME

Then, just as the law appeared to be closing in on Public Enemy Number 1, he escaped, at least temporarily. On the advice of his lawyers, he boldly charged S. D. McCreary, the safety director of Miami, with false arrest, and on May 27 Public Enemy Number 1 appeared in court—not as a defendant but as a plaintiff. He had come to testify against his tormentor.

Public Enemy Number 1 told the court, "I saw Mr. McCreary at the [police] station when they tried to take my valuables. I asked them for a receipt and they said that they didn't give them. Mr. McCreary said, 'Take them off of him and throw him in the jail.' They placed me in one cell . . . and a little later they changed me to a cell that had no air. . . . He left word that I was to have nothing to eat or drink. He told me this in front of three witnesses. He tried to make me miserable. I was not allowed to use the telephone or send out word. They also had orders not to give me blankets," he added, eliciting laughter. (It later emerged that McCreary had thrown Capone's valuables, including more than a thousand dollars, his watch, and other personal items, into a toilet.)

"What did they charge you with?" asked Warren L. Newcomb, a justice of the peace who was acting as judge and, when the mood came over him, as jury.

"Nothing at all," Public Enemy Number 1 shot back.

The following day, the city commissioner, John C. Knight, took the stand; Public Enemy Number 1 had charged him as well as several other city officials with conspiracy to arrest him. On this occasion, Justice Newcomb asked most of the questions, and, in the process, demonstrated that he was not going to permit the plaintiff to be arrested time and again without a warrant just because the newspapers had taken to calling him Public Enemy Number 1. In one charged exchange, Knight explained that he considered the plaintiff a "menace to the community" based on information in newspaper and magazine accounts. At this point, Justice Newcomb subjected the commissioner to a humiliating catechism.

"Do you believe in the Constitution of the United States?" Newcomb inquired.

"Yes, sir."

"You believe it should not be violated?"

"Yes."

"You believe that unless you can place a specific charge against a man he should not be arrested?"

"My feeling about that, Mr. Newcomb, is that if a man has leprosy it thereby creates a menace to the community."

"Where would you suggest this man live?" asked one of Capone's lawyers.

"I don't know," Knight said.

"He is an American citizen, isn't he?"

"I cannot answer that question."

"He has as much right to walk the streets of Miami as you have."

"I cannot tell you."

"Do you believe in mob rule?" asked Justice Newcomb.

"No, sir."

"Do you believe in the law taking its course?"

"Yes, sir."

In that case, Newcomb lectured, "You don't believe that Capone should be arrested and placed in jail incommunicado at any time without having a specific charge against him."

The following day, Public Enemy Number 1 was vindicated when the city manager rescinded the order to arrest the racketeer on sight. To ensure that Capone was not harassed again, Justice Newcomb declared him a "state witness" and warned that anyone who interfered with him would have to answer the consequences. Finally, McCreary was ordered to pay court costs. With that, Capone won a small but significant victory and was able to keep the police at bay in Miami if nowhere else. In the morning, Capone beheld a headline calculated to make him grin, for once: "PEACE JUSTICE MOVES TO AID OF 'CITIZEN AL'."

Within days, the state of Florida attempted to oust Capone by padlocking the Palm Island villa because it was a "public nuisance." Again, Capone made a point to appear in court throughout the hearings, attracting attention if only because of his clothing. "During the five days of the court proceedings," the *Chicago Tribune* noted, "he has worn five entirely different outfits, with motifs of white, tan, blue, green, and gray, respectively." On this occasion Circuit Judge Paul D. Barns ruled that the state of Florida could not carry out its plan because "the only cause of annoyance is the mere presence of Al Capone upon the premises." So Capone the colorful won this case, too, and kept his house open.

The city of Miami immediately retaliated by issuing a warrant for his arrest, with which he was served even before he arrived home to celebrate this latest victory. In this instance, he was accused of perjury. S. D. Mc-Creary, the safety director who, Capone said, prevented him from calling his lawyer and confined him to a cell without blankets, charged that Public Enemy Number 1 was a bold-faced liar. No one paid attention to McCreary's claim, and by now the pattern was clear. The Miami law enforcement authorities would not be able to force Capone to leave their city. It was not supposed to end this way, with Capone hobbling the local law enforcement authorities and a judge lecturing everyone about Capone's constitutional rights, but that is exactly what happened. Again and again he had demonstrated his resourcefulness in the courts.

At the moment of victory, Capone suddenly alienated his lawyer, Vincent Giblin, who had sent Capone a bill for $50,000. This was a lot of money, but not in light of the value of the freedom and peace of mind Giblin had been able to win for Capone. Nonetheless, he refused to honor the debt. Normally, Capone paid substantial fees without complaint to lawyers, doctors, and other professionals. Perhaps on this occasion he failed to understand what Giblin had done to deserve such a large fee; perhaps he simply did not have enough money on hand. In any event, Giblin would not put up with this kind of treatment from Al Capone or anyone else, and one day he simply arrived at the Palm Island villa without warning, rushed over to Capone, and, clutching the racketeer by the shirt, said that if he were not paid that instant he would bash in Al's face. Amazed and, for once, intimidated, Capone reluctantly led the lawyer up to the master bedroom, where Capone stashed his cash in the chest at the foot of the bed. He opened the chest, scooped out a handful of bills, and handed them to Giblin. When he later counted the money, the lawyer realized he had still not been paid in full, and he sued Capone for the rest of the fee.

As a result of this episode, Capone lost the best lawyer he had ever had. Without the benefit of Giblin's vigorous protection, he was vulnerable once again. Since his appointment as a U.S. attorney for Chicago two years earlier, George E. Q. Johnson had devoted his best efforts to assembling a case against Al Capone. During that time, the investigation had grown to include the FBI, the IRS, the Secret Six, the Chicago Crime Commission, and even President Hoover. Despite the countless man hours these agencies had devoted to the cause and the reams of newsprint their efforts had generated, they had come up with next to nothing with which to indict Al Capone. It was true they had gotten Ralph Capone convicted of tax evasion, but Ralph Capone was not Public Enemy Number 1. In fact, neither the U.S. attorney's office in Chicago nor the IRS Intelligence Unit had been able to gather sufficient evidence against Al Capone to obtain an indictment. After two years, they were beginning to look foolish and inept. And the longer Al Capone remained free, the better he looked, stronger and bolder and entitled to his freedom now that he had endured the government's scrutiny.

That situation was permanently altered on June 9, 1930, when a shot rang out in the Chicago Loop. If not heard around the world, the shot made headlines across the country and pitched the city headlong into a new crisis. Not even the St. Valentine's Day Massacre had caused an outcry of such intensity, and the reason for all the shouting was quite simple: for the first time, the victim of a gangland slaying was not a gangster but a reporter, and in this instance the unlucky reporter happened to be Al Capone's friend and contact at the *Chicago Tribune*, Jake Lingle.

• • •

According to one tally, Chicago had been the scene of 530 gangland slayings since the start of Prohibition a decade earlier; set against this statistic was the unwritten but fervently held rule of the era that gangsters shed the blood only of other gangsters. Journalists, like women and children, were strictly hors de combat. At least they were until the afternoon of June 9, when a *Tribune* reporter was assassinated in front of hundreds of witnesses. No one doubted that it was a gangland assassination, and theories inevitably invoked the name of Al Capone. But Alfred "Jake" Lingle, police reporter, was not what he appeared. Although he worked for the *Tribune*, Jake Lingle, in fact, proved the rule that gangsters did kill only their own kind.

Until the shooting, recalls his *Tribune* colleague Walter Trohan, "Jake Lingle was known as a friend of Al Capone's. He could approach Capone and ask what he was doing. In general Lingle was known to have a lot of underworld contacts." Although Trohan and the others at the paper did not consider Lingle dishonest, "he was a ham actor, a show-off. He and another police reporter liked to put on a big act in which they borrowed a hundred or two from each other and paid it back the next day to show they were big shots. We didn't have that kind of money." Another *Tribune* reporter recalls Lingle's swagger at poker games: "He would take money out of his billfold, sometimes a pile of thousand-dollar bills. We'd ask him about this. And we all accepted his story that he had inherited a lot of money from a rich uncle." There was no rich uncle, of course. A journalist who looked into the matter discovered that Lingle inherited just $500 from his father. At the *Tribune*, Lingle made $65 a week, not a bad salary for a reporter but hardly enough to stuff a billfold.

This was Chicago during Prohibition, not the Columbia School of Journalism, and many reporters augmented their meager salaries with money acquired through job-related scams. They quickly realized how to obtain free tickets, free meals, a box of good Cuban cigars, a bottle of imported Scotch, and, on occasion, cash in return for a favorable story. For this reason, reporters got a lot of attention but little respect, especially from other reporters. The prevailing attitude was expressed in *The Front Page*, the 1928 hit play written by two celebrated graduates of Chicago newsrooms, Ben Hecht and Charles MacArthur. "Journalists!" exclaims Hildy Johnson, a character closely modeled on an actual reporter of the day, Hilding Johnson of the *Herald and Examiner*. "Peeking through keyholes! Running after fire engines like a lot of coach dogs! Waking people up in the middle of the night to ask them what they think of Mussolini. Stealing pictures from old ladies of their daughters that get raped in Oak Park. A lot of lousy, daffy, buttinskis, swelling around with holes in their pants, borrowing nickels from office boys. . . .

I don't need anybody to tell me about newspapers. I've been a newspaperman fifteen years. A cross between a bootlegger and a whore." That was a fairly accurate portrait of the real-life police reporter, Jake Lingle.

Bribery was a fact of life in certain Chicago newsrooms. When a young reporter named Vern Whaley came to Chicago "with a lot of hay on my shoulder" and landed a job as the boxing correspondent for the *Chicago Evening Post* at $45 a week, he thought he was doing well until he met a "big, tall Irishman named Jack O'Keefe" who had just read one of Whaley's boxing articles. "I want to shake your hand," he told Whaley, who recalls, "He grabbed my hand, and when I got my hand back there were five $100 bills in it. I said, 'What's it for?' " And O'Keefe said, 'I want you to buy yourself a new hat with that.' 'I could buy a haberdashery with that kind of dough,' I told him." After repeatedly experiencing this generosity, he decided he had better talk to his editor. Whaley confessed that back in Des Moines, where he worked on the *Register* for $25 a week, his superiors warned him against taking money in return for anything he wrote, but here in Chicago, "every time I write something somebody comes up and hands me a bill. And I feel guilty taking this money because I know it's wrong." In only six weeks, he had socked away over $4,000 from the bribes, and he was still a green kid from Iowa, who refused to spend it because he figured he would have to give it back when he was found out. When Whaley finished his story, his editor "looked shocked, as if he'd been hypnotized. He didn't say anything to me. He just got out of his chair, shaking his head, looked out the window at Wacker Drive and didn't say anything. Then he starts to talk, but his back's still to me, and he says, 'Well, Vern, the budget doesn't permit me to give you any more salary right now, but'—and he turns and looks me right me in the face—*'take all you can get.'* "

For Whaley, Lingle, and others like them the opportunities for corruption in Prohibition-era Chicago were endless. Soon after he switched to the *Tribune*, Whaley was invited to a sportswriters' lunch hosted by Al Capone; it was, he discovered, a standing invitation to a weekly gathering. The topic under discussion at these lunches was always the same: who would win the fights. The term for a fixed fight, he learned, was a "Barney," but not all of the fights were Barneys, though many were. And the funny thing was, Whaley says, "some of the best fights I ever saw were Barneys." Soon Whaley, like so many others, fell under Capone's spell. "The booze was good, the meal was great, and at the end, Capone himself got up and passed around this box of Havana cigars. Now those cigars must have cost a buck and a half apiece, they were great big ones, and I was smoking nickel cigars at the time. White Owls. Well, I lit up Capone's cigar and I puffed on it a couple times, and it was exotic, it was so delicious. And as I started to describe the joy of smoking that cigar, the other guys looked at me like I was crazy, and Capone sat at the end of the table, smiling. When I got up to leave, I'm still puffing on this cigar, and he says, 'Here, Vern, here's a gift.' He gave me fifty of those expensive cigars. I could never smoke a cheap cigar again for the rest of my life." Walter Trohan recalled attending another Capone soiree, this one attended by the press and politicians alike in a West Side restaurant. "People were fawning over Capone," he remembers. "They were paying court to him, delighted to go up to him and shake his hand. I got highly indignant and turned around and left, even though the drinks were free."

Although Lingle was only one of many journalists close to Capone, the reporter flaunted the connection. He wore a diamond-studded belt buckle Capone had given him, and he liked to startle his *Tribune* colleagues by claiming he was responsible for fixing the price of beer in Chicago. In reality, Lingle no more fixed the price of beer than Billy Sunday did. Although he was no bootlegger, Lingle *was* an informer, and that was a dangerous occupation in Chicago. Even worse, he had a penchant for double- and triple-crossing those close to him. Says Trohan: "Shortly before he was shot, Jake went to the city editor and wanted him to fire me because he thought I had insulted him. The point was that Jake had come to me and asked me to fix a couple of property taxes for two gals. It was a common thing, like fixing a speeding ticket. I took 'em to an assistant state's attorney, and I said, 'Jake Lingle asked me to have you take care of 'em,' and he said, 'What are they?' and I said in a wisecracking way, 'I don't know—one of Jake's rackets.' When this got back to Lingle, it made him very angry, because he was above the rackets. Or pretended to be. He was on the take, I'm sure. That's why he was so touchy about my remark, but at the time I knew nothing about it."

In addition to accepting money and favors from bootleggers, Lingle also acted as a liaison between the *Tribune* and the Chicago police. In this area he did have some real clout; in fact, he was the man who selected Chicago's next chief of police. "Our managing editor," says Trohan, "was a fine gentleman named Edward Scott Beck, who greatly helped to build the *Tribune* into a powerful paper. He was then in his seventies and lived on the Near North Side. Whenever he'd hear of a gambling joint, a speakeasy, or a house of prostitution in the neighborhood, he'd go to Lingle and say, 'Have the chief of police raid this place and close it.' And that was what Lingle would do." At this time, according to Trohan, a real estate scandal erupted at City Hall, and the *Tribune* came to play a major role by exposing it. As a result, John Stege, the chief of police who had engaged in so much pointless verbal sparring with Capone, resigned; to mollify the paper, the Thompson administration, being run by Samuel Ettelson, the corporation counsel, in Thompson's absence, allowed the *Tribune* to select Stege's successor. The *Tribune* editors in turn went to their police reporter, Jake Lingle, for a recommendation. "He picked a fellow named Bill Russell," Trohan recalls, "who had been a copper in his neighborhood when he was a kid. He was a good man, a nice fellow. Crime was important news, and it was very important for the *Tribune* to have a friendly chief of police and get a fair break." That was how deals were struck in Chicago; the interested parties—in this case the Police Department, the *Tribune*, City Hall, and the Capone organization—worked together through middlemen and arrived at compromises. Thus, through his man Jake Lingle, Al Capone was able to approve the city's next chief of police. Lingle had done a great service for Capone; he had earned his keep. That was why he could afford to live in the Stevens Hotel, own a country house, and drive a flashy car. That was why he could bark at Ralph Capone on the telephone. Only in Chicago could a man function as a kingmaker in the Police Department and the confidant of gangsters—and have his byline in the newspaper.

But Lingle wanted more. His influence made him feel invulnerable when in fact his position was extremely vulnerable. Acting as a double agent or even a triple agent was too thrilling to resist. Not satisfied with playing this extremely tricky role, he agreed to inform on Capone for the federal government. On June 8, Frank Wilson, the dogged IRS investigator, visited the publisher of the *Tribune*, Robert McCormick, to request an interview with Jake Lingle, "whom I heard had many underworld contacts." As Wilson wrote in his autobiography, *Special Agent*, "Colonel McCormick was cooperative and promised me an interview with Lingle inside of forty-eight hours." McCormick went so far as to promise Wilson, "I'll get Lingle to go all the way with you." The appointment was scheduled for June 10.

One day before his appointment with Wilson, Jake Lingle left the Stevens Hotel bound for the *Tribune*, where he advised his editor that something was stirring in Chicago's rackets, something on the North Side: "I've been trying to find 'Bugs' Moran—he'd tell me, I think, what the dope is." Go to it, said his boss. Since the St. Valentine's Day Massacre had decimated its ranks, the Moran outfit had continued to function in a reduced capacity, still controlling bootlegging in a tightly circumscribed territory on the North Side, and while Moran's clout could not compare to Capone's, "Bugs" was still a presence in Chicago.

It was a fine day, and Lingle strolled through the Loop toward what was known as "The Corner," the intersection of Clark and Randolph, reputedly a meeting place for racketeers, but he soon forgot all about "Bugs" Moran and the North Side and decided he would do what he liked best, which was to fritter away the afternoon at the track. He headed for the Illinois Central Railroad station, where a train bound for the Washington Park racetrack was scheduled to depart at 1:30 P.M. He broke his jaunty stride long enough to purchase a racing form, then entered an eighty-five-foot long pedestrian tunnel running beneath Michigan Avenue to the train terminal. A thin young man, well turned out, began to follow him, and as Lingle neared the end of the tunnel, the young man produced a revolver, closed in on Lingle, and, holding the gun inches from the back of the reporter's head, fired once. Lingle fell to the ground, the racing form in his hand and a lit cigar clenched between his teeth. He was thirty-nine years old at the time of his death. The shot echoed throughout the tunnel, the killer fled up the staircase, and a woman screamed. Several bystanders chased the killer along Randolph Street, through an alley, onto Wabash. Policemen joined the race, but in the end the killer got away, though not before dozens of people had seen him.

The next day, the murder of Jake Lingle dominated all the Chicago newspapers, but his employer, the *Chicago Tribune*, was now itself a part of the story. And when people in Chicago referred to the *Tribune*, they usually meant its imperious publisher, Colonel Robert Rutherford McCormick.

Even by the rather extravagant standards of Chicago tycoons, McCormick qualified as a great eccentric. He was, in all likelihood, the only newspaper publisher who buried his wife with full military honors, the only newspaper publisher ever to have made a habit of walking the streets of his city disguised as a blind man, accompanied by a Seeing Eye dog. He was an intimidating presence. Nobody called him "Bob," "Robert," or even "Mr." He was always known as "the Colonel." He came by his high estate as the scion of not one or even two but *three* dynasties: the Medills, the Pattersons, and the Mc-Cormicks. Born in 1880, he attended Groton and Yale before taking his place in the family business, which he successfully administered. In a 1934 analysis of McCormick's paper, *Fortune* magazine proclaimed, "The *Tribune* is a great money-maker. It dominates the Chicago newspaper field in circulation and advertising linage. Its circulation (except on Sunday when the Hearst paper is still ahead) is about two and a half times that of its only morning competitor, the *Herald and Examiner*. Almost twice as many people buy the *Tribune* as buy the Chicago *Daily News*."

Those who worked for the Colonel held him in awe, even as they chuckled at his eccentricities. "He was a great man in the sense that he was trying to educate his readers instead of pandering to them," said Walter Trohan, echoing the sentiments of many. For instance, McCormick insisted the paper heed his idiosyncratic notions of grammar: no *s* in "island," only one *z* in "jazz"; "freight" became "frate," and "clue" "clew," "synagogue" "synagog," and so on through the language. Some said McCormick inherited his linguistic ideas from his grandfather; others believed he was taking revenge on one of his Groton masters. More significantly, he made the *Tribune* into a forum for his convictions about everything from world affairs (the paper was notoriously isolationist) to Prohibition (the paper vehemently opposed it).

At the time the Lingle scandal broke, McCormick, the man who inherited an empire, had already had one memorable encounter with Capone, the man who'd stolen an empire. The occasion was a threatened strike by the Newsboys' Union, which was allied with the Capone organization, in early 1929. In his account, McCormick related how he headed off the strike personally and put Capone to flight.

> The publishers called a meeting to hear the demands. I arrived late. As I entered an outer office, I saw several swarthy, evil-looking men who eyed me coldly. Inside I saw to my amazement that Al Capone brazenly had invaded the meeting with the aim of terrorizing those present. I ordered Capone to leave and to take his plug-uglies with him. I knew his reputation but I also knew he had never killed anyone himself and I didn't think he'd start then. Capone got out. He didn't muscle in on the newspapers. We continued to expose him.

The truth was more complicated. Capone happened to be present at the meeting because his man in Mayor Thompson's City Hall, Daniel Serritella, was also the head of the Newsboys' Union. Although McCormick tried to give the impression that he dealt with the mob-controlled union against his will, he did employ Moe Annenberg's brother Max as the director of circulation for the *Tribune*. Max owed his job to his ties to both Serritella and Capone, and he used those connections to assure the *Tribune*'s commercial success.

In light of this arrangement, Serritella's eyewitness account offers a more plausible version of the meeting between Capone and McCormick and highlights Annenberg's role, which McCormick had conveniently omitted:

> A little over two years ago, Max Annenberg, director of circulation of the *Chicago Tribune*, . . . told me the *Tribune* was having some trouble with their chauffeurs and drivers. . . . Annenberg said he wanted to treat the [news] boys right and that he wanted to reach someone who could get the executive committee to fix the strike up.
>
> I told him that as president of the newsboys' union there was nothing I could do. Then Max Annenberg said he would call up Capone and see if he could do anything in the matter, which he did and made an appointment with Capone to meet him in the *Tribune*'s office. I attended this meeting, at which Capone agreed to use his influence to stop the strike, which prevented the same. Max Annenberg then brought in Robert McCormick, editor and publisher of the *Chicago Tribune*, and introduced McCormick to Capone. McCormick thanked Capone for calling off the strike for the *Tribune* and said, "You know, you are famous, like Babe Ruth. We can't help printing things about you, but I will see that the *Tribune* gives you a square deal."

As a result of these negotiations, the *Tribune* found itself in the peculiar position of denouncing Capone even as it relied on his "muscle" to facilitate its circulation. But the idea of maintaining an arm's length relationship with Capone made McCormick uneasy and fearful of assassination. Coping with the threat in the manner to which he was accustomed, he purchased a bulletproof Rolls-Royce to ferry him between his office in the *Tribune* tower and his 800-acre estate in Wheaton, Illinois.

Insulated by his wealth and position, McCormick lived in a different world from that of his reporters. At the time of Lingle's murder, he let the impression stand that he had never heard of the man and had no idea that anyone so closely involved with the Capone organization worked at the *Tribune*. Fred Pasley, the *Tribune* reporter, claimed in his early book on Capone, "[Lingle's] obscurity was such that Colonel Robert R. McCormick, editor and publisher, was unaware of his identity." This excuse was widely accepted, in part because McCormick seemed so remote, but it was false. Days earlier, Frank Wilson of the IRS had approached McCormick about Lingle; the two men had discussed Lingle's contacts with Capone, and in the end, the publisher himself had offered to produce Jake Lingle. And Lingle was killed the day before he was to keep an appointment with the IRS that McCormick had arranged. All of which meant that McCormick had known all along who Jake Lingle was. Furthermore, McCormick knew that Lingle maintained close contacts with the Capone organization—as did anyone who saw his diamond-studded belt buckle and read his newspaper articles. But it wouldn't do for the publisher of the *Chicago Tribune* to admit that he knowingly employed a reporter closely connected to the Capone organization, not when the paper had been crusading *against* Capone with ferocious headlines and damning editorials. Crime was the big story in Chicago at the time, and the *Tribune* stood to lose all credibility on that issue if the truth came out. That was why Lingle's murder was so alarming to McCormick and the *Tribune*; it threatened to expose how one of the the paper's most influential reporters had closely collaborated with Al Capone. It was bad enough that the paper had to rely on the likes of Max Annenberg and Capone to ensure its circulation; to hint that Capone controlled its reporting as well would have been devastating.

McCormick chose the safer course of feigning ignorance and taking refuge in a display of shock, dismay, indignation—the emotions befitting the publisher of a great newspaper. Vern Whaley, who by now had moved to the *Tribune*, remembers that on the morning after Lingle's murder, "Colonel McCormick called a staff meeting in the city room, and he was livid with rage. He addressed the whole editorial staff, a hundred and fifty people. The place was jammed. I thought he was going to have a stroke, but he swore in strong language that the *Tribune* was now going to avenge Jake Lingle's death. He would take care of that crime syndicate. It was a hell of a meeting."

In life, Lingle had been a fixer for the Capone organization; in death, McCormick portrayed him as a martyr to the Capone organization. The *Tribune* posted a reward of $25,000 "for information which will lead to the conviction of the slayer or slayers," and other Chicago dailies also kicked in, more than doubling the amount. McCormick's paper backed the reward with furious words, beginning with an editorial devoted to the Lingle murder.

THE CHALLENGE

The meaning of this murder is plain. It was committed in reprisal and in attempt at intimidation. Mr. Lingle was a police reporter and an exceptionally well-informed one. His personal friendships included the highest police officials and the contacts of his work made him familiar to most of the big and little fellows of gangland. . . . What made him valuable to his newspaper marked him as dangerous to killers. . . . It is war. There will be casualties, but that is to be expected, it being war. . . . The challenge of crime to the community must be accepted. It had been given with bravado. It is accepted and we'll see what the consequences are to be. Justice will make a fight of it or it will abdicate.

In its splendor and pageantry, the funeral of Alfred Lingle was worthy of a dignitary, indeed, it was worthy of any gangster, not excepting Dion O'Banion. The Police Department, the Fire Department, the American Legion, even the Navy all sent delegates to march through the streets of Chicago. Prominent judges, aldermen, and prosecutors appeared in the procession, and Bill Russell, whom Lingle had arranged to be appointed the chief of police, served as the head pallbearer. Born a Jew, Lingle was buried as a Catholic at Mt. Carmel Cemetery, the final resting place of so many other racketeers; it was only a few paces from his tombstone to the elegant obelisk commemorating Dion O'Banion. At the graveside, recalls Walter Trohan, "The priest delivered a sermon that Lingle was a hero, having been killed by gangsters, but many people thought the priest had his fingers crossed when he gave that sermon, that even *he* suspected that Jake wasn't so good."

The investigation into Lingle's murder turned up evidence that the slain reporter was indeed not "so good." For this, the credit belonged not to the *Chicago Tribune*, which continued to mourn Lingle as a martyr, but to the *St. Louis Post-Dispatch*, which hastened to publish details of Lingle's career as a fixer, the Capone belt buckle he proudly wore, and his prodigal spending. And the *Post-Dispatch* had received its information from Frank Wilson of the IRS. Lingle, it will be recalled, was supposed to meet with Wilson on

June 10, the day after the reporter was murdered. Just after Lingle's death, Wilson questioned Frankie Pope, who managed gambling dens in Cicero for Capone, and Pope told Wilson that Lingle was not what he seemed. "Jake," said Pope, "was a fixer." Wilson passed this lead on to to a reporter at the *Post-Dispatch*, John T. Rogers, who began investigating Lingle's double life. The resulting exposé sent shock waves through Chicago, especially its newspapers, and the *Tribune* in particular, for just prior to publishing his article, Rogers called McCormick to tell him of its disturbing contents. McCormick reacted with a show of outrage, but he was powerless to stop the *St. Louis Post-Dispatch* from going forward. "It was not Lingle's career as a reporter on which the searchlight of investigation has been focused," Rogers wrote. "It was his life of ease, enjoyment and plenty, and the power he wielded in police affairs, that has aroused the curiosity not only of the new police commissioner but of the *Tribune* itself, and turned the inquiry for the moment on the man and the mysterious sources of the large sums of money that passed with regularity through his bank account."

A separate investigation into Lingle's finances yielded disturbing details of his shady practices. In a period of two years, he had accumulated nearly $64,000 in his account at the Lake Shore Trust and Savings Bank, and he had plunged heavily into stocks in partnership with his friend, Police Chief Russell. But Lingle always needed more money; at the time of his death he had lost a quarter of a million dollars in the stock market. The growing tide of scandal and corruption forced the resignation of both Lingle's friend Bill Russell, the chief of police, and the deputy chief, John Stege, who had uttered so many memorable and empty threats against Capone. The revelations also brought grief to Colonel McCormick, and his rivals were quick to embarrass him. "Big Bill" Thompson, whom the *Tribune* had vilified for years, seized the opportunity to mock the newspaper. At press conferences, he made political hay out of the *Tribune*'s misery by calling the paper the "Lingle Wrecking Crew" or the "Lingle Evangelistic Institute." The lines drew hearty laughter from reporters toiling for rival papers.

In the end, McCormick was forced to repudiate Lingle. It would no longer do for his newspaper to build the slain reporter into a martyr; the *Tribune* suddenly denounced him as a scoundrel who had deceived everyone around him. "Alfred Lingle now takes on a different character, one in which he was unknown to the management of the *Tribune* when he was alive," the paper claimed. "The reasonable appearance against Lingle now is that he was accepted in the world of politics and crime for something undreamed of in his office and that he used this in undertakings which made him money and brought him to his death." In its defense, the *Tribune* lamely argued, "There are weak men on other newspapers and in other professions, in positions of trust and responsibility greater than that of Alfred Lingle."

Pressing the attack on racketeers to deflect attention from its own sins, the *Tribune* initiated a splashy antigangster campaign. McCormick assigned Lingle's boss, Robert M. Lee, the city editor, to enlist the support of Judge John Lyle, who remained eager to see his name in the headlines. "Is the law helpless against the gangsters?" Lee asked the judge. "Can't some way be found to haul them into court and make them answer questions under penalty of prison if they lie?" And then Lee spoke words certain to endear the cause to Lyle: "You can be sure that the newspapers, the civic organizations and all the decent people will line up solidly behind you." It had long been Lyle's dream to run for mayor of Chicago, so the carrot of support Lee dangled was naturally most attractive. Lyle agreed and immediately swung into action, meeting regularly with *Tribune* representatives and assigning law clerks to dig up statutes to be used against the gangsters. In the end, they unearthed obscure ordinances concerning "vagrancy" and "vagabonds," two extremely elastic terms. Lyle conveyed the impression that the idea of trying Capone and the other Public Enemies as vagrants was an original one, when in fact the state of Florida had already tried the same tactic, but with little success. However, he was convinced that Capone could be convicted as a vagrant in Chicago. Once convicted, he would not spend much time in jail on a vagrancy charge—the law called for only modest fines and sentences—but Lyle predicted banner headlines and great publicity. And from there it would be only a short step to the mayor's office.

The judge was thrilled with his own cleverness. "I held within me a warm, tingling sense of satisfaction as I reviewed the possibilities in the law in the case of, let us say, Al Capone," he wrote in his autobiography, *The Dry and Lawless Years*. Those possibilities were enough to make Lyle cackle with judicial glee:

> If Capone, arrested on a vagrancy warrant, declined to answer questions he would automatically fail to disprove the allegations. I could find him guilty of vagrancy and fine him $2000. If he tried to pay the fine he would have to explain where the money had come from. He could be sentenced to the House of Correction to work out the fine.
>
> Were he to recite the sources of his income he would be opening the door to criminal charges. And any claim to legitimate employment would launch an investigation that would conceivably result in perjury charges.
>
> There was also the possibility that a vagrancy hearing would assist the treasury agents in their efforts to develop an income tax case against Capone. . . . Under cross-examination in my court the mobster might make admissions at variance with the statement he had given the government.

Lyle immediately met with his old friend Henry Barrett Chamberlin of the Chicago Crime Commission, whose "keen eyes sparkled as I outlined the vagrancy attack." Barrett took the plan to Frank Loesch, who gave his approval.

The judge issued warrants for the arrest of Al Capone and the rest of Chicago's Public Enemies on vagrancy charges. The *Tribune* gave the campaign ample publicity, and Lyle suddenly found himself center stage in the city's crime drama. He made a point to carry a gun with him now at all times; yes, he assured reporters, it was a necessary precaution, he had been receiving threats, his life was in danger. This was rough justice, but with the public's fear of gangsters running higher than ever, Lyle was able to get away with his posturing and his legal maneuvering. Ultimately, all the "vagrants," including Al Capone, were tried and convicted, with the exception of "Spike" O'Donnell, who received some helpful legal advice from Trohan "for the sake of a good color story." (Even Trohan was learning how things were done in Chicago.)

The legal victory proved illusory. In the end, the state Supreme Court overruled the convictions, and the vagrancy campaign fizzled out. All along, it had been nothing more than an attention-getting device for Lyle and the newspapers, especially the *Tribune*, a way of assuring the public that they were doing something big and bold about the gangsters. In fact, they had accomplished nothing. In the end, only Judge Lyle benefited from the crusade. Exploiting the favorable press he had received, he did run for mayor, opposing "Big Bill" Thompson himself in the primary.

Meanwhile, the search for Lingle's killer continued to preoccupy Chicago. Theories abounded as to who had killed the journalist and why. Newspapers speculated that Lingle had double-crossed Capone, who then ordered his death, but no proof was forthcoming. Colonel Calvin Goddard, the ballistics expert, examined the bullets and weapons supposedly used in the murder, but even he was stumped. At the *Tribune* Walter Trohan had been working constantly on the Lingle case, and as he immersed himself in the details of the slain reporter's career, Trohan became convinced he knew who was responsible. The culprit was not Al Capone, as so many people assumed, but Capone's longstanding rival, "Bugs" Moran, who was highly displeased with Lingle's selection of Bill Russell as the chief of police. As Trohan and others had begun to realize, Lingle cooperated with both Capone and Moran—a dangerous practice. In all likelihood, Moran, believing that Lingle had betrayed him both to Capone and to the police, ordered Lingle's death. From Moran's point of view, the murder of Jake Lingle was the perfect crime, for Moran knew that the blame would fall on Capone, as did the blame for McSwiggin and, of course, the St. Valentine's Day Massacre.

Although Trohan came closer than anyone else to the truth by implicating

Moran in the death of Jake Lingle, Moran himself did not pull the trigger. To find out who did, the *Tribune* formed and funded a committee to investigate the matter; the most prominent members were Charles F. Rathbun, a lawyer who worked for the newspaper; Patrick T. Roche, an investigator for the state attorney; and John Boettiger, a *Tribune* reporter. As might be suspected, the committee became more interested in covering up the *Tribune's* involvement with Lingle than in uncovering the truth. After more than a year of delays, the committee named an unlikely suspect, Leo Vincent Brothers, a thirty-one-year-old gunman out of St. Louis, where he ran with the Egan's Rats gang. When Brothers was brought to trial, the evidence against him proved to be less than compelling. For instance, fourteen witnesses testified that they had seen Lingle's murderer fleeing the scene of the crime, but only half of them named Brothers as the assassin. Brothers himself refused to comment on the killing or to reveal who, if anyone, had hired him to kill Jake Lingle. Still, he looked the part of a killer, surly and snarling, and in the *Tribune's* version, he was the man who had killed Lingle. In the end, a jury found him guilty, but given the inconclusive nature of the evidence against him, he received the minimum sentence, fourteen years, with time off for good behavior. Defiant to the end, Brothers jeered, "I can do that standing on my head." His conviction satisfied no one but McCormick and the *Tribune's* editorial writers, who loudly proclaimed that justice had been done, the newspaper's honor avenged. But many in Chicago, including the impartial Chicago Crime Commission, remained convinced that Brothers had been framed and that Lingle's killer was still at large.

· · ·

Al Capone watched the Lingle drama unfold from the relative safety of his Miami Beach retreat. He finally broke his silence on July 18, when he invited Harry Brundidge of the *St. Louis Star* to Palm Island and spoke with the reporter about Lingle for three hours as, Brundidge wrote, "the beams of a tropical moon danced on the waters of Biscayne Bay."

Brundidge found Capone in good spirits, brimming with "typical Latin effusiveness," which meant that Capone placed his hand on the reporter's shoulder to emphasize a point. Despite the revulsion he felt, Brundidge could not bring himself to dislike the affable racketeer. "He has a dark, kindly face, big sparkling eyes, and dark curly hair that is thinning from the brows," Brundidge observed. "His whole demeanor is that of an overgrown boy. The long scar on his left cheek adds to his appearance; his personality is exceptionally pleasing, and it requires no vivid imagination to understand the reasons for his huge success in his chosen field. A stranger, knowing nothing of his past, might characterize him as 'a playful, lovable chap, as harmless as a St. Bernard dog.' "

Capone turned somber when Brundidge brought up the murder that had shaken Chicago. "Was Jake your friend?"

"Yes," Capone replied, "up to the very day he died."

"Did you have a row with him?"

"Absolutely not."

"It is said you fell out with him because he failed to split profits from handbooks."

"Bunk. The handbook racket hasn't really been organized in Chicago for more than two years and any one who says it is doesn't know Chicago."

Brundidge brought up another subject of intense public interest: "What about Jake's diamond belt buckle?"

"I gave it to him," Capone said.

"Do you mind stating what it cost?"

"Two hundred and fifty dollars."

"Why did you give it to him?"

"He was my friend."

Brundidge fed Capone another soft question. "What do you think of newspaper men who turn their profession into a racket?"

"Newspapers and newspapermen should be busy suppressing rackets and not supporting them. It does not become me of all persons to say that, but I believe it."

"How many newspaper men have you had on your pay roll?"

Capone's reponse was calculated to cause consternation in Chicago news-rooms: "Plenty."

The two men had been speaking on the porch. Capone now treated Brundidge to a tour of the house, and as they went from room to room, the racketeer tried to make light of his recent legal difficulties in Miami. "A little clique . . . has tried to run me out of town, but I refused to be chased. They have arrested me repeatedly, tried me unsuccessfully on a perjury charge which was trumped up and tried to padlock my home because I kept a drink here for myself, as who in Miami doesn't?" he explained. "I am out of all rackets. I will make Miami my home and will go to Chicago only occasion-ally. I had my success, saved my money and now I'm through with the rackets."

Capone had said this before, and he would say it again, but no matter how persuasive his tone, he was *not* through with the rackets, nor were the rackets through with him. Capone knew better than any one else how difficult it was to abandon *la mala vita*, and when a man was as notorious as he, it was virtually impossible. Even if he made his peace with his colleagues, the federal government would never leave him alone. The guns, the fear, the stigma—the whole seductive, glamorous, hellish business of the gangster life—would hound him to the grave.

CHAPTER 9

Secret Agents

THE SUMMER OF 1930 HAD BEEN LONG, hot, and frustrating for Frank J. Wilson, who led the IRS investigation of Al Capone. Wilson had watched the murder of Jake Lingle induce paroxysms of dread in Chicago, and he was crestfallen when the ensuing scandal failed to smoke out Capone. Rather, it made everyone realize that Capone's tentacles reached everywhere, not only into the city's gambling dens, brothels, nightclubs, and saloons, not only into City Hall and the Police Department and the town of Cicero, but into the city's newsrooms. Isolated by the fear that corruption would taint his office as well, Wilson had spent the last two years studying countless ledgers and bank statements, but he had failed to uncover any concrete evidence of Capone's income. "He had bought himself a Florida Palace on Palm Island, imported a chef from Chicago and was spending $1,000 a week on banquets. He tore around in sixteen-cylinder limousines, slept in $50 French pajamas, and ordered fifteen suits a time at $135 each," Wilson reminded himself, "and I couldn't show that this satrap of Chicago earned more than $5,000 a year!"

Wilson received countless leads developed from newspaper stories and informers, but in every case he came up empty-handed. "Everyone was hostile," he found. "They were a hundred times more afraid of being killed by Capone guns than they were of having to serve a prison term for perjury." Although Wilson's snooping placed him squarely in harm's way, his anonymous, peripatetic existence protected him better than conventional security. Lurking in the shadows of Capone's empire, he looked like Everyman—gangly, balding, bespectacled, attired in a wrinkled white shirt and tie—and he lived a makeshift life of last-minute train rides, short stays in rundown rooming houses, smoking an endless stream of cigarettes as he placed calls from public phones. He was willing to track down any lead, no matter how inconsequential. At one point he was reduced to exploring a rumor that Capone controlled the miniature-golf racket, such as it was, in Chicago. "Investigation of this merely improved my putting," he tersely noted of the result. It defied reason that one of the most powerful men in Chicago, perhaps *the* most powerful, left no fiscal fingerprints, yet there it was: Public Enemy Number 1 was financially invisible.

Desperate for a productive lead, Wilson turned to outside sources. He traveled to St. Louis, where he saw John T. Rogers, the reporter whom he had assisted with the exposé of Jake Lingle in the *Post-Dispatch*. Now Wilson wanted a favor in return. Rogers invited Wilson to lunch at the Missouri Athletic Club, where they were joined by a third man, who claimed he was in position to know something about the Capone organization's gambling income. His name was Edward O'Hare. As a young man he had gone into business with the inventor of a patented mechanical rabbit used to start dog races. Track owners paid a small percentage of their take for the right to use the device, and over the years O'Hare, by controlling these rights, made a considerable amount of money. That was not his only source of income; in 1923 he was convicted of a bootlegging-related offense. The conviction was overturned on appeal, and O'Hare's ability to negotiate around the law earned him the sobriquet "Artful Eddie." He subsequently began operating dog tracks across Illinois, soon attracting the interest of Al Capone, who wanted a piece of this particularly lucrative business. (Dog racing was a racketeer's dream because it was easy to fix; all you had to do was feed the dogs you wanted to lose a large meal shortly before the start of the race.)

Initially, O'Hare resisted Capone's overtures and operated the Lawndale Kennel Club in competition with Capone's Hawthorne Kennel Club. A supremely self-confident man, O'Hare warned that he would refuse to allow the mechanical rabbit to be used on any tracks if Capone tried to hurt him or his business. In response, Capone proposed a meeting, and the two men, though rivals, took a liking to one another. In the end, Capone suggested that O'Hare could make more money than he thought possible if their dog tracks merged. At the moment, dog racing was all the rage, and the tracks were said to net $50,000 during a good week. O'Hare was under no illusions about Capone, but "Artful Eddie" persuaded himself he could handle the perils involved. "You can make money through business associations with gangsters, and you will run no risk if you don't associate personally with them," he explained. "Keep it on a business basis and there's nothing to fear."

O'Hare kept his distance from the Capone organization; he was never seen in Capone's company or at a Capone-controlled gambling den, but there was no way out of the arrangement, and by the time he met Frank Wilson, O'Hare had come to realize he had made a pact with the Devil. "Eddie realized too late that Capone was so powerful . . . he couldn't operate the dog track without accepting this new silent partner," Wilson noted. "I sympathized with O'Hare as I realized the serious predicament into which he had unconsciously been thrown." As the lunch proceeded, it became apparent that the light of Eddie O'Hare's life was his son, twelve-year-old Butch. Father and son shared a dream that one day little Butch O'Hare would attend the U.S. Naval Academy at Annapolis. Wilson liked the genial O'Hare, but he could not imagine why O'Hare would jeopardize his life, as well as his son's, by testifying against Capone. However, only days after he returned to Chicago, Wilson received a phone call from his friend Rogers, who announced that O'Hare was prepared to tell what he knew. Wilson remained skeptical: "I hope he doesn't have too much blood on his hands and that we can depend on him."

"I've known him twenty years," Rogers assured Wilson. "He never got drawn directly into any of the gang wars. He limits his activity to legitimate dog tracks and has no connection with the Capone booze and vice rackets. He has wanted for a long time to get away from Capone, but once the organization sucks in a businessman they just don't let him retire." But why, Wilson asked, was O'Hare willing to talk? "He's nuts about that boy Butch," Rogers explained. "He's dead set on getting him into Annapolis and he figures he must break away. But he can't do it while Capone is on the throne. I told him you were making headway and that if he helped, the big shot might be on his way to the penitentiary a little quicker."

"Does he realize that in helping me put Scarface on the spot he is taking his life in his hands?"

"Hell, Frank, if Eddie had ten lives to live he'd jeopardize every one of them for that boy Butch."

From that time forward, Rogers served as an intermediary, passing information from the compromised businessman seeking redemption to the IRS investigator intent on obtaining Al Capone's conviction.

· · ·

Confident that Judge John Lyle's outstanding warrant for his arrest on vagrancy charges was meaningless, Al Capone celebrated his return to Chicago with a banquet at the Western Hotel. Days before, on July 29, the assassination of Jack Zuta, a pimp and accountant for the old Moran gang, briefly raised the hopes of law enforcement authorities who thought they might be able to prove that Capone was somehow involved. Because the police had questioned Zuta a month before his killing, the newspapers speculated that he had implicated Capone in any number of crimes ("The vice monger was a softie," explained the *Chicago Tribune*'s Fred Pasley. "Gangland had him pegged as yellow and a squawker.") and that Capone had killed him in retribution. However, this theory, like so many others concerning the inner workings of Chicago's rackets, sounded dramatic but lacked a basis in fact. Of greater interest were the financial records found among Zuta's effects; these showed that the Moran gang, for which he worked, practiced precisely the same type of bribery of elected officials as the Capone organization. The documents suggested that Zuta had tried to cultivate the late, unlamented Frankie Yale and lesser known Capone allies. In a letter dated June 1927, Louis La Cava, who worked for Capone before fleeing to New York, wrote to Zuta about trying to defeat the Capone organization: "I'd help you organize a strong business organization capable of coping with theirs in Cicero. You know you have lots of virgin territory on the north side limits border line, and they are going to try and prevent me from lining up with you and keep starving me out until I go back to them, begging for mercy." Although Zuta's records contained many such fascinating tidbits, they did not, by themselves, present a comprehensive picture of either the Moran gang or Al Capone's criminal behavior.

Throughout the uproar over Zuta's death, Capone gave the appearance of luxuriating in peaceful retirement. He devoted most of August to the pursuit of a lower handicap at the Burnham Wood golf course, where, between churning up divots, he casually transacted business with "Greasy Thumb" Guzik and "Machine Gun" McGurn. It was just like old times, the betting, the cheating, the rude camaraderie of the boys as they whiled away the late-summer afternoons playing gangster golf. "He's all right, if you ask me," a waitress said of Capone, "and he and the boys always play a full eighteen holes, too."

In September, a French newspaper, Le Journal, assigned a reporter to question Alphonse Capone, who was known throughout Europe as the preeminent American gangster. The Chicago Police Department claimed they had no idea of Capone's whereabouts, but the correspondent, who had never been to Chicago, readily found him. Like all Europeans, the French were appalled by Prohibition and inclined to view bootleggers sympathetically, and the resulting interview made headlines in both the United States and Europe, for the racketeer had brought all his formidable charm to bear on the journalist, who painted a vivid, bilingual portrait of the racketeer challenging his critics:

Lifting his shoulders, amplifying his voice, he exclaims:
   "Hypocrites, hypocrites! This country has really too many of them. . . . I am sick of that game (c'est un jeu qui me rend malade). There are people who vote dry and who are wet. . . . And then there are the politicians who wear a mask of respectability and who are only crooks (des canailles). . . . They say they despise those they call gang-

sters, but they are glad to take their money to fatten their campaign funds. . . . How can you expect me not to despise these persons? I would rather share my breakfast with a stool-pigeon than with them."

"With a stool-pigeon?"

My guide then explains that in gangster's slang a stool-pigeon means a police indicator (*un indicateur*). . . .

"In any case, I hope that you won't call me a 'gorilla.'

"So long . . . (*Adieu*). This winter, if you come to Florida, pop in (*passez chez moi*). You will see my beautiful flowers."

And the man of fifty corpses gives me, always smiling, his hand, fine and very white.

Capone sounded confident, even indignant, because he was convinced he was out of danger. Judge Lyle could say whatever he liked about gangsters to try to get himself elected mayor, Al Capone would not pay attention; that was what his lawyers were for. And he was also convinced that the Internal Revenue Service would never indict him for tax evasion. After years of investigation it was apparent the IRS had failed to find enough evidence to persuade a grand jury to return an indictment. If they continued to harass him, he would take the IRS to court, he would take the whole United States to court, if necessary, just as he had taken the safety director of Miami to court and watched him squirm as the judge lectured him about constitutional guarantees of freedom. Yes, Capone would enjoy his revenge on his antagonists; even better, it would be perfectly legal.

• • •

At the time, Frank Wilson agreed with Al Capone: the IRS had little to show for its two-year-long investigation. Wilson's field agent, Art Madden, had once warned that Wilson might as well try to "hang a foreclosure sign on the moon" as nail Capone for income tax evasion, and Madden's prophecy had proved depressingly accurate. By the end of the summer, Wilson was on the verge of giving up his futile investigation. "I am known as a cold and calculating character," he noted, but "after two years I was in a sweat."

Wilson had further cause for anxiety when he received word that the Capone organization was planning to kill him. Until this time, Wilson had taken reasonable precautions regarding his personal safety, but he had not feared for his life. The message came from an informer named De Angelo, but that was not his real name. It was the alias of Mike Malone, an undercover agent Wilson had assigned to gather intelligence on Capone nearly two years before. In Wilson's estimation, Malone was "the greatest natural undercover worker the Service has ever had. Five feet, eight inches tall, a barrelchested, powerful two hundred pounds, with jet black hair, sharp brown eyes underscored with heavy dark circles and a brilliant, friendly smile, Mike could easily pass for Italian, Jew, Greek or whomever the occasion demanded. He was actually 'black Irish' from Jersey City." Malone was married, but after the death of his infant daughter in a car accident, he and his wife had split up, and he had little interest in anything other than his work. As such he was a natural candidate for a prolonged, demanding, hazardous assignment.

In preparation for going undercover, Malone fabricated a long, involved history for himself as a hoodlum from Brooklyn and thus a suitable candidate for the Capone organization. In this role he registered at the Lexington Hotel, where he happened to be given room 724, adjacent to Philip D'Andrea, one of Al Capone's bodyguards. During the next few weeks Malone, under the name De Angelo, made himself conspicuous in the hotel lobby until he was approached by one of Capone's men, who asked him his business. "I'm a promoter," De Angelo said. "Know anybody who'd be interested in buyin' some gold bricks?" Maintaining his cover, De Angelo spoke of his Brooklyn past and mentioned his involvement in a shooting incident. He even claimed to have been a member of the Five Points gang, the spawning ground of so many racketeers. With this bold talk (all of it carefully contrived) he won the confidence of the Capone organization and eventually earned a job as a croupier in a Cicero gambling house. Throughout, De Angelo had always been scrupulous about keeping his distance from his real boss, Frank J. Wilson of the IRS. As the months passed he received regular promotions, until he became the head croupier of the joint. During his off-hours, De Angelo ate and drank with the Capone men, and he duly reported his findings, such as the remarks one hoodlum made to him concerning "The Enforcer," presumably Frank Nitti: "He keeps everything in line for Al. Somebody gets out of line, Al tells the Enforcer. The next thing you know, a couple of guys get off a train from Detroit or New York or St. Louis, and the Enforcer tells them who has to go. The guys do the job and go home." In contrast to the imported assassins, said the hoodlum, "Al don't like his guys to do no shootin' unless its absolutely necessary. And they gotta be quiet. That's what happened to Scalise and Anselmi. I don't want Al givin' me no banquets. I see him give a guy a banquet one night, and when the guy gets up to take a bow, Al reaches for a baseball bat and beats the guy's brains out right in front of everybody." Shortly afterward, De Angelo received an invitation to attend just such a banquet, a birthday party Al was throwing for the Enforcer himself, Frank Nitti, at the New Florence restaurant.

De Angelo had his doubts about the wisdom of attending, but he knew Al Capone would attend, and he was eager to see Public Enemy Number 1 in action. He alerted other special agents to station themselves outside the restaurant where the celebration was to be held, and then went inside to watch Capone, McGurn, and other insiders drink themselves into oblivion. No bathtub gin for them; only the best imported champagne was served. Wearing a tuxedo, Capone maintained his dignity throughout the evening. He wielded no baseball bat on this occasion, and he even gave De Angelo a reassuring pat on the shoulder. If Al suspected that a spy for the IRS was present, he gave no indication.

However, De Angelo became convinced that Capone's chef tried to poison him. The offending morsel was a piece of steak; when De Angelo swallowed, the meat burned his mouth and tongue, and he suddenly felt short of breath. He shouted for water, only to hear in reply, "What the hell do you want water for, with all this champagne around?" De Angelo lamely explained that his ulcers prevented him from drinking. After he drank a pitcher of ice water and recovered somewhat, he asked the man sitting next to him, Paul "The Waiter" Ricca, another prominent member of the Capone organization, what kind of meat they were eating. "Spiced steak," Ricca said. "Don't you like it?" The red-hot peppers turned out to be the most violent aspect of the party. And the cake was lovely: "Happy Birthday Frank," it said.

After several months, De Angelo was joined in his game of deception by another undercover agent who went by the name of Graziano. Together, they happened to overhear a troubling conversation between two Capone gunmen. "Snorky's gonna have that fella taken care of," said one. "Where's he livin'?" asked the other. And the first man replied, "The S.P." As everyone in Chicago knew, the initials stood for the Sheridan Plaza, where Wilson and his wife resided under assumed names. De Angelo and Graziano immediately related this information to Wilson, who passed the grim news along to *his* boss, Elmer Irey, the head of the Special Intelligence Unit. Irey came up with an even darker theory. What if Capone had known all along that Graziano and De Angelo were spies for the IRS? If so, he might be feeding them misleading information. And if Capone *knew* the men were spies, he would not hesitate to order their deaths whenever it suited him. Irey relayed his theory back to De Angelo, who, avoiding the phone for fear of wiretaps, replied by letter. "I feel very certain that the [Capone] gang has no inkling as to my real identity," he wrote. "Since they are not on to me, they are not on to Graziano either. I have talked this matter over with him very thoroughly and he feels the same way as I do. We want to see this thing through."

No sooner had De Angelo mailed the letter than he received further indication that Wilson's life was in imminent danger, and the undercover agent broke all the rules of his trade by placing a call directly to Wilson at his room in the Sheridan Plaza. "This is an emergency," he said when Wilson answered. "You've got to get out of the hotel right now." In a near panic, Wilson did as De Angelo advised. When they met, De Angelo explained that

Capone's men had been tailing Wilson for days, and when the IRS man became skeptical, De Angelo stunned him by describing the lunch Wilson had ordered the day before, right down to the $5 bill with which he had paid for the meal. "I wanted to get you out of the Sheridan Plaza," De Angelo said, "because they were going to kill you when you walked back to the garage for your car in the morning. . . . A couple of guys were going to let themselves into your car during the night. . . . When you got behind the wheel they were going to give it to you with a rod equipped with a silencer, and then when you slumped over they'd drive off with you, weight your body and toss it into the river."

Listening to De Angelo describe how the Capone mob planned to do away with him, Wilson chewed on a nickel cigar. He released a cloud of smoke and said, "I'll get the evidence on Capone if I never live to do another thing."

But first, Wilson and his wife moved out of the Sheridan Plaza. As he checked out, he made of a point of telling the management that he was returning to Kansas. He and his wife then took a three-block taxi ride to his car and drove to an apartment house. Wilson got out, rang a doorbell, and then returned to his car. Next, he went to Union Station. He lingered there briefly and drove on to another hotel in Chicago, the Palmer House, where he checked in, convinced that his erratic movements had befuddled any Capone operative trying to tail him. In the meantime, the *Chicago Tribune* had learned of the threat against Wilson's life and to his dismay ran a report on the front page. "I was much disgusted when I read the story this morning about the public disclosure of the plans of Capone to bring four gunmen to Chicago from New York," he wrote Irey. "By that breach of confidence the lives of our informants [De Angelo and Graziano] may be in jeopardy, and our chances of obtaining further help from this source may be eliminated."

Shortly afterward, undercover agent Graziano fed Wilson another lead. It was just a scrap of a conversation, and it seemed small, almost insignificant, but it would eventually become the first concrete evidence that Al Capone did in fact enjoy a vast, unreported income. The lead developed as Graziano lounged about the Lexington Hotel and fell into a conversation with yet another Capone employee, who claimed to possess inside information concerning the police raid on the Hawthorne Smoke Shop five years earlier, shortly after the murder of William McSwiggin, the young assistant state's attorney. "They walked out with a nice book of figures from the smoke shop that they could've used against the Big Boy," the employee said, "only they overlooked it." Graziano could not be certain what this intelligence signified, but he dutifully reported the conversation in a letter to Irey, who immediately realized that a ledger *already in the custody of the IRS* contained vital information about Capone's finances. Irey became so excited that he left Washington and went to Chicago to discuss the matter with his agents.

Wilson, who had spent the better part of two years examining such ledgers, recalled nothing that fit Graziano's description, but, he promised, "I'll look through everything again."

Wilson looked for hours and then for days. By midnight on the last day of his review, he concluded he had been wasting his time and prepared to go home. As he was storing the papers, he recalled, "I uncovered a ledger. It had been lying there in that file for about five years and the label on it didn't mean a thing to me. But curiosity made me open it. As soon as I looked inside that book I knew we had our case." What Wilson had discovered were the records Graziano had heard about, records the IRS had had in its possession all along, records that Capone had long feared the government might one day use against him. "I snipped the string and found myself holding three ledgers, black ones with red corners," Wilson continued. "The first one didn't mean much. The second I spotted as a 'special column cashbook.' My eye leaped over the column heading: 'Bird Cage,' '21,' 'Faro,' 'Roulette,' 'Horse bets.' " Wilson gave up any thought of going home that night and went to his cubbyhole of an office to study the ledgers and make a few calculations, and when he was finished, he realized he was going over the books of a business with net profits of over half a million dollars during an eighteen-month period, and that was four years ago, when Capone's operation was much smaller. Even better, the ledgers showed *income*; Wilson and his crew had done yeoman's work spotting Capone's *expenses*, but to make the tax case really stick, it was vital to demonstrate Capone's earning power.

The next step was to connect the information contained in the ledgers to Al Capone himself, and for once Wilson knew where to turn: Fred Ries, the cashier whom Nels Tessem had identified as a crucial link in the chain of Capone's finances. But Ries had vanished. Wilson frittered away a week in search of his quarry, until he received a tip that the man in question could be found in St. Louis. Wilson and Tessem immediately boarded a train bound for that city. "We found out from the Post Office inspectors that a special-delivery letter was about to be delivered to him, so we simply tailed the messenger boy and I crossed Ries's palm with a federal subpoena," Wilson said of the arrest. The man from the IRS also found a letter from one Louis Lipschultz to Ries, advising the cashier to head further west, all the way to California; money for travel was enclosed. Lipschultz, Wilson knew, was Jack Guzik's brother-in-law, so there was one more tie between Ries and the Capone gambling empire.

Ries was indignant as only the guilty can be, and more than that, he was afraid for his life. "Who are you?" he demanded of his unexpected visitors. "If you are government men show me your badges!" Wilson and Tessem had no badges to display. "I never squawked or squealed on Capone in my life," Ries protested. "You have me all wrong. I never saw the Pinkert State Bank.

I've never been to Cicero." As Ries continued to proclaim his ignorance and innocence, Wilson realized that the cashier required a little more encouragement before he implicated the most feared racketeer in Chicago. Wilson was prepared to face just this problem. Through his network of informers, he had learned that Ries had an absolute horror of insects; on opening a burlap bag of cash, which happened to be infested with cockroaches, the cashier had recoiled in pathological dread at the sight of the little brown bugs scampering away. Wilson put this knowledge to immediate use by arranging to place Ries, now a material witness in the Capone case, in an obscure, rundown jail in Danville, Illinois. "In it was a little room on the third floor especially designed for Fred Ries," Wilson recalled. "He took one look and gasped, 'This ain't fit for a dog!' Cockroaches and other wildlife were virtually holding a convention on the premises."

"If you don't like it here," Wilson told Ries, "just tell the jailer you are willing to play ball." Wilson tossed a pack of cigarettes into the cell and departed, leaving the cashier to contend with his worst nightmare. The idea of torturing Ries with bugs appealed to Wilson; after two years of frustration, he enjoyed his power over the cashier. He told Tessem how Ries was probably going out of his mind right about then, and the two men "chuckled." After enduring five days of torture in his filthy cell, Ries capitulated and summoned Wilson. "The bedbugs are eating me alive," he wailed. "I haven't eaten a decent meal or slept in five days. Take me out of here! . . . I'm nearly crazy. I'll play ball—I'll explain those cashier's checks. But for God's sake, get me away from these bugs!" Wilson toyed with his captive for a while, then freed Ries from Danville and spirited him into Chicago, where, before a grand jury convened in the middle of the night amid great secrecy, Ries explained how the Ship was rigged so that the house always won, how he converted the winnings, nearly $100,000 on a good night, into cashier's checks, which he then turned over to Jack Guzik, how the cashiers skimmed salaries for themselves off the top of the house take, and finally, how he forwarded the largest cut of the profits to the "Big Fellow," "Snorky," "Scarface," Public Enemy Number 1, call him whatever they liked, to Al Capone himself. Wilson was overjoyed; Ries's testimony "sounded like the Gettysburg Address to me." Largely on the strength of Ries's testimony, the federal grand jury indicted Jack "Greasy Thumb" Guzik for tax evasion; the trial was set for November.

·   ·   ·

When Fred Ries testified before the grand jury, the federal government's case against Al Capone suddenly began to come together. But the very next day, September 19, 1930, the case nearly fell apart when J. Edgar Hoover—the man who would later make a career out of boasting that he and his bureau had been responsible for bringing Al Capone to justice—refused to cooperate with George E. Q. Johnson in the hazardous business of prosecuting gangsters. Hoover begged off by claiming his bureau was understaffed and overworked, and in case those excuses failed to sound convincing, he also maintained that it was simply not the responsibility of the FBI to get Capone or any other racketeer. In a lengthy, combative memorandum to the assistant attorney general, Hoover complained:

> I think it is manifestly unfair and unreasonable for this Bureau to be expected to assign Agents to matters that do not come within this Bureau's jurisdiction, particularly when the work of this Bureau is as congested as it is at the present time. We have primary jurisdiction in Bankruptcy, National Bank cases, White Slave violations, Antitrust violations, Motor Theft violations, and innumerable other major violations of the Criminal Code. . . . Our investigative force is totally inadequate for the performance of the Bureau's regular duties, but it becomes an impossibility to properly function at all if we are going to be called upon to work on cases for which other Governmental investigative agencies have been created.

In other words, Hoover was saying, if Al Capone happens to steal a car, the FBI will look into it; otherwise please don't even think of bothering us, we're drowning in work as it is.

Over Hoover's strenuous objections, the Department of Justice prevailed on the Chicago office of the FBI to arrest Frank Nitti, the "Enforcer," who had been in hiding since he had been indicted for tax evasion in March 1930. One reason the FBI reluctantly came around was the discovery, in late September, of a list of thirty-one racketeers scheduled to be arrested by one federal agency or another. The list turned up when two IRS agents, Art Madden and Clarence Converse, staged a raid on the Carleon Hotel in Cicero, in reality a thirty-five crib brothel owned and operated by Dennis Cooney on behalf of Al Capone. In the previous weeks, Converse had taken to disguising himself as a gandy dancer, a track laborer, and asked around about Nitti, who he heard was staying at the Carleon. When they raided the hotel, the agents went from room to room, rousting the disgruntled women out of bed, but Nitti had fled. Instead, Madden confronted a Capone spear carrier named Tony Tagenti, who claimed to be down with the flu. Searching for a weapon, Converse overturned Tagenti's pillow, revealing a list. As the agents began to read, Tagenti strenuously denied any knowledge of it; he had no idea whatsoever how it had come to be under his pillow. Tagenti was taken down to police headquarters to be fingerprinted, while agents placed copies of the list in the hands of the city's newspapers, going over the heads

of corrupt police who would surely have destroyed it, for this was a remarkable list, containing both the names of the racketeers to be arrested on
vagrancy warrants as well the police officers assigned to each man. Although
Madden had yet to find Nitti, the IRS agent had exposed yet another example
of the close cooperation between the Capone organization and the police,
cooperation that made the Feds' task extremely difficult to accomplish.

Embarrassed into action by the latest scandal, a team of FBI agents located
Nitti in a roadhouse called the Roamer Inn, outside Michigan City, Indiana,
on October 11. When the agents, shorn of identification, entered the restaurant, they discovered a supply of bootleg booze and prostitutes eager for
business. The Roamer Inn, it seemed, was a typical Capone brothel. Rather
than arresting Nitti on the spot, the agents shadowed him until the end of the
month. By that time, a detail consisting of two FBI agents and no less than
fifteen Chicago policemen was following his movements in Berwyn, the
town adjoining Cicero, where Nitti and his wife lived quietly under assumed
names. The agents wanted to arrest Nitti at home, but they lacked his exact
address.

Pat O'Rourke of the Treasury Department finally succeeded in tracing
Nitti to his current address by following his wife home from the beauty parlor
one afternoon. To determine the correct alias and apartment number, the
Treasury agent resorted to a ruse. One night he pushed Nitti's car in front of
a fire hydrant and then set off a nearby alarm to summon the Fire Department. When the firemen found a car blocking the hydrant, they traced its
owner, and in this way O'Rourke learned that Nitti lived in apartment 3D
under the name Belmont. The agent staked out the apartment for two days,
and when he was certain he had seen Nitti come home for dinner, he
summoned police backup and pounded on Nitti's front door. "There must be
some mistake," Nitti shouted. "My name's Belmont. I'm the well-known
Belmont," adding, sotto voce, "you son of a bitch!" The police broke down
the door and arrested the well-known Mr. Belmont-Nitti.

Now that they had Nitti in custody, the federal agents realized to their
embarrassment they knew next to nothing about him or his actual connection to Capone. Unlike every other principal in the Capone organization,
Nitti had no criminal record. That was all about to change; from now on
Nitti would have a record, "if for no other reason than his association with
the celebrated gangster [Al Capone]," in the words of an FBI memorandum.
Under questioning, Nitti revealed he had been born in Angri, Italy, on
January 27, 1888. He also supplied a wan little autobiographical sketch of a
typical immigrant boyhood, omitting any reference to Capone or racketeering. In his version he was no enforcer, merely a humble barber who, he
wrote, "worked at various jobs in Brooklyn, . . . giving my earnings to my
mother to support the family."

In the wake of the arrest, Nitti's photograph appeared in all the Chicago papers, and the entire city became familiar with the dapper little man who sported a neatly trimmed mustache and whose brow seemed furrowed in perpetual worry. Despite Nitti's lack of a criminal record, Ries's testimony proved that Nitti had been making secret deposits for Al Capone at the Schiff Trust and Savings Bank, and on that basis the U.S. attorney pressed charges. Confronted with the evidence against him, Nitti lost his mettle; indeed, he seemed to have lost his will to live. Dispirited, he pleaded guilty, and in exchange for his cooperation was given a relatively light sentence of eighteen months in jail.

George E. Q. Johnson received still more good news days after Nitti's arrest. On November 19, 1930, a federal jury, after hearing evidence for a week and deliberating for six and a half hours, returned a guilty verdict against Jack Guzik for failing to pay his income tax in 1927, 1928, and 1929. During the trial the government had contended that Guzik had earned about $1 million during those years but had paid only $60,240 in taxes out of the $250,000 he actually owed. Fred Ries, the Capone accountant, was the government's star witness, and his testimony implicated not only Guzik but Capone, who had yet to be indicted. Ries told the court that Jack Guzik was his "immediate boss" and that he had others, namely, "Al Capone, Ralph Capone and Frank Nitti." He explained that a typical Capone gambling operation netted about $25,000 a week, "when business was good," that the house never lost money, and that he delivered the profits, in the form of cashier's checks, to Guzik's chauffeur.

Following his conviction, Guzik went through another round of appeals, all denied, and Judge Charles E. Woodward sentenced him to five years in Leavenworth Federal Penitentiary and ordered him to pay a fine of $17,500. Guzik staved off the inevitable with more appeals until, on April 8, 1932, the fat little pimp whom all Chicago had come to despise finally began to serve his jail sentence.

In his testimony implicating Guzik, Nitti, and Capone, Ries had performed splendidly for the government, but the Capone organization had posted a reward for information leading to the cashier's whereabouts (or worse). Since it would be many months until Ries would be required to testify again, there was every reason to believe that he might not survive. Having personally apprehended Ries, then tormented him with confinement in a vermin-infested cell, and finally made him a prime target for Capone's assassins, Frank Wilson came to feel a measure of responsibility toward Ries, whose life was now in constant peril. At the time there was no Witness Protection Program, no formal way at all to safeguard the government's key witness, so Wilson improvised a solution of his own: "I packed my scowling little treasure off to South America with government agents to guard him until we needed him in court." Wilson even persuaded the Secret Six, the group of wealthy financiers dedicated to cleaning up Chicago, to pick up the tab for Ries's enforced vacation.

With Frank "The Enforcer" Nitti, Jack "Greasy Thumb" Guzik and Ralph "Bottles" Capone all convicted, the U.S. attorney's office in Chicago could now count three large, if belated, victories against the Capone organization. So Johnson had reason to take heart, for the case against Al Capone himself, Public Enemy Number 1, was becoming stronger with every passing month, and later, as events began to crowd one another, with every passing week.

• • •

The world of the rackets was changing quickly, and Capone was struggling to keep pace. Since the start of his outlaw career, he had survived because he recognized that the greatest threat he faced came not from the law but from other gangsters. Now he was slow to realize that the situation had changed. He was the "Big Fellow," the dominant racketeer in Chicago, and he had little to fear from his former rivals—he had defeated them all. In their place he faced a newly invigorated law enforcement establishment. Even his time-tested weapon in dealing with lawmen—the bribe—did not work with the new breed of zealots. Meanwhile, as Ries testified and Frank Nitti pleaded guilty, Al Capone decided to try his case in the court of public opinion.

"120,000 MEALS ARE SERVED BY CAPONE FREE SOUP KITCHEN," the *Chicago Tribune* headlined on December 5. " 'Vagrant without Support for Self or Family,' " as Judge Lyle's warrant described Capone, "Spends $12,000." During the last weeks of 1930, Al Capone's soup kitchen became one of the strangest sights Chicagoans had ever seen. An army of ragged, starving men assembled three times a day beside a storefront at 935 South State Street, feasting on the largesse of Al Capone. Toasting his health. Telling the newspapers that Capone was doing more for the poor than the entire U.S. government. Why, he was even offering some of them jobs. Capone milked his good works for all the favorable publicity they were worth. He came down and walked among the men, the wretched of the earth, offering a handshake, a hearty smile, and words of encouragement from the great Al Capone. He wondered aloud why the government was wasting its time trying to prosecute a benefactor and employer like him when it had so many more pressing concerns, such as feeding the hungry.

During November and December, Al Capone's soup kitchen kept regular hours, serving breakfast from 7:00 A.M. until 9:00 A.M., lunch from 11:30 until 2:00, and dinner from 4:30 until 6:30—early enough for his homeless patrons to find themselves a flophouse or a park bench for the night. Thanksgiving Day 1930 was a particular public relations triumph for Capone. On that day he could boast that he fed more than 5,000 hungry men, women, and children with a hearty beef stew. He made certain to publicize the fact that he had bought and paid for 1,250 pounds of beef. No politician running for office could have handled this particular social program more nimbly than Capone. The regular publicity given to the soup kitchen generated a torrent of favorable mail, much of it addressed simply to "Al Capone, Chicago, USA" or "Al Capone's Soup Kitchen." Many of the letters beseeched Al Capone, the vagrant and Public Enemy, to help them get back on their feet. Even more remarkably, Capone's soup kitchen appealed to the rich and influential as well as the poor and disenfranchised. "I met a lovely member of Chicago's four hundred who spoke to me with tears in her eyes of Capone," wrote Mary Borden in *Harper's Monthly*. "I was already getting rather sick of the Scarface, but this suddenly made me feel quite ill, this sentimentality frightened me. I had heard, of course, of the Capone fans—he had more adorers, so I'd been told, than any movie star—but I had not expected the friends of my childhood to be numbered among them. That the hungry and ragged army of unemployed waiting in the street to partake of his bounty should, with a catch of the throat, mumble the maudlin words, 'Goodhearted Al' seemed natural enough, but that the petted and pampered daughters of Chicago's old families should be moved to tears by the spectacular display of the bootlegger's big heart was startling. It seemed to indicate . . . the spread of some moral intoxication or fever." Borden left Chicago deeply troubled by what she had seen and heard; she was convinced that Capone's organization was, as everyone had described it to her, "a government within a government."

To counteract the favorable publicity the soup kitchen generated for Capone (and to boost his candidacy for mayor), Judge Lyle participated in a raid on Capone's hideaway on South Austin Boulevard in Cicero on November 30. The information as to Capone's whereabouts was woefully out of date; he hadn't used the place in several years, but his absence did not stop the federal agents from ogling the luxurious furnishings. As they searched the place, they came across a dozen pairs of silk pajamas monogrammed "A.C.," but they came no closer to Capone that night. Even if they had found him lolling in his bed, the agents could have done little more than hold him briefly on Lyle's vagrancy warrant, which was itself of doubtful legality. The raid proved an embarrassing anticlimax.

Meanwhile, the soup kitchen continued to serve thousands of meals a week, and Capone was still at large. Exasperated beyond reason, Lyle insisted that if Al Capone ever appeared before him in court he would send the racketeer straight to the electric chair. The occasion for this startling declaration was a banquet held by the Chicago Corset Manufacturers' Association at the Hotel La Salle, with Judge Lyle as the guest of honor. The city's assembled corset manufacturers listened respectfully as he was introduced as

"Chicago's most distinguished jurist," and, more to the point, "Chicago's next mayor." At the podium, Lyle took the occasion to denounce Al Capone to the corset manufacturers. "Capone has become almost a mythical being in Chicago," Lyle told them. "He is not a myth but a reptile. He is more than a concentrated crime wave. He is a real and powerful political force. He sent one of his men to the legislature at the last election when a Democrat was crowded from the field. He has one mouthpiece in Congress and another in the City Council. . . . He must go, both as a criminal force and a political force." Lyle came to a rousing conclusion: "We will send him to the chair if it is possible to do so. He deserves to die; he has no right to live." To bolster this conclusion, Lyle proceeded to blame the racketeer for the death of "Big Jim" Colosimo in 1920, well before Capone arrived in Chicago. The corset manufacturers applauded heartily, assured that Judge John H. Lyle would keep their industry safe from the depredations of racketeers. Of course, Lyle's reckless disregard for due process and for the rights of the accused made him sound foolish, but people understood the motive behind his tirade. The man was running for mayor; he couldn't help himself.

As Lyle's hysterical remarks suggested, a climate of fear surrounded Capone wherever he went, even in the soup kitchen. The potential for violence was always present, as Mike Rotunno, a press photographer, discovered when he was sent down to the soup kitchen to get a picture of Capone distributing food to the poor. Rotunno knew Al from various Chicago courthouses, where he photographed the racketeer, and, during lulls, played cards with him, and in his experience Al was always a cooperative subject. Rotunno knew that if he photographed only the right side of Capone's face, omitting the scars, he would receive a $50 "tip" for his trouble. On this day Rotunno went about his business, but as he snapped his picture, the flash powder exploded in a bright puff of smoke, and everyone ran for cover. Rotunno tried to explain that no gun had gone off, no assassins had tried to kill Capone, it was merely the photographic apparatus, but the fear was so great, he recalls, that "for a couple of minutes I thought there was going to be bloodshed."

The tide of emotion obscured certain facts about the soup kitchen. Although Capone stated that the soup kitchen cost $10,000 a month to operate, he probably did not pay its costs himself; he "encouraged" local bakeries, meatpackers, and coffee roasters to donate to his cause, and what Al Capone told them to do, they did. More importantly, at the same time that he fed the poor, he raised the wholesale price of beer in Chicago. For as long as anyone could remember it had been $55 a barrel, but in the early weeks of December, when the soup kitchen was at its height, it went to $60 a barrel, with the increase being passed along to the customer. Meanwhile the cost of producing the suds remained constant, at about $4 a barrel. Even as Capone gave to the poor with one hand, he took with the other, yet because he had timed the maneuver to coincide with the soup kitchen, he managed to escape criticism.

Indeed, by the end of 1930, his popularity was as high as it had ever been. At the Medill School of Journalism in Chicago, a student poll of the ten most "outstanding personages in the world" generated the following list: Benito Mussolini, Charles Lindbergh, Admiral Richard Byrd, George Bernard Shaw, Bobby Jones, Herbert Hoover, Mahatma Gandhi, Albert Einstein, Henry Ford, and Alphonse Capone. As this register suggested, the 1920s had been a decade of heroes—athletes, scientists, explorers, industrialists—but the decade just beginning would have a different tone; the 1930s would be an era of tyrants and dictators and demagogues. Capone managed to straddle both extremes; he had the unique ability to play the villain and the hero simultaneously, the Robin Hood who was also Public Enemy Number 1, the "vagrant" who fed thousands of hungry, law-abiding citizens. Capone appealed to Americans because he combined several persistent popular mythologies. To some, he was an urban outlaw, Jesse James in Chicago's canyons of steel and stone, a man asserting his identity in a world of ciphers. To others, he was a bandit with a social conscience, a romantic figure stealing from the wealthy to help the poor. Playing Robin Hood, he had the courage to confront America's impersonal, rapacious corporate culture. All that was required to seal his reputation was his martyrdom.

Capone's soup kitchen was distinct from his earlier generosity, which had always been private and capricious, although equally dedicated to his self-glorification. He had thrown money from a car, bestowed cash on widows at weddings, left extravagant tips, and in general enjoyed playing the "Big Fellow." In this case, however, his soup kitchen was carefully calculated to rehabilitate his image and to ingratiate himself with the workingman, who, he realized, had come to regard him as another unimaginably wealthy and powerful tycoon. Although his maneuvers gave his reputation a temporary boost, he missed the opportunity to transcend himself by establishing other social services for the customers who frequented his soup kitchen or leaving the rackets as he had so often said he would. That promise, once sincere, if unrealistic, fell victim to his fear and his notoriety. As Public Enemy Number 1, he was no longer free to return to the legitimate world; about the best he could expect was to forestall the inevitable reckoning waiting for him at the end of *la mala vita*.

Capone described his position this way: "The men with power are the men with money or the will to take it. They break down into just two classes: the squares and the hustlers. I am a hustler, but I got respect for squares." By squares, Capone meant Henry Ford or Thomas Edison, "a guy with brains and determination and a willingness to work for what he wants." A typical hustler, on the other hand, was a "stock market speculator, a guy who wants to make money out of money instead of producing something people want and need." And Capone had "no respect" for such people, he said. "They are greater crooks than hustlers in the underworld. At least an underworld hustler has the guts to go out and take it at the point of a gun." Through such statements Capone attempted to convey the impression that he was actually leading a workingman's revolt against the bankrupt, hypocritical Establishment, but the argument was cynical and self-serving. The working class supplied the bulk of his customers, but he had no genuine interest in helping them, preferring to reap the rewards of their expenditures on vice. To the extent that Capone had political power, it was based solely on corruption. Although he did a fairly efficient job of redistributing some wealth, it was also true that this particular Robin Hood stole as much from the poor as he did from the rich—possibly more. Indeed, the disenfranchised were his natural victims, and the wealth he displayed in Florida came largely from the pockets of workingmen who had succumbed to the temptation to drink, gamble, or avail themselves of a prostitute. Although Capone aspired to a higher condition, and argued that his magnanimous ends justified his brutal means, he had no political plan or goals, no theory of social justice, only an undying contempt for the law coupled with an inexhaustible cunning.

• • •

In the afterglow of his soup kitchen triumph, Capone wanted to do even more to burnish his image. He decided the time had come, as it does to all great men of affairs, to publish his autobiography. In his spare time he had been reading Fred Pasley's sensationalistic portrait, *Al Capone: The Biography of a Self-Made Man*, growing angrier with every page he turned. He saw the book as nothing more than another attempt by a journalist to smear him by linking him to every gangland killing in recent memory. In contrast, his autobiography would highlight his good works, his charitable contributions, his love for his son, and his loyalty to his mother, whom he called every day, no matter what. He lacked only a skillful ghostwriter to give the book its proper form, and after due consideration he dispatched an emissary to speak with Howard O'Brien of the *Chicago Daily News*. The go-between contacted O'Brien, informing him that he had been "thoroughly investigated" and was a "square guy" as far as Al was concerned—"Mr. Capone or his advisers had read everything I had ever written and there seemed to be no detail of my life which had escaped their scrutiny," O'Brien recalled—and if he was interested in writing Capone's authorized autobiography he should appear the next afternoon at the Lexington Hotel, one o'clock sharp, for Mr. Capone was a busy man and did not like to be kept waiting.

Intrigued, O'Brien followed orders, and "exactly on the stroke of one at the lobby entrance of the drugstore a young man appeared. He was straight out of a gangster movie, impeccably dressed, and with the inevitable pearl-gray hat." The man nodded and ushered the reporter into Capone's corner office. "Capone, as starched and pressed as a fashion plate, wearing a double-breasted brown suit, rose to greet us. He was heavily built with an obvious tendency to fat. His manner was suave, his voice gently modulated." O'Brien studied the surroundings: the filing cabinets, the view of Chicago, and the portraits of Washington and Lincoln—"and between the two was a drawing of Capone himself wearing knickerbockers and holding a golf club." O'Brien found the setting appropriate to that of any corporate tycoon. Capone began by making small talk about golf, and then, getting down to business, he complained bitterly about Pasley's book, calling it "libelous" and threatening the author. Alarmed, O'Brien said that few had troubled to read it. "Not at all," Capone told him. "That book has sold seventy thousand copies in Chicago alone." O'Brien assured him the figure was vastly inflated; the book hadn't sold that many copies "in the entire solar system." Capone excused himself to take a phone call. "From Washington," the racketeer said by way of explanation.

In his absence, Jack Guzik, who had been listening to the conversation, declared: "There is the difference between a Jew and a Italian. To a Jew seventy thousand is a big number."

When Capone returned, O'Brien laid out his ideas for the book, but he found that whenever he asked a "pointed question" his subject refused to cooperate. For instance, O'Brien wanted to know, was it true that Al had actually bludgeoned Scalise, Anselmi, and Guinta with a baseball bat? Capone dismissed such questions with a wave of the hand and the cryptic reply, "I can't tell you that. It wouldn't be fair to my people." It quickly became apparent that Capone was far more interested in making money from the book than he was in clearing his name; in fact, he expected to earn "millions" from his life story. O'Brien tried to explain that very, very few books earned millions, but Capone brushed the thought aside. At the end of the meeting he signed a letter of agreement designating O'Brien as his authorized biographer and agent.

O'Brien took the first train to New York, where he made the rounds of magazine and book publishers, telling them that he would have the benefit of Capone's full cooperation and would write about an Al Capone dramatically different from the public's impression of him. Why, the man even called his *mother* every day. But the editors balked at the idea of an "authorized" Capone biography. Still, the idea of writing his autobiography appealed strongly to Capone's vanity and his hunger for status, so even without a contract he continued to meet frequently with O'Brien, endlessly making plans for the phantom book.

They usually met in Capone's office in the Lexington, where Al habitually stood by the big bay windows, gazing down on the site of the Century of Progress Exposition, where ground had recently been broken. The event, designed to celebrate the city's history and replenish its exhausted coffers, was scheduled to open in 1933, and the city was betting heavily that it would revive Chicago's economy, which the Depression had battered, as well as its image, which gangsters, Capone especially, had tarnished. To Al the world's fair meant one thing, more paying customers for beer, and he had been lobbying unsuccessfully for a piece of the action. "I'd give anything for the beer concession," he said to O'Brien, who expressed the opinion that Capone should be content with the millions he earned from his current bootlegging activities. "Yes, but that has to be split so many ways," Capone patiently explained, "and there's so much murder and bloodshed and general trouble that goes with it. I'd much rather be in a legal business." In the weeks he spent observing Capone administer his organization, O'Brien discovered to his surprise that racketeering, though illegal, had its own stringently enforced laws. "I got the impression that most of the gangland killings were in reality executions, and in a strange sort of way, legal." In contrast to the legitimate world, where people could seek justice in court, "in the extralegal occupations, gambling, prostitution and bootlegging, the victim of an injustice has no recourse to a court. The only way he can make a man pay a bill and keep honest accounts is to threaten him with death if he fails. It was my impression that if a man in the rackets behaved with reasonable honesty he was as safe as he would be in any stratum of society." O'Brien would soon have occasion to test this theory as it applied to his own case.

In all the time they spent together, O'Brien found Capone to be even tempered and businesslike, except for a lunch when he promised his biographer that real, imported Parmesan cheese would be served. When an inferior American substitute arrived, O'Brien was startled by the sudden change in Capone: "I thought he'd tear the waiter in two. He behaved like an angry leopard." This was the only time O'Brien glimpsed the rage boiling within Capone, the only time the journalist found it conceivable that his generally affable and businesslike host was capable of battering three men with a baseball bat. When Capone regained his composure, O'Brien tried to forget the incident, but it continued to trouble him.

Other disquieting events followed. As he spent his days with Capone, O'Brien became familiar with three men, "shadows," he called them, who periodically appeared in the office and ordered Capone around. Apparently this was the powerful Chicago Heights contingent—Roberto, Emery, and La Porte—to whom Capone owed his position and for whom he served as figurehead. O'Brien was astonished: Al was supposed to be the big boss of Chicago, but in this context he appeared to be just a "cog in the machine and not a ruler." O'Brien thought he was gathering material that would make for a fascinating book, but then the three shadows with their shoulder holsters and pearl-gray fedoras began menacing him, throwing him "the look." Later, Capone rather carelessly confided in his amanuensis: "You know, sometimes I lose my temper, and I say, 'Gee I wish somebody would bump that guy off,' and then one of these young punks who wants to make a name for himself goes ahead and does it. And then I have to pick up the pieces."

On hearing that confession, which may also have been an indirect threat, O'Brien realized he had gotten *too* close to Capone, and the stories he had heard could send him to his grave. In the name of self-preservation he decided to relinquish the project, daring to publish his recollections only after Capone was safely dead. Once O'Brien withdrew, Al gave up any more thought of writing his autobiography and the millions it might have earned.

• • •

As 1930 drew to a close, Al Capone was able to look back over the last several months with a sense of satisfaction. The IRS and Judge Lyle had left him alone, and, since his return to Chicago, he had significantly enhanced his reputation with his widely heralded soup kitchen. To assert his status as the city's leading racketeer, if not its leading citizen, he gave his eighteen-year-old sister Mafalda a wedding Chicago would long remember. On Sunday, December 14, she married John Maritote, twenty-three, at St. Mary's Church in Cicero, a locale, noted the *New York Times*, "in the Capone domain but reasonably distant from the battle zone." Four thousand guests attended the ceremony and another 1,000 bystanders gathered outside the church on that wintry afternoon, all of them proud to be seen and associated with the public benefactor whom some called Public Enemy Number 1. Mafalda's new husband was inevitably linked to the rackets; in fact, this was a marriage joining two underworld dynasties. Although the groom listed his occupation as "motion picture operator," he was, more importantly, the younger brother of Frank Diamond, another Public Enemy.

Chicago had witnessed many opulent gangster funerals over the last ten years, but nothing equaled the splendor of Mafalda's nuptial ceremony. The bride wore an ivory satin wedding gown, complete with a twenty-five-foot train. In her ample hands she grasped a bouquet comprised of 400 lilies. Five bridesmaids, wearing matching pink taffeta gowns and blue slippers, formed the wedding party. During the ceremony, an organ played softly, but, according to one account, "there was an air of furtive repression upon many within the edifice, and detectives, unbidden guests, quietly removed five uneasy men, each of whom was carrying a pistol." Ralph Capone, convicted tax evader, gave Mafalda away. As Mafalda left the church on the arm of her new husband, the mother of the bride, Teresa Capone, dwarfed in a mink coat, dabbed her eyes with a handkerchief. It had been a perfect afternoon, with one significant exception. Although the wedding guests and journalists alike looked for him everywhere, Al Capone, fearing arrest, was nowhere to be seen.

• • •

Al Capone was fortunate in his antagonists. Although they were well funded and powerful, they were not especially popular. Among the most powerful were President Hoover, who had been discredited by the Depression, and the director of the FBI, J. Edgar Hoover, who was reluctant to take him on. There were others, such as the evangelist Billy Sunday, who railed against him, but they preached to the converted. Having enemies such as these actually worked in Capone's favor and elicited some sympathy for his plight. To many, if a man was going to have enemies, he could do worse than to have Billy Sunday and Herbert Hoover crusading against him. Pledging their support of Prohibition, they had proved themselves friends of hypocrisy. A man with enemies like those might even have something going for him.

Capone's youngest enemy, Eliot Ness, was different. He was as much a showman in his own way as Al Capone was in his. Ness cultivated a reputation as the college boy who raided breweries in the morning, played tennis in the afternoon, and dodged bullets at night. Yet in the months since Capone had been out of jail, Ness had made little headway against the racketeer. Perhaps his chief accomplishment thus far had been to refuse an envelope containing a $2,000 bribe. However, Ness did make a point of telling anyone willing to listen that he had done so. Unlike his elders, Frank Wilson and George E. Q. Johnson, who habitually avoided publicity, Ness was a glory hound; if he could not actually get Capone, he at least wanted to be seen trying. He wanted everything to happen in the open, under the glare of photographers' lights. He was a young man in a hurry because he had jumped on the anti-Capone bandwagon rather late, near the end of the journey, when Prohibition was about to become obsolete.

In November 1930, Ness's unflagging zeal earned him a promotion within the U.S. attorney's office. "I was instructed by the U.S. District Attorney to report to William Froelich, who came in from Omaha as special Attorney General," Ness recalled in his original memoir. "It was my job to ruin the income possibilities for the Capone mob. After conference with Froelich, I was allowed to pick a number of agents from any government service that I wished. I was to have a squad of about 12 men who would work with me directly under the authority of the U.S. Attorney and the assistant Attorney General." The actual number of men in Ness's group at any given time fluctuated between six and twelve, and original members of the "Untouchables," as Ness came to call his group, included Martin Lahart, Jim Seeley, Samuel Seager, Lyle Chapman, Barney Cloonan, Thomas Friel, Paul Robsky, Michael King, William Gardner, and Joseph Leeson, who, at thirty, was the oldest among them. Having the combined forces of the Untouchables at his command gave Ness a greater sense of power and potency than he had ever known. Furthermore, the existence of the group became a terrific publicity device. Once the press picked up the name of the Untouchables and wrote up their exploits, Ness was finally able to taste a bit of the fame he had craved for so long.

"Our first move was to make an analysis of how we could hurt the Capone mob and its income the most," Ness wrote of that heady time. "If this group of 12 were to make a dent where 250 Prohibition agents and quite a few thousand police had not, a different kind of game would have to be played. . . . I was later to learn that Capone breweries were manned only about 40 minutes during a 24 hour period. The first observation we made was that the barrels had to be used over and over again, and that if we could successfully follow a beer barrel from a speakeasy, we would wind up locating a Capone brewery." Two of the Untouchables, Leeson and Seeley, picked up the trail of barrels at a large saloon in the Loop. No detective work was required to ferret out its existence, for the place operated as if Prohibition had never existed. Hiding behind the saloon, Leeson and Seeley watched a crew of Capone men retrieve the empty barrels to take them to the brewery to be refilled. The Untouchables jumped into their Ford coupe and followed the truck on its rounds through the South Side. "When the truck was full," Ness wrote, "it made its way to 38th and Shields, to an old factory building near the Chicago White Sox Kaminski [sic] Park." Believing they had found a genuine Capone brewery, Leeson and Seeley rented an apartment nearby to conduct surveillance, only to discover they were mistaken. "The Capone gang," they realized, "in its typically efficient manner, had specialized operations. This plant was used for cleaning barrels (which was done by a steam process)." The Untouchables discovered other cleaning plants and estimated that the Capone organization was selling at least $140,000 of beer each day in Chicago. As they found additional sites, they revised the figure upward, to $13 million a year—truly a big business.

As their investigation continued, Leeson and Seeley followed the barrels from the cleaning plant to another fleet of trucks, heavily guarded. Initially concerned that they would be caught, the agents soon realized the Capone sentries had become so accustomed to going about their work without interference that they were extremely lax. Without being detected, the two Untouchables discovered that the barrels typically were driven from the cleaning plant at about 3:00 A.M. to another address, 1632 South Cicero Avenue. Once again, Ness and his group were convinced they had located a Capone brewery. Staking out the site, they observed trucks entering and leaving the building "laden down with their new load." At last, Ness wrote, "We were now ready to make a Federal raid."

The Untouchables' first major raid on a Capone brewery took place on the morning of March 11, 1931, under Ness's direction. By then he had taken a fancy to another one of his men—in this case an agent he had recruited from the Prohibition Bureau to participate in the raid. His name was Bill Gardner, and he was, according to Ness, a "full blooded Indian, who was a very handsome boy, and a fashion-plate. Bill must have weighed about 240 lbs. and he was all muscle." This was Ness's idea of a real man, and he plainly enjoyed Gardner's company, his looks, and the sense of masculine power he exuded.

Although the raid was fraught with hazard, Ness, ever the jaunty college boy, planned it as a "football play," with the emphasis on play. As the play unfolded, however, Ness confronted unanticipated obstacles and hazards, as he related in his memoir.

> I had a truck with a huge steel bumper on the front of it. No prisoners had ever been taken during a Capone brewery raid; it was our plan not to give them a chance to escape, so it was decided that we would drive the truck through the doors of the brewery; five of us riding in the truck and 10 in two other cars. . . . We put the truck into low gear, up the street and—wham—through the doors. The doors fell with a great loud clap, and at that moment my heart sank. There was no brewery! What I was looking at was a wooden wall, painted black, about two truck lengths away from the front of the building, thus giving the illusion of a vacant garage. We soon found swinging doors in this wooden wall and were on the necks of five operators in less time than it took to tell it.

The raiders' haul proved impressive: two trucks, including a glass-lined "tank truck," and five men, most notably a brewmaster named Steve Svoboda who was, according to Ness, "Capone's ace brewer, for each time [he was arrested] he would get out on bond and go back to brewing beer." Once the men were arrested, Ness took in the surroundings. "This brewery was capable of turning out 100 barrels of brew daily. Seven 320 gallon vats were placed in a line in the room which was automatically cooled so that each morning 320 gallons of wort, unfermented beer, were brought in a tank truck. One hundred barrels would be filled with beer, the fermentation period being two weeks. In addition . . . the beer was spiked with carbonated gas." To add to Ness's sense of satisfaction, the raid received newspaper and newsreel coverage, and this publicity began to spread the story of the courageous young special agent and his incorruptible band of Untouchables. It was precisely the sort of publicity that Al Capone's own brother, "Two-Gun" Hart, had received during the height of his Prohibition raids, tales of brave men risking their lives to capture stills. And, like Hart, Ness reveled in the attention. The sole disappointment of the raid was that his handsome young friend, Bill Gardner, quit the Untouchables immediately afterward. According to Ness, Gardner returned to his former boss, and said, "If the job is anything like THAT, I'm through!"

Undeterred, Ness devoted the next four months to a series of raids. In the account he wrote in his later years, he claimed to have raided no less than twenty-five Capone breweries and seized no less than forty-five delivery trucks. However, in a lengthy report to his boss, George E. Q. Johnson, dated March 26, 1932, much closer to the actual events, Ness offered a more realistic assessment of his accomplishments:

> From the inception of the organization of the special group . . . six breweries with total equipment valued at $140,000 were seized. Observation of the workings of these breweries indicated that the total income based upon the wholesale [price] of beer manufactured would have totalled $9,154,200 annually. Five large beer distributing plants were seized in addition to the breweries. The total amount of beer seized in the breweries and plants was approximately 200,000 gallons having a wholesale value to the Capone organization of $343,750. Twenty-five trucks and two cars were seized, the value of which totalled approximately $30,950. Many of these trucks were large trucks exceeding ten tons and some of them were specially constructed. Four stills were seized with an approximate value of $12,000. 403,500 gallons of alcohol mash were seized in connection with these stills, value of said mash approximating $4,000.

Even without Ness's subsequent inflation of these figures, it was apparent that the Untouchables had compiled an impressive record.

Ness was less satisfied, however, when he calculated the effect of his Untouchables on the Capone organization itself. In his 1932 report, he noted, "The attitude of the persons arrested has . . . changed from one of kind indulgence such as was shown in the beginning of 1931 to despair and violence . . . as these individuals realize that their backs are to the wall and that the United States Attorney plans to go through with the drastic seizures and arrests to its complete obliteration. It is interesting to note in this regard that it was apparent that the Capone organization felt the presence of this small United States Attorney's group more acutely than any other organization."

As he conducted the raids, Ness gained an appreciation for Capone's methodical and professional approach to the business of bootlegging. "Each raid was made in exactly the same way," he noted in his original memoir, "and each brewery was found to be erected on the scale of 100 barrels of beer a day. . . . Everything the Capone gang did was on a large scale and specialized basis. They had a sales office where the telephones rang without let-up with orders from speakeasies for beer and liquor. Another office was head of distribution—the dangerous business of getting the illicit product to the consumer. Another division was production; only the best brewing barons in the country could have so expertly designed and laid out various breweries . . . for 14 day fermentation." Ness made the most of his findings by placing taps on the telephones of the Capone sales office, and when the sales office moved to a new location Ness followed, placing new taps within a matter of days. "In a short period of time," he concluded, "it became almost impossible for them to deliver beer without a good risk of being knocked off by us."

Eventually, the forty-five delivery trucks seized by the Untouchables during their raids would be sold at public auction, but before that occurred, Ness wanted to use them to taunt Capone. Thus, he boasted in *The Untouchables*, "I evolved a brilliant psychological counterstroke." If not precisely "brilliant," Ness's plan *was* theatrical. He ordered the entire fleet of trucks to be cleaned until they gleamed. He then assembled them into a long convoy, really a parade, made longer still with the addition of several police cars to afford protection and to prevent hijackings. When all was ready, Ness arranged for the trucks to be driven along Michigan Avenue, past the Lexington Hotel. Just before the "parade" was to begin, so Ness relates in *The Untouchables*, he placed a call to the Lexington Hotel. "Put me through to Mr. Capone," he told the switchboard operator, and when another voice growled, Ness said, "Let me talk to Snorky."

"Who's callin'?" the voice at the other end inquired.

"None of your God-damned business. But if you know what's good for you, you'll put him on here damned quick." And when Capone himself did come on the line, Ness said, "Well, Snorky, I just wanted to tell you that if you look out your front windows down onto Michigan Avenue at exactly eleven o'clock you'll see something that should interest you." And with that, Ness hung up.

The drivers started their trucks, and one of the stranger parades ever seen in Chicago got under way. The trucks lumbered through the morning traffic, staying together with difficulty, as Ness, riding in the lead car and armed with a sawed-off shotgun, looked out for hijackers who might mistake the unusual convoy for easy prey. When the parade reached the Lexington Hotel, Ness was pleased to note "an even better 'house' than I had expected" as the captured trucks lumbered past the Capone stronghold. Brandishing his shotgun, Ness perused the sea of pearl-gray fedoras for the familiar scarred face and concluded that Capone was watching from his office window on a high floor. He looked up, noting the heads poking through the windows, but he saw no sign of Capone himself. Still, Ness was convinced that "Snorky" was up there somewhere, strangling on the humiliation the Untouchables had inflicted on him. Or so Ness imagined.

As the last of the trucks turned off Michigan Avenue, the parade gained speed and returned to a secure garage.

• • •

"In February 1931, I stood by the rail at Hialeah and looked into the boxes at the man I had been stalking for nearly three years," recalled Frank Wilson. At the moment, the IRS investigator was not a well man. Deprived of sleep for months on end, smoking ever more heavily, he had begun to suffer from mysterious pains in his teeth and gums and other symptoms of nervous strain. His boss, Elmer Irey, concluded that the best solution was to send Wilson to Florida, where he could recover his health *and* continue his research into the finances of Al Capone, who had recently returned to the warmth—and comparative safety—of his Palm Island villa. In Miami Beach, Capone again frequented the Hialeah racetrack, posing as another carefree high roller enjoying the warm weather and fast horses. The role made Wilson bridle. "Scarface Al Capone sat with a jeweled moll on either side of him," the man from the IRS continued, "smoking a long cigar, occasionally raising his binoculars to his eyes, greeting a parade of fawning sycophants who came to shake his hand like a veritable Shah of Persia." It was as if Wilson were gazing upon the devil himself: "I looked at his pudgy olive face, his thick pursed lips, the rolls of fat descending from his chin—and the scar, like a heavy pencil line across his cheek. When a country constable wants a man he just walks up and says, 'You're pinched.' Here I am, with the whole U.S. government behind me, as powerless as a canary."

In frustration Wilson did the next best thing to arresting Al Capone. Visiting a local dog track, he located an elusive bookkeeper for the Capone organization. This was Leslie Shumway, the man who had actually entered the figures into the registers Wilson had discovered that hot summer night in Chicago. Shumway was a major find; if he became a government witness, his testimony could conclusively tie Capone to the profits from the Cicero gambling clubs. The trick was to capture Shumway rather than frighten him into silence, and Wilson brought a certain amount of guile to the task. Within twenty-four hours Shumway was served with a subpoena to testify about a certain "White Steel Company." Shumway protested that he had never heard of the company, and the agent who served the summons readily agreed that it was probably a mistake, but he encouraged Shumway to appear anyway, if only to clear up the confusion and to receive an apology. When Shumway did appear, the trap set by Wilson swiftly closed around the book-keeper. The White Steel Company was fictitious, the subpoena a ruse. Instead of the expected apology, Shumway found himself face to face with Frank J. Wilson of the IRS, who produced the register of Al Capone's gambling income, the register Shumway had compiled. (Actually, Shumway had employed two distinct types of handwriting to confuse investigators, but Wilson had caught on to the gimmick.)

Even when presented with this evidence, Shumway strenuously denied any knowledge of Capone. "Leslie," Wilson said at last, "I know you're in a helluva spot. You have only two choices: If you refuse to play ball with me, I will send a deputy marshal looking for you at the dog track. . . . You get the point, Leslie. As soon as the gang knows the government has located you . . . they will probably decide to bump you off." Alternatively, Shumway could "come clean" by agreeing to explain the entries in the captured reg-ister. Wilson promised to protect Shumway, as Wilson had previously prom-ised to protect Ries, or, as the IRS agent put it, "I'll guarantee that Mrs. Shumway will not become a widow." Faced with the inevitable, Shumway agreed to betray Capone to the federal government.

Before Wilson had a chance to enjoy his victory over the Capone orga-nization, Elmer Irey received word from one of his undercover operatives that Al had kept watch over Shumway, had learned that the bookkeeper had talked to Wilson, and, exactly as Wilson predicted, planned to kill Shumway in retaliation. Irey's first instinct was to pick up the phone and relay the warning to Wilson down in Miami, but the IRS operatives had also notified Irey that the phone in the rooming house where Wilson was staying had been tapped—not by the government, but by Capone's men. Irey got around the problem by placing the call but first warning the operator not to say it was long distance, thereby alerting anyone listening in on the conversation that it was out of the ordinary. When Wilson got on the line, Irey recommended that Shumway leave Miami immediately, in the company of Wilson. Within thirty minutes, Wilson and Shumway were on their way to Peoria, Illinois, where they were met by Art Madden. Throughout the journey, Shumway supplied details of Capone's gambling operation and explicated details of the register.

Leslie Shumway appeared before a federal grand jury in Chicago on March 13, only forty-eight hours before a statute of limitations would have ruled his testimony out of bounds. When he was finished, he took an enforced "va-cation" paid for by the Secret Six. Accompanied by an IRS agent, the bookkeeper left for Oregon, one of the few states in the Union beyond the reach of Capone's tentacles, and remained there until May. With the addition of Shumway's testimony, the case against Public Enemy Number 1, after years of delay, was fast becoming overwhelming.

His nerves frayed to the breaking point by the stress of the investigation, Wilson had cut his investigation close, *very* close; had Capone's lawyers realized the circumstances under which the IRS had obtained its evidence from Shumway, they would have howled, but secrecy worked in Wilson's favor. In his willingness to bend the rules as far as he dared, he proved himself to be just the sort of zealot who was actually capable of damaging the Capone organization. Although he dealt only in financial matters, the trail of lucre led inevitably to vice, bootlegging, and gambling. Had Wilson investigated only bootlegging, or only murder, he would have had only a partial, distorted view of the Capone empire. By following the money he saw the big picture. The money was the most sensitive aspect of the Capone organization; Al knew how to deal with accusations of murder (he gave an interview proclaiming his love of family) and with accusations of bootlegging (he pointed out the hypocrisy of Prohibition), but he had no defense against the charge that he had failed to pay taxes on his immense income. As he knew, after the booze was served and the blood was shed, money was what it was all about; money was power—power to bribe, power to buy political influence, power to deny reality. Money—not bullets—proved to be Capone's main tool of business. As he pieced together the details of Capone's finances, Wilson was probing the essence of the Capone organization and the ultimate source of all his power. For that reason, he, more than any other man, more than J. Edgar Hoover, more than Eliot Ness, grasped the inner workings of the Capone organization; thus he, more than any other man, lived in constant peril.

Wilson was not the only representative of the federal government who traveled to Florida to conduct covert surveillance of Al Capone. George E. Q. Johnson, the U.S. attorney who was assembling the evidence collected by Wilson and the other agents into a case, also made the pilgrimage to Miami Beach, ostensibly to recover from a nasty bout of bronchitis brought on by the merciless Chicago winter. Even as Johnson kept watch on Capone, the racketeer's hirelings kept tabs on the prosecutor and his son. "We picked up Secret Service agents in Miami," recalls his son, George Jr., who accompanied his father, "and we arrived by train and went straight out to Palm Island to see the Capone mansion. It was a gorgeous place. I was a young man at the time, and I was impressed, because back in Chicago my life was restricted. Apparently word got around the gang that we were there, and there were cars and strange, tough-looking people hanging around our hotel. The hotel management was less than happy about our being there, not because we were disorderly but because of the activity our presence created around the hotel. The other guests were afraid they'd be caught in the crossfire of my father's assassination."

                                    •   •   •

With both Frank Wilson and George E. Q. Johnson tracking his movements in Miami, Capone decided that he would be safer in Chicago, winter weather or not. Two urgent matters required his presence, the mayoral primary and a new summons for his arrest, and both were scheduled only days apart. First, the election. Of the utmost importance to Capone was the defeat of Judge Lyle, the dangerous, publicity hungry reformer who had staked his campaign on the effort to jail Capone for vagrancy. That left "Big Bill" Thompson, the Republican incumbent, who was entrenched, thoroughly discredited, but nonetheless willing to do Capone's bidding. Lyle was determined to make Thompson's ties to Public Enemy Number 1 the sole campaign issue. "If Mayor Thompson is renominated, the newspapers of the United States and Europe will herald the news with headlines saying, 'Capone Wins,' " he told a rally. "Four years ago it was not generally known that Capone was behind the Thompson scenes. Now his face can be seen plainly peering from the wings, looking over the crowd to see whether his star performer is getting away with it." But Thompson wasn't getting away with much in this campaign. Lyle and the Chicago Crime Commission both declared that they had proof that Capone had contributed to Thompson's campaign; sums varying from $25,000 to $150,000 were mentioned.

On February 21, four days after Lyle leveled his charges and four days before the election, Capone, accompanied by his brother Ralph, took the Dixie Flyer from Miami to Danville, Illinois, and proceeded to Chicago, where the primary was entering its final frenzy. Thompson emerged from the seclusion that had marked most of his term as mayor to clobber his opponent with crudely entertaining rhetoric. In campaign speeches he called Lyle a "monkey," a "chimpanzee," and "the greatest liar." In exasperation, he growled, "That lily-livered reformer has attacked my integrity. That's too much. I'll knock him down and jump on his face and kick hell out of him. You watch Big Bill Thompson." Rising to this dubious challenge, Lyle replied, "People have grown tired of this blubbering jungle hippopotamus, defending his gangsters, his crooked contractors, and lazy blood-sucking jobbers by slobbering insults against the people of Chicago." The voters loved the fray; this was politics, Chicago-style—part street brawl, part circus. It was generally assumed that Thompson would easily defeat Lyle and that Chicago was destined to succumb to four more years of "Bigbillism," with all its attendant corruption and spectacle. The prospect suited Capone, who had long profited greatly from the status quo.

As the rhetoric dazzled the public, private discussions proved more revealing of the extent of Capone's involvement in the election. Shortly before the primary, Judge Lyle encountered Tony Cermak, the likely Democratic candidate, at a wake.

"Notice anything strange about that fellow?" Cermak asked him afterward, meaning the corpse.

"I think he was wearing a wig," Lyle said.

"Shotgun slugs took off the top of his head," Cermak explained. "He used to work for the Genna brothers. Then he went out on his own as an alcohol cooker. He killed two Capone men who had been assigned to kill him."

Lyle considered this information and demanded that Cermak, his former boxing partner, get to the point.

"John," Cermak told him, "you were put on the spot at that wake. You were pointed out to at least eight members of the Mafia. They're scheming to kill you. . . . My man says the Capone . . . leaders have been meeting to discuss what to do about you. They know the straw votes show you running ahead of Thompson 4 to 1 and in some places 8 to 1. They don't want you nominated because they know that if you're elected you'll run 'em out of town." Cermak advised Lyle not to travel anywhere without a full complement of bodyguards and expressed the hope that Lyle would defeat Thompson in the primary. Of the Capone organization, Cermak confided, "They don't know how I feel about them. I think I can get some support from the mob in the campaign. I'll take it. But after the election I'll boot them out of town."

Lyle was astonished by Cermak's remarks. First he had threatened the judge, then he had denounced Capone, and finally he had implied he had formed a secret alliance with Capone. "In effect he was announcing his intention to double-cross the Capone mob," Lyle realized. "It was, I reflected, a dangerous game to play with cutthroats."

Despite Cermak's prediction of a Lyle victory, Thompson swept the primary, much to Capone's relief. The victory demonstrated that "Big Bill" Thompson and by extension Al Capone remained the dominant power in Chicago's Republican machine, but at the same time the prospect of Thompson's infesting City Hall for four more years inspired fresh public scrutiny of his racketeering affiliations. On that point, at least, the defeated Judge Lyle had been absolutely correct. And because the notorious Al Capone was involved, an obscure primary election in the American Midwest attracted not just national but international attention. Hours after declaring victory, Thompson was on the phone with the *London Daily Express*, defending his record, claiming he had nothing to do with Capone, in short, lying. It was all "newspaper talk," he declared. "I don't know anything about Al Capone. . . . I don't know where you folks get that stuff, but I can tell you that the statistics published by the United States Government show that there are only sixty-eight other cities in this country with a population of more than one hundred thousand that have less crime than Chicago." Did that make everything perfectly confused? If so, Thompson was happy.

With his defeat, Judge Lyle's effort to "get Capone," which had always been driven more by publicity and emotion than by logic or the law, ground to a halt. The vagrancy case on which the judge had staked his reputation as a gangbuster ("Capone deserves to die like a reptile") was quietly dropped because the assistant state's attorney claimed he "was unable to find any policemen who would give evidence of illegal activities of Al Capone, public enemy No. 1, within the last 18 months."

Then there was the matter of the summons for Capone's arrest. As the city went to the polls to vote in the primary, Capone appeared before Federal Judge James J. Wilkerson to face a charge of contempt of court. The accusation stemmed from Capone's ignoring a subpoena in March 1929, shortly after the St. Valentine's Day Massacre, to appear before a grand jury in Chicago. At the time, Capone claimed that he was suffering from pneumonia and was too weak to travel all the way from Miami to Florida. The FBI subsequently gathered over a dozen affidavits from witnesses who saw Capone enjoying himself in Miami at the time he claimed to be deathly ill. The contempt trial was set for February 24, the day of the primary.

Appearing on the steps of the Federal Building in a conservative blue suit, spats, the inevitable pearl-gray fedora, and a gold watch chain studded with countless diamonds stretching across his vest, Capone appeared preoccupied with politics. "The election?" he remarked, "I was the goat, but Judge Lyle made me look silly when he said I put up $150,000 for the mayor's campaign." Then he turned to the subject of his autobiography, claiming that someone—he did not say who—had bid $2 million for his life's story, including "moving picture rights, serial rights and book rights." However, he maintained that he refused the offer; he was not going into "the literary business" even at that price because, he said, "that would be cutting in on the work of the boys who are writing about me." As for the Pasley biography, he said he'd read the first ten pages and decided the book was "about someone else," not Al Capone. "I don't belong in this book anymore than I belong in a book by Horatio Alger."

Concluding his diverting, if daft, remarks, Capone exchanged the early spring sunshine for the gloom of Judge Wilkerson's courtroom, where the racketeer, in the words of the *Tribune*, "settled his porcine bulk—235 pounds—in his chair at the counsel table and presented the complacency of a milk fattened shoat lolling in a mud puddle." To Capone and his lawyers, Nash and Ahern, this court date was a minor matter, a legal skirmish with no real consequences. They could not have been more mistaken, for James H. Wilkerson was a federal judge; unlike Lyle, he was not running for mayor, and he was not subject to Capone's usual manipulation. He was determined to teach the racketeer a lesson about the federal courts. Adding to the intensity of the confrontation was the expectation that if and when Capone was indicted for income tax evasion he would be tried in Judge Wilkerson's courtroom, and as a result Wilkerson inflated this initial encounter between gangster and magistrate into a dress rehearsal for the day of reckoning.

One by one, the government's witnesses told the court of seeing Capone in various locales throughout Miami, everywhere except at home, in bed, where he said he had been. As the hearing continued, it became apparent that Capone had in fact suffered from pneumonia; the only problem was that he'd been sick about six weeks earlier than he claimed and had exaggerated the length of his convalescence to dodge the subpoena. The hearing began on a Tuesday, and by Friday Judge Wilkerson was prepared to make his ruling. Summarizing the government's case, he said, "The evidence shows . . . frequent attendance at the race tracks; it shows a trip in an airplane; it shows a boat trip, and taking all of the evidence it is perfectly clear that at least after the 2nd of February [1929] it could not be truthfully stated that the respondent [Capone] was confined to his bed." Convinced that Capone had lied, Wilkerson proceeded to lecture him that he was not in a municipal courtroom this time, where he was able to bribe and intimidate everyone from the judge down to bailiffs; he was now in a *federal* court. "Now the Court deals with litigants, with witnesses, with jurors in only one way," Wilkerson explained, "and that is through the process of Court. . . . It is to be respected, it is to be obeyed, it is not to be trifled with, it is not to be flaunted; and . . . when an attempt is made to interfere with the execution of the process of the Court, when an appeal is made to the Court to relieve a party from obedience to the process of the Court, the Court is entitled to the fullest, the fairest and most complete disclosure of all the facts." As Wilkerson's words reverberated throughout the courtroom, Capone, who had been placid during the week's proceedings, anxiously fidgeted in his chair, and he appeared to be startled when the judge, to the surprise of no one, pronounced Public Enemy Number 1 guilty as charged.

Silence fell across the courtroom. "And as punishment for the contempt," the judge continued, "the respondent shall be confined to the Cook County Jail for a period of six months." No sooner had the judge pronounced what he intended to be a harsh sentence that would make an example of Capone than the guilty party leaned back in his chair and smiled, and as the grin spread across his face it became apparent that he was chewing gum, for he realized that a sentence of six months was no sentence at all. His lawyers

would appeal the ruling, he would post bail—$5,000 or some other incon-
sequential amount—and he would never see the inside of the Cook County
Jail. For all his lecturing and his reliance on the powers of the federal court,
Wilkerson had revealed himself to be a paper tiger, at least in Capone's
estimation.

As he left the court, Capone was surrounded by reporters demanding to
know how he felt about the onerous sentence the judge had just pronounced.
Summoning a gravity appropriate to the situation, he said, "If the judge
thinks it's correct, he ought to know. You can't overrule the judge." Al went
straight to the Lexington Hotel to celebrate both his deliverance from Wilkerson's wrath and the victory of "Big Bill" Thompson at the polls. All in all,
his first week back in Chicago had been hectic but exhilarating.

• • • •

George E. Q. Johnson was also delighted with the outcome of the case.
The U.S. attorney saw it as a victory for the federal court and a demonstration that Judge Wilkerson was capable of handling Capone when the time
came to try the racketeer for income tax evasion. In a generous gesture, he
immediately contacted the local FBI representative to express his appreciation for the work the bureau had done in preparing the affidavits proving
Capone a liar, and the agent in turn reported the discussion to J. Edgar
Hoover in Washington: "Johnson . . . stated that he was very much elated
with the outcome of this case, and desired to congratulate this Bureau in
connection with the obtaining of evidence and the work performed during
the trial of this case." But Hoover read this simple declaration of gratitude
with a jaundiced eye, for he detested anyone, even a U.S. attorney, who
dared to take credit for bringing criminals, especially famous ones, to justice.
Although Johnson had specifically requested cooperation from the FBI and
had been refused, Hoover rewrote recent history and claimed that he, not
Johnson, had led the effort to get Capone. To make certain that his version
of events was handed down to posterity, Hoover scrawled this startling comment on the bottom of the report from his agent in Chicago:

> The U.S. Attorney's enthusiasm is rather amusing. It has taken us
> nearly two years to force him to bring this matter to an issue. 3/1/31
> J.E.H.

Three days later, a selection of newspaper clippings hailing Johnson's early
triumph over Capone landed on Hoover's desk, further enraging the director.
His pathological jealousy and reckless disregard for the truth is evident in the
comment he wrote on this occasion:

Well of all the bunk, this takes the prize. It took us 2 years to get him [Johnson] to try Capone & now he basks in the sunlight of the effort which he did everything to avoid. J.E.H.

Both of Hoover's statements were, of course, blatantly false. It was *Hoover* who had done all he could to avoid the task of bringing Capone to justice. And it was *Johnson* who had devoted more than two years to the effort, risking his life and those of his family. It was Johnson who had tried to get the FBI involved, and Hoover who had refused. In trying to thank the FBI for the limited assistance he had received, Johnson had inadvertently made himself a powerful new enemy—not a gangster, but J. Edgar Hoover himself.

The episode marked the beginning of Hoover's disparaging and subverting the entire government effort to bring Capone to justice. From this time forward, he saw to it neither Johnson nor anyone else involved in the case would have the benefit of the FBI's assistance. More than that, he did his best to block the efforts of Johnson and his men (such as Eliot Ness) to further their careers. Long after Johnson and the others had forgotten they had once rubbed Hoover the wrong way, Hoover would remember. The director never forgot a slight, even when it was purely imaginary.

•   •   •

"Hell, Colonel, I'd know you anywhere—you look just like your pictures."

"Hell, Al, I'd never have recognized you—you are much bigger than you appear to be in photographs."

The scene was the Lexington Hotel, "Al" was naturally Al Capone, and his guest this wintry day was an unusual one: Colonel Robert Isham Randolph, the head of the Secret Six, the vigilante organization comprised of some of the wealthiest men in Chicago to be found outside the rackets. The reason for the meeting was simple: the colonel wanted to see Public Enemy Number 1 in the flesh, and Capone, convinced he would prevail over the Secret Six, was happy to oblige.

"May I use your telephone?" Randolph inquired. "You see, your name has been used to frighten women and children for so long that Mrs. Randolph is worried about me."

After Randolph called home to reassure his wife, Al presented him with a beer and a question: "What are you trying to do to me?"

"Put you out of business," Randolph explained.

"You know what will happen if you put me out of business?" Capone asked. "I have 185 men on my personal payroll, and I pay them from $300 to $400 a week each. They're all ex-convicts and gunmen, but they are respectable businessmen now, just as respectable as the people who buy my stuff and gamble in my places. They know the beer, booze, and gambling rackets. . . . If you put me out of business, I'll turn every one of those 185 respectable ex-convicts loose on Chicago."

"Well, Al, to speak frankly, we . . . are burned up about the reputation you have given Chicago."

"Say, Colonel, I'm burned up about that, too. Chicago's bad reputation is bad for my business. It keeps the tourists out of town. I'll tell you what I'll do: If the Secret Six will lay off my beer, booze, and gambling rackets, I'll police this town for you—I'll clean it up so there won't be a stickup or a murder in Cook County. I'll give you my hand on it." Randolph refused the offer, preferring to imbibe another forbidden beer. As the meeting drew to a close, Capone turned the topic of conversation to politics, specifically, April's mayoral election.

"Should I come out for Cermak or ride along with Thompson?" Al inquired.

"I think you had better stick with 'Big Bill,' " said Randolph. As Capone considered the advice, the colonel requested the pistol that he had yielded on entering the hotel. When it was returned to him, Al remarked as they parted, "So even respectable people carry those things?"

The next respectable person to visit Capone at the Lexington Hotel was the socialite and journalist Cornelius Vanderbilt Jr., who boasted that he had met and dined with "every major crowned head of Europe" by the time he turned sixteen. Now he had come to call on the royalty of the Chicago rackets. Like all visitors to the Capone headquarters, he was thoroughly searched, and after waiting in what appeared to be a large office, he was startled when a man approached him and stuck out his hand to introduce himself. "I was taken aback," Vanderbilt wrote of the encounter. "He was much taller than I had expected. There was nothing noisy in his attire: a conservative single-breasted blue suit, plain blue tie, white soft shirt. And his voice was quite pleasant: well modulated and clear. Only the famous scar gave him away. Otherwise he could have passed easily for a substantial merchant of Greek or Italian descent."

After they entered Capone's office, and Vanderbilt had an opportunity to study the view and the portrait of Lincoln, his host began speaking. "Here I am, Public Enemy No. 1, the meal-ticket of shyster lawyers and bum reporters," Capone told the young man, "and who am I with all of it? Just a piker. The real graft goes to the bankers, to your dad's friends. Isn't it true?"

"It depends on what you call 'graft,' " the young Vanderbilt replied, noting that Capone, despite his lack of formal education, sounded more like a left-leaning politician than a gangster, especially when he challenged his wealthy guest.

"Why should you live on Fifth Avenue and sail a yacht while millions of

Americans sleep on benches and in flop-houses?" Vanderbilt groped for words. "Do you know how many people there are on my payroll?" Capone inquired.

"I suppose quite a few."

"Over five thousand."

"All in the beer-running business?"

"Beer, beer and beer. That's all I hear. Why, hardly five percent of my income comes from beer."

"And the rest?"

"From the rackets. All sorts of rackets."

"You are very frank," Vanderbilt said, and Capone proceeded to deliver an hour-long denunciation of corruption and hypocrisy in the federal government. "They are only trying to scare me. They know very well there'd be hell in this city if they put me away. Who else can keep the small-time racketeers from annoying decent folks."

When Capone finally fell quiet, Vanderbilt asked one final question: "Do you have to kill many people?"

Capone threw his head back and roared. "I knew it was coming," he said. "Well, believe it or not, I personally never killed nor wounded a single person."

"And your men?"

"They kill only the rats and they do it on their own. I find out about it from the papers. . . . Let me explain to you how I work." Whereupon Capone pressed a buzzer on his desk and instructed an office boy to bring in "the documents." Within seconds a pile of ledgers, bills, receipts, and correspondence—all the records of a sophisticated, large-scale business—landed on his desk. Capone, who had worked briefly as an accountant when he was about Vanderbilt's age, began to thumb through the documents, studying the columns of figures, until the phone interrupted him. He scowled as he listened to the message, then handed the receiver to Vanderbilt. "Police headquarters. They think I kidnapped you." After assuring the police that he was safe, Vanderbilt took his leave with the greatest reluctance, for he had been "having the best time of my life" chatting with that charming tycoon, Al Capone.

•   •   •

As Colonel Randolph had advised, Capone stuck with "Big Bill" Thompson right up until the election, on April 8, when his candidate was soundly beaten by the underdog, Democrat Tony Cermak. The changing of Chicago's political guard reflected the transformation wrought by the Depression throughout the nation, and it meant the beginning of the end of Capone's stranglehold on City Hall. At first, a sense of euphoria overtook the city freed at last of a mayor who was not only corrupt, which was understandable given the nature of Chicago politics, but a national laughingstock, which was not. The morning after "Big Bill" 's humiliating defeat, the *Tribune*, his longtime adversary, published a furious denunciation of the Thompson legacy:

> For Chicago Thompson has meant filth, corruption, idiocy and bank-ruptcy. He has given our city an international reputation for moronic buffoonery, barbaric crime, triumphant hoodlumism, unchecked graft and a dejected citizenship. He has ruined the property and completely destroyed the pride of the city. He made Chicago a byword for the collapse of American civilization.

The jubilation inspired by Thompson's defeat was tempered by the knowl-edge that his successor, Tony Cermak, was no reformer. Unlike Chicago's last Democratic mayor, the honorable but ill-starred William E. Dever, Cermak was a traditional machine politician, a product of the Illinois Dem-ocratic organization. Coming up the hard way, he learned early in the game not to go around taking controversial stands, such as denouncing gangsters or supporting Prohibition; he knew the value of rewarding supporters with pa-tronage; and as he had confided to Judge Lyle during the primary, he was perfectly willing to accommodate the Capone organization, if that was what it took to get elected. For all these reasons, a wave of reaction to the election condemned Tony Cermak in advance as a second-rate political hack and influence peddler. In an article headlined "Chicago Goes Tammany," the *Nation* argued, "To the practical and unprejudiced observer it appears that Chicago has simply swapped one evil for another. Indeed, it is clear that the great crusade has had one net result: the people of Chicago, by electing Tony Cermak, have made him the most powerful political boss in the United States today. The power that lies in his hands is greater than that possessed by any other boss anywhere in the country; it may eventually prove greater than that of any other boss in American history, barring not even Tweed, Platt, Penrose, or Mark Hanna." Fueling the fear surrounding Cermak's elevation to the mayor's office was a considerable amount of ethnic prejudice and ethnic envy, for the new mayor was cut from a different cloth than William Hale Thompson. For all his buffoonery, "Big Bill" came from an old, moneyed New England family, while Cermak had been born in Prague, the son of a miner, and had emigrated to the United States as a child. To his opponents, a foreigner had become the mayor of Chicago.

Once Cermak took office, the crucial issue he faced, as the newspapers incessantly reminded him, was Chicago's gangsters, specifically Al Capone. Most publications predicted failure. "He stands completely helpless before the gangsters and racketeers, and he will continue helpless, granting that he is sincere in saying that he is opposed to gangster rule, so long as the operation of the gangs and racketeers remains profitable to so many of the important people in the city," said the *Nation's* correspondent, who went on to warn, "I have heard in the last few days from the lips of more than one speakeasy proprietor and more than one Capone henchman that far from fearing anything in the way of a genuine Cermak offensive against the gangsters, these men actually supported Cermak on election day in the belief that he is helpless to move against them."

In reality, Cermak's situation was not quite so dire. By now the federal government's campaign to get Capone was so advanced that Cermak did not need to do much on his own; the momentum generated by Johnson, Wilson, and the other federal agents carried him along. Furthermore, Prohibition, it was now generally conceded, was on the way out, along with Herbert Hoover. Spared the thankless choice of defending or subverting the law, Cermak managed to avoid the one issue that could undo his administration. Which is not to say that the advocates of the Temperance movement had given up. The WCTU, the Anti-Saloon League, and all the other drys continued to proclaim Prohibition a great success and to argue that the only cure for violations of the law, which were universal, was stronger enforcement measures, yet the jails around the country were already swollen with the ranks of bootleggers; there was nowhere to put convicted offenders, whom judges were increasingly quick to let off with a warning and wink. It was 1931, and the drys were sounding not like voices from another decade but from another century, as indeed they were, and few politicians, Cermak included, troubled to listen to them anymore. Even President Hoover suspected the cause of Prohibition was futile, yet it was too late for him to adapt to new political and economic realities, for that would have meant abandoning his political base.

·   ·   ·

To hear Eliot Ness tell it, by the spring of 1931 he had succeeded in destroying Al Capone's empire. As a result, "I was now receiving a great deal of newspaper publicity, and gradually becoming known as a 'gangbuster.' " However, publicity, like beauty, is often in the eye of the beholder. It was true that his name appeared from time to time in the Chicago newspapers, but only because George E. Q. Johnson made a point to tell reporters what a fine job young Eliot Ness was doing, going around in the dead of night raiding stills and generally distracting Al Capone while the federal government carried on the real business of assembling enough evidence to obtain indictments for income tax evasion. A typical account of his activities, appearing in the *Chicago Tribune* on April 11, 1931, read, "U.S. DRYS RAID BIG BREWERY OF CAPONE; NAB 5. Agents Batter Down Door with Truck; Seize

$100,000 Equipment." The name of Eliot Ness, misspelled, did not appear until the third paragraph. Even that much attention was too much, for Ness was supposed to maintain a low profile in the performance of his duties.

Addicted to the limelight, Ness ignored the need for secrecy—and for safety. As Capone's men became familiar with the identity of their principal antagonist, Ness became the subject of numerous threats. On one occasion, he noticed something amiss with the hood of his car as he happened to balance his briefcase on the fender. "Very cautiously I raised the hood," he wrote. "Attached to the wiring system just under the thin panel separating the driver's seat from the motor was a dynamite bomb. I carefully lowered the hood and called the police. 'If you had touched that starter,' said the Police Department explosives expert as he gingerly removed it [the bomb] from the car, 'you'd have been blown to kingdom come.' "

For once, even Ness was frightened, and he sat for a long time afterward in his car, trembling.

•   •   •

A month after taking office, Mayor Cermak confounded his critics by launching a major offensive against the Capone organization. The move was prompted by the discovery of the charred torso of Mike "de Pike" Heitler, a pimp who had, not long before his death, talked to the police about Al Capone. The state's attorney brought in no less than nine Capone lieutenants for questioning, including Phil D'Andrea, Capone's principal bodyguard, and Tony Accardo, now rising quickly through the ranks of the organization. Cermak himself declared that Al Capone was also wanted for questioning in the murder of Heitler. It was a bold move, perhaps a suicidal one, at least in Judge Lyle's estimation, but with it Cermak demonstrated that he had established a new political order in Chicago.

Capone was by now expert at distancing himself from gangland violence, and he knew the outcry over Heitler would soon fade—and so it did. Instead, he was preoccupied with strengthening his position on the national racketeering scene. His vehicle for doing so was the first major racketeering conference since the Atlantic City gathering two years earlier. Then, Capone had been in disgrace following the St. Valentine's Day Massacre, and his jealous rivals, especially from New York, had conspired to transfer control of the Chicago organization from his trigger-happy hands to Johnny Torrio's steadier grip. The plan had never been implemented, and Capone's dominance of the nation's rackets, especially bootlegging, had grown during that period to the point that he now played host for the new conference, which took place at the end of May.

The conference had been called following a vicious gangland war in New York, a struggle with national reverberations. Known in gangster chronicles as the Castellammarese War after the Sicilian village where many of the participants had been born, the conflict erupted on April 15, when Giuseppe Masseria, the leading Mafia boss in New York, was assassinated in a Coney Island restaurant. His death upset an uneasy balance of power among the city's rival Mafia clans. Capone's boyhood acquaintance "Lucky" Luciano took on the role of "boss of bosses" in New York, and he moved quickly to organize the clans into five Mafia "families" that survive to this day. Luciano himself took over the leadership of what later became known as the Genovese family, Joseph Profaci remained in charge of what is now known as the Colombo family, Philip Mangano became chief of the early Gambino family, Gaetano Gagliano assumed leadership of Lucchese family, and finally Joseph Bonanno gave his name to the former Maranzano family. At the beginning of the bloody conflict Capone had sent money to Masseria, but he wisely heeded a warning from Masseria's enemies to avoid doing anything rash, such as sending gunmen. As a result, when the smoke cleared Capone was on good terms with the survivors; indeed, they now looked to him as an established boss to whom they could turn for advice and connections, even though he was an outsider, a *Napolitano* among *Siciliani*. Thanks to this gang war, Capone was poised to win the acceptance he had always been denied by the New York Mafia.

Among the racketeers who converged on Chicago that May was the young Joseph Bonanno, in the company of Salvatore Maranzano, who had assumed *his* position on the death of Giuseppe Masseria. "Capone was an extravagant host," Bonanno later recalled in his popular memoir, *A Man of Honor*. "He picked up the tab for everyone's accommodations and provided the food, the drink and the women. He sent Maranzano a gold watch studded with diamonds. Capone also gave us his unimpeachable assurance that the police would not meddle in our business while we were at the hotel. . . . Despite his grisly reputation, now that I met him . . . I found him to be a rather jolly fellow, at least on this occasion." As the conference got under way, Maranzano related the travails of the Castellammarese War and then introduced the new heads of the New York families. "Maranzano spoke glowingly about Capone," Bonanno wrote. "Although Capone used to be of the Masseria faction, . . . he now wanted peace and the enjoyment of a society of friends. In so many words, therefore, Maranzano recognized Capone as the head of the Chicago Family. All clapped." Capone in turn gave a speech in praise of Maranzano.

Until this conference, Capone and the Mafia had often been mortal enemies. By the standards of the secretive Mafia, Capone's organization was too public and included too many non-Italians. The differences had been insuperable until now, when Capone and the Mafia finally met as equals rather than rivals. To be accepted by the men of the Mafia, to be invited into their secret society, meant new opportunities for Capone to expand his racketeering network into the once hostile territory of New York, and, of even greater importance, it diminished the likelihood that Mafia gunmen would hunt him down. To be accepted by the Mafia now was a high honor indeed.

Despite all the toasts, tributes, and outward signs of harmony, old rivalries and insecurities threatened to surface. At the final banquet, the heads of the various families offered a traditional tribute to Luciano in the form of cash-filled envelopes, but Luciano, concerned that his position made him vulnerable to assassination, wisely chose to refuse the gifts. "Why should you be payin' anythin' to me when we're all equals?" he told the others.

The exuberant Capone failed to grasp this Sicilian subtlety. "Maybe it's all right to break down them old traditions," he said to Luciano, "but why do you have to break that kind of tradition? . . . Why get rid of a good thing?"

"It ain't a good thing," Luciano said. "It makes them feel like I'm the boss and I don't want that. There ain't gonna be no more gifts, no more envelopes, nothin' like that." In private, Luciano said, "I think I really made Capone sick. His face turned green."

Even as the other racketeers welcomed Capone into the fold, they were acutely aware that he would be indicted for income tax evasion at any moment, and, given the federal government's perfect record of convictions for that offense, it was obvious to everyone—except, that is, to Capone himself—that the head of the Chicago "family" was bound for jail. The prospect of Capone's departure from the racketeering scene raised the vexing question of succession. Capone favored his brother Ralph as his second-in-command, but "Bottles" lacked Al's fighting spirit and leadership capabilities. Furthermore, he had been convicted of income tax evasion, and although he was free on appeal, he could be sent to jail at any time. Meanwhile, a group of younger members of the Capone organization vied for power; among the most prominent were Tony Accardo and Murray Llewellyn Humphreys—or, as he was known, "Murray the Hump," and by extension, "Murray the Camel." He was, incredibly, a Welshman, probably the only Welsh gangster to be found in America's gangland. He was skinny and dapper and handsome in a sinister sort of way, a representative of the new breed of racketeer, part thug and part businessman. And he enjoyed Capone's favor. "Anybody can use a gun," Al said of his protégé. "The Hump uses his head. He can shoot if he has to, but he likes to negotiate with cash when he can. I like that in a man."

•   •   •

As the nation's most powerful racketeers hailed Al Capone, the federal government's investigation of Public Enemy Number 1 nearly came undone.

The first sign of a problem occurred when Frank Wilson received another unexpected phone call from Mike Malone, the IRS agent living undercover at the Lexington Hotel as De Angelo, the small time hood from Brooklyn. This time, Malone was calling to warn that Capone had brought in five gunmen to assassinate Wilson, Art Madden, Elmer Irey, and everyone else of consequence at the IRS. "I suppose Al figures it'll scare the jury to death," the undercover operative offered. Once again, Wilson and his wife moved, only to receive further word from Malone that Capone had changed his mind and dismissed the hired killers.

Irey himself was the next target. When a Capone functionary visited the head of the IRS Intelligence Unit, hinting at the possibility of an enormous bribe, Irey, who had been waiting for this moment, sternly lectured his guest: "I don't happen to share the fear that Al Capone throws into a great many people. There is no reason whatever why he should be treated differently than any other man who has criminally violated the statutes of the Unites States Government. I might add that so far as I am concerned Al Capone is just a big fat man in a mustard-colored suit. There is one thing I want to make clear to you, and I will appreciate it if you will make it clear to Capone. We know for a fact that Capone does not hesitate to order the murder of anyone who stands in his way. Now, if anything happens to any of our agents or witnesses at his trial I can guarantee you that the whole force of the United States Government will be brought to bear against those who are responsible." The Capone delegate departed without a deal, and Irey returned to his business with renewed zest.

Finally, George E. Q. Johnson also became a target of Capone's manipulations, which nearly derailed the government's painstakingly assembled case against him. Two months earlier, on March 13, a grand jury had actually taken the fateful step of returning an indictment of Al Capone for income tax evasion, but Johnson had decided to suppress it to avoid publicity and because Wilson, Irey, and the other agents had recently discovered new information on Capone's income. In April, Johnson empaneled a new grand jury, which he expected to return a more thorough and damning indictment. By then Capone had learned of the suppressed indictment, and in May his lawyers, Thomas Nash and Michael Ahern, paid a call on Johnson, startling him with an alarmingly thorough account of the grand jury's supposedly secret activities. They went on to claim that it would be impossible for Capone to receive a fair trial in Chicago, where he had received so much bad publicity over the years. Once they had concluded their legal posturing, they came to the point. Their client, Al Capone, was ready to make a deal with the U.S. attorney. In Johnson's words, "If reasonable sentence were imposed he would be willing to enter a plea of guilty to the present indictment and to the indictments which he expected to be returned." This simple offer, essentially a plea bargain, placed Johnson in a complex dilemma. If he refused the bargain and went to trial, he would inevitably face the possibility of jury tampering, especially in Chicago, where it was common. Whether or not members of the jury had been influenced through bribes or intimidation, there was a real chance that Capone would be acquitted, and for Johnson, that eventuality would be a disaster. On the other hand, if Capone actually went to jail on a plea bargain arrangement, there was a good chance he would be freed in time for the Chicago World's Fair. That would be another disaster for the Feds, who worried that he would control unions and scare away tourists. For Johnson, the *only* acceptable course was a trial by a jury ready, willing, and able to convict Capone. Johnson had one powerful ally in this matter: Judge Wilkerson. From the way he had handled Capone in the contempt trial, it was obvious that the judge would, if given half a chance, prescribe the maximum sentence for Capone. Yet this course was risky indeed. If the jury acquitted Capone, there was little that Wilkerson, Johnson, Wilson, or any one of the dozens of other men who had dedicated themselves to bringing the racketeer to justice could do. Ultimately, Johnson was faced with a roll of the dice, and it seemed likely that Capone's attorneys had loaded those dice.

At that point, Johnson should have told Capone's silver-tongued lawyers there would be no deal; instead, he hesitated and explained he would have to discuss the matter with the Department of Justice. He left immediately for Washington, where he conferred with the attorney general, who also equivocated and instructed Johnson to wait. On his return to Chicago, Johnson and Ahern met again, and this time Capone's lawyer proposed a jail term of, say, eighteen months. Johnson refused; the sentence was too short.

The next person to hear of the secret negotiations in which Capone proposed to plead guilty in exchange for a reduced sentence was Judge James Wilkerson. Johnson expressed his opinion that the proposed sentence was too short; the U.S. attorney's office had gathered evidence of Capone's failure to pay income tax each year from 1924 through 1929. Wilkerson was horrified that Johnson was even *thinking* of agreeing to a deal. No matter how long or short the proposed sentence, Wilkerson would permit no deal, now or ever. As a result, Johnson was finally free to press his case. Meanwhile, Capone's lawyers labored under the misapprehension that they were was still negotiating a plea bargain.

At this delicate moment, June 5, 1931, the United States finally indicted Al Capone on twenty-two counts of income tax evasion, and the headline in the *New York Times* briskly summarized the long-delayed breakthrough.

CAPONE IS INDICTED IN INCOME TAX CASE

Gangster Surrenders and Posts Bail
on Charge of Evading
Payment of $215,080.

FACES FIVE-YEAR TERM

Chicago Aides Are Said to Have Revealed
His 1925-29 Revenue
Was $1,038,654.

"Scarface" Alphonse Capone, number one among Chicago's "public enemies" and reputedly the wealthiest of gangland leaders, surrendered to the government this afternoon and was released on $50,000 bail following an indictment by a Federal grand jury on charges of wilful evasion of income taxes amounting to $215,080.48.

George E. Q. Johnson, United States Attorney, whose assassination Capone was said to have plotted in an effort to forestall the indictment, stated this evening that he was ready for the court battle to send Capone to Leavenworth Penitentiary. Mr. Johnson has not yet failed on a gangster case.

The indictment ran to sixty-five pages, but the heart of it was the government's record of the amount Capone earned from 1924 to 1929, and the income tax he owed on that amount, according to the 1927 Supreme Court ruling that even profits from illegal business such as gambling and bootlegging were taxable.

Year	Net Income	Tax Owed
1924	$123,101.89	$32,489.24
1925	257,285.98	55,365.25
1926	195,676.00	39,962.75
1927	218,056.04	45,557.76
1928	140,535.93	25,887.72
1929	103,999.00	15,817.76
TOTAL	$1,038,654.84	$215,080.48

Johnson hastened to point out that the amount was by no means Capone's total income during this period, merely the amount the government's legion of investigators had been able to prove. No doubt Capone's actual income was much, much greater.

It is worth noting that, at the time, relatively few people were required to pay federal income tax. In 1920, for instance, only 7 percent of all U.S. citizens earned enough to qualify for filing. There were no withholding taxes; nor did the tax form automatically arrive in the mail. The taxpayer had to apply to an accountant, lawyer, or the local IRS office for it. In Capone's case, the government planned to emphasize his lack of formal financial records, as if the omission offered evidence of his hiding his income. However, there was less bookkeeping in those days, especially because most people did not have checking accounts. This chaotic situation led Will Rogers to observe, "The Income Tax has made more liars out of the American people than Golf has. Even when you make one out on the level, you don't know . . . if you are a crook or a martyr." Capone was both, for the law required that the government demonstrate willful failure to pay income tax, yet Capone had, in the end, offered to pay up. Despite all these flaws in the government case, the fact was that the same strategy had worked against Guzik and Ralph Capone, both of whom had been convicted for income tax evasion.

As soon as the indictments were announced, Clarence Converse, one of the Treasury's special agents, planned to have the satisfaction of going to the Lexington Hotel and arresting Al Capone for income tax evasion. Meanwhile Capone startled all Chicago by turning himself in within hours of the announcement, posting $50,000 bail, and leaving. Disappointed that he had missed his chance to make a little bit of history, Converse broke down in tears.

The following week, Capone was indicted *again*, this time for Prohibition violations resulting from the evidence gathered by Eliot Ness and the Untouchables. The indictment was, in the words of Ness, "a sensation." However, "sideshow" or "distraction" was a more accurate description of this legal maneuver, for the truth was that the evidence collected by Eliot Ness wound up in the newspapers, but the evidence collected by Frank Wilson of the IRS would be used in court against Capone. Yet the sheer amount of evidence against Capone that Ness and his Untouchables had amassed was undeniably impressive, alleging over 5,000 offenses, 4,000 of which stemmed from the transportation of beer in delivery trucks. However, Johnson, who was Ness's boss, realized it would be futile to attempt to convict Capone for bootlegging. Instead, the U.S. attorney gave this fine young man, Eliot Ness, a public pat on the back and immediately returned to the important business of Capone's taxes.

Ness actually received more coverage in the *New York Times* than he did in the Chicago newspapers, which still misspelled his name, when they even mentioned it. On the morning of June 18, for instance, New Yorkers read a lengthy account of the Untouchables' numerous raids. "FACED MANY PERILS

IN CAPONE ROUND-UP," the headline declared. "Squad of Seven Young Dry Agents Credited with Successful Drive on Chicago Gangster. LEADER ONLY 28 YEARS OLD. Impervious to Threats of Death and Bribes, They Have Been Styled 'Untouchables.' " The *Times* portrayed Ness as a rarity among law enforcement agents, for he was young, possessed a sense of humor, college-educated, and becomingly modest ("What of the offers of bribes and the threats of death that came the way of Eliot Ness and his youthful assistants? Ness is reluctant to talk about them. He calls them side incidents in the larger task of doing a job and doing it well.").

That was New York. In Chicago, journalists were neither charmed by his sense of humor nor impressed by his degree from the University of Chicago. "Ness was considered not quite a phony but strictly small time," recalls Tony Berardi, the veteran newspaper photographer. Indeed, when Ness later tried to recruit a Chicago journalist to help him write his version of the effort to get Capone in *The Untouchables*, he found no takers. The reporters he approached had lived through the Prohibition era in Chicago, they had known and covered Capone, and the idea of writing a book about how Eliot Ness, of all people, destroyed Al Capone struck them as ludicrous. If they recognized the name at all—and many of the journalists could not—they knew that Ness had played only a minor role in the multifaceted effort to bring Capone to justice.

Indeed, there many who came forward to assert their claim to the title "The Man Who Got Capone," some with more reason than others. There was J. Edgar Hoover, for one, although he had done all he could to keep the FBI from becoming involved; his claim was, if anything, even more exaggerated than Ness's boasting. Then there was President Herbert Hoover, who also believed he deserved some credit, and indeed he did. But most of the credit belonged to two lesser-known men, Frank Wilson of the IRS, who actually did the investigative work, and George E. Q. Johnson, the U.S. attorney who devoted five years of his life to the quest and who coordinated the contributions and balanced the conflicting claims of all the parties involved. Of them all, Johnson was most deserving of the title "The Man Who Got Capone," for without him Capone would have remained at large indefinitely. Yet of all those who claimed responsibility for bringing Al Capone to justice, Johnson was among the least boastful, the only one to resist the temptation to write books or articles recounting his exploits and singing his own praises. It is one of the ironies of the entire history of the effort to get Capone that Eliot Ness, whose role was rather small, ultimately received more credit than any of the others because he gave himself the opportunity to play between the covers of a book the heroic role that real life denied him.

• • •

Now that Capone had finally been indicted, the Chicago press gleefully predicted his defeat and humiliation. On June 15, a front-page cartoon in the *Tribune* depicted a roly-poly Capone sitting on the shoulders of a stooped, beleaguered Chicago. Meanwhile, a large hand labeled "U.S. District Attorney Johnson" reached from behind to yank Capone from his perch. As a crown fell from his head and a gun dropped from his hand, a startled Capone heard a voice of doom warn: "King Alphonse, you are about to lose your throne."

However, it would not be quite that easy to depose "King" Capone. At the time of the indictment, the racketeer had abandoned his throne in Chicago and retreated to Benton Harbor, Michigan, the quiet lakeside community where so many of his principal lieutenants had built large, secluded homes. Capone spent his days at a nearby golf course and his nights at the Vincent Hotel, where he and his men occupied an entire floor. "Every time Al's fleet of big sedans, carrying his 'gorillas' and guests, draws up in front of the hotel," an observer noted, "Manager Dan O'Connor greets him from the front door, bowing and rubbing his hands, while Al marches down a nodding file of unctuous bellhops to the clerk's desk." The reason for the bowing and scraping was that the honored guest distributed the largest tips ever seen in Benton Harbor: $10 for the manicurist, $5 for the bellhop. Impressed by this bounty, the mayor, Merwin Strouk, pronounced Capone a "perfect gentleman," and, he added, "I know our citizens have no objections to his presence."

Meanwhile, his lawyers were wheeling and dealing on his behalf in Chicago. Ahern and Nash believed—or said they believed—that they had previously reached an agreement with Johnson whereby their client would plead guilty and receive a reduced sentence. With this understanding Capone formally pleaded guilty as charged, immediately thereafter declaring that he had made a deal with the government to serve two and a half years in jail. Although the government would later deny his claim, the fact was that Capone had struck a bargain. On July 24, the attorney general of the United States wrote to Johnson,

> Your proposal to make a recommendation to the Court as to the sentence to be imposed on Alphonse Capone has my approval. I understand the recommendation will be that on his pleas of guilty to the several counts in the indictments charging violations of the income tax laws he be sentenced to a term of two and one-half years in the aggregate, to run concurrently with the sentence that is imposed upon him under the indictment charging conspiracy to violate the National prohibition act. The maximum sentence which could be imposed under the latter indictment, as I understand, is two years.

In other words, the deal covered both the tax evasion and bootlegging indictments. All things considered, it was, for Capone, an attractive proposition. He was only thirty-two at the time, and he would be out of jail before his thirty-fifth birthday, able to look forward to decades of racketeering.

> While the sentence recommended seems a moderate one [the Attorney General continued], the Treasury Department informs me that it would be more severe than any other that has been imposed on an income tax case on a plea of guilty. . . . I believe we are all agreed that the public interests would best be served by the immediate imprisonment of Capone for a substantial term in the penitentiary, rather than by incurring all the risks and delays of a contested trial in the hope that after a year or two a more severe punishment would be inflicted.

That the federal government was willing at this late a date to forgo a trial and make a deal with Capone should have cast a pall over Chicago. It did come as a disappointment for those who had dedicated themselves to getting rid of Capone permanently. "There is a very distinct undertone of dissatisfaction," wrote Frank Loesch to President Hoover of the proposed deal. "I have had many expressions to the effect that 'Well, you got your man, you got him by law; that is better than his being murdered by gangsters.'" That was a minority opinion. In contrast, the press and public interpreted Capone's guilty plea as an indication that he was so overwhelmed by the indictments that he was finished. "The abject refusal of Capone to fight against the mountain of evidence piled up by the government was regarded as his farewell to power and perhaps the actual breaking up of the entire criminal business organization he and his predecessors had built up in ten years of ruthless effort," the *Tribune* commented. Premature valedictories appeared, bidding adieu to the "Last of the great gang monarchs," and sounding the "Knell of super crime." Newspapers confidently predicted that he would enter Leavenworth before the month was out. George E. Q. Johnson traveled to Springfield, Illinois, where Herbert Hoover was attending a ceremony rededicating Lincoln's tomb, to receive the congratulations from the president himself on a job well done, and when Johnson returned to Chicago he paused for a picture with his wife and son in front of their home. J. Edgar Hoover's reaction to the lionizing of the U.S. attorney can only be imagined.

The extraordinary excitement signified that more than a legal proceeding was at stake. The effort to bring Capone to justice represented the collective catharsis of Chicago and, by extension, the entire nation as it emerged from its Prohibition-era stupor into the austere reality of the Depression. Chicago had never witnessed anything like this outbreak of reformist zeal, nor had the country, and certainly no racketeer had ever seen anything like it before. As recently as 1929, Capone's flouting of federal tax regulations was condoned and tacitly approved by many. During the reckless twenties, everyone from President Calvin Coolidge to Mayor "Big Bill" Thompson was looking the other way, but the thirties were another matter; the shattering of the economy introduced a sober, conscience-stricken tone in public life, and now Al Capone, who had thrived on laissez-faire and corruption, appeared to be a genuine criminal, a menace to society, the Public Enemy the Chicago Crime Commission had long insisted he was. Public tolerance and sympathy for him vanished; almost overnight he went from being a colorful emblem of the era, part fixer and part Robin Hood, to a pariah. He had built an empire based on social hypocrisy surrounding the consumption of alcohol and, by extension, sensual indulgence and pleasure; now a new social order was set to destroy him.

At the end of July, Capone returned to Chicago, where the populace suffered under 100-degree temperatures, and held one last press conference at the Lexington Hotel. It was a bizarre scene. Capone, perspiring profusely, attired in black satin pajamas, rambled on about his impending stretch in Leavenworth and declared his intention to go absolutely straight upon his release. He switched to the subject of gangster movies, a genre gaining sudden popularity. "Why, they ought to take all of them and throw them in the lake," he insisted. "They're doing nothing but harm to the younger element. . . . You remember reading dime novels, maybe, when you were a kid. Well, you know how it made you want to get out and kill pirates and look for buried treasure—you know. Well, these gang movies are making a lot of kids want to be tough guys, and they don't serve any useful purpose"— certainly not when the gangsters slumped over dead, as they did at the end of nearly every motion picture.

The next day, July 30, Capone, having exchanged his black pajamas for a green suit, appeared before Judge Wilkerson to enter his guilty plea in expectation of a reduced sentence. Spectators were waiting to catch a glimpse of Capone as he swiftly left his car and walked into the Federal Building under police escort. Waiting for him in the courtroom were, among others, George E. Q. Johnson and Eliot Ness. Capone refused to acknowledge the presence of either man. The day's drama began as his lawyer, Michael Ahern, raised the subject of a reduced sentence, and Judge Wilkerson became infuriated. "The parties to a criminal case may not stipulate as to the judgment to be entered," he told Ahern. "It is time for somebody to impress upon this defendant that it is utterly impossible to bargain with a Federal court." As the judge spoke those words, it seemed to reporters that Capone wilted; suddenly he looked defeated, shabby, his hair in disarray, his brow damp, his complexion ashen. So there would be no deal, no plea bargain. Capone changed his plea to "not guilty."

For the next several days all of Chicago reverberated with Judge Wilkerson's eloquently stated principle. "I cannot put upon paper . . . the thrill that went over the city of Chicago when Judge Wilkerson said he would not be bound by any such bargain as that," said Frank Loesch, who had considered the idea of sending Capone to jail for only two and a half years "abominable." Once Wilkerson ruled, everything changed. The government joined the battle, potential jurors were summoned, and preparations for what the newspapers were already calling "the trial of the century" went forward with a new sense of purpose and urgency. The trial date was set for October 6.

• • •

During the languid, late summer weeks Al Capone once again dropped from public view to visit his summer hideout in Lansing, Michigan. It was his last opportunity to stroll down to the little cottage by Round Lake, where Virginia, his golden-haired mistress, or her equivalent, waited for him. For the last time he was free to picnic with McGurn and the boys and to walk along a dusty country lane with them, laughing and talking. In the ways that mattered most, this was the last summer of his life, even though he had sixteen years left to him. As the days shortened, the weather turned cooler, and the leaves flared up into brilliant colors and began to carpet the unmarked country roads, Al continued to pretend that once he got the unpleasantness of the tax trial behind him, he would return to Lansing the following summer, and the summer after that, and everything would be the same as it had been.

Late in September, Capone surreptitiously returned to the Lexington Hotel. As usual, no one in Chicago, with the exception of a handful of intimates, knew where he had been during the late summer weeks, how he had spent his time, or how he had acquired his tan. Not even Ness, who prided himself on his detailed knowledge of Capone, had any idea of his whereabouts—only that he had inexplicably gone into hiding. The great fear was that he would flee the country, and the United States would have to begin tedious extradition proceedings, but Capone surprised both his lawyer and his adversaries by returning to Chicago as nonchalantly as he had left. Immediately he faced a rumor that had gained wide currency in his absence. Capone's men, so the story went, had been shaking down every bookie in Chicago to raise a huge war chest to pay for his defense, to which he responded, "Just the old story of Capone this and Capone that. . . . The charge that I have been trying to raise money from bookmakers is silly. It has for its purpose, though, the poisoning of the minds of those who may be called as jurors in my case. . . . Give me the fair trial that I am entitled to. If I lose, I won't complain about it." But as the trial drew closer, his tone became more urgent. "I'm being hounded by a public that won't give me a

fair chance," he complained to journalists. "They want a full show, all the
courtroom trappings, the hue and cry, and all the rest. It's utterly impossible
for a man of my age to have done all the things with which I'm charged. I'm
a spook, born of a million minds. Yet if Al Capone is found guilty, who is
going to suffer—a masquerading ghost or the man who stands before you?
You're right—it'll be me who goes to jail. I'd much rather be setting in a box
watching the world baseball championships. What a life!"

Although Capone sounded resigned to his fate, his entire organization was
in fact engaged in an all-out, last-minute effort to ensure his acquittal by any
means possible. Fortunately, Wilson's carefully cultivated network of secret
agents was still in place and relayed news of Capone's latest activities. On
September 23, just two weeks before the trial was scheduled to begin, Eddie
O'Hare contacted Wilson, insisting they meet immediately. When they
came face to face on a street corner in a remote Chicago neighborhood,
O'Hare conveyed disturbing news. "Capone's boys have a complete list of the
prospective jurors," he said. "They're fixing them one by one. They're passing out $1,000 bills. They're promising political jobs. They're giving out
tickets to prize fights. They're giving donations to churches. They're using
muscle, too."

Every figure involved with the case recognized that jury tampering was the
chief threat to the effort to get Capone behind bars, but Wilson refused to
become concerned, at first. "Eddie," he said between puffs on a cigarette,
"you've been reading too many detective stories. The judge and the U.S.
attorney don't even have the jury list yet. I asked about it today." At that,
O'Hare flourished a list of ten names, complete with addresses. They covered
prospective jurors numbers 30 to 39. Wilson's cigarette fell to the pavement
as he snatched the list from O'Hare's hand. He went directly to Johnson's
office in the Federal Building. The U.S. attorney, normally calm and controlled, took one look at the list and whacked his desk. "So Capone's even got
the Court under his thumb!" he shouted in a rare display of temper. "Some
skunk probably got a few thousand dollars for selling Capone that list."
Wilson and Johnson then went to Judge Wilkerson's chambers, where they
showed the list to the judge, who reacted with circumspection. "I do not have
my jury list yet. I do not believe it wise for me to ask for it, lest I engender
suspicion," he said. "I shall call you gentlemen when I get it."

At their next meeting, O'Hare supplied further details to Wilson: "Capone
and his gang are not worrying about the trial, Frank. They've got the entire
jury list parceled out in lots of five and ten names. Some of the biggest shots
in town have their quotas to work on. When they get through, every prospective juror on the panel will be either beholden to Capone or so scared
that the trial will be over before it gets started." Wilson was devastated; he
believed the government, after all its work, would finally lose because the

jury was fixed. The next day, Johnson and he again met with Wilkerson to impress the seriousness of the situation on the judge, but once again Wilkerson appeared unperturbed. "Bring your case into court," he told them. "Leave the rest to me." Wilson hoped the judge knew what he was doing.

•   •   •

On Saturday, October 3, three days before his trial was scheduled to begin, Al Capone decided to venture forth. Accompanied by "Machine Gun" Jack McGurn, the architect of the St. Valentine's Day Massacre, he attended a football game between Northwestern University and Nebraska in Evanston, Illinois, the home of the Women's Christian Temperance Union and the seat of the Prohibition movement. Being around McGurn made Al feel good; after all, McGurn had killed so many men and gotten away with it. Why shouldn't Al get off easy for failing to pay his income tax?

The two men arrived after the kickoff. As they took their seats they were subjected to hostile stares. Capone did his best to ignore them, for he loved sporting events of all kinds, and he expected respectful treatment wherever he went. But those days were gone. Before the end of the first quarter, a few hesitant groans were heard, followed by a chorus of boos, and as the game progressed the vocal disapproval of Capone grew steadily until it seemed that all 40,000 spectators were watching Public Enemy Number 1 rather than the game. Finally, at the end of the third quarter, Capone could stand the humiliation no longer. He left the stadium, trailed by McGurn and a daring troupe of Boy Scouts who ran behind chanting, "Al, Al, Al." The rest of the crowd cheered his departure from the scene.

The following week, the university's student newspaper, the *Daily Northwestern*, published an editorial written in gangster lingo. "Get this, Capone," it began, "you are not wanted at Dyche Stadium nor at Soldier Field when Northwestern is host. You are not getting away with anything and you are only impressing a moronic few who don't matter anyway." Capone was not accustomed to this type of rude treatment, but then what did a bunch of college kids know? Come Tuesday, he would face a more mature audience: a judge and jury.

CHAPTER 10

The United States of America
vs.
Alphonse Capone

"THE COURTROOM! HOT! CROWDED! Policemen everywhere!" cried the man from *Collier's* magazine as the trial of Al Capone for income tax evasion finally began. The excitement surrounding the event was palpable—as feverish, contagious, and debilitating as influenza. On the first morning of the hearing, a detail of forty policemen assembled to greet Capone as he emerged from his car, smiling incongruously at the throng. "There he was," a reporter marveled, "the boy who had 'come out on top' in the Chicago struggle between gangsters." And the crowd surged forward, hoping for a brief glimpse of his famous face, the scars, the fedora, or any other sign of his presence before the police escorted him into the gloom of the Federal Building.

Located at the corner of Dearborn and Adams, this monument to civic dreariness was only a short drive from his Lexington Hotel headquarters. Its monolithic solidity recalled an era when Chicago was a fort imposing itself on a lawless wilderness: a place of confinement in the midst of nothingness. If the exterior of the building presented unrelieved solemnity, the interior was slightly less forbidding. Visitors passed through an impressive lobby, whose high ceiling created a large space echoing with the murmur of business. Upstairs, on the sixth floor, the courtroom of Judge James Herbert Wilkerson abounded in patriotic and legal imagery. The walls were finished with white marble, accented by columns soaring toward the ceiling, whose tops were decorated with gilded scrolls. Some walls were devoted to large murals depicting the Founding Fathers. But time had darkened the murals to the point where their noble subjects were scarcely discernible, and few of the people who passed through this room would have been able to identify them. Everything about the setting evoked the tarnished state of the law in Chicago at the time.

As he made his first appearance in the courtroom, Capone was besieged by reporters who noted that he looked well rested and well dressed in a blue serge suit with a white handkerchief neatly stuffed in the breast pocket, a brown-and-white tie, and a thin gold chain studded with tiny diamonds stretching across his generous abdomen. "He wore no rings," one journalist said in disappointment at the lack of the gaudier gangster accoutrements, "and the two scars on his left cheek were barely visible."

Some of the best journalistic talent in the country had converged on Chicago to cover the trial of Al Capone for income tax evasion. The Hearst chain assigned the defendant's boon companion Damon Runyon to cover the proceedings. A man who lived by the motto "Get the money," Runyon approached the legal contest with the same bemused irony that informed his celebrated stories of gangsters' uncouth charm. *Time*, in contrast, gloated at the spectacle of "greasy, grinning" Capone, mopping his "fat head" as he prepared for his legal comeuppance. Even the *Christian Science Monitor*, which normally eschewed coverage of gangsters' uninstructive behavior, was there. *Collier's* became positively breathless at the prospect of the imminent legal Armageddon. "The Battle of Chicago is still raging," the magazine informed its readers. "Public Enemy No. 1 and a supporting army of gangsters and racketeers have taken the first three trenches: city, county and state forces could not stop them. Now they are facing the fourth trench—our national government." The *New York Times's* Meyer Berger proved a more even-handed commentator; he recognized that although society had changed in reaction to economic catastrophe, Capone himself was perfectly consistent. The Chicago papers, however, had a vested interest in the outcome of this trial. For them, the trial was more than a legal proceeding, it was a referendum on Capone's life and crimes, a crusade to rescue the city from its hoodlums. "It will be the most famous of all prosecutions of gang chieftains," the *Tribune* predicted. "Agents of the intelligence unit which developed the income tax case against Capone expressed themselves as certain of a conviction."

The reporters all posed the same question: was Capone worried?

"Worried?" he answered with a broad grin, "Well, who wouldn't be?" At the moment, however, he was feeling quite confident. He assumed that his organization had gotten to the jury and all that was required of him was to show up in court each day, appearing polite and respectful, until his inevitable acquittal. And even then he would be sure to act magnanimous and tell the press that there were no hard feelings on his part, he knew the government boys were just doing their job. His roving eyes landed briefly on his brother, Matthew, and his sister, Mafalda, both of whom huddled un-obtrusively at the back of the courtroom, Mafalda's anonymity heightened by the dark veil covering her face. Far more prominent in the courtroom were the members of the government's prosecution team. First there was George E. Q. Johnson himself, tall, wearing gold-rimmed spectacles and his familiar mop of unruly hair uncertainly parted in the center; the presence of the U.S. attorney signified that the government considered this a case of the utmost importance. He was surrounded by his team of prosecutors: Dwight Green, Jacob Grossman, William Froelich, and Samuel Clawson—all of whom would take turns questioning witnesses. As the U.S. attorney, Johnson was Capone's main antagonist in the courtroom, but throughout the trial the two men never spoke to one another, although they sometimes stood only a foot apart. Their proximity invited comparison between them: "Capone's thick-featured face, the roll of flesh at the back of his neck, presents a contrast to the attorney's lean face, his shock of gray hair, and his general appearance of wiriness," in the words of one correspondent.

Capone's confident façade crumbled the moment Judge Wilkerson en-tered the courtroom. "Judge Edwards has another trial commencing today," Wilkerson suddenly said. "Go to his courtroom and bring me the entire panel of jurors. Take my entire panel to Judge Edwards." With that, the men who were supposed to sit in judgment on Capone left the courtroom, where they were replaced by a new set of prospective jurors whose names had not appeared on any list and who had not been approached with bribes or threats from the Capone organization. Throughout the shuffling of jurors, Capone remained rigid in his chair, his smile hardening into mask. His lawyer, Michael Ahern, was caught completely off guard by the switch and hardly bothered to challenge any of the prospective jurors. When the final selection process was finished, the jury who would decide the guilt or innocence of Al Capone consisted primarily of white rural men; their number included a retired hardware dealer, a country storekeeper, a real estate agent, and a farmer; all of them were over forty-five. The sole exception to the jury's rustic, Protestant cast was Louis Woelfersheim, a retired grocer who came from Chicago. Judge Wilkerson's switch did not completely end the threat of jury tampering, since the Chicago newspapers dutifully printed the names, addresses, and occupations of all jurors. The practice, unthinkable in a trial involving organized crime today, exposed them to bribes and threats. To minimize the chance of the Capone organization's getting to a juror, the judge was determined to keep the trial as short as possible. And he ordered the jurors to be confined at night. Although they could be effective, neither of these precautions guaranteed an impartial jury.

"Capone is to have no trial by his peers in Chicago," the *Tribune* com-mented. "It is to be by the men who reflect the opinions of the countryside, whose minds are formed in the quiet of the fields." More bluntly, Runyon dismissed the jurors as a bunch of ignorant hayseeds, "horny-handed tillers of the fruitful soil, small town store-keepers, mechanics and clerks, who gazed frankly interested at the burly figure of the moon-faced fellow causing all this excitement and said, 'Why, no: we ain't got no prejudice again Al Capone.' "

After the jury was empaneled, Judge Wilkerson addressed Capone's counsel.

"What is the plea?"

"Not guilty," Michael Ahern responded firmly.

A native of Chicago, Ahern was just short of his forty-third birthday. He had benefited from a rigorous Jesuit education, and during the nearly twenty years he had been practicing law, he had become, along with his partner Thomas Nash, one of the city's best known criminal lawyers. Ahern was tall, with an amiable presence; his low-key, precise manner of speaking belied the fact that he had represented some of Chicago's most notorious hoodlums, in addition to Capone.

"Is the defendant in court?" Wilkerson asked.

Capone rose and faced the judge, and later entered the witness box, so that the jury would be able to identify him, as if that were necessary.

Court was adjourned, and the great room emptied.

•   •   •

Wednesday, October 7: Every place in Judge Wilkerson's sixth-floor courtroom was occupied for this, the first day of testimony. At least twenty-five reporters were present. In the hall outside, telegraph instruments clicked quietly, guards patrolled the corridors, and marshals occupied strategic corners of the floor. Within the courtroom, a clerk called the court to order, and *United States vs. Alphonse Capone*, the culmination of a four-year effort to put Capone in prison, was finally under way. Judge Wilkerson managed the proceedings with crisp efficiency. He did not wear a robe, preferring instead a somber business suit, but his air of rigid authority was no less intimidating. Having already refused Capone's attempt to plea bargain, he brought a brusque, adversarial manner to the proceedings.

The legal skirmishing commenced immediately as Michael Ahern—the slim, well-dressed, agile defense counsel—seized the initiative to complain about the circumstances surrounding his client's guilty plea, stressing that it had been entered with an understanding that the court would treat Capone leniently, and now the arrangement had been abrogated. Ahern managed to get his objection on the record, but the trial went forward.

As the prosecution outlined to the jury the case against Alphonse Capone for willful evasion of income taxes, Capone, a "bloated figure in the dark suit leaned indolently back in a swivel chair, facing Judge Wilkerson," said a reporter. "The thick lips formed a constant smile that sometimes widened to a grin. The fat, powerful fingers, covered with dark hair, drummed on the counsel table. The thick, hair-covered wrist flicked at the leather straps of a high-priced brief case which the gangster carries."

As its first major witness, the prosecution called an insurance agent named Chester Bragg, whose testimony proved suggestive enough, though it harked back six years, long before Capone was actually vulnerable to the charge of income tax evasion. Leading the questioning was Dwight Green, of the prosecution team.

"Do you know Alphonse Capone?" Green began, ritualistically.

"Yes," replied Bragg.

"Point him out, please."

Bragg pointed as he spoke. "The gentleman with the dark suit and blue tie."

"Describe your first meeting with Capone."

"In 1925 I was with a group from the West Suburban Ministers' and Citizens' Association on a raid at 4818 West Twenty-second Street, Cicero. It was the Saturday of Derby Day, in the month of May."

"Did you have any conversation with the defendant?"

"Yes."

"Who was present?"

"A number of people of the raiding party and some of the employees of the place, inside the saloon."

"Describe the conversation."

"Well, my job was to watch the front door and keep anybody from going in or out. A big powerful man tried to get in and finally forced the door open. I got sore and asked him, 'What the hell do you think this is, a party?' And he said, 'Well, it ought to be party, I'm the owner of this place.' So I said, 'Come on, Al, we're waiting for you.'"

"What did the defendant do then?"

"He went upstairs with Mr. Morgan, one of the raiding party."

"Did you have any later conversation with the defendant?"

"Well, I was present at several conversations. One was upstairs when Capone asked Mr. Morgan and the Reverend Mr. Hoover why they were always picking on him. 'Why don't you lay off me in Cicero?' he said, and Mr. Hoover said they were not picking on him. 'This is the last raid you'll ever pull on me,' Capone said."

"Describe what you saw upstairs."

"There were roulette wheels, pool, billiard and crap tables, and a chuck-a-luck outfit."

"Did you see Capone again?"

"Yes, when Judge Hamilton of LaGrange, who was with us, was asked to issue a warrant for him. Shortly after that Capone disappeared."

Green ended his questioning, and Capone's lawyer quickly began cross-examining the witness, picking at a small but telling point.

"What's chuck-a-luck?" he asked Bragg.

"I don't know."

"Then you can't say whether there were chuck-a-luck outfits there."

"I mean I don't know exactly. It's something like a parrot's cage and dice roll in the center.

"In how many raids have you taken part?"

"I was in on another one in Stickney."

"Was there any attempt made to arrest Capone in the raid at 4818 West Twenty-second Street?"

"I don't know. I didn't see any."

"Were others arrested?"

"Warrants were drawn for the minor help."

"You saw no warrant drawn for the man who said he was the owner of the place?"

"There was a demand made for the warrant, and I saw a man start to draw it, but before the warrant was ready Capone was gone."

"Why was the warrant not served?"

"I don't pretend to know the intricacies of the law in such cases."

Ahern shifted his tone of voice to disparaging sarcasm. "Oh, you suspect that there was skullduggery, do you?"

"I know it was a rotten job not to go through with the arrest."

After successfully suggesting that the raid could have been fixed, Ahern stumbled. All trial lawyers face the hazard of probing too deeply, of asking one question too many, and that is what Ahern did next.

"How do you have such a distinct recollection of this raid?"

"Well, if you had your face busted like I did you wouldn't forget it for awhile."

"Oh, you were beaten up? Where was that?"

"Outside, as I was leaving. My nose was broken by a blackjack or a brass knuckle."

Ahern stopped pressing for answers.

After Bragg stepped down, the prosecution called another witness, David Morgan, to corroborate the details of the raid, which Morgan did almost verbatim, suggesting that he and Bragg had been carefully coached about their testimony. "He was unshaven," said Morgan of Capone's appearance during the raid. "He looked as though he had about a day's growth of beard, dark complected, and some kind of rough shirt on; he didn't have a tie and a collar on, not dressed at all."

At this point Morgan underwent a cross examination by Capone's cocounsel, a tax specialist who had come out of retirement especially for this trial. His name was Albert Fink, and he was in every way Ahern's opposite. Where Ahern was tall, graceful, and smooth of speech, Fink was short, feisty, and blunt, and he tore into Morgan with a will. Under Fink's questioning, Morgan described himself as an "investigator for the Western Suburb Ministers and Citizens Association"—but an investigator whose powers of observation were limited, at best.

"That was an organization of the good people of that town to put down vice, I suppose?" asked Fink about Morgan's employer.

"Of several suburbs, yes, sir."

"What did they pay you for your services?"

"Forty dollars a week."

"And how long were you in their employ?"

"Perhaps a year."

After drawing Morgan out on his earlier career as a machinist for Western Electric, which operated an enormous plant in Cicero, Fink remarked, "Well, you have been a machinist all your life until you became a detective, is that right?"

"Well, I wouldn't call it exactly detective."

"What would you call it?"

"I was in investigation work."

After that, Fink did what he could to demonstrate to the court that the machinist-turned-investigator was not much of a detective.

"Do you know Ralph Capone?" he asked, referring to Al's older brother.

"I've seen him," Morgan replied.

"What is your best recollection as to the number of times you have seen him?"

"Probably about the same as Alphonse."

"What was the comparative size of Ralph and Al in 1925 when you knew them both? Was Al larger or smaller than Ralph?"

"Well, they had different shapes; I wouldn't say he would be larger or smaller in appearance."

"Which was the taller of the two?"

"I wouldn't state for sure."

"Which one weighs the most?"

"That is also pretty hard to judge."

"As a matter of fact," Fink concluded, "you didn't know them apart."

Fink's statement brought Green to his feet, objecting. The defense lawyer then tried to undo the damage Ahern had done concerning the beating received by the raiders as they were leaving.

"Nobody hit you with a blackjack or a pair off brass knuckles, did they, that day?"

"Yes," Morgan said, "I got about the same as Mr. Bragg did."

"Hit you on the nose?"

"Yes."

"Al didn't do it?"

"No, he didn't."

The procession of government witnesses continued with Leslie Shumway, one of Frank Wilson's prized sources, who returned from his Oregon "vacation" to give details about the Capones' Hawthorne Smoke Shop.

"Who were the managers of the place?" Jacob Grossman asked.

"Mr. Penovich and Mr. Pope."

"And just what kind of a place was that gambling establishment? What did they have there?"

"Well, they had the horses, and all kinds of gambling games, a wheel, craps, 'Twenty-one,' bird cage."

"Was it a pretty complete establishment?"

"Why, yes, sir, I should say so."

At that point Shumway presented thirty-four loose-leaf books documenting the Hawthorne Smoke Shop's gambling activities. Jacob Grossman began to leaf through them, pausing to ask Shumway if he had actually seen Capone on the premises.

"Yes, sir, I have seen him in there."

"Where did you see him?"

"Well, it would be in the office, because I never would be anywhere else."

"Did you see Al make any bets in that establishment on horses?"

"No, sir."

"Do you know whether he ever made any bets there?"

"Well, he has made some over the wire, but he didn't make any in the establishment."

"Did you ever see Al Capone's name on the wire record as having made bets over the wire?"

"Yes, sir."

"Now, how many places did you operate in, do you remember?"

"Yes, I would say five or six. I don't know."

"Right in the immediate neighborhood there, is that right?"

"Yes, all around within a couple of blocks or so."

"Well, where was the money kept?"

"The money was kept in a big safe in a nearby vacant building."

Grossman tried again to tie Capone to the gambling business, but the prosecution still failed to prove the crucial point, that Capone was deriving *revenue* from the venture. "Did you any time after that have any conversation with Al Capone about carrying the money over there?"

"Yes, it was some time later that Al asked me what I would do if I got stuck up, and I told him, I says, 'I would just let them take it,' and he says, 'That is right.' "

Shumway stepped down from the stand, and as their next witness the prosecutors presented Capone's primary self-appointed adversary, the Reverend Henry C. Hoover himself. The thirty-five year-old Hoover had succeeded in making himself into a celebrity in Chicago; even those who disagreed with him dared not criticize a man of the cloth. The newspapers liked Hoover, he made good copy, as crusaders went, he liked to be quoted, he made things simple—good versus evil, as in the Bible—and they took to calling Hoover "The Raiding Pastor." The name stuck. It was Hoover who had been the first guardian of the public morals to call attention to Capone's nefarious activities in Stickney and Cicero, and who had first generated negative publicity for Capone by proclaiming him the king of Chicago's rackets—all this in 1925, a year before the McSwiggin killing brought Capone under official scrutiny for murder as well as racketeering. The nagging Hoover was a man ahead of his time; few paid him heed while the money and liquor flowed, but now in a time when God seemed to be visiting judgment on American society in the form of the Great Depression, the pastor suddenly acquired authority as the man who had warned Chicago all along about the dangers of worshiping the Golden Calf.

Dwight Green of the prosecution began questioning the Raiding Pastor.

"What is your occupation?"

"Minister of the Gospel."

"Do you know the defendant Alphonse Capone?"

Hoover looked at Capone, who quietly, insolently, chewed gum. Through his pince-nez, the Raiding Pastor glared at Capone and pointed him out with his right hand.

"When did you first see him?"

"On a Saturday afternoon in May 1925 at 4818 West Twenty-second Street, Cicero. That was a gaming establishment."

"Where in this establishment did you see him?"

"In the main gambling hall, on the second floor, and later back behind the partition, in a back room."

"Describe the second floor."

"It was a large hall, with gambling apparatus, chairs, and racing forms, and then to a rear a partition shut off a back room."

"Where on the second floor did you first see the defendant?"

"I was in the larger hall. I saw him first when he came up the stairway, into the hall, and disappeared into the back room. . . . I followed him into the back room. When I saw him then he was taking the money out of the till and putting it into his pockets." He was, said Hoover, "dressed as though he had just gotten out of bed, with a pajama shirt and a suit of clothes. He was unshaven."

"Did you talk with the defendant at this time?"

"Yes. I said to Lieutenant Davidson, 'Who is this man?' and Mr. Capone raised his head and replied, 'I'm Al Brown, if that good enough for you.' I said, 'Oh, I thought it was someone like that, someone more powerful than the president of the United States.' " The reverend's bitter jest fell flat in the courtroom, but his implication that the federal government, if no one else, had jurisdiction over Capone's unchecked racketeering was not lost on the members of the jury, who did not know much about the law but did respect authority.

"What else did the defendant say?" Green asked his witness.

"He said, 'Why are you fellows always picking on me?' I told him this was not a personal matter, that we were simply trying to uphold the law in the western suburbs."

"Did you see the defendant at a later time on the same day in this establishment?"

"Yes."

"What did he say, if anything?"

"He said, 'Reverend, can't you and I get together—come to an understanding?' I asked him what he meant, and he said, 'If you will let up on me in Cicero, I'll withdraw from Stickney.' "

Hoover's improbably formal rendition of Capone's speech drew laughter from the courtroom, even from the Raiding Pastor himself, who turned purple as he continued his account: "I said, 'Mr. Capone, the only understanding you and I can have is that you must obey the law or get out of the western suburbs.' "

As Hoover told this story, Capone poked his lawyers in the back and appeared to find it so funny that he had to restrain himself from laughing in the Raiding Pastor's thin-lipped face. Hoover happened to be precisely the sort of self-righteous, self-promoting zealot Capone detested. Nor was Capone the only one who had his doubts about Hoover. The *Times*'s Meyer Berger spoke for many in the courtroom when he noted his reservations about Hoover's testimony. "The thought of this pale-faced minister dictating terms to a man who is supposed to have a legion of machine gunners and quick trigger men to do his bidding seemed incongruous." Although Capone, in Hoover's account, sounded more like a harried businessman than Public Enemy No. 1, the testimony did link Capone to the gambling house: a crucial point in the government's circumstantial case. "Capone had so cleverly hid himself in his operations, keeping no bank account, holding no property in his own name, signing no checks, always working through others, that he was almost invisible and invulnerable," Johnson wrote soon after the trial. However, even Johnson's good luck of stumbling across the Raiding Pastor was highly qualified. "The raid was five years old," he explained. "It was a question whether it was outlawed by the statute of limitations. This law holds that after a certain time a crime cannot be prosecuted. . . . We took our chance and went ahead." Johnson waited for Ahern and Fink to bring up the issue and try to have Hoover's testimony thrown out of court. "We on the Government's side expected them to do so. It would have been almost the obvious thing. However, to our utter astonishment, Capone's counsel failed to plead the statute of limitations!" And, he realized, "once having let slip the opportunity . . . Capone could not recover it again."

Once Hoover concluded his testimony, which entered the record without being challenged, Judge Wilkerson declared court adjourned. It had been a long day, but Capone lingered in the courtroom, flanked by his two lawyers and his bodyguard, Philip D'Andrea, who, with his gold-rimmed spectacles, quiet suit, and somber mien, looked like just another lawyer as the entire group posed for photographs. "The impression gathered from watching Capone playing hide-and-seek through corridors and entrances of the federal building, grinning at the crowds, and tirelessly posing for photographs," noted the Chicago Tribune, "is that the gangster is enjoying himself immensely."

•   •   •

On the second day of testimony, October 8, the prosecution seized the advantage by introducing a series of letters that seemed to prove that Capone had avoided paying his taxes. The background of the letters was this: In 1930, Capone, concerned about an impending indictment for federal income tax evasion, had asked a lawyer in Miami, Lawrence Mattingly, to handle the situation. At the time, this seemed to be a prudent move, especially since his brother Ralph was about to convicted for the same offense. However, the resulting correspondence was about to be used against him in court. As evidence, these letters cut both ways. On the one hand, they demonstrated that Capone was pursuing the matter rather than trying to shirk his obligation; on the other hand, since he never did take Mattingly's advice to pay the taxes, the Mattingly letters could also be used to prove that Capone couldn't claim ignorance in this matter.

Had Capone's lawyers worked harder and relied less on their client's proven ability to tamper with a jury or bribe a judge, they would have done all they could to make sure these letters were excluded from the trial. And if they had been excluded, the case against Al Capone, lacking proof that he was aware of his obligation to pay federal income tax, would have been far weaker.

The first letter introduced in evidence was from Mattingly to an IRS agent named C. W. Herrick in Chicago:

Dear Sir:

Mr. Alphonse Capone, residing at 2135 South Michigan Avenue, Chicago, Ill. [the Lexington Hotel], has authorized me to make an exact computation of income tax liability for the year 1929 and prior years, the amount of which he will pay as soon as determined. Mr. Capone has never filed income tax returns.

Next, the court heard a transcript of an April 17, 1930, discussion Capone and Mattingly held with the IRS agent about the matter.

HERRICK: Now, Mr. Capone, just so we all understand the situation, you and Mr. Mattingly are here in an effort to clean up your income tax liability. I want to say this, in order that there may be no misunderstanding, that any statement you make here will naturally be the subject of such investigation and verification as we can make.

MATTINGLY: Mr. Capone is here to cooperate with you and work with you. It isn't my purpose here, I don't feel that I can, in justice to my client, permit him to make any statement or admission that might subject him to criminal prosecution.

HERRICK: What records have you of your income, Mr. Capone—do you keep any records?

CAPONE: No, I never did.

HERRICK: Any checking accounts?

CAPONE: No, sir.

HERRICK: Do you own any property in your own name?

CAPONE: No, sir.

HERRICK: How long, Mr. Capone, have you enjoyed a large income?

CAPONE: I never had much of an income, a large income.

HERRICK: I will state it a little differently, an income that might be taxable?

CAPONE: I would rather let my lawyer answer that question.

MATTINGLY: Well, I tell you, prior to 1926, John Torrio, who happens to be a client of mine, was the employer of Mr. Capone and up to that point it is my impression his income wasn't large. He was in the position of an employee, pure and simple. That is the information I get from Mr. Torrio and Mr. Capone.

HERRICK: Prior to 1926? At that rate, the years under consideration would be 1926, 1927, 1928 and 1929?

CAPONE: That's it exactly.

MATTINGLY: I should like to say further that Mr. Capone will hold himself in readiness to appear at any time you may call upon him.
WILSON: Have you ever filed income tax returns?
CAPONE: No.

The transcript was no more forthcoming on the subject of Capone's income *after* 1926. When it came to his Miami house, he would admit only that he had bought the property for $10,000 in cash, and obtained a mortgage for $30,000. He refused to admit owning any racehorses or to explain how he had managed to pay his legal fees over the years.

In September, the court heard, Mattingly appeared at the Federal Building in Chicago to relay Capone's accounting and an offer to pay income tax. "Mr. Mattingly sat down across from me at the desk and said they had done the best they could to get the records," Frank J. Wilson, the IRS agent, testified. "He took some papers out of his inside coat pocket and in turning them over he would look out the window and talk very slowly, deliberately. Finally he threw the papers over to me. There was a two-page letter with carbon copies, held together with a paper clip. He says, 'This is the best we can do. Mr. Capone is willing to pay tax on these figures.' "

In what became the decisive moment of the entire trial, Fink objected to the letter, which was certain to contain proof that Capone knew he was supposed to pay his taxes and hadn't. The letter was so convincing that the newspapers took to calling it the "confession letter," and it was now apparent that Capone was, in all probability, facing conviction and a jail sentence, following the example of his brother Ralph and Jake Guzik.

To hear the matter out, the judge excused the jury, and the lawyers went at it. "This is the last toe," Fink wailed at the bench. "They have got him nailed to the cross now. This is just putting the last toe on him. I think in justice to the defendant that your honor ought to let the whole thing go in now, because there are some things in this letter that indicate that the lawyer was crazy."

"Well, I don't think so," said Clawson. Neither did the judge, who eventually permitted the letter to be read into the record. It was an awkward document, trying to harness the astronomical and carelessly counted winnings of a racketeer with the strict accounting demanded by law:

Sir:

The taxpayer is now 31 years old, and has continuously lived with his wife since his marriage in 1917. He has one child, a son, now nearly 12 years old. Since 1922 he has been the principal support of his widowed mother and his sister and brother, now 19 and 21 years of age, respectively.

Prior to the latter part of the year 1925 he was employed at a salary which at no time exceeded $75 per week. During the years 1926 to 1929, inclusive, he was the recipient of considerable sums of money, title of which vested in him by right of possession only. . . .

The only attorneys employed by the taxpayer personally during this period were Nash & Ahern, Ben Epstein and Capt. Billy Waugh, all of Chicago, Ill. The so-called bodyguards with which he is reputed to surround himself on the occasion of infrequent appearances in public, were not, as a general rule, his personal employees, but were, in fact, employees of the organization which participated in its profits. Several of these employees stopped at the same hotel with the taxpayer while he was in Chicago. . . .

The furniture in the home occupied by the taxpayer while he was in Florida was acquired at a cost not in excess of $20,000. The house and grounds have been thoroughly appraised and the appraisal has been heretofore submitted to you. There is a mortgage against the house and grounds of $30,000. His indebtedness to his associates has rarely ever been less than $75,000 since 1927. It has frequently been much more.

Notwithstanding that two of the taxpayer's associates from whom I have sought information with respect to the taxpayer's income insist that his yearly income never exceeded $50,000 in any one year, I am of the opinion that his taxable income for the years 1925 and 1926 might fairly be fixed at not to exceed $26,000 and $40,000 respectively and for the years 1928 and 1929 not to exceed $100,000 per year.

With the damning proof offered by the Mattingly letters now on the record, the prosecution had made the heart of its case. Even Capone, who had been a model of affability throughout, looked shaken by the revelation. A reporter noted, "The fatuous grin began to disappear and his pudgy fingers toyed nervously with the diamond-studded watch chain that glittered on his paunch."

•   •   •

While Capone sank under the weight of his tax burden, Eliot Ness boldly continued to arrest the men who ran Capone's bootlegging operation. Now holding the title of assistant chief of special Prohibition agents in Chicago, Ness arrested a Capone henchman named Nick Juffra (alias Frankie Rose), who had once worked for Joe Fusco, one of Capone's lieutenants. Juffra became the sixty-ninth Capone bootlegger whom Ness arrested.

However, despite the aura of derring-do which continued to cling to Ness, he had lost the public's attention. All anyone cared about these days were the events unfolding in Judge Wilkerson's courtroom.

•   •   •

On Friday, October 9, the government moved from strength to strength, producing its showiest evidence of Al's lavish expenditures on luxury items. The prosecution had a serious purpose; by demonstrating how much the accused spent, the government could infer how much he earned, but Damon Runyon, for one, found the premise ridiculous: "Your Uncle Sam argues that if a man spends a raft of money he must necessarily have a raft of money to spend, a theory that sounds logical enough unless your Uncle Sam is including horse players." As even Runyon had to admit, the tactic made for good courtroom theater. "LAVISH CAPONE LIFE AND $5 TIPS BARED— HIS ATTORNEYS RESENT 'SPANISH INQUISITION,' " the *New York Times* trumpeted. The government was pursuing a time-honored trial tactic, to sway the jury by making them envious of the accused with little things, concrete things, things like expensive shirts and suits and ties and shoes, things the jurors could never afford to buy for themselves. In the process, the jury and the public acquired a window on Capone's private life.

The prosecution turned its attention to Capone's gambling and business interests in Miami to prove that he had earned huge sums of undocumented, unreported income. Their first witness was a Florida state attorney, who revealed how concerned local officials were that Capone would introduce gambling to Miami and described a 1928 meeting he had with the accused and his lawyer at the time—presumably Lawrence Mattingly. "Capone and a partner of his came in," he recalled. "I said I wanted to talk to Capone about what he proposed to do in Miami. He said he was there to rest. I asked him what his business was but his attorney objected. I said that if I couldn't ask him what I pleased, the conference was off so far as I was concerned. Capone then said, 'I'll answer that question. I am in the cleaning business in Chicago.'

" 'What else?' I asked.

" 'I am also in the real estate business,' he said.

" 'As a matter of fact,' I asked, 'aren't you in the gambling business?'

" 'I have an interest in a racetrack in Cicero,' he said.

" 'As a matter of fact, isn't gambling your chief occupation?' I asked.

"Capone hesitated, and said, 'Yes, it is.' "

Dwight Green handled the prosecution's next witness, Parker Henderson, the Florida hotel manager whom Capone had befriended and used. Dressed in a stylish brown suit accented by faint white stripes, Henderson seemed ill at ease on the stand; he obviously feared the consequences of testifying against Al Capone, but the defendant tried to reassure him with a broad smile.

As the questioning began, Henderson said he had first met Capone in Miami in January 1928. "I was called to the defendant's room by a Miami man named George Downs, and I was introduced to a fellow named Nick Sorello," he explained, referring to a Capone bodyguard. "I was introduced to him as Al Brown. Mr. Downs said that they were some friends of his from Chicago, and that they were going to be there throughout the winter, and wanted me to take care of them. Some time during the conversation, Mr. Brown told me that his name was Al Capone." The following day, Henderson said, he accepted a dinner invitation with Capone. The racketeer sent his black Lincoln to pick him up.

"Who was present?"

"Sorello's wife, Mr. Capone's wife, Sorello, Mr. Capone, myself, and I think Denny Cooney and his wife." Cooney ran several brothels controlled by Capone. Henderson went on to testify that he proceeded to see Al nearly every day throughout the winter of 1928–29.

After drawing all that he could from Henderson on the subject of Capone's receiving wire transfers of money, the prosecutor asked about the curious way the defendant had purchased his Miami estate.

"Some real estate agents called me at the Ponce de León Hotel and wanted me to get in touch with Mr. Capone in regard to selling some property," Henderson explained. "This was in March or April, 1928. I was closely connected with Mr. Newton Lummus, then mayor of Miami Beach, and I told him that these real estate men were figuring on selling Capone some property and asked him what he thought about it. Lummis said that if anybody sold Capone any property he and I should try. So I asked Al if he was interested in buying any property and he said he was, in buying a winter home. So we made an appointment with him and carried him out and showed him several places. This place on Palm Island he seemed to like very much. Later he told me had decided to take it. He gave me money to put up the binder." The amount was $2,000, to which Capone later added $8,000, and the deal was done. However, Capone did not buy the home in his own name. To avoid publicity, the sale was listed in the name of Parker Henderson, who kept possession for several months before quietly deeding it to Capone's wife, Mae.

The deed was now admitted in evidence, and then Lummus himself took the stand, corroborating Henderson's story.

"Mr. Parker Henderson was over to see me one day," he informed the court, "and told me that Mr. Capone was interested in the purchase of a home, and he wanted to know if I could run the sale through our office, which we agreed to, and I went around and took a look at several places on

Miami Beach, and after looking at them several days later Mr. Henderson advised me that Mr. Capone was interested in a place on Palm Island that was later purchased." Under questioning by the prosecution, he gave further details of how Capone accomplished the sale: "The purchase price was $40,000. A $2,000 binder was made at that time, and I saw that payment; it was paid by Mr. Parker Henderson. The balance of $8,000 in cash, at the closing of the transaction, was paid in our office, and I witnessed the deed to Mr. Parker Henderson from Mr. Popham, the owner of the place. The balance of the purchase price was represented by three mortgages of $10,000 each, due on or before one, two and three years respectively." As explained by Lummus, Capone's machinations, while deceptive, were not in themselves illegal or the subject of the indictment; the idea was to prove that he had enough money to buy the Palm Island house. To demonstrate this point, the prosecution now produced no less than three Miami-based Western Union operators, who collectively described money transfers to the Capone family of nearly $40,000.

The prosecutors were not quite finished. Next, McLean Smith, a clerk at the Metropole Hotel, where Capone had lived in 1925, took the stand, and under much prodding he reluctantly provided further clues to the vast amounts of cash Capone controlled. Questioned by Jacob Grossman, Smith told of Capone's five-room suite on the fourth floor and another suite consisting of six rooms.

"I ask you if you ever saw these sheets," said Grossman, producing the hotel's records.

"I made them out," Smith replied. "When they paid me money, I put it down."

"Here's a record for $1,500, dated March 25, 1927, for the rooms occupied by Mr. Capone, is that right?"

"Yes."

"Under what name did Capone register?"

"Under the name of Mr. Ross."

"Here's an entry for Mr. Ross," Grossman continued, "on September 4, 1927, $150 for rooms and $650 for incidentals. Was that in cash?"

"Yes."

Capone's attorney Albert Fink protested that Grossman was merely trying to show how much Capone spent, but that, Judge Wilkerson reminded him, was precisely the point. "If there's money going out," the judge insisted, "there is a presumption that it is coming in."

Grossman resumed his line of questioning, showing that there was, indeed, plenty of money coming in. "Here's an entry for Mr. Ross on September 28, 1927, an entry of $1,633. What was that for?"

"For a party of friends."

"Ever see Jack Guzik there?" asked Grossman, referring to the man who doubled as Capone's accountant and brothel supervisor.

"Yes."

"How would Capone pay his bills?"

"In cash."

"What denominations?"

"The ordinary denominations used by Uncle Sam," the clerk shot back, amid laughter.

"Well, how large?"

"Oh, $100 bills, sometimes $500 bills."

"Ever see Al distribute any tips?"

"Oh, yes, he distributed small gratuities."

"How much?"

Smith's reply caused a visible—and, to the prosecution, a gratifying—reaction among the jurors. "Oh, $5 or so." With that, Smith stepped down from the stand.

Although the details of Capone's myriad financial transactions had an irrefutable logic about them, from the jury's standpoint they proved to be less than compelling. The droning testimony, the methodical questioning, and the gathering air of inevitability about the outcome of the trial all combined to lull several jurors to sleep. The prosecution's mission was not to entertain but to instruct, however. So long as the jury understood and accepted the premise that proof of expenditures equals proof of income, the government had succeeded in mounting an effective, if bloodless, case against the accused. In sum, the *Chicago Tribune* announced, "Al Capone last night found himself caught in a net of his own weaving."

.   .   .

That day a Capone confidant also found himself entangled in the snares of the law. The debonair Sam "Golf Bag" Hunt, Al's former bodyguard and boon companion, stood before Judge Matthew Hardigan in another Chicago courtroom.

The charge against him, that of obliterating the serial number on a pistol, stemmed from an arrest fully two years earlier, when Chicago police discovered an abandoned automobile, raked with bullets and spattered with blood, in Grant Park near the Art Institute, a tranquil neighborhood where gangsters did not normally pursue their nefarious activities. The police arrested Hunt and another man they discovered fleeing the scene. No proof of any murder surfaced, however, so the only crime involved the discovery of a pistol with defaced serial numbers, but the evidence proved sufficient to convict Hunt.

As he listened to the sentence being pronounced—ninety days in jail, an insignificant penalty compared to what Capone faced—Sam Hunt burst into tears.

•   •   •

October 10 brought nasty weather. Sheets of rain fell across the city, sending pedestrians scurrying for shelter and keeping curiosity seekers at bay; less than a dozen were on hand this gloomy morning to observe the brief Saturday morning session. "The outside murkiness had worked into the halls of justice, as it will on rainy days," said one reporter, "making the white marble walls seem gray as parchment, adding an air of deeper tarnish to the gold scroll column tops, driving the figures in the gloomy wall paintings into gloomier retreat." In contrast to the oppressive weather, Capone was resplendent in a double-breasted suit of a deep green hue, an immaculate white handkerchief peeking from his breast pocket, a white fedora, green tie, and black shoes.

On this foul day the government turned to documenting Capone's personal expenditures: a task involving fifty witnesses, primarily tradesmen and merchants who testified about the value of the goods and services they had furnished to him over the years. There was the Miami real estate agent who testified that he had rented a house to Capone on Indian Creek Drive in 1927 for six months; Capone had always paid the monthly rent of $2,500 in cash; there was the builder who testified seeing money wrappers designated for $1,000 strewn about the house; the butcher who said Capone paid him approximately $6,500 a year—in cash, always in cash when you were dealing with Mr. Capone; another builder who received nearly $11,000 from Capone for improvements on a garage at the Palm Island estate; the contractor who garnered $6,000 for work on the boathouse; the interior decorators who received $1,725 and $1,500 respectively for their work; and the department store manager who testified receiving $800 in cash in 1928 for linen and glassware with which to set the table in the Capone household. When Capone paid by check rather than cash, the testimony revealed, he turned to the ever present, ever-useful Guziks; they wrote the checks—on one occasion $7,000 for some furniture for the Capone household—and Capone reimbursed them. The evidence that Capone had enjoyed a fantastic income, well in excess of the $100,000 his lawyer Lawrence Mattingly once claimed, was overwhelming.

The day's real excitement began once Judge Wilkerson declared court adjourned until Monday. The courtroom emptied, and Capone headed down the corridor to the elevator, "a powerful figure, . . . quick in stride for a man who tips it at 220 pounds," in Berger's words.

"Just a minute," someone said. Instantly two policemen isolated Philip

D'Andrea, Capone's constant companion and bodyguard throughout the trial. Under orders from Judge Wilkerson himself, the cops frisked D'Andrea; one slipped his hand under the bodyguard's coat and to absolutely nobody's surprise found a .38-caliber pistol. Wilkerson was certain that D'Andrea's mere presence in the courtroom had been sufficient to intimidate several witnesses who had already testified. Actually, the loaded weapon he carried was only part of the aura of menace he introduced into Judge Wilkerson's court. He had also whiled away the hours throwing "the look" at various witnesses, the menacing expression warning them to shut up or else. D'Andrea had not been subtle, for even Judge Wilkerson from his vantage point high on the bench had noticed the chilling effect of the bodyguard's murderous scowl on various witnesses whose memories suddenly became vague and confused under its malevolent influence.

Now it was D'Andrea's turn to tremble; as the police detained him, his face turned white, and Capone instantly complained to his lawyers. "Capone without a guard seemed a flustered Capone," Berger observed. Suddenly D'Andrea produced a shield; it was shaped like a star and read: "Deputy bailiff of the Municipal Court."

"No good," a policeman said to D'Andrea. "That's expired. You can't carry a gun on that and certainly not in a courtroom." The bodyguard remained in custody.

Ahern and Fink tried to locate the judge and lodge a complaint, but Wilkerson had already departed, bound for a football game, rain or shine. As D'Andrea was led away, Capone glumly left the building, weaving his way "through the usual lane of policemen and gangster-worshipers." He climbed heavily into cab, which sped off in the pouring rain.

At four in the afternoon, Wilkerson returned to court and ordered D'Andrea to appear before him without any lawyers present. "It is not necessary to have counsel here today," Wilkerson told him. "I do not intend to dispose of this case now. There is a rule of the federal court of long standing, in the disposition of cases of this kind. In the case of Sharon vs. Hill it is stated that any man or counsel or witness who comes into court armed should be punished. This also applies to the lawyers who allowed it." With that, D'Andrea was locked up in the county jail until Monday morning, when he would face a charge of carrying a concealed weapon into the courtroom. Nothing could have been more calculated to alienate and infuriate Wilkerson than the presence of an armed associate of the defendant. As a result of the incident, Capone seemed less a celebrity and more a Chicago hoodlum reflexively resorting to violence.

The unmasking of D'Andrea received considerable attention in the press, partly because he seemed to be a new face in the Capone crowd. Actually, he was a longtime Capone confidant and insider, a quieter version of "Machine Gun" Jack McGurn but no less dangerous when provoked. D'Andrea lived in a splendid estate in Benton Harbor, Michigan, not far from the lake. He had long cherished his anonymity and was furious about losing it; in fact, nothing irritated him more than the journalists who would proceed to brand him as a gunman, and especially the photographers who jostled to take his picture as he moved through the corridors of the Federal Building. As D'Andrea discovered, one of the photographers, Tony Berardi, the amateur boxer, proved as tough as any gangster; the only difference was that the weapon he wielded happened to be a camera, which in its own way could be as deadly as a gun. Once the photograph was published in the paper with an appropriate caption, it could do irreparable harm to the subject's reputation. "I was the first guy ever to take a picture of D'Andrea," Tony Berardi later boasted. "I took the only clear picture ever made of the guy, and he threatened me, the little shit." *Nobody* threatened the feisty little Berardi, not even Capone himself, and certainly not an unknown bodyguard. "I picked him up and put him right against the wall and said, 'You little son of a bitch, I'll kill you first!' " This was normal Chicago talk, phrased in terms D'Andrea could understand. He backed off, the photographer got his picture, and came away unharmed.

• • •

Columbus Day is normally a holiday of particular pride to Italian-Americans, but as if to emphasize his lack of sympathy for that group, Judge Wilkerson insisted court would be in session on that date: Monday, October 12. Capone looked rested after the weekend, and he arrived wearing a luxurious tan overcoat. He took his seat and listened to the prosecution resume its tally of his personal expenditures—"Capone's trail of gold," the newspapers took to calling it.

Capone's lawyers remained mute until the prosecution introduced Capone's phone bills as evidence. The debate began when a representative of Miami's telephone company stated that Capone had paid $955.55 in telephone tolls in 1928, an almost unbelievable $3,141.40 in 1929, $3,061.29 in 1930, and $1,226.64 for the first five months of 1931.

"Now what in the world have 1930 and 1931 to do with this lawsuit?" demanded Fink.

To which Grossman replied with devastating effectiveness: "The bill payments show that money was available to pay taxes."

"And they used it to pay telephone bills with," Judge Wilkerson interjected.

"We were trying to pay the taxes," said Fink with an acquiescent smile, "and apparently the Government wouldn't take them and had us indicted."

The judge smiled right back at the counsel for the defense. "Because you did not want to pay enough."

After the phone bill had been dealt with, the prosecution detailed Capone's disbursements in Chicago, and again the scale of living described by the merchants he had done business with was sufficient to startle the jury. Capone had paid $3,500 for a rug for his mother on Prairie Avenue, and another $800 for rugs in the hotels where he himself had lived. He bought a $4,500 McFarlan automobile for Mae back in 1924; even then, the dealer testified, Capone was able to pay in cash, as he did for another McFarlan in 1926 and a Lincoln in 1928. (The automobile Capone purchased for his wife was a custom-designed cabriolet, similar in style and quality to a Cadillac, manufactured by the short-lived McFarlan Motor Corporation of Indiana.) In 1928, testimony also revealed, Capone paid a jeweler on Wabash Avenue $4,000 in cash for sterling silver and glassware. Then there were the glittering diamond-studded belt buckles he bestowed on his friends and allies: trophies that by the end of the 1920s had turned into badges of corruption. Jake Lingle had been wearing one at the time of his death. The jurors heard that Capone had purchased thirty of them at $275 apiece.

A salesman from Marshall Field testified about Capone's clothing expenditures, symbolically stripping the defendant to his silken underwear before the court. In 1927 and 1928, he had bought himself twenty-three suits and three topcoats from this store alone, sales that totaled $2,635 the first year and $1,080 the next. The shirts, which went for $18 to $30, he bought literally by the dozen, as he did the neckties, the collars, and the handkerchiefs. Then of course there were the union suits, the undershirts and shorts, and finally the very special union suits made out of "Italian glove silk," which sold for $12 each.

"Italian glove silk," Fink asked the witness. "What is that?"

"A knitted silk, very fine, similar to ladies' gloves, a knit glove."

"Is it warm?"

"No, it is just a nice suit of underwear."

Capone laughed in embarrassment. Hearing merriment coming from all directions, he turned his head, and as he did so, he blushed, and the twin scars on his left cheek suddenly appeared freshly emblazoned as he tried to laugh along with the spectators. They all laughed at Al, at the man who swaddled his privates in Italian glove silk. The revelation caused Meyer Berger, for one, to regard Capone in a new and unexpected light. Sinister around the edges but soft at the center. The reporter, nobody's fool, decided that this fearsome Capone was actually "soft," "home-loving," and even "naïve," a man with "distinctly feminine traits," as evidenced by his "passion for colored-silk underwear." Compared to Jack "Legs" Diamond, another gangster whom Berger had also studied in court, Capone seemed as appealing and affable as a "jovial Italian opera singer." So Berger became one of the few outsiders to recognize that Capone was not exactly a psychopath, cold-blooded killer, or an evil genius. He was, in fact, highly congenial and touchingly eager for the good opinion of all those with whom he dealt, and Berger concluded, "The previous conception of Capone, as gleaned from newspaper stories of his gang's massacre of seven rivals in one shooting, does not fit in with the smiling, good-natured Capone trying to find a place for himself and his wife in a fashionable Florida community."

"What is the price of those now?" Fink continued, referring to the silk union suits.

"Ten dollars a garment."

"Came down $2."

(Said Runyon: "It looked for a moment as if he had a sale.")

Few citizens of Chicago could afford to pay $12 for Italian glove silk union suits in good times, and even fewer could afford $10 with the Depression at hand. It was in homely details such as these that the jury gained an appreciation of the extent of Capone's wealth. At the same, the image of Capone spending his time at Marshall Field rather than in some seedy roadhouse or gambling den made a strong impression. "The testimony revealed Al as rather a busy and shrewd shopper," Runyon felt. "While he is usually pictured as a ruthless gang chieftain, he was today presented as a domesticated sort of chap going around buying furniture, and silverware, and rugs, and knickknacks of one kind and another for his household. . . . Moreover Al appears to have been somewhat conservative in his big household purchases, considering the amount of plunder he is supposed to have handled."

Finished at last with tales of Capone's shirts and underwear, the prosecution summoned a clerk named Walter Housen, who had worked at both the Lexington and Metropole Hotels, Capone's principal headquarters in Chicago. Housen proceeded to offer fresh instances of Capone's evasiveness as well as his seemingly limitless supply of money.

"What did his bills average a week?" asked Jacob Grossman.

"Oh, twelve to fifteen hundred."

"Did he ever give any banquets?"

"Well, there was one after the Dempsey-Tunney fight that lasted two nights."

"Did you get paid for it?"

"Yes."

The prosecution went on to establish that Capone moved from the Metropole to the nearby Lexington Hotel on July 30, 1928. Several days after moving out, he paid his tab of over $2,000 in cash. The move involved both Capone and as many as twenty members of his gang, all of whom registered at the Lexington under the incongruous designation "George Phillips and family." This strange state of affairs aroused the suspicions of Judge Wilkerson, who demanded of the witness, "Now, just what do you know about the relation of this defendant to that party?"

"All I know is," Housen meekly replied, "they came in for rooms that were engaged, and I couldn't get anybody to register for the rooms, and I took it upon myself, because I had to have something to show for the rooms."

"Is it in your handwriting?" asked Jacob Grossman of the prosecution's team.

"Yes, sir."

"And one of that group was the defendant Alphonse Capone?"

"Not at that time, no sir."

"Well, when did he come in?"

"Well, he might have come in that day, and he might have the next day."

"What room did the defendant Alphonse Capone occupy?"

"Two thirty," the clerk said.

"And how does that room compare in size with the other rooms?"

"Well, that is a suite; that is, three rooms in one group."

As the government lawyer badgered the witness, it became apparent that Housen was lying—not bold deceptions, but small evasions designed to save the skin of a frightened hotel clerk, who was terrified of testifying against the "Big Fellow."

In the afternoon session, a builder named Henry Keller, who had worked on Capone's Palm Island dock, took the stand, but to the prosecutors' chagrin, his testimony, rather than damning Capone, painted the racketeer in a sympathetic, if not entirely innocent light. "There was one day early in July," Keller began. "We were sitting together having lunch at his house and we started a conversation in a casual way, and as it drifted around he said, 'Dad, where are you from?' I said, 'I am from New York, born in the Tenth Ward, 1863.'"

Bewildered, Ahern demanded to know where Keller's testimony was leading.

"What *do* you expect to prove?" Judge Wilkerson asked the prosecution.

"Oh, just trying to show that the defendant started in a very humble way in New York, and didn't have any money when he started, and comparing that with the vast amounts of money that he spent in Florida, is some indication that he must have gotten some, or earned it; he didn't inherit it," Jacob Grossman explained.

"He started in a humble way like Hoover and Andrew Jackson and a number of other people who have risen to some distinction in the country," said Fink in defense of his client.

"Well, he didn't start in *exactly* the same way," Grossman pointed out.

After the skirmish, Keller resumed his testimony. "The conversation then finally drifted around to what I had done when we first started in, and in the natural course of the conversation, I says, 'What did you start at?' He said, 'My first job was tending bar at Coney Island.' "

At that point, Grossman abruptly terminated Keller's testimony, lest Capone seem too sympathetic, too much the self-made man. Had he been quicker on his feet, Grossman might have taken this moment to point out the speed with which Capone had acquired his uncounted wealth. At the time Keller talked with Capone, approximately 1927, only nine years had elapsed since Capone had held his first job as a bartender at the Harvard Inn on Coney Island, and only seven years separated that job from his taking over the Chicago rackets from Johnny Torrio. Such was the velocity of the 1920s.

• • •

All eyes were on Capone to see what color suit he would wear on October 13. He had clothed himself in a different hue for each day of the hearing. Today he wore a blue suit, with thin stripes, and to the surprise of some, no garters; instead, he wore his socks rolled down, collegiate-style, as it was called. He remained silent throughout this day as he had every other day of the trial. Rumors rushed to fill the vacuum created by his silence, and a story circulated that Johnny Torrio would take the stand today to testify against his former protégé, but the rumor turned out to be groundless and Torrio failed to appear, much to the relief of Capone and his lawyers.

However, the prosecution planned to call five other witnesses to testify against Capone. The most important member of the roster was Fred Ries, the gambling cashier with the pathological dread of insects, whom Frank Wilson of the IRS had virtually tortured into testifying. His testimony had already helped to put Jack Guzik away for five years, and the government expected Ries to do even worse damage to Capone. Ries was a tall, stooped figure, nearly bald, his face partly obscured by thick horn-rimmed glasses. He looked exactly like the bookkeeper he was and nothing at all like a gambler or a gangster. He wore a light brown suit, and as he sat in the witness box, he constantly shuffled his feet, "as if operating an invisible sewing machine," noted a reporter. This nervous mannerism was a manifestation of the fear the high-strung Ries felt at having to testify against Capone, a fear that was well placed. "They say, here, that the trigger men of the Chicago gang have been trying to find Ries since he testified as one of the key witnesses at the Guzik trial," Meyer Berger remarked, sharing the widespread assumption that Ries was a marked man.

"Mr. Ries," Grossman began, "were you in 1927 cashier of a gambling house called the Subway in Cicero, Illinois?"

"Yes, sir."

"Who was the manager of that institution?"

"A man by the name of Pete Penovich."

"Do you remember the address of the Subway?"

"I think it was 4738 Twenty-second Street."

"In Cicero, Illinois?"

"Yes, sir."

"Did that gambling house have any competition there in Cicero?"

"No, sir."

"Now Mr. Ries, as cashier did you have charge of all the finances of the gambling house?"

"Yes, sir."

"I show you a cashier's check from the Pinkert State Bank, Cicero. Tell us about that check."

"I bought it with cash representing profits from the house and turned it over to Bobby Barton," he replied, referring to Capone's chauffeur, but the connection eluded the prosecutors, and Grossman turned his attention to establishing a link between the money and Capone. "Did you say you operated at the Ship?"

"Yes, sir."

"Did you operate at the Ship before or after you operated at the Subway?"

"We operated the Ship early in '27 and also in September '27."

"Now, did you see the defendant, Alphonse Capone, on the premises of the Ship?"

"Yes, sir."

"When?"

"January 1927."

"Tell us about where he was on the premises at that time."

"Well, he was right at the telegraph operator's office talking to Mr. Guzik."

"And was the telegraph operator's office a part of the main establishment where the public usually congregated?"

"The telegraph office was right next to the main office. The public didn't congregate at the telegraph office as a rule, no, nobody is supposed to be there, no outsiders."

"No outsiders," Grossman repeated for emphasis. "Is that the first time you saw the defendant Capone at that place?"

"Yes, sir."

"Did you operate a place called the Radio?" asked Grossman, referring to another of Capone's gambling parlors.

"Yes, sir."

"Did you ever see the defendant Capone at that place in 1927?"

"Yes, sir."

"Well, where was he at that time when you saw him?"

"Well, I was taking bets at the counter and he would come by, and he said, 'Hello, Ries,' and I said, 'Hello, Al.' "

"Yes. Where did he go?"

"He went back to the office."

"Now referring to this check for $2,500, Mr. Ries, you say that J.C. Dunbar, the payee thereof, is you?"

"Yes, sir."

"And as cashier for the gambling establishment you had charge of the finances there, you say?"

"Yes, sir."

"And if profits were made what would you do with the profits?"

"I would turn them over to Jack Guzik in the shape of a check."

Grossman prompted him. "You would take the profits and buy . . ."

"I would buy cashier's checks and turn them over to Bobby Barton, and he would turn them over to Jack Guzik." Barton was Capone's chauffeur.

"Do you know the approximate total that you turned over to Jack Guzik in 1927?"

"I think around $150,000."

"Now, Mr. Ries, who was operating the place known as the Ship in early 1927?"

"Jimmy Mondi was the manager there."

"Was there any change?"

"At the Subway there was a change of manager."

"What happened at that time?"

"Ralph came down one day."

"Ralph who?"

"Ralph Brown or Ralph Capone," said Ries, referring to the alias frequently adopted by the family. "And he came down there with Pete Penovich one day and said Pete Penovich was taking charge. He said Mondi was out."

"I show you here forty-three cashier's checks. Tell us about them," said Grossman, bringing out a series of exhibits.

"They represented profits above the bankroll of $10,000 we always kept and above all expenses which I paid out. I bought the checks and gave them to Bobby Barton." The checks came to a total of $177,500 for 1927 and $24,800 for the following year—all of it profits from gambling.

Capone's lawyers tried to have this evidence ruled out of bounds. At the same time, they conceded that their client was unquestionably a professional gambler. In response, Jacob Grossman traced the path of the profits from Capone's gambling establishments through layers of accountants and bookkeepers: a paper trail so complex that it almost but not quite obscured Capone's involvement.

Wilkerson predictably sided with the prosecution. "This defendant enjoyed an income in excess of the amount which made it obligatory for him to return and pay a tax to the United States. . . . The government has offered in evidence tending to show what might be characterized as negative evidence: evidence tending to show there were no memorandums, no books of account, no records, no bank account; evidence tending to show the defendant on many occasions was in the possession of large sums of money; . . . evidence tending to establish that this defendant had undertaken to build around him a stone wall so that those who sought to learn his condition as to financial affairs would find him inaccessible. In view of that situation the government is relying upon a chain of circumstances. I think it is proper evidence," he finally declared. "Overruled."

But Michael Ahern wanted to make one last point concerning this damning chain. How one interpreted it, he said, depended on whether one looked at the transactions individually or collectively. Separately, they signified nothing, and even taken together, they made for a very weak presumption. "On top of that," Ahern continued, "they build another presumption, that Capone knew Ries just because he said, 'Hello, Ries,' and Ries said, 'Hello, Al.' " Ahern shook his head in dismay. "Why, I venture to say that all of these newspaper boys here in the courtroom would be able to say to me, 'Hello, Mike,' and yet I could not call them by name." Ahern resumed hammering away at the chain, trying to find the weak link to smash. Perhaps it was the Guzik connection. "Let us take the statement in 1928 when he cashed a check and somebody asked him who Jack Guzik was. Well, just as much as to say, 'That is none of your business,' he might say, 'That is my financial secretary,' or 'my social secretary.' But did he say that?"

"The testimony is that he did say Guzik was his financial secretary," said Judge Wilkerson.

Ahern pounced. "When did he say it? If he said it at all he said it in 1928. Then that was subsequent to those transactions that are here sought now to be introduced, and an admission in 1928, if you consider it so, that 'he is my financial secretary,' does not make that run backwards."

"You cannot take a chain of circumstances and rule them all out merely because each one stands alone," Wilkerson concluded. "Objection overruled."

The checks were entered into the records, along with the Mattingly letters and the testimony of fifty government witnesses about the tens of thousands of dollars Capone had paid for goods and services over the years.

With a final flourish, the prosecutors flipped over one of the checks, in the amount of $2,500, and pointed out the endorsement, containing the signature of the defendant himself, not an assistant or an employee: proof that Capone himself had received the money. The check was stamped as being paid on June 3, 1927. In this case, at least, the jury would not have to presume anything about the defendant's reaping the profits of the gambling establishments.

George E. Q. Johnson, the U.S. attorney, rose and addressed the court for the first time. It was 2:20 in the afternoon, and his carefully chosen words startled everyone:

"If it please the court, at this time the government rests its case."

*   *   *

The unexpected announcement created an uproar. The courtroom emptied as reporters dashed to the telephones to get the news to their respective city desks: Prosecution rests its case. Ahern looked up in astonishment. "What?" he was heard to say to his partner. Both he and Fink had been taken completely by surprise. In terms of outmaneuvering the other side, Johnson's prosecutors had just accomplished a considerable coup.

Relishing the obvious confusion in the Capone camp, Judge Wilkerson turned to Fink and asked, "Are you ready to proceed?"

The lawyers huddled at the bench, as Capone leaned forward in his seat, straining to hear what was said.

"Well, if Your Honor please," Fink stammered, "this is kind of a surprise. We would like a little time to get ready for our defense. Your Honor said, I think, that if during the course of the trial we were not prepared to meet what the government offered, you would be a little indulgent with us for a while."

Wilkerson excused the jury, and the defense lawyers continued to complain. Convinced of government treachery, aware that they were unprepared to mount a defense of their client, they pleaded with the judge for more time. Flushed with passion, Fink argued that the government's team of four lawyers had been assembling its case against Capone for the better part of four years, while he and Mr. Ahern, toiling all alone, had but a few weeks to prepare. It simply wasn't fair to hurry the defense.

"We have a jury confined here," Judge Wilkerson reminded the defense lawyers, and he gave them until the following morning to present their case.

"If Your Honor thinks it fair to put this man to defense at 10 A.M. tomorrow, I'll be here. I'll do the best I can," said Fink, sounding deeply offended. "If we offer no evidence, what time may we have for arguments?" Fink pleaded for ten hours to present his closing argument.

"Ten hours?" said the judge, his wiry eyebrows shooting up.

The two haggled, and in the end, Ahern and Fink were granted four hours in which to attempt to exculpate their client. With that, court was adjourned.

*   *   *   *

The curiosity seekers, whose number had been dwindling, returned to the courthouse with a vengeance on Wednesday, October 14, to behold a pair of celebrities: Al Capone, the nation's best known gangster, and Edward G. Robinson, Hollywood's best known gangster actor. "Little Caesar" (the role he played in the hit movie earlier in the year) came to study his original in the flesh; art was imitating life.

The hastily assembled defense of Al Capone they all heard that day was an embarrassment—a laughable parade of gamblers whose testimony might have been scripted by Damon Runyon. The "shiny-shoed" gamblers he called them, men with suspicious tans and carefree manners acquired in Florida, who looked wholly out of place in Chicago, to which they had been summoned to testify in Capone's defense. They formed part of Ahern and Fink's ill-conceived strategy: they would attempt to prove that whatever he *earned* by gambling, he *lost* by gambling, usually at the track. Even if true, and there was a grain of truth to it, this was as much an indictment of their client as a defense, but they doggedly pursued it anyway, and if the strategy failed to save Al Capone from conviction, it did offer an analysis of his reckless gambling behavior—as well as a few good laughs at the expense of the "shiny-shoed" gamblers. "The gambler witnesses prove a naïve lot, their mental outlook formed in a world of which the rural jurors could have little conception," the *Tribune* warned. "They have a code of strict honor applied to their own business. They have little sense of being outlaws, or of doing wrong in the accepted sense. To circumvent 'the law' is part of their life, a sort of game." But now the law had caught up with them.

Calling his first "shiny-shoed" witness for the defense, Albert Fink examined a bookie by the name of Milton Held.

"Have you had any transactions with the defendant, Alphonse Capone?" Fink began.

"Yes, while I was taking oral bets at Hawthorne in 1924 and 1925. I would take a bet and settle the next day."

"Did he win or did you?"

"He lost, I judge, about $12,000."

Dwight Green of the prosecution then subjected the bookie to a brief cross-examination by asking a spiraling series of questions.

"What was your first transaction with the defendant?"

"At Hawthorne in 1924," Held said.

"Name the first horse he bet on."

"I can't do that."

"Name any horse he ever bet on."

"I am not able to that."

"How did you arrive at the amount of $12,000 which you say he lost?"

"That was just an estimate."

"Are you positive he lost?"

"Absolutely."

"How much did Capone bet at a time?"

"Three or four hundred dollars."

"How many customers did you have who bet that much?"

"Two or three."

"Did he have much of a roll when he paid you?"

"Yes, he usually had quite a lot of money, mostly in $100 bills. Sometimes in $500 bills."

As Green's questions implied, Held's testimony, vague as it was, offered further circumstantial evidence of his vast, untaxed income; in its own way it was as revealing as the stories of the Marshall Field salesman.

Green proceeded to cast suspicions on Held's legitimacy as a witness. "Where did you discuss your testimony first?" he asked.

"At the Lexington Hotel, Monday night. Somebody called me up and I went there. Mr. Fink, Mr. Capone, Mr. Ahern and a lot of bookmakers were there."

"Who rang you up?"

"I don't know. One of Al's boys."

"Did you discuss the case again?"

"Well, I went back last night at eight o'clock and Al asked me if I'd be here this morning at ten o'clock."

"Did you treat that as a demand?"

"I don't think so."

"Who are some of Al's boys?" Green inquired.

"I don't know."

In any event, Green had effectively managed to suggest that Held was testifying under duress. (But so, of course, were several government witnesses, notably Fred Ries, the cashier.)

After another bookie, Oscar Gutter, took the stand and testified that Capone lost about $60,000 through him, Green again subjected him to a searching cross examination.

"How did you remember that he lost $60,000?"

"My ledger showed that at the end of the season."

"I thought you didn't keep any books."

"Well, I kept them from month to month so I could pay my income tax," Gutter stated, as if he were telling the truth, which was highly unlikely. He was simply trying to avoid being prosecuted for failing to pay taxes himself.

"Why didn't you keep them permanently?"

"Well, it was an illegitimate business."

"Did you pay the defendant in checks or currency when he won?"

"I always paid him in currency, because he requested that. I called at the Metropole Hotel and paid him if he won or collected if he lost."

More damage to Capone's case. Gutter stepped down from the stand.

As its next witness, the prosecution called Pete Penovich, the Capone employee and stalwart. Burly, somber, dark-visaged, he was plainly not a man to trifle with.

"You are the Pete Penovich who has been referred to in the testimony in connection with the Smoke Shop gambling house?"

"Yes, sir."

Fink showed him a chart listing the owners of the Hawthorne Smoke Shop, followed by the percentage of the business they held. But Penovich's testimony did nothing to advance the defense case. However, under cross examination by the prosecution's Clawson, Penovich divulged more details of the organization of the Hawthorne Smoke Shop than the jury had previously heard.

"Did you have anything to do with horse bets?" Clawson asked Penovich.

"It was all a part of the business, excepting the wire bets, and that was handled by Frankie Pope."

"Well, was Frankie Pope under you, then?"

"No, Frankie Pope was the man I was supposed to take orders from. He and Ralph Capone."

"Who handled the money during the period from May until November 1924?"

"I handled the money in the operation of the business. I received the checks, and I banked the money, and after I had accumulated a profit of $10,000 or $15,000, it would be turned over to Frankie Pope."

"Did you have an interest in the place?"

"Well, my interest varied. Originally I was supposed to have an interest of 25 percent."

"You were one of the partners? Was Frankie Pope one of the original partners?"

"Yes, sir."

"And how much was he to get?"

"I believe his interest was to be twenty-five, too."

"When did he become your boss?"

"Shortly after we opened in May 1924. Ralph Capone told me there would be a different disposition of money and to go along, and that he would take care of me."

"You started as a full partner, did you not?"

"Yes."

"Did it suit you to be cut down, to be made an underling?"

"No. I told Ralph I wanted to know why I was cut down, and he said,

'Well, we had to make different arrangements,' and for me to go along with him, and that he would see that I would be taken care of."

"What did you say about being under Frankie Pope?"

"Well, I condescended to it," replied Penovich, to laughter.

Clawson continued to press him for information on Capone's gambling establishment.

"How did you happen to go into this Hawthorne Smoke Shop at all?"

"I had a bad location; my location was at a railroad crossing. There were railroad tracks and no business activities."

"Just a moment," Clawson interrupted. "It was so bad you that you had to use ten men to help you run it?" he asked in disbelief.

"Well," Penovich explained, "in the operation of a gambling house ten men are very few help."

"So what did you do about it?"

"I spoke to Ralph about changing my location and getting up near the Western Electric plant." The idea was to be convenient to the plant's well-compensated employees, who could stop by and gamble away their earnings before they reached home and turned the money over to their wives, mothers, and children.

"Why did you speak to Ralph?"

"Because I understood Ralph was the boss, and he could do the fixing for me in Cicero."

"Fixing with whom?" inquired Clawson.

"With the powers that might be in a position to let me go along without being molested."

"What powers?"

"Political powers, the police departments, anybody that might be in a position to stop me. I thought maybe, if I would be left alone, I would make some money near the Western Electric plant."

"What else were you afraid of?" asked Clawson, trying to suggest that Penovich had no choice in the matter of selecting a site for his gambling house because the Capone brothers controlled Cicero.

"Well, I wasn't afraid of anybody in particular."

"And the only reason you spoke to Ralph was so that you could get the political powers to allow you to run?"

"That was one of the main reasons."

"Is it not a fact, Penovich, that the main reason you had to talk to Ralph was that the gang or the organization that was out in Cicero would not let you run unless you talked to him?"

"The main reason was that I felt that I could make more money at Twenty-second and Forty-eighth Avenue than I could at Fifty-second Avenue and Twenty-fifth Street."

"Why did you not first open up there, then?"

"I didn't know how to make the connections."

"What connections?"

"Connections whereby I could run without being molested by the authorities."

"What authorities?"

"Police officers, the state's attorney, the mayor, sheriff—authorities that are in a position to arrest you if you have a place of business where you operate gambling."

"What did you think Ralph could do with those connections?"

"I thought he could fix me so that I would be able to run without being molested."

"What made you think that Ralph could do you any good?"

"From what I heard he could do lots of good in that respect. I heard it from Ralph himself. He seemed to be prosperous, and he was catered to. Every place he went he was welcomed; he was pointed out, in theaters, cafés, places of amusement."

"Pointed out by whom?"

"People that I had been with, people that I had seen in the lobby, who talked to him."

"Did he tell you he had such connections?"

"Yes, he told me I would be left alone. He said, 'Stay here until after the election and I'll take care of you, so you can make money.' "

"Now, Penovich, isn't it a fact that there was an organization or syndicate in control of Cicero at that time, and of its gambling activities?"

"No, sir."

At that point, Clawson pointed out that Penovich was contradicting testimony he had earlier given to a grand jury; he was impeaching himself. The claim touched off a donnybrook involving the lawyers from both sides; the arguing persisted until Judge Wilkerson declared court adjourned. Penovich stepped down from the stand. He had revealed much but kept even more to himself. He had not even hinted at the Capone brothers' involvement in prostitution, bootlegging, and the violence associated with them, or the smell of gunpowder wafting along the streets of Cicero.

· · ·

The next day saw testimony from more gamblers and bookies—some of them "shiny-shoed," others decidedly scruffy. They talked about the money Al had lost by placing wagers with them, the $500 bets and the $3,000 bets, all of them on losing horses. The most impressive testimony came not from a Chicago bookie, however, but from Budd Gentry, "a breezy sort of personality," according to one journalist; Gentry worked, or at least passed his days, at Hialeah, the Miami track where Capone spent as much time as he possibly could whenever he was in Florida. Hialeah was as close to high society and respectability as Capone ever came, but now Hialeah, in the person of Gentry, was coming back to haunt him.

Fink began the morning by inquiring about Gentry's activities during 1929.

"What was the bankroll of your book?"

"Thirty thousand dollars. I believe Mr. Capone put up 60 percent of it and Mr. Cohen [Gentry's boss] 40 percent."

"Did you make a profit that year?"

"Yes, about $13,000 in cash and $8,000 in markers," which, he noted for the rural jury, were the promises bettors made to satisfy bets they had lost: in other words, IOUs.

"What was the highest amount he ever bet?" asked Fink, referring to Capone.

"The highest he bet was $10,000 on one horse. And there were several $10,000 bets."

"Do you recall if he was winner or loser at the end of the season?"

"He lost about $100,000," Gentry answered.

"Did you ever see the defendant play poker that season?"

"Yes, sir. Stud poker. I played in the game."

When Fink and Judge Wilkerson pressed him to name the other participants in the game at Capone's Palm Island estate, Gentry's mind went conveniently blank. "There was always lots of people there, but I just can't recall their names," he offered lamely and lapsed into a daze. ("For a long time Gentry studied the frescoes on the ceiling, his head shaking as if he were trying to squeeze things out of his brain," observed a journalist.) "I'm trying to concentrate," the bookie lamented, "I've got five or six names in my mind, but they won't come out." Eventually his enfeebled memory did manage to yield a name or two: Stribling, Sharkey (prizefighters both), and Mrs. Tex Rickard, the wife of a prominent fight promoter. And what about baseball players? No, Gentry replied, the group consisted not of sports stars but of "sporting people."

The prosecution's Dwight Green cross-examined Gentry, emphasizing the witness's flawed memory to discredit him.

"What horses did the defendant bet $10,000 on?" Green began.

"Several," said the bookie.

"How much was his first bet with you?"

"I think it was $1,500 or $2,000."

"What were the names of the horses he bet on?"

"I don't remember."

Judge Wilkerson interrupted. "Can you give us the name of just *one* horse that this defendant bet on?"

Gentry, not surprisingly, failed to remember a single losing horse on which Capone bet during the 1929 season; for a bookmaker two years might as well have been two centuries. With that unconvincing performance, Ahern and Fink rested their singularly inept defense. Their effort to demonstrate that Capone gambled away his taxable income amounted to no defense at all; in fact, the testimony of the witnesses for the defense, if credible, only served to discredit Capone.

Watching this awkward scene unfold, Runyon, who knew the pitfalls of betting on the horses from long and bitter personal experience, could scarcely contain his laughter at the evidence of his friend's profligacy. "Your correspondent cheerfully yields the palm he has borne with such distinction for lo these many years as the world's worst horse player to Mr. Alphonse Capone," he declared. "Yes sir, and ma'am, Al wins in a common gallop, if we are to believe the testimony brought up in his support today."

The gentlemen of the jury might have wondered how Capone had managed to amass his immense fortune while at the same time gambling it away with infantile abandon. The glaring inconsistency in his behavior throughout the late 1920s went unremarked throughout the trial; neither the judge nor the jury, certainly not Capone himself, would have been able to recognize the underlying cause of his bizarre gambling behavior. His medical history strongly suggests it was his latent neurosyphilis, still undiagnosed but nonetheless present in the frontal lobes of his brain, where it slowly but inexorably distorted his personality. One common manifestation of the disease's ability to exaggerate behavior and induce grandiose fantasies is its victims' tendency to gamble away huge sums of money—just as a dozen bookies testified Capone had. "Patients of this type are euphoric and develop delusions in which they figure as exceptional persons endowed with superhuman strength, immense wealth, or other magnificent attributes," noted Sir Russell Brain, in *Diseases of the Nervous System*, of the psychological effects of syphilis. "They readily act on these delusions and may order large quantities of goods or write their physician a cheque for a million pounds, and they see no discrepancy between their imaginary attributes and their debilitated and unfortunate condition." It was just this kind of behavior to which Judge Wilkerson's courtroom had been exposed for over a week. At the time, it was perceived as the overindulgence of an unimaginably wealthy gangster, but it was also a symptom of Capone's steadily worsening case of neurosyphilis.

The trial had thus far consumed seven exhausting days, and to the jurors the parade of witnesses, all of them carefully rehearsed, their presence in the courtroom representing thousands of hours of preparation, began to fade into a blur of assumptions and presumptions. Here and there the odd detail stuck out: the price of Capone's union suits, for instance, or Pete Penovich's dogged loyalty to his masters, but the significance of it all remained obscure, contradictory, puzzling. Capone had never taken the stand himself, had never uttered a word before the court. It would have been too dangerous for him to do so, because once he was subjected to cross examination by the prosecution, there was no telling what stories and surprises might have come tumbling forth. Soon the jurors—all men, only one from Chicago itself—were going to decide on his guilt or innocence, and what they had seen of the accused was a man who wore a succession of flashy, expensive suits, whose own lawyers claimed he was a gambler (as if that were a defense), and who had brought a gunman into the courtroom; Capone had not, on balance, presented a picture of innocence.

Despite the shambles his lawyers had made of his defense, Capone's legal position was justifiable. A competent defense team, for instance, could have pointed out to the jury that until 1927 earnings from illegitimate activities such as gambling and bootlegging were *not* taxable. After the Supreme Court of the United States ruled otherwise, saying that income from such activities had to be paid even if it incriminated the taxpayer, Capone did make a bona fide attempt through his lawyer Lawrence Mattingly to pay his income taxes. He even met with agents of the IRS. Although he was absent from Chicago, he was generally available at his home in Florida; he was not in hiding. Most important, from Capone's point of view, the government *refused* to accept his belated offer to pay taxes because it preferred to prosecute him. The government was, in effect, plea bargaining with Capone; instead of convicting him for a major offense such as violating the Volstead Act, it prosecuted him for the lesser offense of income tax violations. Ahern and Fink should have made each of these points, but they did not. The jury never had the chance to consider them, and to decide whether they cast a reasonable doubt on the government's charges. Without an adequate defense, the trial amounted to an elaborate charade, a legalistic lynching of Al Capone.

•   •   •

It was the task of the closing arguments for each side to bring a persuasive clarity to bear on the facts that had been revealed in the courtroom. The first oration, for the prosecution, was delivered by Jacob Grossman, who, after reviewing the government's case, pointed out how damning even the testimony mounted by the *defense* was to Capone. "He himself produced witnesses to show that he got a revenue," Grossman reminded the jurors. "His defense witnesses said he lost large sums in race bets in four of those years.

These losses totaled $217,000. Where did Capone get this money? At the start we find a man living on a fine estate in Florida, spending money like a baron and with the lavishness of an Italian prince. We have heard of jewels, and fine furnishings—everything bought with cash. The Florida people were interested in where all this money came from, and they asked Capone. He told them. He said he was a gambler in Cicero and Chicago and was in the real estate and cleaning and dyeing business and added that he had an interest in dog tracks.

"We see, furthermore, by going to his office in the Metropole or Lexington Hotels that he was surrounded by an organization of men who use assumed names. They pushed the register aside. Most of the organization appeared on the witness stand. You saw men who testified that when Capone called them and said, 'Come to my office,' they went. He pulled a string and they came running. These witnesses could remember nothing save that Capone lost money. The Florida people who came here to testify before you included some who fronted for Capone. There was Parker Henderson, who cashed Capone's checks and tried to disguise his handwriting when he did so. He bought Capone's home with Capone's money, and later it was transferred to the name of the defendant's wife. Everything was cash with Capone."

Samuel Clawson resumed arguing the government's case the following day, Friday, October 16, carefully explaining for the jurors the damning implications of the Mattingly letter and the transcript of the meeting between Capone and the IRS agent in Chicago, C. W. Herrick:

"Mr. Herrick told him that any statements that could be used against him probably would be used. He didn't say they might be; he said they would. But when Mr. Herrick asked whether, according to the defendant's statements, the taxable years in question would be 1926 to 1929, Capone himself spoke up. 'That's it, exactly,' he said. That was the most significant thing about the interview: Capone's own admission of liability. Can you, gentlemen of the jury, entertain any serious doubt that Capone knew what this was about? Even though he had lost from $47,000 to $110,000 a year on the races, as the defense has shown us, and his expenditures for luxuries had been enormous, as we have shown, he still had the money and wanted to pay his taxes. Is it conceivable then that he had no taxable income?

"Then, on September 30, 1930, Mattingly brought in the letter. He had consulted with Capone and this was the best they could do—an estimate of taxable income of $26,000 for 1926, $40,000 for 1927, and $100,000 each for the years 1928 and 1929. He had tried to get the revenue agents to say that the admission would not be used against his client; now, in the letter, Mattingly is saying it himself. The letter says, 'This statement is made without prejudice to the taxpayer in any criminal action that may be instituted against him.' Suppose a gambler could tack a little sign on a roulette wheel:

'This device is not to be used as evidence against me.' Suppose a murderer could put a sign on his gun: 'This weapon is not to be used as evidence against me.' What a refuge for criminals that would be! And that is what we have here."

Then it was the turn of the defense to attempt the impossible task of exculpating Capone. The government had set the terms for the trial, and according to those terms Capone was guilty, as his defense lawyers recognized. Their only hope, at this late point in the trial, was to question the fairness of the government's motives and to cast doubt on the integrity of the prosecution's team without actually sounding disrespectful toward the government of the United States. In the end, Michael Ahern tried to suggest that Capone was simply being persecuted, not tried:

"The government has sought by inference, by presumption and by circumstantial evidence to prove this defendant guilty. It has sought to free itself from the law, to convict him merely because his name is Alphonse Capone. In Rome during the Punic Wars there lived a senator named Cato. Cato passed upon the morals of the people; he decided what they should eat, what they should drink, and what they should think. Carthage fell twice, but Carthage grew again and was once more powerful. Cato concluded every speech he made in the Senate by thundering, 'Delenda est Carthago'— 'Carthage must be destroyed.' " Rising to a climax, Ahern declared, "These censors of ours, the prosecutors, the newspapers, all cry, 'Delenda est Capone!' Do you know what that means?"

The fascinated but uncomprehending rural jurors stared blankly at the defense lawyer.

"It means 'Capone must be destroyed!' " Gesturing toward George E. Q. Johnson and his men, Ahern continued, "These censors cry out: 'Capone must be destroyed!' " He pounded on the railing surrounding the jury box, startling the jurors, who recoiled from him. "Why do they seek conviction on this meager evidence? Because he is Alphonse Capone. Because he is the mythical Robin Hood you read so much about in all the newspapers. They have no evidence, or what they have produced here discloses only one thing: that the defendant Al Capone is a spendthrift, that he was extravagant."

Again he spanked the railing.

"But the government itself is also guilty of acts of profligacy. It has spent thousands upon thousands in the investigation and prosecution of this case when it might better have spent that money in these times for the establishment of soup kitchens. If you convict on this sort of evidence," he concluded, "every spendthrift in the country should be imprisoned." Another smack on the railing, and Ahern, breathless, took his seat amid a clearing of throats and a shifting of chairs.

"Capone," said the New York Times of the subject of the impassioned oratory, "drank it all in. A mint kept his ponderous jaws moving. . . . Though there seems to be a reasonable doubt as to whether he grasped the full meaning of it all, it sounded good."

Then it was the turn of Albert Fink to defend the mythical Robin Hood sitting in Judge Wilkerson's courtroom. Where Ahern's delivery was smooth and sonorous, Fink's voice was high-pitched and strained, but his line of reasoning was better grounded in reality than Ahern's oratory had been, emphasizing that Capone had intended all along to pay his income tax just as he would honor any debt. "There is not a man in this court room who doesn't know that Al Capone never had intent to defraud the government of that tax," Fink insisted. "He is not that kind of a man. A tinhorn or a piker might, but no one ever accused Capone of being a piker. If he owed a tax you may be sure he didn't pay it from some motive other than to defraud the government."

As Fink spoke, the *Times* remarked, "a lump bulged in Capone's throat," and "his whole face showed deep self-pity." By the time Fink concluded, he was hoarse, his face flushed, a man who had given his all. The defense rested.

"Quite a gale of oratory zipped around the corridors of the old Federal Building before the day was done," Runyon noted in his summary of the day's marathon, "what with Ahern's remarks, a lengthy outburst by his associate, Albert Fink, and a long lingual drive by Samuel G. Clawson, of your Uncle Sam's team of lawyers. What Ahern and Fink said, when you boiled it down to a nubbin, was that your Uncle Sam hasn't proved all those things said about Al Capone in the indictments, and that he is entitled to his liberty forthwith. What Clawson said, reduced to a mere hatful, is that Al had a lot of income and didn't pay tax on said income, and therefore ought to be put in the cooler."

•   •   •

"FATE OF CAPONE WILL REST WITH JURY TODAY," read the morning's headline in the *Chicago Tribune* for Saturday, October 17. "G. E. Q. Johnson to Close U.S. Plea." The final summation for the prosecution belonged to the man whose crusade this had become: George E. Q. Johnson. In his closing argument, he was bound to restrict himself to proven fact; anything else, any speculation, last-minute theories or evidence could be grounds for contempt. Although he was the august U.S. attorney, Johnson, like most of the members of the jury, hailed from a farm background, and he knew how to speak to this audience, knew their biases, knew, in short, how to get them to convict. He wanted the jury to help him cut Capone down to size.

"Every morning there are thousands of unmarried men and unmarried women who go to their daily work, and every one of those workers must pay an income tax on every dollar that they earn above the sum of $1,500," he reminded the jurors. "The government has no more important function, except in the emergency of war, than to enforce the revenue laws of this government, and if the time ever occurs in the United States when our American people will pay taxes only when the government seeks to find out what they owe, or when it begins an investigation of their affairs to determine their tax, then government will fail; then the Army and the Navy will disband; and our institutions will disappear. Our courts will be swept aside; American civilization will fail; and organized society will revert to the days of the jungle, where every man will be for himself."

He turned his attention to Capone. "I have been a little bewildered in this case at the manner in which the defense has attempted to weave a halo of mystery and romance around the head of this man. Who is he? Who is this man who during the years that we have considered here has so lavishly expended what he claims to be almost half a million dollars? Is he the little boy out of the Second Reader, who succeeded in finding a pot of gold at the end of the rainbow, that he has been spending so lavishly, or maybe, as his counsel says, is he Robin Hood? You will remember how Robin Hood in the days of the barons took from the strong to feed the weak and the starving peasants. Counsel referred to him in his argument as Robin Hood. But was it Robin Hood in this case who bought $8,000 worth of diamond belt buckles to give to the unemployed? Was it Robin Hood in this case who paid a meat bill of $6,500? Did that go to the unemployed? It went to the house on Palm Island. Did he buy these $27 shirts to protect the shivering men who sleep under Wacker Drive at night? No."

It was an effective argument, except that nothing Johnson described in Capone's actions was actually illegal. The jury could not convict Capone for being a lavish spender. Johnson went on to question Capone's character and motives by constructing a profile of his Al Capone. "My friends, let us look at this defendant as he appears to be in this record. The first time we see him is as a bartender at Coney Island. Then we see him later through the witness Belford, alias Slim Jim, the dice man, who meets him at Colosimo's, and then we get a fleeting glimpse again of him as a brothel keeper on 22nd Street, at Johnny Torrio's; and then the next picture we have of him is in 1924. He has risen in influence and power, and we see him buying a car for $4,500. But we see something else; we see a prosperous gambling establishment here at Cicero, a gambling establishment, gentlemen of the jury, which you will find paid a profit in 1924 of $300,000; and even if you take the theory of the opposing counsel, Mr. Fink, that he had only 8 percent; that was $24,000.

"The next picture we have of this defendant is in 1925, and the record tells you this: Mr. Bragg, and Mr. Hoover, that sincere man, who is a minister of the Gospel, who had the courage, testified before you that they had received money. From whom and for what? They wanted to protect their homes in the western suburbs. Bragg told you he was interested because he had some kids to bring up, and there were gambling places in Cicero, and they wanted to protect the reputation of their community. They wanted to close this institution of gambling, which was exercising such a sinister influence upon the life of Cicero. That, gentlemen of the jury, was their interest in this case, and if that did not spring from the highest motives of citizenship, then I do not understand what citizenship in America means."

Johnson continued his review of the government witnesses, explaining how each man's testimony contributed to a pointillist portrait of tax evasion. Then he returned to the question of Capone's character. "Let us see how the halo of mystery and romance fits upon the brow of this defendant. At any time, at any place, has this defendant ever appeared in a reputable business? Have there appeared records such as honest citizens keep? Has there appeared, outside the purchase of the home in Florida, a single instance of contact with reputable business? What a picture we have in this case: no income, but the defendant in the years in question spent—on diamond buckles, on twenty-seven dollar shirts, on furnishings for his home— $116,000 that is not deductible from his income. And yet counsel comes here and argues to you that the man had *no* income."

Johnson then started a bold attack on Ahern and Fink. His manner became, according to the *Chicago Tribune*, "almost evangelical, clenching his fist, shaking his gray head, clamping his lean jaws together as he bit into the evidence and tore into the defense."

"Now," said Johnson, "let me ask counsel some pertinent questions in this case. Why did not the counsel call Jack Guzik, who has been talked about in this case? And they talked about Ralph Capone, or the intimation that it was Ralph Capone who was at the raid when Hoover and his associates raided that place. Could anyone forget the hulking form of this defendant with the flaming scars on his cheek? If it was Ralph Capone, if there was any question about it, why was not Ralph Capone called as a witness?"

"I object to that line of argument," Ahern protested, though with a noticeable lack of conviction. "Both Ralph Capone and Jack Guzik are under conviction and their cases on appeal. He has no right to say they are defendants."

Judge Wilkerson, however, sided with Johnson. "The Court has indulged a very great latitude to the defense in this case," he lectured Ahern.

"But, Your Honor, isn't it a matter of fact that we cannot call a defendant, that he is privileged from testifying?"

"Overruled," Wilkerson declared. "You may note your exception."

Undeterred, Johnson persisted in naming names. "Frank Nitti appears as an endorser on these profit checks, and the name of Sam Guzik appears as a sender of money. May I suggest to you why the government did not call these witnesses. There is a moral responsibility that comes to the attorney. He vouches for the witness who appears on the witness stand, and the government did not care to vouch for these witnesses." But matters were different when it came to the most controversial government evidence of all, Lawrence Mattingly's letter. "So far as this record shows here, gentlemen, Lawrence Mattingly represents the defendant in this case before the Treasury Department of the United States." Even though Mattingly had not testified, his letter was still valid; indeed, Johnson claimed that the other witnesses had virtually corroborated it. "If an artist paints a picture he can put some lines in the face that make the face look like a sage or a fool. And so you can take isolated facts in a record and distort them, and counsel here has sought to give a tortured meaning to the statements of Mr. Clawson and said we admitted we have no case except upon the evidence of Mattingly.

"Gentlemen of the jury, the government in this case asks you not to take a single fact. We ask you to take the whole picture as it is painted to you here. Take every fact and circumstance, and consider, and when you do that, you will find that every page of this record cries out the guilt of this defendant."

Once he had finished buttressing the circumstantial nature of his case, Johnson turned to Ahern and Fink's flimsy defense. "If you believe the words that come out of the mouths of these men," he said of the procession of bookies the defense had presented, "then this defendant lost in the years to which they had testified $327,000 on betting on the horses. Is that a probable story from a man whom they contend had no income?"

Nearing the end of his oration, Johnson again appealed to the jury's leveling instinct. What they heard in his voice with its flat intonations, indelibly marked with the certitudes of life on the prairie, was the anger and indignation of the honest, literal-minded man who has toiled countless hours for meager wages, who has gone without for the sake of others, and who harbors an implacable resentment of the man who has made easy money, dishonest money, and has used it to indulge himself in every conceivable way. "I am going to ask you to think about the thousands of men and thousands of women who go to work, and who earn just a little above $1,500, and who pay a tax to the government of the United States," Johnson said. "Is it reasonable to suppose that it is public clamor that brings this defendant before the bar of justice? This is not a case of public clamor. The United States attorney in this district was never more sincere, or more determined in my five years, than I am in this case. I am asking you to treat this case as though the defendant were John Brown. . . . I agree with counsel that this is a case future generations will remember . . . for the reason that it will establish this: whether any man can be above the law, whether any man can conduct his affairs so that he can escape entirely the burdens of government; and that is the record, gentlemen of the jury, that your verdict will write in this case."

After Johnson returned to his seat, Judge Wilkerson instructed the jury, and in his detailed speech, which lasted over an hour, he gradually revealed his position to be virtually identical to the prosecution's. He explained to the jury exactly how they could find Capone guilty, despite the lack of hard evidence against him. He reminded them that evidence of his great spending in Chicago and in Miami was sufficient under the law to demonstrate that he had a great income, and he paid special attention to explaining the legal technicalities of relying on the prosecution's most damning evidence, the Mattingly letter.

"You are the judges of the weight which is to be given to the testimony of the witnesses who have appeared before you in this case," the judge concluded. "You have had many witnesses here, men from all walks of life. You have had government agents, ministers of the Gospel, business men, and other classes of witnesses. You are not obliged to believe that a thing is so merely because somebody swears to it. Of course, you can't arbitrarily or whimsically put aside the testimony of any witness. You should weigh this testimony calmly and dispassionately, and then reach a conclusion as to how much weight is to be given to his testimony; you are to consider the interest, if any, in the outcome of the case, the manner in which he has testified on the witness stand, the frankness or lack of frankness, his ability to render some things vividly, and his inability to state other things, if that is the case."

The judge finished reciting his instructions. His rasping voice stilled at last, a murmur went up, the disconnected mumbling of the multitude. The members of the press began their vigil, drinking away the anxious hours in a nearby speakeasy. The curiosity seekers went home. Ahern returned to his office. The twelve jurors went to the jury room to begin their deliberations. Al Capone, accompanied by Albert Fink, returned to his suite at the Lexington Hotel, where the mood was subdued. Capone set the tone, saying little. The gloomy October afternoon passed, and then the evening. It would not be a swift decision: the first indication the government might not prevail. The longer the jury was out, the lawyers on both sides knew, the greater the likelihood that they would be unable to find the defendant guilty. As the hours passed, the suspicion among the prosecutors increased that something had gone awry in the deliberations of the carefully chosen and instructed members of the jury.

• • •

Locked away, the jurors took ballots—as many as twenty according to one account. There *was* a problem, as it happened. All the jurors save one wanted to convict Capone on all counts, and the holdout proved stubborn and persuasive. Although his identity was not disclosed, another juror later described what had occurred in the jury room. During the eight hours of deliberation, the dissenting juror argued that the Mattingly letter, rather than damning Capone, actually demonstrated that the man was only trying to pay his taxes. As the hours passed, he managed to convince the other members of the jury to temper their verdict. Which they did, though by how much would not be revealed until the decision was announced.

At 10:51 P.M., after nearly nine hours of discussion, the jurors informed the judge that they had reached a verdict. Capone was summoned from his hotel suite. Twenty minutes later he was battling the throng in front of the Federal Building as he lumbered up the stone steps. He was, as always, wearing his fedora, which he removed as he took his seat in Judge Wilkerson's courtroom. And the legal spectacle reached its climax.

"Have you arrived at a verdict?" the judge asked.

"We have, Your Honor," said the foreman, who handed a piece of paper to the bailiff, who gave it to the clerk, who read the verdict aloud:

"On indictment No. 22852," he said, which referred to Capone's failure to pay taxes for 1924, "we find the defendant not guilty. On indictment No. 23232," which covered the years 1925 through 1929, "we find the defendant guilty on counts 1,5,9,13, and 18 and not guilty on counts 2,3,4,6,7,8, 10,11,12,14,16,17,19,20,21, and 23." The convictions included three felonies and two misdemeanors. The first count, an "attempt to evade and defeat income tax for 1925," meant that Capone had failed to pay Uncle Sam what he owed on $250,000 in income. The second count, another felony, applied to his evading tax on his $195,000 income for 1926, and the third and final felony meant the same for his income of $200,000 in 1927. The two misdemeanors concerned his failure to file for income tax in 1928 and 1929.

Ahern insisted on polling the jury members. "Was this and is this your verdict?" he asked every one of them, and each said it was.

The five counts on which the jury had convicted Capone were serious and foretold heavy penalties: enormous fines and the likelihood of jail. The verdict was a clear-cut defeat for Capone; neither he nor his lawyers would be able to salvage anything from the jury's findings or claim victory. He and his team had bungled the trial, bungled it badly. The combination of a zealous judge, a rural jury immune to bribery, a determined and extremely well-prepared prosecution team, and his own slovenly counsel had proved disastrous. Al Capone was, for once, out-bullied, though it took the government of the United States to accomplish the feat.

Despite the severity of the verdict, neither Capone nor his counsel was wholly surprised. They anticipated he would have to pay heavy fines, and even go to jail for a few years, perhaps as many as five, though with time off for good behavior, he could be out in three years: 1935. He would be only thirty-six, with plenty of time ahead of him. Five years was a manageable amount of time; he could do it, as Leo Brothers had said, standing on his head; and as a VIP prisoner, he would almost certainly be accorded special privileges behind bars—privileges concerning food, lodging, visitors. His experience in Philadelphia had showed him that he could probably transact all the business he needed from jail, and anything he could not attend to personally, Nitti or Ralph could handle. With Prohibition still in force, Capone's syndicate would conduct business as usual. Al's confinement in jail changed nothing, no matter what the Feds believed or what the Chicago papers said about the consequences of his incarceration. He told himself it might be a good thing to spend a little time as a guest of the United States in jail, safe from his enemies, while everyone cooled off or died out. He could be seen as paying his debt to society. This whole tax thing was ridiculous, as everyone knew, and trivial compared to the real crimes he had committed, the lives he had taken, or ordered to be terminated. The worst part was the thought of his son visiting him in jail, knowing his father was a convict, and having to live his young life with that stigma. Nothing Al could do would alleviate that pain; he just hoped that Sonny would learn to understand and to forgive—and never be forced to make the choices his father had made.

•   •   •

"You don't need to be ordering fancy duds," Frankie Rio advised his boss as a tailor took measurements of Capone's swollen physique at the Lexington Hotel. "You're going to prison. Why don't you have a suit made with stripes on it?"

"The hell I am," Al shot back. "I'm going to Florida for a nice long rest, and I need some new clothes before I go." In this irrationally jaunty mood, he ordered two new lightweight suits and made plans for an extended stay at his Palm Island hacienda.

"PRISON?" asked the *Washington Herald*'s headline. "BAH! ME TO FLORIDA, SCOFFS CAPONE."

•   •   •

Just before ten o'clock in the morning on Saturday, October 24, Capone appeared in Judge Wilkerson's court to hear his sentence. He was freshly shaved, wearing a dark purple suit accented by a white silk handkerchief tucked in the breast pocket; he was eager to get on with the business at hand.

The bailiff called the court to order, and Judge Wilkerson entered, looking even grimmer than usual, his bristly, unkempt hair grayer than it had been during the trial. Only seventeen days had passed since he had first called the court to order, but it seemed a lifetime ago. The intensity of the trial had drained all the participants, each of whom had a large stake in its outcome, none more than Capone himself, who had begun this trial with an air of youthful defiance, convinced of his ability to bribe and maneuver his way to freedom, and who was ending it suddenly vulnerable, chastened, and aged.

At the outset Michael Ahern vainly objected to the court's attempting to pass sentence on his client. Capone edged forward to listen to the legal fracas, as the judge quickly dismissed the obstacle and proceeded briskly to the business at hand.

"Let the defendant step to the bar of the court," Wilkerson declared. Capone, composed and tranquil as he had been throughout the ordeal, rose and approached the judge. His hands were at his back, and a marshal stood at his side. "It is the judgment of the Court that on count 1 the defendant is sentenced to imprisonment in the penitentiary for a period of five years, and to pay a fine of $10,000 and all costs of prosecution." Capone did not flinch; this was precisely what he had expected: a series of concurrent sentences. What was $10,000 to him, or $100,000? "On count 5," Wilkerson continued, "the defendant is sentenced to five years in a penitentiary and to pay a fine of $10,000 and all costs of prosecution. On count 9 the defendant is sentenced to five years in a penitentiary and to pay a fine of $10,000 and all costs of prosecution."

Capone had also been convicted of two other counts; these were misdemeanors for failing to file tax returns in 1928 and 1929. For each, Capone received a year in the county jail and a $10,000 fine.

As the judge methodically listed the penalties, "Capone's eyes seemed to harden," a reporter noted, "and his fingers locked and unlocked behind his back. He thrust his hands in front of him and squared himself for what was to follow."

Capone had been sentenced to a total of seventeen years in jail. Wilkerson now came to the crucial matter of how the jail terms were to be served: concurrently, as Capone expected, or improbably, consecutively. "The sentences on counts 1 and 5 are to be served concurrently," Wilkerson declared. "The sentences on the other counts are to be consecutive and cumulative." In sum, Capone would have to pay a total of $80,000 in fines and court costs, and to serve a total of *eleven* years behind bars, ten in a federal penitentiary and one in a county jail. It was a far more severe sentence than anyone, especially Capone, had expected.

"Capone tried to smile again," wrote Meyer Berger of the *New York Times*, "but the smile was bitter. He licked his fat lips. He jiggled on his feet. His tongue moved in his cheeks. He was trying to be nonchalant, but he looked as if he must have felt—ready to give way to an outburst of anger." The money was meaningless to Capone, but the amount of jail time he must serve was staggering. "It was a smashing blow to the massive gang chief," Berger continued. "He tried to take it with a smile, but that smile was almost pitiful. His clumsy fingers, tightly locked behind his back, twitched and twisted. He had hoped for a sentence of not more than three years." Wilkerson's sentence was, in fact, the longest jail term anyone had yet received for income tax evasion, but it might have been even more severe. If not for the lone juror who had argued for eight hours during the deliberation that the defendant had wanted to pay the tax and the government had prevented him, Capone might well have spent the rest of his life behind bars. As matters now stood, Capone was forced to realize the government of the United States had attained its goal: to put him away for as long as possible, no bargains, no deals, no chance to make amends. The legal Lilliputians had finally managed to tie down their gangster Gulliver.

"Eleven years, did you say?" asked Fink, disbelieving his ears.

"Yes," the judge said, insisting that he wanted the convict escorted to Leavenworth Penitentiary, Kansas, immediately—that night, if possible. "He will serve the felony count first, before he serves the misdemeanor count. It is ordered that the marshal take custody of the defendant." Thinking he was about to be shipped off to Leavenworth, Capone suddenly reached out toward Fink; the two men vigorously shook hands good-bye. The lawyers resumed arguing with the judge about the sentence, where and how and if it should be served, and eventually Wilkerson backed down. Capone did not have to leave for Leavenworth tonight; he could stay in the county jail, in Chicago, at least until the following Monday, while his lawyers filed appeals on his behalf.

As he tried to leave the courthouse, Capone faced fresh indignities. In the hallway, a collector for the Internal Revenue Service, a frightened looking little man, approached him and said, "I want to serve this." With that, he handed Capone assessments for delinquent taxes in the amount of $68,644 and a notice that the U.S. government declared its intention to seize the contents of his safety deposit boxes and attach the Palm Island estate, the home into which he had poured so much money, the symbol of his fumbling attempt for respectability, the refuge he would not be seeing for many years. Capone reared back, as if preparing to kick the diminutive yet omnipotent tax collector in the shins, but he quickly regained his self-control and accepted the papers.

He retrieved his coat and hat, and then with the coat slung across his left arm and his fedora clamped down on his head, Capone the convict rode the elevator. Even here lurked another surprise: Mike Malone, the IRS agent who had been living at the Lexington Hotel under the alias De Angelo. Capone took one look him and realized De Angelo was a spy, but the convicted tax evader did not appear to be angry. "The only thing that fooled me was your looks," he told the agent. "You look like a Wop. You took your chances, and I took mine." As they reached the main floor, the door opened, and Capone faced hundreds of citizens of Chicago; the men who had drunk his beer, gambled in his joints, and slept with his prostitutes all strained for a glimpse of him as he bounded down the steps in the raw October air, climbed into a waiting car and, said *Time*, "disappeared into the sprawling city whose thousands of illicit night haunts were his Empire."

● ● ●

Later that evening, Capone entered the county jail, where he paused briefly to talk with reporters, many of whom he knew by name or by sight, some of whom had accepted his gifts and favors and had then helped send him to jail. "What do you say, Al?" one asked.

"I haven't anything to say," he replied with a weak smile, adding, "Well, you can say I decided to get through with it." Capone wasn't angry with the press, he didn't bother to criticize them for his misfortune, but he was deadly serious. "It was a blow to the belt," he said of the eleven-year sentence, "but what can you expect when the whole community is prejudiced against you? I've never heard of anyone getting more than five years for income tax trouble, but when they're prejudiced, what can you do even if you've got good lawyers?" He hurried inside the building, but the photographers were waiting for him in the corridors, hoping to snap a photo of Public Enemy Number 1 behind bars at last. Hoping to catch him growling, cursing, crying, grinning, anything that would satisfy the public's craving to see the conclusion of the drama. As the wardens registered their celebrity guest and led him to a cell, he called out to the camera men: "Think of my family. Please don't take my picture." Most respected his wishes, but as one photographer raised his camera, Capone cried, "I'll knock your block off!" and attempted to hurl a water bucket at the man.

The wardens quickly subdued the infuriated prisoner. Locked in his cell, Capone discovered he had company, a vagrant who was unable to pay a $100 fine for a disorderly conduct charge. The men spoke briefly. "I'm gonna help this guy out," Capone decided; he retrieved a C-note from his pocket and gave it to the vagrant, who used it to pay his fine. So Capone bought himself a little privacy. That night, brooding in his cell as the reality of the situation settled over him, he was served his reformatory repast: a tin plate of corned beef and cabbage. He refused to eat it, restricting himself instead to rice pudding, which he swallowed between gulps of tepid coffee.

As Capone settled into jail, word of his sentence raced along the darkened streets of Chicago, streets smelling of wet fallen leaves, factory exhaust, and hastily brewed beer; it was repeated in homes, amplified on the radio, fixed for posterity in newspaper headlines across the nation: Capone guilty, Capone sentenced, Capone jailed. "CAPONE GETS 11-YEAR TERM; FINED $50,000—PENALTIES MAY MULCT HIM OF HALF A MILLION," announced the *New York Evening Post*, which explained that "Judge James H. Wilkerson dealt the century's most sensational criminal a crippling blow today." "HOODLUM, STUNNED BY OUTCOME, CURSES AS HE FACES TIME IN PENITENTIARY," declared the *Kansas City Star*, with obvious relish. Not all editors were pleased, however; a large sector of the press described the conviction of Al Capone for income tax evasion, of all things, as a legalistic sham, a mere technicality. "It is ludicrous that this underworld gang leader has been led to the doors of the penitentiary at last only through prosecutions on income tax and liquor conspiracy laws," the *Boston Globe* complained, while the *Washington Evening Star* observed, "No matter how satisfactory will be the eventual incarceration of Capone in a Federal prison for the failure to make an income-tax return, as a technical means to the end of getting him in jail, there will remain the sense that the law has failed."

The severity of Capone's term—eleven years—shocked everyone. The smart money had said he would be sent away for two, perhaps three years—long enough at any rate to miss the Chicago World's Fair of 1933. Now it seemed that Al would not go free until 1942. The World's Fair would be long gone, indeed the world would be a different place by then. "No one seemed to believe that the 'Big Shot' was at last on the way to jail," Meyer Berger reflected, "that the man who had controlled the city's warring machine gunners, beer runners, panderers, gamblers and other lawless elements had finally been tripped up and hog-tied. It was the general idea that 'he's much too big for that; got too much money and too much influence.' "

The blunt fact of his conviction ended the secret life of Al Capone, and he began a new life as a convict, shorn of privacy. In its clumsy, incomplete way, the trial had succeeded in piercing the secrecy in which he had always moved. From this time forward, he would be stripped of his social camouflage; his life was about to become one long documentary, everything on the record, the story of a prisoner in the custody of the state, subject to an omnipotent bureaucracy and relentless scrutiny that would eventually leave him paralyzed and powerless.

· · ·

Desperate to keep their client from going to Leavenworth, Ahern and Fink appeared before three judges of the U.S. Circuit Court of Appeals, Seventh Circuit. It was now Monday, October 26.

Fink did most of the talking, filling in the judges on the status of Capone's case. "As you have perhaps read in the newspapers, he was tried downstairs and on Saturday he was convicted," he began. "As soon as the sentence was

pronounced, we filed our petition for an appeal, and Judge Wilkerson allowed the appeal. . . . Unless we can get some relief from the Circuit judges,
the prisoner will go down to Leavenworth tonight to begin his sentence in the
penitentiary. Now, as I view it, there isn't any reason in the world why this
man should be denied bail."

Sidestepping the issue of bail, the judges asked Fink on what grounds he
was appealing. The question suggested they might be more sympathetic than
Judge Wilkerson had, and the prospect of reversing the conviction brought
the elderly little lawyer to life.

"As to the particular counts upon which the verdict has been returned,"
Fink replied, "they charge merely this and nothing else: that the defendant
was a resident of this district and that he had a gross tax and deductions and
should pay so much in income tax. When it comes to the charging part of
the indictment, the count says that the defendant did willfully and fraudu-
lently attempt to evade and defeat said tax, and this is all. To tell a defendant
only that six years ago he made a willful attempt to evade his income tax for
the year before is to tell him absolutely nothing." Fink appeared to gain the
sympathy of the judges, who pressed for more details and legal citations. For
once, Fink's long years of legal experience came into play, and he was able
to mount an impressive display of justification for his position, especially
concerning the three felony counts of which Capone had been convicted.
"The evidence as to any expenditures is very, very meager," he told the
triumvirate, "and I don't think there is any evidence of expenditure for the
years 1925 and 1926, and in 1927, except that the defendant lived at a
hotel—I have forgotten the name of it. What is the name of that?"

"Metropole," Dwight Green interjected.

"Metropole Hotel," Fink resumed, "together with a lot of other fellows,
presumably gangsters, or at least claimed by the government to be gangsters,
and that somebody paid the bills there, and that the defendant paid the bills
himself, and that for the year 1925 he made a statement to two police who
were out there on a raid in their presence that he owned a gambling house.
The fact that he owned a gambling house does not prove he made a profit,
and we contend that, if Your Honors please, there is no evidence on the
record upon which the court should have submitted the case to the jury."

Later in the discussion, Green reviewed the government's case to impress
the weight of the evidence upon the judges. "He stated that he was in the
gambling business," Green said of Capone, "and that Guzik was his business
associate."

"Who stated it?" asked Judge Alschuler.

"The defendant stated that in admissions."

"Did he testify?"

"No, he didn't testify," Green said. "He stated that in admissions to various officials down in Florida. For instance, he said to some of the shopkeepers, one of them at least, 'Guzik is my financial secretary.' And then there were a number of wire transmittals that came from Chicago to Florida that were, as we proved, sent by Guzik, and then we showed that the defendant had an organization here of some kind in Chicago which consisted of at least about eighteen men, who all lived together at the Metropole Hotel, and there on several occasions the defendant himself paid the entire bill."

"Might not that be expenses rather than income?" asked the judge.

Green conceded that might be the case and resumed his review, focusing on Capone's profits from the Cicero gambling houses. "There was Guzik running it, and Alphonse Capone was in the place at the time that the business was conducted, and we show there about $120,000 worth of profits, and we showed the defendant's name on one of the checks."

The arguing went on and on, but at the end of the day nothing had changed. Capone was still guilty and faced the imminent prospect of a decade in Leavenworth.

· · ·

There remained but one loose end for Judge Wilkerson to tie up, which he did two days after the appeal, on October 28. Emboldened by the guilty verdict returned against Capone, Judge Wilkerson made his determination in the contempt charge against D'Andrea, who, despite the marshal's badge he carried as faithfully as a religious medal, belonged to an "organized body of men whose outlaw camp is at the Lexington Hotel. Of this body, defendant Capone was chief. . . . It is perfectly clear from a long array of conclusive circumstances that this band exercises a coercive influence over those with whom it comes in contact, which is nothing less than insurrection against the laws of the United States." The judge was especially unhappy with D'Andrea's murderous scowl. "The court would have been blind if it had not observed the intimidation practiced on witnesses almost under the eyes of the court. It must be borne in mind that this respondent was sitting with his concealed firearms behind the defendant while glaring at witnesses who were on the point of remembering something about the business in which defendant was engaged and which the witnesses could not possibly have forgotten; yet witnesses faltered and failed at the critical point."

The judge proceeded to discredit virtually every defense witness, as well as the defense lawyers, Ahern and Fink, insisting that they all had been coerced—not by D'Andrea, but by Al Capone himself. "To this camp at the Lexington were summoned the witnesses who testified to the defendant Capone's losses on horse races. To that camp were summoned counsel for conferences. And from that camp, under what coercive influences we can only conjecture from what transpired in court, came that array of shocking perjury with which the court was confronted during the closing days of the trial. We had here the spectacle of witness after witness testifying in a way which was psychologically impossible, pretending to remember things which in the very nature of the human mind the witness could not have remembered. . . . It was perjury on its face." *Coercive influences, shocking perjury, psychologically impossible*: with these phrases Judge Wilkerson poured out the weeks of anger and frustration he had endured in the effort to get Capone behind bars. Ahern and Fink strenuously disagreed with his characterization of their dealings with their client. Why, they had never been "summoned" to the Lexington, they declared, and they certainly had never been coerced by Capone or anyone else except, they wished to add, the court.

"I still think if I had been in your place, I would not have gone down there," the judge remonstrated.

Having nothing left to lose, Ahern decided to lecture the judge. "Your Honor, when you are dealing with gamblers you are not dealing with ministers' daughters, and I would much rather interview those gamblers some place else rather than my office."

"I don't blame you," said the judge, unmoved.

As he began to deliver D'Andrea's sentence, Wilkerson dropped his voice. The pistol D'Andrea had carried into the courtroom, said the judge, "was less serious than the perjury." As a result, he recommended a sentence of "six months in the county jail."

D'Andrea's sentence was not so onerous as it seemed, for his cellmate at the Cook County Jail was none other than Al Capone, who was already busy bribing prison officials and arranging extraordinary jailhouse privileges for them both. As the government of the United States was about to discover to its dismay, it was one thing to put Public Enemy Number 1 in jail, but it was quite another to put him out of business.

CHAPTER 11

Circles of Hell

WITHIN DAYS OF HIS ARRIVAL on October 24, 1931, Al Capone transformed the Cook Country Jail into the newest outpost of his fiefdom, and he was soon as comfortably established there as he had been in his suite at the Lexington Hotel. Languishing in his oversize cell throughout the fall, the most famous convict in the nation conducted his affairs almost as if he were at liberty. Even better, the taxpayers now bore the cost of his lodging and upkeep as well as providing that other essential: security.

In those days rank had its privileges, especially in the Cook County Jail, where the warden, presciently named David T. Moneypenny, proved suspiciously eager to accommodate Capone's every whim. He assigned the famous prisoner to a quiet, private, oversize cell on the fifth-floor hospital ward. Over 1,500 prisoners crowded the jail, but Capone's exclusive quarters could have held a dozen or more men. Amid these luxurious surroundings, he slept as late as he liked, and he avoided the common run of criminals. He shared his VIP accommodations with his bodyguard, Philip D'Andrea, and together they enjoyed amenities that the average con would have envied: box spring mattresses, a radio, and an ample supply of Mae Capone's cuisine, which was delivered regularly, still hot; a typical meal consisted of kidney stew, bread, and butter. On Thanksgiving Day, Capone, D'Andrea, and several friends and family members enjoyed a lavish feast served by a black butler.

As winter approached, Capone became ever more entrenched in the Cook County Jail. Conviction or no conviction, he conducted business as usual from his cell; he obtained access to the jail's telegraph system, and he placed calls on the jail's phone to his family, lawyers, bookies, and other well-placed contacts in the city administration. Since he could not get out to see the men he needed to see, they came to him. "Today was visiting day on Capone's floor at the jail and he had some distinguished visitors," the *New York Times* dryly noted. "They included Dan Serritella, State Senator and former city sealer, Alderman William Pacelli, and Harry Hockstein, former city sealer." Before long Pete Penovich, Matthew and John Capone, Murray "The Camel" Humphreys, and other loyalists were also calling on "Snorky" in his new "office" to bring him up to date on the latest take.

Surrounded by activity and friends, Capone remained buoyant, and he expected to go free at any time, following the example set by his older brother. In April 1930, Ralph Capone had been indicted for the same offense, income tax evasion, also in Judge Wilkerson's court, and he was supposed to serve three years in Leavenworth Penitentiary, which, compared to the Cook County Jail, was hard time. Ralph had managed to stave off jail with a barrage of appeals, however, and was still at large in Miami. No one could say whether he was cunning or just lucky. The government, it seemed, had all but forgotten about him, although the zealous Chicago Crime Commission continued to list him as Public Enemy Number 3. Al, who perennially ranked first on the list, saw no reason why he wouldn't fall through the cracks as Ralph had, and he would at last put all this unpleasantness behind him.

Then, without warning, Ralph's number was up. His last appeal—before the U.S. Supreme Court—failed, and he was ordered to report to Leavenworth Penitentiary immediately. "CAPONE'S BROTHER ON WAY TO GIVE UP," the *New York Times* summarized on November 4. "Counsel Calls Him from Florida to 'Come In' and Surrender in Chicago Tomorrow. FURTHER APPEALS FRUITLESS."

Throughout their legal difficulties, as in their family life, Ralph had always led the way, and now he became to the first Capone to serve his sentence for income tax evasion. (The days that Al, currently held without bail, served in the Cook County Jail counted for nothing.) Ralph took the Twentieth Century Limited to Chicago and reported to the Federal Building, where he was fingerprinted, photographed, and interviewed. Coached by his lawyer, he supplied the following personal history, a profile of the man whom the Chicago Crime Commission called Public Enemy Number 3:

Name..Ralph J. Capone
Address...7244 Prairie Avenue
Age..37 years
Height ....5 feet 11 inches
Weight ....215 pounds
Hair...Black
Eyes..Brown

Descent...Italian
How Long in U.S.A..36 years
How Long in Cook County..9 years
Education..Grammar school
Occupation..Race horse owner
Married...Yes
Wife..Valma Capone
Children..............................Ralph, Jr.—14 years old
Father..Deceased
Mother...Theresa Capone
Address..7244 Prairie Avenue

When that grim procedure was concluded, the *Chicago Tribune* reported, "the gangster was taken to the county jail in a taxicab by two deputy marshals, being spared the customary ride in a patrol wagon with narcotic addicts and dry law violators. He was placed in the large receiving cell on the first floor, with a group of Negroes, Chinese, and police court prisoners." Meanwhile, Al lingered upstairs in his fifth floor deluxe cell, and rumors circulated that the two brothers would soon depart for Leavenworth together.

On Friday morning, November 6, Ralph took his leave of the county jail, but not before the ever-obliging Warden Moneypenny permitted the brothers Capone to hold a lengthy reunion. Teresa also arrived to bid her son goodbye, and she left the jail sobbing. Ralph himself was said to be "morose." After he made his final farewell, he was driven away in a police van bound for a train to Leavenworth.

"I'd like to eat in the diner," he told the marshal accompanying him for the journey.

"Can't be done," came the reply.

"Well, then, I'd like to have some food sent in for me and the boys," Ralph said, with a wave of the hand to indicate the other prisoners, "I'll stand the check": a magnanimous gesture to which the marshal readily agreed.

The train reached Leavenworth the following morning, where Ralph traded his custom-tailored clothes for drab gray prison garb, but he did not lack for company in his new home, for the penitentiary housed two of his colleagues: Sam Guzik and Frank Nitti. Sam's brother Jack, Al Capone's accountant, brothel manager, and devoted friend, was scheduled to join the bunch within months. Everywhere Ralph went in the federal penitentiary system, he found himself among close friends and associates. *Campanilismo*, even in jail.

Alarmed at the prospect of the entire Capone gang domiciled together for years, the attorney general ordered the wardens of federal penitentiaries around the country to redistribute them. He received an immediate response from Finch R. Archer, the warden of McNeil Island Penitentiary, located on Puget Sound, off the coast of the state of Washington, vowing to isolate Ralph and to give him no special privileges whatsoever: "Capone will of course be kept from communicating with any member of his gang as far as it can possibly be done. All prisoners received here are treated alike, whether they are bankers or laborers." These arrangements took place in secret as well as in haste. Shortly after his arrival at Leavenworth, on December 10, Ralph received a nasty surprise: he was reassigned to McNeil Island. On the day of his transfer, his lawyers were informed that their client was being moved for "administrative reasons, the importance of which must be fairly plain to you." By the time the lawyers reflexively complained about the hardship the move was certain to inflict on their client and his family, it was too late; Ralph had already arrived at McNeil Island. The presence of a Capone in the Northwest, coupled with rumors that Al himself would soon follow, immediately generated unwelcome publicity. "What an attraction this would be for summer tourists," a local newspaper observed. "Thousands who never heard of this region would visit us every summer during the exile of the kings of gangland. We think the government is right in not wanting to imprison the Caponeites in Leavenworth. It is too common and the scenery is nothing to boast of."

Although Ralph's term lasted until November 6, 1934, he would be eligible for parole within two years, but that was not a likely possibility. Warning that he was a "menace to society" and a "habitual criminal," his parole report recommended against granting him early freedom. "He is a member of . . . the 'Capone Gang' and for years has been engaged in the illegal manufacture, sale, transportation and possession of liquor, the operation of bawdy houses or houses of ill repute, cabarets where the law has been violated and a notorious member of the gambling crowd," the report noted; and, of course, he was the "brother of Alphonse Capone," which might have been his worst offense in the eyes of the U.S. attorney's office. Although Ralph was destined to serve out his full sentence, it was much shorter than what awaited his younger brother.

Ralph was kept active at McNeil, spending his days on a road repair crew, shoveling gravel. "The chill winter fogs that drift across the little island make the sleek gangster keenly appreciative of the heavy winter underwear issued to him," the Tacoma Times remarked with understated glee. The physical activity caused the thirty-seven-year-old racketeer, who weighed over 215 pounds and had a distinctly roly-poly appearance when he arrived there, to lose weight swiftly. Such was the standard procedure for new inmates at McNeil: two weeks on the labor crew followed by four months on a construction crew, and finally reassignment to a less demanding task. A docile prisoner, Ralph was eventually employed as a cook in the prisoners' mess. At Christmas, he decorated his cell with balls of red and green crepe paper, and over his doorway he wrote in chalk "Merry Christmas!" His sole relief that winter from the prison routine was a visit from his wife and mother-in-law. Clad in mink, they traveled by train from Miami, took the ferry to the island, spent a few hours with Ralph, and left as quietly as they had come. By spring he had earned a place on the penitentiary's "entertainment committee," although the opportunities for diversion in this grim little penal colony can only be imagined. But that was going too far for Sanford Bates, the director of the Federal Bureau of Prisons, who promptly insisted that the warden remove him, lest Ralph's position on the committee attract attention. "Mr. Bates would not want Capone to come out of obscurity to even this extent," his assistant explained, adding in grim jest, "I assume that the Wilkerson who is serving on this committee with Capone is not Judge Wilkerson." Archer had no choice but to comply, and Ralph left the committee. The *Tacoma Times* gleefully speculated about how Ralph filled the days and nights in jail. "Possibly he occupies the evenings looking for bedbugs," the paper remarked. "The prisoners are allowed only $10 a month for spending money, and as Warden Archer . . . has offered a reward of $10 for every bedbug captured, the temptation is great. . . . We consider it a very proper life for a great gangster in retirement."

Throughout the cold, dreary months he spent at McNeil Island, Ralph continued to protest his innocence. The record of his initial interview at the penitentiary reveals how in his own mind he deftly rearranged the facts of his case to exculpate himself:

> In 1927 when the Supreme Court decision was handed down that profits from such business were subject to income tax he became fearful that his record might be investigated. Stated that he went to the Federal authorities and offered to pay any such tax that might be due. Told them that he had no way of keeping accurate accounts other than his bank deposit slips. Said that they took these and spread it out over the years of 1922 to 1925. . . . Said he paid the $4,065.75 [tax owed] but that his attorney advised him not to pay the fees and penalties as they could be knocked out because the government had been in error. . . . Said that while this matter was pending that he was indicted.

> Takes rather the attitude that the thing has happened and that his main concern is that of doing his time and getting it over with. Does not blame the government for his trouble, but rather his own attorney.

States that he would like to study Spanish, but that after shoveling all day he feels too tired to study.

Another entry in his prison record notes: "Never did a dishonest thing in his life, he says. . . . Except for the newspapers and politicians, he would never have been prosecuted. They got much publicity because of his brother, Al Capone."

• • •

With both Al and Ralph in jail, a steady drumroll of newspaper headlines in December assured Americans that the Capones' downfall had toppled the careers of many other gangsters, ending their influence for once and all:

CHICAGO'S UNDERWORLD EMPIRE SHAKEN BY THE FALL OF CAPONE
The Opposing Forces of Gangland and the Law as They are Now
Arrayed, and New Elements that Have Entered the Contest

DRIVE ON GANGS SENDS GUNMEN TO U.S. PRISON

CAPONE "FORT" RAIDED, YIELDS TRIO OF CHIEFS

CAPONE ALLIES SEIZED; MAY BE DEPORTED BY U.S.

The dispatches made for gratifying but wholly misleading reading. Judge Wilkerson, who continued to watch Capone's progress with special fascination, discovered the real situation to be exactly the opposite of the newspapers' jubilant accounts. Days after Ralph's departure for Leavenworth, on December 2, he received an anonymous telegram leveling dismaying charges of corruption in the Cook County jail:

WISH TO INFORM YOU THAT AL CAPONE IS USING THE COUNTY JAIL FOR HIS LIQUOR BUSINESS AND TRANSACTS FROM THERE POSSIBLY AS MUCH IF NOT MORE THAN HE USED TO AT HIS OLD HEADQUARTERS AT THE LEXINGTON HOTEL. HIS VISITORS SEEM TO BE COMING ALL DAY LONG AS WELL AS IN THE EVENING. I AM EMPLOYED AT THIS BRANCH OF SERVICE AND CAN NOT UNDERSTAND WHY EVERY PRIVILEGE IS EXTENDED TO HIM AND NONE TO THE OTHERS. PLEASE INVESTIGATE.

Outraged by the special treatment Capone was apparently receiving behind bars, Wilkerson forwarded the telegram to the Chicago office of the Federal Bureau of Investigation on December 3, 1931.

At about the same time, the U.S. attorney, George E. Q. Johnson, received the identical telegram, and it became apparent that a major scandal was brewing. Suddenly it seemed as if all the years of work he had devoted to catching Capone were being undone; the man was a recurring nightmare. The uncomfortable truth was that sending men to jail changed nothing in the Chicago syndicate; the booze and bribes flowed as freely as ever. Judge Wilkerson, U.S. Attorney Johnson, Director of the FBI J. Edgar Hoover, and President Hoover himself could redistribute the members of the "Capone gang," they could execute every gangster on the Chicago Crime Commission's list of Public Enemies, if they wished, without affecting the status quo, for the government's strategy had been flawed from the start. Federal prosecutors had fastened on Al Capone, making him into a potent symbol of lawlessness and corruption, but they had failed to realize that he was, for all his wealth and influence, merely a big bright cog in the Chicago rackets machine, which was driven by Frankie La Porte, who, unknown to the FBI and unheralded by the Chicago Crime Commission, continued to do business from a safe remove in Chicago Heights. The FBI remained unaware this little city served as the epicenter of Chicago racketeering. Even those law enforcement agents who kept an ear close to the ground, men such as Eliot Ness and his band of Untouchables, considered the Heights merely an outpost of bootlegging.

Responding to the charges contained in the anonymous telegram, M. A. McSwain, a Chicago-based FBI agent, began a thorough inquiry and discovered no end of risqué tales of Capone's life behind bars. He heard that Capone kept gallons of whiskey in his cell, serving it to his guests; that a pimp named "Bon-Bon" Allegretti furnished Capone with a steady supply of prostitutes, who on one occasion put on an "obscene performance"; that a woman named Marion, who was supposedly Capone's mistress, had been sequestered with him; and finally, that he bribed Warden Moneypenny and other prison workers.

Dreading the newspapers' airing of these allegations, Johnson decided to investigate personally. It was highly unusual for a U.S. attorney to intervene in the running of a county jail, but these were unusual times. Johnson went to the Cook County Jail, avoiding Capone but subjecting Moneypenny and his assistants to a thorough inquiry. The warden, according to Agent McSwain's report of the matter, explained that

> visitors seeing Al Capone must talk to the latter through wire mesh, and none other than his attorneys and possibly Capone's mother and sister are permitted to actually enter the hospital. . . . Likewise, Mr. Moneypenny denied any knowledge of any women visiting Capone's quarters other than Capone's mother and sister. . . . Mr. Moneypenny did

state that food was sent in twice a day from the outside for Capone, but this is not an unusual practice, as all prisoners are permitted to receive food from the outside.

Half a dozen other prison employees, from the assistant warden to the night watchman, vouched for this account, and after a week of worry, Johnson's informal but thorough investigation persuaded him that most of the allegations were groundless. However, Capone, if he wished, could conduct business from jail, so new measures were instituted to restrict the flow of visitors. "Henceforth," the report concluded, "no persons shall be allowed to visit Alphonse Capone in the Cook County Jail without a pass from the United States Marshal."

The newspapers made the most of the developments. Where they had recently tolled the death of gangland, their headlines now related a much different tale. "CAPONE RUNS UNDERWORLD FROM CELL, U.S. REVEALS—Gangster's Daily Visitors at Jail, Tipster Wires Washington; Al Living in Luxury—Warden and Aides Questioned; Politicians Linked; Ban on Passes Ordered by Marshal," announced the *Chicago Herald and Examiner*. To those familiar with Chicago politics, none of this came a surprise—considering Capone's massive clout, how could it be otherwise?—but the headlines were a revelation in Washington. Under pressure from the White House, the Department of Justice applied greater pressure on Johnson to move Capone to a federal penitentiary, where he would be less likely to have the run of the place.

Only two days later, on December 22, a fresh scandal broke with the appearance of this headline in the *Chicago Daily Times*: "BARE WARDEN'S CAPITOL TRIP IN AL CAPONE'S MOTOR CAR." Although David Moneypenny had recently told George E. Q. Johnson, the U.S. attorney, that Al Capone was receiving absolutely no preferential treatment in jail, it was now apparent that the *warden* had been receiving preferential treatment from his celebrated inmate. Moneypenny would have gotten away with using Capone's car—a spiffy sixteen-cylinder Cadillac—had he not suffered a mechanical breakdown while driving from Springfield, Illinois, to Chicago. Waiting impatiently at a garage for repairs to be completed, Moneypenny tried to impress the mechanics with the importance of his position. They fixed him, instead, by alerting reporters, who quickly traced the sleek Cadillac to Mae Capone, in whose name it was registered. When the reporters confronted him with their discovery, Moneypenny lamely insisted he had no idea who owned the car, but the incident served as a convincing demonstration that he had, despite his hot denials, accepted favors if not outright bribes from Capone.

Warden Moneypenny's luckless drive through the Illinois countryside in Mae's Cadillac backfired for Al as well. Once the news hit the papers, the scandal redoubled the government's determination to remove Capone from his privileged position at the Cook County Jail, but they were still frustrated by Capone's unending appeals. For months, his lawyers had toiled behind the scenes, attempting a series of legal maneuvers aimed at obtaining the release of their notorious client. None of the stratagems they employed had a remote chance of succeeding, but they had the less spectacular effect of delaying their client's transfer to Leavenworth.

As the weeks of confinement slipped past, Capone continued to lead his comfortable jailhouse existence, hold court, and pursue his interest in boxing. He called his friend "Doc" Kearns, the fight promoter, to request fifty seats for his men at the upcoming Jackie Fields–Lou Brouillard heavyweight title fight, specifying that Kearns deliver the tickets in person to the Cook County Jail. Instead of the grim prison setting he expected to find, Kearns came upon this cozy scene: "Al had a radio playing softly. There was an expensive quilt neatly folded at the bottom of his cot and there was a small table which openly bore several bottles of whiskey next to a cut glass, silver-topped humidor filled with cigars." Once Kearns handed over the tickets, Capone summoned a turnkey, who obediently fetched a bucket of ice, while the prisoner prepared highballs with a masterful touch. After several drinks, the two men relaxed, and Kearns become sufficiently emboldened to ask Capone what he planned to do if he were convicted of income tax evasion.

"I got no idea," said the racketeer with a frown. "I guess if it ain't too stiff a rap, why the organization would sort of hold together until I got back. 'Course, you never know what a difference a few years make and there's no tellin' how things might be, one way or another, when I finally got out. Hell, the booze racket's about shot to hell right now the way the Feds have been cracking down." Capone took a gulp from his drink, adding, "Why'd you ask, 'Doc'?"

Under the influence of the jailhouse liquor, Kearns finally came out with his grand scheme to rehabilitate Capone in the public mind and, doing well by doing good, to reap a large profit in the process. "You'd be sensational as an evangelist," he informed the astonished racketeer. "You know this here Billy Sunday?" Kearns said, referring to the baseball player who had become a popular preacher. "If he can be an evangelist, why not you?"

"It sounds wacky to me," Al said.

"You don't understand," Kearns insisted, on his feet with excitement. "You'll get reformed, see. Everybody has heard about you and all the evil things you've done. . . ."

"Now justa minute, God dammit," Capone shouted as he shot to his feet, ready to punch out Kearns.

"I ain't knockin' you, Al. I'm your friend," Kearns told him. "If they stick you in the big house you'd have lots of time to study up on the Bible." Al sat and poured himself another drink as Kearns continued to explain his scheme. "I'd take you on tour and you'd be a national hero."

"For Christ's sake," Capone protested, "I'm national now. Maybe not a hero, but they know Capone everywhere—you can get a bundle on that."

Kearns took another drink. "We'd make a million bucks when I took you on tour."

Now it was Al's turn to take another drink. Under the influence of the alcohol, he warmed to the scheme. Publicity was always a pleasing prospect for Capone, and he remained eager for the public to think well of him. "You know, 'Doc,' " he said, "maybe you got somethin' there, at that. I could always talk real good, even without some of my boys alongside me to keep my audience listening real close." To demonstrate his evangelical speaking style, Capone puffed out his chest and began declaiming: "Crime don't pay and I'm the guy who can tell you good people about it, and you damned well better listen! You got to lead a good Christian life and don't never knock nobody off, like the one time . . ." Al paused, muttered that he had better skip over that incident, and resumed his tirade. "The devil gets inside of you when you don't take care of yourself in a good Christian manner, and run around and drink that God-dammned booze." Again he caught himself and muttered, "No use knockin' booze until I know it's legal." He helped himself to another drink, and told his friend, "They'd listen to Al Capone, or, by God, they'd wish they had."

Kearns drunkenly agreed, but then remarked that evangelists, "although I ain't no authority on 'em," probably refrained from taking the Lord's name in vain during their sermons. The mild criticism provoked a further outburst from Capone. "Now if I'm gonna manage this God damned tour," Kearns lectured him, "you're gonna have to listen to some suggestions without getting hot under the collar every time I turn around." Capone relented, and his would-be manager brought up the financial aspects of their partnership. "This deal is fifty-fifty," he announced. Capone, he recalled, "looked like I'd stabbed him."

"Nobody gets 50 percent of any of my deals," Al said, before dissolving into alcoholic laughter. Finally he agreed to the terms, declaring, "It's worth it to be a national hero and preaching religion."

Kearns left the Cook County Jail that day with a drunken glow and the prospect of an important new client, but as the weeks and months passed, it became apparent that Capone would never obtain the freedom necessary to allow him to pursue a career as a crusading evangelist. Although Kearns's wild scheme came to nothing, the promoter had planted the seeds of an idea in Capone's mind, the idea being public rehabilitation. Brooding on his situation during the long days in jail, he soon devised another way to make himself into a national hero.

At the beginning of March 1932, Capone, along with the rest of the nation, reacted with horror and fascination to the kidnapping of Charles Lindbergh's infant son. Since his solo transatlantic flight five years before, the "Lone Eagle" had been among the most famous and fortunate of Americans, his prowess and daring celebrated both at home and abroad. He had seemed touched with grace, invulnerable, but his life entered a darker chapter when his infant son was kidnapped from the Lindbergh estate in Hopewell, New Jersey, on March 1. The event triggered national hysteria as well as a massive hunt to find the missing child and his abductor. It quickly became symbolic of a larger evil abroad in the land, a truly malevolent force. Capone seized on the tragedy as an example of unmitigated evil, compared to which his bootlegging and tax dodging were relatively benign, victimless crimes. He knew he was not wholly innocent—there was too much blood on his hands—but he thought of himself as pragmatic and resourceful, a *necessary* evil. He instinctively identified with Lindbergh as a victim of fame and could easily imagine a similar tragedy befalling thirteen-year-old Sonny, whose photograph adorned his father's cell. Kidnapping had always struck Al as the most despicable of all crimes. It was one thing to kill a man—sometimes the harsh reality of the rackets left no other choice—but to harm a child was monstrous, inexcusable. Eventually Al's compassion gave way to his megalomania and his cunning. He hatched a plot of his own, one that cast him as a hero and would, he hoped, to spring him from jail at last. It began with a request to see Mr. Arthur Brisbane, the most influential editor in the Hearst newspaper empire.

On the morning of March 10, Brisbane—tall, thin-lipped, balding, with horn-rimmed glasses—entered the Cook County Jail. Escorted to Capone's jumbo-sized cell in the hospital ward, he found the most celebrated gangster of the day sitting alone at a table, engrossed in a game of solitaire. Once Brisbane took a seat, Capone asked for the latest news of the Lindbergh kidnapping and proceeded to divulge his plan: if the authorities would let him out of jail, he would use all his powers to find the Lindbergh baby. "I will give any bond they require if they are interested in the child," Capone explained. "I will spend every hour of the night and day with Thomas Callaghan, head of the United States Secret Service. The Government knows that it can trust him, I think, and I will send my young brother to stay here in the jail until I come back. You don't suppose anybody would suggest that I would double-cross my own brother and leave him here, if I could get away from Callaghan?" Capone did not invoke the name of Thomas Callaghan lightly. In fact, the IRS learned that Callaghan had recently visited Capone in jail three or four times, and Capone probably thought he had Callaghan's blessing. But when it came to specifics concerning his attempt to recover the Lindbergh baby, Capone became vague and confused, talking of the "angles" he would pursue on the outside and promising to do his best.

Like nearly every journalist who interviewed Al Capone, Brisbane became fond of the man and listened attentively as the prisoner turned the subject to his own plight. "I handle beer," he said, "and beer never did anybody any harm. Everybody is a bootlegger nowadays, either selling it or buying it. The man that buys it violates the law as much as the man that sells it." As he spoke, Al wove elaborate fantasies tinged with paranoia, and his deteriorating mental condition became increasingly apparent: "I am only 33 years old, and they tie me up with things that happened 25 years ago, talking about mobs I never heard of. When I came to Chicago 11 years ago, I only had $40 in my pocket. I went into a business that was open and didn't do anybody any harm. They talk about the unemployed. I have given work to the unemployed. At least 300 young men, thanks to me, are getting from $150 to $200 a week, and are making it in the harmless beer racket, which is better than their jobs before. I have given work that has taken many a man out of the hold-up and bank robbery business." Of course, the hundreds killed in Chicago since the inception of Prohibition demonstrated that the beer racket was anything but "harmless," but Capone was appealing to the emotions, not logic. He concluded on a political note: "I have always been a Republican, and my young men are 100 percent Republicans. But we don't ask for any profit out of politics. That isn't our racket. I don't see why they should crucify me."

Brisbane was hardly the first to hear the offer; in fact, Capone had been trying out the ploy on journalists for weeks with little success. The *New York Times* had run a brief account several days earlier, but it was buried deep in the paper and went unnoticed. And when Will Rogers came a-calling at the Cook County Jail in search of material to flesh out his newspaper column, Capone spent two hours discussing his offer with the humorist, who against his better judgment wound up in Capone's thrall. "There was absolutely no way I could write it and not make a hero out of him," Rogers wrote in his diary of Capone's offer. "What's the matter with an age when our biggest gangster is our greatest national interest?"

Brisbane had no such scruples. The journalist knew he had a scoop of major proportions. It was not his place to find fault with Capone's self-serving and irrational remarks. In the morning, Hearst papers around the nation repeated and amplified Capone's offer in banner headlines. Joining two of the most famous Americans of the day, the aviator and the gangster, the story offered just the sort of sensationalism on which the Hearst press thrived.

Art Madden, one of the savvier government agents in Chicago and a keen student of Capone, dismissed the offer. "Capone could be useful only if the kidnapping was perpetrated by underworld characters," he advised his superiors. "Even if that were the situation, there is reason to believe that Capone, under an eleven-year sentence, has necessarily lost much of his influence." If any underworld character could help, Madden discovered, it was Lucky Luciano in New York. Remarkably, Lindbergh was desperate enough to give serious consideration to Capone's offer, and he discussed it at length with Elmer Irey and Frank Wilson, the dogged IRS agents who had built the tax evasion case against Capone. Visiting Lindbergh in New Jersey, they prudently advised the aviator to ignore the outlandish and distracting proposal. (Police finally discovered the badly decomposed body of the Lindbergh baby in May.) Assessing Capone's empty ploy and the enormous publicity it received in the Hearst press, *Time* magazine concluded: "The whole affair was a typical Hearstian exploit—shrewd, bold, and precisely on the borderline of journalistic integrity."

By now Capone, his bluster gone and his desperation obvious, had become a figure of fun in the press. Only a year before, political cartoonists had depicted a giant Capone standing astride a miniature representation of Chicago. Now they depicted a rail-thin Uncle Sam lording over a fat, cowering Capone, kicking him into a jail or lecturing about the importance of paying taxes. One artist imagined Capone sitting at a desk in a jailhouse schoolroom, taking grammar lessons. "There ain't no gat on this here table," he tells his instructor, who replies, "That's ungrammatical, Mr. Capone. You must say there is no gat on this table." Now that Capone was fair game, a humorist and screenwriter named Homer Croy invited the racketeer to create his own "advance epitaph" for an anthology Croy planned to publish, and in case nothing came to mind, Croy proposed several: *Gone but not forgotten, Excuse me for not coming to the door,* or *Anyway, I don't have to worry about my income tax anymore.* "I think they are all rather amusing," Croy wrote, but an official of the Federal Bureau of Prisons who intercepted the letter thought otherwise. "I wonder why you did not realize that there is nothing very humorous about an eleven year sentence," he admonished Croy. "I would not ask Capone or any other prisoner to try to view such a situation humorously."

One final appeal now stood between Capone and the start of his actual jail sentence in a federal penitentiary, and that was his petition before the Supreme Court of the United States for review of his case. It was extremely unlikely that the Court would consent to review, but the action delayed Capone's removal from the Cook County Jail for another six weeks or so. Finally, on May 2, came word that Capone's petition, his last resort, had been rejected without a word of comment from the bench. With that decision, Capone's time in the purgatory of the Cook County Jail, his legal maneuvering, his appeals, and his false hopes of winning an early release all came to an end. When he heard the bleak news, Capone fell into a deep gloom and began pacing his cell with nervous, angry steps. A journalist pressed his nose against the wire mesh separating Capone from the rest of the world, wanting to know how he felt, now that he was sure to serve his sentence. Summoning all his self-control, Capone replied in a low growl, "Nothing to say." His lawyer, Michael Ahern, dejected and exhausted from the long legal battle, finally gave up; it was, he said, "the end of three bitter years for us and the end of Al Capone."

The end of Al Capone: ominous words, ones that Capone himself dismissed, but Ahern, who had seen more of the criminal justice system than his client had, knew better. This *was* the end of Capone's career. The public Capone, the biggest bootlegger in the nation, the well-heeled gambler, the self-styled Robin Hood and celebrity, was finished, but as for the man himself, he was about to embark on the most bizarre and difficult part of his life. His battles from now on would be private ones—with himself, his health, and his sanity—rather than with gangs and prosecutors and glory-seeking Prohibition agents, and they would prove to be the most discouraging battles he had ever fought.

The wheels of the legal system had ground slowly and deliberately since Capone's trial, but once he had exhausted his last appeal, the machinery abruptly lurched into high gear. Within hours of the Supreme Court ruling, the U.S. marshals were ready to deliver him to a federal penitentiary. Capone expected to join his buddies at Leavenworth, but without warning the attorney general decided to send him to a more remote location, where he would be less likely to encounter his colleagues: the federal penitentiary in Atlanta, Georgia, reputed to be the meanest prison in the entire system. It was also among the most crowded; designed to house 1,800 prisoners, it now held more than 4,000. With time off for good behavior (ten days a month), he would not be out until January 19, 1939, at the earliest, the day after his fortieth birthday. His son would be twenty-one years old by that time, a fully grown man in his own right; would he be able to recall his father as anything other than a convict?

· · ·

On the afternoon of May 3, 1932, Al bade farewell to the Capone clan: Mae, Sonny, his mother and sister, and his brother Matthew. He then packed his clothes, and readied himself for the journey to a lower circle of hell. As darkness fell, he began his trip to the Atlanta Penitentiary under extremely heavy security.

To make certain that the prisoner actually reached the train taking him to his final destination (and, one suspects, to gratify his own desire for vindication), Eliot Ness rode shotgun, accompanied by the rest of the Untouchables. "I was determined to see there would be no 'rescue' or that no assassin's bullet would cheat the law," he wrote of the scene.

We arranged a five-car caravan to escort "Snorkey" from the Cook County jail to the old Dearborn Station. Lahart, Seager and I were to ride in the first car. Behind it was to be the car with Capone, followed by Robsky, Cloonan and King in another, followed by two automobiles carrying Chicago policemen. All of us were heavily armed: my crew was ready with sawed-off shotguns, revolvers and automatics loose in shoulder holsters. . . . As Capone was led into the warden's office, the shouts of other prisoners echoed down the jail corridors.

"You got a bum break, Al!"

"Keep your chin up, Al—it ain't so tough!"

"You'll own the joint before you're there very long, Al!"

Two marshals proceeded to handcuff Capone to another prisoner, Vito Morici, bound for a Florida prison. Morici began to put on his overcoat, and Capone advised him to drape it over their manacled wrists to conceal the handcuffs. At that moment, Eliot Ness stepped forward.

I led the way into the jail's inner courtyard where a horde of photographers went into action, their flashbulbs exploding with blinding frequency. Capone, who had been surly for days in his jail cell, made no attempt to cover the scar on his face but strutted forward toward the photographers.

"Jeez," he said, a proud note in his voice, "you'd think Mussolini was passin' through."

The jail's gate swung open, and the caravan left, the crowd parting before it. "After that it was every driver for himself. Fenders and bumpers clashed and pedestrians were trampled in the stampede to avoid being hit by the fast moving officials' motors," a reporter said of the commotion. "Police officials described the ride to the Dearborn station as the wildest and noisiest in their experience."

Sirens wailing, the cars drove along Ogden Avenue to Clark Street, where the St. Valentine's Day Massacre had occurred two years before. Pausing at a stoplight, Capone gazed at the dark, hulking form of the Federal Building, where he had lost his tax case. Minutes later the caravan pulled up at Dearborn Station, where they were besieged by another crowd of journalists, detectives, deputy marshals, and curiosity seekers. Capone and Morici, still shackled together, awkwardly climbed out of their car and lurched into the crowd, cursing and elbowing photographers away, but they discovered it was not an entirely hostile gathering, not by any means. The boys in Chicago Heights had arranged for Capone's friends and family members to be at the station to wish him Godspeed.

Clearing the throng at last, Capone and Morici, manacled and stumbling, were led to the Dixie Flyer, a regularly scheduled Pullman train bound for Atlanta. After the Untouchables had thoroughly searched its eight cars, the prisoners entered, followed by photographers, flashing away. Inside his car, Capone regained his composure and made a point of presenting a *bella figura* for the cameras. He removed his coat, took his seat, and lit a cigar. Though manacled, he was *smiling*—the same sickly smile he had displayed during his tax trial, and when the cameras moved in for a close up of his famous scars, he did not flinch from their scrutiny. "I don't know much about Atlanta," he said to the reporters. "For one thing, it'll be hot." He tried to make the best of a bad situation, saying he hoped to lose a little weight and join the prison baseball team, claiming he was a "pretty good pitcher and first baseman, if I do say so myself."

In the midst of the tumult his eyes fell on a vaguely familiar form, a slim young man with blue eyes and hair parted in the center. It was Eliot Ness, the man who had done so much damage to his bootlegging business and humiliated him by parading captured delivery trucks up Michigan Avenue. "Well, I'm on my way to do eleven years," he told Ness. "I've got to do it. I'm not sore at anybody. Some people are lucky. I wasn't. There was too much overhead in my business anyhow, paying off all the time and replacing trucks and breweries. They ought to make it legitimate."

"That's a strange idea coming from you," Ness said. "If it was legitimate, you certainly wouldn't want anything to do with it."

Capone glared at his young antagonist, who slowly backed down the aisle to the end of the car, then turned and jumped to the platform. It was the last time he ever saw Al Capone. "There goes two and a half years of my life," he thought as he watched the Dixie Flyer creak to life. Sensing the movement, Capone glanced out the window; he wouldn't be seeing Chicago again for years. The procession of cars gathered speed, and he settled into a game of poker with his grim captors.

"I felt as if a terrific weight had been lifted from my shoulders now that the shadow of 'Scarface Al' no longer hovered over Chicago—and over us," Ness recalled. He thought briefly of all the other hoodlums still at large in Chicago, men like Jack McGurn and "Bugs" Moran, but, he decided, "None possessed the genius for organization which had made Al Capone criminal czar of a captive city." Now Capone himself was finally in captivity, but despite their last, bitter exchange, Ness, who thrived on causes and who had defined himself against everything he believed Al Capone represented, felt empty rather than triumphant. As the Dixie Flyer shrank to a pair of glowing red lights and the crowd dispersed, Ness left Dearborn Station, pondering one final thought:

"Only then did it come to me that the work of 'The Untouchables' was finished."

• • •

The Dixie Flyer bearing Capone rumbled south through the night, and radio stations broadcast hourly bulletins of its progress and itinerary. As the gleaming cars passed through whistle-stops in the light of dawn, crowds appeared, hoping to catch a glimpse of the celebrated ganglord within. "They pressed alongside the Pullman cars and peered into the window," the *New York Times* reported. "Capone answered their waves with broad smiles and the gesture of a handshake. In some of the small towns, little Negro boys stood well back from the train and pointed at the car in which they thought Capone was a passenger, seemingly afraid."

Agitated and unable to sleep, Capone held a marathon press conference with reporters accompanying him for the ride, and he continued to complain that the federal government had singled him out for unfair treatment. "I'll be made an issue in the next Presidential campaign," he insisted. " 'We sent Capone to the penitentiary,' they'll be saying. It wouldn't seem so bad if they didn't use the income-tax law for political purposes. There's a lot of big men in Chicago who beat the government out of most of the taxes they ought to pay and they get away with it. I tried to settle with the government and they used it against me. I don't think that's playing fair, but they've got me and I'll have to take the medicine." He went on to discuss his bootlegging, claiming that the government had exaggerated his profits. Even in his best months, he never managed to move more than 5,000 cases of whiskey, and what with overhead, payoffs, and raids, he could never clear more than $10 a case. It was a lousy business, bootlegging—couldn't the IRS understand that?

As Capone rationalized the hours away, passengers from other cars occasionally walked past his seat, hoping to catch a glimpse of the celebrity about whom they had read so much. The bolder among them stopped to offer their best wishes, to shake Capone's hand, to receive a gift from the gangster in the form of a twenty-five-cent cigar. Even the engineer conveyed his kind regards to the celebrated prisoner. Meanwhile, the conductor, one James A. Brown, recalled previous trips the racketeer had made on the very same Dixie Flyer, bound for Florida during the lush times, when the whiskey and jazz never quit. In those days Capone had taken over the entire train for private parties and distributed lavish tips. Now he was manacled to a petty thief named Morici, at the mercy of marshals, hounded by the press. How the times have changed, Brown said with a sigh, how the times have changed us all.

Capone arrived at the Atlanta Penitentiary via a rail spur, and the marshals who had accompanied him from Chicago surrendered their charge to prison officials. After walking a flight of stone steps into the prison, he entered the receiving office, where the warden, A. C. Aderhold, startled him by asking, "What is your name?" His registration papers noted the bare facts of his prison term; his complete sentence or "full time" lasted until May 3, 1948, but with time deducted for good behavior, his "short time" extended until "only" January 19, 1939. His previous criminal record, as listed in the papers, was dismayingly long, with no less than seventeen entries between 1919 and the present. After registering, Capone was ordered to strip. He yielded his clothes (a tailor-made suit, silk underwear, and his immaculate fedora), a fountain pen, a rosary, and $231 in cash. He bathed, and then, for the first time, he donned a denim prisoner's suit. He had left Chicago as Alphonse Capone, and twenty-four hours later, at the Atlanta Federal Penitentiary, he became convict number 40886.

At the time he entered Atlanta, the federal prison system was a relatively new aspect of American law enforcement. As recently as 1895, federal offenders had been sent to state prisons, their upkeep paid by the federal government. In the years to come, the Department of Justice established five federal penitentiaries, an equal number of reformatories, as well as prison camps, reform schools for juvenile offenders, and other correctional institutions. With the advent of Prohibition and an influx of convicted bootleggers, the federal penitentiary system experienced its first serious overcrowding; of 18,000 federal inmates, 6,000 had to be farmed out to state prisons. The overcrowding precipitated riots, scandals, and a congressional investigation. Now, the federal penitentiary system faced a new challenge: Al Capone.

The Atlanta Penitentiary suffered from the ills afflicting other facilities in the organization. Charges of corruptions swirled constantly around the guards and reached all the way to the warden's office, but Warden Aderhold himself was known as a remote, incorruptible public servant determined to treat all his prisoners exactly the same. There would be no chance of Capone influencing him with the promise of a spin in Mae's shiny Cadillac. The prison's population was swollen with bootleggers; they came from the South, generally from rural areas, where they had brewed their moonshine, but the revenuers had caught up with them as surely as they had caught up with Capone. Aware that the biggest bootlegger of all had at last become one of them, the other convicts cheered and jeered when Capone entered the prison, but he had nothing to do with them, at first. Like all new arrivals at the penitentiary, he passed his first three weeks in quarantine, undergoing medical examinations and inoculations. There were no more interviews, no more headlines, and no more lawyers; from now on his relatives would have to assume responsibility for directing his long-shot legal appeals. There was only the promise of occasional visits from immediate members of the family, as long he was on good behavior. With the exception of a prison baseball game on Sunday afternoon and a movie shown to prisoners on Sunday night, years of endless days stretched before him, each one precisely the same as the others.

In quarantine, Capone was questioned by Warden Aderhold's young assistant, Myrl E. Alexander, who later rose to become head of the Federal Bureau of Prisons during the Kennedy administration. Alexander was concerned and open-minded, as prison officials go, and he was willing at first to take an unbiased view of Capone. "When he entered my office I saw that he wasn't the short, pudgy man I thought he seemed to be," Alexander later recalled. "He was rather tall, slightly balding, smiling as he entered, but obviously the Capone pictured in the newspapers. As we went through the usual questions about family, education, and so on, he responded promptly and intelligently. Then, as we discussed his sentence and his offence of violating the Income Tax Code, he had no problem acknowledging his bootlegging activities. But he hotly denied the allegations of prostitution and narcotic activities. He staunchly declared his respect for his mother, sister, and wife as evidence of his 'hatred' for prostitution and other activities."

"Sure," Capone told Alexander, "money was made in the bootlegging business. The public demanded booze and I supplied it. Lots of it. But I also spent a lot of money in helping the poor, supplying food kitchens, and making jobs for the unemployed." Angered by Capone's characterizing himself as the "major welfare agency in Chicago" and running out of patience with his ranting, Alexander terminated the interview. A week later, Alexander received an explanation of Capone's puzzling and unpleasant behavior, his rapid shift from calm deliberation to megalomania, in the form of the results of Capone's medical examination. His Wassermann blood test conclusively demonstrated that he suffered from "Central nervous system syphilis." This was the first time Capone's neurosyphilis had been officially diagnosed. After years of latency, the disease had finally erupted into the tertiary stage. The jail's medical staff began treating convict number 40886 with one of the standard procedures of the day, bismuth therapy, but the disease was incurable, and Capone's illness amounted to a death sentence, one that would take years to reach its culmination. Until then, it would slowly take over his brain, further distort his personality, and destroy his memory.

Nor was syphilis Capone's only serious medical problem. The examination revealed that he also suffered from chronic prostatitis. At thirty-three, he was far too young to have prostatic hypertrophia, a condition commonly afflicting older men, so the likely cause of Capone's condition was gonorrhea. It was certainly possible for him to have *both* syphilis and gonorrhea at the same time; they were caused by different bacteria: *Treponema pallidum* for syphilis, and *Neisseria gonorrheae* for gonorrhea. But he acquired the diseases from the same source: prostitutes. Gonorrhea generally has far more serious consequences for women than for men, and Capone's case did not attack his central nervous system the way syphilis did. Typically gonorrhea causes a burning sensation and discharge from the penis, after which it disappears, only to return from time to time. It leaves behind scars which, if untreated, can create a urethral obstruction. To alleviate the obstruction, the prison administered a standard medical treatment in the form of weekly prostate massages, which appeared to help. His urine, which had been cloudy at the time of his admission, eventually became clearer, but remained discolored. "The prostate soon quieted down, and at this time he had a large, boggy, soft prostate that is easy to massage," noted the prison's urology consultant after several months of treatment. "This patient should continue on prostatic massages, followed by bladder irrigations at least once weekly until such time as the pathology clears."

Despite all his medical problems, Capone could still function more or less normally, and after his quarantine ended he joined the general prison population, which could only have come as a relief after the confinement and isolation he had endured since his arrival in Atlanta. He was assigned to share a cell with a popular convict named Red Rudensky, a small-time safe cracker. "Rusty," as he was known, was short and powerfully built; his impish face and impossibly large nose seemed better suited to a comic than a retired robber. In prison, he was earnestly trying to reform himself by studying the Bible and Koran. He also dreamed of becoming a writer some day, and he later published an autobiography entitled *The Gonif* (Yiddish for "thief"), which included his years in the Atlanta Penitentiary. During his career as a small-time hood, Rudensky had been on the fringes of the Capone organization, as well as its Detroit affiliate, the Purple gang, and he was absolutely astounded to learn that he would now room with Al Capone himself. Although he remained genial, Rudensky had seen enough of prison life to predict that "Atlanta would soon strip Capone down to the bare essentials—mainly guts and patience—and if he didn't have one or the other he'd be in trouble after his high living and days of czarship."

When the new man appeared, the two shook hands, and Capone was quick to remember Rudensky by his street name: "Hey, Rusty, how's it with you?" From the start, Rudensky, having heard rumors of Capone's syphilis, was apprehensive about his cell mate's condition. "Al's complexion was pale, almost sheet-white, and his eyes seemed tired and beady, but he had the inner radiation of someone who's been through it all." Not surprisingly, Capone was on edge, and he was unable to sleep during their first night. He lay on his bunk, smoking cigars, and when that no longer pacified him, he woke Rudensky. "How the hell am I gonna take it?" he asked and began weaving fantasy and reality into a diatribe. "Imagine, some creep gets me in a damn tax rap and now I suppose they'll be cutting each other up on the outside for splits. Here I am with a million bucks in half a dozen banks and I'm sitting in a hole like this. Ain't it a helluva deal, Rusty?" So it went night after night, Capone obsessively complaining about his lot. Nor did he find respite in sleep, for nightmares made him scream "No! No! No!" or whimper in agony. On one occasion, he became so distraught that Rudensky jumped on top of Capone and slapped his scarred cheek to wake him from tormented slumber.

Although sympathetic to his cell mate's misery, Rudensky failed to realize that Capone was suffering from more than the pangs of confinement in jail. He was undergoing withdrawal from cocaine. Given the freedom he had enjoyed in the Cook County Jail, it is entirely possible that he had been able to smuggle the drug into that prison, but here in Atlanta it was impossible for him to continue his addiction. Unlike heroin, cocaine does not inflict an easily identifiable withdrawal syndrome on the user; there is no classic process of going cold turkey. Psychologically, however, withdrawal from cocaine can be agonizing, often accompanied by feelings of depression, weakness, hallucinations, and paranoia. Even when these symptoms relent, and life becomes bearable again, the desire for the drug does not completely abate. So, deprived of his cocaine, Capone was destined to be inwardly tormented even though he suffered no physical symptoms.

In time the balance between the two men changed. Rudensky had expected to function as Capone's subordinate and errand-runner; instead, he became Capone's confessor and guardian. In fact, Rudensky, unlike the newcomer Capone, ranked fairly high in the convict hierarchy, as he soon demonstrated. Within weeks of his arrival, Capone had became a target for other prisoners, "grubby two-bit nonentities" as the loyal Rudensky described them, who would shout out, "Where're the broads and booze now, fat boy?" Nor was the contempt limited to a few prisoners. Another inmate, Bryan Conway, recalled that "Capone was unpopular in Atlanta . . . because he was a weakling and he couldn't take it"—meaning the constant harassment and threats. Fearing Capone would crack up under the pressure, Rudensky cautioned the hecklers to lay off. Two convicts disregarded the warning, and as Rudensky delicately put it, "I sent word out to lean on them a little, not too hard but enough to let them know I meant business. My subordinates unfortunately were a little over-zealous and put the creeps in the infirmary with broken ribs and fractured jaws."

After that unpleasant episode, Capone's life in jail stabilized. With Rudensky's help, he assembled a small contingent of prisoners who served as his protectors. "It was right comical to see Capone exercising in the yard surrounded by his guard," said Conway, evidently one of the Capone-haters.

"Of course they weren't armed with machine guns, as his Chicago bodyguard was, but every man had a long knife or a blackjack. Such weapons were plentiful in Atlanta at the time." The question of whether the men were, in fact, armed would eventually become a source of controversy in Atlanta, with profound ramifications for Capone. Even if they were not armed, as was probably the case, the mere existence of a group of prisoners looking out for his safety proved to be a fecund source of stories that Capone was indeed receiving preferential treatment in Atlanta, not as lavish as the treatment he had received in the Cook County Jail, which had required the collusion of Warden Moneypenny, but visible enough to attract notice at the highest bureaucratic levels.

Despite the threat of violence that hung in the air like a gunpowder haze, Capone proved to be a placid prisoner. He spent his days working in the shoe shop, cutting and sewing leather, repairing soles. "A hulking figure in cheap, baggy cotton clothing, swart-skinned, sits hunched over a whirling electric stiching machine," wrote a reporter who saw Capone at work. "Hands once soft from a life of luxurious ease, Oriental in its splendor . . . , now calloused, deftly fit a heavy strip of sole leather on a bulky, shapeless show upper. . . . The machine thumps and pounds. The heavy needle bites into the coarse leather. He snips away the loose ends of waxed cord and passes the shoe on to another denim clad figure, then picks up another shoe upper and sole block. Then another. And another. Eight hours a day. Forty-four hours a week." Despite the tedium, he proved to be a patient, methodical worker and, one suspects, grateful for the distraction the manual labor afforded him.

Rudensky, for his part, held a more visible and sensitive position writing editorials for the prison's newspaper. Since he burned to practice journalism on the outside some day, he pursued his job with feverish dedication. "Just seeing your idea down in print, it gives you the best damn feeling. You should try it, Al," he would urge, but Capone demurred.

"Hell, Rusty, I have trouble writing a letter home. A pencil seems to weigh a ton."

Writing was an ordeal for Capone, and as his illness progressed, his facility with language deteriorated. In July 1932, he wrote this barely coherent note to the warden: "My wife sent to me five pictures of herself and my Baby all different poses and I was call and was informed that I could only receive one and that I would have to send the other four back home telling me that with your permission I would be allowed to have the other four. Sir rather than send them back and infere they may get lost. Sir if I am not allowed to have then wish you would send for me so I may have them distroyed in your presents as I dont want them to go astray as some New's paper may get them." (Capone never did get the extra photos.)

As the months dragged on, Rudensky became ever more fond of Capone, outbursts of temper and all.

It wasn't hero worship but something else [Rudensky wrote in *The Gonif*]. I could understand him being hateful or vitriolic but he wasn't. Oh, he'd storm over the inefficiency of his latest attorneys. He'd confide to me, "They're overpaid dumb bastards who couldn't spring a pickpocket. They should have had me out of here three weeks ago."

But his flare-ups . . . died quickly. He'd spend hours mulling over letters from his family or reading papers and sports magazines. Despite his sinister reputation, Capone was a family man and religious too. He showed me his son's picture and asked, "How in hell can a fat dago like me have a son that good lookin?"

When not brooding or ranting, Capone gave way to irrational episodes of high spirits. He and Rudensky often listened with earphones to the hit comedy series on radio, *Amos 'n' Andy,* and after hearing a particularly amusing routine they started laughing uncontrollably. Ripping his earphones off, Al shouted, "I've just thought of the funniest damn thing you'll ever hear. I'm supposed to be the big shot, and I've wound up in the shoe shop. You're supposed to be a safe cracker, and now you write goddamn editorials. What kind of a screwed up, lousy world is this?" After they speculated on what would happen if they pursued these trades on the outside, Rudensky recalled, "I fell into Al's arms and we held each other like two kids celebrating First Communion. I whispered in his ear, 'Al, it's not so much that I can read and write, it's just that you know so damn much about shoes!' "

The two of them fell to the floor; their raucous laughter brought a guard running to the cell, demanding to know what they thought they were doing. Capone bellowed in reply: "Just a couple of sweethearts meeting after the prom, you dumb bastard." At moments like these, Rudensky, against his better judgment, fell helplessly under Capone's spell. He was, after all, the great "Scarface." Rudensky brought up the St. Valentine's Day Massacre, just to get a reaction, but Capone only laughed at the mention of the most famous slaying in the history of gangland. "Those silly Irish bastards," he wailed. "They have more guts than sense. If we'd only hooked up, I could have been president."

That was the Capone bravado—endearing and outrageous. Throughout all his months in the hot, claustrophobic Atlanta Penitentiary, he remained a great hoper and believer in himself, in the future, and in the one twist of fate that would spring him from jail. A *deus ex machina* in a gray flannel suit. Fate appeared to cooperate with Capone when the U.S. Supreme Court amended some of the laws applying to his case. The revision was purely technical, but Capone, desperate for any source of hope, eagerly clutched at it. At the time of his trial, federal statutes specified that prosecution for tax violations could include offenses no older than three years, except for schemes "defrauding or attempting to defraud" the government, in which case the limit extended to six years. Capone's indictments went back as far as 1925, and the most recent offense occurred in 1927—four years earlier. Then, in the spring of 1932, the Supreme Court ruled that avoiding federal income tax was actually not "fraud" after all, and the three-year limit applied. By this reckoning, Capone's tax violations had occurred *outside* the new time frame. Once he grasped the significance of the ruling in his own case, Capone decided to jettison Ahern and Fink, who had proved so inept in defending him, and from his cell in Atlanta he ordered his family to hire two new lawyers in Washington. Tax specialists, they filed a writ of habeas corpus before Federal Judge E. Marvin Underwood of Atlanta, Georgia.

Freedom seemed tantalizingly closer when Capone appeared in court as part of the legal initiative. He gained his first headlines in months, but they told a pathetic tale. "AL CAPONE MAKES NEW LIBERTY PLEA," declared a representative headline in the *New York Times* of September 22, 1933. "HE APPEARS IN HANDCUFFS. Gangster, Thinner and Subdued, Spends Five Minutes in Court while Hearing is Set on Writ." In addition to the handcuffs, he was manacled. He had lost over forty pounds during his stay in prison and now weighed 215 pounds. Capone listened to his lawyers make their arguments, and within three hours of his court appearance, he returned to his cell, where he had to wait until December for the judge's ruling. The last thing this judge wanted was to be known as the man who set Al Capone free on a technicality, even though the government had put him in jail on a series of technicalities. So Judge Underwood peered deeply into the wording of the relevant statute, which stated in part, "The time during which the person committing the offense is absent from the district wherein the same was committed shall not be taken as any part of the time limited by law." On that basis, he ruled that the months and years Capone had spent away from Chicago—in Florida, in Philadelphia—could be *deducted* from the limit, and thus Capone was still fully accountable for his failure to pay taxes. With that, Judge Underwood dismissed Capone's plea for freedom.

·   ·   ·

As Al Capone encountered one legal frustration after another, the Chicago Police Department and U.S. government agents made steady progress against the Capone organization. One brother, Albert, was arrested in connection with the bombing of the home of Cicero's mayor; he was the youngest of the Capone boys, and prior to the arrest he had no police record, but after he was

Brooklyn's "Prince of Darkness,"
Frankie Yale, Al Capone's mentor,
partner, and, ultimately, victim.
(Chicago Historical Society, ICHi-23877)

Jack "Greasy Thumb" Guzik, notorious
pimp and accountant to the Capone
organization, in a rare photograph.
(Chicago Historical Society, DN-8761)

Frank "The Enforcer"
Nitti (center) ran the
Capone organization
during the years Al was
in jail. *(Chicago Historical
Society, DN-93637)*

Al Capone (center) with friends and associates during a picnic in Chicago Heights. The dapper Frankie La Porte, the only racketeer from whom Al Capone took orders, is seated at left; Jim Emery, another Capone racketeer active in the Heights, reclines on the grass at right. Emery's daughter Vera sits between La Porte and Capone, who was her baptismal godfather. *(Collection of Jon Binder)*

Al Capone's mother, Teresina Raiola Capone, with one of her many grandchildren. *(Collection of Maxine and Mona Pucci)*

Ralph Capone's only child, Ralphie, who later committed suicide after Senate hearings exposed his father to national scrutiny. As a child, Ralphie was almost a second son to Al Capone. *(Collection of Maxine and Mona Pucci)*

George E. Q. Johnson, the United States Attorney who led the prosecution of Al Capone for income tax evasion. *(Collection of George E. Q. Johnson, Jr.)*

Frank Wilson, the intrepid IRS agent who investigated the finances of the Capone organization. *(Chicago Historical Society, ICHi-23876)*

As Cleveland's director of public safety, Eliot Ness (right) traded on his reputation as the onetime scourge of Al Capone. *(Cleveland Press Collection, the Cleveland State University Archives)*

Al Capone attends a baseball game in Chicago in 1931, not long before his trial for income tax evasion commenced. The boy sitting beside Capone, often thought to be the racketeer's son, is a stand-in. *(Chicago Historical Society, DN-96548)*

Capone's soup kitchen, intended to win sympathy for him as the Depression tightened its grip on Chicago. *(Chicago Historical Society, DN-93842)*

A smiling Al Capone in an immaculate pearl-gray fedora on the way to his trial for income tax evasion. *(Chicago Historical Society, DN-97013)*

Capone at his trial, flanked by his lawyers, Michael Ahern (left) and Albert Fink (right). *(Chicago Historical Society, DN-97061)*

Alcatraz Federal Penitentiary as it looked during the years Capone was incarcerated there. *(San Francisco Maritime National Historical Park, Don Devevi Collection)*

Three heavily guarded railroad cars bearing Al Capone and other prisoners arrive at Alcatraz in August 1934. *(San Francisco Maritime National Historical Park, Don Devevi Collection)*

Al Capone's wife, Mae, hiding from reporters who besieged her car after she visited her husband at Alcatraz in 1938. *(UPI/Bettmann)*

After his release from Alcatraz, Capone, his mental faculties impaired by neurosyphilis, returned to Palm Island in Miami Beach, Florida, where he spent most of his time in a fog. He is shown here with a trainer. *(Historical Association of Southern Florida, Miami News Collection)*

An apparently robust Capone in the summer of 1944 at his brother Ralph's hideout in Mercer, Wisconsin. *(Harry H. Hart)*

As Al lay dying in his Palm Island villa, his brother Ralph entertained reporters who maintained a vigil with bulletins and, appropriately, bottles of beer. *(Historical Association of Southern Florida, Miami News Collection)*

The pool and pool house Capone added to his villa on Palm Island, as they look today. (*Author's collection*)

The entrance to Al Capone's Palm Island villa. (*Author's collection*)

Al Capone died in this simple room in his Palm Island villa on January 25, 1947. (*Author's collection*)

freed, he was constantly watched. Soon after, another brother, John, was ordered to testify before a federal grand jury investigating the liquor rackets. Meanwhile, President Hoover, in the waning days of his administration, rewarded George E. Q. Johnson, the U.S. attorney who had prosecuted Al Capone, with an appointment as a federal judge, and his assistant, Dwight Green, received a promotion. Later, Green was given to gloating over Capone as convict. "He behaves so well in Atlanta that the other inmates are beginning to think he is a milksop," he announced. "He has been trying unsuccessfully to get a place on the prison baseball team. He is a model prisoner, and obeys every order the second it is given. His face is bronzed and his figure has become trim and lost its paunchiness. He has now become a valuable worker in the prison shoe factory." As the prosecutors discovered, jousting with Capone was an excellent career move: Johnson later devoted himself to a lucrative private law practice, and Green went on to win election as governor of Illinois.

Their ascendance did not mean the end of lawlessness and violence in Chicago. Quite the opposite. Unknown to them all, Frankie La Porte continued to dominate the rackets from his base in Chicago Heights, and his nearly invisible supervision of the syndicate helped make it possible for other members of the Capone organization to pick up where they had left off before they went to jail. One by one their sentences ran out, and the men, having paid their debt to society, regained their liberty. In February 1934, Ralph Capone's lawyers paid a $10,000 fine, and he finally left the McNeil Island Penitentiary, where he had been confined for a little more than two years. He was able to leave early thanks to time off for good behavior. He had passed the time cooking (although prisoners complained he used too much spice), playing baseball (working his way up to starting first baseman for the prison team), and learning a little Spanish. "Capone became a model prisoner after he learned that no one in this prison gets anything unless he earns it," said Warden Archer on the occasion of Ralph's release. "At first he complained about the hard work and his lack of privileges. When he understood the situation, he turned to and worked." Ralph's wife, Valma, was there to greet him when he reached the mainland, and the two of them departed in a limousine. The next morning, the newspapers taunted him, claiming Ralph Capone would be out of work in post-Prohibition American society, but the newspapers were wrong; his old job as a racketeer was waiting for him. Although he had lost nearly thirty pounds in jail and had grown a thin mustache, Ralph was basically unchanged; he still liked the horses and still carried the nickname "Bottles," and he slipped quickly and comfortably back into his old life. Unlike his younger brother, Ralph was blessed with an easygoing temperament; his prison sentence instantly became one more unpleasant experience he put behind him.

Frank Nitti also returned to freedom. In January 1931, he had begun serving his sentence for income tax evasion at Leavenworth. Several months later, his wife wrote to the parole board to plead for her husband's early release, her letter a compilation of half-truths and wishful thinking. "Frank and I have been married for three years and this is the first time he has been away from me," she told them. Implying that he would have nothing further to do with the Capone organization, she went on to explain, "We both agreed that to return to Chicago, where he is known and everyone aware that he has been in the penitentiary would be the wrong thing to do. He has been offered a job with the Forest Dairy of Kansas City, Mo. at a wage sufficient to maintain us in comfort. As soon as he is released I will join him in Kansas City, make him a home, and keep him on the straight and narrow path in the future." Her plea and promise to move to Kansas City failed to win her husband his early freedom, however, and Nitti served his full sentence, though he did receive time off for good behavior. After little more than a year in jail, he returned to Chicago (so much for the job in a Kansas City dairy "on the straight and narrow path") and resumed his place in the Capone organization. Although he earned the nickname "The Enforcer," as if he were the Capones' hit man, in reality Frank Nitti was too quiet and nervous to engage in violence. He enforced his will not with a machine gun but with a telephone and a pen, and as the Capones languished in jail, he served as custodian of the organization.

Jack Guzik—Orthodox Jew, pimp, and accountant to the syndicate—was the next to go free. Having done his time at both Leavenworth and Lewisburg, Pennsylvania, he received his discharge on December 15, 1935; he was another model prisoner, presumably reformed, who immediately resumed his former duties. A year later, Murray Humphreys, the youngest member of the Capone syndicate to serve time for income tax evasion, graduated from Leavenworth and returned to his rightful place in the rackets.

Even though they were at liberty, it was a different world for the old gang now. They were ex-cons, for one thing, and the prison experience had marked them, made them more secretive and fearful, and it had branded them as outlaws, inflicting psychic scars on both them and their families. They now bore a lifelong stigma. It was harder for ex-cons to buy judges and politicians, and the glamour of *la mala vita* was gone, a casualty of the Depression economy and a sea change in society's values. The racketeers still drove their big sixteen-cylinder Cadillacs, and their wives still wore furs and diamonds, but there was less ostentation now—and less money. Their customers had less to spend on gambling and brothels, and once Prohibition was repealed in 1933, the syndicate's largest source of income dried up.

Prohibition had been a mixed blessing in the end, for bootlegging had been a far more vicious and volatile business than any of them had expected, and far more visible. Given the nature of their business, they were always more comfortable on the margins of society, but bootlegging had dragged them center stage. As Capone himself had noted, the process of manufacturing, importing, and serving alcohol had brought them into contact with virtually every level of society, from the spacious penthouses along Lake Shore Drive to the crowded shacks on the South Side, but that heady visibility had, in the long run, proved to be a tremendous liability, exposing them to unprecedented legal scrutiny. It was as if Prohibition had been a giant trap set by the federal government to ensnare the racketeers, and they had all taken the bait and suffered the consequences. Had they never entered the illicit liquor trade, they might well have escaped notoriety and jail. Frank Capone, the handsomest, the most daring of all the brothers, might still be alive. For all these reasons, then, many racketeers were actually *relieved* by the prospect of repeal. Those who wished to remain in the liquor trade simply went legitimate, while the others returned to their core businesses: gambling and vice. Furthermore, the rise of labor unions offered the syndicate new worlds to conquer. All in all, the rest of the 1930s held promise for those racketeers who knew where and how to take their chances.

·   ·   ·

As his friends and brothers flourished on the outside, Al Capone remained in the Atlanta Pententiary. Cobbling shoes. Brooding on the failures of his lawyers. Out of touch. Slowly losing his mind. Without hope of imminent legal rescue, his second year in Atlanta proved to be even more depressing and difficult to bear than the first had been. Speaking from experience, Rudensky warned Capone that he was entering the most trying period of all; if he could get through it, he would come out OK. Capone responded by seeking refuge in grandiose fantasies. He constantly muttered about big people, well-connected lawyers and politicians, who would free him from jail any day now. There was a man in Washington, or so he said, to whom he paid $2,000 for just that reason. Often as not, he would wind up blubbering and lay his head on his cell mate's shoulder and murmur, "Rusty, where the hell are all the guys you expect so much from?"

The poisonous combination of Capone's increasing frustration and decreasing mental abilities led to a spate of disciplinary incidents during 1933. The most serious concerned an apparent plot to escape. A guard discovered eight sheets fastened to Capone's bunk, some of them tied together; apparently convict number 40886 planned to lower himself from a window via a bedsheet ladder. It was a peculiar violation, more indicative of Capone's disordered mental state than his cunning. In all, the incidents numbered about half a dozen, and after Capone received his reprimands, they were filed away and forgotten. But far more public charges of Capone's receiving special favors surfaced early the following year, and these allegations, which were serious enough to warrant an FBI investigation, proved embarrassing both to Warden Aderhold and the Federal Bureau of Prisons, and they would have drastic consequences for Capone himself.

Many of the stories originated with other prisoners, snitches motivated more by jealousy than a desire for justice. Fearing for their lives—so they said—they hid behind pseudonyms as they claimed Capone had devised a system to bring money into the Atlanta Penitentiary, which he used to bribe guards and win preferential treatment. It is possible that Capone himself unwittingly started some of the rumors with his constant, delusional claims that he had "fixed" anyone who had power over him. Although the FBI's investigation team found no substantiation for the stories, they entered the record and, even though unproved, cast a long shadow.

In the midst of these investigations, a veritable compendium of Capone's special privileges came to light in the form of a mysterious, anonymous manuscript entitled "The Biography of Al Capone's Life in the Atlanta Penitentiary." The FBI looked into that, too, and the report of the investigating agent, E. E. Conroy, suggests the yarn's smarmy tone: "There is an allegation to the effect that Capone would knock a tennis ball over the prison wall while playing tennis, and immediately afterward a different tennis ball would be returned over the wall from the outside. There is a suggestion that the substituted tennis ball contained narcotics." Another scene depicted Capone receiving drugs contained in a tea bag concealed in the underwear of a visiting relative, and still other passages detailed at wearying length Capone's attempts to obtain extra food and offer thousand-dollar bribes to incredulous guards. With its plethora of detail and malevolent air, the manuscript, nearly 250 pages long, had the earmarks of an inside job. The writer, who refused to come forth and identify himself, possessed enough knowledge of the prison's day-to-day operations, as well as access to Capone's records, to concoct a plausible scenario.

However, the FBI found the truth to be altogether different. As for the drugs concealed in tennis balls, "My knowledge of the prison and surrounding terrain leads me to believe that this allegation is ridiculous in the extreme," agent Conroy concluded. Subsequent FBI inquiries turned up convincing evidence that Capone, rather than bribing others with fistfuls of cash, was actually the *victim* of extortion attempts made by other prisoners, who assumed he was wealthy and afraid and thus would yield to their demands. The threats Capone received, according to one report, included "death and bodily harm while at Atlanta Federal Penitentiary."

Despite all these findings to the contrary, the suspicion persisted that Capone was somehow using his influence to obtain special privileges, as he had in the Cook County Jail. The rumors concerning his treatment reached a crescendo in the U.S. House of Representatives, where lawmakers heard allegations based on newspaper articles written by an ex-convict named Lee Molnar, who claimed that Capone had bribed his way into a life of well-fed ease in the Atlanta Penitentiary. Warden Aderhold denied all of Molnar's charges, the most inflammatory (and far-fetched) being that Capone continued to wear his silk underwear, custom shoes, and tailor-made suits behind bars. No, said Aderhold, Capone wore only regulation underwear, suits, and shoes manufactured in the prison's shop.

Oblivious to the public controversy surrounding him, Capone remained locked in the tight little world of the penitentiary, becoming ever more dependent on his level-headed cell mate Red Rudensky for emotional support. With a little help from "Rusty" he was learning to tolerate life behind bars, and as long as they were together Capone figured he could last until that bright day in 1939 when he was scheduled to be freed. Rudensky's fund of convict lore gave the Atlanta Federal Penitentiary a human face, and Al, in turn, promised to take care of his buddy when they got out. Despite his announced determination to go straight, the former safe cracker found himself seriously tempted by the prospect of living the sumptuous life as a member of Capone's inner circle. Their plans were all fantasy, of course. Had Capone possessed the mental acuity to read the signals, he would have realized that far worse awaited him in prison.

On May 27, 1934, the new attorney general of the United States, Homer S. Cummings, visited the Atlanta Penitentiary; this was the AG's first visit to a federal prison, and although the occasion had no announced purpose, he did make it a point to observe its most celebrated inmate, Al Capone, and to investigate the rumors of preferential treatment. Cummings caught sight of Capone walking from his cell to the dining area. Chewing tobacco and slouching, convict number 40886 looked nothing like a fearless gangster. It seemed he was not receiving special favors, but of course one could never tell from mere appearances, and Cummings remained suspicious. As it happened, the AG was just then bursting with plans for a new addition to the federal penitentiary system: a restored military garrison designed to house irredeemable prisoners. Located in San Francisco Bay, the maximum security facility had become Cummings's pet project. It was called Alcatraz.

Rudensky, with his years of prison experience, was sharp enough to read the ominous signs and to guess what they meant for his cell mate. "The pile is like a giant poker game if you begin to read the faces," he wrote. "You begin to play your hand by the atmosphere and begin to smell and sense the action. That's the way it was on the hot, windless, Saturday afternoon of August 18, 1934. Call it a long nose . . . or a hunch, but I knew something was going to happen."

Returning to the cell block before dinner that day, Rudensky found Capone in a characteristic pose, lolling on his bunk, staring at Sonny's photograph.

"Rusty," he sighed, "did you really ever see a better lookin' con's kid?"

"I guess not, Al," said Rudensky in reply to a question his cell mate had asked countless times. "How the hell many cons' kids do you suppose I've seen?"

"I'm getting damn lonesome just looking at shoes and these damn guards," Capone continued. "I mean I'm getting anxious to get out."

Without warning, he turned "purple," Rudensky recalled, and "slammed the picture back down on his bunk, almost shattering it."

"Damn it, Rusty," Capone shouted, "I want action! Where the hell are my big friends? What are those high paid lawyer sons of bitches doing?"

Another con, annoyed by the uproar, called out, "Knock it off, Al."

Capone quieted down and, sitting with crossed legs on the edge of his bunk, idly toyed with a cigar. In the summer heat, his underarms were damp with perspiration, and the veins in his neck twitched with every beat of his heart. "At that moment," wrote Rudensky, "I couldn't picture him the leader of scores of sharpies, guys who sliced up the biggest gangland empire in history." Pitying Capone, he spoke soothing words, suggesting that he give his big-shot lawyers just a little more time.

After dinner, a guard came by the cell to summon Capone. "Nobody's taking me any damn place unless I tell them where I'm going," Capone said.

Three more guards—"bulls" or "screws" in prison parlance—formed a line in front of the cell, waiting to escort the prisoner. "You're going to see the Warden, Al," said one. "Take it easy."

Suddenly someone called out, "You're going to the Rock, Al, a nice long ride to Alcatraz."

The words instantly galvanized Capone. Astonished, Rudensky saw "all the fire and hate and strength and torment erupt suddenly. He was all power and anger as he leaped at the nearest guard, shouting obscenities."

The bulls drove the seething prisoner to the wall of the cell, fixing him with their weight. For a moment Capone stopped screaming for the lawyers and people with pull in Washington, glanced at his friend and cell mate, and pleaded, "What the hell are they doing to me, Red?"

Summoning his immense strength, Capone threw the bulls off him, grabbed the precious photograph of Sonny, and hurled it at the face of one of his tormentors, screaming, "You'll never take me out of here!" Rudensky joined the fray, and another bull struck him a blow that sent him sprawling to the floor, unconscious. When he woke, Capone was gone. Rusty never saw his friend again.

"Capone, to me, wasn't a big shot gangland giant in the end but a tired, sick, lonely man," he later wrote. "Guided in other directions, his imagination, drive and fearlessness might have made him a heroic general, captain of a fleet or a mighty business mogul. He had a brilliant knack for organization, which, channeled in the proper direction, would have made him a success in any business operation."

So much for what might have been; instead, he carried the memory of Capone's last words: "My God, you don't come back from the Rock."

·   ·   ·

As the real Al Capone languished in the federal penitentiary system, his fictional counterparts grew in potency and allure. Although the U.S. government was determined to keep him from view, the public simply could not get enough of the man, especially with the Depression at hand and disillusionment with American institutions on the rise. Angry, bored, frustrated, Americans became a receptive audience for fictional accounts of Capone's exploits. They applauded him on Broadway, hissed him at the movies, and read about him in pulp magazines. The newspapers' banner headlines had made him famous, but Hollywood, especially, built him into a legend. As Capone languished in jail, a sick, defeated man, the legend gradually supplanted the reality.

During Capone's rise to power in the 1920s, gangster melodramas proliferated on stage; among the most popular was *Broadway* (1926), which played for well over a year on the Great White Way. The following year, Edward G. Robinson portrayed a Capone-like killer named Nick Scarsi in a Broadway hit called *The Racket*. Ironically, "Big Bill" Thompson prevented a touring company from presenting the play in Chicago and sullying that city's pristine reputation. So *The Racket* went west to Los Angeles, where it became the basis of a movie starring Louis Wolheim in the role Robinson had created on stage.

Gangster melodramas achieved their greatest popularity on the screen. Indeed, the film industry had relied on violent, sensational crime as a prime subject ever since Edwin S. Porter's 1903 short film, *The Great Train Robbery*, baptized the American public into the secular religion of moviegoing. Early gangster movies of the 1920s included *Chicago After Midnight*, *Lights of New York*, *Me Gangster*, and *Underworld*, the latter directed by Joseph von Sternberg. There were many others as well, so many that they elicited protests from politicians in New York and Chicago, who claimed their fair cities were being unfairly smeared, and from various self-appointed guardians of public morality. In October 1928, the *New Yorker*, taking note of the gangster movies' popularity, remarked, "Women's clubs and mother's clubs throughout the land are protesting the output of underworld pictures." As the 1920s staggered to a close, gangster movies disappeared briefly from the nation's screens, only to reappear in 1930 in greater numbers than ever. By

1931, fifty-one new gangster films reached the theaters, almost one per week. The rigors the Depression visited on Americans made the gangster life appear both tantalizing and understandable, and the new breed offered harsh, realistic depictions of criminal figures, presenting the criminals with a measure of sympathy. In *Born Reckless*, to name one instance, the director John Ford told the story of a racketeer who tries to leave his life of crime behind and go legitimate, but who finds no work and faces the prospect of annihilation. At the time, millions of dispossessed Americans were prepared to endorse the film's anger and disillusionment.

In search of authenticity, several movies in the new cycle attempted to evoke Al Capone, although any resemblance to the *real* Capone was purely coincidental. Among the first was *Doorway to Hell*, which opened in November 1930, almost a year before the tax trial that sent him to prison. In this melodrama, Lew Ayres played a racketeer known as Louis Ricarno who is slain by a rival gang. Since the movie showed Ricarno moving to Florida, as Capone had, and participating in a racketeer's convention in Atlantic City, just as Capone had, there could be no doubt as to the movie's source of inspiration.

Although *Doorway to Hell* was a hit in its day, the next Capone-influenced film, *Little Caesar*, became a lasting popular phenomenon. Its pedigree was slightly more authentic than its predecessors', for the movie originated as a popular crime novel by W. R. Burnett, who as a young man left his native Ohio for Chicago, determined to make his name as a writer. On his first night in Chicago, Burnett was awakened by a "terrific explosion across the street" that threw him out of bed. He stumbled to the lobby of his hotel to inquire what had happened, but the blasé clerk told him some garage owners were waging a price war, and the interested parties had resorted to tossing "pineapples" to make their points. Heady stuff for a young man from Ohio. "On me, an outsider, an alien from Ohio, the impact of Chicago was terrific. It seemed overwhelmingly big, teeming, dirty, brawling, frantically alive," Burnett recalled. "Capone was King. Corruption was rampant. Big Bill Thompson, the mayor, was threatening to punch King George in the 'snoot.' Gangsters were shooting each other all over town." Burnett yearned to get all this excitement and destructive energy into a novel, which he planned to write in the "illiterate jargon of the Chicago gangster." He came to know a small-time hoodlum, an embittered man, cynical and alienated, who served as the model for the book's protagonist, Rico Bandello. The author never intended Rico to represent Capone; he left that to another character, a mob boss named "Big Boy," which happened to be one of Capone's many nicknames. Burnett had no idea what he had wrought in his terse, violent novel; "I was afraid I was giving birth to a monster," he later confessed, but *Little Caesar* turned out to be a profitable monster indeed. Published by the Dial

Press in June 1929, it became an immediate best-seller. As the economy worsened—almost 2.5 million Americans were out of work by the spring of 1930—the book's bleak view of human nature grew in appeal. It soon came to the attention of Jack Warner, the movie producer. Erroneously assuming the character of Rico was based on Al Capone, he bought the story for his studio and immediately put it into production.

Little Caesar, the movie, opened in January 1931, highlighted by Edward G. Robinson's stinging portrayal of Rico. Robinson had made a specialty of playing gangsters, and when audiences imagined how they really talked and acted, they thought of Robinson's tight, nervous mannerisms and staccato speech rhythms. It was generally assumed that Robinson had modeled his mean, snarling little Italian hood on Capone, and for years after, people assumed that Capone himself was a snarling little man. The fact that Capone was actually large and affable often came as a surprise to those encountering him for the first time. Further blurring the line between fantasy and reality, the movie version combined Rico's dramatic assassination—and his memorable but fictional last words: "Mother of Mercy, is this the end of Rico?"—with a gangster funeral that employed newsreel coverage of Dion O'Banion's last rites.

For all its embellishments, *Little Caesar* was accepted as a realistic portrayal of Capone and Chicago's gangland. The critics praised Robinson's sullen, controlled performance, and it drew huge, excitable audiences. In New York, a crowd of 3,000 stormed a theater at Broadway and 47th Street, shattering glass and assaulting the box offices. The movie proved especially popular with children; a 1933 survey found that impressionable young boys from poor neighborhoods were prone to identify with the doomed Rico. As they watched it over and over, the boys absorbed a gangster lingo coined in Hollywood; expressions such as "You can dish it out, but you can't take it" and "Take him for a ride" immediately entered the language. Although audiences took Rico's tragic fate for Capone's, Burnett knew better—or so he told himself. He had never intended his Rico to be anything more than just another small-time hood, an urban American anti-hero. But Capone himself, he said, "is immune. He has a villa in Florida; he is a millionaire; his name has become a household world. The old pre-prohibition slogan 'you can't win' is shown to be nonsense." Burnett wrote those words in 1930; within a few short years, they no longer rang true, except in Hollywood.

Although *Little Caesar* was in the final analysis a generic gangster movie, it succeeded primarily because it evoked the special Capone aura. Scores of other gangsters—Yale, O'Banion, Torrio, McGurn, and Weiss, to name but a few of that bloody fraternity—had attained a measure of notoriety during the 1920s, and their lives and spectacular deaths might have inspired hit movies. Instead of those men, Capone, with his love of press conferences, his brash conduct during his income tax trial, and above all the row of scars on his left cheek, became virtually synonymous with gangland in the mind of the American public. He came to incarnate the dual spirit of the age, representing both the amiable lawlessness of the 1920s, that flouting of Prohibition's flimsy hypocrisy, and the angry, disillusioned tenor of the 1930s, when times were so hard that a life of crime came to seem not just justifiable but inevitable.

With every passing month Capone's fame and popularity grew, in Hollywood if not in Washington, D.C. Inevitably, a producer planned a feature film unashamedly based on Capone's life, and it wasn't just any producer, but Howard Hughes, who would in later years become a reclusive billionaire sequestered in his Las Vegas lair, every bit as fabled a character as Al Capone. At the time, though, Hughes was a wealthy aviation engineer and test pilot desperately trying to buy his way into Hollywood. He had purchased the film rights to a crime novel called *Scarface*, written by Armitage Trail, but little of that work survived the screenplay by Chicago's best-known journalist, Ben Hecht. Prolific, poetic, coarse, and versatile, Hecht was a veritable writing machine who had learned his trade at several of the city's daily papers before turning his ferocious energy to short stories and novels. Following the money, Hecht moved to Hollywood, where he ground out gangster screenplays with equal verve. By the time Hughes hired him, Hecht was able to command a fee of $1,000 a day for his services, payable in cash. It was a deal that Capone himself would have envied.

Hecht and the director, Howard Hawks (another highly capable professional), decided to graft the grit of Capone's story onto a gaudy background inspired by the Borgia dynasty. That was their theory; in reality, the notion meant they invented an unconsummated incestuous relationship between their Capone stand-in, whom they rechristened Tony Camonte, and his sister, Cesca. To make their tale of Camonte's violent rise come alive, the film's makers were extremely fortunate in their casting choices. Paul Muni imparted an irresistibly sinister appeal to the role of Tony Camonte, in part because he avoided obvious gangster mannerisms. Of course, he sported scars on his cheek, although these were X-shaped instead of Capone's parallel stripes. Ann Dvorak played the sister who is the object of Muni's lust, George Raft his companion Rinaldo, who is given to cutting out paper dolls. His secret marriage to the vivacious Cesca prompts Tony, who has shot and killed his way to the top, to turn on Rinaldo and kill him, as well. The other major death scene depicts the assassination of Camonte's rival Gaffney (played by Boris Karloff) in a bowling alley; just as Gaffney makes a strike, the machine guns roar, and he and the bowling pins fall in unison. At the end of the movie, Camonte, like so many other Capone stand-ins, meets a violent end. The film's closing scene shows him sprawled on the street beneath a huge electric sign flashing the message "The World Is Yours." Of course, the real Capone lived on, but the world no longer belonged to him.

When production began in the summer of 1931, there were a few unorthodox elements. In his zeal for realism, Hughes hired a retinue of underworld types as "technical advisers," and the machine guns used in the shootouts fired live ammunition. *Scarface* shared with other cinematic depictions of gangland a tendency to sermonize, in large part to placate Hollywood censorship represented by the newly established Hays Office. In fact, the Hays Office was so infuriated by *Scarface's* violent excesses that it forced Hawkes to soften the edges of the story and to add the clumsy subtitle *The Shame of the Nation* to ensure that audiences disapproved of what they had paid to see on the screen. The Hays Office in its wisdom even forced Hawkes to include a preposterous scene at the picture's conclusion. In it, an extra representing Camonte—Muni would have nothing to do with the alteration—submits to a harangue insisting that crime does not pay, and then he is hanged. When the movie finally cleared the Hays Office and opened in May 1932, it had two different endings: Hawkes's original for the big cities, and the anticrime sermon for the rural regions where censorship was tight. No matter what version they saw, audiences came away from *Scarface* thinking they now knew Al Capone: he was a thin man with a wan smile who had shot his boss to death, stolen his blonde moll, lusted after his sister, killed his best friend, and had recently been gunned down on the streets of Chicago. (As for Capone himself, he sat wasting in his cell in the Atlanta Penitentiary.)

On the strength of its violent spectacle, the movie ranked as one of the year's ten most popular films, and it earned critical praise. *Variety* claimed *Scarface* "bumps off more guys and mixes more blood with rum than most of the past gangster offerings combined." Little moments were even more chilling than the bloodbaths: Muni fondling his machine gun, Raft toying with his paper dolls. Here was a gallery of psychopaths who wanted to rule the world—and almost did. In its mixture of psychology and gore, the movie was horrifying but also witty. No matter how the Hays Office meddled, *Scarface* glorified Capone in particular and gangsters in general; they were rich when most folks were bust, they claimed and cast aside women as they pleased, and they got away with murder. Anyone who read the newspapers knew that crime *did* pay. Both movies and newspapers, illusion and reality, suggested that the United States, land of the free, was also the land of exploitation, inequality, and despair. Gangsters seized the popular imagination because they thrived on desperation: the belief that it was impossible to change anything in society, to right wrongs, to rise above one's caste.

As *Scarface* played to rapt audiences across the country, the public was inundated with accounts of Capone's exploits in hastily published biographies of dubious authenticity, pamphlets, and souvenir booklets. Filled with photographs of dead or dying gangsters, these booklets created a pornography of death and violence. They were printed in large quantities on cheap paper, and they circulated primarily in the Chicago area, where they quickly became collectors' items. Adults read them, showed them to friends, and hid them away from the prying eyes of children. Among the most popular in this shady category was Richard T. Enright's *Al Capone on the Spot*. Enright's commentary was vigorous, ripe and portentous, in the best pulp magazine manner:

> Al Capone is not dead—yet.
> But Al lives every day with death and knows that it will get him in the end.
> The world has put the finger on him. He is on the spot and—today, tomorrow, next week or next month, perhaps next year—sometime the gats will spit, the machine guns rattle, or the sawed-off shotguns roar.
> And then the world and gangland will make holiday while the costliest coffin is borne behind the longest parade of flower-laden limousines and Al Capone will ride in the Last Parade. . . .

The descriptions of murder and mayhem that followed paled beside the booklet's grisly illustrations. Readers were confronted with a full-page photograph of the dead Frank Capone, the bullet holes visible in his chest; another shot showed the bodies of Scalise, Anselmi, and Guinta lying beneath sheets in the morgue, with only their heads visible; in his portrait, Frankie Yale sprawled in a pool of blood beside the car in which he had tried to elude Capone's hit squad (which had consisted of Scalise and Anselmi); and there were gory shots of other, lesser gangsters lying in roadside ditches or slumped behind the wheel of a car, their straw boaters tilted at a fatal angle.

Other artifacts of the rapidly growing Capone cult were outright frauds, but their popularity testified to the racketeer's hold on the world's imagination. In Germany, Peter Omm's *Alkoholkrieg in U.S.A.* purported to be a true account by a Chicagoan calling himself Lemon Scoots. After returning from the Great War, Lemon wrote, he became a saloon keeper and bootlegger, rising to become a lieutenant of Capone himself. Said one reviewer of this work, "Anything glaringly improbable in the account is easily explained by the unfathomable gullibility of the Americans." A more successful hoax flowed from the pen of an English writer, Hugo C. K. Baruch. Under the nom de plume of Jack Bilbo, he concocted *Carrying a Gun for Al Capone: The Intimate Experiences of a Gangster in the Bodyguard of Al Capone*. Published in both England and the United States by Putnam in 1932, the work became a best-seller and remained in print until 1948, yet no one seemed to realize that the author, who had never laid eyes on Capone, wrote the book entirely out of his imagination. The English, particularly, were fascinated by Capone at the time; his notoriety inspired Owen Collins, a journalist, to write a well-intentioned study in 1932 entitled *King Crime: An English Study of America's Greatest Problem*. Edgar Wallace, the English mystery writer, visited Chicago for four days during Capone's tax trial, long enough to decide Capone was the victim of a witch hunt and to find inspiration to write a play about him on the transatlantic crossing home. The result, called *On the Spot*, became a hit in London and Paris.

It was but a short step from these bloody, simplistic dramatizations to the comics. Among the best known was Chester Gould's innovative daily strip, *Dick Tracy*. Gould's strip began appearing in the *Chicago Tribune* and other papers in 1931, when the comics habitually relied on fantasy heroes such as Tarzan and Buck Rogers or tame domestic satire. Gould, in contrast, took his inspiration from the news of the day, especially the newfound fascination with crime as an expression of social outrage that was characteristic of the Depression. Gould brought the criminal ethos to life through the character of a detective who remorselessly punished the wicked. "Big gangsters were running wild but going to court and getting off scot-free," he observed. "I thought: why not have a guy who doesn't take the gangsters to court but shoots 'em?" According to Max Allan Collins, the writer of the present-day version of the strip, Gould's inspiration for his detective came from Eliot Ness, whom he envisioned as a latter-day Sherlock Holmes, a man both fearless and technologically adept. Ness took the direct action that Gould calculated would appeal to his readers. Having chosen his model, Gould confronted his contemporary detective with an array of contemporary crimes to solve; he pursued kidnappers as well as gangsters. (Gould's retelling of the Lindbergh kidnapping gave the real-life tragedy a happy ending.) But Dick Tracy was no sentimentalist; he was as hard and remote as his victims, a sleuth whose style reflected the hard-boiled school of detective writing forged by Raymond Chandler and Dashiell Hammett. And Tracy was a trained professional; in his strip Gould regularly provided tidbits of information about fighting crime; he instructed readers on the proper procedure for photographing suspects, for instance, or taking fingerprints; the times demanded no less. True, *Dick Tracy* was only a comic strip, but it revealed a new way of thinking and feeling about daily life in crime-ridden cities. Gould's art work contributed to the strip's emotional appeal; panels were arresting to the eye: cinematic, menacing, blotted with black silhouettes of distorted human forms toting machine guns. Scenes of stark confrontation occurred in claustrophobic dark alleys or in the blinding glare of headlights. Gould transformed the gory photos of gangland slayings into comic book art for children to imbibe along with their milk and cereal.

In the guise of a character named Big Boy, Capone appeared in *Dick Tracy* early in December of 1931, not long after his tax trial had made him a front-page staple across the nation. In Gould's story, Big Boy is spending his idle time listening to a moll inspired by Texie Garcia, a popular speakeasy entertainer, play the piano. Tracy knocks on the door. Big Boy instructs the moll to continue playing ("He's pecking the ivories—he doesn't suspect anything," Tracy remarks) and fires a volley of shots through the door, hitting Tracy's sidekick. Tracy breaks down the door, only to find the moll alone in the flat; Big Boy has vanished into the night, and not even Dick Tracy can capture him.

Gangster fantasy found a home on the airwaves as well as in the comic strips. The radio version of *Dick Tracy* was broadcast early enough for children to tune in, as was the crime show, *Gangbusters*. In *The Shadow*, another popular radio series, Orson Welles portrayed Lamont Cranston and spoke chillingly of the evil lurking in the hearts of men. Crime fantasies were everywhere: in the newspapers and magazines, on the air, and on the nation's movie screens; and directly or indirectly, they reinforced the impression that Capone was the archvillain of the day. The plays and movies and comics succeeded because audiences wanted to believe that Al Capone was omnipotent, that he was evil incarnate, and they enjoyed projecting their fantasies onto him. In the realm of popular culture, he became the eternal Other. In the United States, Capone's alien nature was often thought to derive from his Italian immigrant origins. Surely the foreign blood coursing in his veins explained why he turned to a life of crime. But in Europe, Capone became a distinctively *American* phenomenon, the culmination of democracy's tendency to spawn a demotic, gangster culture. Capone was among the most readily identifiable of all Americans, the gangster who ruled Chicago, that quintessentially American city. Despite their diversity, all these representations of Capone shared one important element: they described a man who never was.

As Capone's reputation became bloated with myth and pseudofacts, a fresh roster of criminals captured the attention of the American public and fed its appetite for crime. They were a new breed, this group—not gangsters, but loners, outcasts, and misfits. Capone was a creation of the 1920s—the flashy, amiable, and highly sociable bootlegger. His immediate successors were different, distinctly products of the Depression. They were WASPs from rural backgrounds or small cities, places that were not supposed to be breeding grounds for criminals, places that honored American values, that had been dry before, during, and after Prohibition. Far removed from the Gowanus Canal or Chicago Heights, they were places where people studied and feared the Bible—the "real" America. But it made no difference; the farms and small towns of the Midwest proved just as liable to spawn criminals as the tenements of the East Coast. And some of these criminals were women, shattering another cherished stereotype. The new breed made no pretense about being Robin Hoods; they never even got rich. Capone, in comparison, was a tycoon of crime. This ugly crew fascinated Americans for one reason in particular: they robbed banks in an era when banks ruthlessly dispossessed so many farms, homes, and businesses. Many law-abiding citizens felt like robbing banks themselves, but these people went out and did it. In contrast, Capone never robbed a bank in his life, preferring to control them quietly, from behind the scenes.

Their number included "Baby Face" Nelson, "Ma" Barker, "Pretty Boy" Floyd, Bonnie Parker and Clyde Barrow, but above all there was John Herbert Dillinger. He resembled a nightmarish version of Clark Gable: thick hair, neat mustache, perpetual snarl, and chilling, feral eyes. He was a loner, a thrill seeker, and a renowned lover. Popular lore had it that his penis was extraordinarily long, but there is no evidence to support the claim. However, there is no doubt that this Indiana farm boy was extraordinarily violent. His short career in crime implicated him in ten bank holdups, ten shootings, and three jailbreaks: a one-man crime wave. Borrowing the concept of a public enemies list from the Chicago Crime Commission, the FBI's chief, J. Edgar Hoover, named Dillinger as the most wanted criminal in the country. The attention only served to glorify him. This was the Depression; Americans were suspicious of the federal government, and they rooted for underdogs like Dillinger, seeing him as an engine of social justice. "Dillinger does not rob poor people," explained an Indianapolis fan. "He robs those who become rich by robbing poor people. I am for Johnnie." Even the *New York Times* editorialized about his "charmed life." Had John Dillinger never existed, it would have been necessary to invent him, for he acted out a populist fantasy of revenge on the big business interests that had brought the country to its knees. In contrast to Capone, the organizer and insider, Dillinger was an outsider, and more than that, he was an outcast. Capone had maintained his own code of conduct: do things his way, and he would take care of you. With Capone morality was relative, everything painted in shades of gray, good and evil cooperating and compromising, one hand washing the other, and perhaps soiling it in the process. He was that quintessentially social phenomenon, the racketeer. At bottom, all his businesses operated on the principle of organizing people, bringing them together and extracting money from the interaction. In the process, he became virtually a government unto himself. But Dillinger was a loner. There was no subtlety about him; everything was black and white. An anarchist to the core, he despised the system; he was thoroughly, bracingly misanthropic and rebellious.

His final, most uproarious spree began in January 1934, when federal agents arrested Dillinger in Arizona and sent him home to Indiana and a murder trial. Foiling his captors, he escaped from a jail that was thought to be highly secure, assembled a small gang, and resumed robbing banks with gleeful abandon. In response, Homer Cummings, the attorney general, pressed Congress for anticrime bills, manpower, and machinery to cope with Dillinger and his like. "I think we ought to have a reasonable number of cars—cars that can go as fast as the devil," he said. "And we ought to have two or three armored cars." Despite Cummings's enthusiasm for the latest techniques in law enforcement, there is no evidence that more cars, laws, and money would succeed where society as a whole had failed. By the spring, 5,000 law enforcement officers were involved in trying to capture Dillinger, as their quarry eluded them, driving across the country from the sheltering arms of one girlfriend to another. Movement was his element: the headlights flickering across darkened country roads, the sound of insects filling the night, the click of weapons being loaded, the dry fear mounting at the back of the throat.

In May, federal agents tracked him to a roadhouse located in the north woods of Mercer, Wisconsin. Hearing their barking dogs, Dillinger leaped from a second-story window to temporary safety at the last possible moment. Since Ralph Capone was then in the process of converting Mercer into a refuge from his notoriety in Chicago, there is a strong possibility that Dillinger received assistance and shelter from the Capone organization. Later that summer, Dillinger slipped into Chicago, where he continued to elude the police, despite having one of the best-known faces in the country. He did take steps to disguise himself; he dyed his eyebrows black, wore glasses, and treated his fingertips with acid to obscure his fingerprints. Again, there is suspicion that he relied on the Capone organization to protect him in the city it still controlled.

For the previous five months, the FBI's chief agent in that city, Melvin Purvis, had been obsessed with capturing the new Public Enemy Number 1. Just thirty at the time, Purvis was more trigger-happy than other FBI agents; his approach to law enforcement was to kill violent criminals, not arrest them. On July 22, he received word that Dillinger had been spotted at the Biograph movie theater on North Lincoln Avenue in the company of two women: Polly Hamilton Keele, a pretty redhead who was one of Dillinger's girlfriends, and Anna Sage, a onetime madam. It was Sage who would betray Dillinger to the FBI; by prior arrangement, she wore a skirt of a conspicuous shade of bright orange, her signal to Purvis's men that she was with Dillinger. The trio bought tickets to see, appropriately enough, a gangster film starring Clark Gable, *Manhattan Melodrama*, and went inside the theater. Meanwhile, Purvis and several other agents quietly converged on the Biograph, trying to look inconspicuous; just before assembling, they had received an order from J. Edgar Hoover himself to shoot Dillinger only if he drew his gun. Chicago was in the midst of a stunning heat wave at the time; the day before, the temperature had reached 108 degrees. Over twenty agents had staked out the theater by the time the movie ended and the audience dispersed into the hot night. Among them was a surprisingly nonchalant Dillinger, who left the theater with his two female companions. As he walked to the former madam's apartment, he passed Purvis, looked at him, in fact, without recognizing him. Overcoming his paralyzing fear, Purvis managed to signal the agents to move in on Dillinger.

Polly was the first to notice that something was dreadfully wrong, that they were being followed. She poked him in the ribs, and Dillinger, who had narrowly eluded the police so many times in the previous months, once again ran for his life. Disobeying Hoover's orders, the agents drew their weapons and began to fire (they could always say they thought they had seen Dillinger produce a weapon). All at once, four bullets entered the body of John Dillinger, including one in the back of the neck, and he fell dead in an alley. He was only thirty-one years of age. A little later Anna Sage, having changed her dress, returned to the scene of the shooting, where passers-by stooped to dip their handkerchiefs in Dillinger's blood. (Later on, when the story of the betrayal came out, journalists employed a bit of poetic license and christened Sage "The Woman in Red.") His body was then taken to the Cook County Morgue, where attendants found $7.70 in his pocket along with a .38-caliber pistol; the safety catch was still on.

During the next few days over 20,000 curiosity seekers turned out to pay their last respects to his bullet-ridden corpse despite temperatures that continued to hover around the 100-degree mark. Eventually his remains were shipped home to be buried in Crown Hill Cemetery, Indianapolis, under heavy police protection. In Chicago, the alley where John Dillinger had died quickly became a tourist attraction, and in his memory, an unknown memorialist wrote on a nearby wall:

> Stranger, stop and wish me well,
> Just say a prayer for my soul in Hell.
> I was a good fellow, people said,
> Betrayed by a woman all dressed in red.

In the Gangster Summer of 1934, as Dillinger flashed across the consciousness of America like a comet trailing blood in its wake, Al Capone continued to serve out the remaining eight years of his prison sentence in near anonymity. Comparing him to Dillinger, the *New York Times* referred to Capone in a new way, the past tense. "Al Capone," the paper editorialized, "was significant because he was obviously the product of a whole environment, social and political." Significant, yes, but also a has-been. Al

Capone had begun the decade as an internationally notorious figure who, despite his conviction for income tax evasion, commanded a vast racketeering empire, but by the summer of 1934 he was broken in mind, body, and spirit, and nearly forgotten by the organs of publicity that had once outdone themselves to celebrate and condemn his career.

•   •   •

As midnight tolled the arrival of Sunday, August 19, a contingent of forty-three prisoners secretly left the Atlanta Penitentiary to board an armored train. They were accompanied by Warden Aderhold and a corps of heavily armed guards. No one would confirm the train's destination, though everyone knew they were bound for the West Coast and Alcatraz. At 6:10 A.M. the train, distinguished by its barred windows, pulled away from the penitentiary, coasted along the rail spur to the main line, and as the sun rose over the South, headed west. Despite the attorney general's refusal to reveal the identities of the prisoners on board the special train, there was widespread suspicion that Al Capone was among them, and as the train rumbled across the tracks of the Southern Pacific through Texas, spectators gathered to watch it pass; they were frightened away, however, by a guard who threatened to shoot.

Capone was indeed on board the train; as the newest, most formidable penitentiary in the country, Alcatraz had been designed expressly with his kind in mind. He had just become part of the federal government's latest experiment in crime deterrence. The name of the game was isolation; deprive a convict of the glamour endowed by publicity, ran the government's theory, and you have drawn his fangs. There was one other pressing reason for the veil of security covering Capone's transfer to Alcatraz: the fear that remnants of his gang might hijack the train, liberate Al, and kill his captors. Although the scenario appeared to be far-fetched, Warden Aderhold took it seriously indeed; in an era when Dillinger could elude thousands of federal agents, he believed that one could not be too careful. For reasons of security, then, Capone spent the entire journey confined to the car, his legs shackled in irons, his wrists manacled. When he went to the bathroom, a guard accompanied him. He was kept away from the barred windows, shrouded in darkness, unable to see the passing countryside. The sweltering heat made the confinement all the more unbearable, and since it was deemed unsafe to let the convicts wash, the cars carrying them were soon reeking. As the train neared Yuma, Arizona, Capone, extremely restless, stretched his legs and inadvertently opened a radiator valve with his foot; suddenly his car filled with scalding steam. Once the damage was repaired, he broke out in a rash, and guards cooled him down with an alcohol sponge bath.

On the morning of August 22, the prison train arrived at its destination, the small town of Tiburon, California, at the edge of San Francisco Bay. As the train approached the station, a group of about 200 spectators cried out for Al, but they received no reply, at least not from the convicts themselves. A child watching the spectacle was reported to have asked a guard, "Are there men as bad as Al Capone on that train? Ma says there are."

To which the guard responded, "Listen, there's no Capone or anybody by any name on that train. They may have been Capones once, but they're just numbers now."

The armored train creaked to a halt under the watchful gaze of heavily armed agents of the Department of Justice. Warden Aderhold, who had accompanied the prisoners on their cross-country journey, formally transferred custody of the men to James A. Johnston, the newly appointed warden of Alcatraz Island. The convicts were not allowed to disembark; they remained confined to the railroad cars, which were transferred to a waiting ferry. As a Coast Guard cutter trained guns on the vessel, the heavily loaded ferry, now bearing Warden Johnston and three armored cars containing forty-three prisoners, cast off from its dock and slowly entered the swirling waters of the bay.

"Alcatraz Island is the most striking natural object in the bay of San Francisco. In its commanding position between two great bridges it impresses with its boldness and beauty," wrote Johnston, who waxed rhapsodic about the penal colony he was about to command.

> To bay area residents viewing it at night from hilltop homes it looks like a huge ship at anchor. To ocean travelers approaching it through Golden Gate it looks like a stern sentinel thrust up by nature to protect the treasures of the inner harbor. . . .
>
> Men of the sea regard its circling light as a beacon to signal and guide ships safely into the docks that project out from the embarcadero and its bellowing buoy and blasting fog horns as warning to avoid the rocks.
>
> The perpendicular cliffside of the Island, exposed to the Golden Gate, is rough, barren, jagged and scarred, showing erosion from the bashing and thrashing of incoming tides, but above the water line there is a profusion of plants and flowers to which the moisture in the air gives luxuriance.
>
> Most of the time the weather is fine and the ocean breezes give the air a tang and zip that is refreshing and invigorating. Then there are days when a filmy, wispy fog comes and goes around it like a gossamer veil, and nights when wet, cold fog envelopes it like a shroud.

As the warden and unchallenged master of Alcatraz Island, Johnston was in a better position than the men in his custody to appreciate its unique setting. Arriving prisoners regarded the island with unmitigated loathing, expecting their time there to be tantamount to a death sentence. "The convict's dread of Alcatraz is due to adroit propaganda of 'the law' in American prisons regarding the terrors of 'the Rock,' " explained Bryan Conway, the Capone-hating convict who followed his enemy from Atlanta to Alcatraz. "The build up makes Alcatraz pretty bad, but the reality is worse." Another early Alcatraz inmate never forgot the hideous sense of foreboding that swept over him as he approached the island for the first time. "All of a sudden a feeling came over me that I would never cross this water again," he wrote. "On my forehead and between my shoulders blades I could feel beads of cold sweat. . . . I was feeling the sweat of fear. I had been afraid before in my life, but not afraid with the kind of fear I was feeling now."

As the ferry laden with its grim cargo of armored railroad cars approached the island, the men could discern the most prominent features of its twelve acres: the abandoned military garrison, the loading dock, the lighthouse, and, most impressively, the newly constructed cell house, an incongruously large edifice perched awkwardly at the summit of the rocky hill. Arriving at the dock after their brief, terrifying ride, Capone and the other convicts were at last freed from the leg irons which had painfully encircled their cramped limbs, though they still wore handcuffs. They emerged from the car in which they had spent the better part of three days. Slowly and stiffly, their ankles swollen from the leg irons, they marched up a series of switchbacks to the cell house, where the inmates lived. (Capone belonged to the second consignment of prisoners; eleven days earlier fifty-three men had come from McNeil Island.) It was a steep climb, equivalent to twelve stories, and each turn disclosed a more striking view than the last. In one direction, the men could see the graceful expanse of the Golden Gate Bridge, now under construction; in another the reaches of San Francisco Bay; and finally, most painfully, the city of San Francisco itself, spread before them in all its splendor, less than a mile distant. Separating them from this glittering city bursting with all that freedom and life had to offer was a stretch of exceedingly dangerous water. Prisoners were told that man-eating sharks infested the bay, and even if an escapee managed to avoid those predators, the treacherous crosscurrents would drown him in a minute.

Winded from the steep climb, the men reached the summit, where they immediately entered a large, dark, stone edifice: the cell house. It was here, in the cold depths of this building, that Capone would pass each day of all the years he would remain in Alcatraz. Along with the others, he was given his 3-by-5-inch card containing his name, number, cell number, and the work detail to which he belonged. He was now convict number 85, one of little more than 100 prisoners on Alcatraz, a group the Federal Bureau of

Prisons considered to be the most dangerous and incorrigible in the entire system. He was then assigned to a guard, who carefully escorted him to the basement, where he took a much-needed bath. He received supplies consisting of a blue wool coat and trousers, two wool shirts, two pairs of brown shoes (one for Sundays), two suits of underwear, six pairs of socks, cap, belt, handkerchief, and his daily uniform—blue-gray overalls. Each item was marked not with his name but with his number, 85. As Capone immediately discovered, the guards and officers never called him by name; from now on, he was simply "Number 85" to them all. In fact, talking of any kind was rare. Warden Johnston had imposed a rule of silence on Alcatraz, and convicts were not to talk to each other, and to a guard only if absolutely necessary.

Capone, like all new arrivals, submitted to a rectal examination and a Wassermann test, which reconfirmed his neurosyphilis. Warden Johnston was well aware of the indignity of the medical exams; in fact, he considered the humiliation they inflicted on the men a vital part of breaking them down. "I never saw a naked man yet who could maintain any sort of dignity," he claimed. "There is very little egotism left in a man when you parade him before other men in a birthday suit." Despite these insults, Capone's ego was intact and struggling for recognition, as Johnston noted in this vignette of the first encounter between warden and convict:

> I didn't have any trouble picking him out when he was lined up for identification his first day in Alcatraz. I had seen his pictures in the papers many times in poses that featured flashy jewelry and sporty suits. He was wearing coveralls that day instead of the Polo Coat that seemed so much a part of his press pictures in Chicago, but there was no mistaking the features. He was a big man. His fat face bore the marks that got him the nick name of "Scar Face." His thick black hair was balding. His neck was thick and his lips were thick and his middle was paunchy but not so oversized as it was in his luxury-living days in Florida.
>
> Before I called him to the desk for instructions I could see him nudging the prisoners near him and slipping them some corner-of-the-mouth comment. I signaled him when it was his turn. As he walked toward me he flashed a big, wide smile. He wanted to talk to me, but I didn't want to talk to him because it was no time for unnecessary conversation. It was apparent that he wanted to impress other prisoners by asking me questions as if he were their leader. I wanted to make sure they didn't get any such idea. I handed him a ticket with his number, 85, gave him the instructions I had given to every other man, and told him to move along.

Although Johnston was determined to treat convict number 85 in precisely the same way as he did numbers 84 and 86, the fourth estate insisted on obtaining news of Al Capone. Johnston finally confirmed what the world at large suspected, that Capone *had* been transferred to Alcatraz, but the cautious warden sought refuge in a general description of the strict regimen in his penal colony. "They are not even going to have an opportunity to know what goes on outside," he insisted. "Those men were sent here because the government wants to break their contacts with the underworld. That is going to be done."

Capone proceeded to his cell. Although it was new—the paint still shiny green, the metal bars and locks gleaming—the cell house had an oppressive, military atmosphere. Each prisoner had his own cell, the better to enforce isolation and prevent conspiracies. The cells rose three stories above a wide, echoing passageway named Broadway; at the far end, a single, stark clock told the time—the irretrievable minutes and hours, days and years of the convicts' lives. Capone's cell was on the second tier; it was exactly the same as the others: a five-by-nine-foot room made all the more oppressive by its low ceiling. It contained a narrow folding bunk bed attached to the wall with chains, a thin mattress covered with two white sheets, a blanket, and, at the foot of the bed, two additional blankets. Each cell had its own toilet (without a seat) located against the rear wall. The lack of privacy meant that prisoners used their toilet facilities in full view of the others; often a man sitting on his toilet would face another con across the way sitting on *his*. The cell also had a small tin sink with a lone spigot, a fold-down tabletop holding an aluminum drinking cup, a razor case, a cake of shaving soap, a toothbrush and tooth powder, a comb, and nail clippers. Capone and the other prisoners were also issued a corncob pipe, a sack of Stud tobacco, toilet paper, a green eyeshade, a broom, shoe polish, and the warden's highly detailed book of rules and regulations governing all aspects of life at Alcatraz. A twenty-watt bulb cast a dim light over the cell's contents.

During the brief intervals when he was not confined to his cell, Capone had access to a small library, another barred room stocked with a limited and closely monitored supply of books and magazines, but for him and the rest of the convicts, by far the most important room was the cafeteria. It was also the most dangerous, for it was here that the convicts handled cutlery, and trusted prisoners on kitchen duty had access to knives in connection with their chores. They were stored in a large, locked cabinet with silhouettes indicating the proper position for each knife. It was also the only location in the cell house where all the prisoners—at times as many as 200—congregated. Against the possibility of a riot, the cafeteria ceiling was honeycombed with canisters of tear gas; prisoners were told that the moment they became disorderly, lethal fumes would spew over them. As a result, the convicts christened the cafeteria the Gas Chamber. Despite the grim surroundings and constant rule of silence, the food, surprisingly enough, was edible; more than that, it was plentiful. Recognizing that prisoners often come to resent the monotonous, tasteless food more than any other aspect of penitentiary life, the Alcatraz administration was determined to make meals varied and appetizing. Prisoners could eat as much as they liked (the better to keep them docile), but they *had* to eat. If they refused three meals in a row, they were placed in D block—isolation.

Known by various euphemisms—Segregation or the Treatment Unit—D block occupied its own wing of the cell house and contained special isolation cells designed to break the will of an unruly prisoner. Five of the fourteen cells afforded total isolation, designed to punish the most serious offenders. Their massive iron doors swung shut after the prisoner, sealing him in total darkness. Nor could the men confined to isolation eat in the cafeteria; they remained in their cells twenty-four hours a day, seven days a week and received spartan "meals" consisting of bread and water pushed into them through a narrow slot designed for that purpose. Their sole respite came when they were permitted to leave for ten minutes, once a week, to shower, and then they marched swiftly back to isolation and darkness. Minor infractions of the prison's rules earned a prisoner three days to a week in solitary; an assault on a guard could lead to weeks of this terrible treatment. A spell in isolation often produced hallucinations, and a few prisoners reportedly lost their minds. In fact a quotient of Alcatraz's convict population men went quietly insane each year, the routine of daily life sufficient to push them over the edge. Guards dragged them off to the prison hospital, and they were never seen again. One day a prisoner performing his assigned chores on the island's dock suddenly took his ax and began to chop off the fingers of his left hand; by the time the guards overpowered him, he had severed them all and was pleading with the guards to chop off his right hand. He, too, was never heard from again, and the convicts simply referred to him as number 284 and shook their heads whenever he was mentioned. Indeed, *all* the men were crazed to some extent from the confinement and regimentation. "Men slowly go insane under the exquisite torture of routine," an inmate who survived the ordeal explained.

Confined to his tiny cell immediately after dinner, Capone did not sleep well. Nights were the toughest to endure. The guards took target practice within the confines of the cell house, and the prisoners could hear the crack of their rifles reverberating throughout the building. "The guards always shot at dummies made in likeness of the human form," an inmate recalled, "and these were left sprawled along the walkway with bullet holes in vital spots, as silent object lessons to cons who might be thinking of making a break for freedom." Once the gunfire subsided, it was replaced by the snoring, coughing, and gurgling of the convicts in the other cells, unseen but all too close. Add to that the insistent, throbbing warning of the foghorns in the bay and the squeal of tires or the wail of a siren wafting across the water from the mainland, and effect must have resembled the sound track of hell.

Whenever Capone nodded off into a light, troubled sleep, he was soon awakened by the sound of the passing guard's footsteps, the creaking of leather soles on the waxed floor. Lying on his cot, he brooded ceaselessly during these wretched hours. On his son. The unfairness of his punishment. The whole country was making fun of him; he, Al Capone, who had given his money to widows and orphans, was even in the *comic strips*. Outside of his family members and a handful of friends, no one really knew him. Didn't they realize he had tried to keep the peace during the gang wars in Chicago? That he voted Republican? Ran soup kitchens? That without him Chicago would have been a far more dangerous place? If they could only see him now, sick, helpless, miserable, and lonely, would they be so quick to laugh at Al Capone?

Roused by a 6:00 A.M. wake-up bell, he began to acquaint himself with the prison's daily regimen. He had twenty minutes to dress, and could shave only three times a week; on prearranged days, he balanced a matchbox on the cell door, and a passing guard placed a blade in the box. Capone and the forty-nine other prisoners permitted to shave that day had to work quickly, for within fifteen minutes the guard returned to retrieve the blades. The blades were then sterilized and placed under lock and key until the following day, when they were issued to another set of prisoners. At 6:30 the guards commenced the day's first count of the prisoners, a process they repeated throughout the day at thirty-minute intervals. Breakfast ensued: coffee, coffee cake, cereal, and, on occasion, pancakes. There was even butter on the table, a luxury unknown elsewhere in the federal penitentiary system. Although Warden Johnston prohibited talking, Number 85 discovered the men could converse sotto voce.

It was here, in the cafeteria, that he had his first look at the complete convict population. He immediately recognized Bryan Conway, whom he remembered from Atlanta, but Conway refused to talk to him. "Dummy up, Al," he told him, "dummy up." After a slight hesitation, Capone replied, "OK, pal."

Capone was hardly the only notorious criminal confined to the Rock. An unexpected result of Attorney General Cummings's plan to ship all the worst and most notorious convicts there was that the roster of Alcatraz prisoners became a *Who's Who* of the decade's most wanted—and most celebrated—outlaws. In addition to being the most feared jail in the country, Alcatraz became the most glamorous; simply being an inmate there conferred a fleeting celebrity on a con. More dangerous than any mob on the outside, the gang of inmates sequestered at Alcatraz included "Doc" Barker, the son of "Ma" Barker; Volney Davis; Harry Campbell; Albert Bates; a Dillinger cohort named Bobby Sherrington; "Machine Gun" Kelly, the well-heeled bootlegger and bank robber; John Paul Chase, late of the "Baby Face" Nelson gang; a kidnapper named Harvey Bailey; Roy Gardner, briefly renowned as a train robber; Charles "Limpy" Cleaver; John Stadig, an erstwhile counterfeiter in San Francisco; and a throwback to a bygone era, Mack Smith, known as the "Wyoming Bad Man." Most had never met before they reached the Rock; they had only read one another's press notices: the headlines announcing their latest robberies, shootings, trials, convictions, and sentences. But now, day in and day out, they ate together, worked together, exercised together, swapped information, laid plans for jobs they would pull and gangs they would form on the outside after their release; the possibilities were endless. After all, the Camorra, predecessor of the Chicago syndicate, had begun in the jails of Naples, where prisoners had had ample opportunity to conspire. Penal colonies came and went, but the rackets went on forever.

After eating and mumbling his way through breakfast, Capone and the rest of the convicts devoted the morning to work. At first Capone pushed a broom. Later he toiled in the laundry, but when a soldier stationed on the island wrote home to boast that Al Capone himself was washing his dirty clothes, number 85 was abruptly reassigned to cleaning the bathhouse. During his entire time on Alcatraz, the most dignified labor he was permitted to perform was ferrying books and magazines between the library and the cells. At other times, he belonged to the bucket brigade; the sight of Capone's tall, slumped form slowly pushing a mop became so familiar to the other convicts that they took to calling him "The Wop with the Mop," and the name stuck with him through all his years at Alcatraz.

The men broke for lunch at 11:30, a heavy meal consisting of pot roast and beans, as well as more coffee. Afterward, they returned briefly to their cells, and then resumed their menial, repetitive, mindless work assignments. As they marched back and forth in the cell house during the day on their rounds, they frequently underwent the scrutiny of a metal detector designed to sound an alarm if a convict carrying a hidden weapon passed through it, but the device was notoriously fickle, ringing loudly when unarmed men walked through but allowing the occasional knife to pass unnoticed. The men ate dinner at 6:30, often chili with apples for dessert and ample coffee. They then marched back to the rows of cells, each man waiting in front of his while the guards performed their final count of the day. On completion, a whistle blew, and the guards locked the men in their minuscule cells for the night. Capone could read if he liked, but the prison library eschewed crime magazines in favor of Westerns, and even the *Saturday Evening Post* was heavily censored, the offending pages snipped out before the convicts could see them. He became fascinated by magazines, and, taking advantage of a loophole in prison regulations, he eventually subscribed to eighty-seven periodicals, including *Harper's Monthly* and the *American Mercury*. Subsequently the *American Mercury* ran an impassioned denouncement of Alcatraz entitled "America's Torture-Chamber." The writer, Anthony M. Turano, declared that Alcatraz existed solely to inflict a "special social vendetta on the gangsters" and stood as a "monument to human stupidity and pointless barbarity."

The prison staff censored the convicts' mail even more stringently than they did the magazines. A prisoner never received an original, handwritten letter from the outside. Before it reached his hands, a clerk carefully reviewed, abridged, and copied it, substituting an impersonal typewriter for the individuality of the handwriting of a wife or brother or son. The same procedure applied to all outgoing correspondence. Because of the work involved in recopying letters, inmates were permitted to send just one letter a week, and their correspondence had to be addressed to immediate family members only. The warden permitted no letters to lawyers, girlfriends, or even in-laws. Inmates were not even permitted to use nicknames in their letters; all the people about whom they wrote had to be named in full. Since the guards retyped incoming and outgoing mail, every word the inmates wrote and received was fully known to the administration and provided an endless supply of gossip for the guards. From the moment he set foot on the island, then, Capone was under a microscope.

Despite the severe restrictions on writing, the Alcatraz experience turned everyone from the warden to the guards and inmates into diarists and autobiographers. Some of these accounts found their way to popular magazines such as the *Saturday Evening Post*, while others appeared in books produced by little-known publishers, sprinkled with inexact spelling and punctuation, and all the more convincing for those lapses. Nearly all these records offered detailed observations on Capone in captivity, for he quickly became the institution's most famous test case.

Although it took the presence of Al Capone to confer lasting, widespread fame on Alcatraz, the small, rugged island had already endured a long and bloody history as a fort and a military penal colony. It received its original name, Isla de los Alcatraces—Island of the Pelicans—as early as 1775, when two Spanish explorers, Captain Juan Manuel de Ayala and his pilot, José Canizares, sailed close enough to the island to remark on the countless pelicans it harbored. During the Civil War, "Fort Alcatraz," as the island was then called, became a prison when the Union confined a handful of captives there. In the early years of the twentieth century, the island served as a military prison for a fluctuating number of soldiers and aliens until Homer Cummings, sailing past its rocks rising out of the waters of San

Francisco Bay, decided that Alcatraz would make a splendid site for the newest federal penitentiary. Cummings liked the drama of the place because he intended the new maximum security facility to demonstrate to all Americans—especially gangsters—that the U.S. government would not tolerate lawlessness and violence, although those are exactly the elements that Alcatraz, with all the publicity it received, popularized for a new generation of Americans coming of age in the Depression.

Once Cummings took control of Alcatraz from the War Department in 1933, he moved swiftly to place his imprint on the institution. The federal government expended several hundred thousand dollars refurbishing the island's existing facilities and renovating its penological pièce de résistance, the monolithic cell house. On October 12, 1933, Cummings explained the purpose of the new super prison in a national radio broadcast, stating, "Here may be isolated the criminals of the vicious and irredeemable type so that their evil influence may not be extended to other prisoners who are disposed to rehabilitate themselves."

The fanfare with which Cummings introduced Alcatraz served to focus public attention on the penitentiary and churned up controversy as well. San Francisco's chief of police, William J. Quinn, its Board of Supervisors, and the *San Francisco Chronicle* all denounced the idea of creating a prison designed expressly to house gangsters. They warned that the island was nowhere near as secure as Cummings liked to believe; by some accounts, as many as twenty-three desperate military prisoners had escaped successfully, either by swimming or commandeering a boat. To prove the point, two young women, Doris McLeod and Gloria Scigliano, swam out to the island on different occasions, and if they could accomplish this feat as a lark, surely desperate prisoners could brave the bay's waters as well.

None of these arguments and demonstrations, convincing though they were, deterred Cummings from the pursuit of his goal to establish a super penal colony in San Francisco Bay, but he did increase its security, equipping guards with an arsenal consisting, in part, of Thompson machine guns, hand grenades, and tear gas guns. On January 2, 1934, he appointed James A. Johnston as the first warden of Alcatraz. Now the super penal colony required a supply of super criminals equal to its reputation. John Dillinger would have been among the first to be assigned there, but he was already dead, as were so many other gangsters and badmen who had inspired Cummings to create Alcatraz in the first place. In their absence the slightly older Capone filled the bill quite nicely.

• • •

During his first months at Alcatraz, Capone repeatedly tested his status as a prisoner during highly charged interviews with Warden Johnston—"Pussyfoot," to the inmates. Johnston's appearance was deceptively mild: a "friendly, ruddy-faced, white-haired perfect gentleman," in the words of a visitor, "just about the last person in the world you would pick on appearance to herd the toughest, meanest, most dangerous collection of criminals in the land." But Johnston was tougher than he looked. He had spent two decades in California prison administration, first at Folsom and later at San Quentin. Along the way, he developed a succinct formula for the handling of incorrigible prisoners: "examination, classification, and segregation." In essence, it meant removing the most dangerous criminals from a prison population and confining them under relentless scrutiny. The scheme had helped maintain order at Folsom and San Quentin, and now, as warden of Alcatraz, Johnston was employing it again, in its toughest test of all.

Such was the man to whom number 85 poured out the thoughts he was forced to keep to himself at all other times. "You're my Warden now," Capone announced one day, "and I just thought I better tell you I have a lot of friends and I expect to have lots of visitors and I want to arrange to see my wife and my mother and my son and my brothers."

The warden explained that Capone could receive visitors, *except* for his brother Ralph, an ex-convict. "And only two persons may visit at the same time."

"Warden, I got a big family and they all want to see me, and I want to see them all," number 85 complained.

"They cannot all come at the same time because the regulations limit the number of visitors to two relatives at one time. That rule will apply to you as it will govern all other prisoners. When you write to your wife tell her what I have just told you. Also tell her to advise me when she wants to visit and I will send her a pass with full instructions."

With that, number 85 "shrugged his shoulders, smiled a sick sort of smile and walked away," Johnston recalled. As he left, the prisoner had a parting thought:

"It looks like Alcatraz has got me licked."

If Johnston thought he was finished with Capone, he was mistaken, for the following day number 85 returned, and this time he indulged in flights of megalomania, the consequence of his neurosyphilis. "Don't get me wrong, Warden, I'm not looking for any favors," Johnston recalled the convict saying, "but maybe some of these older cons ain't got any friends, but I gotta lot of friends. Maybe you don't know it, Warden, and maybe you won't believe it, but a lotta big businessmen used to be glad to be friends with me when I was on top and they wanted me to do things for them."

"What kind of businessmen . . . would need or require any help from you?" asked the startled warden.

With that, number 85 flew into a tirade. As transcribed by Johnston, the stream-of-consciousness recollection of his late, great days in Chicago serves as a harsh but poignant portrait of Capone hovering on the threshold of psychosis.

> Warden, you musta heard about how the big Chicago papers were always fighting, you know what I mean, fighting each other for business. Talk about gangs, talk about rackets, talk about battles, them guys didn't stop at nothing. Them circulation fights sure was murder. Just the same the top guys were all smart guys. They knifed each other like hell and they didn't give a damn what happened and you wouldn't think they'd speak to each other till somebody outside the circle, you know somebody that didn't belong to their own gang, was getting in their hair and then they yelled murder and hollered for help like when the newsboys went on strike. Them newsboy strikes and them newsboy raids on different papers sure were tough battles. They sure had the big boys worried. And who do you think settled all them strikes and fights?
>
> *Me, I'm the guy that settled all their strikes and all their circulation raids.*

Capone was shouting now, banging on the warden's table, bringing armed guards padding to the office like faithful dogs.

Mesmerized by his uncanny presence, Johnston threw caution aside and challenged number 85. "You mean to tell me that the circulation managers of the papers asked you to help them settle their labor troubles?"

"No, Warden, you don't get me. Warden, I never did any business with any managers. I was no piker and I didn't do any business with pikers. I didn't butt in. I waited for the high-ups to send for me, and when I call 'em high-ups I mean the highest top guys that own the newspapers send for Al whenever they were in trouble. . . . And Al always delivered, and Al never got anything for doing what he did for them. The big boys always sent for Al and they were glad to talk to Al when they needed Al, but they sure put the boots to me when they got me down."

Number 85, his face flushed, his breath coming in rasps, concluded his speech and waited for Johnston's reaction to these astonishing revelations. Silence reigned, but eventually the warden did reply, his tone as icy as Capone's had been fiery.

"That is very interesting," he said. "You may want to tell me some more sometime."

A perverse bond formed between the two men; it was based more on mutual loathing than respect, but it was nonetheless real for that. It was the bond between a kidnapper and his prize hostage. Almost every day, it seemed, number 85 was in the warden's office to ask for special favors, permission to lend money to the other prisoners, to bend the rules, only a little, when it came to visits. In every case, the answer was, inevitably, no, but that did not discourage Capone from asking. Johnston became fascinated by the power he held over this man, once the most feared criminal in the nation, the former Public Enemy Number 1 who was now merely his convict number 85. It was literally a power of life or death; he could with complete freedom consign Capone to the torture chamber of the isolation ward, as he did on several occasions. It was within his power to drive his prisoner mad or to keep him sufficiently content to remain rational.

Capone, for his part, came to treat the quietly sadistic warden as his father confessor, whom he alternately tried to cajole, flatter, and impress. "I made the dough, plenty of it," he boasted during another of their sessions. "I got mine. I never denied it, but I didn't put it into a sock, I put it out, I spent it, I gave it away, I kept it circulatin'. I took care of my family and I took care of my friends and their families. Nobody went hungry or wanted for anything when Al was around. You oughta heard 'em. It was Al gimme this and Al gimme that and Al donate and Al contribute and Al subscribe and Al buy tickets and Al they need something for the hospital and Al they need something for the church and Al they want you to put up the dough for a soup kitchen and Al never said no. I always came through." So it went, week after week, Capone bursting into the warden's office to spew out his pent-up reflections and fantasies and Johnston listening in chilly silence, the two of them locked in an embrace of penance.

•   •   •

In December 1934, number 85's first significant breach of the prison's rules occurred. At the time, he was working in the laundry, feeding clothing into the mangle, a machine consisting of two rollers that pressed and smoothed out the cloth. The job was one of those boring, pointless, infuriating activities of which daily life at Alcatraz consisted. His partner in this task was William Collyer, number 185, a soldier sentenced to life for murdering an Army officer. Usually, Capone was affable on the job, and when the guards were not around to enforce the rule of silence, he kept up a constant patter about his exploits in Chicago. In fact, one of his coworkers was so impressed by the relentless boasting that he decided Capone "must have put the go into ego." On one occasion, however, Collyer's laggard behavior infuriated Capone, who hurled a wad of wet laundry at him. Collyer responded by throwing a bench at Capone, and the two came to blows. The transgression earned both men confinement in leg irons and a night in an obscure part of Alcatraz known as the Dungeon, a holdover from the days when the island had served as a garrison for the Spanish.

Collyer demonstrated to the other cons that you could take on Capone in

Alcatraz, man to man, with bare fists, and live. The fight with Collyer taught number 85 something, as well: he would receive no special favors from the warden or anyone else. He was not the only big shot criminal on the Rock, as he had been in Atlanta; he had to compete with "Machine Gun" Kelly and other men whose names had been more recently in the news and on the lips of Americans; he could consider himself their equal and no more. It was not like the outside; as the warden himself never tired of repeating, every man was equal on the Rock, which, translated into the lingo of the con, meant that every man was vulnerable, especially Al Capone. While number 85 tried to fit in as best as he could, obscure punks transferred from Leavenworth and McNeil caused most of the ruckuses, assaulting the guards, throwing food, and muttering about insurrection. They had been nobodies on the outside, and they desperately wanted to prove they could be Somebody on the inside. From then on, the testing of Capone's mettle began. At first the treatment fellow prisoners accorded him was mild, a shove here, a slur there. Since Capone was easily excitable, these slights infuriated him. For petty insults, nothing matched the treatment he received on the baseball team. "Pussyfoot" Johnston permitted prisoners on good behavior to play indoors a modified form of baseball. Like everyone else, Capone wanted to play on the team; more than that, he wanted to manage it, but as first baseman he proved so clumsy that he was relegated to the outfield, and then to the bench. His self-esteem wounded, he stormed off the field, and he consoled himself by tossing horseshoes. If another con beat him at that game, Capone refused to talk to him afterward.

Unable to defend to himself, Capone attracted a new tormentor named Jimmy Lucas, an ornery little (140-pound) hard case, as his prior record demonstrated. Serving a life sentence for murder, he had escaped from the Huntsville, Texas, penitentiary; while on the loose, he robbed a bank, was recaptured, and sent to Leavenworth; and from there he had been transferred to the Rock in January 1935 to serve a thirty-year sentence. There Lucas joined forces with another inmate, Cecil Snow, and together they laid a trap for Capone. The bait came in the form of a secret escape plan. They confided to Capone that they could sneak a cache of machine guns onto the Rock; they would then blast their way out of the cell house and escape aboard a waiting speedboat. If Capone wanted to participate in the jailbreak, he would have to contribute $15,000 toward expenses. Seeing the preposterous plan for what it was—extortion—Capone refused to have any part of it, but he was unable to rid himself of Lucas's tactics of intimidation. Lucas belonged to an entrenched clique of inmates from Texas and Oklahoma; to the man, they hated Capone, and they vowed to get him any way they could. The clique, known as the Texas Cowboys, started spreading rumors that Capone was ratting on the other inmates. Was a guard accepting favors from a prisoner? Capone was said to have turned them in. Was an inmate some-how found to have concealed a bottle of whiskey in his cell? Capone had told the guards. There was no truth to the rumors, but their mere existence polarized the inmates into pro- and anti-Capone factions. Al Best, number 107, belonged to the small group who remained loyal to Capone. "Outside of losing his head so easily and bragging about what he has done, Capone has a heart as a big as a house," Best wrote after he was freed in 1937. "He wanted to do his time in Alcatraz as easy as he could—but the majority of the men had it in for him and were out to get him."

Despite all these difficulties, Capone learned to accept his place within the structure of the prison's rituals and routines with less complaint than the average inmate did. Although he was confined to a prison undeniably mean and miserable, Capone patiently stuck it out and did his time. In fact, his first few years at Alcatraz were remarkable for their absence of trouble; warden, guards, and inmates alike discovered that the mighty Capone, the ruthless, feared ganglord who had once brought an entire city to its knees, was gen-erally amiable, docile, and touchingly eager for the good opinion of all. One young newcomer to the rock was startled when Capone sidled up to him and shook his hand. "Anything I can do for you," he said in the manner of an unctuous major domo, "don't hesitate to call on me." Of course there was nothing number 85 could do for the new member of the Alcatraz men's club, or, for that matter, himself.

Number 85 had changed, physically as well as mentally. He was no longer the shrewd, occasionally temperamental Capone of old. His relentlessly advancing case of neurosyphilis, two years in the Atlanta penitentiary, and the regimentation of Alcatraz had all taken their toll on mind and body, and as 1934 slipped into 1935, he was a shabby counterfeit of the man he had once been. Some of the changes were superficial—the receding hairline, the prison pallor, the shrunken gut—but other, more insidious changes sug-gested his inner decay: his sunken eyes ringed by frighteningly dark circles, his stooped posture and shuffling gait, and his increasingly slurred speech. Number 85 spent ever more time in his own world, muttering to himself, staring into space, singing softly, detached from the brutal reality of Alcatraz and its tough crew. Rather than foment rebellion and shout defiance at the authorities, as was expected of him, he preferred to lose himself in pristine reveries of his wife and child and to pursue an improbable new ambition: he wanted to start a band consisting of Alcatraz inmates.

This was no transient daydream for number 85; it was an obsession that took hold of his disintegrating mind and which he pursued relentlessly during 1935. At first he approached Warden Johnston with the idea of purchasing instruments for the inmates. Money was no obstacle; he would pay whatever it cost. The sound of clarinets, flutes, trombones, gleaming brass, and throbbing drums would emanate from the island of the damned to mingle with the foghorns. No, the warden said, that would not be possible. After all, prisoners were not even allowed to *speak* in this prison, much less play marching songs. Number 85 did not let the matter rest there, however. A band would be good for morale, he said. Finally, after a year of campaigning, Warden Johnston yielded slightly, allowing the prisoners to form a band. They could practice for up to twenty minutes a day. However, Capone was absolutely forbidden to buy instruments for others; prisoners were required to use their own funds. To emphasize that the band would not be a Capone enterprise, the warden placed another inmate, number 199, in charge of the band. Known as Arthur Charrington in his previous life, he had spent his nights playing in an orchestra in Chicago and his days helping Dillinger rob banks.

Capone then decided he would play the banjo. He had not previously played this or any other instrument, nor is there any evidence that he was able to read music prior to jail, but he patiently familiarized himself with the rudiments of music theory and was eventually able to decipher musical notation and to pick out a few simple tunes, softly singing along. At first the members of the Alcatraz band managed to cooperate with each other, Capone plucking on the strings of his banjo, "Machine Gun" Kelly banging the drums, and a young kidnapper named Harmon Waley blowing on sax. The seeds of conflict were sewn, however, when Capone exchanged his banjo for its Old World counterpart, the mandolin. Other convicts whispered that Capone's new instrument cost $600 and that his sheet music consisted of original orchestrations shipped directly from Europe. Matters came to head during one weekend practice section when Capone complained that Waley was blowing his saxophone too close to his—Capone's—head. Suddenly Capone lost his temper, swearing at the young man, who silently waited for Al to turn his back. The instant he did, Waley smashed his saxophone into Capone's head, knocking him from his stool. The two of them fell to the floor, pummeling each other, until the guards broke up the fight, which earned the participants a week in isolation. With that fight, number 85 dropped another notch in the convict hierarchy. Shunned by jealous inmates, he henceforth played—and sang—by himself.

Although music afforded Capone solace and respite from the constant threats he now received, it could not offer him physical protection. At the beginning of January 1936 a convicts' strike brought him even closer to danger. The inciting incident involved the death of an inmate, Jack Allen, who had been complaining for days of severe stomach pains without receiving medical attention. The doctors assumed that Allen was fabricating symptoms, and the inmate was thrown into solitary for his trouble. In the morning, he was found unconscious, and he died soon after on the prison's operating table of a perforated ulcer. Best observed, "This death of Allen really hurt everyone."

The inmates immediately began to organize themselves for a strike, but Capone refused to participate. He was sympathetic to their cause, but, as "Machine Gun" Kelly reminded him, the moment Capone joined the strike, the guards and prison officials would assume he was organizing it, and, at the very least, his sentence would be lengthened by several years. Other prisoners took Capone's determination to sit out the strike as an excuse to abuse him. "Phony Capone," they called him, as they shouted threats to kill him, his wife, and son. Capone was so frustrated, infuriated, and unnerved by their taunts that he retreated to his cell, pulled the blankets over his head, and cried.

Guards and inmates alike remarked on Capone's childish and erratic behavior; unaware of his neurosyphilis, they assumed he was going crazy from too much time in stir. The strike went forward without his involvement and against formidable odds. "It is difficult to organize a prison mutiny, even among the men of the high average intelligence of those at Alcatraz," another convict observed. "You can't trust everybody, and sometimes even the strong weaken and reveal the secrets of their crowd. Alcatraz either brings out all the strength of a man or it breaks him into a sniveling snitch and a coward." For five days the prisoners refused to perform their work assignments. The warden dispatched the leaders to D Block, where in the darkness of their solitary cells they began a hunger strike, which ended only when prison doctors started to force feed them with a rubber tube. If an inmate refused to allow the tube in his mouth, guards held him down, and the doctors inserted the tube into his nose. The crude procedure proved effective, and at last the strike was broken. In the end, the protest accomplished nothing, but the inmates continued their talk of rebellion, although it was now an empty threat. Throughout the grim ordeal, Capone managed to keep clear of trouble.

Over the next several months the Texas Cowboys attempted to ambush the man who had cried in his cell. Desperate men, many of them serving life sentences, they had but a single intention: to kill Al Capone. To avoid them, number 85 tried to hover near a guard, but it was only a matter of time before he forgot himself and left an opening. The inevitable confrontation occurred on June 23, 1936. That morning he had just received a new mandolin in the mail, and now in the clothing supply room, he was showing it off to one of the guards. In the next room, overhearing Capone, was his enemy Jimmy Lucas, getting his monthly haircut from a convict barber, another Texas Cowboy who went by the name of "Hard Rock." As Capone continued his boasting in the next room, "Hard Rock" unscrewed his steel barber shears and slipped Lucas a lethal weapon in the form of one of the blades.

The two of them waited for Capone to leave the supply room and return to the bathhouse, where he was mopping floors, but as their mark continued to talk, Lucas finally lost patience and charged into the adjoining room. Before the guard could move, Lucas sank the shaft of sharp steel into the soft flesh of Capone's lower back. The two of them fell to the ground, struggling, Lucas repeatedly stabbing Capone until the guard suddenly struck the young Texas Cowboy in the head with a blackjack, knocking him out. Al Best, who had been only several feet from the fight, ran to the aid of the bloodstained victim. "The dirty shit stabbed me," Capone said as he tried to regain his footing. "Please take me to the hospital."

"I helped Capone to quiet down and then helped him upstairs to the hospital," Best recalled. "When the shirt was removed they saw all the stab wounds, including one real bad one near the kidneys. The officer brought the half shear up to the doctor, and they noticed that the tip was broke off. I went downstairs and swept the floor, but I couldn't find it. The doctor then X-rayed Capone's body to try to find the missing piece. It turned out this piece of steel was embedded in his thumb. Capone must have put up his hand to shield his eyes. They removed the small piece of steel and put Capone to bed in the hospital."

The fight's aftermath was swift. Capone burst into the headlines after an absence of two years, and newspapers carried a full account of the stabbing, implying heavily that the appalling conditions of Alcatraz were the underlying cause. Johnston questioned Capone in the hospital; the warden learned that Lucas had been trying to extort money from Capone, and when he refused to pay, Lucas began spreading rumors that Capone was an informer. As Johnston pursued his inquiry, the U.S. attorney in San Francisco and the FBI both launched investigations into the attack, an inquiry that subjected Warden Johnston's regime to its first real scrutiny from the outside world. An FBI agent traveled to Alcatraz to interview Johnston, who described the attack in detail and explained that Capone's multiple stab wounds were "not serious, and that he would be ready for release from the Prison Hospital in a short period." There was talk of prosecuting Lucas in a federal district court, but as the FBI and Johnston reviewed the problems involved in maintaining security for both Lucas and Capone, they concluded, as the FBI report put it, "a chance of escape would be eminent," and the matter was dropped. On his own, Johnston meted out severe punishment for Lucas; his thirty-year sentence was lengthened by twelve additional years, and he was ordered to spend six months in isolation. Inmates agreed among themselves that just nineteen days was the absolute limit of human endurance in isolation. "Anyone who stays in solitary longer than this time-tried limit is tempting death," noted one. Lucas managed to survive the half year in darkness, but the experience left him mentally unhinged—"stir bugs," the cons called it.

Even before the attack, a series of newspapers articles had questioned the wisdom of Alcatraz's unforgiving regimen. "Just a Life of Hell—That's Felon's Alcatraz Story— Monotony Breaks Spirit," declared the headline of a representative account, which had run the previous February in the *San Francisco Chronicle*. "Why, a man can talk only six minutes a day in that place," said a convict named Alfred "Sailor" Loomis, a counterfeiter who had recently been released. "It's the 'island of mistreated men.' Soon it will the 'island of mad men,' " he warned, and he proceeded to relate appalling tales of the Gas Chamber, the Dungeon, and the entire dark side of Johnston's all-men-are-equal regime. Yes, the inmates are bad, Loomis argued, but conditions at Alcatraz made them even worse.

Two months later, in April, "Dutch" Bowers, a post office safe cracker, became the first inmate to attempt to escape the Rock. He had previously tried to commit suicide—which amounted to the same thing as attempting to escape Alcatraz—by breaking his glasses and slashing his throat. Once he recovered, he was assigned to a work detail at the incinerator; one afternoon he started chasing a windblown piece of paper and suddenly broke for the barbed wire surrounding the perimeter of the island. Guards shouted for him to halt, but he ignored them and hauled himself up the wire, above the rocks and pounding surf. Two guards fired on him, and he fell fifty feet, breaking his neck. The inmates saw in the foolish escape attempt proof that Bowers had gone "stir bugs." That horrifying death and Capone's stabbing generated further publicity, all of it portraying Alcatraz as a penal colony of men pushed to the brink of sanity, an unimaginable hell located right in San Francisco Bay. A growing sector of the public viewed Alcatraz as an exercise in government-sponsored sadism rather than the last word in criminal deterrence.

•   •   •

No one worried more acutely about the welfare of Al Capone than his family. News of his stabbing sent shock waves through the Capone clan. During his months in Alcatraz, they had rarely visited because, as they knew only too well, their journey to Alcatraz was certain to bring the newspapers hovering like vultures. The government had succeeded in permanently stigmatizing not only Al but the rest of his family, who lived like exiles and outcasts in their own country. Mae rarely left the grounds of the Palm Island hacienda; she spent her days in isolation, worrying about Sonny's welfare, trying with a complete lack of success to live down the notoriety of being married to Al Capone.

It appeared that even the house, her last refuge, would soon be taken from her. In October, the government announced its intention to auction it off to the highest bidder as part of the penalty for Capone's failure to pay taxes. On October 20, newspapers carried word that "The stucco mansion, the tiled swimming pool and the extensive grounds on Biscayne Bay will be sold to satisfy a Federal Tax lien of $51,498.08 recently filed against the gangster's wife." Ralph took the lead in trying to head off the IRS, assisting Mae, and keeping Al abreast of the painful developments, especially the imminent loss of the Palm Island estate. As Ralph explained in a letter to his brother, "We had them beat until they served notice on Mae as transferee and would have beat them only for the fact that when Mae was originally assessed in 1931, she did not protest the assessments. The law provides that the assessment must be protested within ninety days or lose the right to. . . . I am sorry this had to be the final outcome of everything, but we did our best and it is all due to another mistake on the part of your attorneys." Days later, Ralph wrote again, this time with a much brighter assessment: "Well you need have no more worries about the Florida home. I paid the whole thing in Jacksonville last Saturday, the total amount was $52,103.30. We have obtained a complete release and there is no further claim against the home by the Gov. I obtained a mortgage on the house for $35,000." Ralph explained that he borrowed the rest of the money required to satisfy the claim, and his easy access to cash, not to mention a mortgage, suggests how well established he had become after his own release from prison. Sounding like a member of the Miami Chamber of Commerce, Ralph went on to paint a cheery picture of the local scene for Al: "Everything points to a big season in Miami. . . . They built 37 new hotels in the past six months."

In contrast to Ralph's even temper, Mae was overwrought from the ordeal of nearly losing her home. She sent an urgent telegram to Warden Johnston beseeching him for permission to visit her husband. She then wrote a long, frenzied letter to Al himself to tell him of her impending arrival. She began by marking a solemn anniversary, her tone veering eerily between Victorian homily and gangster tough talk:

> 93 Palm Island
> Miami Beach, Fla.
> Saturday, Oct. 24, '36

My Dear Husband:

Honey five years ago today, you were taken away from us, it was a dreadful and sad day, and dear this five long years has been cruel and terrible not only that you were taken away and moved from place to place, but everything in general has come up to annoy and make you and your dear ones have a heavy cross to carry—but darling you have been grand, took it all like a major, and in spite of all have gone through this crisis, and held your own. . . .

Honey I sent a wire to the "Warden" last night asking for permission for Mattie [Al's younger brother Matthew] to come along with me, so most likely I will get the answer today. I called him last night and he was overjoyed and happy to go with me, so dear as soon as I get his answer I shall make different train arrangements as I have my ticket bought. . . . I spoke to your mother on the phone today, she sent me some fresh Italian sausage. . . . Well sweet I will close, no more to say, take care of yourself and never give [up], grit your teeth and grin always, you know Honey it really hurts people to see they can't get us down, so I don't mean maybe. I will see you soon. "God" bless you. Love and kisses. I love you.

Forever your loving Wife and Son.

Capone's joy at the prospect of seeing his wife again can well be imagined, but at the same time the restrictions surrounding visits made them extremely frustrating and painful experiences for inmates and relatives alike. After taking a ferry to the Rock, visitors walked up the switchbacks past the breathtaking views of the Golden Gate Bridge and the San Francisco skyline to the cell house, where they had to clear the metal detector, and were then ushered into a special room separated from Broadway by a thick steel wall. As number 85 learned, visits were brutally brief—no more than twenty minutes' duration. Nor could the inmate hold, touch, or even stand in the same room as the visitors who had, in all probability, traveled halfway across the country to see him. In the presence of a guard, the wife, mother, or son of an inmate peered through a three-by-nine-inch hole in the wall, hardly large enough to reveal a face, covered with inch-thick glass. On the other side, the inmate, also in the company of a guard, walked to the far end of Broadway, where the peep holes were located. There he was allowed to glimpse the face of the family member who had come to see him. They could try to talk, if they wished, through a small panel to the left of the glass window, but screens made communication so difficult that convicts had to shout to be heard, and in Alcatraz, with its rule of silence, every word a convict said to his visitor reverberated throughout the cell house, obliterating privacy. Such were the infuriatingly impersonal conditions under which Al and Mae "visited" that day in October 1936.

•   •   •

Capone received additional news of the world beyond Alcatraz from a new prisoner, Alvin Karpis. After Capone, "Creepy" Karpis was the most notorious inmate of Alcatraz. As the leader of a gang he had formed with Freddie Barker, Karpis had the distinction of succeeding Capone and Dillinger as Public Enemy Number 1. In its inglorious heyday, the Karpis-Barker gang had pulled off two spectacular kidnappings. First they nabbed William Hamm Jr., the president of Hamm Brewing of St. Paul, Minnesota, a job netting the gang a $100,000 ransom; subsequently they took a bank president named Edward Bremer, for whom they received a $200,000 ransom, only to discover that the bills were marked. The gang disintegrated when Freddie and "Ma" Barker were shot to death, and "Creepy" himself was captured. When Karpis arrived at Alcatraz in August 1936, a few days before his twenty-eighth birthday, he was perhaps the only man *relieved* to be confined to the Rock; otherwise, he figured, he would have been executed for one of the various murders in which he had been involved during his hectic career. He ultimately spent twenty-five years at Alcatraz: a testament to his tenacity no less than his wickedness.

From the start, Karpis was among friends on the Rock. No fewer than nine members of the Karpis-Barker gang served sentences at Alcatraz simultaneously, a melancholy reunion of kidnappers, robbers, and murderers. On first catching sight of Capone, he was astonished by the changes time and disease had wrought. Number 85 seemed a "pale, shrunken figure," albeit "calm and controlled." On reflection, Karpis decided that Capone was ill-equipped to survive at Alcatraz; most of the prison's population consisted of small-time criminals. Capone, on the other hand, was a racketeer, a businessman surrounded by street fighters. One could call him a white-collar criminal, except that in his case the collar was stained with blood.

Eventually the two men found a way to meet and discuss their common concerns. The rules of silence had been relaxed slightly, but private conversation remained a hard-won rarity. With the cooperation of another con acting as a lookout, Karpis and Capone were able to hold a fleeting conference in the shower room. There Capone immediately voiced his most urgent concern, the welfare of his stand-in, Frank Nitti, the organization's hapless enforcer. Capone knew only that Nitti had recently been involved in a violent altercation with the law. "Why was Frank Nitti shot by that detective?" he immediately asked.

Karpis revealed that he had seen Nitti several months after the shooting in Benton Harbor, Michigan, where many of the Capone racketeers had their summer homes. At the time, Karpis was staying in the house of the former mayor of Cicero, that grim Chicago suburb which had served as a Capone stronghold. Talking with Nitti on a beach beside the sparkling waters of Lake Michigan, Karpis learned that the detective was named Walter Lang, and even though Nitti had taken the bullet in his neck, he had recovered fully.

"Nitti told me the guy shot him over a personal grudge," Karpis told Capone. "Something left over from years before."

"Did he tell you what it was about?"

"I didn't ask." It was the correct response—discreet, responsible. It was apparent that Karpis operated strictly on a need-to-know basis.

Recognizing that he was dealing with a fellow professional, Capone briskly moved on to other pressing matters, inquiring as to the reasons behind the killing of Willie "Three-Fingers" White, who had once belonged to the Capone organization.

"Whenever someone in your outfit is killed, you guys always claim he was caught talking to the FBI," Karpis told him. "Sure enough!" The scuttlebutt, according to Karpis, was that White had talked to Melvin Purvis, head of the FBI's Chicago office. Karpis thought he knew which syndicate gunman had killed White, and he was bursting with other gangster gossip as well, but fearing Capone's reaction to it, he decided to keep his intelligence to himself. Capone thanked him, and their clandestine conference ended before the guards discovered it.

Number 85's next contact with the outside world occurred in a wholly different context, an interview with the new director of the Federal Bureau of Prisons, James V. Bennett. On assuming his position, he decided to act, in his words, as "the talent scout for Alcatraz." He took it upon himself to "review the records of all the men in the various federal prisons and decide who would be sent to 'the Rock.' I also had to supervise the performance of the men on Alcatraz and help determine who was ready to be sent back to prisons on the mainland." An announcement that the director himself intended to visit Alcatraz and interview inmates lifted the hopes of the prisoners, nearly all of whom requested a hearing with him.

Arriving at Alcatraz in the spring of 1937, Bennett discovered he had come to a prison unlike any other he had ever visited. He set up a desk in a "drafty, cheerless, half-lit corner" of the cell house, where he received inmates who one after the other requested transfer to prisons on the mainland; even the Lewisburg or Atlanta pen seemed a welcome alternative to the rigors of life at Alcatraz. As the prisoners spoke with Bennett, two armed guards kept a vigil, one pacing the floor, the other aiming his rifle at the prisoner's chest. The show of firepower unnerved Bennett, and he ventured to complain to Johnston that the "men might not feel free to speak their minds" under these circumstances, but the warden reminded him that Alcatraz housed "the most desperate men in the world, and they might regard it as an accomplishment to assault the prison director."

Among the first petitioners was number 85, who took his seat and whose manner, despite the rifle leveled at him, took Bennett by surprise. "He did not snarl, as most of the movies, books, and plays about him had led me to expect," the director observed. Instead, Capone smiled and attempted to ingratiate himself with the one man who might possibly ease the rigors of his sentence. He pointed out that he was serving the longest sentence ever given for income tax evasion and had been tried not for that offense, in reality, but for his notorious reputation. "I'm not lily white," he explained, "but most of the stuff the newspapers reported about me was the bunk and they knew it."

Bennett described his flippant response: "I told him he was by his own admission certainly guilty of cheating the government out of its taxes and that he must have done more than sing loud in church to get all his money."

Maintaining his composure under these trying circumstances, Capone subjected Bennett to a familiar litany of protests and boasts, insisting he had given thousands of dollars to charity, fed the hungry, sheltered the homeless, and given jobs to the unemployed. Once again he invoked the newsboys' strike as an example of his power in Prohibition-era Chicago, claiming that he had received $100,000 for his role in settling the dispute, which he had promptly donated to a hospital. Finally, number 85 raised the issue of obtaining a transfer to a prison on the mainland, where he could serve out the remaining three years of his "short time."

Until this point, Capone had given a credible simulation of sanity, but he lapsed into irrationality when he offered to cut a deal with Bennett. Capone promised "exclusive rights" to a book based on his life; he would tell the director of the Federal Bureau of Prisons everything he knew about gangsters and gang wars. "I'll tell you who to see and where you can check on every-thing I say," number 85 added. "It'll sell and I'll throw in movie rights." In return, all Bennett had to do was transfer Capone to another prison. Taken aback, Bennett demurred. "I'm not trying to bribe you," number 85 assured him. "All I want is for people to know the facts." Bennett quickly terminated the interview. Later, the director learned that Capone, rather than expressing bitterness at the outcome of the meeting, "vowed he would see to it that James V. Bennett was the next attorney general of the United States, perhaps because I could not be bought."

In the end, Bennett's visit to the island proved a bitter disappointment for Capone and for all the other inmates who had pleaded for leniency or better conditions, for once he was safely on the mainland again, Bennett held a press conference and declared, "The convicts in Alcatraz are nothing but a bunch of cry babies who already have more privileges than they deserve. Alcatraz will remain a place of maximum security and minimum privileges." When rumors of his inflammatory remarks reached the cell house, the inmates called another strike, this one heavily influenced by Communist ideology. Johnston retaliated by vowing to starve the inmates who did not return to their assigned tasks immediately; most strikers caved in at this point. Despite the tensions roiling the cell house, the warden persisted in his habit of standing watch unarmed in the cafeteria as the men filed past him after meals. One recalcitrant convict, a bank robber named Barton "Whitey" Phillips, suddenly broke ranks, slugged Warden Johnston in the jaw, knocked him to the ground, and stomped on his head. The blows sent several of the warden's teeth flying. Once the guards finally restored order, the rebel paid dearly for his attack. The bulls beat him mercilessly, and the warden consigned him to months in the darkness of an isolation cell. Phillips emerged a broken man.

Capone was one of the few prisoners to resist the temptation to participate in the strike, but he appeared destined to remain at Alcatraz, imperiled by violent and jealous inmates, until the end of his sentence in 1940. He resumed his monotonous life, spending his days in his cell, making and unmaking his bed, singing softly to himself, and from time to time engaging in conversation with imaginary individuals. As the weeks passed, he became ever more passive and withdrawn, until February 5, 1938, when everything changed for him.

The inmates were on their way to the Gas Chamber for breakfast that chilly winter morning when the food line abruptly stopped. One man was refusing to move. Karpis recorded the scene in his diary: "The obstacle is Al Capone, causing a bottleneck of traffic as everyone stares as they pass him." Everyone in the cell house stopped to watch Capone and to murmur about his bizarre behavior.

> Capone is in a daze [Karpis continued]. I can see he has no idea where he is; the guard on duty is watching him closely. He's dressed for the yard, not the mess hall. His work gloves have been shoved in his back pocket at the last moment and protrude from his coat.
>
> Continuing into the mess hall and sitting down with my meal, I see the end of the line coming through the cell-house door. In the last position, alone and disoriented, Capone shuffles down the middle aisle toward the steam table. Under the strict regulations here no one is ever permitted to be out of his regular position in line.
>
> About halfway down the aisle, Capone staggers, turns looking for help where none exists, and vomits on the dining-hall floor. Two screws escort him upstairs to the hospital. He never returns to population.

Karpis and the other inmates did not understand why Capone was acting this way, but they knew he was suffering from more than a simple case of "stir bugs." It was, in fact, the most violent symptom yet of his advancing case of neurosyphilis. His breakdown signaled that the disease had finally seized control of his nervous system, and he would no longer be able to function normally. Since his arrival at Alcatraz four years before, Capone himself had refused to acknowledge that he was suffering from the disease, but now even he had to admit that something was seriously wrong.

The warden found Capone in the hospital, acting calmly, apparently lucid once again. "What happened to you this morning?" he asked.

"I dunno, Warden," Capone answered, "they tell me I acted like I was a little wacky."

Capone remained in the prison hospital, where a consulting psychiatrist by the name of Dr. Edward Twitchell diagnosed the patient as suffering from "paresis"—paralysis caused by neurosyphilis, and a term that became a euphemism for the disease itself. The doctors told Capone of the diagnosis, who calmly permitted them to perform a spinal tap, the one sure way to confirm his illness. When the fluid was checked (actually double-checked both at Alcatraz and in a San Francisco hospital), the results were unequivocally positive.

Capone's breakdown created an enormous problem for the prison administration. Warden Johnston could say whatever he liked about all prisoners being equal, but number 85 *was* the most famous convict in Alcatraz, and his health problem had to be handled delicately, especially in an era when the word *syphilis* was still not mentioned in polite society, if at all. He was too sick to return to the prison population, but, at the same time, Johnston did not want to let Capone leave Alcatraz. For the moment, he remained under observation in the prison's small hospital ward, located in another wing of the cell house. Word of his condition began to leak out, and after three days of silence from Alcatraz, newspapers received the following terse communication: "It was announced at the Department of Justice today that on February 5, 1938, Alphonse Capone, an inmate of the United States Penitentiary at Alcatraz, became ill. Since that time he has been confined to the prison hospital on the Island. He is still under observation but the doctors have not made a definite diagnosis of the case."

A day later, Warden Johnston received a telegram from a frightened Mae Capone: "DUE TO THE RUMORS WOULD LIKE TO LEAVE AT ONCE SO I COULD BE NEAR MY HUSBAND IF ANYTHING SHOULD HAPPEN THAT HE WOULD NEED ME BUT WOULD NOT LIKE TO MAKE THE TRIP AND FIND THAT HE HAS ALREADY BEEN TRANSFERRED/ KINDLY PLEASE ADVISE ME BY RETURN WIRE COLLECT WESTERN UNION/ RESPECTFULLY YOURS/ MRS ALPHONSE CAPONE/ 93 PALM ISLAND."

In his reply, Johnston tried to allay her anxieties, but he pointedly ignored her request for permission to visit: "HAVE JUST HAD REPORT FROM PHYSICIANS ADVISING ME THAT YOUR HUSBAND IS QUIET, COMMUNICATIVE, COOPERATIVE, APPARENTLY COMPREHENDS HIS CONDITION AND NECESSITY OF FOLLOWING DOCTORS ORDERS AND THUS IT IS NOT NOW NECESSARY TO RESTRAIN HIM THEREFORE DISCOUNT RUMORS/ HOWEVER, THEY CANNOT DEFINITELY DETER-

MINE WHAT CHANGES MAY OCCUR AND THEY DO NOT WANT TO PREDICT/ IN THE
CIRCUMSTANCES I SUGGEST YOU AWAIT FURTHER ADVICE AND IN THE MEAN-
TIME KEEP IN TOUCH WITH DIRECTOR OF BUREAU, WASHINGTON, TO WHOM
REPORTS WILL BE FORWARDED/ J A JOHNSTON."

As word of Capone's breakdown generated headlines in Chicago and across
the country, Johnston tried to contain the growing demand for more detailed
information. Mae and other family representatives called repeatedly to urge
Capone's release, arguing that he was obviously too sick to serve any more
time at Alcatraz. "I had to convince them that he couldn't be released,"
Johnston wrote, "but that he would be given good medical care."

As Mae fretted in Florida, her husband remained confined to the Alcatraz
prison hospital, where he underwent a full battery of medical and psychiatric
tests. It was this examination that revealed, among other things, his perforated septum, the result of his repeated use of cocaine years before. In sum,
the confidential results showed that the Al Capone who had arrived on the
Rock four years before, the man who had been convicted of income tax
evasion, who had been the most visible bootlegger of the Prohibition era, the
nation's most celebrated and feared gangster, Public Enemy Number 1—that
Al Capone was no longer; he had been overtaken by syphilis and was now a
frail and desperately ill man.

UNITED STATES PUBLIC HEALTH SERVICE,
U.S. Penitentiary, Alcatraz, California.
Neuro-Psychiatric Examination.

#85-Az.—CAPONE, ALPHONSE   Informant: Inmate.

White. Male. Married. Age 39. Received at Atlanta in 1932 to serve
11 years for Income Tax Law violations. Transferred to Alcatraz
1934. . . .

Physical: He is a well nourished white man who is 5 ft 10-1/4 inches
tall and weighed 215 pounds on admission in 1934 but has
lost weight recently. His hair is curly and very thin on top.
His complexion is dark and features are regular and definitely Italian in type. There are two linear scars, two and
three inches long, on the left cheek and neck which resulted from knife wounds many years ago. He was treated
for many months in Atlanta for Prostatic trouble. He denies the use of Narcotic Drugs and there are no needle
scars on the body. He has a perforated nasal septum. He
has had two courses of Anti-syphilitic treatment since 1934
and is now taking a third course. His heart action is normal

and his lungs are clear and there are no physical complaints except some headaches which he attributes to Sinus trouble but X ray plates do not bear out that explanation. His neurological examination shows some loss of the normal lines of facial expression. There is a very pronounced dysarthria or defect in articulation which is most noticed on test words such as "Methodist Episcopal" "Roman Catholicism" "Truly Rural" "Massachusetts Legislature" Etc. etc.

The deep reflexes are equal and the knee-jerks are present but diminished. Romerg sign negative. Pupils are unequal and do not react to light but contract very slightly to accommodation. The right pupil is irregular in outline. Station and gait normal. No Babinski. No Gordon. No Oppenheim. No clonus.

On February 5th 1938 he suffered a sudden disturbance of consciousness described as a fainting attack or possibly a Hysterical episode. Very shortly after that he had a definitely convulsive attack described as Epileptiform which lasted several minutes and was followed by stuporous sleep and later mental confusion. During the next few days he became quite disturbed, noisy, restless and twice soiled his room. Within about five days however he became much quieter, regained partial orientation and was tractable. He is at present looking quite clear and is feeling quite well.

Mental: He comes to the examining room willingly and is cooperative and orderly. He appears to be properly oriented. His memory is good except for a period of five or six days recently during which he suffered convulsive attacks. His intellectual development is normal but Psychiatric tests were not undertaken because of the evident loss of ability to concentrate as well as much distractibility. His reasoning ability and judgement show considerable loss of acuity. His voluntary speech is free and circumstantial. He is definitely expansive in mood and has developed extensive plans as to his activities after his release. He is going extensively into Charity work and will build factories and industries etc to furnish employment to everyone needing it. He takes a great deal of pleasure in perfecting these plans and relating them. His mood is happy and he has no enemies he cannot excuse readily for their mistaken views etc etc. He still has some disturbances of consciousness at times as his mind wanders and he hears God and the Angels verbally reply to prayers etc. He however retains partial insight into these and says that he probably imagines some of the things he hears. These experiences are pleasant and he enjoys them and feels friendly toward those about him although he is very unstable and easily aroused by any excitement or confusion taking place on the Ward.

Diagnosis: Psychosis with General Paralysis of the Insane: Expansive type.

June 4, 1938   /s/ Romney M. Ritchey, Surgeon (R), Psychiatrist

.   .   .

Later that summer, prison doctors deemed Capone well enough to receive a visit from his family. It was preceded, as always, by an elaborate letter from Mae asking permission and a terse response from Warden Johnston granting the privilege. The visit was scheduled for August 3, 1938, seven months after Capone's breakdown.

When number 85 was escorted to the visiting area and looked through the peep hole that day, he received perhaps his biggest surprise of his five years in jail, for there, through the glass, he saw a tall young man who bore his features and yet looked almost wholly unfamiliar. It was his boy, Sonny, now nineteen years old. No longer the sweet-faced child in the photograph Capone displayed in his cell, Sonny was a young man, poised and remote. A college student, he was attending Notre Dame under an assumed name. Before he lost his mind, Capone had dreaded this moment: the idea of his son seeing him confined to jail, powerless, had struck him as the ultimate indignity, and for that reason Sonny had never visited him at Atlanta, let alone Alcatraz. But now, when they finally did meet, Capone was no longer capable of feeling shame; in all probability he did not even recognize this young man peering back at him through the glass. Sonny wore a light-weight summer suit, and he was tanned. He had a collegiate air about him; in fact, he looked like any prosperous businessman's son. The last time he had seen his father, Sonny was fourteen, and Capone the king of the Cook County Jail. "He knew his father then as a fastidious dresser, a 'business man' who was flanked by a retinue of eighteen bodyguards," wrote a journalist who had been tipped off to the meeting. "Father and son played together on the floor of the Capones' luxurious apartment. The boy had been lavished with gifts while being kept in seclusion with his mother. But Capone was no longer dressed in finely woven, pearl gray business suits . . . The son looked at a man wearing an ill-fitting prison uniform issued by the toughest prison in the country, and said, 'Dad.'

"Capone reached forward to embrace him. But bars and nonshatterable prison glass separated them. 'My boy,' he said."

In these circumstances, communication was impossible. The visit ended almost before it began. Sonny and Mae were led from the visitors' chamber, past the metal detector, down the switchbacks, and onto the ferry bound for the mainland. "I tried to keep all this from the kid when he was little," Capone later reflected. "I tried to be a good father. I didn't want him to know about me. Now he comes and sees me here, like this. It must have hit him between the eyes."

During his months in the prison hospital, to which he was now confined, number 85 was locked in one of its three "bug cages" for mentally unstable inmates. The cages occupied a corridor running off the ward, and since they were made of wire, they permitted communication between the inmates confined to them, unlike the regular cells with their thick walls. Confined in the bug cage adjoining Capone's was a bank robber named Carl Janaway, formerly the "Terror of the Ozarks." He had gone "stir bugs" shortly after arriving at Alcatraz and had been in the cage ever since. With nothing better to do, Capone and Janaway passed the time haranguing each other.

"When we both get out of here, I'm going to give you millions of dollars, Janaway. I'm going to make you a millionaire," Capone would say, to which the "Terror of the Ozarks" would reply from the safety of his cage:

"Fuck you, Mr. Millionaire!"

And Capone would respond with a taunt: "Bug House Janaway, the millionaire."

Then the shouting would start. "Don't call me that! Don't call me that!" Janaway ordered. "You goddamn dago!"

But Capone repeated the taunt: "Bug House Janaway! Bug House Janaway!"

Overhearing one of these fights, Alvin Karpis could only compare it to the behavior of "two six-year-olds in a sandbox." The next development startled even him, and he found himself witnessing a scene from hell. Janaway picked up his bedpan, reached inside, grasped a handful of feces, and hurled it at Capone. "The missile hits the hog wire separating the two cages," wrote Karpis, "splattering throughout Capone's cell and freckling the body of Scarface like a volley of lead from a machine gun."

Capone howled with anger, quickly retrieved the bedpan in his cell, and threw a handful of his own feces at Janaway. Again it spattered on the wire and covered the victim with stains. Gleeful in their madness, the two prisoners threw one handful of feces after another at each other. "Everything within range slowly changes color as sickly green-brown lumps land indiscriminately, changing the room," Karpis recorded. Two orderlies appeared, but they were reluctant to intervene and became soiled themselves. By this time the cells of both Janaway and Capone had become so fouled that the men were slipping on the floor. At last, when they had exhausted themselves and emptied their bedpans of waste, the orderlies entered the cages, hosed down the "bug cages," and led the men to the showers to cleanse themselves.

•   •   •

By hurling his feces at another prisoner and completely fouling himself, Capone in his madness finally achieved what his family and lawyers could not: his transfer from the Rock. The episode persuaded Warden Johnston that it had become too difficult to maintain number 85 at Alcatraz. The warden asked Dr. Ritchey to reexamine number 85, this time with a view to transferring him to a penitentiary on the mainland. "I now feel that if it could be arranged he should be transferred to Springfield or Leavenworth before the expiration of his time here," Ritchey wrote to Johnston on November 19. "He is in good physical condition and there appears to be no medical objection to his transfer. He is now taking routine treatment [for syphilis] which can be continued in any Institution until his release." Ritchey concluded his evaluation on a resounding note of irony: "He is ambulatory and cooperative and insists he is in better condition than at any time since his confinement." Although the warden now had the medical rationale to transfer Capone, he was still concerned about the impression the move would make; he did not want to appear soft on a notorious criminal and thereby set a damaging precedent. Alcatraz's reputation remained intact, however, because the American people heard a much different version of Capone's situation. On December 20, the headline in the New York Times announced: "ILLNESS OF CAPONE BARS HIS RELEASE—Federal Officials to Hold him and Will Consult Family on Future Steps—HIS CONDITION DANGEROUS."

There was one other element critical to Capone's transfer from Alcatraz, and that was his testifying against his beloved mentor, Johnny Torrio. At the time, the U.S. government was preparing a tax evasion case against Torrio similar to the one Capone had faced. After years of travel and dabbling in real estate, the grand old man of the rackets now lived in obscure but wealthy semiretirement in White Plains, a large suburban community north of New York City. However, the Internal Revenue Service had continued to track him down the years, and the IRS paid special attention to a tip that Torrio maintained a concealed interest in a wholesale liquor dealer—precisely the lucrative sinecure a retired Prohibition-era bootlegger would be expected to hold. Agents promptly appeared at the distributorship's headquarters in White Plains, where they found a man they thought might be Torrio. But the agents weren't sure what Torrio actually looked like (so effective were his efforts to avoid publicity), and the man in question insisted his name was "J. T. McCarthy." Anyone who knew Torrio well would have realized that McCarthy was his wife's maiden name, and the J. T. stood for Johnny Torrio. Eventually the agents figured this out, and further investigation disclosed that Torrio was using his hidden partnership in an otherwise reputable firm to conceal his income and thus to avoid paying federal income taxes.

At this point, Torrio, assuming he was about to be indicted for tax evasion, applied for a passport. Fearing he would flee to Europe at any moment, the IRS became desperate. "We asked the State Department to mail Johnny his passport," wrote Elmer Irey, who led the operation against Torrio, "and when he came to pick it up at the Post Office we arrested him on what are generally described as 'trumped up' charges." Just four hours later, Mrs. Torrio posted bail in the amount of $100,000 cash and freed her loving husband. Meanwhile, the IRS was involved in a paper chase, trying to link Johnny Torrio to an old but incriminating check in the amount of $109; only a nearly invisible bookkeeper's note, "J.T.," tied Torrio to the check, which suggested that Torrio actually bankrolled the liquor dealer for whom he worked under the name J. T. McCarthy.

The government claimed that far more compelling evidence against Torrio came from Al Capone himself. The revelation that Capone, while still at Alcatraz, had become a stool pigeon generated both headlines ("U.S. Reveals Capone Squealed on Torrio," "Capone Aided U.S. in the Torrio Case") and misunderstanding. The facts were these: Capone agreed to give a lengthy deposition to an assistant U.S. attorney named Seymour Klein. The timing suggested strongly that, by cooperating with the Feds, Capone expected to win an early release from Alcatraz, or, failing that, a transfer to another penitentiary. But there was much less to his "squealing" than the government implied. Since Capone had recently been diagnosed as psychotic by Dr. Ritchey and claimed to be on speaking terms with God and the angels as well as inquisitive attorneys, the information he divulged was of dubious value. The fact that he willingly testified against Torrio, whom he had revered and shielded for thirty years, was itself a symptom of mental instability. Klein traveled to Alcatraz twice during January 1939 to conduct his interviews with Capone, but the sessions proved to be a disappointment. The psychotic prisoner spent hours in rambling conversation, contradicting himself, telling Klein whatever he wanted to hear. In the end, the deposition, which ran to fifty pages, was useless. Even without Capone's "assistance," however, the IRS pressed its case in federal court. Torrio eventually pleaded guilty to evading almost $87,000 in taxes, threw himself on the mercy of the court, and spent the next two and a half years at Leavenworth. After his release, he continued to live in obscurity in White Plains, one of the ablest and most notorious racketeers of the century, now an old, forgotten man.

In his epic poem, *The Divine Comedy*, Dante described a hell consisting of twenty-four circles. At the outermost ring were arrayed the lesser sinners; at the innermost, the greatest. Capone's eight-year journey through the federal penitentiary system, from Atlanta to Alcatraz, had been a journey through a modern-day hell. Of all his prison experiences, Capone's betrayal of Johnny Torrio ranked as the most bizarre, the most unlike him. Even in jail, Capone had always been recognizably himself, until this time. In his vision of hell, Dante recognized the gravity of such treachery, for he made the bottom of the pit of hell a frozen lake, reserved for traitors—to their family, their country, their rulers. It was at this state that Capone himself finally arrived. His journey there had been so slow that no one recognized how far he had declined until it was too late to effect a rescue.

On January 6, 1939, several weeks after he gave his capricious deposition about Torrio, Capone was released from the "bug cage" to which he had been confined almost continuously since his final breakdown a year earlier. During that time, he had lived as if he were a laboratory animal, without privacy and without the freedom to do the simplest things for himself; by comparison even his earlier years among the general convict population at Alcatraz had been comparatively unfettered and even luxurious. There appears to be little justification for having confined him to the "bug cage," for he was not prone to violence; in fact, he proved remarkably docile and compliant. That he was not considered especially dangerous at the time of his release can be inferred from the light security on hand during his transfer; instead of the armed guards and armored railroad cars in which he had arrived at Alcatraz four and half years earlier, only an associate warden was present. The convict walked slowly down the switchbacks from the cell house for the last time, looked out across the fog-shrouded bay as sea gulls wheeled overhead, occasionally diving at the waves, and stepped from the prison dock into a launch waiting to carry him across the choppy waters of San Francisco Bay to Oakland.

•   •   •

One of the strengths of the Capone family was that throughout the ordeal of Ralph's and Al's jail sentences it remained a *family*, intact and functioning, if not thriving. In effect, they managed the family business as best they could, and their strength came from their numbers. Al had no less than *five* siblings looking out for his interests; whenever one was incapacitated, the others filled in, and if none of the other Capones was as charismatic, theatrical, personable, persuasive, and intuitive as Al, they were Capones nonetheless. They had already survived the disappearance of the oldest son,

Vincenzo, and they had overcome their grief over the death of Frank at the hands of the Cicero police, but the removal of Al from the field of battle, not to mention his mental deterioration, limited the family's ascent and dynastic ambitions. No one else could quite take his place. The younger brothers—John, Mattie, and Albert—were ambivalent, at best, about devoting their lives to the rackets, for they had seen the price such a life could demand. As for Ralph, easy-going, accommodating Ralph, he simply lacked Al's drive and daring, that thirst for innovation; he was content to be merely a racketeer, hanging around the racetrack and the nightclub, tending to his interests. His equanimity had enabled him to do his time in jail and to resume his life where he had left off. (He also had the good fortune not to suffer from tertiary syphilis.) That was not Al's destiny, though. His drive and cunning were unique, to say nothing of his immense ego. An ego that would never let him rest, that tormented him during his days in jail as it had during his nights on the lam. No one was more acutely aware than Al that he had once been king of the Chicago rackets, the bootlegger to society, the best-connected fixer in the entire city. There was only one Al Capone, as Capone knew better than anyone else. But there was no way he would be able to resume his role, not with the government prepared to hobble him for the rest of his life, and certainly not with his illness.

Although he had finally rid himself of Alcatraz, he had to complete one last year of his sentence. Judge Wilkerson had ordered Capone to serve the time in the Cook County Jail, but the idea of exposing him to a new round of publicity, to say nothing of the potential for further corruption within the jail, prompted the Department of Justice to permit him to serve his final months in the Federal Correctional Institution, Terminal Island, near Los Angeles. Once again, he boarded a launch to reach the island prison, his legs shackled, but with Capone partly disabled from the neurosyphilis, there was little likelihood of his attempting to escape or behaving violently. On arrival, he immediately came under the care of the prison's chief medical officer, George Hess, who ordered him confined to a hospital cell for observation. "During the first few days this patient was definitely confused, indifferent and somewhat depressed," Dr. Hess took care to note. "The depression was punctuated with periods of irritability but he was at all times the same cooperative person as always. His stream of thought was superficial and the speech was slurring in character. . . . His treatment at the time consists of Tryparsamide and Bismuth, each once a week." These medicines could slow the progress of the disease, though Capone's neurosyphilis was far too advanced to be cured.

Under the care of Dr. Hess, Capone's months at Terminal Island passed in a daze. In June, the doctor performed a spinal puncture to check the progress of Capone's neurosyphilis and confirmed that it had advanced far into the tertiary stage. By October, Capone was indulging in paranoid fantasies concerning William Randolph Hearst, the newspaper publisher. "He brands Hearst as a degenerate and claims that Hearst is the one who is the cause of all the adverse publicity in his case," Hess observed. "He then makes the remark that Hearst will not bother him again because they have run him out of the country and have sold his papers." Capone also threatened to expose Hearst in the *Miami Times*, which he claimed to own.

Unlike other prison doctors, Dr. Hess took a proprietary interest in Capone and his welfare. Shortly after the October report, he spoke sternly with Al's youngest brother, John, who with his wife visited Terminal Island. "I have impressed them with the necessity of keeping the patient's activities suppressed at all times," he wrote Bennett. Dr. Hess also offered John Capone advice on treating Capone's neurosyphilis after jail, suggesting that the family investigate the outstanding facilities of the Johns Hopkins Hospital in Baltimore, Maryland. For now, the plans were kept secret; even Al had no idea where he was going after his release. The physician spoke vaguely about a "private institute," and left it at that. He proffered more explicit advice to James Bennett on the best way to handle the logistics of Capone's release from prison: "I would like to volunteer a suggestion that we do not go via Chicago, chiefly because of the possibility of going from one station to another. I believe it would be better to go via St. Louis or any other route where a change of trains would not be necessary."

Days later, Director Bennett briefed the attorney general on the final plans for Al's release and postprison life: "Ralph has now agreed to place his brother under the case of Dr. Joseph E. Moore in the Johns Hopkins Hospital. Dr. Moore is an outstanding specialist in the treatment of general paresis and is also a consultant to the United States Public Health Service on venereal diseases. . . . Dr. Moore, however, is most anxious to avoid publicity with respect to the case. . . . He [Capone] is not to be admitted under his own name and no reference is to be made to the fact that he is to go to Johns Hopkins. I believe that it would be decidedly to the advantage of the Government to cooperate in this matter and therefore suggest that Capone be transferred just prior to the completion of his sentence from Los Angeles to . . . Lewisburg, Pennsylvania, . . . thus avoiding the publicity which would follow were he discharged in California."

Although the prison authorities knew the extent to which neurosyphilis had diminished Capone's mental capacity, the FBI, the Department of Justice, and even the attorney general himself persisted in regarding Capone as a prized source of information about the current state of racketeering. Their stated reason was that despite his condition he provided valuable leads. However, the transcripts of Capone's remarks reveal no usable leads at all, and a more likely reason for the interviews was that none of the authorities

could resist the chance to visit with the infamous Al Capone himself. Even
Attorney General Frank Murphy traveled all the way to California to chat
with the mad oracle of Terminal Island. Needless to say, no racketeer in his
right mind would ever want to meet, much less help such people, but
Capone, having little idea of the consequences of his words and actions, and
flattered by the attention, was happy to oblige. He talked with one and
all—various FBI agents, the attorney general, *anybody* who was willing to
listen. Nor did he merely respond to questions in a tight-lipped evasive
manner; he told the authorities everything he could recall, which was not
much, and went on to weave fantastic stories for them, essentially tales told
by an idiot.

On October 25, 1939, to cite one instance, FBI agent D. W. Magee
traveled to Terminal Island, purportedly to discuss groundless rumors that
Mae Capone planned to divorce her husband. The conversation soon turned
to a current target of FBI scrutiny, the Chicago Motion Picture Operators
Union, which had become infiltrated by Capone syndicate operatives Nick
"Nickelodeon" Circella, Willie Bioff, George E. Brown, and Tommie Malloy. To judge from the FBI's confidential record, the meeting contained
more black comedy than serious inquiry. "Al Capone seemed in high spirits
during the course of the interview," the agent dutifully recorded, "and stated
that he knew NICK (NICKELODEON) CIRCELLA well; that he remembered
GEORGE E. BROWN, but could not place WILLIE BIOFF. . . . He suggested that
his brother RALPH CAPONE would be more in a position to furnish information
on these individuals, and stated that TOMMIE MALLOY had been one of his
men, but MALLOY got out of line and subsequently was killed in an automobile accident, giving Agent a confidential wink of his left eye while making
his statement." Capone proceeded to make even wilder claims, boasting he
had made $10 million during Prohibition, "but stated that he had never been
interested in any vice racket," unlike Johnny Torrio. Capone's statements
appeared clear-cut, but he often became fuzzy and disconnected. He repeatedly asked the FBI agent, "What are we talking about?" and Agent Magee
would have to remind him of the topic under consideration. Later in the
conversation, he boasted about his close friendship with Jack Dempsey and
lashed into William Randolph Hearst. "On one occasion," Capone insisted,
"HEARST had encouraged DEMPSEY to bring him, CAPONE, to HEARST's beach
residence at Santa Monica, California, where CAPONE claims to have witnessed various sexual activities which disgusted him."

Only when he talked about his family, the agent noticed, did Capone
seem happy, especially when it came to Sonny, but even on this subject
Capone's mind teemed with brilliant fantasies, referring to Sonny as a lawyer
and a Notre Dame graduate. "He stated that he received a letter from the
school authorities at Notre Dame informing him that his son was a diligent

student but that he shunned recreation," the agent solemnly noted, as Capone detailed other cherished illusions about his life after his release from prison:

> He stated he was going to his Florida home to join his wife and his son and enjoy a family life. . . . He stated that TOM CALLAHAN, Head of the Chicago Office of the United States Secret Service, was going to accompany him and RALPH CAPONE to Florida. . . .
>
> CAPONE stated that he and RALPH intended to establish four furniture and automobile factories in Florida, and that this would give employment to thousands of people. He stated he did not intend to go to Chicago and neither he nor his brother RALPH was going to engage in any rackets. He stated he and the family owned a lot of stock in the Pabst Brewery; that they had extensive interests in greyhound racing establishments; that he still owned the Colosimo Cafe and the Metropole Hotel in Chicago. . . . He stated they had paid over $300,000 income tax last year.
>
> He continually stated that RALPH CAPONE was making all the plans. He spoke of other connections in the past, naming CLARENCE DARROW as one of his former attorneys. When conversing on old activities and racketeering connections, CAPONE gave confidential, sly winks of his left eye at frequent intervals.

Winking and smiling his way through the interview, Capone could no longer distinguish between truth and falsehood; almost nothing he said was accurate. He had no relationship with Clarence Darrow, nor did he own any part of the Metropole Hotel, which had once served as his base of operations in Chicago. Although Sonny had attended Notre Dame, he had failed to graduate and was not a lawyer. Furthermore, Ralph *did* continue to play a major role in the Chicago rackets. As for the $300,000 in taxes the family had recently paid, that was the amount the IRS recently declared Al *owed* on his release from prison. Agent Magee noted, "CAPONE, during the course of interview, seemed to have plenty of courage and spoke in big figures," but the calculations and bravado came from a man who had lost his mind, if not his heart.

·   ·   ·

"Do you feel the need of prayer?" asked the Reverend Silas A. Thweat of the convicts during the Sunday service at Terminal Island.

Al Capone raised his hand.

"Are any of you here feeling the need of a savior?"

Al Capone stood.

• • •

As the expiration of Capone's sentence approached, his new lawyer in Chicago, Abraham Teitelbaum, made final arrangements, but the actual date of release remained in doubt, for in late October the government reminded Teitelbaum that his client still owed an additional $20,000 fine for income tax evasion. Relying on Ralph's ready access to cash, Teitelbaum paid the full amount "under protest" on November 3 and smoothed the way for Al's emancipation.

The Federal Bureau of Prisons selected November 16, 1939, as the final day of Al Capone's jail sentence. In the morning, his train from Los Angeles arrived at the Lewisburg, Pennsylvania, federal penitentiary, where the Department of Justice, the FBI, and the Federal Bureau of Prisons, in their combined wisdom, had decided to release him. Ralph arranged for a limousine to transport Mae and Sonny to the prison but, wanting no part of prisons and wardens himself, kept his distance. The convict Mae and Sonny retrieved from the Lewisburg Penitentiary bore only a superficial and haunting resemblance to the sleek, confident, well-dressed Capone who had entered the Cook County Jail that long-ago day in October 1931. The man who stood before them now, grinning lopsidedly, a trail of spittle trickling from the corner of his mouth, had the demeanor of a jailbird, timid and wary. He wore drab, shapeless, prison-issue clothing. And then there were the shoes: heavy, dark, clumsy, and institutional. To look at them was to feel the dehumanizing effects of the eight years he had spent in confinement. He had lost weight, but he did not look fit. Only forty, he seemed at least a decade older, his hair thinning, his posture stooped. The glint in his gray eyes had vanished, replaced by an apprehensive dullness. At least his voice was reassuringly calm, but as soon as he spoke it was apparent that his pronunciation was indistinct, his thoughts disconnected. He sounded as though he were babbling in his sleep, and he had only vague recollections of where he had been for the past eight years; in the weeks to come Capone would startle his family with his constant praise of the federal penitentiary system, especially the splendid care Warden Johnston had lavished on him at Alcatraz.

Before they could leave the prison, the Capones had to endure a brief meeting with a prison administrator, in this case Myrl E. Alexander, who as a young warden's assistant had interviewed Capone years before, on arrival at Atlanta. Since Capone was non compos mentis, it was Alexander's assignment to make certain that the family understood that the prisoner's release was conditional and subject to parole regulations. Alexander reviewed the formal conditions of release for the uncomprehending Capone, who sat beside Mae, radiantly happy to see her husband again, and Sonny, dressed incongruously in a white summer suit. Quietly and expectantly they waited for the moment of Capone's freedom as Alexander attached various bureaucratic strings. The parole would last until May 3, 1942, Alexander carefully explained. Until then, the prisoner—they still called him that—would have to report regularly to a parole officer, avoid alcohol and drugs, and so on and so forth, including the condition that he "shall not associate with persons of bad reputation." The clause gave the government considerable leeway in administering Capone's parole, for it could, without stretching a point, conclude that his brother Ralph, formerly Public Enemy Number 3, was a person of bad reputation. Mae and Sonny were afraid to complain about the conditions, and the prisoner himself was too befuddled to understand them. "Capone didn't seem to realize exactly where he was at the time of our final interview," Alexander said later, "and it was obvious that he probably had some memory loss and was not fully aware of his surroundings or the full content of our conversation. He was indeed a different kind of person than the one I had interviewed earlier in Atlanta. That final day at Lewisburg he seemed more pathologically foolish and disoriented."

At the end of the interview, the Capones rose in unison. Mae left the warden's office first, followed by Sonny, and finally Al himself. They walked out of the prison's front gate to the waiting limousine, just like that, without guards, guns, or manacles. "They departed in a limousine parked outside the front entrance to the prison," Alexander recalled, "and that was the last I ever saw or talked with Capone."

Had Capone been able to comprehend his new condition, how he would have savored those first moments of freedom. The cruel paradox of his situation was that once he finally obtained his freedom after eight harrowing years of imprisonment, he could no longer appreciate his deliverance. For the rest of his life, he would be a captive of his severely impaired mental state, unable to function on his own, unable to comprehend, except in the simplest ways, what was going on around him.

Once the limousine bearing the reunited Capone family drove away from the Lewisburg Penitentiary, Al disappeared from public view. Few Americans realized that he suffered from any major health problems, let alone "paresis" or neurosyphilis. At the time of his release, *Look* magazine published a sensational article titled "When I Get Out of Prison: Al Capone Talks," which portrayed him as confident, robust, and ready to go back to work, actually strengthened in mind and body from the ordeal of jail. "Capone is sane," the magazine declared. "He is mentally and physically adjusted to re-enter civil life." The article left the impression that he would shortly return to his Palm Island estate and resume his racketeering. The new attorney general, Frank Murphy, lent the authority of his office to the cover-up, telling reporters that he had visited Capone only last June and found him "physically in perfect condition; he was in much better health than any one

I see in this room." Though he knew perfectly well that Capone was Baltimore-bound, Attorney General Murphy talked glibly of keeping tabs on him in Miami, "where there is already some indication that unsavory characters are assembling, perhaps in anticipation of Capone's visit," the *New York Times* suggested. By spreading these misleading stories, the Department of Justice avoided speculation that his dismal health resulted from his treatment in jail.

The truth was that the Capone family, as they had planned all along, drove Al directly to Johns Hopkins Hospital in Baltimore, where they committed him to the care of Dr. J. Earle Moore, the eminent syphilologist. There Al Capone the ex-convict—a frail, docile man, ignorant of his own predicament—embarked on an unusual course of treatment. While medical opinion decreed his illness was irreversible, the Johns Hopkins doctors were experimenting with advanced drugs and other techniques for treating syphilis. Perhaps a miracle would occur. There was always hope, if nothing else.

CHAPTER 12

After Capone

RICHARD "TWO-GUN" HART was not a religious man by any stretch of the imagination, but when he looked back over his life it seemed an invisible hand had controlled events. When he was a young man, the hand had pointed him westward, away from his family, especially his younger brother Al. Later, as he entered middle age, the hand prodded him back to his past, the family he had renounced, and even the identity with which he had come into this world. The changes occurred slowly, imperceptibly, by degrees that eventually described the arc of his destiny.

After serving as a bodyguard to President Calvin Coolidge during the summer of 1927, Hart spent the next four years wandering from one Indian reservation to the next across the Northwest, chasing bootleggers, getting himself in and out scrapes with the law and the Indians alike. He stood trial at least once more, this time for shooting an Indian fugitive to death. The jury acquitted him, and his reputation as a fearless lawman remained intact. Of all the Capones, he, not Al, was the most violent. Everywhere he went, people knew who he was—or thought they did. The legend of "Two-Gun" Hart was so well known in the Northwest that in the spring of 1930, when he was in Tekoa, Washington, the post office was able to deliver to him a letter bearing no address, merely the word HART and a sketch of two revolvers.

Wherever he went, his ability to contain lawlessness made a memorable impression. He appeared at the Bonner County fairground in Sandpoint, Idaho, in the summer of 1930, where various Indian tribes from northwestern states were holding their annual meeting which was, essentially, a five-day-long party. "They came with ponies, some dragging teepees, buggies, and old Model-T Fords," recalls one observer, Harold Hagen. "They set up their camps in the woods and fields surrounding the fairground. Mostly what they did was gamble, usually blackjack. They spread blankets on the ground, and when night came they hung Coleman lanterns on sticks and kept right on." Only one lawman was there to police the 500 or so Indians who had assembled: "Two-Gun" Hart. As Hagen remembers, "He was dressed Western-style, with his two guns. He didn't mingle much, but he was always in evidence. He appeared to have an easy relationship with the Indians, who seemed to like him. There was a small platform with a four-piece band, and Hart would pick up a fiddle and join in. There was no boozing. Occasionally an argument would start, but before anything got very far someone would threaten to call 'Two-Gun' Hart, and that would end it. In retrospect, I realize the Indians knew all about Hart and had good reason to mind their manners when he was around. But I didn't hear a word of griping about him the times I visited their big pow-wows. I had a real sense they liked and trusted him."

Hart returned to the wrinkle in the prairie he called home later in 1931. The Depression had preceded him. "I just remember the hard times. Real hard times," says his youngest son, Harry. Jobs were scarce in Homer, the winters colder than ever, and with Prohibition heading toward repeal, it looked like "Two-Gun" would soon be out of a job. He was approaching his forties, putting on weight, no longer a young man ready to endure physical hardship for the sake of catching a few bootleggers, and he had a wife and four children to support. But he had few prospects. The flow of newspaper articles recounting his adventures slowed to a trickle; law enforcement was no longer the glamour game it once was. If gangsters and bootleggers died young and rich, it was said, lawmen lived long and died broke. Hart was just beginning to learn the bitter truth of that observation. Indeed, the rest of his life would consist of an often humiliating struggle to make ends meet. He accepted a position as a justice of the peace in Homer, but the pay was low, and he soon found himself accepting the sort of odd jobs he had taken when he had first arrived years before. At various times he painted houses, worked as a paperhanger, and maintained a fish camp. Folks from Sioux City came to the camp, caught fish, and held fish fries. "There was nothing else to do, no work, nothing," recalls Harry of the lean years. "Eventually we got on relief. I used to pick up the commodities in my little wagon."

So the early years of the Depression were not kind to Al Capone's adventurous older brother; in fact, the entire decade would be humbling. There were at least some rewards, however, as his life began to come full circle in ways that seemed determined by divine prestidigitation. The underemployed Hart filled the empty hours with music. "He could make the piano just vibrate," says another family member. He also played the violin, but the mandolin held the most fascination for him. This was an exotic instrument for these parts and one of the few clues to his Italian origins. "He used to sit down on Main Street and play and play, and the old timers who didn't have that much to do would listen," according to Harry. "And I would sing along with him." At about the same time, Al Capone, confined to Alcatraz, was also consoling himself with the mandolin's sweet strains, playing soft tunes to himself by the hour.

Although his mean streak was often in evidence on the job, Hart was indulgent toward his children, especially his youngest. "Things were tough, but he treated me very good," Harry says. A former roustabout, Hart retained his fascination with carnivals, and every Fourth of July found him participating in Homer's festivities, which not even the Depression managed to dampen. Hart also remained on intimate terms with firearms, which continued to play an important role in the family. "I would always go pheasant hunting with him," Harry recalls, "and he was a very good shot. The first time I ever went out with him my dad had a pump shotgun, and he got up and bing-bing-bing he got three of them before the other guy even got off a shot. He was that good. He taught me how to shoot a gun, how to handle guns. You don't point it at anybody, and I've always taught my grandkids how to handle guns because I've been around guns all my life."

Occasionally Hart returned to playing the role of lawman and exhibited flashes of his former intensity, which made a lifelong impression on Harry. "Gypsies used to come to Homer every year on horseback. They always had their caravan, quite a few wagons. There's a place south of town where they always stayed. My dad knew the head guy real well at the Gypsy camp. Old man McKinley, who lived near the camp, got to hollering about them. 'Dick, Dick,' he said to my dad, 'those so-and-so's they got my billfold.' My dad got ahold of the head Gypsy and told him, 'You give that billfold back to him. If I catch you. . . .' Dad, he made 'em give it back." On another occasion Hart brought his passion for justice to bear on one of his children. "My brother Bill used to get these lids off coffee cans, and you know he'd sail them. He sailed one out and hit a guy's car across the street. The guy complained, so my dad put Bill right in the jail cell and locked him in for a day.

"I can remember one of the guys in the jail telling my dad that if he didn't have these two guns on him he wouldn't be so tough. When he heard about that he took everything off, the handcuffs and everything, got in the jail cell, had the guy lock the jail cell, and then he went ahead and showed the guys how tough he was with his fists. The other guy was going to whip him and beat the hell out of him, but he didn't get the job done. My dad didn't back down from anybody. The other guy didn't wake for a while."

By 1933, everyone in Chicago and for that matter throughout the Midwest was in a froth of excitement over the new world's fair. For Chicago, the exposition was squarely in the best tradition of boosterism, announcing the beginning of a new era, one that had nothing to do with the Depression or racketeers. If Al Capone symbolized the old Chicago, a city of gangsters and corruption and violence, the world's fair symbolized the airy promises of the future. For a city and a nation badly in need of good news, it proved a whopping success, attracting over 5 million visitors. Among them was Richard "Two-Gun" Hart, who paused to have his photograph taken in full Western regalia: sitting tall in the saddle, wearing a buckskin jacket and riding boots. When he left the exposition, he donned more conventional clothing and made the pilgrimage to his mother's house at 7244 Prairie Avenue and accepted a contribution from Ralph to help him get through the year. From then on, he returned to Chicago from time to time, and Ralph always came through. Thanks to this money, "Two-Gun" Hart was able to feed his family, to keep a roof over their heads, and to outlast the ravages of the Depression. He was still on the family dole, still living with his family in Homer, Nebraska, when his younger brother Al was finally released from prison in November 1939.

· · ·

"Al Capone, the eminent Chicago racketeer, is a patient at the moment at the Union Memorial Hospital. He is suffering from general paresis, the end result of a syphilitic infection," noted H.L. Mencken, the writer, editor, and critic, in his diary on November 29, 1939, two weeks after Capone arrived in Baltimore. The announcement that Capone had finally won his freedom had inspired newspapers across the nation to commemorate the events with overstated and inaccurate headlines—"Capone is Free After Seven Years—Al Has Lost Even His Hair," "Al Capone, the Greatest Gangster of Them All, Comes Out," "Capone Smuggled to Freedom: Disguise Worn to Dodge Rival Gangsters"—but Mencken was much closer to Capone and to the truth of the racketeer's plight. Himself an eminent hypochondriac, Mencken happened to be a good friend of the physician who treated Capone, Dr. Joseph E. Moore, an associate professor of medicine at the Johns Hopkins Medical School, and Dr. Moore confided details of Capone's medical condition to the writer, who reviewed the tragic course of the racketeer's syphilis.

> Capone says that he was infected very early in life and assumed for years that he had been cured. . . . His wife has apparently escaped infection. The symptoms of paresis began to show themselves in Capone during the early part of his imprisonment. He was then locked up in Atlanta. The medical officers there wanted to make a lumbar puncture to ascertain his condition accurately, but Capone refused. In 1937, after he had been transferred to Alcatraz, he suddenly developed convulsions.

They are often the first sign of paresis. He was put on malaria treatment, but after nine chills the convulsations [sic] returned and became so alarming that the treatment was abandoned. By that time Capone, who is not unintelligent, had been convinced that his condition was serious and so he made arrangements for intensive treatment after his release. Dr. Moore was recommended and hence Capone came to Baltimore.

Mencken was above all a brilliant iconoclast, and he had long railed against the follies and hypocrisies of Prohibition, so for him Capone was not simply a gangster to be reviled and discarded; he was, at the least, an interesting case history, and possibly considerably more than that, as much a product of the American way of life as Charles Lindbergh or Henry Ford. However, many members of the medical community felt differently and took the unorthodox position of refusing to treat Capone.

Dr. Moore [Mencken wrote] planned to enter him at the Johns Hopkins Hospital and Wilford Smith, the superintendent, consented, but the lay board of trustees made objections and so Capone was sent to the Union Memorial Hospital instead.

Almost the same thing happened there. The medical board was in favor of receiving him, if only on the ground that a first class hospital should take in every sick man and waste no time upon inquiring into his morals. . . . After Capone got to hospital the women of the lay board began setting up a row, led by Mrs. William A. Cochran, whose husband is a pious Prohibitionist and wowser. As I write this row is still going on, but Capone remains at the hospital. The lady uplifters argue that his presence is keeping other patients out of the place. The medical board replied that that is unfortunate but unavoidable. It argues that a hospital as a matter of ethics can't refuse any sick man who applies for treatment.

Moore has put Capone on the malaria cure and at the moment it seems to be working very well. Capone has already developed a temperature as high as 106 degrees.

The "malaria cure" Capone received was generally reserved for only the most serious cases. Dr. Moore inoculated his patient with the expectation that malarial fevers would raise the body's temperature and destroy or at least inhibit syphilis. This particular treatment had a fairly exotic pedigree. Decades earlier, Russian physicians noticed that nearly all their officers who returned from duty in the Caucasus Mountains had syphilis. However, none of the men who also had malaria developed the deadly tertiary syphilis. Of course Capone already had tertiary syphilis, so the treatment, while dramatic and seeming to offer relief in the short run, offered no long-term benefits.

When Mae learned that the hospital was actually giving Capone malaria, she became hysterical and claimed the doctors there were trying to kill her husband. Because this treatment involved allowing the fever to persist so that it could counteract the syphilis, her fear, while misplaced, was understandable. The usual treatment involved giving the patient tertian malaria, which produced a fever and chills every other day. However, it became apparent that Capone was immune to that particular version of malaria because he already had been inoculated with it in jail. Instead, he received inoculations for quartan malaria, which produces symptoms every fourth day. Even this treatment produced limited success; it killed the spirochetes that had been slowly eating away Capone's central nervous system and turning his brain to jelly, but there was no way to reconstruct the nerve cells destroyed by neurosyphilis. It was beyond the ability of any physician to restore his mental abilities and his personality.

Mencken continued:

I am told that he bears the accompanying discomforts very philosophically and is, in fact, an extremely docile patient. His mental disturbance takes the form of delusions of grandeur. He believes that he is the owner of a factory somewhere in Florida employing 25,000 men and he predicts freely that he'll soon be employing 75,000. This factory is, of course, purely imaginary. Otherwise Capone's aberrations are not serious. He is able to talk rationally about his own condition and about events of the day.

He is occupying two rooms and a bath at a cost of $30 [a] day. He sleeps in one room himself and the other is a sort of meeting place for his old mother, his three brothers and his wife. The brothers spend the days playing checkers, with occasional visits with the patient. They made an effort lately to rent a house in Guilford but were refused when their benefactor became known.

The mother, an ancient Italian of the peasant type, can barely speak English. The brothers, all of them apparently born in this country, are relatively intelligent fellows. The wife, who is ignorant but apparently no[t] unintelligent, moves a cot into Capone's room every night and sleeps there. He has two night nurses and one day nurse. He is naturally very popular with the hospital staff and especially the orderlies, for he is not only a good patient, he is also likely to leave large tips.

His chills come on every second day and Moore plans to keep him in bed here until he has had fifteen of then. He will then be transferred to Miami. The Federal Bureau of Investigation has notified Moore that so far as it knows there is no project on foot to kill Capone. Thus no guard upon him is maintained and any visitor to the hospital is free to barge into his room.

Capone's syphilis treatment at Union Hospital sounds like a medically sanctioned, premature hell, as if he were getting a head start on atoning for his sins. Actually, the reason for the apparent medical madness inflicted by Dr. Moore on Capone was simple enough: raising the body's temperature helps to kill infection, just as having a fever does. The fever treatment caused a temporary neurologic remission, and physicians noticed that patients afflicted with syphilis seemed to improve when they had a fever. The procedure, which had been around since the First World War, involved placing the patient in a so-called fever box, in which the heat steadily rose until the body temperature reached 105 degrees. The treatment amounted to nothing more than a glorified sweatbox, and while it might have helped Capone behave better, it could not cure his neurosyphilis.

There was one other treatment for syphilis, and researchers in the field had been aware of it since the 1920s: penicillin. While it was known that the penicillin mold could inhibit the growth of bacteria, specific medical applications did not develop until World War II, when the U.S. government supported research in this area as part of the war effort. Thus several more years would pass until Capone finally received the most effective syphilis treatment of all, but even if he had been given penicillin from the day he arrived at Union Memorial Hospital, the outcome of his treatment would have been precisely the same, for penicillin can only arrest the disease; it cannot not reverse its effects.

If any good came out of the agonizing treatments Capone underwent at Union Memorial Hospital, it was that his health ceased to decline. There were no more breakdowns, and he recovered his emotional equilibrium, although the improvement might have been the result of his leaving prison. Once Capone's condition stabilized, he moved from the hospital, where, as Mencken noted, he was vulnerable to intruders, to a secure rented house in the Baltimore neighborhood of Mt. Washington. Even though he was living once again under the same roof as his family, the ordeal of his syphilis treatments continued. Once a week, Dr. Moore's junior partner, Dr. Paul Padget, arrived to give Capone a spinal puncture to test his spinal fluid for the presence of spirochetes. The procedure involved inserting a needle between the vertebrae in the lumbar region and drawing the spinal fluid. Dr. Padget performed the procedure in the presence of several Capone bodyguards, who dumbly observed the pathetic spectacle of the once-great "Snorky" reduced to a state of affable helplessness. The results of these tests demonstrated the inevitable: after a certain point, the treatments failed to improve Capone's condition. By this point, he lacked the mental capacity to evaluate the meaning of these results or to care for himself. Still, he was capable of basic functions. He could talk. Walk. Eat. Recognize people well known to him. When he hallucinated he usually kept his visions to himself and those around him were not aware of his departures from reality. He was generally genial and cooperative, no longer subject to wild mood swings or outbursts of violent temper. Nor did he complain or indulge in self-pity, partly because he was unable to comprehend that he *was* permanently disabled, which in a way was a mercy.

As Capone underwent his syphilis treatments, James V. Bennett, the head of the federal penitentiary system, continued to harass his former inmate. On December 21, he wrote to Dr. Moore to warn that Capone would have to satisfy his tax bill before the doctor could receive his fee. "I presume you realize that the government has been trying to collect $300,000 in back income tax from your client," Bennett advised. (Actually, the amount the government claimed Capone owed was $201,347.) "They have not succeeded in finding any property on which the levy can be made. He has had some rather intelligent attorneys, and I dare say it will be terribly difficult to find anything tangible in the records of the Treasury Department." The letter failed to discouraged Moore or the hospital from treating Capone, whose medical expenses were paid by Ralph out of his share of the proceeds of the rackets in Chicago.

After four months of syphilis treatment in Baltimore, Capone and his family bade farewell to Dr. Moore and the other men in the long white coats, and Al was driven to Florida, to the house on Palm Island where he had always planned to retire from the rackets. When he arrived on March 22, 1940, he readily adjusted to his comfortable new surroundings, though he gave no indication that he remembered them from his previous life. "Although the former gang leader must stay in bed most of the day," the *Miami Herald* reported, "he is able to sit in the sun and walk around for short periods behind the high walls of his estate. However, he cannot go out sightseeing or even go swimming in his ornate tiled swimming pool, because all forms of exercise are forbidden. While he lies in beds and fights to regain the cocksure energy that pushed him to the top of the racketeering in the prohibition era and afterwards, Capone's chief diversions are reading and listening to the radio. He avidly reads newspapers, particularly the stories concerning himself."

When he regained his strength, he tried to play a little tennis on the lawn, but he was not really up to the game anymore, and golf was out of the question for a man in his condition. Now and then he played pinochle with "the boys," but it was painfully apparent that the calculations demanded by the game were beyond him, and the other players were careful to give him every advantage. When he was inadvertently beaten, the old Capone briefly flared. "Who's this smart guy?" he shouted. "Tell the boys to take care of him." No one lifted a finger anymore; everyone realized the poor old man was out of his head. Still, Al appeared content, sitting on the dock overlooking Biscayne Bay, dressed in pajamas, his hair graying and unkempt, a fishing pole stuck in his powerful hands, to all appearances an old man passing the time, each day an exact replica of the one that had come before it and the one that would come after it. He was forty-one years old.

Since the day the police had shot his brother Frank to death on the streets of Cicero, Al Capone believed himself doomed, but he was mistaken about the form of the ruin that would be visited upon him. Assuming that he would die like Frank, Al had spent most of his adult life on the run, living with a fear that drove him to take security measures the likes of which no other racketeer took. Because of his caution, and his luck, he contrived to escape the doom he knew—sudden death from gunfire—only to fall victim to the doom he at first refused to acknowledge and later failed to comprehend because it had destroyed his mind: slow death from tertiary syphilis. In this way Capone finally did fulfill his vow to quit the rackets—but at a steep price. He had to lose his mind before he was able to find peace.

Even if Capone had not been afflicted with syphilis, even if he had come out of jail stronger and sharper than ever, it was a different world now, and he would not have been able to return to business as usual. Law enforcement agencies were far more sophisticated in their understanding of how the rackets operated. Prohibition—the nation's great gift to gangsters—was long gone, and the racketeering landscape had changed. Once Capone's domain had included most of Chicago, as well as bootlegging and racketeering networks reaching all the way from New York to the western states. He had residences throughout the city, as well as hideouts in Chicago and in Lansing, Michigan. Wherever he went, his mistresses, bodyguards, and flunkies were ready to do his bidding. He administered his empire with the meticulousness of an accountant and the ruthlessness of a gunman. He befriended entertainers of every description and bankrolled Chicago's booming jazz scene. But all that was over now, part of the past, a memory, a yellowed newspaper clipping. While the Capone family still owned the little house on Prairie Avenue, Al rarely returned to that address, and he never again visited the little cottage at Round Lake, near Lansing, or the Burnham Wood golf course, where he had whiled away the sultry summer days playing crooked gangster golf. Nor did he return to the haunts of his Brooklyn boyhood, now the spawning ground of a new generation of racketeers. His large suite at the Lexington Hotel, decorated with portraits of Lincoln, Washington, and that other distinguished public servant, "Big Bill" Thompson, was long gone. His world had shrunk to the Palm Island villa, which Ralph had managed to snatch from the jaws of the IRS.

As Al passed his days deep in delusion, oblivious to the world at large, the press still covered the Capone phenomenon, though with a new ghoulish fascination. As a former inmate of Alcatraz and a victim of syphilis, he was doubly stigmatized. Even the newspapers were reluctant to print the word *syphilis*, preferring to use the gentler term *paresis* to describe his condition. There was talk of his "brain paralysis" and "chronic nervous system ailment." To respond to journalist inquiries, the family selected John "Mimi" Capone to act as spokesman. Two years younger than Al, John had only a marginal involvement in the rackets. As the most nearly legitimate member of the Capone family, he was thus the most respectable and presentable. John discharged his awkward assignment capably enough, telling curious reporters that Al was "tickled to death" to be back home in Florida and explaining, "We arrived . . . after driving straight through in about twenty-eight or thirty hours. We left secretly because we didn't want anything to happen that would aggravate Al's condition"—a polite way of saying that the family did not want Al to be killed now, after the long years in prison.

Although the Capone family lived peacefully and privately, the Miami office of the Federal Bureau of Investigation kept the compound under surveillance and reported its findings to J. Edgar Hoover. FBI agents interviewed neighbors, and unnamed members of the Capone household who were in position to observe Al at close range. The result of their prolonged investigation was a lengthy file that painted a full portrait of Al Capone in his premature dotage, surrounded and protected by his extended family. The household, according to the FBI report, included Al, his wife, Mae; his son; Mae's sister, Muriel; and Muriel's husband, Louis Clark. "It was determined through informants that Muriel and Louis have the complete confidence of Al and Mae Capone and are fully aware of the past and present activities of the Capone family," the report observed, noting the presence of two domestics, a "houseman" named "Brownie" Brown and a maid known as Rose. The Capones maintained an unlisted phone number, 5-5050, and just one automobile, a "1941 aquamarine colored Pontiac sedanette . . . which is used as the family car." There was no sign of any weapons on the property, no rifles, revolvers, or machine guns, only an "old, but exceedingly alert small fox terrier dog . . . which barks when anyone approaches the gates."

The FBI also maintained a permanent vigil over the other members of the Capone family living in the vicinity, especially Capone's only child Sonny, who was beginning to make his way in the world. Albert Francis Capone was still hard of hearing, the legacy of his father's syphilis; despite his disability he had entered Notre Dame in 1937, going by the name Al Brown, which was, pathetically enough, one of his father's old aliases. He was living out the highest ambition of Al Capone and many other racketeers: to see their sons grow up and attend college, become real Americans, and enter business, politics, one of the legitimate professions—in short, to *assimilate*. The irony was that Sonny was unable to follow this path precisely because his father was "Scarface" Capone. Not long after the young man entered Notre Dame, his true identity was discovered, and the embarrassment forced him to drop out. All the love and concern Al had lavished on his son could not protect Sonny from the notoriety of the Capone name. Through this inescapable stigma the sins of the father were visited on the son.

Returning to Florida, Sonny entered Miami University under his own name and worked haphazardly toward a degree in business administration, which he finally received in 1941. The following year, according to the FBI account, he moved from Palm Island to his own home with his wife, Ruth, and their two children. At the same time he became involved with the war effort even though he was classified 4-F because of his deafness. The report continued: "He operated a floral shop on Miami Beach from September 1941 to March 1942 and is presently employed by the War Department at the Miami Air Depot, having entered on duty there August 9, 1943, as a mechanic's learner at a salary of $1,200 per annum. He is now employed in the aircraft engine line assembly at a salary of $2,680.00 per annum, attached to the maintenance division." The inevitable question was whether Sonny Capone would become a racketeer himself, but for the moment the FBI was satisfied that the young Capone was completely legitimate, exactly as his parents wished. Their report stated:

> An examination of his personnel record at the Air Depot reflects that he is viewed as a conscientious employee who has at no time exhibited any tendencies to be other than a normal, law-abiding citizen. . . . From all sources it was determined that ALBERT [i.e., Sonny] has never been involved in any illegal activities, gangsterism, or enterprises of his father. It is known that both AL and MAE have made a determined and conscientious effort throughout the life of the boy to shield him from such influences that surrounded AL and to preclude any possibility of his, ALBERT's, falling into a life of crime. It is apparent that MAE has exerted a great deal of effort to see that ALBERT led a clean life.

Nonetheless, Sonny remained attached to his parents, as the family life unfolded under the watchful eye of the FBI:

> There is an extremely close bond between AL CAPONE, his wife, ALBERT, and ALBERT's family. It is, of course, well know than the CAPONE family

is a closely knit unit. AL and MAE make numerous visits each to AL-
BERT's home, and on days which these visits do not take place, ALBERT
and RUTH usually have dinner with AL and MAE several nights a week.
It is known that one of the paramount interests in AL's present life is the
welfare of ALBERT's two children, for whom he is constantly purchasing
gifts. This feeling, of course, is equally shared by MAE who supplies
RUTH with money on numerous occasions to augment the income of
ALBERT. RUTH is presently expecting another child. . . . It is known
that RUTH M. CASEY, mother of ALBERT's wife, is a chronic alcoholic,
causing considerable embarrassment to the entire family, but she has
no interest in attempting to remedy her present condition. . . . Al is a
habitual cigar smoker, preferring 25 cent Coronas. He leaves the house
almost daily, sometimes attends to the shopping and accompanies his
wife to drive up to his son's home for frequent visits.

So much had changed in the Capone family since Al's parents—Gabriele,
a barber, and Teresa, a seamstress—had emigrated from Naples to New York
half a century earlier—so much violence, notoriety, and tragedy—but one
thing had not changed. The Capone family endured, and *campanilismo*
endured. Indeed, on Palm Island the definition of *campanilismo* expanded to
include various members of the Coughlin family, who braved the Capone
stigma to be at Mae's side. Mae's brother, Danny Coughlin, had business
interests strongly suggesting that he was at least on the fringe of the rackets in
Miami, for he was associated with the local Bartenders' and Waiters' Union
and ran a couple of restaurants, Winnie's Little Club and Winnie's Waffle
Shop—both named for his wife Winifred. "It is known," the FBI reported,
"that police characters, confidence men, hoodlums, and visiting gangsters
are habitues of both establishments." How much Danny understood is open
to question, for he was afflicted with a severe drinking problem, to the
chagrin of the Capones and the Coughlins alike.
    For all its tranquillity, life on Palm Island was not quite so pleasant and
innocent as it seemed. A constantly changing cast of racketeering characters
came down from Chicago to visit the Capone family. They made small talk
with Al and did business with Ralph and John Capone, who continued to
look after the family interests. Even when it knew the names of the visitors,
the FBI was frequently unable to identify their role in the post-Capone
rackets. Then there were the suspicious phone calls to Chicago, of which the
FBI was also aware through its extensive wiretapping of the Capone household, but once again the purpose of these messages eluded federal agents.
Attempting to learn more, they would "interview" Mae from time to time,
but she did an admirable job of feigning ignorance and blocking the course
of their inquiries even as she presented the appearance of wanting to help.

One thing was certain, however. Every week Ralph Capone sent a registered letter to Mae from his hunting lodge in Mercer, Wisconsin. Each letter contained a check in the amount of $600 made out to Mae Capone. As far as the FBI could tell, this was her only source of income, and no doubt it was but a tiny fraction of the organization's revenue from the Chicago rackets.

Like Mae, everyone in the Capone home lived in fear of further inquiry into those rackets, especially by federal agents. "The CAPONE family hold no particular regard for local law enforcement agencies, but have an exceedingly respectful fear of any Federal investigation, particularly one conducted by this Bureau," the FBI boasted.

In the spring of 1944, the Capones' relatively peaceful existence in Florida was shattered when one of the younger boys, Matt, got into a bad scrape up in Cicero. Of all the brothers, he had seemed the most likely to escape the racketeering environment and make something of himself in the legitimate world, but he had failed to live up to those aspirations. Now thirty-six, Matt spent his days running the Hall of Fame Tavern in Cicero and putting on weight; he might as well have hung a sign around his neck reading "No-account younger brother of a once-famous gangster." On April 18, two employees at the Tavern, Jens Larrison and Walters Sanders, got into a brawl over a $5 bill supposedly missing from the till. There were perhaps twenty people in the tavern at the time, and as they later told police, they saw Sanders push Larrison into the back while Matt looked for something in a drawer. Next thing they knew, the place reverberated with the sound of gunfire. Matt took off, and police found Larrison's corpse in an alley far from the scene of the crime. Wanted for questioning, Matt compounded his problems by going into hiding, and his absence gave law enforcement officials an excuse to go snooping through the Capones' affairs all over again. They turned up nothing of interest, and the case against Matt Capone collapsed when the star witness, Sanders, also disappeared. After a year, Matt resurfaced, his aspirations to legitimacy thoroughly discredited. From then on, law enforcement authorities all knew Matt Capone had once been involved in a murder, and the event would shadow him for the rest of his life.

Notably absent from Palm Island—and from the FBI files—were Capone's mother, Teresa, who continued to reside on Prairie Avenue in Chicago, and Mafalda, the only Capone sister. She remained in Chicago, where she ran a bakery and catered weddings and other family affairs. In her later years, she became, in the words of a Capone family intimate, "a rough customer. Ornery. She cussed a lot. She was altogether different from Al, who was cool, calm, and collected, at least until he got his dander up. She ran the show, not her husband. She was heavy, but still good-looking."

In contrast to the profane Mafalda, Mae Capone became increasingly pious as time went by. She rarely ventured out by herself except to attend

Mass, which she did at least four times a week at St. Patrick's Cathedral in Miami Beach. One can only surmise what blessings, what forgiveness, what mercy she requested in her prayers. Of all the Capones, she was the most diligent observer of the code of *omertà*; not once did she yield to the temptation to give an interview in defense of her husband.

At the beginning of 1945, Al Capone became one of the first civilians to receive penicillin as a treatment for syphilis, although, as his doctors knew, his disease was too advanced for him to gain any real benefit from the treatment. In April, the ever-vigilant FBI noted his continuing disintegration: "Al speaks very rapidly, slurring his words together with a slight Italian accent and is exceedingly difficult to understand. . . . He constantly hums, whistles and sings while engaged in conversation, and it is difficult for him to coordinate his thoughts, moving rapidly from one subject to another in disconnected fashion. He has become quite obese but is very active, walking with jerky movements. . . . He is, of course, shielded from the outside world by Mae." In sum, the Capone family considered Al to be "mentally ill and incapable of handling serious or weighty problems, and efforts are made on all sides to humor him as far as possible. He is pampered to a considerable degree and is believed to still view himself as the underworld king he once was in Chicago, becoming greatly excited and irritated when his every wish is not immediately fulfilled."

As the Capones adjusted to exile in Florida, their old allies and enemies in the Chicago rackets made news, beginning with the spectacular murder of Edward J. O'Hare, one of the government's most valuable informants. It was O'Hare, Capone's silent partner in dog tracks, who had warned Frank Wilson that the jury set to hear the income tax case was fixed, thereby prompting Judge Wilkerson to bring in a new jury. Had O'Hare kept silent, there is every reason to believe that the original jury would have acquitted Capone. Since the trial, O'Hare had conducted his dual career as a racket-backed sports promoter and as a government informer, and he had prospered. He continued to manage racing interests for the Capone organization—with the end of Prohibition and bootlegging, those interests had become more important than ever—and in return for his loyalty he had been appointed president of Sportsman's Park in Stickney, and he had secretly become a director of the newly formed Chicago Cardinals football team, for whom he negotiated and affixed his signature to a lucrative radio contract. Although it was no secret that O'Hare maintained close ties to the Capone organization—the information cropped up every so often in the *Tribune* and other newspapers—he escaped prosecution in part because he honored his deal to keep Wilson supplied with information and in part because he conducted himself like a legitimate businessman rather than a hoodlum. Not only that, but his adored son, Butch, had made it to Annapolis, graduating as the specter of another world war loomed. The other important person in O'Hare's personal life was his mistress (his "fiancée," in the newspapers), Sue Granata, whose brother rather conveniently sat in the state legislature. In token of their relationship, O'Hare wore a treasured memento she had given him: a watch inscribed "*Amor Sempiternus* [Love Everlasting] Ed–Sue."

During the days just prior to Capone's release from jail, O'Hare had been carrying a pistol, a .32-caliber automatic, suggesting that he feared reprisal for having become a snitch. Although none of the other government witnesses in the Capone tax trial had been killed, O'Hare's case was special, for he alone had voluntarily come forward, and his warning to Wilson that Capone's men had gotten to potential jurors had undoubtedly altered the course of the trial. Still, O'Hare went about his business as usual. On Wednesday, November 8, eight days before Al Capone was released from jail, O'Hare left his office at Sportsman's Park, entered his car, and was driving himself along Ogden Avenue, a busy Chicago thoroughfare. He was planning to leave for Florida, where he was developing new racetrack ventures. His pistol lay on the seat beside him, and his wallet contained just $53. Suddenly a car sped past him, and one or more gunmen fired two rounds of buckshot, instantly killing O'Hare, whose car veered out of control, jumped the curb, and charged along a set of trolley tracks, finally crumpling against a trolley pole. In all respects, the murder of Edward J. O'Hare had been the work of professional assassins, and despite intensive investigation their identities were never discovered. After his death and the revelations that O'Hare had been both a front man for the Capone organization and an informer, it was suggested—through never confirmed—that his death was intended as a gruesome "gift" to Capone on his release from jail.

After his father's death and the wealth of scandal it generated, Butch O'Hare, now a Navy fighter pilot, was determined to redeem the honor of the family name. His great moment arrived in the early, desperate days of World War II. On February 20, 1942, while piloting a Grumman F-4 "Wildcat" over the Pacific, he encountered nine Japanese twin-engine bombers. Taking his plane through a series of dives and loops, he managed to shoot down five of the Japanese bombers and to disable a sixth; the other three were downed by aircraft carrier fire. This feat of bravery earned him the distinction of becoming one of the first true heroes of the war, and in April he received a Medal of Honor; President Roosevelt described Butch O'Hare's actions as "one of the most daring, if not the most daring single action in the history of aviation." Edward O'Hare did not live to see his son's medal, nor did he ride beside him in the parade Chicago gave for him, nor did he witness the strange coda to these events. When the cheering died away, Butch startled everyone by returning to action in the Pacific, always seeking another moment of heroism, although it seemed to some that he wanted more than mere heroism, that because of the exceptional burden his father had placed on him, he was seeking martyrdom. He finally found it on November 26, 1943, when his plane was shot down in the South Pacific, never to be recovered. He was twenty-eight years old at the time of his death, and he received a fitting memorial. In 1949, Chicago's newly expanded airport, known as Old Orchard Field (a name that survives only on Chicago-bound baggage tags marked "ORD"), was renamed for O'Hare, whose father's involvement with Capone had been forgiven or forgotten by then. The dramatic christening ceremony was highlighted by a mock bombing raid and a skywriter spelling out his name in the air. The prime mover in the campaign to name the airport after Butch O'Hare was none other than Colonel McCormick, the publisher of the *Chicago Tribune*, who had once waged an earlier campaign against Butch's father's business partner, Al Capone.

The violent death of Edward O'Hare offered convincing proof that gang warfare persisted in Chicago and that Capone himself—or those around him—had good reason to fear for his safety. There would always be the possibility that some enemy of his who had been lying in wait for eight years, or longer, was now preparing to avenge some wrong by taking aim at him. Furthermore, even though Al had retired from the rackets and from the world in general, the Capone *family* certainly had not. Ralph continued to act as the nominal head of the clan, and he continued to exert influence in Chicago. Although the Capones had long ago quit the Lexington Hotel, which had fallen on hard times, Ralph owned interests in nightclubs and hotels throughout Chicago, especially on the South Side and in Cicero, those traditional Capone strongholds, and in Mercer, Wisconsin, where he maintained a bar. Age had mellowed "Bottles," and he was now known not as Al's loutish, insecure brother but as an elder statesmen of the rackets, a link by virtue of his name to the late, great Prohibition era. In fact, the entire period was coming to be seen with increasing tolerance and even a touch of nostalgia, as if its murderous gangsters—"Scarface," Dion O'Banion, "Hymie" Weiss, Jack "Greasy Thumb" Guzik, Frank "The Enforcer" Nitti, Fred "Killer" Burke, "Big Jim" Colosimo, "Machine Gun" Jack McGurn, "Bugs" Moran, "Schemer" Drucci, and so many others—were no more than colorful scoundrels, their lives a bloody vaudeville.

Jack McGurn's last years illustrated what happened to gangsters who outlived their time. After Al went to jail, life was not the same for McGurn. Although he had orchestrated the St. Valentine's Day Massacre, arguably the crime of the century, he no longer enjoyed the patronage of the Capone organization. He fell on hard times, and Louise Rolfe, the "Blonde Alibi" whom he had married to escape prosecution for his role in the St. Valentine's Day Massacre, abandoned him. The day before Valentine's Day, 1936, found him at a bowling alley at 805 Milwaukee Avenue in Chicago. Two gunmen burst in and shot him to death in front of twenty witnesses. The timing of the event strongly suggested that the assassination was "Bugs" Moran's revenge for the Massacre, but the killers were never caught, although they left a calling card in the form of a crude poem placed in McGurn's lifeless left hand.

> You've lost your job
> You've lost your dough
> Your jewels and handsome houses.
> But things could be worse, you know.
> You haven't lost your trousers.

Frank "The Enforcer" Nitti also fell on hard times. While Capone was in jail, he had been shot and nearly killed during a quarrel with two policemen. Once he recovered, he ran afoul of the Feds, who reindicted him for tax evasion, along with the surviving members of the Capone organization, all of whom were prepared to offer him up to the government as a sacrificial lamb. Isolated from friend and foe alike, Nitti cheated them all by shooting himself to death on March 19, 1943, the only Capone racketeer of any consequence to commit suicide.

Exactly one year later, "Big Bill" Thompson, the most colorful and corrupt mayor Chicago had ever seen, died of pneumonia shortly after waging an unsuccessful campaign for governor of Illinois. At the time of his death, it was revealed that this dedicated public servant, who had never earned more than $22,500 a year as the mayor of Chicago, left an estate worth nearly $2 million, most of it in banknotes and gold certificates crammed into strongboxes.

"Bugs" Moran, who had escaped his appointment with death at the St. Valentine's Day Massacre in 1929, lived on and on, although his career was much diminished. He reverted to the petty burglaries of his youth, and in 1956 the FBI finally caught up with him and arrested him for a bank robbery he had committed years before. Moran died in Leavenworth Penitentiary in February 1957 of lung cancer and was buried in the prison's cemetery.

Many other racketeers managed to dodge the law as nimbly as they ever had. Under the leadership of younger Capone lieutenants such as Murray "The Camel" Humphreys, who succeeded Al as Public Enemy Number 1, the rackets continued to thrive in Chicago. Of course the nature of the game had changed, along with the rest of American society; bootlegging no longer figured in the racketeering equation, but many former bootleggers had become semirespectable liquor distributors and saloon owners. Gambling and prostitution still flourished under the management of the rackets, and political payoffs, while more discreet, remained a fact of public life in Chicago.

The racketeers had become more sophisticated in their business dealings with the passage of time; they now sought to control unions and financial institutions, and many of them—or their sons—passed into the legitimate sphere altogether, bidding farewell to the old ways, even the old neighborhoods, and, no doubt, the old thrills.

The complicated network of overlapping rackets formerly known as the Torrio organization, later as the Capone organization or the syndicate, was now called the Outfit, the name by which the Chicago rackets are known today. In many ways, the Outfit resembled its predecessors. For one thing, it was based in Chicago Heights, Al Capone's old refuge, and the ultimate boss was still Frankie La Porte. Now that Al had lost his mind, La Porte wanted all the Capones to remain quiet and out of sight. That was the way La Porte preferred to do business; he had learned the lesson Johnny Torrio had known by heart, that in the rackets publicity led to disaster. It proved to be a successful strategy, for only those in the rackets guessed at his importance. As for the inhabitants of Chicago Heights, Frankie La Porte intimidated them all into silence. They were afraid to speak his name, let alone reveal his identity to the police. Under his leadership, the Outfit reverted to the traditional racketeering style. Once again it became secretive and clannish, with little of the flamboyance that had marked Capone's reign. No one would ever make a movie about Frankie La Porte, for he avoided publicity with the zeal that Al Capone had once displayed in seeking it, but he remained the most powerful and capable racketeer of them all, the true heir of Johnny Torrio's embattled empire.

•   •   •

In Homer, Nebraska, things had gone from bad to worse for Richard "Two-Gun" Hart. By 1940 he was so broke that he could not afford to pay the light bill, and the power company was threatening to shut off the electricity. Once again he had to swallow his pride and appeal to his brother Ralph Capone for financial assistance. Instead of money, he received an invitation to visit Ralph at his summer retreat in Mercer, Wisconsin. It was a long drive from Homer, Nebraska, to the woods of northern Michigan, but Hart had no choice.

When he arrived in Mercer, Hart was welcomed by Ralph, a few of the boys from the old days in Chicago, and, unexpectedly, his mother. It was quite a homecoming, and, to judge from the new clothes he bought for himself, quite profitable, too. When Hart returned to Homer he wore a spanking new Panama suit, and his pockets were stuffed with $100 bills. His transformation astonished his sons. They had never seen a $100 bill before, and now their father had an entire roll of them. When they asked where he had come by all this money, he suddenly grew stern and secretive, telling them he had taken a job with the government, but he could not reveal what it was, since the nature of his work was a military secret.

In the months to come, Ralph continued to forward money to the lost Capone brother, and when Hart ventured north to Wisconsin the following summer he was in for a shock, for there was Al himself, tan and robust. The brothers had not seen one another since well before Al went to jail, and Hart noted that his younger brother did not seem to be all that sick and weak from "paresis." In fact, he looked healthy and happy; he just didn't have much of a memory. But, the Capones rationalized, who would after spending all those years in Alcatraz? No doubt the guards had beaten him silly while he was there, and that was the real reason why he was a little funny in the head.

Later, Hart brought three of his boys, Bill, Sherman, and Harry, who were teenagers now, to visit the Capone family in Wisconsin, and the family spent the whole summer together. When Hart and his children reached Mercer, they were met by their Uncle Ralph, who had a surprise in store for them. "We drove down a highway quite a bit," Harry recalls, "way back into the timber, and then we came to a gate, and I started to get out an open it, but Ralph said, 'Wait a minute.' Pretty soon a guy comes walking out, and he opens the gate. We close it and go on in. It's like a resort town in there, a beautiful place, all cabins, and it's nice and everything, and then I was sitting at a table between Uncle Ralph and Uncle Al"—Al Capone, the uncle he had never met but knew only through rumor and legend and who, the boy began to realize, was the ultimate source of his father's mysterious, newfound riches. "We were in a great big room," Harry continues, "and there were about twenty people or so sitting around the table and in the middle there was a lazy Susan turning with all the food on it, and if you wanted anything you just turned to it. I didn't know it at the time, but I was sitting with all the bigwigs from Chicago that night. They were having a big meeting."

As the Hart boys came to know their Uncle Al, they discovered that he was nothing like the Al Capone in the movies and newspapers. He was no gangster, he was a stocky, gentle man who wore khaki pants and a work shirt and had always had a kind word. Just a great big gentle lovable bear of a man. (Several years later a reporter asked Harry if he was afraid of the notorious Al Capone. "Why should I be?" Harry replied. "I had no reason to be scared of him. He was my uncle.") The boys used to wrestle with Al in the lodge, all the kids piling on top of Uncle Al, one after the other, trying to hold him down. He didn't realize his own strength. And then when they were still gasping for air he would give the boys a $100 bill, tell them to go and buy him some cigars, and keep the change. They couldn't help but like him. Nor were they aware that he was a sick man; to the young Harry, he looked "the picture of health." And a friend whom Harry took along on the trip to Mercer came away with this impression of Al: "He was a big man, very friendly and outgoing. He was in a fine mood, very happy. He did not appear to be in poor health; he looked just fine." Despite these impressions, Al's health was more precarious than it appeared; he was incapable of tending to himself and still lived in a perpetual daze.

After the weeks in Mercer, Harry traveled to Chicago to become acquainted with another part of his lost family, his grandmother Teresa, who still lived in the house on Prairie Avenue, where he spent three of the strangest, most fascinating weeks of his life. The name of the street was about the only thing that reminded Harry of home, however, for, as he quickly realized, he was among virtual foreigners. His grandmother Teresa knew a few words of English, but she mainly spoke Italian, which he couldn't understand, since he had not realized until recently that his father came from Italy. Occasionally Richard would say, "Now mother, talk English so we understand you."

So the Capone family survived, and, for Teresa, surely, the best part was having all her children together again, not just Ralph, Matt, Mimi, Mafalda, and Albert, but also Al, who slipped into Chicago now and then to visit her, and Richard, who with every passing year was becoming less of a "Two-Gun" Hart and more of a Vincenzo Capone. Of course, in a family gathering of this size, there were bound to be strains. Mafalda, for instance, made no secret of her dislike of Vincenzo, that traitor and deserter, posing as a marshal and a Prohibition agent, of all things, when the real family interests lay on the other side of the law, and she also resented Ralph's generosity. The way she looked at things, the more money Ralph gave Vincenzo, the less would be left over for her.

There was also a "little tension," as Harry recalled, between Al and his lost brother, but how could there not be, when the two of them had spent their lives on opposite sides of the law? Vincenzo expressed no remorse for having abandoned the family as a teenager, nor would he admit that he had lived a lie since then. And when Ralph pointed out some of the good things racketeers did, how they fed hungry Italians (including Vincenzo) during the Depression and supported churches and other charities, all from the proceeds of a little harmless gambling and other vices in which people would engage regardless, Vincenzo refused to go along with this line of reasoning. For him, the law was the law, and he liked enforcing it. When his brothers pointed out that it was the law, the Chicago police, to be exact, who had killed Frank Capone as he walked down a street in Cicero in broad daylight, Vincenzo had nothing to say. Prohibition was over, so what difference did it make? Nothing would bring back Frank. The other Capones hoped Vincenzo's sons wouldn't turn around and become cops. No, their father assured his brothers, the boys had their own ideas. Now that they were all reunited, the

Capone family would try to stay that way, because that was how they started out, and, in the end, all they had was each other.

· · ·

Ever since that day in 1932 when he had seen Al Capone off to the Atlanta Penitentiary, it had been Eliot Ness's fondest wish to become an agent for the Federal Bureau of Investigation. And why not? What better candidate than Ness, with his degree from the University of Chicago and his experience as a Treasury agent in Chicago during the last years of Prohibition, collecting evidence of Capone's bootlegging activities? He was truly a scholar-policeman.

Only one man blocked the fulfillment of that dream. He was J. Edgar Hoover, the director himself. Awaiting his appointment to the FBI, Ness drifted from one law enforcement position to the next. 1933 found him in Cincinnati, Ohio, working in the local Prohibition agency, but with repeal now a reality, the job was a dead end. He was thirty, the Depression had eliminated jobs in the private sector, and he was growing desperate. At this point he contacted his former boss, George E. Q. Johnson, the U.S. attorney in Chicago, to write a letter of recommendation to J. Edgar Hoover. Unfortunately, Ness had no way of knowing that Hoover still harbored a dislike of Johnson, based on the irrational belief that the prosecutor had stolen the FBI's thunder during the effort to put Al Capone in jail. In any event, the U.S. attorney wrote to Hoover. "During the Government's investigation of the Capone case," Johnson said of Ness's work with the Untouchables, "he had a special division working which reported to the United States Attorney; under his direction these men did a splendid piece of work. His integrity was never questioned and I recommend him to you without reservations." Few things could do more damage to Ness's prospects at the FBI than a letter from Johnson, and inevitably Ness's application was not approved. But that was not the end of his involvement with the Bureau. Now that Hoover associated him with Johnson, the FBI regarded Ness as a troublemaker and began to maintain a confidential file on his activities, as it would with any other individual suspected of breaking federal laws. As the years went by, the file expanded to include Hoover's numerous handwritten comments, mostly warning his men to have nothing whatsoever to do with Ness. "Beware of Ness," he advised. It was Hoover's eternal frustration that Ness was widely assumed to have spent at least part of his career as an FBI agent, and Hoover went out of his way to assure everyone that Ness never worked for the Bureau. But Hoover's interests went beyond setting the record straight. The critical tone of his comments about Ness and the FBI reports on his activities make it clear that Hoover regarded Ness not as a lawman but as a dangerous

and reckless vigilante, and for the rest of his life the director waged a propaganda war against Ness and his reputation as a gangbuster.

Having put his dream of working for the FBI aside, Ness accepted a
position as director of public safety in Cleveland, Ohio, on December 12,
1935. Just weeks before, a reform mayor, Harold Hitz Burton, had taken
office, and he quickly made his most important appointment, that of Eliot
Ness. The choice proved an immediate success, for the corruption-weary city
was delighted to have the young, handsome former Treasury agent who
billed himself as the nemesis of Al Capone. "CLEVELAND: MEET THE MAN WHO
BROKE CAPONE," declared a newspaper headline. Taking office on a wave of
reform, Ness was charged with the task of driving the rackets out of town and
reviving its tired police department. He now had responsibility for the safety
of the nation's seventh-largest city, with a population of just under a million.
At the time, Cleveland was known as a haven for racketeers, most of whom
had used the profits of bootlegging and gambling during Prohibition to
purchase political power. Although Cleveland had no one to equal Al Capone, the city was honeycombed with brothels and gambling dens, and its
police department was widely acknowledged to be corrupt and ineffectual, its
equipment obsolete. For all these reasons Ness faced daunting challenges on
taking office, but he delighted Clevelanders with the bold measures he took
during his first months on the job. He transferred half the sergeants on the
force and more than a third of the patrolmen. He fired officers for drunkenness and ordered weapons to be brought up to date. He staged raids—
highly publicized in the papers, of course—on local roadhouses and
gambling dens. Because he was young, handsome, and married (to Edna
Staley), Ness became known as a man on the go in Cleveland, achieving the
celebrity that had eluded him in Chicago. He cultivated close relationships
with reporters, especially Ralph Kelly of the *Cleveland Plain Dealer* and
Clayton Fritchey of the *Cleveland Press*. In fact, he became so close to
Fritchey that the editor of the *Press*, Louis B. Seltzer, allowed the reporter to
work with Ness on a full-time basis as an investigator. In return, the newspaper received a never-ending series of exclusives. The unorthodox arrangement allowed Ness to reach Clevelanders without submitting to the scrutiny
of an independent journalist. It meant that every article concerning his
activities amounted to a press release. And it meant that no one challenged
Ness. In a city battered by the Depression, Eliot Ness's latest exploits against
local racketeers always made for colorful, upbeat reading, and the newspapers all spelled his name correctly now. After only six months, the *Cleveland
News*, reviewing Ness's report to the mayor, editorialized, "There is one
interesting—very interesting—paragraph in the report of Cleveland's safety
director. We quote a simple sentence: 'Cases of vandalism totaled 89 this year

as against 300 for the same period last year.' For that single sentence, Mr. Ness, you are entitled to take a bow."

Ness's youth and good looks helped his popular appeal. Still slender, his hair full, and his eyes glimmering, he looked like a hero as he gave his interviews and feigned modesty. Even as he went about the serious business of flushing out Cleveland's gamblers, prostitutes, and crooked policemen, Ness cultivated his image as a gangbuster by addressing impressionable audiences, for whom he inflated his deeds in Chicago to heroic proportions. "Thousand Young Dick Tracys Thrill and Cheer As Ness Tells How G-Men Got Capone Gang," ran a representative headline in the *Cleveland News*. The audience consisted of children, who, before receiving their Dick Tracy badges, had to submit to a lecture by Ness about his exploits on the trail of Al Capone. When Ness finished, and they received their souvenirs at last, Ness told the cheering throng, "You have a badge just like mine, only maybe yours is a little smaller. When you grow up to be a man with long pants perhaps your badge will grow up with you, and when that time comes I'd like to have you all working for me as real detectives." Thus Ness indoctrinated a new generation. According to a reporter who was present, "The enthusiasm was uncontrollable."

The defining moment of Ness's early career in Cleveland occurred on the frigid night of January 10, 1936, when he was summoned to a raid in progress on the Harvard Club in Newburgh Heights, one of the city's best-known gambling dens. The county prosecutor, Frank T. Cullitan, had begun the exercise earlier that evening by trying to break down the club's steel door, but he and his men were driven off by James "Shimmy" Patton, one of the owners, who wielded a machine gun with conviction. Cullitan and his men retreated to a nearby gas station, where the prosecutor called for backup, only to be refused by local law enforcement agents. In desperation Cullitan called the safety director, Eliot Ness, and when Ness tried to assemble a raiding party, *he* met with the same reaction, obviously the result of payoffs and politics-as-usual in Cleveland. Even Harold Burton, the reform mayor responsible for appointing Ness, refused to assist because the prosecutor was a Democrat while the mayor happened to be a Republican. Undeterred, Ness went to a nearby police station, recruited a group of twenty-seven volunteers (an ad hoc Untouchables), and drove to the Harvard Club, pausing only to tip off reporters that he was about to generate headlines for the morning edition.

When all was in readiness, he strode to the barricaded doorway, knocked, and announced, "I'm Eliot Ness. I'm coming in with some warrants." As Ness liked to tell it, he then summoned all his expertise in jujitsu and with a mighty kick broke down that steel door, charged inside and, once more drawing on his skill in the martial arts, knocked down a gunman about to blast him to kingdom come, whereupon the Harvard Club emptied. According to the *official* version, however, after Ness knocked on the door, he and his men stood around in the freezing cold for five minutes or so, until the door opened (without a kick), and a man wearing a tuxedo approached Ness and demanded, "Who the hell are you?" Ness replied by flashing his badge and walking past the bouncer. The only violence, according to the official report, was a scuffle between one of the club's employees and a couple of reporters. Since more than five hours had elapsed since Cullitan had begun the raid, its patrons were long gone, taking most of the gambling apparatus with them. Nevertheless, the newspapers told of the safety director's heroism as he took the notorious gambling den by storm, adding another episode to the fast-gathering legend of Eliot Ness. He was now the most visible public servant in Cleveland, his reputation eclipsing even that of Mayor Burton. It was only a matter of time, people said, until young Ness ran for mayor of Cleveland.

In his lust for publicity, he traded on his reputation as a former Untouchable by establishing an elite cadre of undercover agents in Cleveland whom he dubbed the "Unknowns," and he set them to work wiretapping and shadowing elected officials and police suspected of corruption. Since the Unknowns operated behind a veil of secrecy, their mere existence gave them extraordinary power to intimidate; they became, in effect, his secret police. Yet their investigations turned up relatively little in the way of scandal and corruption, and in the end the only public official forced to resign was Ness's own assistant, John Flynn.

To make matters worse, Ness also failed to solve Cleveland's most notorious crime problem: the so-called torso murders. Over a period of two years, a serial killer had murdered and dismembered at least six victims in the Cleveland area. Although each corpse had been mutilated, the dead were a varied lot: male and female, black and white. The lack of a common thread hindered investigation, although each murder caused a sensation and inspired a massive manhunt for the culprit. Through it all, Ness failed to make a useful contribution. Although he was quick to tip off reporters to flashy raids and investigations of police corruption, he ducked questions concerning the torso murders. His behavior suggested that he had no interest in a matter of public safety, even one as pressing as the torso murders, unless he could use it to reap personal publicity.

By 1938, the reputation of Eliot Ness, once the darling of Cleveland, or at least its newspapers, had entered a decline. His stock sank even lower when he announced that he and Edna were getting divorced; his terse public comment on this sensitive issue—"We both realized a mistake was made, and we set out to correct it"—alienated many of the city's Catholics. His name was mentioned in connection not with police work but with the women with whom he had been seen even before the announcement of his divorce. In fact, Ness was spending an increasing amount his time at two posh watering holes, the Bronze Room at the Hotel Cleveland and the Vogue Room at the Hollenden Hotel, where the management reserved a table for their prominent regular, who was generally with a pretty young companion. Indeed, women adored him. Marion Hopwood Kelly, who was married to Ralph Kelly, Ness's good friend, remembers him as "the sexiest man I'd ever known. He used to say to me, 'I'll never forget the first time that I saw you. You were wearing a red dress.' I was just so flattered that anybody remembered me for anything." It was not his virility that appealed to women or even his good looks so much as a certain lost boy quality about him; women did not want him to make love to them so much as they wanted to mother him.

Ness's romantic dalliances were invariably linked to alcohol—lots of it— for only when he drank did he feel relaxed enough to lower his guard, a guard he had learned to maintain since childhood, when his mother and sister had ruled his fate. He consumed six or eight drinks in the course of an evening, and like many an alcoholic, his tolerance was high, and he rarely appeared drunk, merely relaxed, pleasant, and flirtatious. Yet the spectacle of the city's safety director (and former Prohibition agent) spending night after night in a lounge, drinking with an ever-changing cast of women, created the wrong impression. His newspaper pals told him to ease the pace of his drinking and dating, which by Cleveland standards bordered on the scandalous, but he ignored their well-intentioned warnings, preferring to divert himself with bizarre practical jokes. One night he invited the governor of Ohio, Martin L. Davey, and Dan Moore, another state official, to join him for a drink. While the men chatted, a man in the lounge began to cause a stir by trying to sell drugs. In reality, Ness had hired an actor to play the dope pusher, who took to his role with a will, provoking another patron to violence. Appalled by the sordid doings, Governor Davey fled the scene, climbing down a fire escape to make sure no one saw him. Ness enjoyed his prank, but his behavior was completely at odds with his professional responsibilities and his reputation. On another occasion he bugged his apartment just before hosting a party for about two dozen of his friends. Among the guests that night was Marion Hopwood Kelly. "When the party was nearing the end," she recalls, "he told us what he had done, and he began to play back the recording. On it, we heard women talking with other women's husbands. He managed to pick up quite a lot, and even though it stopped short of scandal, it wasn't a very nice thing to do. People were not amused. They were not amused with that at all."

There were other lapses in judgment, all the more surprising to those who witnessed them because they ran counter to the image Ness took pains to project. A particularly embarrassing episode began when he ran a red light in Cleveland's Italian district and one of the residents shouted abuse at him. Ignoring police procedure, Ness pulled over and got out of the car. His antagonist approached him and suddenly slammed Ness's head between the car and its door. Assisted by a policeman, Ness went to nearby University Hospital for stitches, but he refused to file a complaint against his attacker, even though the cop urged him to take action. No, said Ness, he didn't want this kind of publicity, and he didn't receive it. The local reporters remained loyal to their friend, and they kept all mention of this and similar incidents out of the papers. Even so, the word got around that the safety director was capable of strange behavior, and the talk about Eliot Ness running for mayor died away.

In late 1938, Ness, now thirty-five, returned to form, at least for a while, by directing a series of raids uncovering the largest numbers racket in the city. The leads produced by these raids led him to investigate the inner circle of Cleveland's rackets, the Mayfield Road gang, led by Morris Barney "Moe" Dalitz, who had served his apprenticeship with the Purple gang in Detroit, where he had distinguished himself as a bootlegger and bookkeeper. Arriving in Cleveland, Dalitz quickly rose to the top echelon of the Mayfield Road gang, which, as everyone in town knew, maintained headquarters in suite 281 at the Hollenden Hotel. The reign of the Mayfield Road gang came to an abrupt end in April 1939, when Ness appeared before a grand jury, which in turn indicted no less than twenty-three racketeers—men such as Charles Polizzi, "Big Angelo" Lonardo, and "Little Angelo" Scirrca. The Mayfield Road gang was never the same after that. Many of its members, including Moe Dalitz, fled Cleveland, which was a victory for Ness. However, as the years passed, they moved west, not stopping until they reached Las Vegas, where under the direction of Moe Dalitz they transformed that desert hamlet into a gambling empire.

By this time Ness was seen most often with a woman named Evaline McAndrews, an illustrator and former model. Evaline was twenty-seven, alluring, divorced, and a former student at the Art Institute in Chicago; in fact, some said she had originally met Ness during those days. On October 14, less than a month before Al Capone was released from Terminal Island, Ness and McAndrews wed secretly in Greenup, Kentucky. "Ness' Bride to Keep House—and Career, Too," declared the *Plain Dealer* on their return. The newlyweds moved into an apartment on Lake Avenue, and when Eliot returned to his office in City Hall, Evaline resumed her job at Higbee's department store, where she drew fashion illustrations. For a time, the union was blessed with happiness. "Evaline liked being Eliot's wife when he was a famous and influential public official," a friend once explained. "She liked his prominence and power and fame. He loved her, no question about that.

He always called her 'Doll.' " Theirs was not a conventional household, for they were often joined by another woman, who acted as Evaline's bodyguard. She looked the part, tall and muscular, and had once worked as a bouncer in Florida, and, as a publicity stunt, married a dwarf. The three of them—Eliot, Evaline, and the female bodyguard—were often spotted around Cleveland, raising eyebrows wherever they went. This arrangement was altogether too Bohemian for Cleveland, whose citizens expected Ness to live up to his fair and square reputation.

Two days before Capone won his freedom, Ness's boss, Mayor Harold Burton, won reelection and shortly thereafter launched a successful campaign for senator. (In 1945, President Truman appointed Burton to the U.S. Supreme Court.) Under Burton's replacement, Edward Blythin, Ness was rarely heard, rarely seen, and nowhere near as active in public affairs as he once had been. He and Evaline moved into a showy boathouse in Lakewood, and Ness frittered away his time attending parties and drinking; he was much more likely to be seen in a tuxedo than wearing a shoulder holster. Behind his genial façade, Ness was a man haunted by ghosts of the past, especially the shade of Al Capone. Entering his late thirties, no longer the boy wonder of law enforcement, Ness began to reminisce about his days in Chicago chasing Public Enemy Number 1 and the vanished world of the Prohibition era. The more he reminisced, the more he embellished his tales until it seemed that he had managed to knock off the Capone empire singlehandedly.

Capone's malady also haunted Ness, who launched a crusade against syphilis at a time when the disease was still not discussed in polite society. Growing restless with his job and with Cleveland, Ness yearned to move on to better things, but he was blocked at the FBI by Hoover's intransigence. In his boredom, he pursued this public health issue in the hope that it would lead to a new career. He became a consultant to the Federal Social Protection Program. The position allowed him to travel to Washington and establish contacts designed to further his career. Borrowing a tactic from the Chicago Crime Commission, he began calling venereal disease "Military Saboteur Number 1." Although Ness's concern was foresighted, his zeal struck his friends and coworkers as quixotic and more than a little peculiar. "Most were genuinely puzzled as to why a man with Eliot's virtues—a brilliant mind, an engaging personality, a reputation for integrity—would commit his time and talents to a cause as unconventional and unrewarding as curbing the spread of social diseases," writes Steven Nickel in *Torso*, an account of Cleveland's most famous unsolved murder case—a case, incidentally, that remained unsolved at the time Ness undertook his public health crusade. By 1941, his indifference to public safety became an issue, and when a Democratic mayor took over City Hall, rumors circulated that Ness's days in office were numbered. His enemies, and he had acquired many by this time, insisted on replacing him with someone who enjoyed the blessing of J. Edgar Hoover and the cooperation of the FBI.

Ness had come to a difficult pass in his life, and it was then that he self-destructed in a spectacular manner. On the night of March 4, 1942, he chose to mark the publication of a lengthy article on syphilis in the *Annals of the American Academy of Political and Social Sciences* by drinking the night away at the Vogue Room with his wife and another couple. When the lounge closed, the revelers repaired to a hotel room for more drinking, and not until 4:30 in the morning did Ness and Evaline leave for home. Tired and drunk, Ness drove quickly along Bulkley Boulevard (now West Memorial Shoreway), trying to negotiate the icy road in the dark. He lost control of his car, went into a long skid, and crashed into another car, injuring the driver, twenty-one year-old Robert Sims. Ness staggered from his car, determined that Sims was still alive, and left the scene of the accident, refusing to give his name, although Sims had the presence of mind to note the license plate: EN-3. This distinctive vanity plate was known throughout Cleveland, and police quickly tracked down Ness.

For once his friends on the newspapers were powerless to protect him, and the scandal of Eliot Ness, director of public safety, involved in a hit-and-run accident while under the influence of alcohol filled the city's dailies. After maintaining silence for several days, he held a press conference in which he offered lame excuses for his behavior. Yes, he had been drinking. No, he was not drunk. And as for the accident, "It was very slippery and the thing happened just like that." He did further damage to himself when he claimed he had planned to follow the injured driver to the hospital but was distracted by his wife, who'd had the wind knocked out of her. In sum, he insisted, "There was no attempt at evasion in any particular." Few believed him, and a cry for his resignation went up. Ness successfully maneuvered to avoid prosecution for the accident, but on April 30, 1942, he resigned in disgrace. One of the few voices raised in his defense belonged to Clayton Fritchey of the *Press*, whose farewell assessment attempted to put the Ness record in the best possible light. "Cleveland is a different place than it was when Eliot Ness became the safety director under former mayor Burton late in 1935," Fritchey reminded his readers.

For instance:

POLICEMEN no longer have to tip their hats when they pass a gangster on the street.

LABOR racketeers no longer parade down Euclid avenue in limousines bearing placards deriding the public law enforcement in general.

MOTORISTS have been taught and tamed into killing only about half as many people as they used to slaughter.

During his seven years as its safety director, Cleveland had seen many sides of Eliot Ness: his thirst for publicity and his bold raids, as well as his curious lapses, his drinking and skirt chasing. In the end, his vices outweighed his virtues, and his law enforcement career in Cleveland, once so promising, so full of excitement and headlines and raids and Dick Tracy badges, came to an ignominious end. Hailed as a gangbuster by the time he was twenty-nine, he seemed destined to accomplish great things in law enforcement. At thirty-nine, he was looking for work.

He persuaded Evaline to move with him to Washington, D.C., where he successfully lobbied to become the director of the Federal Social Protection Program. The couple lived there during the war years, trying to maintain their marriage until, in 1944, Evaline moved to New York and resumed her career as an illustrator. As the end of the war approached, Ness returned to Ohio without fanfare, this time to manage the Diebold Safe & Lock Company, located in Canton. Initially, he made a favorable impression in his new post, restructuring the company and overseeing a merger with a competing entity, but he was constantly plagued by marital problems.

Even before Evaline divorced Ness on grounds of gross neglect and extreme cruelty he became involved with Elizabeth "Betty" Anderson, another woman with an artistic bent. She was a graduate of the Cleveland Institute of Art; like Ness, she was divorced and, like Ness, a heavy drinker. Betty became Ness's third wife on January 31, 1946, and they later adopted a son whom they named Robert Warren Ness, but fatherhood did not prove to be a happy experience for him. By now Ness had left Diebold, left Cleveland altogether, and moved with Betty and the child to New York, where he became an executive with an import company. He had an office in Rockefeller Center, an annual income of $24,000, and a lingering reputation as a former law enforcement wunderkind, sufficient even now to bring him publicity in magazines such as *Fortune*, which noted that he "carefully avoids the appearance of being a young man in a hurry." Yet he was still given to boasting. "My business affairs are in such excellent shape that I do not have to worry about a livelihood," he explained to Richard Maher of the *Cleveland Press*, adding, "I have some ideas about public service—and I want to try them."

In July 1947 Ness reappeared in Cleveland to run for mayor as a Republican. In explaining his reasons for seeking the office, he declared that at the time he resigned as director of safety five years earlier, Cleveland was a "vibrant, spirited city, interested in accomplishment and improvement. . . . I have returned to find it, by comparison, a tired and listless town; its air filled with soot and smoke; its streets dirty and in a most deplorable condition; its transportation system noisy, inadequate, and approaching insolvency. The equipment of its police and fire department is poorly maintained; its traffic moves painstakingly and with confusion; newspapers indicate that Cleveland streets are unsafe after dark. . . . Cleveland is going backward instead of forward." Although he had been absent for a long spell, Ness's candidacy was backed by such old friends as Ralph Kelly and Clayton Fritchey, whose newspapers rehashed the highlights of the candidate's career as safety director while downplaying any reference to the hit-and-run accident that had brought about his resignation, his failure to find the torso murderer, or his several marriages. He amassed a war chest estimated at $150,000—three times greater than that of the Democratic candidate, incumbent Thomas A. Burke—and plastered the city with his campaign slogan, "Vote Yes for Eliot Ness." He was always a man of promising starts, and his candidacy proved to be another example of that phenomenon. As the campaign wore on, he appeared to lose interest in the contest. His speaking appearances were notably lackluster, and his drinking had taken its toll on his demeanor and his appearance. The once-agile Ness looked flabby, ill at ease, and distracted during the final phase of the campaign. He continued to fraternize with pals in the opposing camp, such as Al Sutton, who now held Ness's old job. "He'd come up to my office," Sutton says of Ness's strange behavior, "and I'd say to him, 'What are you doing here?' You're running for mayor and I'm Safety Director for Tom Burke [Ness's opponent]. He's about fifty feet from here. Will you get out of here and don't come back!' "

Then came election day. Although Ness had outspent his rival by more than a three-to-one margin, he received only 86,000 votes as compared to Burke's resounding 168,000. It was a disgraceful showing for Ness, who failed to understand how he could have lost by such a wide margin. He tried to give the appearance of taking defeat in stride, even to the point of attending Burke's victory celebration, where he personally congratulated his rival. In the next instant, bitterness overcame him, and he remarked, "Who'd want an honest politician, anyway?"

Although he was only forty-three when he lost his bid to become mayor of Cleveland, Eliot Ness never recovered from the humiliation. He tried and failed to return to one of his former positions in business. There was talk of his becoming police chief of Detroit, but he lost the job because of his political ambitions. A year after the election, he returned to Cleveland for the fourth time to ask about an opening that paid only $60 a week, a fraction of his former salary. Ness did not get even this humble position. He moved from job to job, from bar to bar. He never put down roots, he always moved around, as if he were trying to find himself, or run away from himself.

• • •

Al Capone's health remained strong enough for him to see the end of World War II, though he displayed little comprehension of what that struggle had been all about, even though one of his nephews, "Two-Gun" Hart's boy, Richard Jr., had been killed in the Philippines in 1944. During the war years Capone occasionally went to restaurants with his wife and a bodyguard or two in the Miami area, looking dapper in a white straw hat, with a rose stuck in his lapel. There was a time that Capone would have taken over an entire restaurant, or commanded the attention of every patron when he arrived surrounded by a retinue of gunmen, but the times were changing, the country was entering the post-World War II era, and people barely noticed him now. Those who recognized him were often surprised that Al Capone was still alive; they thought he had died in jail years ago. They remembered the movies about his life, especially *Scarface* and *Little Caesar*, better than the man himself.

But there were some who did remember. In 1946, his former protégé from Chicago Heights, Sam Pontarelli, happened to be visiting Miami on his honeymoon when he was unexpectedly approached by a stranger who told him, "Al wants to see you."

"I'm on my honeymoon," Pontarelli replied. "Don't bother me."

"Look, I got my orders."

Pontarelli relented. "Okay," he said. "Give me an hour."

"Get all your clothes," the man said as he left.

When he arrived at the Palm Island villa, Capone was there to greet him. Like Harry Hart and others who saw Capone during this period, Pontarelli was struck by how *healthy* he appeared. "The man was in good shape. He had all his marbles," Pontarelli recalls. "He grabbed me and kissed me," Pontarelli recalls. "Gave me a big bear hug. 'You stay here,' he says, meaning in a carriage house adjacent to the main building. Then he says, 'We're gonna go eat tonight at the Tropicana.' Next day, we went fishing on his boat, then skeet shooting. Three days go by, and it's time for me to go home. My wife tells Mae we're leaving in the morning. Al threw a nice going-away party for us, and then he grabs me, takes my hand, and I felt something. 'What are you doing?' I say to him. I look and it's $500." Pontarelli came away with a renewed admiration for Capone. The man had been to hell and back, and he still remembered the people who were with him all along. Sure he had been in the rackets, he had been a bootlegger, and maybe a few other things, as well, though not everything they called him in the newspapers, but Pontarelli did not fault Capone for that. "The man did what he had to do," Pontarelli says today, "and he knew how to do it. He did it the right way. If there was a dollar to cut up, he cut it up fifty-fifty, not sixty-forty."

Sam Pontarelli was one of the last emissaries from the world beyond the walls of Palm Island to see Al Capone. After that visit, Al went into a decline, not all at once, but slowly, unmistakably. He usually slept by himself in a plain, small bedroom, not much larger than his cell at Alcatraz had been.

The room held two narrow beds and a night table. A window overlooked the front lawn of the house; from it the palm trees and houses across the quiet street were visible, and when there was a breeze, as there often was across Biscayne Bay, he would hear the palm fronds sway and softly scrape against one another. Even in this tranquil setting, he did not sleep well. By three o'clock in the morning a light went on in his room, and he was up and about the house. His grasp on reality became more tenuous than ever.

On January 18, 1947, he quietly celebrated his forty-eighth birthday. It was, by the standards of his milieu, a great age, and he had outlived almost everyone from the days in Chicago—with two notable exceptions. "Bugs" Moran was still at large, a small time hoodlum robbing banks and engaging in other forms of petty crime; and Johnny Torrio, Capone's true mentor, lived on in quiet retirement in White Plains, New York. Shortly after his birthday celebration, Capone suffered a stroke and slipped into a coma. He remained in his small bedroom, attended by Dr. Kenneth Phillips (the physician who had exaggerated the length of Capone's bout with pneumonia in 1929), as well as a staff of round-the-clock nurses. Fearing that his brother's condition was serious, Ralph came down from Mercer, and other Capones converged on Palm Island from Chicago. Throughout the week, Capone's condition worsened. He contracted pneumonia, and a high fever further weakened his body. Now his family, including Sonny, Ralph, Mae, Teresa, Mafalda, Matt, and Mimi, were all in constant attendance, crowding the little bedroom at the top of the stairs, hoping he would live even as they knew they were watching him die.

The endless, sleepless week dragged on until, at 7:25 in the evening on Saturday, January 25, the best-known, least understood gangster of all died in the presence of his immediate family. Beyond the gates of the house, a small group of reporters, keeping a death vigil, waited patiently for news from within the walls. As soon as Dr. Phillips closed the deceased's eyes, Mae, realizing that after twenty-eight years of marriage to Al Capone she was now alone, collapsed. She required medical attention herself. Later, Capone's physicians appeared before the reporters to give them the news for which they had been waiting. "As word of the death spread," wrote the correspondent for the *Miami Herald*, "a procession of automobiles began to arrive at the high-walled home where Capone had lived out his anti-climactic years. More callers than the villa has ever had, even in the lush times when gangsters used it as a holiday retreat, were admitted through the gates. A block-long line of sleek, black limousines was parked outside." A little later a hearse pulled up to the house and took the body to the Philbrick Miami Beach Funeral Home.

The following day, his body, looking "shrunken and colorless in a massive bronze casket," was seen by about 350 visitors, who first had to submit to the scrutiny of guards stationed at the entrance of the mortuary. The last outfit Capone ever wore consisted of a new double-breasted suit of a somber blue hue, a white shirt, black tie, and white "sport shoes." Although Capone was still enough of a name to command a crowd at this, his final appearance, his last rites were extremely modest compared with the great gangster funerals Chicago had witnessed during the Prohibition era, several of which Capone had instigated by sending the victim to his grave. But there would be no processions for Al Capone, no flags flying at half mast, no hundred-car-long cortege, no throng jamming the streets or any other reminder that the deceased belonged to gangland. Even the lavish floral tributes that had marked the last rites of so many other gangsters, including Al's own brother Frank, were absent. The family's plan was to give Al his send-off with the least amount of fuss possible. In Chicago, his lawyer, Abraham Teitelbaum, announced that Al Capone had died penniless: "As far as I know, Capone didn't leave any money or any will. I think he died broke and I'm sure it is untrue that he was fabulously wealthy. I think he lived on the generosity of his brothers and other members of his family. He still owed the Government money, and the Florida home in which he lived was heavily mortgaged." As Teitelbaum implied, the thriving Chicago Outfit continued to funnel money to Capone's immediate family.

Because Capone had died on a Saturday, his passing became grist for Sunday newspapers across the country, and their obituaries vied for the honor of kicking dirt on his grave. The *New York Times* described his death as the "end of an evil dream," and drew the following moral: "Though 'Scarface Al,' once Public Enemy No. 1, died in bed in the midst of luxury, his career ended in mental and physical horror. Among the funeral wreaths his old gangster associates will doubtless shower on his bier there should be at least one inscribed, 'The wages of sin is death.' "

The Chicago papers all summoned the specter of the gang lord who once ruled their town. "In the days of his power there were fantastic tales about him," explained his old enemy, the *Chicago Tribune*, as if Capone had never been quite real, more a creature of the popular imagination than a historical figure.

His "syndicate" was credited with doing business of 25 million dollars a year and he was reputedly many times a millionaire; there was even a story that he had personally lost $7,500,000 in a few years of gambling. With awe, it was related that the armored car in which he rode weighed 7½ tons and that he went about always with at least a dozen "torpedoes" [armed bodyguards] to protect his life.

Dozens of murders were attributed to him and his gang: murders for which no one was ever tried. There were many accusations, most of which no one troubled to deny, that he and his cohorts practiced bribery of public officials and policemen on a large scale. Capone was astute enough to realize the great money-making possibilities in labor rackets, and some of his underlings were still prospering in them long after he retired. He began toward the end of his sovereignty to understand the power of the ballot, and there were territories in which only his candidates could be elected.

Although the *Tribune* presented a fairly comprehensive account of Capone's public career, the newspaper omitted the one episode that demonstrated how closely the newspaper and the racketeer were linked: the murder of Jake Lingle, the *Tribune* reporter who doubled as a Capone racketeer.

In his lifetime, Capone had enjoyed ties to newspapers and journalists not only in Chicago but throughout the country. He had always sold copies, and he had cultivated a number of prominent journalists, including Damon Runyon, Harry Read, and Jake Lingle. Surveying the reaction of the press, A. J. Liebling, that connoisseur of street life, was underwhelmed. In the glossy pages of the *New Yorker* he alone waxed nostalgic for Capone and dared to make fun of the censoriousness surrounding his death. Perhaps, thought Liebling, Capone had simply outlived his time, and people no longer appreciated him or his era. If he had died fifteen years earlier, Liebling wrote, "the event would have rated more space than a World Series, and I suppose it is a sign of having my particular age that I was astonished at the restraint with which most papers handled the news of his death in Miami Beach."

Liebling neglected to mention that Capone, in a manner of speaking, had died a thousand deaths in the newspapers over the years. They had declared him finished, washed up, a has-been every time he was hauled in for a major murder investigation; they wrote premature obituaries when he was indicted for income tax evasion and again when he was convicted of the charge; they wrote him off when he went to the Atlanta Penitentiary and later when he was sent to Alcatraz. They declared him as good as dead when he was released at the end of 1939. "Death had beckoned him for years, as stridently as a Cicero whore calling to a cash customer," as *Time* put it. No matter what they wrote about Capone, he kept coming back, a bit frailer in every incarnation, but still alive. So when the end came quietly, almost imperceptibly, it seemed an anticlimax to Liebling and to many other Americans, for the event occurred without benefit of the gallows, the electric chair, or the machine gun. No one had taken Capone for a ride, leaving his body to be found in three inches of freezing ditch water. At home, in bed, surrounded by grieving relatives, Al Capone died the death of a family man, not a gangster. It was not the end that Americans, conditioned by over two decades of violent gangster movies, expected; nor was it the end that law enforcement authorities wanted. The former preferred him to die in a hail of bullets, the latter in jail. Capone had managed to outwit everyone and everything—with the exception of syphilis.

The family arranged for the body to be shipped to Chicago, and on the afternoon of February 4 the mortal remains of Al Capone were laid to rest in Mt. Olivet Cemetery. It was a bitterly cold day, the ground was covered with snow. In keeping with the trappings of his funeral, even the Capone head-stone was understated, as if to minimize his notorious reputation. The small slab read:

Qui Riposa
Alphonse Capone
Nato: Jan. 17, 1899
Morto: Jan. 25, 1947

Only a handful of mourners were present to pay their last respects to Capone and gaze on these words. Among them were Jack "Greasy Thumb" Guzik and Capone's suave heir apparent, Murray "The Camel" Humphreys. One other mourner went unrecognized; he was Timothy Sullivan, Capone's old caddie. Sullivan was under no illusions about Capone's deeds, but, he recalled, "I remembered another side and I mourned him. I wanted him somehow to know I was there because, as a boy, I never had a better friend. Nobody had ever treated me or my family with such kindness." He remembered the gifts Capone had lavished on the family, especially his sister Babe, who became Al's mistress, and he remembered the wild rounds of gangster golf he had caddied.

Once the men had assembled at the graveside, they stood about in the snow, stamping their feet, trading gossip, looking out for undercover FBI agents. When Capone's widow, mother and sister arrived, all the men doffed their hats. They watched tearfully as Capone's coffin, all but obscured be-neath a blanket of orchids and gardenias, was carried to the waiting, gaping grave. At this moment a few reporters ventured close to the canopy marking the grave, only to be reprimanded by Ralph. "Why don't you leave us alone?" he barked. The reporters moved back, but only slightly; they had a job to do. Then Monsignor William J. Gorman, who was the chaplain of the Chicago Fire Department, made the following remarks: "The Roman Cath-olic Church never condones evil, nor the evil in any man's life. But this ceremony is sanctioned by our archbishop as recognition of Alphonse Ca-pone's repentance, and the fact that he died with the sentiments of the Church." As the women sobbed and the men glared at the reporters, the priest continued. "I never knew Alphonse Capone in life, but during the years that I was pastor of St. Columbanus Church on the South Side, I knew and respected his mother for her unfailing piety. So far as I know, she never missed a mass a day of her adult life. . . . She asked me to conduct this service today." After that, the priest read a few prayers. The mourning racketeers recited their Hail Marys, and when they were done, the coffin was lowered into the grave. Father Gorman knelt and scattered a handful of frozen earth after it. By now the short winter afternoon was nearly over, and it was growing dark and gloomy in the graveyard. The women entered the waiting limousines, followed by the men, and gradually the cemetery emptied of its visitors.

In his forty-eight years, Capone led many lives, public and private, valiant and contemptible. At various times he was a pimp, a loving husband, a murderer, a bootlegger, martyr, role model, antihero—Public Enemy Number 1. He left behind so many lasting, unexpected impressions: the young boy who retrieved a widow's stolen washtub (*"We are the boys of Navy Street and touch us if you dare!"*) . . . the trustworthy young apprentice to Johnny Torrio . . . the successful racketeer attired in a pink apron, cooking spaghetti and declaring his intention to retire . . . paying the hospital bill for Robert St. John, the crusading young journalist his goons had beaten . . . flinging coins from his car as he drove through the streets of Chicago Heights . . . cowering before Frankie La Porte . . . telling Sergeant Anthony McSwiggin to shoot him if he thought Capone was actually responsible for murdering his son, William McSwiggin . . . playing Pied Piper to a group of young children as he took them for ice cream in Lansing . . . assenting to "Machine Gun" Jack McGurn's plan for the St. Valentine's Day Massacre . . . murdering three would-be traitors with a baseball bat . . . warning a youthful admirer never to enter the rackets, or "I'll personally kill you" . . . ordering a doctor to save a young black musician's severed finger . . . skimming along Biscayne Bay in his powerboat with Sonny at his side . . . holding hands with his girlfriend, Babe, at the movies . . . raging at a waiter who dared serve him domestic Parmesan cheese . . . running a soup kitchen to feed thousands of unemployed men during the Depression . . . fitting a new suit during his tax trial . . . clutching his hands behind his back as Judge Wilkerson sentenced him to eleven years in jail for income tax evasion . . . journeying through the summer heat to Alcatraz, his legs shackled . . . hiding under his blanket during a prison riot . . . teaching himself to play the mandolin . . . roughhousing with his estranged brother's boys . . .

Acts of grace and mortal sins, one leading inexplicably yet inevitably to another.

In his forty-eight years, Capone had left his mark on the rackets and on Chicago, and more than anyone else he had demonstrated the folly of Prohibition; in the process he also made a fortune. Beyond that, he captured and held the imagination of the American public as few public figures ever do. Capone's fame should have been fleeting, a passing sensation, but instead it lodged permanently in the consciousness of Americans, for whom he redefined the concept of crime into an organized endeavor modeled on corporate enterprise. As he was at pains to point out, many of his crimes were relative; bootlegging was criminal only because a certain set of laws decreed it, and then the laws were changed. He also cunningly promoted the notion that the criminal, or, to employ his euphemism, the racketeer, redistributes wealth, taking it from the rich, who scarcely miss it, and giving it to the poor, who cannot come by it any other way. Finally, there was the symbol most closely associated with him—the machine gun. Although there is no evidence that Capone himself ever used one, it belonged to his way of life, *la mala vita*.

      •   •   •

In his last, liquor-sodden years, Eliot Ness entered a spiral of decline. In 1948 he returned to the Diebold Safe Company, commuting forty miles from his rented home in Cleveland to Canton. However, he spent more time on the road, drinking, than he did in his office. Each day he would stop in Kent, Ohio, for more than a few drinks. While drifting through town, he became intrigued by the local automobile dealership, a Lincoln-Mercury agency; there Ness struck up a friendship with the manager, Jack Foyle, who was almost twenty years younger. Theirs was almost a father-son relationship. "He was a very lonesome man looking for a friend," Foyle came to realize. "He was totally depressed by his defeat in Cleveland for mayor. He took it very hard. He was ostracized." Eventually Ness bought a car from Foyle; it was a "jazzed-up Mercury coupé, dark green. He wanted a car with all the fancy things you could buy—the spotlights and the chrome and the bumper guards, all the trimmings." Although Ness was chronically short of money, he paid $2,000 for his new car, all of it in cash. "I remember specifically he counted out the cash for it," says Foyle.

Even after the purchase, Ness never failed to stop for a drink with young Jack. "He would drop by about 3:30 or 4:00 o'clock in the afternoon on his way home, and we went down to the Kent Hotel. I would have two drinks, and he would have twenty-two. He would drink 'em like water." But then, when it was time to leave, Ness could not pay because he did not have his wallet with him—or so he claimed. In fact, Foyle discovered that Ness almost never had his wallet with him. "Then all of a sudden he'd have money, and he'd pay for the drinks with a twenty-dollar bill and say to the waitress, 'Keep the change.' " Since Ness drank so much, Foyle was naturally concerned about the drive home, but Ness insisted he was able to make it back to Cleveland. "He was a typical alcoholic driver," Foyle told himself.

"The car knew where to go." Then one evening Foyle received a call from the local police station. It turned out that a man claiming he was Eliot Ness had been picked up for driving while intoxicated, but he had no wallet, no identification, and insisted the police call Foyle, who would be able to identify him. "I went down to the police station," Foyle recalls, "and the chief of police said, 'Are you sure this is Eliot Ness?' I said I knew goddamn well it was."

After that incident, the two became even better friends and drinking partners, and Ness passed the drunken afternoons reminiscing about the good old days in Chicago and especially Al Capone. He even took to calling Foyle "Al Capone," and the two of them would kid about it, Al and Eliot having a drink, and even the waitresses and the bartender got in on the joke; they all started to call Foyle "Al Capone." But when the laughter died away, Ness would be consumed by self-pity, the lost opportunities, the vanished hopes. He was haunted by the unsolved "torso" murders that had plagued his tenure as safety director in Cleveland and by his repeated failures in the business world. He complained of his treatment at Diebold. "They're putting me out to pasture," he would say, his voice filling with resentment. Were it not for a little driving mishap, he told himself, he could have been mayor of Cleveland, and after that, who knows? Senator Ness. Governor Ness. But it was not to be. He blamed J. Edgar Hoover for his defeat, without explaining why. For a time he'd had it all, a beautiful wife, a glamorous job, but then the life of this one-time Prohibition agent became a page from a WCTU tract concerning the evils of drink.

"You had to blame most of his conversation on alcohol," Foyle insists. "I wouldn't say all of it, but a good deal. He wanted praise, and he wanted someone who would listen to his stories with great compassion. And I was that person." Ness's wife, Betty, apparently was not. "From what I could tell he did not get along too well with his wife," says Foyle. "He was reluctant to go home. Whenever he'd leave he'd say, 'I'm gonna get killed when I get home. I'm gonna be murdered. She's gonna be unhappy.' In my book, he was kind of a womanizer. I never saw him actually picking up a woman, but he did a lot of cocktail party talk. He was a very lonesome person."

Ness had some comprehension that his drinking had become a serious problem. When he was settled in his den, he would remark to his housekeeper, Corinne Lawson, that he was "writing an article about alcoholism," but he was only kidding. He did not summon the will to seek treatment. Since Lawson observed Ness at close hand, she became increasingly aware of his drinking and the profound sadness underlying it, a sadness that Ness would attempt to dispel with a stream of lighthearted patter. He would tell her about Al Capone, boasting that "Scarface" shot at him nine times in all, but he outran the bullets. The line was good for a laugh but not much more.

"We had such sad times," Lawson recalls of those days. "One time the butcher told us that they couldn't extend credit to us any more, and I began to wonder what was going on. Then they wanted to buy a home in Shaker Heights. Well, Mr. Ness sent a check for $3,000, and a month later they sent it right back because the owners didn't want any part of him. They didn't want Mr. and Mrs. Ness to buy because they drank too much." Even the owner of the house Ness rented no longer wanted any part of him. She wanted the Nesses out because they left cigarette burns on the carpet and the furniture, including the grand piano.

By 1953, Ness had left Diebold. He now worked for the Guaranty Paper and Fidelity Check Corporation, a subsidiary of the North Ridge Industrial Corporation of Cleveland. His salary came to $150 a week, much of which he drank away. The company was then experimenting with a new process of watermarking checks to prevent forgery, and Ness decided to invest in the company, but ultimately the process proved too expensive to be practical, and his division headed toward insolvency. Ness was staring at failure once again. To attempt to generate interest in his product, Ness, accompanied by a colleague, John Phelps, visited New York in 1955. On this trip Phelps happened to meet Oscar Fraley, then a sportswriter with United Press International. By this time, Ness had been trying without success to find someone to collaborate with him on his book about how he brought down Al Capone. Phelps sold Fraley on the idea: "You'll have to get Eliot to tell you about his experience as a Prohibition agent in Chicago. . . . Maybe you've never heard of him but it's real gangbuster stuff, killings, raids and the works. It was plenty dangerous." And, to look at Ness now, a sad, sweet-natured drunk, it also seemed plenty unlikely. Ness mumbled something to the effect that it had been dangerous, he supposed, and he spent the rest of the night gradually reliving the era—or, rather, his version of it, with Eliot Ness cast in the starring role reality had denied him—for the benefit of Fraley. When he was done, the young sportswriter suggested that Ness write a book about his adventures. "You might make some money with it," he advised.

"I could use it," Ness said. Thereafter he devoted his spare time to the project, writing down stories, collecting old scrapbooks. "He told me the reason why he wrote that book was that he didn't have any insurance," Lawson remembers. "In fact, he didn't have any money. He was broke, and he didn't know what was going to happen to Bobby, the boy he and his wife adopted." To add to his woes, he had a heart murmur.

Unable to afford living in Cleveland, Eliot and Betty Ness moved with their young son to a comfortable old home in Coudersport, Pennsylvania. It was 1956, and Ness worked in an office on Main Street. He lived a small-town life, with fixed routines and few of the distractions that had marked his time in Cleveland, to say nothing of his youth in Chicago. He spent much time at a local bar, where he became known as the fellow with the broken-down car who spent his days drinking and talking about how he got Al Capone. His listeners indulged him, but few believed him, for Ness looked like the aging businessman he was, not the daring federal agent he claimed to be. Occasionally Fraley visited, and work on the book, now called *The Untouchables*, proceeded at a measured pace. Ness and Fraley eventually found a publisher, Julian Messner, who was willing to gamble on the project. Ness received an advance of $200, the market value of his dreams. At the end of April 1957, the galleys arrived from New York, and the book was scheduled to appear in the fall. He eagerly awaited publication; it was something to live for.

On May 16, 1957, Eliot Ness came home from work early, as usual, and went straight to the kitchen, where he prepared a scotch and soda. It was to be his last taste of liquor. Betty was in the garden at the time. She called to him, and he failed to answer. At about 5:15 she entered the kitchen and found him lying on the floor, the remains of his drink sprinkled around him. Eliot Ness was dead of a heart attack. He was just fifty-four years old.

At the time of his death Ness was nearly $10,000 in debt, and the cost of his funeral—$350—added to his widow's burden. His assets were few. He left just $273 in his checking account, and his thousands of shares of the troubled Guaranty Paper Corporation would fetch only a few hundred dollars. Although *The Untouchables* became a popular success and the basis of the hit television series on ABC beginning in 1959, Betty Ness, also handicapped by alcoholism, had precious little to show for it. She received some royalties, but the checks were infrequent and small, $32 here, $28 there. When she finally ran out of money in the midsixties, she moved in with Corinne Lawson, the woman who had been their housekeeper in Cleveland, although Betty did not view the arrangement quite that way. She explained to Corinne that she wanted to stay for just a few days or perhaps weeks while she looked at hotels in Cleveland. The stay lasted three full years, and Betty Ness continued to drink throughout that time. "I would find bottles under her bed and everywhere," says Lawson, "but she and Mr. Ness had done so much for me and had been so nice that I didn't care about that." Meanwhile, Eliot Ness's widow lived on food stamps—"just like all the rest of my friends around here," Lawson recalls. "Sometimes I would go and get the food stamps for her."

She died soon after, and a few years later, their adopted son, Robert, died of leukemia. It was not the end Eliot Ness would have wanted for his son nor for his attractive, talented third wife. Nor was his own death, hastened by alcohol, one he would have chosen for himself. No doubt Ness would have reveled in the celebrity the television version of *The Untouchables* posthumously conferred on his name and reputation, even if most of its tales sprang from fancy rather than fact, for he loved publicity above all else, with the possible exception of pretty young women—and his badge. If F. Scott Fitzgerald had ever troubled to write about the life of a detective, he might have taken Eliot Ness as his model, for his life, with all its unfulfilled promise, illustrated one of Fitzgerald's favorite axioms, that there were no second acts in the lives of Americans.

•   •   •

Mt. Olivet Cemetery was not the final resting place for the earthly remains of Al Capone. The family was not pleased with the location of the grave. According to some reports, it was located on unhallowed ground. Then, too, it had become a magnet for curiosity seekers, and the family looked on them with disfavor, as well. In life, Al Capone had been highly superstitious about tombstones and abhorred the thought of desecration. For this reason, the body of Al Capone was exhumed amid great secrecy and moved to the broad expanses of Mt. Carmel Cemetery, where so many of Al Capone's enemies and allies, everyone from Dion O'Banion to William McSwiggin, slumbered sub specie aeternitatis. The Capone family purchased a spacious family plot in Mt. Carmel. It was here that Al Capone was reburied, where Frank Capone was reburied, where Gabriele Capone, after being disinterred from his burial ground in New York, was reburied, where Teresa would be buried when she died in 1952, and where the other Capones would all eventually be buried. The grave of each family member was marked by a small, simple stone lying flat on the ground, containing the name of the deceased, the year of birth and of death, and the legend "My Jesus Mercy." No stone was larger than another. Even in death, *campanilismo* ruled the lives of the Capone family.

Like many Italians, the Capones did not bury their dead and forget them; they practiced ancestor worship. At the cemetery, the inherently matriarchal character of Italian families came to the fore. The women did most if not all the work of weeping, wailing, and the protracted business of mourning, as if they alone possessed the emotional intensity equal to the task. On a hot weekend, Italian families from Chicago often sought refuge under a shady tree at Mt. Carmel Cemetery. Families lavished so much attention on the grave and visited so often that it became an annex, practically a new address, where they ate from carefully prepared picnic baskets and lovingly tended the grave sites, weeding them, planting flowers, watering the grass over their beloved, all the while mumbling to themselves, or to the deceased, finding at last the words they were never able to utter when the deceased was still alive. In this way ancient family quarrels reached posthumous resolution.

•   •   •

There would be no resolution in the federal government's quarrel with the surviving members of the Capone family, however. In 1950 Ralph Capone was summoned to Washington to appear before Senator Estes Kefauver's widely publicized special committee investigating organized crime. There "Bottles" enlightened the members of the committee about various obscure aspects of the bootlegger's trade, beginning with the size of his "organization," which, he said, consisted of "two fellows and myself. That was all I needed."

"Did you have trucks?" the committee inquired.

"No," Ralph patiently explained, "the beer was delivered to me. I was given $2 a barrel for the beer. The beer was not mine. I got a commission to sell it for $2 a barrel."

"You never even saw the beer?"

"That is true." But he was less forthcoming when the committee asked him to name other members of the "Capone gang," and when Ralph balked, they supplied some for him. They mentioned Jack Guzik, whom Ralph admitted he knew "very well," as did his late brother, Al. And they mentioned Murray Humphreys, and, yes, Ralph said he also knew him "very well." The same went for two other former Capone bodyguards, Philip D'Andrea and Louis "Little New York" Campagna. The committee also wanted to know how Ralph spent his time in Miami Beach. At the dog tracks, Ralph admitted. "When you showed up they rolled out the red carpet for you, didn't they?" asked a committee member.

"Not necessarily," Ralph testified. "When I went there they were out of red carpet."

When the subject turned to the Mafia, Ralph turned as silent as a stone. All he knew about the Mafia, he claimed, was what he read in the newspapers. As flimsy as the claim sounded, there was some truth to it, for Ralph Capone had nothing to do with the Mafia, and the Mafia had nothing to do with him. But the committee had little comprehension of the subtleties of organized crime; to them the Mafia was synonymous with the rackets, and they made no distinction between the Outfit in Chicago and the Mafia's five families in New York. After Ralph stepped down, John Capone, who also had some marginal involvement in the Outfit, appeared before the committee, where he spent hours parrying Kefauver's questions. It made for good theater, but John and Ralph admitted very little that was new. But the inquisition helped to ensure that the stigma of the Capone name would not fade. All the while, unknown to the members of the committee, the real head of the Outfit, Frankie La Porte, remained in secure anonymity in Chicago Heights,

If Ralph ever believed that his appearances before the Kefauver committee would earn him some relief, he was soon disabused of that notion. A few months after the hearings, his son, Ralph Jr., crushed by his father's disgrace, committed suicide. In his Chicago apartment he washed down a mouthful of pills with a quart of scotch, and as the lethal mixture took effect, he wrote a pathetic note to his girlfriend, a singer named Jeanne Kerin. "I love you," he managed to scrawl. "I love you. Jeanie only you I love. Only you. I'm gone—" He wrote no more and lived no more.

Soon after this tragedy, his father faced new legal challenges. On March 16, 1951, the government leveled fresh charges of income tax evasion against him. Since he had already been convicted of that offense, the indictment posed an especially serious threat. Ralph's lawyers attempted to arrive at a compromise, but the Internal Revenue Service refused even to discuss the matter. Ralph Capone owed $96,679 income tax, said the IRS. They claimed to have twenty-five agents continuing to work on Ralph's case, and they were bound to come up with still more evidence of income tax evasion. Ralph was now fifty-seven years old, and it appeared that he was destined to spend the rest of his days trapped in the coils of the tax code.

· · ·

The intensive IRS investigation of Ralph Capone yielded one surprising result. The agents examining his finances followed a strange trail leading from his retreat in Mercer, Wisconsin, all the way to Homer, Nebraska, and a man known as "Two-Gun" Hart. Ralph was no smarter now than he had been twenty years earlier, when the government first began investigating him, and in a move that Al Capone, had he been alive to see it, would surely have prevented, Ralph listed their "lost" brother, "Two-Gun" Hart, as the title holder of Recap Lodge, Ralph's primary place of business in Mercer. Since Hart had rejoined the Capone family by this time, although keeping his assumed name, federal agents made short work of establishing his true identity. In September 1951, a grand jury in Chicago heard the startling news that the "Two-Gun" Hart who held title to the Recap Lodge was actually Ralph's brother—and the brother of Al Capone. By now the reputation of "Two-Gun" Hart, once the most feared and violent Prohibition agent west of the Mississippi, had faded into distant memory, but Al Capone remained fresh in the mind of the public, and any brother of his was newsworthy, especially one who had once been a lawman himself. After decades of obscurity, Hart burst into the headlines again, not for rounding up bootlegging suspects or drunken Indians, but for playing a minor role in the Capone family's finances. It seemed to him as though the invisible hand was at work again. First it had led him back to his family, and now it prodded him to shed the disguise he had worn since his youth and to reveal his true identity to the U.S. government.

Served with a subpoena to appear before the grand jury investigating Ralph

Capone's tax problems, Hart and his wife journeyed by train from Homer to Union Station in Chicago, where reporters caught up with him. The man who appeared before them bore only a faint resemblance to "Two-Gun" Hart in his prime. Suffering from diabetes, he had become obese, and he walked slowly and hesitantly, with the aid of a cane. He was balding, and he wore glasses, but even with them his eyesight was severely impaired. He looked nothing like the man who had once tracked Indians for days across the wilderness, nor did he resemble a gangster. He appeared, instead, to be a retired civil servant, which was what he was. The following day, Hart spent five hours before the grand jury, reminding them of his unusual life story, his reasons for changing his name, and his memorable exploits as a marshal and Prohibition agent. As for his ties to Ralph Capone, all he would say was that they were brothers.

As soon as he finished testifying, he and his wife left Chicago and returned to the wrinkle in the prairie that had been his home for many years. He died in Homer of a heart attack on October 1, 1952, at the age of sixty. Because of the recent publicity he had received, his passing was widely noted. Although the ruse he had sustained throughout his adult life had finally been exposed, the newspapers sympathized with his efforts to distance himself from his family. "The very name Capone recalls an era," the *Lincoln* (Nebraska) *Star* editorialized. "Al rose to the head of a crime empire that owned official Chicago and ruled the underworld throughout America. . . . Now comes to light that there was another Capone, a brother named James. Ashamed of his four gangster brothers, James went to Nebraska and became a law enforcement officer. He called himself Harte [sic] and was so stern that lawbreakers called him 'Two-gun' Harte. He was so fine a man that he was named district commissioner of the Boy Scouts of America. Let no man bemoan his handicaps. A Capone became a leader for good in his community!" Although newspaper editorials sought to differentiate Hart from the other Capones, he had more in common with his brothers than their sermonizing suggested. Throughout his life, in so many ways, he had been Al Capone's hidden doppelgänger, bringing many of the same tactics to law enforcement that Al brought to the rackets.

As death depleted the ranks of the Capone family, Ralph soldiered on. Spending most of time in Mercer, Wisconsin, he dealt at arm's length with the IRS throughout the fifties. The interest and penalties on the taxes more than doubled the amount he owed, but in the end he paid up and retained his freedom, as well as a measure of privacy.

The same could not be said of Al's only child, Sonny, who drifted along in Miami. He avoided the temptation to enter the rackets, where his name alone would have guaranteed him a position, largely to honor his mother's wishes. Indeed, at one point a representative of the Chicago Outfit approached him with an offer to play a more active role, but when he told his mother, she would have none of it. "Your father broke my heart," she told Sonny. "Don't you do it, too." In need of money, Sonny opened a restaurant in Miami, where he was often seen in the kitchen, preparing the sauces. The FBI, keeping him under discreet scrutiny, learned that Sonny was not quite as removed from the Outfit as Mae would have wished, for he did receive a modest annual allowance from the boys in Chicago—La Porte, Humphreys, and their colleagues. It was the Outfit's policy to keep the widows and orphans of its deceased members on a stipend, never a large one, but enough to get along. In return, the Outfit demanded loyalty and silence. Any recipient who started to cooperate with the FBI, for instance, was cut off immediately. The stipend was, in effect, hush money. Yet there was a limit to the Outfit's generosity. At one point Sonny asked to borrow $24,000 to expand his restaurant, but the Outfit refused his request.

Sonny was stripped of whatever dignity he had left in August 1965, when he was arrested for shoplifting in the Kwik Chek supermarket in North Miami Beach; he was a regular at the store, well known to the management. Nonetheless, he was charged with stealing two bottles of aspirin and a package of flashlight batteries, whose value came to all of $3.50. "Everybody has a little larceny in them," he said by way of explanation when he was arrested. Since The Untouchables had recently been a hit on television, public awareness of Capone was once again high, and Sonny's appearance in court before Judge Edward S. Klein to answer the charge of shoplifting generated a flurry of interest. Neatly dressed, balding, looking even older than his forty-five years, Sonny pleaded no contest and received two years' probation. At the time of this incident, he was in the midst of his second divorce, and his pathetic little venture into the world of crime sounded very much like a cry for help, but help never came, at least not from the world at large. Sonny responded by legally changing his name from Albert Francis Capone to Albert Francis, the name by which he is known today.

As the years passed, death took more members of the Capone family. Ralph died on November 22, 1974, in a rest home near Mercer, Wisconsin, where he had spent his last years. The cause of death was listed as cardiac failure. He was eighty years old. Al's widow, Mae, lasted until April 16, 1986, when she died at the Hollywood Hills Nursing Home in Florida. She was eighty-nine. Mafalda, the sole Capone sister, died in Michigan on March 25, 1988, at the age of seventy-six. It was said that her tongue remained sharp until the end of her life.

· · ·

Harry Hart, Al Capone's nephew, has spent his entire life in Homer, Nebraska, population 560, where he lives in his father's house. He is a gentle, softspoken man who resembles his famous uncle only vaguely, mostly around the eyes, which are searching, intense, wary. His accent is as flat as the prairie, his manner soft and considerate. He is a civic leader in that part of the state, playing prominent roles in the Boy Scouts of America and the Lutheran Church.

Not long ago Harry and his wife Joyce visited a large old home reputed to be Al Capone's hideout in Wisconsin. The current owners have turned the place into a tourist attraction. As he took the tour, Harry was amused as the guide pointed out the nests and dungeons that Capone and other gangsters supposedly used in their day. Near the end of the tour, another member of the party asked the guide if Al Capone had any descendants. "I heard he had a son or a brother who was a lawyer," the tourist said, and the guide agreed this was so. Joyce poked her husband in the ribs and encouraged him to speak up and correct the guide, but Harry, in his self-effacing way, preferred to chuckle silently. This was just one more piece of misinformation about Al Capone floating around. He was content in the knowledge that he had come to know and appreciate his uncle. Unlike the crowd of tourists relishing tales of murder and mayhem, he knew who Al Capone really was.

Acknowledgments

I HAVE NEVER BEFORE WRITTEN about someone who differed so sharply from his reputation as Al Capone—with the possible exception of Eliot Ness, that man of many shadows.

When I began work on this book, I received warnings that it might be difficult to conduct research, and initially I encountered my fair share of *omertà*, the code of silence shielding underworld activities. Especially in Chicago—Al Capone's main arena—people who are in a position to know, but who are now quite respectable, often sought to divert me from the subject of my inquiry. They expressed pride in the city's Art Institute, the Symphony; why, they asked, did I want to dredge up old stories? As I got beyond such reservations, I came to realize that Al Capone is as much a fact of Chicago life as Lake Michigan.

As my research progressed, I gradually abandoned conventional assumptions of guilt and innocence, right and wrong. Time and again, I found, the good guys behaved like bad guys, and the bad guys behaved like good guys. Capone himself confounded clear-cut definitions of good and evil; surrounded by a hypocritical establishment, he improvised a code of behavior that allowed him to do business in the legitimate sphere as well as the illegitimate. In the process he became a target of anti-Italian prejudice and a scapegoat for the failure of Prohibition. Eventually it became apparent to me that the life of Al Capone was more than the story of a gangster; it is also a story about American society, American culture, and the American legal system—the dark side of the American democratic dream.

Many people helped to make this book a reality. Andrew Wylie, my literary agent, believed in the idea from the start, and he has my deepest thanks for all he has done. At the Wylie, Aitken & Stone office, the inde-

fatigable Deborah Karl has been a mainstay throughout. Thanks also to
Sarah Chalfant, Bridget Love, and to Gillon Aitken in England.

At Simon & Schuster, Michael Korda, my editor, gave me the encouragement and support necessary for a project of this scope. I would also like
to thank Eric Rayman for his legal counsel and Gail Winston. Chuck Adams
has been meticulous in preparing the manuscript. At Macmillan London,
Roland Philipps, Felicity Rubinstein, and Catherine Hurley brought their
enthusiasm to this book.

My search for the real Al Capone took me from Chicago to Miami; Los
Angeles; San Francisco (Alcatraz); Cleveland; Brooklyn; Washington, D.C.;
Nebraska; and several cities in Michigan. I went in search of government files
and records, little-known books and periodicals, historic sites, and most
importantly, people who had known, were related to, or had done business
with Capone.

Interviews form a crucial part of this book. I conducted more than 300 of
them, talking with certain individuals as many as a dozen times. Some of the
most intriguing and productive encounters occurred in the summer of 1991,
when I traveled to Lansing, Michigan, to talk with members of an extended
family about the Al Capone they had known. It was the first time they had
ever discussed him with an outsider, the first time they revealed closely
guarded, cherished family secrets. Throughout their lives they feared the
stigma of close association with Capone, but it became strikingly apparent
that the Capone they described with such vividness and affection was almost
unknown to the world at large.

In the following months, I met with other members of this family in
locations as different as a diner on a bleak, windy highway outside Chicago
Heights and a lavish home in Southern California. At their request, I have
given pseudonyms to this group of individuals. They include: Giovanna
Antonucci, Grazia Mastropietro, Sam Pontarelli, and Anthony Russo.

Later that summer, I found myself sitting across a kitchen table from Al
Capone's nephew, Harry Hart, in Homer, Nebraska, where I heard still more
about the unknown side of Capone. Homer—pop. 560—doesn't appear on
the maps they give out at car rental counters. I doubt its dusty, abbreviated
main street has changed much in half a century. As I pulled up to Harry's
house in my rented car, his son and grandchildren were leaving. The interior
was immaculate, adorned with church and scouting awards. As the afternoon
gave way to evening, this reserved and gentle man proceeded to tell me
whatever he could about the incredible career of his father, Richard "Two-
Gun" Hart (born Vincenzo Capone), who was Al's oldest brother, and about
Uncle Al himself. Over tall glasses of iced tea, Harry produced photographs,
letters, and yellowed newspaper clippings documenting the life of "Two-
Gun": a legendary marshal, presidential bodyguard, and Prohibition agent.

All the while, his younger brother was the largest bootlegger in the country. Listening to Harry, I began to realize that Al Capone was a character far more rich and strange than I had previously imagined. It was evident that the Capone family contained vast potential for both good and evil.

I am equally grateful to all the other individuals who generously shared their recollections and put up with my frequent prodding for more information and elucidation. They include: Mike Aiello, Myrl E. Alexander, Jim Bacon, William Balsamo, John Bean, Tony Berardi, Philip R. Bergen, Barbara Botein, Jim Brindisi, Rio Burke, Irving Burstein, Harry Busch, Jackie Cain, Mona Pucci Clemens, Max Allan Collins, Lou Corsino, Jack Cranall, Sharon Ness Darkovich, William Dale Dunlap, Jack Foyle, Dolly Galter, Michael Graham, Dick Grose, Harold Hagen, Dr. Richard Hahn, Joyce Hart, Harry Hart, William S. Hart, Kenan Heise, William Helmer, Milt "Judge" Hinton, Mona Hinton, Art Hodes, Charlie Hopkins, Henry Jacoby, Louise Jamie, George E. Q. Johnson Jr., Nate Kaplan, Marion Hopwood Kelly, Gera-Lind Kolarik, Donald Knox, Roy Kral, Bill Lambie, Andrea Andrews Larkin, Corinne Lawson, Mark Levell, Raymond Longwell, John Madigan, Jonathan Margolis, Virginia Marmaduke, Terence F. MacCarthy, Dr. Victor McCusick, Rebecca McFarland, Alan McKee, Henry Morrison, George Murray, Richard Van Orman, John Pegoria, Stanley Pieza, Nicholas Pileggi, Rick Porrello, Leslie L. Potts, Maxine Pucci, William F. Roemer Jr., Mike Rotunno, James L. Simon, Lloyd Wendt, Robert St. John, Henry A. Schaefer, Walter Spirko, Al Sutton, Walter Trohan, Dr. Thomas Turner, Vern Whaley, Al "Wallpaper" Wolff, and Artha Woods.

A significant number of other individuals talked with me off the record, and they also have my thanks.

Documents pertaining to Capone's life and career proved abundant, thanks in part to five decades of press scrutiny, Senate hearings, FBI investigations, court records, prison files, wiretaps, and loquacious informers. At times I was nearly overwhelmed by the sheer quantity of detailed information available on Capone in particular and the supposedly secret subject of organized crime in general. Would that we were as well-informed about the inner workings of some of our *legitimate* institutions.

Because of the federal government's extensive surveillance of Capone and his family, he proved well suited to Freedom of Information Act (FOIA) inquiries. In many cases, I have been the first to draw on these documents for publication. The following government agencies provided information to me under this act:

In Washington, D.C., the Federal Bureau of Investigation made available approximately 2,500 pages of documents from their permanent file on Al Capone, as well as their files on Frank "The Enforcer" Nitti and Eliot Ness.

My thanks to J. Kevin O'Brien and Gerry Brovy of the FBI's Records Management Division for their cooperation with my numerous requests for copies of these once confidential dossiers. At the Internal Revenue Service, Criminal Division, Johnnie Nix, Edwin R. Ward, and Bill Woolf of the FOIA/ Privacy Section supplied a transcript of the tax trial of Al Capone; Shelley Davis, the IRS historian, contributed additional material. At the Department of Justice, Pamela Jones and J. Brian Ferrel of the Tax Division cheerfully supplied extensive documents pertaining to Al Capone and his associates. I also wish to acknowledge the Great Lakes Region branch of the National Archives and archivist Donald W. Jackanicz for access to additional documents pertaining to Al Capone's tax trial, and Vicki Herman, the librarian of the Federal Bureau of Alcohol, Tobacco and Firearms in Washington, D.C., for information on Eliot Ness.

I found federal prison files for so-called "Notorious Offenders" especially valuable because they contain detailed and reliable medical, biographical, and psychological information on their subjects, as well as correspondence, parole proceedings, and even a comprehensive list of the inmates' visitors. At the National Archives and Records Administration in Washington, D.C., Sue McDonough provided the extensive "Notorious Offenders" prison files for Frank "The Enforcer" Nitti and Jack "Greasy Thumb" Guzik. The National Archives Trust Fund Board in Atlanta, Georgia, furnished the "Notorious Offenders" file on Ralph Capone. John W. Roberts, the archivist of the Federal Bureau of Prisons in Washington, D.C., went to great lengths to locate Al Capone's prison file; my thanks to him for all his help.

In addition, I wish to extend thanks to a number of institutions in and around Chicago, where I conducted much of the research for this book. The Chicago Historical Society proved to be an exceptional resource, and I am grateful to its staff, including Eileen Flanagan, Russell Lewis, Archie Motley, and Corey Seebohm, for their assistance with my studies of the intertwined subjects of Capone, organized crime, Chicago history, and Prohibition. I also wish to thank the Newberry Library, the Regenstein Library of the University of Chicago, the Chicago Public Library, the Chicago Heights Public Library, and the Chicago Museum of Broadcast Communications. At the Chicago Crime Commission, Jeannette Callaway and Jerry Gladden patiently answered my questions and provided access to their archives. Joseph Saccomonto of the American Police Center and Museum furnished photographs and other information. Terence F. MacCarthy, the executive director of the Federal Defender Program and a defense lawyer for Al Capone in the ABA's 1990 retrial, supplied documents from the original hearing as well as a cogent analysis of it. Bryan Goggin and Jerry Sciaraffa led me to Cook County court documents pertaining to Capone's early criminal career. The Italian Cultural Center in Stone Park, Illinois, graciously provided access to its oral history project documenting the experiences of Italian-Americans in Chicago, and Professor Dominic Candeloro added perspective. In St. Joseph, Michigan, Bea Rodgers of the Maud Preston Palenske Memorial Library assisted. Special thanks to Douglas Bukowski of the University of Illinois for sharing his copy of the FBI files on Al Capone with me. Mark Levell acted as my guide to the grave sites of Capone, his family, and several of his victims. My appreciation goes to the staff of the Omni Ambassador East Hotel, where I stayed during my research trips. I must also acknowledge the assistance of the Merry Gangsters Literary Society, whose members provided countless leads and companionship that warmed the winter weeks I spent in Chicago.

The apparent "success" of Prohibition in the 1920s had the bitterly ironic effect of making the rise of bootleggers such as Al Capone not just possible but inevitable. The Temperance and Prohibition movements generated an extraordinary outpouring of material: journals, broadsides, and privately published memoirs. In my search for the lost literature of Temperance, I was fortunate to visit the National Headquarters of the Women's Christian Temperance Union in Evanston, Illinois. There Rachel Kelly, the president, and Alfred Epstein, the librarian, generously permitted me access to the unique trove of Temperance and Prohibition literature in the Frances E. Willard Memorial Library. Thanks also to the Evanston Historical Society, where Mark Burnette furthered my understanding of Evanston's place in the annals of the Temperance movement.

In New York, I am grateful for the assistance of the staffs of the New York Society Library; the Police Museum of the New York Police Department; and the Othmer Library of the Brooklyn Historical Society. At the Museum of Modern Art, Mary Corliss furnished stills from movies inspired by the Capone legend. On Staten Island, I furthered my research on the Italian-American experience at the Center for Migration Studies, whose librarian, Diane Zimmerman, helped me to make the best use of the collection.

In Cleveland, where the records of Eliot Ness's career are located, I wish to thank Artha Woods, clerk of council, and Martin Hauserman, archivist of the Cleveland City Council, for their help. Ness's papers, including thirteen of his personal scrapbooks, are to be found at the Western Reserve Historical Society, where Kermit J. Pike, Anne Sindelar, and Barbara Henritze offered guidance to this revealing material. My thanks as well to the Cleveland Police Historical Society and its curator, Anne T. Kmiek, and to Rebecca McFarland of the Rocky River, Ohio, Public Library.

Other archives across the country furnished additional information. I wish to acknowledge the assistance of Dwight M. Miller and Jennifer Pederson of the Herbert Hoover Library in West Branch, Iowa; Nancy McCall and the Johns Hopkins Medical Archives; Joan Ferguson of the Nebraska State His-

torical Society; Nancy Neumann of the Sioux City Public Library; Kathy
Scheetz of the South Sioux City Public Library; Erica S. Toland and Irene
Stachura of the San Francisco Maritime National Historical Park (Alcatraz
Island); Pamela D. Arceneaux and Carol Bartels of the Historic New Orleans
Collection; Widener Library (Harvard University), and the New York City
Department of Records and Information Services. In Baltimore, Marion
Elizabeth Rodgers, a biographer of H. L. Mencken, alerted me to material
in Mencken's papers concerning Capone, and Averil J. Kadis of the Enoch
Pratt Free Library provided the relevant documents. In addition, I wish to
acknowledge the Baltimore Sun library; the New Orleans Times-Picayune
library; Broward County, Florida Vital Statistics Office and Court Archives;
Dade County, Florida Records Library; the Miami Dade Public Library; and
the Historical Society of Southern Florida.

Several research assistants made significant contributions to this book.
Sarah Koenig tracked down leads in Chicago, San Francisco, and Miami.
Kathy Cantor located documents in Chicago, as did Dave Auburn, who also
visited Capone's backwoods retreat in northern Wisconsin. Ken Lauber, Erin
Donovan, and Lesley Alderman transcribed my tape-recorded interviews.
Bryan Hammond sent material from London. Lea Saslav located elusive
books. Three resourceful genealogists pieced together the complicated and
far-flung Capone family tree: Marsha Saron Dennis in New York, Steven W.
Siegel in New York and Miami, and Kay Ingalls in California. It was Marsha
who noticed that an oft-reproduced draft registration for Al Capone actually
belonged to another man with a similar name, and who then located the
correct document. Once again, Susan Shapiro proved to be an invaluable
researcher, host, and sounding board. My profound appreciation for all she
has done.

Other individuals, friends, and family members contributed to this book in
a variety of ways. Sidney Abrams, my father-in-law, came through with
several vital leads; both he and my mother-in-law, Bernice Abrams, provided
generous hospitality during my visits to Cleveland to conduct research on
Eliot Ness. Thanks also to Scott Anderson; William Balsamo for his running
commentary on the Brooklyn underworld; Edward Baumann; Irwin and
Cecile Bazelon; my brother John Bergreen for photographic reproductions;
Jon Binder; Max Allan Collins for sending his colorful Eliot Ness mystery
novels; Lou Corsino for the wide-ranging tour of Chicago Heights; Sharon L.
Darkovich; Nathaniel Deutsch; Daniel Dolgin for his wisdom and legal
advice; Alexandra Dworkin; Dr. Ron Dworkin; my sister-in-law Joan Freeman and her husband Robert Alden for their hospitality in Los Angeles;
Gerry Greenbach of Two Bunch Palms in Desert Hot Springs, California;
Charles Halevi; Maureen and James Houtrides for their detailed knowledge
of Brooklyn; Tom Hollatz; George E. Q. Johnson Jr. (the son of the U.S.

attorney who prosecuted Al Capone) for providing several hundred pages of documents from his personal collection relating to the tax trial; Anne Johnston; Gera-Lind Kolarik for the tour of those former Capone strongholds, Berwyn and Cicero, Illinois; Don Kurdziel; Steve Kurdziel; Gene Lees, for his knowledge of jazz in the Capone era; Eric Levin; Richard C. Lindberg; Matthew Luzi, for sharing his expertise on the history of Chicago Heights; James T. Maher, who was always there with a kind word and thoughtful advice; Lieutenant Monty McCord of the Hastings, Nebraska, Police Department for material about Richard "Two-Gun" Hart; Vivian and Lloyd Moles; John O'Brien; J. David Roellgen; Barney Rosset; Rich Samuels; Bruce Stark and Costa Rodis of Computer Tutor for hi-tech help; Tom Stroobie; Ion Trewin; and Ned Whelan.

Dr. Jack Shapiro contributed a great deal to my understanding of Capone's syphilis as well as the social climate surrounding the disease. Capone's cocaine habit, an important aspect of his life in the 1920s, had been overlooked until Dr. Shapiro examined the medical records and brought it to my attention. My thanks to both Dr. and Mrs. Shapiro, as well, for their hospitality during my stay in Michigan.

I also wish to acknowledge the contribution of Monte McLaws, who has spent years researching the life of Al Capone's oldest brother, Richard "Two-Gun" Hart. When ill health caused him to abandon the project, he contacted me and generously offered to share his research; my sincere appreciation to him and his wife, Emily, for doing so.

Special thanks to Bill Roemer, author of *Roemer: Man Against the Mob* and one of the best-informed people around on the subject of organized crime. Since Bill served as an FBI agent in Chicago with considerable distinction for many years, he was the only person I dared ask the probably ridiculous but possibly vital question: Is there any danger in writing about Al Capone today? Drawing on his experience, he said, he was 90 percent certain I would be safe. I intend to hold him to those odds.

My wife, Betsy, and our children, Nicholas and Sara, sustained me throughout the years I worked on this book and have contributed much to it. For all this I owe them more than I can say.

Notes on Sources

Abbreviations for archives and frequently cited sources:

Archives and Other Collections:

CCC Chicago Crime Commission. Chicago, Illinois.

CHS Chicago Historical Society. Chicago, Illinois.

GEQJ Personal Collection of George E. Q. Johnson, Jr. Chicago, Illinois.

HHL Herbert Hoover Library. West Branch, Iowa.

MC Mencken Collection, Enoch Pratt Free Library. Baltimore, Maryland.

MM Personal Collection of Monte McLaws. Salt Lake City, Utah.

NAGL National Archives and Records Administration—Great Lakes Regional Office. Chicago, Illinois.

WRHS Eliot Ness Collection, The Western Reserve Historical Society. Cleveland, Ohio.

Files Obtained Through the Freedom of Information Act:

FBI-AC FBI Permanent File for Alphonse Capone. FBI, Washington, D.C.

FBI-EN FBI Permanent File for Eliot Ness. FBI, Washington, D.C.

FBI-FN FBI Permanent File for Frank Nitti. FBI, Washington, D.C.

BP-AC Federal Bureau of Prisons' file for Al Capone. Federal Bureau of Prisons, Washington, D.C.

BP-RC Federal Bureau of Prisons' "Notorious Offenders" file for Ralph Capone. National Archives Trust Fund Board. Atlanta, Georgia.

DJ Department of Justice, Tax Division. Washington, D.C.

NA-JG "Notorious Offenders" prison file for Jack Guzik. National Archives and Records Administration. Washington, D.C.

NA-FN   "Notorious Offenders" prison file for Frank Nitti (alias Nitto). National Archives and Records Administration. Washington, D.C.

TRAN   Transcript of the trial of Al Capone for Federal income tax evasion, Chicago, Illinois, 1931. Internal Revenue Service, Criminal Division. Washington, D.C.

Publications:

    NYT   *New York Times*
     CT   *Chicago Tribune*

Notes

Prologue:
page 17 All I know: Author's interview with Anthony Russo.

Chapter 1: *Campanilismo*
page 20 "You who only": *CT*, May 18, 1929.
     21 "equal to one-tenth": Lodge, "The Restriction of Immigration," *North American Review*, January 1891.
     21 "We have the right": *ibid.*
     21 "paupers and criminals": Lodge, "Lynch Law and Unrestricted Immigration," *North American Review*, May 1891.
     21 "We are overwhelmed": *New York Herald*, December 5, 1892.
     22 "Steerage passengers from Naples": Ross, "Italians in America," *Century Magazine*, July 1914, in LaGumina, ed., *Wop!*, pp. 138–141.
     22 "promptly reproduces conditions": Riis, *How the Other Half Lives*, pp. 36–39.
     23 the numbers exploded: Nelli, *The Business of Crime*, p. 22. Nelli's source is U.S. Department of Commerce, Bureau of the Census, *Historical Statistics of the United States, Colonial Times to 1957*, pp. 56–57.
     24 Teresina Raiola: Certificate of Death, State of Illinois, #82971.
     24 "There is nothing": Hutton, *Naples and Southern Italy*, p. 1.
     24 Proverbs dear to the peasantry: Nelli, *The Business of Crime*, p. 4.
     25 "levied blackmail": *ibid.*, p. 18.
     25 The various forms: Koren, "The Padrone System and Padrone Banks," *Bulletin of the Department of Labor*, p. 113.
     25 The Camorra played: Nelli, *The Business of Crime*, p. 19.

25 The Camorra succeeded: Iorizzo, ed., *An Inquiry Into Organized Crime*, p. 7.

25 Naples was divided: Nelli, *The Business of Crime*, pp. 18–20.

27 42,977 Italians: *ibid.*, p. 22.

27 Raffaele: State of Wisconsin Certificate of Death, #74 034707.

27 *campanilismo*: Candeloro, "Suburban Italians: Chicago Heights, 1890–1975," in Holli and Jones, *Ethnic Chicago*, p. 244.

29 "a slum that faces": Miller, *A View from the Bridge*, p. 88.

29 The Capone family: Author's interview with Angela Pitaro.

29 Rents in the district: Kobler, *Capone*, p. 18.

29 "tall and handsome": Pitaro interview.

30 The subject states: December 14, 1931, *BP-RC*.

30 Senate investigation committee: *Hearings Before the Special Committee to Investigate Organized Crime in Interstate Commerce*, pp. 1239–1240.

31 January 17, 1899: Registration Card for Alphonse Capone. Order number A2840. Local Board for Division #48, City of New York, State of N.Y. Brooklyn, Kings County, September 12, 1918.

31 infant mortality rate: Kobler, *Capone*, p. 20; Pilat and Ransom, *Sodom by the Sea*, p. 273.

31 February 7: Baptismal Certificate, St. Michael and St. Edward's Church. The author thanks William Balsamo for obtaining this document.

31 "Depart from": Weller, *The Roman Ritual*, pp. 43–61.

32 street festival: Kobler, *Capone*, pp. 23–24.

32 U.S. census: 1900 U.S. census, State and City of New York, Kings County, Borough of Brooklyn Enumeration District 159; page 5A, lines 9–16.

33 May 25, 1906: Petition to Become a Citizen of the United States: County Court, Kings County, Brooklyn, vol. 331, p. 202.

33 New York City: Tomasi and Engel, *The Italian Experience in the United States*, pp. 138–141.

34 "The Italians are": *ibid.*, p. 167.

34 "They were a": Mulvaney, "A Brooklyn Childhood," *The New Yorker*, December 18, 1943.

34 "Hey, you long-legged": Kobler, *Capone*, pp. 25–26.

35 "When Al Capone": Pitaro interview.

37 "best and dearest": Asbury, *Gem of the Prairie*, p. 321.

37 "As an organizer": *ibid.*, pp. 320–321.

38 simple test: Russo interview.

38 Paolo Antonini Vacarelli: Sifakis, *Mafia Encyclopedia*, p. 121; Kobler, *Capone*, pp. 31–33.

39 youth gangs: Author's interview with William Balsamo.

41 Mafalda: State of Michigan Certificate of Death, #015597.

41 the eldest Capone boy: *BP-RC*; author's interview with Harry
    Hart.
42 the only Capone to enter: Hart interview. Photograph in possession
    of Hart.
42 Capone family knew nothing: Pitaro interview.
42 gonorrhea: *BP-RC*.
42 On October 20, 1915: *BP-RC*; Ralph Capone's Affidavit for License
    to Marry and Certificate and Record of Marriage: New York City
    Department of Records and Information Services, Municipal Ar-
    chives.
43 three years working: *BP-AC*.
43 "something of a nonentity": Fuchs, "Where Al Capone Grew Up,"
    New Republic, September 9, 1931.
43 "Let me say": Sullivan, "I Know You, Al," *North American Review*,
    September 1929.
43 Adonis Social Club: Kobler, *Capone*, p. 36.
44 infected early in his life: *MC*.
44 Estimates of syphilis: Author's interview with Dr. Jack Shapiro;
    Kolmer, "A Social Menace," *Hygeia*, June 1929.
44 Girolamo Fracastoro: Buret, *Syphilis*, vol. 1, p. 27.
44 "Know syphilis": Briskman, "Syphilis—The Unfortunate Disease,"
    Hygeia, March 1931.
45 As he later told: *MC*.
45 "Frequently the initial": Dattner, Thomas and Wexler, *The Man-
    agement of Neurosyphilis*, p. 299.
46 "slicker had stopped in": Sullivan, "I Know You, Al."
47 His original name: Balsamo interview.
47 the ice route: Pilat and Ransom, *Sodom by the Sea*, pp. 273–274.
48 the laundry business: Kobler, *Ardent Spirits*, p. 263.
48 Established in 1916: Pilat and Ransom, *Sodom by the Sea*, pp.
    274–278.
49 "Honey, you have": Balsamo interview. Gallucio related this inci-
    dent to Balsamo in 1959.
50 Salvatore Lucania: Balsamo and Carpozi, *Under the Clock*, pp.
    255–256.
50 Hearing the story: Balsamo interview.
51 He told Capone: Balsamo interview; Kobler, *Capone*, p. 36.
52 Domenica: Author's confidential interviews.
52 Carroll Street: Kobler, *Capone*, p. 36.
52 the Coughlins resided: 1900 U.S. Census, State and City of New
    York, Kings County, Borough of Brooklyn, Enumeration District
    64, Sheet 4A, lines 40–44, Ward 6, Block B.
52 On January 28, 1894: Certificate of Marriage for Michael Coughlin
    and Bridget Gorman, Church of St. Anthony, #1340, vol. 7, p.
    88.

54 On September 12: Registration Card for Alphonse Capone. Order
    number A2840. Local Board for Division #48, City of New
    York, State of N.Y. Brooklyn, Kings County, September 12,
    1918.

54 "When deafness": Dennie and Pakula, *Congenital Syphilis*, p. 370.

54 Even though Sonny's: Dennie and Pakula, *Congenital Syphilis*, p.
    363; Nelson, *Textbook of Pediatrics*, pp. 453–461.

55 On this document: New York State Department of Health, Marriage
    License, December 30, 1918, Kings County, Borough of Brook-
    lyn: New York City Department of Records and Information Ser-
    vices, Chambers Street, New York.

55 "I have not": *ibid*.

55 On December 30: Certificate of Marriage for "Albert Capone" and
    "Mary Coughlin" [sic], St. Mary Star of the Sea Church, Brook-
    lyn, N.Y.

57 "Evidently he was": Author's interview with Mike Aiello.

57 the census taker: 1920 U.S. Census for household of Gabriel Ca-
    poni [sic]. New York City, Borough of Brooklyn, Enumeration
    District 557, Sheet 6, Lines 28–33.

57 "chronic myocarditis": Death Certificate of Gabriel Caponi [sic],
    November 14, 1920, State of New York, Department of Health of
    The City of New York, Bureau of Records, cert. #21742.

58 "He said that he was": Aiello interview.

Chapter 2: *Where the East Meets the West*
 page 59 In the spring: Hart interview.
    59 tribute to his hero: *ibid*.
    61 limited career opportunities: *ibid*.
    61 "Hart pushed": Reprinted in the *Omaha World-Herald Magazine*,
        October 7, 1951.
    61 The Winches had arrived: Hart interview.
    62 On his youngest son's: Birth certificate of Richard Hart Jr. Nebraska
        State Department of Health, #18024. MM.
    63 "Pictures of Hart's raid": Reprinted in the *Omaha World-Herald
        Magazine*, October 7, 1951.
    64 "dim lights flitting": *Bridgeport News-Blade*, n.d., in possession of
        Harry Hart.
    66 "is becoming": Reprinted in the *Omaha World-Herald Magazine*,
        October 7, 1951.
    66 "I wish to commend": letter in possession of Harry Hart.
    66 "You've got": Hart interview.
    67 On the evening of October 23: Deposition of Walter Gumm, Logan
        Lambert, and Richard J. Hart, *State of Nebraska vs. Richard J.
        Hart*. MM. (Hereafter referred to as "Deposition")
    68 "We were satisfied": *ibid*.

68   "Hart discharged": *ibid.*

68   "determined the cause": *ibid.*

69   "Hart and I": *ibid.*

69   "Now the bootleggers": Reprinted in the *Omaha World-Herald Magazine*, October 7, 1951.

69   "the officers accused": Unidentified newspaper clipping headlined, "Slain Man's Widow Sues," MM.

70   "CORONER'S JURY": Unidentified newspaper clipping. MM.

70   "This is not a question": Harry L. Keefe to A. M. Smith, October 16, 1923. MM.

70   "guilty of careless indifference": Mabel Walker Willebrandt to James C. Kinsler, April 19, 1924. MM.

70   "all the shooting": James C. Kinsler to the Attorney General, Washington, D.C., April 23, 1924. MM.

71   *Hog Butcher:* Sandburg, *Complete Poems,* p. 3.

71   "This will be": *Rand McNally Guide to Chicago,* p. 3.

71   *And they tell:* Sandburg, *Complete Poems,* p. 3.

72   In a city obsessed: Statistics for Chicago in the early 1920s come from the *Rand McNally Guide to Chicago, passim.*

74   "All the legal": *Rand McNally Guide to Chicago,* p. 26.

74   "two-fisted": St. John, *This Was My World,* p. 108.

74   "the most intense": Gunther, *Inside U.S.A.,* p. 370.

74   "Here in Boston": St. John, *This Was My World,* p. 109.

75   H. G. Wells: Gunther, *Inside U.S.A.,* pp. 369, 379.

76   *Laughing the stormy:* Sandburg, *Complete Poems,* p. 3.

76   "When I came": *Washington Herald,* March 11, 1932.

77   "First in violence": Steffens, *The Shame of the Cities,* pp. 234–235.

78   For many years Chicago: Landesco, *Organized Crime in Chicago,* pp. 2–4.

78   "conservative estimate": Thrasher, *The Gang,* p. 5.

79   A racketeer may: *Chicago Journal of Commerce,* December 17, 1927, in Asbury, *Gem of the Prairie,* p. 365.

79   "Sexual commerce": Wilson, *Chicago,* pp. 53–54.

80   Cadets' Protective: Kobler, *Capone,* p. 43.

80   Michael "Hinky Dink" Kenna: Pasley, *Al Capone,* p. 13.

81   racketeers mingled: Lindberg, *To Serve and Collect,* pp. 156–157.

81   "Here they could": Harrison, *Stormy Years,* p. 305.

82   On the last day: Burns, *The One-Way Ride,* pp. 13–18.

83   "The murder of James Colosimo": *Chicago Daily News,* May 12, 1920, in Landesco, *Organized Crime in Chicago,* p. 36.

83   "Big Jim": Burns, *The One-Way Ride,* p. 17.

83   A procession: Landesco, *Organized Crime in Chicago,* p. 191.

83   "It is a strange commentary": Asbury, *Gem of the Prairie,* p. 316.

84   The list of suspects: Nelli, *Italians in Chicago,* pp. 150–151.

84   "So long, vampire": Lindberg, *To Serve and Collect,* p. 159.

84 In February 1922: Balsamo and Carpozi, *Under the Clock*, pp. 114–123.

86 William H. Thompson Republican Club: Wendt and Kogan, *Big Bill of Chicago*, p. 237.

86 "Modern crime": Nelli, *Italians in Chicago*, p. 150.

87 organization was making: Wendt and Kogan, *Big Bill of Chicago*, p. 238.

88 "swarthy, heavy-set fellow": Waller, *Chicago Uncensored*, pp. 67–68. Waller dates this incident to the summer of 1923, but by then Capone's days as a lowly street hustler were behind him, and he was running Torrio's vice empire. Thus, the incident probably occurred a year or more earlier.

89 Four Deuces: Asbury, *Gem of the Prairie*, p. 319.

89 "a colorless": McPhaul, *Johnny Torrio*.

89 "They're tortured": Kobler, *Capone*, p. 67.

89 "ALPHONSE CAPONE": Pasley, *Al Capone*, p. 19.

89 Each was devoted: Burns, *The One-Way Ride*, p. 37; Pasley, *Al Capone*, p. 70.

90 Jack Guzik: There is little agreement over how Jack Guzik spelled his name. The newspapers called him Jack, Jake, and Jacob, but he generally referred to himself as Jack. The spelling of his last name also varies; some popular versions are Cusick, Gusick, and Gusik.

90 The parents: 1900 U.S. Census, Illinois, vol. 45, ED 603, Sheet 20, Line 67 (311a Taylor, Chicago, Cook County).

91 precinct captain: *CT*, February 22, 1956.

91 "The Blue Goose": Pre-Parole Investigation. *NA-JG*.

91 December 3, 1917: Chicago Crime Commission to United States Board of Parole, May 16, 1932. *NA-JG*.

93 In August 1922, while drunk: Lyle, *The Dry and Lawless Years*, p. 72.

93 "Alfred Caponi": Pasley, *Al Capone*, p. 20.

94 "To this picnic": Author's interview with Rio Burke.

94 7244 South Prairie Avenue: Pasley, *Al Capone*, pp. 88–90.

95 Only Ralph: *Hearings before the Special Committee to Investigate Organized Crime in Interstate Commerce*, pp. 1227, 1231.

95 The Capones soon became known: Pasley, *Al Capone*, pp. 88–90.

97 "This guerrilla war": Kobler, *Capone*, p. 111.

97 Western Electric plant: St. John, *This Was My World*, p. 178; Mayer and Wade, *Chicago*, p. 250.

99 " 'whoopee' spot": *BP-RC*.

99 In his first: St. John, *This Was My World*, p. 172.

99 "I saw no harm": Kobler, *Capone*, pp. 122–123.

99 It sheltered: Sifakis, *The Mafia Encyclopedia*, pp. 314–315.

100   complicated business: Landesco, *Organized Crime in Chicago*, p. 180.
101   " 'I'm going to Chicago' ": Pitaro interview.
101   "great respect": Cohen and Nugent, *Mickey Cohen*, pp. 24–25.
102   "See, I was": *ibid.*
102   "Are you crazy": *ibid.*, p. 29.
103   "You know, a ten-dollar": *ibid.*
103   "they were just": *ibid.*
103   Peter Aiello was coming: Aiello interview.
104   Robert St. John: Author's interview with Robert St. John.
104   "I started the paper": *ibid.*
104   "harassed my reporters": *ibid.*
105   "Why don't you": St. John, *This Was My World*, p. 173.
105   Once the plan: *ibid.*
106   The experience: *CT*, April 2, 1924.
106   "Polling places": *ibid.*
106   Edmund K. Jarecki: *ibid.*
106   "I noticed a neatly": St. John, *This Was My World*, p. 179.
107   "They tell us": *ibid.*
107   One of the policemen: *Chicago Daily News*, April 2, 1924.
107   "When we rolled": St. John interview.
108   7,878 votes: *CT*, *Chicago Daily News*, April 2, 1924.
108   "When I could get": St. John, *This Was My World*, p. 181.
109   "Practically all": *CT*, April 3, 1924.
109   At the inquest Al testified: *Chicago Daily News*, April 2, 1924.
      In time, the circumstances of Frank Capone's death became embellished with extravagant flourishes. According to Herbert Asbury's *Gem of the Prairie*, Frank stood shoulder to shoulder with his brother Al and other Capone gunmen, exchanging shots with the police. After Frank fell, "Al Capone fled down Cicero Avenue, encountered another group of policemen, and with a gun blazing in each hand fought them off until darkness came to his aid and he escaped." In fact, Al Capone did not fire on the police or anyone else that day, let alone with a "gun blazing in each hand."
110   "GANGLAND BOWS": *Chicago Daily News*, April 5, 1924.
110   "Dressed in their best": *CT*, April 6, 1924.
110   "curious commingling": *ibid.*
110   "He could twist": Pasley, *Al Capone*, p. 45.
110   "Chicago's arch-criminal": Asbury, *Gem of the Prairie*, p. 341.
110   "was banked": Kobler, *Capone*, p. 116.
111   "ground into powder": *Chicago Daily News*, April 5, 1924.
111   "You people": *ibid.*
111   "Scarface": *CT*, April 5, 1924.

112   "Listen, you Dago pimp": Lyle, *The Dry and Lawless Years*, p. 73;
        Chicago Daily News, December 23, 1930.
112   "I am certain": Pasley, *Al Capone*, p. 27.
113   "stooping behind": *CT*, May 9, 1924.
113   GUNMAN: *ibid.*
113   "hanging prosecutor": Lyle, *The Dry and Lawless Years*, p. 73.
114   "I hear the police": Pasley, *Al Capone*, p. 29.
114   "We, the jury": *ibid.*, p. 30.
114   Hawthorne Inn: Asbury, *Gem of the Prairie*, p. 335.
114   "Entrance was": Pasley, *Al Capone*, pp. 62–63.
115   The liquor flowed: Kobler, *Capone*, p. 117.
115   The racketeers' lingo: Asbury, *Gem of the Prairie*, p. 340; Pasley, *Al
        Capone*, p. 37.
115   Al's real retreat: Author's interview with Roy Kral. This building still
        stands, looking very much as it did in Capone's day, as does the
        Anton, but the Hawthorne Inn has long since been torn down.
116   "perforated nasal septum": U.S. Penitentiary, Alcatraz, California,
        Neuro-Psychiatric Examination, June 4, 1938. *BP-AC*.
117   "Ninety-nine percent": St. John interview.
118   "One midnight": St. John, *This Was My World*, p. 182.
118   "All were blasé": *ibid.*, p. 184.
118   The atmosphere: St. John interview.
118   "I had undertaken": St. John, *This Was My World*, p. 184.
118   "Everywhere they went": *ibid.*, pp. 186–187.
120   "angry that the whole": *ibid.*, p. 188.
120   "The brakes shrieked": *ibid.*, p. 189.
121   Capone henchmen kidnapped: St. John interview; St. John, *This
        Was My World*, p. 190.
121   "He was rather dark": *ibid.*, pp. 190–191.
121   "as clean-cut": *ibid.*, p. 191–192.
121   talcum powder: St. John interview.
121   "He was impeccably": St. John, *This Was My World*, pp. 192–194.
123   "Maybe you don't": *ibid.*, p. 195.
123   "I telegraphed": St. John interview.
124   As he was delivering: St. John, *This Was My World*, pp. 196–197.
125   The journalists: Author's interview with Tony Berardi.
126   rumors trailed him: Author's confidential interview.

Chapter 3: *Memento Mori*
page 128   the survey: *CCC*.
128   "Two-thirds": Sullivan, *Rattling the Cup*, p. 49; Allsop, *The Boot-
        leggers*, p. 76.
128   "You can hardly": *Literary Digest*, October 30, 1926.
129   $1 million annually: Asbury, *Gem of the Prairie*, p. 344.

129   "Dion was all right": Sullivan, *Rattling the Cup*, p. 48.

129   Torrio proposed: Asbury, *Gem of the Prairie*, p. 345.

130   "alky-cookers": Pasley, *Al Capone*, p. 49; Allsop, *The Bootleggers*, pp. 76–77.

130   Gennas' homemade brew: Kobler, *Capone*, pp. 90–91.

131   When the Gennas began: Asbury, *Gem of the Prairie*, pp. 345–347.

131   "He was spoiling": Sullivan, *Rattling the Cup*, p. 49.

131   retire from bootlegging: Asbury, *Gem of the Prairie*, pp. 348–349.

133   "Oh, to hell": *ibid.*, p. 349; Pasley, *Al Capone*, p. 50.

133   Don Miguel Merlo: Balsamo and Carpozi, *Under the Clock*, p. 188.

133   Mike Merlo's passing: Asbury, *Gem of the Prairie*, pp. 349–350; Pasley, *Al Capone*, pp. 54–55. Pasley says that the effigy was made of wax rather than flowers.

133   The selection: Kobler, *Capone*, p. 127.

134   "Two of them": *ibid.*, p. 128.

134   "Hello, boys": Burns, *The One-Way Ride*, p. 101.

135   the police did not try: Pasley, *Al Capone*, p. 57.

136   John A. Sbarbaro: *ibid.*, p. 58.

136   "lay in state": Asbury, *Gem of the Prairie*, p. 351.

136   "the Simon Legree": Pasley, *Al Capone*, p. 51.

136   The cortege: *ibid.*, p. 58; Burns, *The One-Way Ride*, pp. 104–105.

137   "Are we living": Allsop, *The Bootleggers*, p. 87.

138   "O'Banion was a thief": Asbury, *Gem of the Prairie*, p. 352.

138   Sylvester Barton: Allsop, *The Bootleggers*, p. 91.

139   Johnny Torrio traveled south: Asbury, *Gem of the Prairie*, p. 353.

139   "Hymie" Weiss: *ibid.*, p. 352.

139   "You'd expect": Kobler, *Capone*, p. 84.

140   "That's a beautiful": *ibid.*, p. 85.

141   Thompson submachine gun: Helmer, *The Gun that Made the Twenties Roar*, *passim*; Levell and Helmer, *The Quotable Al Capone*, pp. 29–34.

141   "Sure Defense": Levell and Helmer, *The Quotable Al Capone*, p. 34.

141   The gun sold: Kobler, *Capone*, p. 97.

142   "That's the gun!": Sullivan, *Rattling the Cup*, p. 37.

142   kidnapped the new man: Kobler, *Capone*, pp. 135–136.

143   On January 24: Asbury, *Gem of the Prairie*, p. 353; Allsop, *The Bootleggers*, p. 92.

144   "loud, checked suit": McPhaul, *Johnny Torrio*, pp. 33–34.

144   "I know you": *ibid.*, pp. 34–35.

145   "most brutal gunman": Kobler, *Capone*, p. 96.

145   When he was: McPhaul, *Johnny Torrio*, p. 215.

145   "I know who": Lyle, *The Dry and Lawless Years*, pp. 111–112; Allsop, *The Bootleggers*, p. 92.

147   the "Terrible Gennas": Asbury, *Gem of the Prairie*, pp. 355–356;
      CT, May 11, 1929.

147   Capone moved: *CT*, October 10, 1931.

148   "The first time": Author's interview with Tony Berardi.

149   Capone appeared: Author's interview with Stanley Pieza.

149   "There was a lot": Berardi interview.

149   "I never saw": *ibid.*

149   "There were roughly": *ibid.*

150   "I used to work": *ibid.*

150   "Kid, how you doing?": *ibid.*

151   The first time: Lyle, *The Dry and Lawless Years*, p. 115.

152   "was a miserable": *ibid.*

152   "This is the last": *CT*, October 8, 1931.

153   "What is your": Pasley, *Al Capone*, pp. 72–73.

153   "The body was": *ibid.*, pp. 78–79.

153   "Preceding the portable": *ibid.*

154   the *schvitz*: Author's confidential interviews.

155   In search of a cure: Balsamo and Carpozi, *Under the Clock*, p. 202.

155   Chicago's supply: Woods, "Was the First Interstate Trucking Pio-
      neer … Al Capone?" *Dunes Country Magazine*, Summer 1982.

156   The plan was: Balsamo and Carpozi, *Under the Clock*, pp. 202–205.

156   Capone, Scalise, and Anselmi: *ibid.*, pp. 206–209.

157   "You can bet": Kobler, *Capone*, p. 164.

157   "I was visiting": *New York Daily News*, August 15, 1982.

158   "Chicago is the imperial": Johnston, "Gangs à la Mode," *The New
      Yorker*, August 25, 1928.

158   After Dion O'Banion: *ibid.*

159   "reign of terror": Allsop, *The Bootleggers*, pp. 100–101; Kobler,
      Capone, pp. 166–167.

160   "The first shipment": Woods, "Was the First."

161   "If Al Capone": *ibid.*

161   Jack Richie: *ibid.*

162   MCSWIGGIN: *CT*, April 29, 1926.

162   on the last day: Spiering, *The Man Who Got Capone*, p. 10.

162   "idolized his brilliant son": Lyle, *The Dry and Lawless Years*, p. 81.

162   "I have an appointment": Burns, *The One-Way Ride*, p. 162.

163   " 'Samoots' Amatuna": *ibid.*, p. 164.

163   " 'Scarface' was at": *ibid.*, p. 165; *Chicago Daily News*, May 1,
      1926.

164   "I saw a closed": Wendt and Lloyd, *Big Bill of Chicago*, p. 452.

164   "Pretty cold-blooded": Kobler, *Capone*, p. 175.

165   "Mrs. McSwiggin was": *Chicago Daily News*, April 28, 1926.

165   Gangsters Turn: *CT*, April 28, 1926.

165   BARE MCSWIGGIN: *Chicago Daily News*, April 28, 1926.

166   wielded sledgehammers: *CT*, April 30, 1926.

166   "such as was": CT, April 29, 1926.
166   The police then invaded: Chicago Daily News, May 8, 1926.
166   "Let him stay": CT, April 29, 1926.
167   "On the way": CT, May 2, 1926.
167   "I thought my life": Spiering, The Man Who Got Capone, p. 13.
168   "He was only": Burns, The One-Way Ride, p. 162.
168   "It will be": Spiering, The Man Who Got Capone, p. 12.
168   "The town is wet": Kobler, Capone, p. 169.
168   "Everybody knows that": Chicago Daily News, April 30, 1926.
169   "When I wanted": Kobler, Capone, p. 173.
169   It has been: Pasley, Al Capone, p. 131.
169   "All of the investigators": Lyle, The Dry and Lawless Years, p. 81.
170   "A conspiracy of silence": Sullivan, Rattling the Cup, p. 141.
170   print their full names: Chicago Daily News, May 3, 1926.
170   cartoon cynically detailed: Chicago Daily News, April 30, 1926.
171   "Why not blame": Chicago Daily News, May 3, 1926.
171   "10,000 gallons": Indictment dated September 1926, District Court
        of the United States of America for the Northern District of Illi-
        nois, Eastern Division. NAGL.
171   For the week: Kobler, Capone, p. 179.
172   "She was the best": Burke interview.
172   "One day my maid": ibid.

Chapter 4: *Round Lake Refuge*

page 176   Angelo Mastropietro: Author's interview with Grazia Mastropietro.
     176   "Life was very hard": ibid.
     176   "The men who worked": ibid.
     178   lavished presents: ibid.
     178   "Al Capone and his family": ibid.
     178   two principal bodyguards: Russo interview.
     178   "We were all thrilled": Author's interview with Giovanna Anto-
            nucci.
     179   The Al Capone he knew: Russo interview.
     180   "When he was angry": ibid.
     181   "He even controlled": ibid.
     181   "In those days": ibid.
     182   "Angelo was": ibid.
     182   "In my personal": ibid.
     183   "He never carried": ibid.
     184   "John O'Brien came": G. Mastropietro interview.
     185   "could be tough": Russo interview.
     185   "When I first": letter from Lloyd Moles to author, January 2, 1992.
     185   Saginaw Street: G. Mastropietro interview.
     185   "He took us kids": Antonucci interview.
     186   "I remember him": G. Mastropietro interview.

186 "My brother and I": Antonucci interview.

186 "You were brought": G. Mastropietro interview.

187 "My mother would say": *ibid.*

188 "There was one family": G. Mastropietro interview.

189 No, Angelo counseled: *ibid.*

189 "Al loved music": *ibid.*

189 the assassination of the superintendent: For a full account of this
        event, see Gambino, *Vendetta*, and Botein, *The Hennessy Case.*

190 the first time: *Organized Crime: Twenty-Five Years After Valachi*, p.
        294.

190 "Who killa": Katz, "The Hennessy Affair," *New Orleans*, October
        1990.

190 "NONE GUILTY!": *New Orleans Daily Picayune*, March 14, 1891.

190 White League: Botein, *The Hennessy Case*, p. 22.

190 Arriving at the prison: Kendall, "Who Killa De Chief?" *Louisiana
        Historical Quarterly*, April 1939; Botein, *The Hennessy Case*, pp.
        111–112.

190 women stopped by: Gambino, *Vendetta*, p. 87.

190 "terribly effective": *NYT*, March 15, 1891.

191 speaking tour: Katz, "Hennessy Affair."

191 "I intend": Gambino, *Vendetta*, p. 162.

191 He began holding: Russo and G. Mastropietro interviews.

192 On July 28, 1926: Landesco, *Organized Crime in Chicago*, p. 19.

192 "We have been talking": Kobler, *Capone*, p. 181.

Chapter 5: *The Return of Al Capone*

page 193 On July 29, 1926: Pasley, *Al Capone*, p. 132.

193 "Of course": Kobler, *Capone*, pp. 181–182.

194 "Why should I": Landesco, *Organized Crime in Chicago*, pp. 19–
        29.

194 "I paid McSwiggin": Kobler, *Capone*, pp. 181–182.

194 "This complaint": Pasley, *Al Capone*, p. 132.

195 "If you think": *ibid.*, p. 134.

196 Thorn Grove: Holli and Jones, p. 240.

197 "was a place": *ibid.*

197 Vincenzo Ammarati: Petition for Naturalization, March 30, 1922,
        Cook County, City of Chicago Heights, Illinois, #1414. His
        petition for naturalization was "Vacated, Cancelled and Set aside"
        in 1932, when he ran permanently afoul of the law.

197 Frankie La Porte: Petition for Naturalization, May 20, 1926, Cook
        County, City of Chicago Heights, Illinois, #1334.

198 Rio Burke: Burke interview.

198 April 14, 1924: *CT*, April 13, 1986.

198 "Dominic made": Burke interview.

198 "Of course Al": *ibid.*

198 "While we lived": *ibid.*

199 violating the Volstead Act: *CT*, April 13, 1986.

199 "*I* became": Burke interview.

200 "shot four times": *Chicago Heights Star*, April 24, 1924.

200 On June 2, 1926: *Chicago Heights Star*, June 4, 1926.

201 "Murder . . . Fades": *Chicago Heights Star*, July 27, 1926.

202 "Even grandmothers": Holli and Jones, p. 263.

202 Vera Emery's life: Author's confidential interviews.

203 "I was in": Author's interview with John Pegoria.

203 "Al came to": Author's interview with Sam Pontarelli.

204 "Since the beginning": *Literary Digest*, October 30, 1926.

204 On August 10: Pasley, *Al Capone*, pp. 120–123; Allsop, *The Bootleggers and Their Era*, p. 119.

205 Six weeks later: Pasley, *Al Capone*, pp. 113–114.

205 Everything happened: *ibid.*

206 "It's a stall": *ibid.*

206 Half a minute: *ibid.*, p. 117.

206 The marauders: *ibid.*, pp. 118–119.

206 "Never saw them": *ibid.*, p. 123.

207 "Capone is very anxious": Burns, *The One-Way Ride*, pp. 188–189. Burns locates this exchange in a subsequent peace conference, at the Hotel Sherman, but since Weiss was dead by then, it is apparent that it occurred earlier, at the Hotel Morrison conference, which only Weiss and Lombardo attended.

207 "I wouldn't do that": Kobler, *Capone*, p. 187.

208 Oscar Lundin rented: Pasley, *Al Capone*, p. 125.

208 the assassins: *ibid.*, p. 126. Saltis was ultimately acquitted of the murder.

208 At The Name: Lyle, *The Dry and Lawless Years*, p. 120.

209 campaign posters: *ibid.*; Allsop, *The Bootleggers and Their Era*, p. 121.

209 array of evidence: Allsop, *The Bootleggers and Their Era*, p. 119; Kobler, *Capone*, p. 189.

209 "Capone played": *Literary Digest*, October 30, 1926.

210 "If there was": Author's interview with Walter Trohan.

210 "is sick today": *Literary Digest*, October 30, 1926.

211 "The *Trib* was": Allsop, *The Bootleggers and Their Era*, pp. 361–362.

213 "the one object": *Literary Digest*, October 30, 1926.

213 "There is enough": *ibid.*

213 emissary to Judge John Lyle: Lyle, *The Dry and Lawless Years*, pp. 19–20.

214 "Here they sat": Pasley, *Al Capone*, p. 142.

215 "I told them": Allsop, *The Bootleggers and Their Era*, p. 125.

215 "Remember that night": Kobler, *Capone*, p. 194.

216   "I'd never have": *ibid.*

216   "Just like the old": *ibid.*, p. 195.

216   For seventy days: Pasley, *Al Capone*, pp. 143–144.

216   January 6, 1927: *ibid.*, pp. 67–68.

217   "I am out": Bennett, *Chicago Gang Land*, p. 81.

218   "Capone lives on": *ibid.*, p. 87.

219   $25,000 yacht: Allsop, *The Bootleggers and Their Era*, pp. 209–210;
        Wendt and Kogan, *Big Bill of Chicago*, p. 13.

219   To exhibit his displeasure: Allsop, *The Bootleggers and Their Era*, p.
        210.

219   "left-handed Irishman": Green and Holli, *The Mayors*, p. 94.

219   immense prestige: *ibid.*, p. 95.

220   "treason-tainted histories": Allsop, *The Bootleggers and Their Era*, p.
        211; Peterson, *Barbarians in Our Midst*, p. 140.

220   "The city is overrun": Lindberg, *To Serve and Collect*, p. 184.

221   contributed $260,000: Allsop, *The Bootleggers and Their Era*, p.
        211; *NYT*, February 17, 1931.

221   "money was ladled": *CT*, February 17, 1931.

221   The Thompson Republican Club: Lindberg, *To Serve and Collect*,
        p. 185.

221   Election eve found: *ibid.*, Wendt and Kogan, *Big Bill of Chicago*, p.
        271.

222   "Drucci said": Allsop, *The Bootleggers and Their Era*, pp. 129–130;
        Pasley, *Al Capone*, p. 160.

222   $400,000 estate: Allsop, *The Bootleggers and Their Era*, p. 130.

223   515,716 votes to Dever's 432,678: *ibid.*, p. 213.

223   aboard his yacht: *ibid.*

223   Capone's ally: Nelli, *Italians in Chicago*, pp. 232–233.

224   "DECIDES BOOTLEGGERS": *NYT*, May 17, 1927.

224   "We are of": *ibid.*

224   "make fabulous profits": *ibid.*

225   the unit toiled in the shadow: Spiering, *The Man Who Got Capone*,
        pp. 43–44.

226   Insull was fired on: Foster, "Dodging Death with 'Emperor' Insull,"
        Startling Detective Adventures, n.d. CHS.

226   Insull contributed: Wendt and Kogan, *Big Bill of Chicago*, p. 276;
        Sargent, "Chicago, Hands Down," *The Forum*, November 1927.

227   Sam Pontarelli: Pontarelli interview.

227   Gabby Hartnett: Berardi interview; Lyle, *The Dry and Lawless Years*,
        p. 115.

228   "He was wearing": Sullivan and Kobler, "Caddying for a Man Who
        Never Shot Par," *Sports Illustrated*, November 6, 1972.

228   Blind Robin: *ibid.*

229   "The boys made": *ibid.*

229   "I would keep": *ibid.*

230 "The bullet plowed": *CT*, September 21, 1928.

230 "After that": Sullivan and Kobler, "Caddying."

230 "One afternoon on the links": *ibid.*

232 "Throughout my career": Ross and Abramson, *No Man Stands Alone*, p. 125.

232 "Al told me": *ibid.*

232 From his two-room office: Brenner and Nagler, *Only the Ring Was Square*, p. 2.

232 "on the day": letter from Vern Whaley to author, August 1, 1991.

232 Among the fighters: Sullivan and Kobler, "Caddying."

233 Dempsey became: Fox, *Blood and Power*, p. 90.

233 Capone bet $50,000: *ibid.*, p. 91.

233 one hundred ringside: Russo interview.

233 "He'd better get": Kearns and Fraley, *The Million Dollar Gate*, p. 226.

234 "To the Dempseys": Fox, *Blood and Power*, p. 91.

234 Damon Runyon: Breslin, *Damon Runyon*, p. 259.

234 "They came in": *CT*, September 23, 1927.

234 "They stood": *ibid.*

235 "savage": *ibid.*

235 "By the time": *Chicago Daily News*, September 23, 1927.

235 After the fight: Breslin, *Damon Runyon*, p. 258.

236 "I quit because": Fox, *Blood and Power*, p. 92.

236 "Capone took over": *CT*, February 17, 1931.

236 "Watching an official": Pasley, *Al Capone*, p. 163.

236 In 1927: *ibid.*, p. 60.

238 Joseph Aiello: Lyle, *The Dry and Lawless Years*, pp. 9–11.

238 311 South Clark Street: *ibid.*, pp. 11–13.

239 "You're dead": Pasley, *Al Capone*, p. 175.

239 "I'm willing": Kobler, *Capone*, pp. 207–208.

240 Richard Hart placed: Hart interview; *Ironwood (Michigan) Daily Globe*, September 6, 1990.

240 "Hart was notified": Unidentified newspaper clipping in possession of Harry Hart.

241 life on a reservation: Hart interview.

241 "TWO-GUNS" SLEUTH: Unidentified newspaper clipping in possession of Harry Hart, *Omaha World-Herald Magazine*, October 7, 1951.

242 "He loved to dress": Hart interview; photographs in possession of Harry Hart.

242 President Calvin Coolidge: Fuess, *Calvin Coolidge*, p. 390.

Chapter 6: *The Jazz Age*

page 245 "Everybody came to Chicago": Author's interview with Milt Hinton.

245 "we wanted our kind": *ibid.*

245   "When Al Capone opened": *ibid.*
246   "alcohol and whiskey": *ibid.*
247   "They took me": *ibid.*
247   He died: Hinton and Berger, *Bass Line*, p. 21.
248   Fats Waller: Waller and Calabrese, *Fats Waller*, p. 62.
249   "Capone's University": Mezzrow and Wolfe, *Really the Blues*, pp. 52–53.
249   "Al always showed": *ibid.*
249   "a sandy-haired": *ibid.*, pp. 53–54.
250   "One of you guys": *ibid.*,
250   After we let: *ibid.*, pp. 52–53.
251   Lewis had become: Messick, *The Beauties and the Beasts*, pp. 26–32.
251   in August 1927: Coffey, *The Long Thirst*, p. 218.
251   "My contract's up": *ibid.*, pp. 218–219.
252   November 9: *ibid.*, p. 221.
252   Thirty minutes later: *ibid.*, pp. 221–222; CT, November 8, 1927.
253   Six days later: Messick, *The Beauties and the Beasts*, pp. 31–32.
254   "Why the hell": Fox, *Blood and Power*, pp. 83–84.
254   "Gangsters were known": Richman and Gehman, *A Hell of a Life*, p. 6.
255   "On opening night": *ibid.*
255   "the ruler": *ibid.*, pp. 8–9.
256   "Instead of going": *ibid.*, p. 10. Richman says Capone was living at the Lexington Hotel, but the racketeer was still at the Metropole at this time; the move would come in the near future.
256   "There was an American": *ibid.*, pp. 11–12.
258   "That's too late": Berle and Frankel, *Milton Berle*, p. 168.
258   "I don't know": *ibid.*
259   "You're a Yid": Adler, *It Ain't Necessarily So*, p. 33.
259   "Look, kid": *ibid.*
261   "the amazing": *Chicago Daily News*, December 6, 1927.
261   "for the latest": CT, December 5, 1927.
261   "sitting comfortably": CT, December 6, 1927.
262   "I'm leaving": *ibid.*
262   "I've been spending": *ibid.*
262   *Chicago Daily News* estimated: *Chicago Daily News*, December 6, 1927.
262   "I could bear": CT, December 6, 1927.
263   "I've never been": *ibid.*
263   "YOU CAN ALL": CT, December 6, 1927; *Chicago Daily News*, December 6, 1927.
264   "I feel almost": CT, December 7, 1927.
265   "This gang war": *Los Angeles Examiner*, December 13, 1927.
265   "I never saw": CT, December 17, 1927.

265   "Why should everybody": *Los Angeles Times*, December 14, 1927.

266   "I will place": *Chicago Herald and Examiner*, December 20, 1927.

266   "CAPONE'S SON": *Chicago Herald and Examiner*, December 15, 1927.

266   "It's pretty tough": *Chicago Herald and Examiner*, December 17, 1927.

267   "Pleased to meet": *ibid*.

267   "Well," said: *CT*, December 17, 1927

268   "They call Al Capone": *New York Sun*, December 21, 1927.

268   December 22: *CCC*.

268   "and tell him": *CT*, December 23, 1927.

269   "the garden of America": *The SunPost* (Miami), February 28, 1991.

269   "only another": *CT*, January 12, 1928.

269   hurricane: *The SunPost* (Miami), February 28, 1991.

269   "CAPONE HUNTED": *CT*, January 12, 1928.

269   "one of the fairest": *NYT*, January 22, 1928.

270   "If he's here": *Literary Digest*, June 15, 1929; *CT*, January 18, 1928.

272   "No record": Robt. H. Lucas, Commissioner of Internal Revenue, to Assistant Secretary Hope, March 19, 1930. *HHL*.

272   "The task": Wilson, "Undercover Man," *Collier's*, April 26, 1947.

272   "completely anonymous": *ibid*.

272   "would be as": *ibid*.

273   "His sources": Pasley, *Al Capone*, p. 87.

273   "It was common": Wilson, "Undercover Man."

273   In the course: Robt. H. Lucas, Commissioner of Internal Revenue, to Assistant Secretary Hope, March 19, 1930. *HHL*.

274   July 11, 1874: Author's interview with George E. Q. Johnson, Jr.

274   federal judges made: *ibid*.

275   "My father said": *ibid*.

275   index-card file: *NYT*, April 3, 1932.

275   "Organized crime was": *ibid*.

276   Guzik family dog: Johnson interview.

276   "Any man": Asbury, *Gem of the Prairie*, p. 366.

276   367 murders: Pasley, *Al Capone*, pp. 151–152.

277   *To the Editor*: *NYT*, January 10, 1928.

277   "CHICAGO BOMBERS": *NYT*, February 18, 1928.

278   In March: Kobler, *Capone*, p. 217.

278   115 bombs: Lyle, *The Dry and Lawless Years*, p. 255.

279   "blown to bits": *NYT*, March 31, 1928; Johnson interview.

279   "You tell": *NYT*, March 31, 1928.

279   "There are fifty": *ibid*.

279   "The bombs are": Allsop, *The Bootleggers and Their Era*, p. 220.

279   "Deneen is filling": Pasley, *Al Capone*, pp. 202–203.

279   "The public is not": *NYT*, March 27, 1928.

280 "King George's": Allsop, *The Bootleggers and Their Era*, p. 221.
280 "most maligned": *NYT*, March 31, 1928.
280 "It costs": Allsop, *The Bootleggers and Their Era*, p. 220.
280 "And what does": Runyon, *The Damon Runyon Omnibus*, p. 238.
281 "a day of sluggings": Pasley, *Al Capone*, p. 217.
281 "ballot rebellion": *ibid.*, p. 218.
281 "Why should I": *ibid.*, p. 220.
281 "The primary brought": *ibid.*, p. 219.
282 the party flew: Sullivan, *Chicago Surrenders*, pp. 86–87.
283 renovation of the Palm Island villa: Author's interview with Henry Morrison.
283 "Don't keep": Kobler, *Capone*, p. 223.
283 Mae favored Louis XIV: Contents of the Capone Palm Island villa described in the April 15, 1992 bulletin of Leslie Hindman Auctioneers (Chicago): "Prohibition Era and 20th Century Crime Memorabilia and Ephemera."
284 "I came to pay": Pasley, *Al Capone*, p. 85.
284 "like a tourist": *Miami Herald*, June 23, 1968.
285 "When I looked": *ibid.*
285 bootlegging arrangement with Frankie Yale: Allsop, *The Bootleggers and Their Era*, p. 276; Pilat and Ransom, *Sodom by the Sea*, pp. 284–285.
286 Capone returned: *NYT*, June 28, 1928.
286 He then approached: *CT*, July 31, August 1, 1928.
287 "would prove a tremendous": *NYT*, June 28, 1928; *Miami Daily News*, June 27, 928.
287 "MIAMI BEACH": *NYT*, June 28, 1928.
287 When the Capones dined: Breslin, *Damon Runyon*, p. 14.
288 Sunday, July 1: Balsamo and Carpozi, *Under the Clock*, pp. 214–216; Pilat and Ransom, *Sodom by the Sea*, p. 103.
289 The funeral took place: Pilat and Ransom, *Sodom by the Sea*, pp. 286–287.
290 The weapons: *CT*, July 31, 1928; August 1, 1928.
290 "YALE DEATH": *CT*, July 8, 1928; July 31, 1928.
291 "eased his bank roll": *CT*, August 4, 1928.
291 On July 30: *CT*, October 15, 1931.
291 bulletproof: Burke interview.
291 "The Lexington": Author's interview with Vern Whaley.
291 To prevent: Kobler, *Capone*, p. 227.
291 His girlfriend: *ibid.*, p. 228.
292 "I love": Murray, *The Legacy of Al Capone*, p. 333.
292 kidnapping: Pasley, *Al Capone*, pp. 229–231.
293 "Like most successful": Allsop, *The Bootleggers and Their Era*, p. 278.
293 two men: Pasley, *Al Capone*, p. 231.

293   $150,000 war chest: *NYT*, June 24, 1928.
293   "All the kidnappings": Allsop, *The Bootleggers and Their Era*, p. 279; Pasley, *Al Capone*, p. 235.
294   "the head center": *CT*, March 25, 1931; Statement of Frank J. Loesch, February 2, 1933. *DJ*.
294   "I found him": *ibid*.
294   "Mr. Capone, gunmen": *ibid*.
295   murder of Pasqualino Lolordo: Pasley, *Al Capone*, pp. 236–238.

Chapter 7: *Slaughter and Sanctuary*
page 300   "No one who": Willebrandt, *The Inside of Prohibition*, p. 15.
300   Leroy Gilbert: *Chicago Daily News*, February 24, 1936.
301   In retaliation: *Chicago Heights Star*, January 8, 1929; *Chicago Daily News*, February 24, 1936.
302   "the revenue": Willebrandt, *The Inside of Prohibition*, p. 151.
303   check for $2,130: *Chicago Daily News*, February 24, 1936; *Chicago Heights Star*, February 28, 1936; Kobler, *Capone*, pp. 272–273.
303   Eddie Waters: Nels E. Tessem to Chief, Intelligence Unit, Bureau of Internal Revenue, February 24, 1932. *BP-RC*.
303   "My client": Kobler, *Capone*, p. 273.
303   The investigation further: Nels E. Tessem to Chief, Intelligence Unit, Bureau of Internal Revenue, February 24, 1932. *BP-RC*.
304   Ralph J. Capone: *ibid*.
306   ruthless bank robber: Pasley, *Al Capone*, pp. 259.
307   Claude Maddox: Helmer, *The Gun That Made the Twenties Roar*, p. 90; Lyle, *The Dry and Lawless Years*, p. 210.
307   "right off the river": Pasley, *Al Capone*, pp. 252.
308   He arranged to be: *CT*, May 27, 1931; Lyle, *The Dry and Lawless Years*, pp. 210–211.
308   Included were: Pasley, *Al Capone*, pp. 252–254.
308   Dr. Reinhart H. Schwimmer: Burns, *The One-Way Ride*, p. 260.
308   At that moment: Pasley, *Al Capone*, pp. 255–257.
309   "Who shot you": *Wisconsin News*, February 15, 1929; Pasley, *Al Capone*, pp. 256–257.
310   In one instance: Trohan, *Political Animals*, p. 24.
310   "I was in": Trohan interview.
311   "I opened the door": *ibid*.
311   "There used to be": *ibid*.
312   "The corpses": Lyle, *The Dry and Lawless Years*, pp. 219–220.
312   "I've got more": Trohan, *Political Animals*, p. 25.
312   "I tell you": *CT*, February 15, 1929.
314   huge rewards: Kobler, *Capone*, p. 247.
314   And on the morning: Lindberg, *To Serve and Collect*, p. 198; Allsop, *The Bootleggers and Their Era*, p. 144. Some accounts place the meeting between Capone and Taylor at Capone's Miami

home, but records pertaining to Capone's trial for tax evasion
reveal that it took place in Taylor's office.

314 "Didn't you ever": Ross, *The Trial of Al Capone*, p. 64.

315 "Only Capone": Lindberg, *To Serve and Collect*, p. 201.

315 fifty hoodlums: *CT*, February 19, 1929.

316 There are sixteen: Inquest on the Bodies of Albert Kachellek, et al., February 23, 1929. *CCC*.

316 Goddard was based: Lyle, *The Dry and Lawless Years*, p. 224.

317 During most of 1929: *St. Joseph Herald-Press*, December 31, 1931.

317 Major Goddard studied: Pasley, *Al Capone*, pp. 262–263.

317 in March 1931: *NYT*, March 27, 1931.

318 $1 a word: Wendt, *Chicago Tribune*, p. 433.

319 "Crime in Chicago": Gunther, "The High Cost of Hoodlums," *Harper's Monthly*, October 1929.

319 "Probably no private": *NYT*, May 26, 1929.

320 "The somewhat portly person": Breslin, *Damon Runyon*, pp. 287–288.

320 the wife of Jack Koefed: Kobler, *Capone*, p. 247.

321 a small airplane: *Tampa Tribune*, January 26, 1969.

322 "they're not touching": Halper, *The Chicago Crime Book*, p. 112.

322 "At once": Hoover, *Memoirs*, p. 277.

322 "Have you got": Lyle, *The Dry and Lawless Years*, p. 197.

323 "Since January 13": Affidavit of Dr. Kenneth Phillips, March 5, 1929. *FBI-AC*.

323 The FBI had: Author's Interview with William Roemer; Salerno and Tompkins, *The Crime Confederation*, p. 280.

323 "as a personal": Memorandum from Mabel Walker Willebrandt for Mr. Hoover, March 22, 1929. *FBI-AC*.

324 In one affidavit: Report of J. J. Perkins, April 3, 1929. *FBI-AC*.

324 "Previous to": J. J. Perkins to Director, Bureau of Investigation, March 27, 1929. *FBI-AC*.

324 "There is no": W. A. McSwain to J. Edgar Hoover, May 14, 1930. *FBI-AC*.

325 "It would be dangerous": *CT*, March 10, 1929.

325 "In dealing": George E. Q. Johnson to Mr. J. Edgar Hoover, March 27, 1929. *FBI-AC*.

325 "Capone is popularly": Memorandum for the Attorney General, November 8, 1930. *FBI-AC*.

325 "They say": *CT*, March 6, 1929.

325 Indeed, the Feds: *CT*, March 19, 1929.

326 On March 19: *CT*, March 20, 1929.

326 "Capone will be": *ibid*.

326 "split any difference": *CT*, March 21, 22, 26, 1929.

326 seized records: *CT*, March 27, 1929.

326 The U.S. Attorney explained: *NYT*, March 27, 1929.

326 "The income": Kobler, *Capone*, p. 274.
327 "This is": *Washington Herald*, March 28, 1929.
327 "My hydro-aeroplane": *CT*, March 6, 1929.
327 He visited Nassau: *NYT*, March 27, 1929.
328 *WALTER WINCHELL: Washington Herald*, October 29, 1931. The visit to Capone's Florida residence described in this column took place at least two years before it was published. Winchell dared to print it only after Capone had been sentenced to a long jail term for income tax evasion.
329 At the end: United Press dispatch, April 25, 1929.
329 "I am the most": Allsop, *The Bootleggers and Their Era*, p. 148.
330 three traitors: Pasley, *Al Capone*, pp. 331–332.
330 three disfigured corpses: Lyle, *The Dry and Lawless Years*, pp. 221–222; Pasley, *Al Capone*, p. 332.
331 Three days after: *NYT*, May 16, 1929.
332 "From what I hear": Runyon, *The Damon Runyon Omnibus*, p. 200.
332 "to pick": *NYT*, May 16, 1929.
332 Accardo betrayed: *Chicago Sun-Times*, November 2, 1953.
333 "I think you": Gosch and Hamner, *The Last Testament of Lucky Luciano*, pp. 105–106.
334 "There are two": Messick, *Lansky*, p. 59.
334 where the "delegates": Gosch and Hamner, *The Last Testament of Lucky Luciano*, pp. 106–107; Fox, *Blood and Power*, pp. 104–105.
335 Robert T. Loughran: *Literary Digest*, June 15, 1929.
337 "I extended": *CT*, May 19, 1929.
337 "I had a most": *Literary Digest*, June 15, 1929. Capone's remarks are rearranged slightly for the sake of coherence.
337 By dawn: *Time*, May 27, 1929.
338 "QUAKER JUSTICE": *CT*, May 18, 1929.
338 90725: *CT*, May 18, 1929.
338 diamond ring: *ibid.*
338 "It's enough": *NYT*, May 19, 1929.
338 "the Capone conviction": *CT*, May 18, 1929.
339 "I've arrested Capone": Pasley, *Al Capone*, p. 328.
339 "Their living room": *CT*, May 18, 1929.
340 "a radiant hostess": *ibid.*
340 Eastern Penitentiary: Pasley, *Al Capone*, p. 333.
340 "I could have": Kobler, *Capone*, pp. 262–263.
341 "CAPONE CRIES": *CT*, September 22, October 5, 9, November 1, 7, 27, 1929.
341 Six of the indictments: Allsop, *The Bootleggers and Their Era*, p. 315.
341 October 8: Messick, *Secret File*, p. 44.

342   fresh contingent of investigators: Ness and Fraley, *The Untouchables*, pp. 105–106.

Chapter 8: *Public Enemies*
page 345   "The ladies": Author's interview with Louise Jamie.
346   In about 1928: Ness Collection. *WRHS*.
346   "The trouble": *ibid.*
347   early raids: *Chicago Herald and Examiner*, May 4, 1929.
347   "the handsomest man": Ness Collection. *WRHS*.
347   "rum-runners": *ibid.*
347   "One time": Pontarelli interview.
348   Martino was: *ibid.*
348   "he hanged himself": *ibid.*
349   "we always travelled": *ibid.*
349   "I got a message": Ness and Fraley, *The Untouchables*, p. 175. In his book, Ness suggests the incident involving the dumdum bullet occurred later, after the formation of the Untouchables. But in his original (and more accurate) manuscript, he placed the episode somewhat earlier, during his career in Chicago Heights. This is the chronology I have followed.
350   "His hands": *Chicago Heights Star*, November 30, 1928.
350   twenty shotgun deaths: *Chicago Heights Star*, December 1, 1928.
350   "81 INDICTED": *Chicago Herald and Examiner*, May 4, 1929.
351   "It was necessary": Ness Collection, *WRHS*. Ness tells the same story, but more breathlessly, in *The Untouchables*, p. 113.
351   "I've got two": Ness and Fraley, *The Untouchables*, pp. 120–121.
352   "We arrested": *ibid.*, p. 122.
352   "there was a bright": *ibid.*, p. 123.
352   "offered a lot": *Chicago Herald and Examiner*, June 15, 1931.
353   "It's funny": *ibid.*
353   Goddard had come: *NYT*, September 8, 1929; *CT*, September 7, 1929.
353   "Of course, we cannot": Pasley, *Al Capone*, p. 334.
353   To avoid a crush: *ibid.*, pp. 346–347; *CT*, March 18, 1930.
354   "We certainly stuck": *CT*, March 18, 1930.
354   *Time* magazine: *Time*, March 24, 1930.
354   "No. 1 underwordling": *ibid.*
354   "Poor little rich": Pasley, *Al Capone*, p. 355.
354   "a book that": *CT*, March 23, 1930.
355   "We're up": Allsop, *The Bootleggers and Their Era*, p. 311.
355   "Jesus, Ralph": Kobler, *Capone*, pp. 264–265.
355   the Lexington Hotel: *CT*, March 22, 1930.
355   "I burned it": Allsop, *The Bootleggers and Their Era*, p. 312.
356   Al, what do you: *CT*, March 22, 1930.
356   "All I ever did": Pasley, *Al Capone*, pp. 349–350.

357 Frankie Frost: Ness and Fraley, *The Untouchables*, pp. 128–130.
357 "Acquiring the poise": *ibid.*, p. 128.
358 On the night of June 13: Nickel, *Torso*, p. 37.
358 begun to bribe telephone: Ness and Fraley, *The Untouchables*, p. 136.
359 "They said": *ibid.*, p. 138.
359 "Listen, and don't": Nickel, *Torso*, p. 37.
359 "Machine Gun" Jack: Pasley, *Al Capone*, pp. 353–354.
359 raided Capone's Palm Island estate: *CT*, March 21, 1930.
359 Like the charges: *Chicago Daily News*, December 25, 1936.
360 Nitti's concealed income: *NYT*, March 23, 1938.
360 "In reference": Telephone message from Mr. Youngquist, March 31, 1930. *HHL.*
361 "What was": Wolfe, *Of Time and the River*, pp. 420–421.
361 "Mismanagement by Mayor": Allsop, *The Bootleggers and Their Era*, pp. 196–197.
361 he visited Burnham: Sullivan and Kobler, "Caddying."
362 "We practically lived": *ibid.*
362 "I'm sick": Burns, *The One-Way Ride*, pp. 210–312.
363 The trial of Ralph Capone: To United States Board of Parole from Milton H. Summers, June 15, 1932, *CCC*; Allsop, *The Bootleggers and Their Era*, p. 316; Messick, *Secret File*, p. 44.
364 "You got caught": Tully, *Treasury Agent*, p. 39.
364 By May: Associated Press dispatch, May 6, 1930; Messick, *Secret File*, p. 46.
364 "There is nothing": A. P. Madden to Chief, Intelligence Unit, April 28, 1930. *HHL.*
365 "Mr. Mattingly": *ibid.*
365 "The American people": *NYT*, March 23, 1930; Fox, *Blood and Power*, pp. 133–134.
365 "I had the operating director": Statement of Frank J. Loesch, February 2, 1933. *DJ.*
366 the order Loesch ranked: *Criminal Justice* (Journal of the Chicago Crime Commission), May 1930.
366 "The purpose": *ibid.*
367 Secret Six: Lyle, *The Dry and Lawless Years*, p. 197; *Chicago Herald and Examiner*, February 23, 1930; Hoffman, *Business vs. Organized Crime*, p. 13.
368 "To an energetic youngster": *Collier's*, March 7, 1931.
368 "Capone is": Hoffman, *Business vs. Organized Crime*, p. 26.
368 "I'm going": *NYT*, May 25, 1930.
368 President Hoover: *Time*, May 19, 1930.
369 "seizing, arresting": Kobler, *Capone*, p. 284.
369 On arrival: Associated Press dispatches, April 20, 21, 1930.

370   FLORIDA SUES: *NYT*, May 9, 14, 15; *CT*, May 10, 19, 30; *Miami Herald*, May 11, 1930.

371   "I saw Mr. McCreary": *Miami Herald*, May 28, 1930; *CT*, June 14, 1930.

372   "Do you believe": *Miami Herald*, May 29, 1930.

372   Capone won: *Miami Herald*, May 30, 1930.

372   "PEACE JUSTICE": *Miami Daily News*, May 28, 1930.

372   "During the five": *CT*, June 14, 1930.

372   "the only cause": *CT*, June 15, 1930; *Miami Herald*, June 15, 1930.

373   bill for $50,000: Kobler, *Capone*, p. 284.

374   "Jake Lingle was known": Trohan interview.

374   "He would take": Whaley interview.

374   Another *Tribune* reporter: Pasley, *Al Capone*, p. 277.

374   job-related scams: Whaley interview.

374   "Journalists!": Hecht and MacArthur, *The Front Page*, p. 40.

374   Hilding Johnson: McPhaul, *Deadlines & Monkeyshines*, p. 227.

375   "big, tall Irishman": Whaley interview.

375   "The booze was good": *ibid*.

376   fixing the price: Pasley, *Al Capone*, p. 267.

376   "Shortly before": Whaley interview.

376   "Our managing": *ibid*.

377   "whom I heard": Wilson and Day, *Special Agent*, p. 31; Wilson, "Undercover Man."

377   One day before his appointment: Boettiger, *Jake Lingle*, pp. 15–22.

378   walking the streets: Nash, *People to See*, p. 192; McPhaul, *Deadlines & Monkeyshines*, p. 138.

378   "The *Tribune* is": "The Chicago *Tribune*," *Fortune*, May 1934.

378   "He was": Trohan interview.

378   notions of grammar: Gies, *The Colonel of Chicago*, pp. 5–6.

379   "The publishers called": Waldrop, *McCormick of Chicago*, p. 189.

379   Capone happened: Fox, *Blood and Power*, p. 105.

379   A little over: Waldrop, *McCormick of Chicago*, p. 187–188.

380   bulletproof: "The Chicago *Tribune*," *Fortune*, May 1934.

380   "Colonel McCormick called": Whaley interview.

381   reward of $25,000: Pasley, *Al Capone*, p. 266.

381   THE CHALLENGE: Allsop, *The Bootleggers and Their Era*, p. 156.

381   The Police Department: Boettiger, *Jake Lingle*, p. 37; Pasley, *Al Capone*, p. 275.

381   "The priest": Trohan interview.

382   Wilson questioned: Kobler, *Capone*, pp. 290–291.

382   "It was not": Pasley, *Al Capone*, pp. 282–283.

382   A separate investigation: Allsop, *The Bootleggers and Their Era*, p. 163.

382   "Lingle Wrecking": McPhaul, *Deadlines & Monkeyshines*, p. 271.

382   "Alfred Lingle now": Pasley, *Al Capone*, p. 293.

383 "Can't some way": Lyle, *The Dry and Lawless Years*, p. 232.

383 If Capone: *ibid.*, p. 233.

385 "the beams": *CT*, July 19, 1930.

386 "Was Jake": *ibid.*

Chapter 9: *Secret Agents*

page 387 "He had bought": Wilson, "Undercover Man."

387 "Everyone was hostile": *Baltimore Sun*, March 20, 1932.

388 "Investigation of this": Wilson, "Undercover Man."

388 "You can make": Kobler, *Capone*, p. 236.

388 "Eddie realized": Wilson and Day, *Special Agent*, pp. 31–32.

389 "I hope": *ibid.*

389 "The vice monger": Pasley, *Al Capone*, p. 301.

390 "I'd help you": *ibid.*, p. 309.

390 "He's all right": *CT*, August 20, 1930.

390 Lifting his shoulders: *CT*, October 10, 1930.

391 "hang a foreclosure": Wilson, "Undercover Man."

391 Wilson had further cause: Hynd, *The Giant Killers*, pp. 31–44.

391 "the greatest natural": Wilson and Day, *Special Agent*, p. 33.

392 "I'm a promoter": Hynd, *The Giant Killers*, p. 37; Tully, *Treasury Agent*, pp. 40–41.

392 "He keeps everything": Spiering, *The Man Who Got Capone*, pp. 89–90.

392 He alerted: *ibid.*, pp. 95–96.

393 "What the hell": *ibid.*, pp. 97–98.

393 "Snorky's gonna have": Hynd, *The Giant Killers*, p. 49.

393 "I feel very certain": *ibid.*, pp. 51–52.

393 "This is an emergency": *ibid.*, pp. 52–53.

394 Wilson and his wife: Wilson, "Undercover Man."

394 "I was much disgusted": Spiering, *The Man Who Got Capone*, p. 138.

395 "I uncovered a ledger": *Baltimore Sun*, March 20, 1932.

395 "I snipped": Wilson, "Undercover Man."

395 "We found out": *ibid.*

395 "Who are you": *ibid.*

397 I think it: Memorandum for Assistant Attorney General Youngquist, September 19, 1930. *FBI-FN.*

397 Carleon Hotel: *CT*, September 26, 1930.

398 Roamer Inn: F.B.I. Case Report, October 18, 1930. *FBI-FN.*

398 movements in Berwyn: FBI Case Report, November 11, 1930. *FBI-FN.*

398 "if for no": Memorandum for the Director, December 15, 1932. *FBI-FN.*

398 "worked at various": *NA-FN.*

399 On November 19, 1930: Milton H. Summers (Chicago Crime

Commission) to United States Board of Parole, May 16, 1932.
NA-JG.

399   "immediate boss": Kobler, *Capone*, p. 276.
399   "I packed my scowling": Wilson, "Undercover Man"; *Chicago Evening Post*, October 24, 1931.
400   During November: *CT*, November 14, December 5, 1930.
401   "I met a lovely": Borden, "Chicago Revisited," *Harper's Monthly*, April 1931.
401   raid on Capone's hideaway: *CT*, December 1, 1930; Dillard, "How the U.S. Government Caught Al Capone," *The Master Detective*, February 1932.
402   "Capone has become": *CT*, *NYT*, December 19, 1930.
402   "for a couple": Author's interview with Mike Rotunno.
403   Medill School: Kobler, *Capone*, p. 306.
403   "The men with power": Murray, *The Legacy of Al Capone*, p. 343.
404   "thoroughly investigated": O'Brien, *All Things Considered*, pp. 60–62.
405   "I can't tell you": *ibid.*, pp. 62–63.
406   "I thought he'd tear": *ibid.*, pp. 63–64.
407   "in the Capone domain": *NYT*, December 15, 1930.
408   In November 1930: Eliot Ness to George E. Q. Johnson, March 26, 1932. *GEQJ*; *FBI-EN*.
408   "I was instructed": Ness Collection, *WRHS*.
409   "When the truck": *ibid.*
409   "The Capone gang": *ibid.*
410   "laden down": *ibid.*
410   "full blooded Indian": *ibid.*
410   I had a truck: *ibid.*
411   From the inception: Eliot Ness to George E. Q. Johnson, March 26, 1932. *GEQJ*; *FBI-EN*.
411   "The attitude": *ibid.*
412   "Each raid was made": Ness Collection, *WRHS*.
412   "I evolved": Ness and Fraley, *The Untouchables*, pp. 196–198.
412   "an even better": *ibid.*, pp. 199–200.
413   "Scarface Al Capone": Wilson, "Undercover Man."
414   Elmer Irey received: Hynd, *The Giant Killers*, pp. 68–70.
414   March 13: Messick, *Secret File*, p. 51; Hynd, *The Giant Killers*, p. 74.
415   "We picked up": Author's interview with George E. Q. Johnson, Jr.
416   "If Mayor Thompson": *NYT*, February 17, 1931.
416   On February 21: *NYT*, February 22, 1931.
416   "monkey": *NYT*, February 24, 1931.
417   "Notice anything strange": Lyle, *The Dry and Lawless Years*, pp. 259–262.
418   "was unable": *CT*, April 4, 1931.

418 $2 million: *Chicago Daily News*, February 25, 1931.

418 "settled his": *CT*, February 26, 1931.

419 "The evidence": Opinion, *United States vs. Capone. NAGL.*

419 "And as punishment": *CT*, February 28, 1931.

420 "If the judge": *ibid.*

420 The U.S. Attorney's: R.C. Harvey to Director, February 27, 1931. *FBI-AC.*

421 Well of all: March 4, 1931. *FBI-AC.*

421 "Hell, Colonel": Hoffman, *Business vs. Organized Crime*, p. 35.

422 "I was taken": Vanderbilt, *Farewell to Fifth Avenue*, pp. 172–174.

424 For Chicago Thompson: *CT*, April 9, 1931.

424 "Chicago Goes": *The Nation*, April 22, 1931.

424 "He stands": *ibid.*

425 "I was now": Ness Collection, *WRHS.*

426 "Very cautiously": Ness and Fraley, *The Untouchables*, pp. 223–224.

426 major offensive: *NYT*, May 3, 1931.

427 the conflict erupted: *Organized Crime: 25 Years after Valachi*, pp. 299–300.

427 "Capone was an extravagant host": Bonanno, *A Man of Honor*, pp. 128–129.

428 "Why should": Gosch and Hamner, *The Last Testament of Lucky Luciano*, p. 147.

429 "I don't happen": Hynd, *The Giant Killers*, p. 76.

429 Two months earlier: George E. Q. Johnson to the Attorney General, December 31, 1931. *GEQJ.*

429 "If reasonable sentence": *ibid.*

430 Judge James Wilkerson: *ibid.*

431 CAPONE IS: *NYT*, June 6, 1931.

431 government's record: *CT, NYT*, June 6, 1931; *NAGL.*

432 Clarence Converse: Irey and Slocum, *The Tax Dodgers*, pp. 56–57.

432 "a sensation": Ness Collection, *WRHS*

432 5,000 offenses: *CT*, June 13, 1931.

433 "Ness was considered": Berardi interview.

433 The reporters: Author's interview with George Murray.

434 "Every time Al's fleet": *CT*, July 18, 1931.

434 Your proposal: Attorney General to George E. Q. Johnson, July 24, 1931. *GEQJ.*

435 "There is": Frank J. Loesch to President Hoover, June 29, 1931. *HHL.*

435 "The abject refusal": *CT*, June 15, 1931.

435 "Last of": *CT*, June 17, 1931.

435 Springfield, Illinois: *CT*, June 19, 1931.

436 "Why, they ought": *Time*, August 10, 1931.

436 "It is time": *NYT*, July 31, 1931.

437   "I cannot": Statement of Frank J. Loesch, February 2, 1933. *DJ*.

437   "Just the old": *NYT*, August 8, 1931; *CT*, August 10, 1931.

437   "I'm being hounded": Allsop, *The Bootleggers and Their Era*, pp. 340–341.

438   On September 23: Spiering, *The Man Who Got Capone*, pp. 157–158.

439   On Saturday: *NYT*, October 4, 1931.

Chapter 10: *The United States of America vs. Alphonse Capone*

page 440   "THE COURTROOM!": Shepherd, "Can Capone Beat Washington, Too?" *Collier's*, October 10, 1931.

441   Damon Runyon to cover: Clark, *The World of Damon Runyon*, p. 222.

441   "greasy, grinning": *Time*, September 21, 1931.

441   "The Battle of Chicago": Shepherd, "Can Capone Beat Washington, Too?"

441   "It will be": *CT*, October 7, 1931.

442   "Capone's thick-featured": *CT*, October 9, 1931.

442   names, addresses, and occupations: *CT*, October 7, 1931.

442   "Capone is to have": *ibid*.

443   "horny-handed tillers": Runyon, *Trials and Other Tribulations*, p. 226.

443   "bloated figure": *NYT*, October 8, 1931.

444   "Do you know Alphonse Capone?": *CT*, October 8, 1931.

445   "He was unshaven:" *TRAN*.

447   "Who were the managers": Ross, *The Trial of Al Capone*, pp. 47–50.

448   "The Raiding Pastor": *CT*, October 8, 1931.

448   "What is your occupation": *ibid*.

449   "The thought": *NYT*, October 8, 1931.

450   "The impression": *CT*, October 8, 1931.

451   Mr. Alphonse Capone: *TRAN*.

451   HERRICK: *NYT*, October 9, 1931.

452   The taxpayer is now 31: *CT*, October 9, 1931.

453   "The fatuous grin": *ibid*.

453   Eliot Ness boldly continued to arrest: *ibid*.

454   "Your Uncle Sam": Runyon, *Trials and Other Tribulations*, p. 235.

454   "LAVISH CAPONE LIFE": *NYT*, October 10, 1931.

455   "I was called": *CT*, October 10, 1931.

455   "Mr. Parker Henderson": *TRAN*.

457   The droning testimony: *NYT*, October 10, 1931.

457   "Al Capone": *CT*, October 9, 1931.

457   Sam "Golf Bag" Hunt: *CT*, October 10, 1931.

458   "The outside murkiness": *NYT*, October 11, 1931.

458 "a powerful figure": *ibid.*
459 "It is not necessary": *CT*, October 11, 1931.
460 "I was the first": Berardi interview.
461 "He bought a $4,500": *TRAN*.
461 A salesman from Marshall Field: *ibid.*
461 Meyer Berger: *NYT*, October 18, 1931.
462 "It looked": Runyon, *Trials and Other Tribulations*: p. 239.
462 "The testimony revealed": *ibid.*
463 "Now, just what": *TRAN*.
463 "There was one day": *ibid.*
464 "as if operating": *NYT*, October 14, 1931.
464 "They say, here": *ibid.*
464 "Mr. Ries:" *TRAN*.
468 "If it please": *NYT*, October 14, 1931.
468 "Are you ready": *CT*, October 14, 1931.
468 "We have a jury": *NYT*, October 14, 1931.
469 Edward G. Robinson: Runyon, *Trials and Other Tribulations*, p. 244.
469 "The gambler witnesses": *CT*, October 15, 1931.
469 "Have you had any transactions": *ibid.*
470 "How did you remember": *ibid.*
471 "You are the Pete Penovich": *TRAN*.
473 "a breezy sort": *NYT*, October 16, 1931.
474 "What was the bankroll": *ibid.*
475 "Your correspondent": Runyon, *Trials and Other Tribulations*, p. 242.
475 "Patients of this type": Brain, *Diseases of the Nervous System*, p. 429.
476 "He himself produced witnesses": Ross, *The Trial of Al Capone*, pp. 94–96.
478 "The government has sought": *NYT*, October 17, 1931.
479 "a lump bulged": *ibid.*
479 "Quite a gale": Runyon, *Trials and Other Tribulations*, p. 245.
479 "Every morning there are thousands": Closing argument by Mr. Johnson on Behalf of the United States. *GEQJ*.
481 "almost evangelical": *CT*, October 18, 1931.
483 "You are the judges": *TRAN*.
483 All the jurors save one: *NYT*, *CT*, October 19, 1931.
484 "Have you arrived": *CT*, October 18, 1931.
485 "You don't need": *Washington Herald*, October 19, 1931.
486 "Let the defendant step": *NYT*, October 25, 1931.
486 "Capone's eyes seemed": *ibid.*
488 "The only thing": Irey, *The Tax Dodgers*, p. 65.
488 "disappeared into the sprawling city": *Time*, October 26, 1931.

488   "Think of my": Ross, *The Trial of Al Capone*, pp. 111–112; *CT*, October 25, 1931.

488   "I'll knock": *CT*, October 25, 1931.

488   corned beef: *ibid*.

489   "CAPONE GETS": *Chicago Evening Post*, October 24, 1931.

489   "HOODLUM": *Kansas City Star*, October 24, 1931.

489   "It is ludicrous": *Literary Digest*, October 31, 1931.

489   "No matter how satisfactory": *ibid*.

489   "No one seemed": *NYT*, October 25, 1931.

489   "As you have perhaps read": *United States of America vs. Alphonse Capone*, Application for Supersedeas and Enlargement on Bail, October 26, 1931. *DJ*.

491   "organized body of men": Oral Announcement of Judge Wilkerson in *United States vs. Philip D'Andrea*, October 28, 1931. *GEQJ*.

492   "I still think": *United States vs. Philip D'Andrea*, October 28, 1931. *DJ*.

Chapter 11: *Circles of Hell*

page 493   David T. Moneypenny: *NYT*, October 26, 1931; *Washington Herald*, March 11, 1932.

494   "Today was visiting": *NYT*, October 30, 1931.

494   personal history: *BP-RC*.

495   "the gangster was taken": *CT*, November 5, 1931.

495   "I'd like to eat": *CT*, November 7, 1931.

495   The train reached Leavenworth: *NYT*, November 7, 1931.

495   attorney general ordered: *BP-RC*.

496   "Capone will": Finch R. Archer to Sanford Bates, December 6, 1931. *BP-RC*.

496   "administrative reasons": *BP-RC*.

496   "What an attraction": *ibid*.

496   "menace to society": Parole Report by United States Attorney. *BP-RC*.

496   Such was the standard procedure: Finch R. Archer to Director, Bureau of Prisons, September 9, 1932. *BP-RC*.

497   At Christmas: *Chicago Herald and Examiner*, December 18, 1931.

497   His sole relief: *Tacoma Daily Ledger*, February 8, 1932.

497   "Mr. Bates": A. H. MacCormick to Finch R. Archer, April 7, 1932. *BP-RC*.

497   In 1927: Ralph Capone's Social Record, December 14, 1931. *BP-RC*.

498   "Never did": Ralph Capone's Medical Record, December 10, 1931. *BP-RC*.

498   CHICAGO'S UNDERWORLD: *NYT*, November 29, 1931; *CT*, November 13, 1931; *Washington Herald*, October 30, 1931; *CT*, November 8, 1931.

498 WISH TO INFORM: *BP-AC*.

499 risqué tales: *ibid.*

499 visitors seeing Al Capone: *ibid.*

500 "BARE WARDEN'S": *Chicago Daily Times*, December 22, 1931; *CT*, December 22, 1931.

501 "Al had a radio": Kearns and Fraley, *The Million Dollar Gate*, p. 253.

501 "You'd be sensational": *ibid.*, pp. 254–257.

503 "I will give": *Washington Herald*, March 11, 1932.

503 Capone did not invoke: Messick, *Secret File*, p. 74.

504 "I handle beer": *Washington Herald*, March 11, 1932.

504 "There was absolutely": Rogers, *The Autobiography of Will Rogers*, p. 277.

504 "Capone could be useful": Messick, *Secret File*, pp. 74–75.

505 Lindbergh was desperate: *ibid.*, pp. 76–77; Wilson, *Special Agent*, p. 58; *New York Daily News*, April 26, 1932.

505 "The whole affair": *Time*, March 21, 1932.

505 "There ain't no gat": *Daily Mirror*, August 28, 1932.

505 "advance epitaph": Homer Croy to Al Capone, April 7, 1932. *BP-AC*.

505 "I wonder why": A. H. MacCormick to Homer Croy, May 13, 1932. *BP-AC*.

505 One final appeal: *CT*, March 23, 1932.

505 Finally, on May 2: *NYT*, May 3, 1932.

507 "I was determined": Ness and Fraley, *The Untouchables*, p. 244–254.

507 "After that it was": *NYT*, May 4, 1932.

508 "Well, I'm on my way": Ness and Fraley, *The Untouchables*, pp. 247–249; *CT*, May 4, 1932; AP dispatch, May 4, 1932.

509 "I'll be made": *NYT*, May 5, 1932.

510 His registration papers: *BP-AC*.

At the time of his arrival at the Atlanta Penitentiary, Al Capone's rap sheet, containing various omissions and errrors, read as follows:

Admission: 1919; Arrested at N.Y. City. Disorderly Conduct. (Fighting) Discharged.

1923,? Arrested, Chicago, Ill. Traffic Violation (Collision) Dismissed.

1923,? (Denied) Fined $150.00. Operating disorderly House, Gambling at Chicago, Ill.

9–5-23; Arrested. Pistol in Car. Discharged.

3–5-24; (Denies) Arrested, Chicago, Ill. Witness—Johnnie Duffey. Murder. Released.

5–8-24; Arrested, Chicago, Ill. Witness—murder Joe Howard.

1925,? Arrested, Olean, N.Y. (Denied) Disorderly. Released.

6–7-26; Indicted at Chicago, Ill. Viol. Nat'l Pro. Act.—Dismissed.

7–15–26; Indicted, Stickney, Ill. Vote Fraud. Dismissed in Dec, 1926.

7–28–26; Arrested, Chicago, Ill. Murder. Charge withdrawn.

10–1-26; Indicted, Chicago, Ill. Viol. N.P. Act (With 78 others) Dismissed.

11–12–27; Arrested, Chicago, Ill. Refusal to Testify. Dismissed.

12–22–27; Fined $2600.00, Joliet, Ill., with 5 other Henchmen. Concealed weapons.

May 17, 1929; Received at Eastern State Pen., Philadelphia, Pa. to serve 12 months for Concealed Weapons. Disch. by Exp. Sentence 3–17–30.

5–8-30; Arrested at Miami, Fla. Suspicion. Kept in jail over night and released.

May 1930; Arrested several times at Miami, Fla., from May 8th to May 17th. Suspicion, Vagrancy, Perjury. Consolidated and dismissed.

2–27–31; Sentenced at Chicago, Ill. to serve 6 months for Contempt. Appealed the case. Conviction affirmed (part of this sentence)

Indictment pending, Chicago, Ill. Cons. Viol. Nat'l Pro, Act.

510   He yielded: *ibid.*
510   the federal prison system: Godwin, *Alcatraz*, pp. 34–35.
510   Like all new arrivals: *NYT*, May 6, 1932.
511   Myrl E. Alexander: *Gainesville Sun*, February 27, 1991.
511   "When he entered" Author's interview with Myrl E. Alexander.
511   The jail's medical staff: Report of Stephen T. Brown, M.D., September 7, 1932. *BP-AC*.
512   "The prostate soon": *ibid.*
512   During his career: Rudensky and Riley, *The Gonif, passim.*
512   "Atlanta would soon strip": *ibid.*, p. 56.
512   "Hey, Rusty": *ibid.*
512   "Al's complexion": *ibid.*
512   "How the hell": *ibid.*
513   "grubby two-bit nonentities": *ibid.*, p. 57.
513   "Capone was unpopular": Conway, "20 Months in Alcatraz," *Saturday Evening Post*, February 19, 1938. Conway was also in the Atlanta Penitentiary at the same time as Capone.
513   "I sent word out": Rudensky and Riley, *The Gonif*, p. 57.
513   "It was right comical": Conway, "20 Months."
514   "A hulking figure": *Daily Mirror*, April 14, 1934. The article emphasizes that Capone had been working in this manner for the previous two years.

514　"Just seeing your idea": Rudensky and Riley, *The Gonif*, p. 57.

514　"My wife sent": July 26, 1932. *BP-AC*.

515　It wasn't hero worship: Rudensky and Riley, *The Gonif*, pp. 57–58.

516　Judge Underwood dismissed: *NYT*, December 10, 1933, January 26, 1934.

516　One brother, Albert: *CT*, June 6, 1932.

517　President Hoover: *NYT*, July 20, August 10, 1932.

517　"He behaves so well": Allsop, *The Bootleggers and Their Era*, pp. 347–348.

517　He had passed: *Tacoma News*, February 27, 1934.

517　"Capone became a model": *NYT*, February 27, 1934.

518　"Frank and I": *NA-FN*.

519　disciplinary incidents: *BP-AC*.

520　"There is an allegation": *The Biography of Al Capone's Life in the Atlanta Penitentiary*; Report of E.E. Conroy. *FBI-AC*.

520　"My knowledge": *ibid*.

520　"death and bodily": FBI report, March 4, 1935. *FBI-AC*.

521　U.S. House of Representatives: *Congressional Record-House*, January 25, 1933, p. 2647.

521　On May 27: Associated Press dispatch, May 28, 1934.

521　"The pile is like": Rudensky and Riley, *The Gonif*, p. 60.

522　"Rusty," he sighed: *ibid*.

522　"Nobody's taking me": *ibid.*, p. 61.

522　"Capone, to me": *ibid.*, p. 62.

523　gangster melodramas: Peary, *Little Caesar*, pp. 9–13.

523　"Women's clubs": *ibid.*, p. 10.

524　fifty-one new gangster films: Fetherling, *The Five Lives of Ben Hecht*, p. 95.

524　*Doorway to Hell*: Peary, *Little Caesar*, pp. 12–13.

524　"terrific explosion": Burnett, *Little Caesar*, pp. 16–22.

525　Further blurring the line: Peary, *Little Caesar*, p. 17.

525　In New York: *ibid.*, p. 25.

525　1933 survey: *ibid.*, pp. 25–26.

525　expressions such as: *ibid.*, p. 27. In his autobiography, the film's director, Mervyn LeRoy, boasted of the popularity of the expressions introduced in the film.

525　"is immune": Burnett, "The Czar of Chicago," *Saturday Review of Literature*, October 8, 1930.

526　$1,000 a day: Fetherling, *The Five Lives of Ben Hecht*, p. 96.

528　Al Capone is not dead: Cowdery, *Capone's Chicago*, p. 17. (Originally published as *Al Capone on the Spot* by Richard T. Enright, 1931.)

528　"Anything glaringly improbable": *The Living Age*, February 1933.

528　*Carrying a Gun for Al Capone*: Lacey, *Little Man*, p. 313.

529　"Big gangsters": Manchester, *The Glory and the Dream*, p. 95.

529   Max Allan Collins: Author's interview with Max Allan Collins.
529   in his strip: Crouch, *Dick Tracy*, pp. 26, 56–57.
530   In the guise: *ibid.*, p. 34.
531   "Dillinger does not": Manchester, *The Glory and the Dream*, p. 94.
531   "charmed life": *NYT*, May 9, 1934.
532   "I think we ought": *NYT*, April 25, 1934.
532   Mercer, Wisconsin: *ibid.*
532   For the previous five months: Cromie and Pinkston, *Dillinger*, pp.
        1–4, 251–261.
533   "Al Capone": *NYT*, May 9, 1934.
534   As midnight tolled: *NYT*, August 20, 1934.
534   Despite the attorney general's refusal: *NYT*, August 21, 1934.
534   As the train neared Yuma: Kobler, *Capone*, p. 358.
535   As a Coast Guard cutter: *Kansas City Times*, August 23, 1934.
535   "Alcatraz Island is": Johnston, *Alcatraz*, pp. 1–2.
536   "The convict's dread": Conway, "20 Months."
536   "All of a sudden": Ellis, *Alcatraz Number 1172*, pp. 13–14.
536   Arriving at the dock: *CT*, February 14, 1988.
537   I didn't have any trouble: Johnston, *Alcatraz*, p. 31.
538   "They are not": *NYT*, August 24, 1934.
538   Capone's cell: Karpis, *On the Rock*, pp. 34–35.
539   "Men slowly go": Conway, "20 Months."
539   "The guards always shot": *ibid.*
540   brooded ceaselessly: *CT*, February 14, 1988.
540   Roused by a 6:00 A.M.: *ibid.*; Conway, "20 Months."
542   He became fascinated: *CT*, February 14, 1988; Turano, "America's
        Torture-Chamber," *American Mercury*, September 1938; *The
        New Yorker*, March 7, December 19, 1936.
542   Isla de los Alcatraces: Johnston, *Alcatraz*, pp. 3–8; Thompson, *The
        Rock*, pp. 76–77.
543   "Here may be isolated": Karpis, *On the Rock*, p. 15.
543   San Francisco's chief of police: Thompson, *The Rock*, pp. 351–369.
544   "friendly, ruddy-faced": Taylor, "Trouble House," *Collier's*, July
        25, 1936.
544   "You're my Warden now": Johnston, *Alcatraz*, pp. 31–34. In the
        interest of clarity I have made minor alterations in Johnston's
        erratic punctuation.
546   first significant breach: *CT*, February 14, 1988.
547   Jimmy Lucas: *NYT*, June 24, 1936.
548   "Outside of losing": *CT*, February 14, 1988.
548   "Anything I can": *ibid.*
548   he wanted to start: *ibid.*; Ellis, *Alcatraz: Number 1172*, pp. 60–61.
550   "It is difficult": Conway, "20 Months."
550   That morning: *FBI-AC.*
551   "The dirty shit": *CT*, February 14, 1988.

551 "Anyone who stays": Conway, "20 Months."

552 "Just a Life of Hell": *San Francisco Chronicle*, February 25, 1936.

552 "Dutch" Bowers: *Milwaukee Journal*, May 24, 1937; Taylor, "Trouble House."

553 "The stucco mansion": NYT, October 20, 1936.

553 "We had them beat": Kobler, *Capone*, p. 369. In the interest of clarity, I have made minor alterations in the letters' punctuation.

553 My Dear Husband: Mae Capone to Al Capone, October 24, 1936, Earl E. Wallar Collection, HDC # 438. Golden Gate National Recreation Area, Historic Documents Collection, San Francisco, California.

554 "Creepy" Karpis was the most notorious: Karpis, *On the Rock*, pp. 3–4.

555 "pale, shrunken figure": *ibid.*, pp. 58–60.

556 "the talent scout": Bennett, *I Chose Prison*, pp. 98–102.

557 "The convicts in Alcatraz": Karpis, *On the Rock*, p. 85.

557 Johnston retaliated: Kobler, *Capone*, p. 370.

558 "The obstacle is Al Capone": Karpis, *On the Rock*, pp. 101–102.

559 Since his arrival: Bennett, *I Chose Prison*, p. 36. In his memoir, Bennett suggests that Capone refused treatment for syphilis, which would have consisted of bismuth and arsenicals, but his medical records, which are more accurate on such matters, state otherwise. In any event, Capone's condition was incurable, and the treatment then available could not reverse the course of the disease.

559 "What happened": Bennett, *I Chose Prison*, p. 37.

559 "It was announced": *BP-AC*.

559 "DUE TO THE RUMORS": *ibid.*

559 "HAVE JUST HAD": *ibid.*

560 "I had to convince": Bennett, *I Chose Prison*, pp. 37–38.

560 Neuro-Psychiatric Examination: *BP-AC*.

562 When number 85 was escorted: United Press dispatch, August 3, 1936; *FBI-AC*.

563 "When we both": Karpis, *On the Rock*, pp. 118–119.

564 "I now feel": Romney M. Ritchey to Warden, November 19, 1938. *BP-AC*.

565 "We asked the State": Irey, *The Tax Dodgers*, p. 163.

565 Klein traveled: *World Telegram*, March 9, 1939; *New York Post*, March 9, 1939; NYT, March 10, 1939; Messick, *Secret File*, p. 99; Kobler, *Capone*, p. 371.

566 description of Alcatraz: Alcatraz continued to function as a federal penitentiary until 1963, when Attorney General Robert Kennedy ordered it to be shut down. It is currently a part of Golden Gate National Park. Ferry boats regularly carry hundreds of tourists each day to the Rock, where they can tour the cell house, pur-

chase souvenirs, and gaze out over the waters that once separated the most notorious convicts in the country from freedom.

567　"During the first few": George Hess to the Medical Director, Bureau of Prisons, January 16, 1939. *BP-AC*.

568　"He brands Hearst": George Hess, M.D. to James V. Bennett, October 26, 1939; Clinical Record, June 20, 1939. *BP-AC*.

568　"Ralph has now agreed": Memorandum for the Attorney General, October 21, 1939., *BP-AC*.

569　"Al Capone seemed": R.B. Hood to J. Edgar Hoover, October 26, 1939. *FBI-AC*.

570　"Do you feel": Kobler, *Capone*, p. 372.

571　As the expiration: Hoyt King to J. V. Bennett, November 3, 1939. *BP-AC*.

571　parole regulations: Certificate of Conditional Release for Alphonse Capone, January 19, 1939. *BP-AC*.

572　"Capone didn't seem": Alexander interview.

572　"Capone is sane": Murray, " 'When I Get Out of Prison...' Al Capone Talks," *Look*, October 24, 1939.

573　"where there is": *NYT*, November 18, 1939. Murphy knew that Capone was going to Baltimore for medical treatment (and not to Miami) because James V. Bennett had written to Murphy about the trip on October 21. Once Capone arrived in Baltimore, Attorney General Murphy admitted the truth but gave no reason for the change in his story. Soon after, President Franklin D. Roosevelt appointed Murphy to the U.S. Supreme Court.

Chapter 12: *After Capone*

page 574　He stood trial: letter from Harold Hagen to author, April 3, 1992.

574　a letter bearing no address: letter in possession of Harry Hart.

574　"They came with ponies": letter from Harold Hagen to author, April 3, 1992.

575　"I just remember": Hart interview.

575　"There was nothing": *ibid*.

577　"Al Capone, the eminent Chicago racketeer": *MC*; *NYT*, November 17, 1939.

577　"Capone is Free": *NYT*, November 17, 1939.

577　Capone says that he was infected: *MC*.

578　Dr. Moore [Mencken wrote] planned: *ibid*.

578　Dr. Moore inoculated: Author's interviews with Dr. Jack Shapiro and Dr. Thomas Turner.

579　When Mae learned: Author's interview with Dr. Richard D. Hahn.

579　I am told that he bears: *MC*.

580　penicillin mold: Shapiro interview.

580　a secure rented house: Hahn interview.

581 "I presume": James V. Bennett to Dr. J.E. Moore, December 21, 1939. *BP-AC*; *NYT*, February 18, 1941.

581 bade farewell: Hahn interview.

581 "Although the former": *Miami Herald*, March 23, 1940.

582 "Who's this": *Time*, February 3, 1947.

583 "brain paralysis": *Miami Herald*, August 3, 1940.

583 "tickled to death": *Baltimore Sun*, May 23, 1940.

583 "It was determined": TO: Director, FBI, April 13, 1945. *FBI-AC*.

584 "He operated": *ibid.*

584 An examination of his personnel record: *ibid.*

585 "It is known": *ibid.*

585 Attempting to learn: *ibid.*

586 "The CAPONE family": *ibid.*

586 On April 18: Kobler, *Capone*, p. 377.

586 "a rough customer": Author's confidential interview.

587 "Al speaks": TO: Director, FBI, April 13, 1945. *FBI-AC*.

588 On Wednesday: *CT*, November 9, 10, 11, 1939.

588 On February 20, 1942: *Newark Star-Ledger*, February 20, 1992.

589 In 1949: *ibid.*; *CT*, September 18, 1949.

590 At the time of his death: Allsop, *The Bootleggers and Their Era*, p. 375.

591 By 1940: Author's interview with Jonathan Margolis.

592 "We drove down": Hart interview.

592 "the picture": Author's interviews with Harry Hart and Raymond Longwell.

594 "During the Government's": George E. Q. Johnson to J. Edgar Hoover, October 30, 1933. Ness Collection, *WRHS*.

594 "Beware of Ness": H. H. Clegg to Director, December 7, 1943. *FBI-EN*.

595 "CLEVELAND": Jedick, *Cleveland*, p. 43.

595 he became so close to Fritchey: *ibid.*, p. 45.

595 "There is one interesting": *Cleveland News*, June 19, 1936.

596 "Thousand Young": *Cleveland News*, April 4, 1936.

596 the Harvard Club in Newburgh Heights: Nickel, *Torso*, pp. 47–49.

596 "I'm Eliot Ness": *ibid.*, pp. 49–50.

597 "the Unknowns": *ibid.*, p. 100.

597 "We both realized": *ibid.*, p. 150.

598 "the sexiest": Author's interview with Marion Hopwood Kelly.

598 practical jokes: Jedick, *Cleveland*, p. 48.

598 "When the party": Kelly interview.

599 ran a red light: Author's confidential interview.

599 Morris Barney "Moe" Dalitz: Roemer, *War of the Godfathers*, pp. 52–53.

599 Charles Polizzi: Nickel, *Torso*, p. 155.

599 "Ness' Bride": *Cleveland Plain Dealer*, October 26, 1939.

599   "Evaline liked": Condon, "The Last American Hero," *Cleveland*,
       August 1987.

600   Evaline's bodyguard: Kelly interview.

600   "Military Saboteur": Ness, "Venereal Disease Control in Defense,"
       Annals of the American Academy of Political and Social Sciences,
       March 1942.

600   "Most were genuinely puzzled": Nickel, *Torso*, pp. 187–188.

601   March 4, 1942: Condon, "Last American Hero."

601   "Cleveland is": *Cleveland Press*, April 27, 1942.

602   Elizabeth "Betty" Anderson: Nickel, *Torso*, p. 203.

602   "carefully avoids": *Fortune*, January 1946.

602   "My business affairs": Condon, "Last American Hero."

602   "vibrant, spirited city": *Cleveland News*, July 30, 1947.

603   "He'd come": Author's interview with Al Sutton.

603   "Who'd want": Jedick, *Cleveland*, p. 55.

604   "Al wants": Pontarelli interview.

605   Capone suffered: *Miami Herald*, January 22, 1947.

605   7:25 in the evening: Certificate of Death for Alphonse Capone.
       Office of Vital Statistics, State of Florida, State File No. 626.

605   "As word": *Miami Herald*, January 25, 1947.

605   "shrunken and colorless": *NYT*, January 27, 1947.

606   Abraham Teitelbaum: *ibid.*

606   "end of an evil": *ibid.*

606   "In the days": *CT*, January 26, 1947.

607   "the event would": Liebling, "The Wayward Press," *The New
       Yorker*, March 1, 1947.

607   "Death had beckoned": *Time*, February 3, 1947.

608   *Qui Riposa*: *Newsweek*, February 17, 1947.

608   "I remembered": Sullivan and Kobler, "Caddying."

608   "Why don't you": Murray, *The Legacy of Al Capone*, p. 12.

608   "The Roman Catholic Church": *ibid.*

610   "He was a very": Author's interview with Jack Foyle.

610   "He would drop": *ibid.*

611   "They're putting me": *ibid.*

611   "writing an article": Author's interview with Corinne Lawson.

612    $150 a week: Nickel, *Torso*, p. 208.

612   "You'll have to get": *ibid.*, pp. 208–209.

612   "He told me": Lawson interview.

613   On May 16, 1957: Jedick, *Cleveland*, p. 57; Nickel, *Torso*, pp.
       214–215.

613   At the time of his death: *ibid.*; Arruda, "Eliot Ness Revisited," *The
       Investigator*, May 1988.

613   "I would find": Lawson interview.

615   "Did you have": *Hearings Before the Special Committee to Investi-
       gate Organized Crime in Interstate Commerce*, pp. 1226–1247.

616 "I love you": Kobler, *Capone*, p. 380.

616 On March 16, 1951: *Chicago Herald-American*, March 16, 1951; Associated Press dispatch, March 16, 1951.

616 In September 1951: *Lincoln Star*, September 20, 1951.

617 Hart spent five hours: *Sioux City Journal*, September 22, 1951.

617 "The very name Capone": *Lincoln Star*, December 13, 1952.

618 "Your father broke": Balsamo interview.

618 annual allowance: Roemer interview; Roemer: *Man Against the Mob*, p. 90.

618 shoplifting in the Kwik Chek: *Miami Herald*, *Miami News*, August 7, 1965; *Miami Herald*, November 16, 1965.

618 Ralph died: Certificate of Death, State of Wisconsin, Department of Health and Social Services, No. 74 034707.

618 April 16, 1986: Certificate of Death, Office of Vital Statistics, State of Florida.

618 Harry Hart, Al Capone's nephew: Author's interviews with Joyce and Harry Hart.

Selected Bibliography

Abadinsky, Howard. *Organized Crime*. Boston: Allyn and Bacon, 1981.

Adler, Larry. *It Ain't Necessarily So*. London: Collins, 1984.

Albini, Joseph L. *The American Mafia: Genesis of a Legend*. New York: Appleton-Century-Crofts, 1971.

Allen, Frederick Lewis. *Only Yesterday*. New York: Harper & Brothers, 1931.

Allsop, Kenneth. *The Bootleggers and Their Era*. Garden City, N.Y.: Doubleday, 1961.

Amfitheatrof, Erik. *The Children of Columbus: An Informal History of the Italians in the New World*. Boston: Little, Brown, 1973.

Armbruster, Eugene L. *Brooklyn's Eastern District*. Brooklyn, N.Y.: Eugene L. Armbruster, 1942.

Asbury, Herbert. *Carry Nation*. New York: Alfred A. Knopf, 1929.

———. *The French Quarter: An Informal History of the New Orleans Underworld*. New York: Alfred A. Knopf, 1936.

———. *The Gangs of New York*. New York: Alfred A. Knopf, 1928.

———. *Gem of the Prairie: An Informal History of the Chicago Underworld*. New York: Alfred A. Knopf, 1940.

———. *The Great Illusion: An Informal History of Prohibition*. Garden City, N.Y.: Doubleday, 1950.

Balsamo, William and George Carpozi Jr. *Under the Clock: The Inside Story of the Mafia's First Hundred Years*. Far Hills, N.J.: New Horizon Press, 1988.

Barzini, Luigi. *The Italians*. New York: Atheneum, 1964.

Bennett, James. *I Chose Prison*. New York: Alfred A. Knopf, 1970.

Bennett, James O'Donnell. *Chicago Gang Land: The True Story of Chicago Crime*. Chicago: Chicago Tribune, 1929.

Berle, Milton, and Haskel Frankel. *Milton Berle: An Autobiography*. New York: Delacorte Press, 1974.

Blumenthal, Ralph. *Last Days of the Sicilians: The FBI's War Against the Mafia*. New York: Pocket Books, 1989.

Boettiger, John. *Jake Lingle: Or Chicago on the Spot*. New York: E.P. Dutton, 1931.

Bonanno, Joseph. *A Man of Honor: The Autobiography of Joseph Bonanno*. New York: Simon and Schuster, 1983.

Brain, Russell. *Diseases of the Nervous System*, 5th ed. London: Oxford University Press, 1955.

Brenner, Teddy, and Barney Nagler. *Only the Ring Was Square*. Englewood Cliffs, N.J.: Prentice-Hall, 1981.

Breslin, Jimmy. *Damon Runyon*. New York: Ticknor & Fields, 1991.

Bright, John. *Hizzoner Big Bill Thompson: An Idyll of Chicago*. New York: Jonathan Cape & Harrison Smith, 1930.

Bruère, Martha Bensley. *Does Prohibition Work?* New York: Harper & Brothers, 1927.

Buret, F. *Syphilis in Ancient and Prehistoric Times*. 3 vols. New York: AMS Press, 1975. (Originally published 1891.)

Burnett, W. R. *Little Caesar*. New York: Dial Press, 1958.

Burns, Walter Noble. *The One-Way Ride*. Garden City, N.Y.: Doubleday, Doran, 1931.

Busch, Francis X. *Enemies of the State*. Indianapolis: Bobbs-Merrill, 1954.

Casey, Robert J., and W. A. S. Douglas: *The Midwesterner: The Story of Dwight H. Green*. Chicago: Wilcox & Follett, 1948.

Chicago Gang Wars in Pictures: X Marks the Spot. Chicago: Spot Publishing, 1930.

Clark, Tom. *The World of Damon Runyon*. New York: Harper & Row, 1978.

Coffey, Thomas M. *The Long Thirst: Prohibition in America, 1920-1933*. New York: W. W. Norton, 1975.

Cohn, Art. *The Joker Is Wild: The Story of Joe E. Lewis*. New York: Random House, 1955.

Cohen, Michael Mickey, and John Peer Nugent. *Mickey Cohen: In My Own Words*. Englewood Cliffs, N.J.: Prentice-Hall, 1975.

Collins, Max Allan. *Bullet Proof*. New York: Bantam Books, 1989.

——. *Butcher's Dozen*. New York: Bantam Books, 1988.

——. *The Dark City*. New York: Bantam Books, 1987.

——. *Stolen Away: A Novel of the Lindbergh Kidnapping*. New York: Bantam Books, 1991.

——. *True Detective*. New York: Tor Books, 1986.

Condon, Eddie. *We Called It Music: A Generation of Jazz*. Westport, Conn.: Greenwood Press, 1947.

Cooney, John. *The Annenbergs*. New York: Simon and Schuster, 1982.

Cooper, Courtney Riley. *Ten Thousand Public Enemies*. Boston: Little, Brown, 1935.

Cowdery, Ray. *Capone's Chicago*. Lakeville, Minn.: Northstar Commemoratives, 1987. (Originally published as *Al Capone on the Spot* by Richard T. Enright, 1931.)

Cressey, Donald R. *Theft of the Nation: The Structure and Operations of Organized Crime in America*. New York: Harper & Row, 1969.

Cromie, Robert, and Joseph Pinkston. *Dillinger: A Short and Violent Life*. Evanston, Ill.: Chicago Historical Bookworks, 1990. (Originally published 1962.)

Crouch, Bill Jr., ed. *Dick Tracy: America's Most Famous Detective*. Secaucus, N.J.: Citadel Press, 1987.

Croy, Homer. *Country Cured*. New York: Harper & Brothers, 1943.

Dattner, Bernhard, Evan W. Thomas, and Gertrude Wexler. *The Management of Neurosyphilis*. New York: Grune & Stratton, 1944.

Dedmon, Emmet. *Fabulous Chicago*. New York: Random House, 1953.

Demaris, Ovid. *Captive City*. New York: Lyle Stuart, 1969.

————. *The Last Mafioso: The Treacherous World of Jimmy Fratianno*. New York: Times Books, 1981.

Dennie, Charles C., and Sidney F. Pakula. *Congenital Syphilis*. Philadelphia: Lea & Febiger, 1940.

Dobyns, Fletcher. *The Amazing Story of Repeal: An Exposé of the Power of Propaganda*. Chicago: Willet, Clark, 1940.

————. *The Underworld of American Politics*. New York: Fletcher Dobyns, 1932.

Duis, Perry R. *The Saloon: Public Drinking in Chicago and Boston, 1880-1920*. Urbana: University of Illinois Press, 1987.

Edge, L. L. *Run the Cat Roads*. New York: Dembner Books, 1981.

Ellis, Steve. *Alcatraz Number 1172*. Los Angeles: Holloway House, 1969.

Fetherling, Doug. *The Five Lives of Ben Hecht*. Toronto: Lester and Orpen, 1977.

Finley, M. I., Denis Mack Smith, and Christoper Duggan. *A History of Sicily*. New York: Viking Penguin, 1987.

Fox, Stephen. *Blood and Power: Organized Crime in Twentieth-Century America*. New York: Penguin Books, 1989.

Fraley, Oscar, and Paul Robsky. *The Last of the Untouchables*. New York: Pocket Books, 1988.

Fried, Albert. *The Rise and Fall of the Jewish Gangster in America*. New York: Holt, Rinehart and Winston, 1980.

Fuess, Clade M. *Calvin Coolidge: The Man from Vermont*. Boston: Little, Brown, 1940.

Gambino, Richard. *Vendetta*. Garden City, N.Y.: Doubleday, 1977.

Gage, Nicholas. *The Mafia Is Not an Equal Opportunity Employer*. New York: McGraw-Hill, 1971.

Gies, Joseph. *The Colonel of Chicago*. New York: E. P. Dutton, 1979.

Godwin, John. *Alcatraz: 1868-1963*. Garden City, N.Y.: Doubleday, 1963.

Goodspeed, Weston, and Daniel D. Healy, eds. *History of Cook County, Illinois.* 2 vols. Chicago: The Goodspeed Historical Association, 1909.

Gosch, Martin A., and Richard Hamner. *The Last Testament of Lucky Luciano.* Boston: Little Brown, 1974.

Gosnell, Harold F. *Machine Politics: The Chicago Model.* Chicago: University of Chicago Press, 1937.

Green, Paul, and Melvin G. Holli, eds. *The Mayors: The Chicago Political Tradition.* Carbondale: Southern Illinois University Press, 1987.

Gunther, John. *Inside U.S.A.* New York: Harper & Brothers, 1947.

Gusfield, Joseph R. *Symbolic Crusade: Status Politics and the American Temperance Movement.* Chicago: University of Illinois, 1963.

Halper, Albert, ed. *The Chicago Crime Book.* Cleveland: World Publishing, 1967.

Harrison, Carter H. *Stormy Years: The Autobiography of Carter Harrison.* Indianapolis: Bobbs-Merrill, 1935.

Healy, Paul F. *Cissy: The Biography of Eleanor M. "Cissy" Patterson.* Garden City, N.Y.: Doubleday, 1966.

Hearings Before the Special Committee to Investigate Organized Crime in Interstate Commerce. Washington, D.C.: United States Government Printing Office, 1950.

Hecht, Ben. *A Child of the Century.* New York: Simon and Schuster, 1954.

Hecht, Ben, and Charles MacArthur. *The Front Page.* New York: Covici, Friede, 1928.

Helmer, William J. *The Gun that Made the Twenties Roar.* London: Macmillan, 1969.

Hernon, Peter, and Terry Ganey. *Under the Influence: The Unauthorized Story of the Anheuser-Busch Dynasty.* New York: Simon and Schuster, 1991.

Hibbert, Christopher. *The Roots of Evil.* London: Weidenfeld and Nicolson: 1963.

Hinton, Milt, and David G. Berger. *Bass Line: The Stories and Photographs of Milton Hinton.* Philadelphia: Temple University Press, 1988.

Hoffman, Dennis E. *Business vs. Organized Crime.* Chicago: Chicago Crime Commission, 1989.

Hollatz, Tom. *Gangster Holidays: The Lore and Legends of the Bad Guys.* St. Cloud, Minn.: North Star Press, 1989.

Holli, Melvin G., and Peter d'A. Jones. *Ethnic Chicago.* Grand Rapids, Mich.: William B. Eerdmans, 1984.

Homer, Nebraska: A Centennial History, 1875-1975. Homer, Nebraska, 1975.

Hoover, Herbert. *The Memoirs of Herbert Hoover: The Cabinet and the Presidency, 1920-1933.* New York: Macmillan, 1952.

Horan, James D. *The Desperate Years: A Pictorial History of the Thirties.* New York: Crown, 1962.

Hutton, Edward. *Naples and Southern Italy.* New York: Macmillan, 1915.

Hynd, Alan. *The Giant Killers.* New York: Robert M. McBride, 1945.

Iorizzo, Luciano J., ed. *An Inquiry into Organized Crime*. New York: The American Italian Historical Association, 1970.

Irey, Elmer L., and William Slocum: *The Tax Dodgers: The Inside Story of the T-Men's War with America's Political and Underworld Hoodlums*. New York: Greenberg, 1948.

Jedick, Peter. *Cleveland: Where the East Coast Meets the Midwest*. Cleveland: Peter Jedick, 1980.

Jessel, George. *So Help Me: The Autobiography of George Jessel*. New York: Random House, 1943.

Johnston, James A. *Alcatraz Island Prison and the Men Who Live There*. New York: Charles Scribner's Sons, 1949.

Karlen, Harvey M. *The Governments of Chicago*. Chicago: Courier, 1958.

Karpis, Alvin. *On the Rock: Twenty-Five Years in Alcatraz*. Mississauga, Canada: L.B.S. Inc., 1988.

Katz, Leonard. *Uncle Frank: The Biography of Frank Costello*. New York: Drake Publishers, 1973.

Kearns, Jack "Doc," and Oscar Fraley. *The Million Dollar Gate*. New York: Macmillan, 1966.

Kefauver, Estes. *Crime in America*. Garden City, N.Y.: Doubleday, 1951.

Killian, Michael, Connie Fletcher, and F. Richard Ciccone. *Who Runs Chicago?* New York: St. Martin's Press, 1979.

Kobler, John. *Ardent Spirits: The Rise and Fall of Prohibition*. New York: G. P. Putnam's Sons, 1973.

———. *Capone: The Life and World of Al Capone*. New York: G. P. Putnam's Sons, 1971.

Krout, John A. *The Origins of Prohibition*. New York: Alfred A. Knopf, 1925.

Lacey, Robert. *Little Man: Meyer Lansky and the Gangster Life*. Boston: Little, Brown, 1991.

Lagumina, Salvatore J., ed. *Wop! A Documentary History of Anti-Italian Discrimination in the United States*. San Francisco: Straight Arrow Books, 1973.

Lait, Jack, and Lee Mortimer. *Chicago: Confidential!* New York: Crown, 1950.

Landesco, John. *Organized Crime in Chicago: Part III of The Illinois Crime Survey*. Chicago: University of Chicago Press, 1929.

Lee, Henry. *How Dry We Were: Prohibition Revisited*. Englewood Cliffs, N.J.: Prentice-Hall, 1963.

Levell, Mark, and Bill Helmer. *The Quotable Al Capone*. Chicago: Chicago Typewriter, 1990.

Levine, Gary. *Anatomy of a Gangster: Jack "Legs" Diamond*. New York: A. S. Barnes, 1979.

Lewis, Lloyd, and Henry Justin Smith. *Chicago: The History of Its Reputation*. New York: Harcourt, Brace, 1929.

Lewis, Norman. *The Honored Society: A Searching Look at the Mafia*. New York: G. P. Putnam's Sons, 1964.

Lindberg, Richard C. *Chicago Ragtime: Another Look at Chicago, 1880-1920*. South Bend, Ind.: Icarus Press, 1985.

————. *To Serve and Collect: Chicago Politics and Police Corruption from the Lager Beer Riot to the Summerdale Scandal.* New York, Praeger: 1991.

Lyle, John H. *The Dry and Lawless Years.* Englewood Cliffs, N.J.: Prentice-Hall, 1960.

Lynch, Denis. *Criminals and Politicians.* New York: Macmillan, 1932.

Maas, Peter. *The Valachi Papers.* New York: G. P. Putnam's Sons, 1968.

Manchester, William. *The Glory and the Dream: A Narrative History of America, 1932-1972.* New York: Bantam Books, 1990.

Mariano, John Horace. *The Second Generation of Italians in New York City.* Boston: Christopher Publishing House, 1921.

Martin, Ralph G. *Cissy: The Extraordinary Life of Eleanor Medill Patterson.* New York: Simon and Schuster, 1979.

Masters, Edgar Lee. *The Tale of Chicago.* New York: G. P. Putnam's Sons, 1933.

Mayer, Harold M., and Richard C. Wade. *Chicago: Growth of a Metropolis.* Chicago: University of Chicago Press, 1969.

McConaughy, John. *From Cain to Capone: Racketeering Down the Ages.* New York: Brentano's, 1931.

McPhaul, John J. *Deadlines & Monkeyshines: The Fabled World of Chicago Journalism.* Englewood Cliffs, N.J.: Prentice-Hall, 1962.

————. *Johnny Torrio: First of the Gang Lords.* New Rochelle, N.Y.: Arlington House, 1970.

Messick, Hank. *The Beauties and the Beasts.* New York: David McKay, 1973.

————. *John Edgar Hoover.* New York: David McKay, 1972.

————. *Lansky.* New York: G. P. Putnam's Sons, 1971.

————. *Secret File.* New York: G. P. Putnam's Sons, 1969.

————. *The Silent Syndicate.* New York: Macmillan, 1967.

Mezzrow, Mezz, and Bernard Wolfe. *Really the Blues.* Garden City, N.Y.: Doubleday, 1972.

Miller, Arthur. *A View from the Bridge.* New York: Viking Press, 1955.

Molstad, George. *Dakota County, Nebraska.* Dakota City, Nebr.: Dakota County Historical Society, 1982.

Mordden, Ethan. *That Jazz! An Idiosyncratic Social History of the American Twenties.* New York: G. P. Putnam's Sons, 1978.

Morgan, John. *No Gangster More Bold: Murray Humphreys.* London: Hodder and Stoughton, 1985.

Morris, Ronald L. *Wait Until Dark: Jazz and the Underworld.* Bowling Green, Ohio: Bowling Green University Press, 1980.

Murphy, Mary Ellen, and Mark Murphy, eds. *A Treasury of Brooklyn.* New York: William Sloane, 1949.

Murray, George. *The Legacy of Al Capone: Portraits and Annals of Chicago's Public Enemies.* New York: G. P. Putnam's Sons, 1975.

Nash, Jay Robert. *Bloodletters and Badmen.* New York: M. Evans, 1973.

————. *Encyclopedia of World Crime.* 6 vols. Wilmette, Ill.: CrimeBooks, 1989.

————. *People to See: An Anecdotal History of Chicago's Makers and Breakers.* Piscataway, N.J.: New Century Publishers, 1981.

Nation, Carry A. *The Use and Need of the Life of Carry A. Nation.* Topeka, Kansas: F. M. Steves and Sons, 1908.

The National Prohibition Law: Hearings Before the Subcommittee of the Committee on the Judiciary, United States Senate, vol. 1. Washington, D.C.: U.S. Government Printing Office, 1926.

Nelli, Humbert S. *The Business of Crime: Italians and Syndicate Crime in the United States.* New York: Oxford University Press, 1976.

————. *From Immigrants to Ethnics: The Italian Americans.* New York: Oxford University Press, 1983.

————. *Italians in Chicago, 1880-1930.* New York: Oxford University Press, 1970.

Nelson, Waldo E., ed. *Textbook of Pediatrics,* 6th ed. Philadelphia: W. B. Saunders, 1954.

Ness, Eliot, and Oscar Fraley. *The Untouchables.* New York: Popular Library, 1960. (Originally published 1957.)

Ness, Evaline. *Sam, Bangs & Moonshine.* New York: Holt, Rinehart and Winston, 1966.

————. *Yeck, Eck.* New York: E. P. Dutton, 1974.

Nickel, Steven. *Torso: Eliot Ness and the Hunt for the Mad Butcher of Kingsbury Run.* New York: Avon Books, 1990.

O'Brien, Howard Vincent. *All Things Considered: Memories, Experiences and Observations of a Chicagoan.* Indianapolis: Bobbs-Merrill, 1948.

Organized Crime: 25 Years after Valachi: Hearings Before the Permanent Subcommittee on Investigations of the Committee on Governmental Affairs, United States Senate. Washington, D.C.: U.S. Government Printing Office, 1990.

Owen, Collinson. *King Crime: An English Study of America's Greatest Problem.* New York: Henry Holt, 1932.

Pasley, Fred D. *Al Capone: The Biography of a Self-Made Man.* Garden City, N.Y.: Garden City Publishing, 1930.

————. *Muscling In.* New York: Ives Washburn, 1931.

Peary, Gerald, ed. *Little Caesar.* Madison: University of Wisconsin Press, 1981.

Peterson, Virgil W. *Barbarians in Our Midst: A History of Chicago Crime and Politics.* Boston: Little, Brown, 1952.

Pilat, Oliver, and Jo Ransom. *Sodom by the Sea.* Garden City, N.Y.: Doubleday, Doran, 1941.

Pileggi, Nicholas. *Wise Guy: Life in a Mafia Family.* New York: Pocket Books, 1987.

Pitkin, Thomas Monroe, and Francisco Cordero. *The Black Hand: A Chapter in Ethnic Crime.* Totowa, N.J.: Littlefield, Adams, 1977.

Rand McNally Guide to Chicago and Environs. Chicago: Rand McNally, 1924.

Reckless, Walter C. *Vice in Chicago.* Chicago: University of Chicago Press, 1933.

Redford, Polly. *Billion-Dollar Sandbar: A Biography of Miami Beach.* New York: E. P. Dutton, 1970.

Redston, George, and Kendall F. Crossen. *The Conspiracy of Death.* Indianapolis: Bobbs-Merrill, 1965.

Reid, Ed. *The Grim Reapers: The Anatomy of Organized Crime in America.* Chicago: Henry Regnery, 1969.

Reppetto, Thomas A. *The Blue Parade.* New York: Free Press, 1978.

Richman, Harry, and Richard Gehman. *A Hell of a Life.* New York: Duell, Sloan and Pearce, 1966.

Riis, Jacob. *The Children of the Poor.* New York: Johnson Reprint Corporation, 1970. (Originally published 1892.)

———. *How the Other Half Lives.* Cambridge, Massachusetts: Harvard University Press, 1970. (Originally published 1890.)

Robbins, Jhan. *Inka Dinka Doo: The Life of Jimmy Durante.* New York: Paragon House, 1991.

Roemer, William F. Jr. *Roemer: Man Against the Mob.* New York: Donald I. Fine, 1989.

———. *War of the Godfathers.* New York: Donald I. Fine, 1990.

Rogers, Will. *The Autobiography of Will Rogers.* Boston: Houghton Mifflin, 1949.

Ross, Barney, and Martin Abramson. *No Man Stands Alone.* Philadelphia: J. B. Lippincott, 1957.

Ross, Robert. *The Trial of Al Capone.* Chicago: Robert Ross, 1933.

Rudensky, Morris (Red), and Don Riley. *The Gonif.* Blue Earth, Minn.: Piper, 1970.

Runyon, Damon. *The Damon Runyon Omnibus.* Garden City, N.Y.: Sun Dial Press, 1943.

———. *Trials and Other Tribulations.* Philadelphia: J. B. Lippincott, 1947.

St. John, Robert. *This Was My World.* Garden City, N.Y.: Doubleday, 1953.

Salerno, Ralph, and John S. Tompkins. *The Crime Confederation: Cosa Nostra and Allied Operations in Organized Crime.* Garden City, N.Y.: Doubleday, 1969.

Sandburg, Carl. *The Complete Poems of Carl Sandburg.* New York: Harcourt Brace Jovanovich, 1970.

Schiavo, Giovanni. *The Truth about the Mafia and Organized Crime in America.* New York: Vigo Press, 1962.

———. *The Italians in Chicago.* New York: Italian American Publishing, 1928.

Schmidt, John R. *The Man Who Cleaned Up Chicago: A Political Biography of William E. Dever.* DeKalb, Ill.: Northern Illinois University Press, 1989.

Schneider, Jane, and Peter Schneider. *Culture and Political Economy in Western Sicily.* New York: Academic Press, 1976.

Schoenberg, Robert J. *Mr. Capone.* New York: Morrow, 1992.

Selvaggi, Giuseppe. *The Rise of the Mafia in New York from 1896 through World War II.* Indianapolis: Bobbs-Merrill, 1978.

Servadio, Gaia. *Mafioso: A History of the Mafia from its Origins to the Present.* New York: Stein and Day, 1976.

Shapiro, Nat, and Nat Hentoff. *Hear Me Talkin' to Ya: The Story of Jazz as Told by the Men Who Made It.* New York: Dover, 1955.

Sifakis, Carl. *The Mafia Encyclopedia.* New York: Facts on File, 1987.

Sinclair, Andrew. *Prohibition: The Era of Excess.* Boston: Little, Brown, 1962.

Smith, Alson J. *Chicago's Left Bank.* Chicago: Henry Regnery, 1953.

————. *Syndicate City: The Chicago Crime Cartel.* Chicago: Henry Regnery, 1954.

Smith, Dwight C. Jr. *The Mafia Mystique.* Mew York: Basic Books, 1975.

Smith, Henry Justin. *Chicago's Great Century, 1833-1933.* Chicago: Consolidated Publishers, 1933.

Sondern, Frederic Jr. *Brotherhood of Evil: The Mafia.* New York: Farrar, Straus and Cudahy, 1959.

Spiering, Frank. *The Man Who Got Capone.* Indianapolis: Bobbs-Merrill, 1976.

Steffens, Lincoln. *The Shame of the Cities.* New York: Peter Smith, 1948. (Originally published 1904.)

Stead, William T. *If Christ Came to Chicago!* Chicago: Laird & Lee, 1894.

Stuart, William H. *The 20 Incredible Years.* Chicago: M. A. Donohue, 1935.

Sullivan, Edward Dean. *Chicago Surrenders.* New York: Vanguard Press, 1930.

————. *Rattling the Cup on Chicago Crime.* New York: Vanguard Press, 1929.

Talese, Gay. *Honor Thy Father.* New York: Fawcett Crest, 1971.

————. *Unto the Sons.* New York: Alfred A. Knopf, 1992.

Taylor, Robert Lewis. *Vessel of Wrath: The Life and Times of Carry Nation.* New York: New American Library, 1966.

Tebbel, John. *An American Dynasty: The Story of the McCormicks, Medills and Pattersons.* Garden City, N.Y.: Doubleday, 1947.

Thomas, Bob. *Winchell.* Garden City, N.Y.: Doubleday, 1971.

Thompson, Craig, and Allen Raymond. *Gang Rule in New York: The Story of a Lawless Era.* New York: Dial Press, 1940.

Thompson, Erwin N. *The Rock: A History of Alcatraz Island, 1847-1972.* Denver: National Park Service, 1979.

Thrasher, Frederic M. *The Gang: A Study of 1,313 Gangs in Chicago.* Chicago: University of Chicago Press, 1927.

Tiede, Tom. *American Tapestry: Eyewitness Accounts of the Twentieth Century.* New York: Pharos Books, 1988.

Tocqueville, Alexis De. *Democracy in America,* vol. 2. New York: Vintage Books, 1945.

Toland, John. *The Dillinger Days.* New York: Random House, 1963.

Tomasi, Silvano M., and Madeline H. Engel, eds. *The Italian Experience in the United States.* Staten Island, N.Y.: Center for Migration Studies, 1970.

Touhy, Roger, and Ray Brennan: *The Stolen Years.* Cleveland: Pennington Press, 1959.

Trohan, Walter. *Political Animals: Memoirs of a Sentimental Cynic.* Garden City, N.Y.: Doubleday, 1975.

Tully, Andrew. *Treasury Agent: The Inside Story*. New York: Simon and Schuster, 1958.

Van Tassel, David D., and John J. Grabowski, eds. *The Encyclopedia of Cleveland History*. Bloomington: Indiana University Press, 1987.

Vanderbilt, Cornelius Jr. *Farewell to Fifth Avenue*. New York: Simon and Schuster, 1935.

Waldrop, Frank C. *McCormick of Chicago*. Englewood Cliffs, N.J.: Prentice-Hall, 1966.

Waller, Irle. *Chicago Uncensored*. New York: Exposition Press, 1965.

Waller, Maurice, and Anthony Calabrese. *Fats Waller*. New York: Schirmer Books, 1977.

Weller, Philip T. *The Roman Ritual*. Milwaukee: Bruce Publishing, 1964.

Wendt, Lloyd. *Chicago Tribune: The Rise of a Great American Newspaper*. Chicago: Rand McNally, 1979.

Wendt, Lloyd, and Herman Kogan. *Big Bill of Chicago*. Indianapolis: Bobbs-Merrill, 1953.

———. *Lords of the Levee: The Story of Bathhouse John and Hinky Dink*. Indianapolis: Bobbs-Merrill, 1943.

Whitehead, Don. *The FBI Story: A Report to the People*. New York: Random House, 1956.

Willard, Frances E. *A Classic Town: The Story of Evanston*. Chicago: Women's Temperance Publication Association, 1892.

Willebrandt, Mabel Walker. *The Inside of Prohibition*. Indianapolis: Bobbs-Merrill, 1929.

Wilson, Frank J., and Beth Day. *Special Agent: A Quarter Century with the Treasury Department and the Secret Service*. New York: Holt, Rinehart and Winston, 1965.

Wilson, Samuel Paynter. *Chicago and Its Cess-pools of Infamy*. Chicago: Samuel Paynter Wilson, 1910.

Wolfe, Thomas. *Of Time and The River*. New York: Charles Scribner's Sons, 1935.

Wright, Carroll D., and Oren W. Weaver, eds. *Bulletin of the Department of Labor*, vol. 2. Washington, D.C.: U.S. Government Printing Office, 1897.

Year Book: 1949. Philadelphia: American Swedish Historical Foundation, 1949.

Zorbaugh, Harvey Warren. *Gold Coast and Slum: A Sociological Study of Chicago's Near North Side*. Chicago: University of Chicago Press, 1929.

Unpublished Materials

Andrews, Janet. *The Italian Communities in South Brooklyn and Fort Greene: 1880–1917.* Fordham University, 1974. Brooklyn Historical Society.

Botein, Barbara. *The Hennessy Case: An Episode in American Nativism, 1890.* New York University Ph.D. dissertation, 1975.

Bukowski, Douglas. *According to Image: William Hale Thompson and the Politics of Chicago, 1915-1931.* University of Illinois at Chicago Ph.D. dissertation, 1989.

History of Chicago's Gangsters. Monograph in the personal collection of George E. Q. Johnson, Jr., Chicago, Illinois.

Inquest on the Bodies of Albert Kachellek, et al. Cook County, Illinois, February 23, 1929. (St. Valentine's Day Massacre) CCC.

Ness, Eliot. Untitled account of "The Capone Case." WRHS.

Index